THE AUTOGRAPH COLLECTOR

PRICE GUIDE

by Kevin Martin

WITHDRAWN

"Trusted by Collectors and Dealers"

Odyssey Publications Inc.

Publisher : Odyssey Publications Inc.
Cover Design : Type "F" Typography
Editor : Kevin Martin
Interior Design and Layout : Andjelika Martin
Copyright 2000 Odyssey Publications Inc.

Printed in the United States of America
Second Edition, First Printing
10 9 8 7 6 5 4 3 2 1

ISBN # 0-9669710-3-5

Library of Congress Catalog Card Number : #99-075881

Odyssey Publications Inc.
510-A So. Corona Mall
Corona, CA 92879-1420
1-800-996-3977
(909) 734-9636
http://www.Autographs.com

PREFACE

Another year has passed since our last edition and I realize now I was just kidding myself when I thought that each succeeding year would get easier.

It's not easy to update over 70,000 prices but it was more of a joy this year since so many of the nations top dealers took time from their busy schedules to submit prices, mark corrections, write chapters and generally update this edition.

Over 4,000 names were added to this year's "Millennium Edition" that are not in ANY other guide currently..names that may surprise you like Hillary Clinton and Jake Lloyd.

The biggest question we are asked is still from people who do not understand exactly how we arrive at these prices..the confusion seems to exist in the area of "content" which is fully explained again this year in the chapter called "How to Use this Guide".

No other guide on the market gives you as much material that you can USE as our guide..we cover more names accurately and although we know the type style is a bit small it is designed to be easier to carry to shows and auctions.

We designed the guide to be useful to you in many ways from the Tables in the back to birth and death dates and valuable comments at the end of each listing.

I produced a small guide six years ago called the "Autograph Prices Current" that at the time I naively thought would be produced twice a year..in it I listed birth and death dates for the FIRST time in price guide history..others have followed suit..like in so many other areas where we added improvements. I could have added unrealted material to "beef" up the page count in the guide, but in my opinion a PRICE GUIDE should be just that...a PRICE GUIDE.

If you are more interested in other areas such as Facsimiles or how to protect your autographs there are several books on those subjects listed in our Bibliography section.

A reader last year wrote stating that there should be more fascimiles..there are ! In a book of over 2,000 facsimiles called the Autograph Collector Guide to Authenticating (see Bibliography) As I stated previously this is a PRICE GUIDE with some facsimiles and other useful material added and I will continue to work hard to make it the most useful and accurate guide on the market today. For the hundreds who have had only nice things to say last year..Thanks for your support.

Until next year, Have a Happy Millennium and Happy Collecting!

ACKNOWLEDGMENTS

It would be a book in itself to try and thank all of the fine dealers, collectors and historians that made this work possible so if you have been left from my list it is entirely unintentional and without you all this book would not be possible each year but, I will try and hit some high points out there !

My deepest thanks as always goes to Darrell Talbert for continuing to believe in my work and working so hard himself to bring it to print.

Bill Miller, its been a tough year for us both Bill and I am more than a little jealous of how your year is ending up ! Thanks !

Andjelika Martin - my soul mate and the love of my life who continues to inspire and support me in so many projects.

Joanne Lindsey - You are the best and easiest person to work with and a blessing to have on my side.

The experts in various fields who have contributed chapters and upated information in this book : Cordelia and Tom Platt, David Frohmann, Gil Griggs, Tony Urban, Americabilia and David Beach.

Thank You.

Thanks to Lynn Keyes and her significant other for their continued support of the guide..we are certainly proud of their accomplishment this past year as well..ANY good accurate information that ANYBODY gets out to the collectors that help them in their collecting, should be applauded.

A personal thanks to John Reznikoff, Danny Brahms, Gil Griggs, Bob Eaton, and so many others for selling and mentioning our guide in their own publications and catalogs.

And of course a special Thanks to all the top dealers in our field who by placing an advertisement in this book have more than proven their support for what we are trying to do..

Happy Collecting Gang !

Kevin Martin

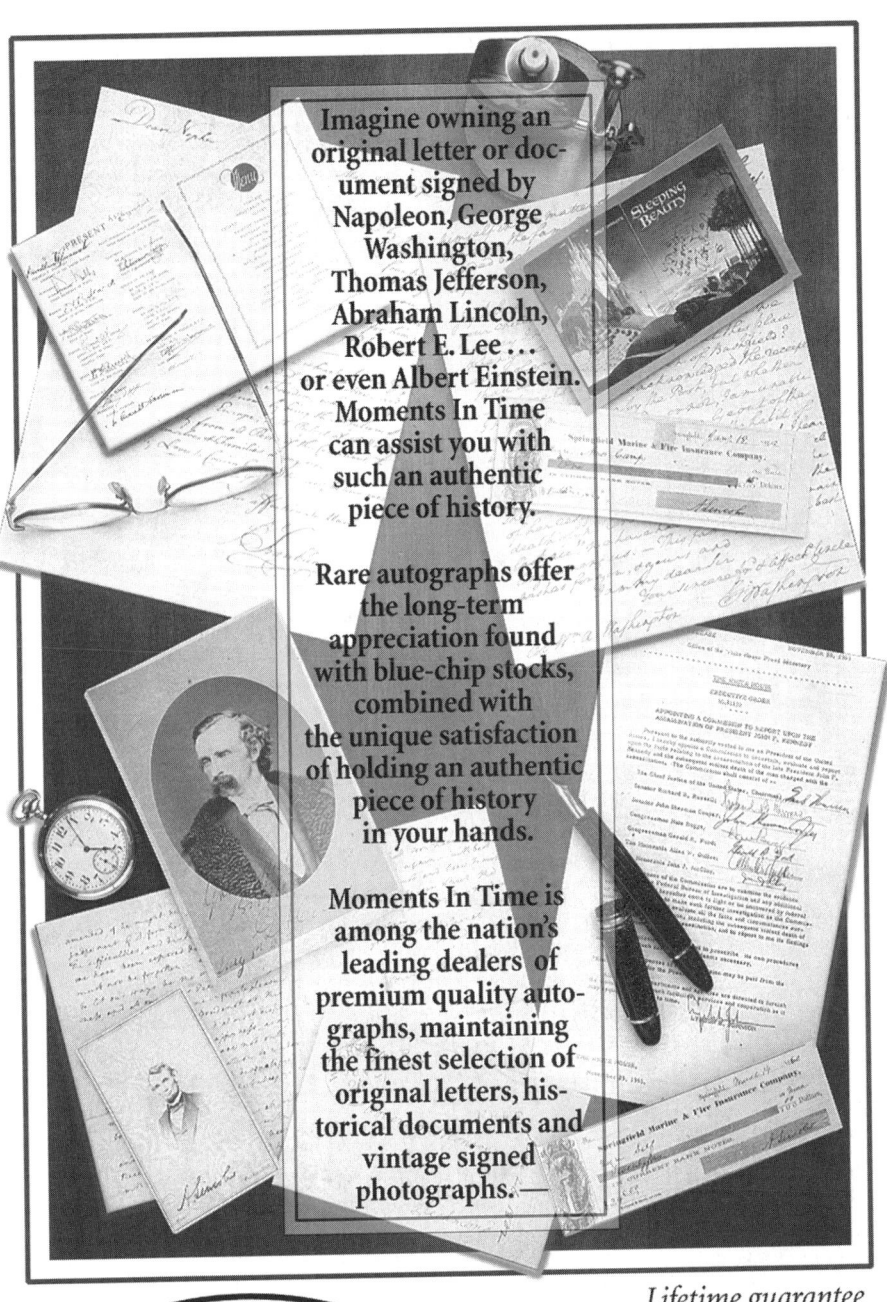

Imagine owning an original letter or document signed by Napoleon, George Washington, Thomas Jefferson, Abraham Lincoln, Robert E. Lee ... or even Albert Einstein. Moments In Time can assist you with such an authentic piece of history.

Rare autographs offer the long-term appreciation found with blue-chip stocks, combined with the unique satisfaction of holding an authentic piece of history in your hands.

Moments In Time is among the nation's leading dealers of premium quality autographs, maintaining the finest selection of original letters, historical documents and vintage signed photographs. —

Moments
In Time

Lifetime guarantee
of authenticity
on all materials.

Phone: 914/497/7373
Fax: 914/496/6367
Web Site: www.momentsintime.com

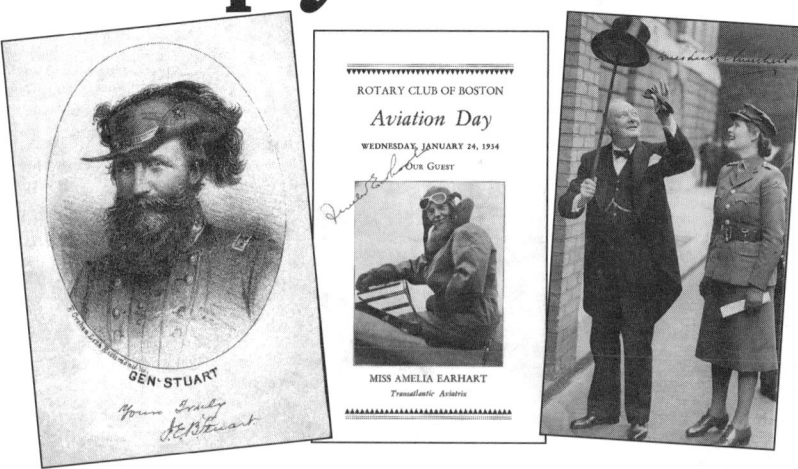

ORGANIZATIONS

IACC/IADA

The International Autograph Collectors Club (IACC) and Dealers Alliance (IADA) established in 1997 is the first autograph organization of its kind. The IACC/DA is a nonprofit organization whose primary purpose is to accurately educate the autograph community around the world and above all to ensure collectors that they will be dealing with IADA members who stand out amongst the rest in credentials, adhering to the hobby's strictest code of ethics.

The club is unique, as it's sole focus is on the field of autograph collecting.

Educational courses are given during our regional shows held around the United States. Notables in our field as Bill Butts, Gil Griggs, Christopher Jaeckel, Steve Koschal, Ken Laurence, Kevin Martin, Bill Miller, Kenneth Rendell, John Reznikoff and Daniel Weinberg have taught these complimentary courses. Each person taking the course receives a certificate of completion signed by the club president and instructor.

To join, collectors need only to fill out a simple application. Our membership dues are the lowest in the hobby.

Not every person who sells autographs can become an IADA member. An existing member must sponsor potential dealer members. They must also have at least two references that are thoroughly checked and in some cases their material is examined before the membership committee votes on their application.

Most importantly, the IACC/DA assures each member that should an ethics complaint arise against any member, that complaint will be acknowledged and acted upon by our ethics board.

Every LKDA member must offer their customers a Lifetime Guarantee with every item sold and a receipt at the time of purchase.

The club is the only one in existence today with a physical headquarters where all members are welcome to visit.

Each club member receives:
a) A membership card.
b) A copy of our Code of Ethics.
c) The IADA Dealers Directory, issued yearly, called by many "The Who's Who In Professional Autograph Dealers."
d) A major signature study. The 1998 study was on Gerald R. Ford, praised by the former president himself. The 1999 study was on Robert F. Kennedy, praised by the John F. Kennedy Library, Autograph Collector magazine and hundreds of collectors. The year 2000 study will be on Neil Armstrong.

Our club issues six magazines a year, The Eyes, Ears And Voice Of The Hobby sent free to our members. It contains up to date information on autographs, timely articles, signature studies and educational information. Each member may place a free 35-word ad in the Bulletin Board section. An unofficial pole ranked our magazine "The BEST educational and informative club magazine in the hobby."

Special private signings are held from which members have the opportunity to purchase autographs at below market prices.

All members have access to a large autograph reference library used by scholars, librarians, collectors and dealers from around the world.

The IACC/DA is the only organization that offers a club authenticating service. Items are examined by a minimum of three experts and a certificate is issued.

You will not simply be joining an autograph club; you will be enjoying an entire autograph experience! To become part of the IACC or IADA family, write for an application to:

IACC/DA
P.O.Box 848486
Hollywood, Florida 33084
USA
    or visit our website: www.iacc-da.com

PADA

The Professional Autograph Dealers Association, Inc. (PADA) is an organization of knowledgeable, experienced, and ethical dealers in historic autograph material. Established in 1995 by many of the nation's leading dealers, PADA is dedicated to maintaining the highest standards of business ethics, professionalism and service in the autograph industry. Its members seek to establish a marketplace for autographs, in which collectors can buy and sell with confidence and receive informed, accurate advice.

PADA has a stringent code of ethics to which its members must adhere. PADA dealers are required to provide a money-back guarantee of authenticity on all the autographs they sell. In addition, they must conscientiously authenticate and accurately describe all autographs; they must conduct their businesses honestly, fairly, and with integrity; and they must make every effort to promote customer satisfaction.

Membership in PADA is limited to dealers who abide by its code of ethics and who have demonstrated expertise and integrity in buying and selling autographs. All applicants for membership are carefully screened. Applicants must have been in the autograph business for at least three years; most PADA members have far more experience than this.

PADA also seeks to encourage interest in and appreciation of autographs. It maintains an informational web site (**www.padaweb.org**) where its complete code of ethics can be found. The site also presents a Monthly Catalogue, a new list every month of autographs offered by PADA members. The Monthly Catalogue provides an excellent sampling of the fine and varied autograph material handled by PADA dealers. The web site also lists all PADA members, along with their areas of special expertise, and it contains links to their individual e-mail addresses and web sites. Further expansion of PADA's web site is planned, including the addition of a library of information that will be helpful for autograph collectors.

Every April, PADA holds an autograph show in New York City that is considered by many the nation's premier autograph show. The organization is planning other shows across the country; details about all PADA shows can be found on its web site. PADA also hopes to issue publications on autographs that will be useful to collectors.

PADA dealers are an unrivaled source for autographs. Collectively, they offer a large and diverse assortment of material, in all price ranges. Among the specialties of PADA members are U.S. history, including Presidents and military leaders; world history; music; literature; the fine and performing arts; science and medicine; exploration; aviation; business and finance; and vintage theater and entertainment.

The members of PADA can provide collectors with other valuable services. With their many years of experience, they can answer questions about autograph collecting and offer advice on all aspects of the field. They can discuss proper methods for storing and displaying autographs and can help locate an expert conservator, when one is needed. Individual members of PADA offer authentication services and appraisals of autographs. They can act as agents for collectors and libraries at auctions.

PADA dealers also represent a significant market for purchasing autographs, whether single items or entire collections. They buy autographs outright, offering a fair price and immediate payment. PADA dealers can also take autographs on consignment, acting as agent for their sale. PADA's code of ethics requires members to adhere to the highest professional standards when they are buying autographs, assuring the seller of courteous and honest treatment.

Whether you are buying or selling autographs, if you do business with a PADA member, you can be sure that you are dealing with a reliable individual who has a commitment to quality, service and integrity. PADA dealers look forward to sharing with you the excitement and rewards of autograph collecting and helping you find the autographs that you will treasure for years to come.

For a free brochure and membership directory, write to:
The Professional Autograph Dealers Association, Inc.
P.O. Box 1729-A, Murray Hill Station
New York, NY 10156
Visit our web site: **www.padaweb.org**

For the only guarantee you will ever need, look for the PADA logo.

UACC

The Universal Autograph Collectors Club, Inc. (UACC) is the world's largest organization for autograph collectors with over 2000 members in over 27 countries. Founded in 1965, the UACC is a federally approved non-profit organization whose purpose is to educate memebers and the public about all aspects of autograph collecting through its publications, shows, conventions and seminars. Unlike other organizations the UACC Executive Board is not made up of dealers but collectors. They are elected by the membership.

By joining the UACC, you will receive our renowned 64-page bimonthly journal, *The Pen and Quill*, which features articles and news on autographs in all areas, including our famous signature studies (articles on authentic, secretarial, autopen, rubber-stamped, facsimile and forged signatures). As well as interesting historical foot notes using collector's documents and stories of in person encounters with the celebrities of the time. This information gives the collector better information in order to make decisions in purchasing good quality material.

To this end the UACC also boasts of the largest Autograph Dealer's registry. Known as UACC Registered Dealers. These 148 individuals or companies have provided information regarding their business for publication including how long they have been involved in the field and if they have any ethics violations. This information is posted on the UACC website at www.uacc.org along with other information important for you to know about each dealer. These dealers are the leaders in the field of autographs and as such fully support the UACC and its goals. We give a Distinguished Dealer Award to one of our dealers each year that excels in service to the industry.

Speaking of the web, the UACC was the first organization to establish a fully interactive website which includes: Autograph news, membership information, Registered Dealer information, the Hall of Shame, Constitution and Code of Ethics, Show schedules and more.

The UACC was also the first organization to institute a Code of Ethics that each member agrees to abide as a condition of membership. Our code is the toughest in the industry and has resolved over 95% of teh complaints filed by the membership. Our extensive ethics files have been used and applauded by numerous law enforcement agencies. Our active Ethics Board works for the protection of the membership.

Each year the UACC gives out a number of awards to individuals that have given of themselves each year for the betterment of the hobby. These include literary awards, collector of the year awards, the president's quality award, and the coveted UACC Distinguished Service Award.

Our members are also given FREE classified ads in our journal as well as opportunities to purchase uncommon autographic material and reference works at affordable prices. There is also our annual auction which benefits the membership.

We sponsor shows around the United States and in Engalnd as well as a yearly convention and are the only organization which accepts Visa and Mastercard for membership or anything elsefor that matter.

Our best resource is our membership. The combined knowledge and experience when shared makes the UACC the best organization for the informed collector.

To learn more about the UACC, send your requests for a brochure and membership information to :

Dept AC
UACC
PO Box 6181
Washington, DC 20044-6181.

OR by visiting our website at **www.uacc.org**.
We hope you will join our universe of fellow collectors soon.

TABLE OF CONTENTS

TABLE OF CONTENTS

Illustrations in Alphabetical Order

HOW TO USE THIS GUIDE

Please read and understand the next couple of pages so you get the most out of using this guide.

CONTENT is the single most important factor after condition to determining value of an item autographed and CONTENT applies to photographs, letters, documents and even in some rare cases, signatures.

Content varies from item to item so it would be inaccurate to try and quantify it in a price guide so we have not tried !

Instead, in each of our fields we have given you the ACTUAL accurate CURRENT recorded average price that the signed piece goes for with NO regard to content.

What exactly does this mean ?

Let's say for example you are looking to buy a George Reeves signed photograph and you look in a dealers catalog and see a lovely 8x10 signed photograph in character as Superman, on of his most famous roles, offered for $2,500.

You then pull out our trusty guide only to find the George Reeves listing for a signed photograph is $1,500...Which is more accurate? The dealer or us?

The answer is BOTH of us are dead on accurate..How?

Our guide lists average, routinely encountered NON CONTENT items in the marketplace. In the case of signed photographs our prices represent an 8x10 black and white signed PORTRAIT like was commonly signed for fans BUT if the star wrote something extraordinary or the image was 11x14 not 8x10 or the image was of their "Signature role" that would constitute CONTENT and be worth more.

Content pieces are the best to buy if you can afford them and should be bought when encountered because they won't last long in the hot market of today !

The same would be true in our document section with a signed typed letter or document concerning a routine invitation, thank you note, tax document etc. being the items we have averaged and placed in our guide under that heading. But, if the document using the above example, were Reeves original contract to play Superman you would throw the guide out the window and hope and pray you can optain the piece before anyone else calls the dealer! A one of a kind item by definition, may never come your way again..and on such items using a price guide of past averages would be pointless.

In our remarks column we have listed career highlights and other comments that will help you determine what may constitute content in that persons life. Under Einstein we list that he was know obviously for his physics theories for one example and a note signed E=MC2 would be worth more than a full letter declining a dinner invitation.

When in doubt, just buy what you like..that way even if it does not apreciate in value it will still always be appreciated - by you !

Kevin Martin

The next time you purchase that wonderful autograph album ... remember that some of the covers are collectable as well.
These are some examples of autograph album covers (usually measuring around 4"x5")

for those of you new to the hobby .. when a dealer says he has a signed album page , he is referring to a page out of a book like the ones pictured here

THE STATE OF OUR INDUSTRY
by Bill Miller & Darrell Talbert

Some People may bristle at our using the term "industry" to describe the hobby of autograph collecting, but as we enter the Millennium and look back over the past ten years, the growth and activity can only be described by using that term.

Collecting autographs has been a favorite pastime and hobby for many, many decades. The last decade, however, has seen a relatively passive hobby springboard into a burgeoning industry, robust with growth, increased values and new technology.

Autograph collecting is unlike the pursuit of any other hobby. Whether you write to celebrities requesting a free autograph or spend hundreds, thousands, or even hundreds of thousands of dollars in your pursuit, the quest is exciting, invigorating and rewarding. Also unlike any other hobby, the autograph collector is "connected" to his or her hero. Where else can you own a letter written by Richard Nixon lamenting the agony of resigning the highest office in our land; or a letter written by Bill Clinton thanking a supporter for his help in electing him to the highest office in the country? No other area of collecting offers such personal, insightful glimpses into the personalities of times present and past.

The industry has grown in all areas, whether it is historical, space, sports or entertainment genres. Prices have steadily increased as a result of new collectors entering the market resulting in competition for material. Full time dealers have increased in numbers tenfold over the past decade. Internet sales and auctions of autographs have further served to expand the market.

Being the Publishers of Autograph Collector magazine allows us unique perspective on this industry. We are privileged to have daily contact with many of the world's finest dealers. These ladies and gentlemen form the backbone of our industry and keep us apprised of all the latest events and trends as they occur. Some operate auction houses, others sell their own material, but when you wrap them all up, they comprise a wealth of knowledge and expertise.

UACC The past decade has also seen the emergence of several new autograph clubs and organizations. In the beginning there was The Manuscript Society and the UACC (Universal Autograph Collector's Club). These two organizations serve thousands of collectors and dealers from around the world. Organizations formed in the past few years include the IACC/IADA (International Autograph Collector's Club and Dealer's Association) and PADA (Professional Autograph Dealer's Association). We're pleased to see all these clubs and organizations formed! They help to educate collectors on the hobby and protect them from the pitfalls therein. You can find information on each of these groups on the pages of this book. We encourage you to support them; they rely on hard-working volunteers and dues to exist.

The Internet has had a major impact on our industry. For the first time, thousands of autographs are being sold by individuals to other individuals. The new buzzwords are "person to person" auctions. What that basically means is that people are trading among themselves, in vast numbers, without the dealer as middleman. While this certainly hasn't put many dealers out of business, it has had a relatively significant impact on many. There are good and bad points to these so-called person to person transactions. The first and most obvious potential benefit is that you might bypass a dealer markup on material. The downside is that by bypassing the dealer, you may have no recourse if you are unhappy with your purchase. What if a well-meaning person in Anytown, Iowa sells you a forgery? You may have no recourse when compared to the recourse afforded you when you have a problem with a known, respected autograph dealer. There have been many reported instances of forgeries being prolific on the Internet; we're not making any sort of judgment call with respect to any of the major auction houses. All we will say is what we've always said: "Buy material only from known, tried-and-true reputable people." Saving a few bucks on an autograph is worthless if you end up with something that is not genuine. As the saying goes: "if the deal seems to good to be true, it probably is..."

The good news is that there are lots of safe ways to collect! If you have dealers who have helped you build your collection and have treated you fairly, support them by continuing to purchase good, fairly priced material they offer you. When bidding in Internet auctions, find out who the seller is. Ask for references and check them out. Any reputable individual or dealer will be more than happy to provide their credentials as well as references. Make sure that every dealer you buy from offers a written, lifetime guarantee of authenticity. If the dealer offers a third-party authentication, insist on a written guarantee from the dealer as well. That's double protection in case anything happens down the line.

So, what's in store for our industry in the coming years? I believe we'll see the hobby continue to grow. Based on all the new collectors and the increased demand for good material, I predict that prices will continue to rise. I also predict a shakeout of person-to-person auctions on the Internet. Like any other industry, the good people will remain on top; the bad will eventually  fade into oblivion. That's just the way it goes, and it's a natural progression in any business.

In the meantime, have fun collecting! Continue to build a collection that has meaning, breadth and scope. The satisfaction of hunting down that long-awaited, special prize offers satisfaction beyond description — and we know; our quest continues each and every day!

Bill Miller
Darrell Talbert
Odyssey Publications

AUTOGRAPH TREASURES OF THE SPACE PROGRAM

by David Frohman

Since the dawn of time, mankind dreamed of one day eloping with the star-filled sky, and departing their Earthly cradle for the cosmos. Indeed, some even thought it possible that Man one day might actually stand on the Moon!

Then, in 1961, thousands of years of dreaming abruptly ended, as two great nations extended their desperate earthbound struggle heavenward, in a frantic race to be the first to plant their flag on the Moon.

What followed, of course, is well known. Barely eight years after John Kennedy tossed down the gauntlet for our nation to conquer the Moon, Neil Armstrong and Buzz Aldrin landed their frail Lunar Module on the dusty Sea of Tranquility, and nothing was ever quite the same again!

As President of Peachstate Historical Consulting, I specialize in obtaining the finest authentic autographs, and artifacts, of the pioneer Mercury, Gemini and Apollo Programs for our clients. I consider these three programs to be central to the golden age of space exploration.

However, I am often asked why I focus with such devotion on what some consider to be a fringe area of history. I usually answer as follows: "Consider, for a moment, the quantum leap made over the course of eleven short years. It began in 1961 with Alan Shepard's fifteen-minute attempt to touch the edge of space, and ending in 1972 as Gene Cernan and Harrison Schmidt actually lived on the moon for three long days!"

Apollo 8 crew-signed earthrise photograph

In the dash for the Moon, technology and resources (the miniaturization of the computer, for example) swiftly evolved, forever changing our world. As you explore the many areas within this invaluable guide, ask yourself a basic question: is there any other field of endeavor, spanning the myriad of human history reflected by the names within these pages, which so radically changed our species in the historical heartbeat of <u>one</u> decade?

Consider for a moment the classic Earthrise photo, photographed and beautifully signed by the first three Homo Sapiens to ever exchange the gravitational field of one world for another: Jim Lovell, Frank Borman and Bill Anders.

I would argue that "Earthrise" is the most important and meaningful, photograph ever taken, and alone justified the entire cost of the space program!

The incredible 1968 Christmastime journey of Apollo 8, our first manned Lunar flight, allowed <u>all</u> mankind to gaze back from afar, for the <u>first</u> time, and see our delicate blue home, suspended in an eternal night!

In short, "Earthrise" suggested a world free of national boundaries, war, or famine. What person would not be moved by this image? And how much more so, I wonder, when it bears the personal autographs of the three representatives of all mankind, captured for the ages in delicate strokes of ink upon mankind's first self-portrait!

Today, the value of an Apollo 8 piece bearing all three crewmembers signatures has risen to nearly $1,000.00, due to Bill Anders reluctance to sign autographs.

Another "stellar" group of voyagers and probably the most famous crew of all time: namely, Apollo 11's Neil Armstrong, Buzz Aldrin, and Michael Collins. Incidentally, many think that skill alone predetermined their historic roles.

Not at all ... in fact, Frank Borman was originally offered the chance to be first on the moon after Gus Grissom's death, but turned the opportunity down. Pete Conrad was then scheduled to be first on the Moon during Apollo 12. However, everything went so well on the preceding flights that the first landing was bumped up one flight, from Apollo 12 to Apollo 11. And which crew was <u>already</u> scheduled in rotation for that flight? You guessed it ...

Apollo 11 crew-signed photograph

Now consider the classic Apollo 11 crew-signed photograph illustrated here. Given Peachstate has sold similar items for $1250.00 - $1500.00 during the past few years, who could have imagined another example bringing $11,500.00 at the September, 1999 Christies Space Auction in New York. Or, a photograph of the Earth, inscribed by Armstrong to a Russian Space Leader, fetching $21,000.00. What pricing conclusions should we infer from these and numerous other huge price increases?

I believe they suggest the pent-up enthusiasm within the <u>general</u> public for American space material, when presented to them for the first time by a <u>mainstream</u> auction house.

Is $11,500.00 a typical price for an Apollo 11 crew-signed photograph? Of course not ... but in the same light, given the untapped enthusiasm I witnessed in the Christies audience, is $1500.00 also realistic anymore? Probably not....

And what of Neil Armstrong? In my article entitled *The Autograph Legacy of Neil Armstrong*, published in the December, 1998 issue of Autograph Collector magazine, I drew a pricing analogy between the autographs of Babe Ruth and Neil Armstrong.

My analogy was drawn at a time when signed 8x10 spacesuit portraits of Armstrong were selling for $100.00, and baseballs signed by Babe Ruth for approximately $3500.00.

Neil Armstrong signed spacesuit portrait

My thinking suggested that numerous parallels exist between the signing histories of Armstrong and Ruth. Both signed freely, and in quantity, during their lifetimes, and each enjoys the best name recognition in their respective fields, along with sustained demand among collectors.

However, compared to space, sports collecting is a fully mature area, perhaps by some fifty years. I thus pondered the possibility that the value of Armstrong's signature might, one day, equal that of Babe Ruth, once space evolved out of its infancy, and reached similar levels of collecting maturity and acceptance.

Since my article appeared, barely over a year ago, the value of that generic Armstrong 8x10 has skyrocket, no pun intended, from $100.00 to over $1,000.00! Further, space artifacts autographed by Armstrong (such as a signed Apollo 11 Final Flight Plan) have sold independently of the Christies sale for over $5,000.00! When I made my pricing projection in 1998, I did not intend, or expect, that my words would be realized within 12 short months!

Other generic, but extremely historic items, such as the Apollo crew-signed Insurance Covers, are also seeing rapid collector appreciation of their historic worth. We are now seeing prices for Apollo 11 covers topping $2,000.00; and covers from later missions, such as

An official Apollo 12 Insurance Cover.

Apollo 12, are now bringing over $500.00!

Recently, all eyes were on Superior Auction Galleries, as they held their semi-annual space auction in late October 1999, to see whether Christie's prices would hold.

Based on the initial sales results, the answer seems to be that prices have returned to strong, but pre-Christies, levels. However, exceptions did occur. An 8x10 inch color signed, but uninscribed, spacesuit portrait of Neil Armstrong brought nearly $2,000.00, while a set of three 8x10s of Armstrong, Aldrin and Collins, each with uninscribed signatures, brought nearly $5,000.00!

Now some other musings....

Throughout recorded history, then have been tens of thousands of Kings, Presidents, Writers, Artists, Musicians, and other notables who have come and gone. A casual glance through this guidebook will confirm that. However, out of this myriad of notables, and the tens of billions of Human beings who have ever lived, only twenty-four have ever flown to the Moon, and of them, only <u>twelve</u> have ever stood on its surface!

In my 1997 Autograph Collector Magazine article *Collecting the 12*

A photograph of the Moon, signed by eight moonwalkers

Apollo Moonwalkers, I stressed the extremely collectable nature of these twelve signatures as a distinct, and desirable, set unto themselves, much as collectors might strive to collect all the signatures of the signers of the Declaration of Independence.

However, I emphasized to my readers that the accomplishment of these twelve human beings transcends all national boundaries, for they stood on another world as representatives of ALL mankind.

Today, I see strong <u>worldwide</u> demand for their material, and my guess is this trend may skyrocket in coming years, as the rest of the world matures in wealth, sophistication, and an appreciation of their wonderful accomplishment.

Today, you might have to pay upwards of $2800.00 for a complete 8x10 set of all twelve, pictured on the Moon, if one could even find them! For example, try finding a signed uninscribed photograph of the most accomplished astronaut of all time, John Young, saluting the flag while leaping two feet off the ground on the Moon in one-sixth gravity on Apollo 16. If you have one, count yourself some $800.00 richer!

However, as much as collectors of the Declaration's Signers also treasure artifacts and letters of each individual signer, especially those with content, the same holds true for letters and artifacts of the Moonwalkers.

For example, I believe that a handwritten narration by Moonwalker Charlie Duke, narrating his voyage to the Moon, differs little from a handwritten letter by John Hancock, narrating the events leading to the Declaration of independence!

Both are extremely rare, and discuss events of enormous historic proportion, yet remain separated by a span of two centuries. Those two centuries of collecting maturity gives the Hancock a $100,000.00 price tag, versus $500.00 for the Duke.

A hand-written narration by moonwalker Charlie Duke, of his voyage to the Moon

However, it is interesting to ponder the pricing possibilities: As space collecting now matures at an ever-increasing pace, and more collectors chasing down fewer available quality space items.

Another area of space collectibles with an autograph connection, which I believe to be greatly undervalued, are artifacts flown in space (or to the Moon) bearing official handwritten certifications by the astronaut who flew them.

Items such as these combine the best of several worlds (no pun intended).

First, they belong to the relatively infinitesimal amount of precious material ever flown into space, much less to another world. I believe collectors, and the public at large, will eventually recognize that human artifacts flown to Lunar orbit, or the Moon's surface, are among the most valuable items on our entire planet, with worldwide appeal.

I suspect, however, that when that day arrives, institutions or collectors with unlimited funds will have absorbed much of the material now available!

However, due to the obvious concern over authenticity of flown mate-

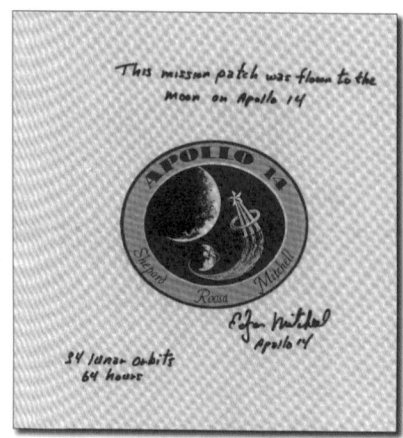

An official astronaut flight-certified Apollo 14 mission emblem.

rial, nothing transforms a simple mission patch from a five-dollar piece of Beta Cloth into a $4000.00 artifact like a simple, but critical, flight-certification by the astronaut who personally carried it to the Moon handwritten on it!

Let me end my discussion of the Moonwalkers with this thought. Of the twelve Moonwalkers, only nine remain with us today. Consider, then, that out of a current world population of six billion, only nine men presently live on our planet who can <u>still</u> describe to you, <u>firsthand</u>, the experience of strolling across the surface of another world!

Eventually, in years to come, there will be only one left among us ....

In conclusion, I believe that collecting space-related autographs and artifacts can be an endlessly fascinating, challenging and rewarding pastime. However, I would also encourage you to invest your hard-earned collecting budget <u>first</u> and foremost in educational reference material, before making sizeable purchases. One of the finest works, to which I am also a contributor, is *Relics of the Space Race*, by Russ Still, now in its second edition.

I would also suggest acquiring back issues of the bi-annual Superior Space Auction Catalogs, with prices realized, to acquaint yourself both with the variety of material obtainable, and price trends. Acquiring an astronaut autopen template set, to help detect machine-generated signatures, would also be a wise investment. Lastly, I urge you to make your space purchases from dealers, who believe in backing up your purchase with an unconditional money-guarantee of authenticity.

I believe that, despite the stirrings of recent price increases, many wonderful buys still exist, and I urge you to begin exploring this truly fascinating, and historic, area today. If current pricing trends continue, we may <u>all</u> look back twenty years from now, and long for the "good-old days"!

Ad Astra!

David Frohman is the President of Peachstate Historical Consulting, Inc. of Atlanta, Georgia, and can be reached, toll-free, at (888) 644-7322, or via e-mail at dfrohman@mindspring.com, and is an advertiser in this price guide.

WHY COLLECT THE CIVIL WAR

By Gil Griggs

Indeed, why does the Civil War remain the hot category in autograph collecting? Why does R. E. Lee, "Stonewall" Jackson and J.E.B. Stuart remain the most sought-after signature on documents and letters? Even CDV's, signed or unsigned, remain on this short list of autographs.

William Barry signature

From the red clay hills of Georgia to the fishing villages of Maine; from Boston Brahmins to wild and woolly cowboys of Texas, they all were involved; they all were passionate as never before and such as may never be again.

Over the last five years in our auction business, we participated in the major Civil War shows throughout the country. When we were in Gettysburg people would ask us about the Pennsylvania Bucktails. In Charleston, SC, they would ask about the Confederate Palmetto. In Nashville we heard, "My grandfather rode with Nathan Bedford Forrest." In Mansfield, "Do you have anything from the 143'd Ohio, Company B? My Grandfather's brother was with them all during the war... What do you have from the Ohio regiments?" In Richmond, we heard, "N4y father told me stories of his father who was in Richmond during the War and once saw General Lee astride his beloved horse, Traveler, and what a grand sight that was!"

Even though we are in the year 2000, the deeds of 1861 to 1865 still thrill us. Look at the success of Ken Bums' documentary and Ted Turner's Gettysburg. We will never forget the pride and the passion. And the issues the North and South fought to resolve are still with us today... too much Federal government, not enough States' rights. Does the Federal government have a right to inflict their will on an issue that the people of a State do not wish? We are still experiencing the bitter passions ignited by the slavery question, and the ramifications of the abolished institution still plague us to this day.

We have to go back to when this great country was being formed, the 13 original colonies who declared themselves independent of England and everyone else. Before the Southern colonies would sign the Declaration of Independence, several lines had to be struck on the position of slavery. The South with their agricultural society felt the institution was key to their way of life. The North led by John Adams and Ben Franklin was opposed to slavery. Therefore a compromise was achieved by deleting the abolition of slavery from the Declaration. Everyone signed the document, including the Southerners.

The Union held together. Over the next 50 years the great debates were enjoined. Daniel Webster of Massachusetts, advocate for the North, John Calhoun of South Carolina, advocate for the South, and Henry Clay of Kentucky, the "great compromiser" rose to national leadership. When they died, there was no one to take their place.

The Republican Party was formed in the North and fielded John Fremont as their first candidate for President of the United States. He nearly won in 1856. In 1860 the new party brought Abraham Lincoln, a man of imposing physical strength and intelligence, but also possessing great strength of character. With great resolve and purpose, he struggled to keep the Union undivided. He was to be tested to the utmost, and his face mirrored the strain month by month and year by year. A true martyr he gave his life for his cause, the preservation of the Union. However, I believe he could have prevented the war. After Fort Sumter fell, if time had been taken to negotiate and let cooler heads prevail, Lincoln might not have called up 75,000 troops as his first act as President. This action and this action alone brought into the Confederacy the wavering States of Virginia and North Carolina. Where would the Confederacy be without these two pivotal States? How far could they go without them? His decision to fire on Fort Sumter of course ignited new passion and strengthened resolve on both sides. The first blood shed on the streets of Baltimore and the mobilizing of troops on both sides sealed the fate of the nation. There was no more compromise.

Beauregard signed CDV

DID THE SOUTH HAVE THE RIGHT TO SECEDE?

In 1866 representatives from every State, including the defeated South, enacted a law that the United States was indivisible. That question was closed forever. But what was the law in 1860? Did each State have a right to leave the Union? With respect to Constitutional law, James Madison often called the architect of the Constitution, was very worried that the northern most states might leave the Union over the shipping embargo with England that had seriously impacted their trade revenue and threatened to rejoin the mother country. Hence the term was coined "New England." Madison knew it was within their rights to leave the Union. If the Northern states had the right to leave the Union, then the precedent would be set for other States to leave if they so desired. In 1860, the question of slavery would be coming to a close. In the next 25 years, most historians agree it would eventually have been abolished as the industrial age overtook the South.

THE WAR BETWEEN THE STATES

This was not a "civil war." The definition of a civil war is that two groups are in conflict for the control of one country. Southern historian Jim Hayes has long led a crusade in naming the war correctly. He freely circulates a printed card, "The Congressional Record of March 2, 1928," which reports Senate Joint Resolution No. 41 wherein Congress recognized the title "War Between the States as proper..."

As to the war itself, the North had all the advantages: more men, more artillery, more rifles, more ships, more factories, more ... more ... more. And a great Yankee pride in getting the job done. European immigrants from Ireland, Scotland and Germany thought the idea of a Union was a cause worth fighting and for which they were willing to lay down their lives.

The South had pride, spirit and a willingness to defend their homes to the last. They also had great leadership: R. E. Lee, T. J. Jackson, J.E.B. Stuart, James Longstreet, A. P. Hill, Pierre Beauregard, Nathan Bedford Forrest, Albert Sydney Johnson, Joe Wheeler and Joe Johnson. These men led by example. In most cases they were outnumbered. Their leadership, zeal and courage won many battles.

John S. Mosby signature

Not until Lincoln got his generals effectively in place did it spell the end for the South Grant, Sherman, and Sheridan. Never was there a more patriotic time. Flags, songs, and newspapers on both sides proclaimed the righteousness of their cause. This passion has never been equaled, and both the North and South were confident they had God on their side. "The Battle Hymn of the Republic" is still a popular spiritual today. The anthem of the South was not "Dixie" even though it was popular. Indeed, the anthem of the Confederacy was "God Save the South."

Most people at that time thought the war would be over within 90 days. However, there were a couple of leaders on both sides who knew it would be a long and bloody affair. W. T. Sherman knew the South would fight and fight well. He believed that in order to win, the war must be waged not only by the destruction of the their army, but also by the destruction of the their cities, roads and trains, that war must be waged against the civilian population so that their will to fight be destroyed. James Longstreet also knew it would be a long war. He knew that with the improvements in rifles and artillery, the man on the defense would be given an edge. No longer would the great Napoleonic attacks be effective. This was dramatically demonstrated at Gettysburg. In all, there were 600,000 casualties out of a country of 30 million. It seemed that everybody lost someone in that tragic conflict,

Philip H. Sheridan signature

COLLECTING THE CIVIL WAR

Innumerable collectors gather everything connected with the war. Autographs of course, but also CDVs, weaponry, camp equipment, letters of obscure soldiers who mention a battle or skirmish, even mundane camp life; also uniforms and buttons, sutler money, the PX script of that time, song sheets and broadsides, even postwar reunion ribbons. As a rule, the Confederate items are three times more expensive- a signature of Lieutenant General "Stonewall" Jackson is ten times more than Lieutenant General James Longstreet is. Jackson was killed in 1862 but Longstreet lived into the next century. An amusing incident occurred in one of our first auctions that well illustrates this point. We offered a pair of US spurs with regimental marks estimated at $100 - $150. They sold at $125. After the auction we received the check and along with it a very strange letter. The buyer informed us that the US markings were spurious. They had been added during the previous year, and there were several other faults. My obvious question to the apparently knowledgeable buyer when I called him was "Why pay for them instead of returning them for a full refund as our lifetime guarantee policy stipulates?" He told me that in fact the spurs were not US but Confederate and worth about five times the sale price. This only goes to prove that in the Civil War collectibles field, as any other, knowledge is everything. My only suggestion is to know the dealer or auctioneer with whom you do business.

William T. Sherman signature

Remember the old joke, "Save your Confederate money; the South will rise again." Well, Confederate denominations right now are higher than current US denominations. A Confederate $1,000 note sold for $15,000 in one of our earlier auctions. The moth eaten uniform of an obscure Confederate colonel with a rusty old sword sold for $23,500. Clearly, the South has risen again.

Don't look for Civil War items to come down in price. It's not going to happen.

There is no reason why such collectibles command such prices or why they will remain high except for the fact that the Civil War was our "American" war. Its seeds were sown in the compromises of the Declaration of Independence and continued to grow over the next 50 years. The Civil War was fought with brother against brother. It was personal then and is personal today. Issues debated then still resonate to this day. This great American conflict still ignites passions like no other.

Happy Hunting for the War Between the States.

Gil Griggs is the owner of "Signature House" an autograph auction company who publishes frequent auction catalogs. "Signature House" is an advertiser in this price guide.

SUPREME COURT CHIEF JUSTICES & ASSOCIATE JUSTICES

by Cordelia Platt

Why this category? These people have been involved with decisions concerning all of us since the Judiciary Act passed by congress on September 24 1789. The first court was made up of one chief justice and five associates. In 1807 the membership was increased to seven, in 1837 increased to nine, in 1863 to ten. Three years later the membership was decreased to seven, but in 1869 it was again raised to nine where it has remained until this day. The tenure of a Supreme Court justice is for life and one can only be expelled by impeachment and conviction. This is covered in the Constitution Article II, Section 4. Only one justice, Samuel Chase, was impeached, and later acquitted. Abe Fortas was accused of having conflicting interests and then resigned due to public pressure.

It is fascinating to read how it all works, why certain cases come to their attention and in some instances their profound decisions astonish us. But a most important fact is written in the 14th Amendment "Nor shall any state deprive any person of life, liberty, or property, without due process of law.

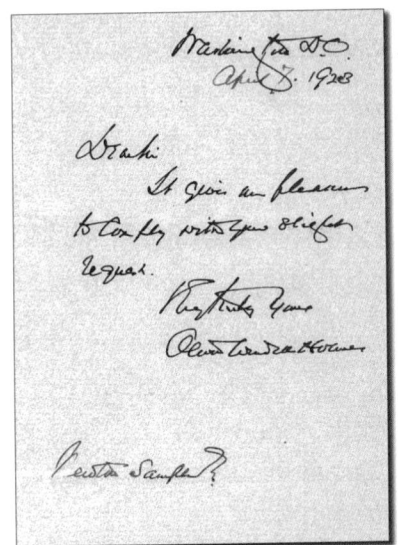

Oliver W. Holmes
Handwritten Signed Letter
(ALS)

Another reason to collect this category is that most of the justices signatures are still quite reasonably priced, especially those of the 20th century. The early justices, of course, are rare and somewhat expensive. In some instances one must be aware that there were men living at the same time with the same name, including fathers and sons. James Iredell is a particularly difficult signature to find. A clip of his would retail for at least $400, but the autograph of his son, who became a congressman, is much less. Their writing is quite similar and it takes a lot of work to make sure you have the one you want. There are some clipped signatures available due to careless collecting of our ancestors, who obviously saved the signatures cut from letters and documents. This happened quite frequently. Another reason that early signatures are scarce is that many justices were prominent in other fields. Collectors would tend to place their signed items in other categories and they would have a way of becoming lost in large collections. In many instances, upon the death of a collector, the collections were donated to museums and the justice signatures were buried even deeper.

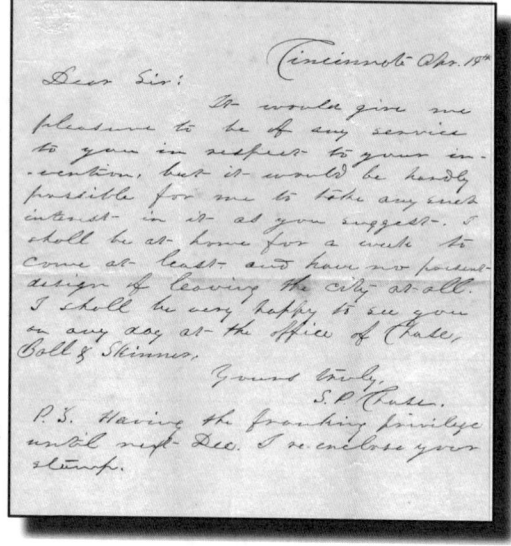

Salmon P. Chase
Handwritten Signed Letter
(ALS)

When collecting the 19th and 20th century justices, we would recommend trying to get the signatures on imprinted supreme court card or supreme court stationary. A letter all in the hand of the justice on Supreme court letterhead would be wonderful and of course the best would be a handwritten letter with content. This is seldom seen. Collectors mostly stick to collecting the signed Sup.Ct.Cards. Also the government prints small biographical booklets about our justices with a small picture next to the bio. Sometimes we can find one or more signatures on the pamphlets. Also a favorite is a picture of any complete court signed by each member. Through the years we have handled a few of these and they are never inexpensive- usually starting at $1,200.00 Most often found are the Warren Court, the Burger Court and the Rehnquist Court. Many engravings and photographs are available of supreme court justices and these lend themselves nicely to creating a matted ensemble.

As in most historical collectibles a lot of enjoyment is in the research. Most supreme court justices led very interesting lives prior to their appointments and you will enjoy studying their lives. A good biographical reference is a publication of the *Commission on the Bicentennial of the United States Constitution,* entitled *The Supreme Court of the United States: Its Beginnings and Its Justices 1790-1991.* Good Luck!

Cordelia Platt founded Cordelia and Tom Platt Autographs and currently resides in Florida where they have a gallery that is open by appointment only.

The following list includes all the justices who have served on the Supreme Court and their dates in office

Henry Baldwin (1830-1846)
Phillip P. Boarbour (1836-1841)
Hugo L. Black (1937-1972)
Harry A Blackmun (1970-1994)
John Blair (1789-1796)
Samuel Blatchford (1882-1894)
Joseph P. Bradley (1869-1892)
Louis D. Brandeis (1916-1939)
William J. Brennan (1956-1990)
David J. Brewer (1889-1910)
Stephen Breyer (1994-Present)
Henry B. Brown (1890-1906)
Warren E. Burger (1969-1986)
Harold H. Burton (1945-1958)
Pierce Butler (1922-1940)
James F. Byrnes (1941-1943)
John A Campbell (1853-1862)
Benjamin N. Cardozo (1932-1939)
John Catron (1837-1865)
Salmon P. Chase (1796-1811)
Samuel Chase (1796-1811)
Tom C. Clark (1949-1967)
John H. Clarke (1916-1922)
Nathan Clifford (1885-1881)
Benjamine R. Curtis (1853-1858)
Peter V. Daniel (1841-1862)
David Davis (1862-1898)
William R. Day (1903-1922)
William O. Douglas (1939-1975)
Gabriel Duvall (1811-1836)
Oliver Ellsworth (1796-1800)
Stephe J. Field (1863-1897)
Abe Fortas (1965-1970)
Felix Frankfurter (1939-1962)
Melville W. Fuller (1888-1910)
Ruth Bader Ginsburg (1993-Present)
Arthur J. Goldberg (1962-1965)
Horace Gray (1881-1902)
Robert C. Grier (1846-1870)
John M. Harlan (1877-1912)
John M. Harlan II (1955-1972)
Oliver W. Holmes (1902-1932)
Charles E. Hughes (1910-1916,
                   1930-1941)
James Irdell (1790-1799)
Howell E. Jackson (1893-1895)
Robert H. Jackson (1941-1955)
John Jay (1789-1795)
Thomas Johnson (1791-1793)
William Johnson (1804-1835)
Anthony M. Kennedy (1988-Present)
Lucius Q.C. Lamar (1888-1893)
Joseph R. Lamar, J (1910-1916)
Brockholst Livingston (1806-1823)
Horace H. Lurton (1909-1914)

John Marshall (1801-1836)
Thurgood Marshall (1967-1991)
Stanley Mathews (1881-1889)
Joseph McKenna (1889-1825)
John McKinley (1837-1853)
John McLean (1829-1862)
James C. McReynolds (1914-1941)
Samuel F. Miller (1862-1890)
Sherman Minton (1949-1956)
William H. Moody (1906-1910)
Alfred Moore (1799-1804)
Frank Murphy (1940-1949)
Samuel Nelson (1845-1872)
Sandra Day O'Connor (1981-Present)
William Paterson (1793-1806)
Rufus W. Peckham (1895-1909)
Mahlon Pitney (1912-1923)
Lewis F. Powell (1972-1988)
Stanley F Reed (1938-1957)
William H. Rehnquist (1972-Present)
Owen J. Roberts (1930-1945)
John Rutledge (1789-1791)
Wiley B. Rutledge (1943-1949)
Edward T. Sanford (1923-1930)
Antoin Scalia (1986-Present)
George Shirras, Jr. (1892-1903)
John P. Stevens (1975-Present)
David Souter (1990-Presnet)
Potter Stewart (1958-1981)
Harlan F. Stone (1925-1946)
Joseph Story (1811-1845)
William Strong (1870-1880)
George Sutherland (1922-1938)
Noah H. Swayne (1862-1881)
William H. Taft (1921-1930)
Roger B. Taney (1991-Present)
Smith Thompson (1823-1845)
Thomas Todd (1807-1826)
Robert Trimble (1826-1829)
Willis Van Devanter (1910-1937)
Fred M.. Vinson (1946-1953)
Morrison R. Waite (1874-1888)
Earl Warren (1953-1969)
Bushrod Washington (1798-1830)
James M. Wayne (1835-1867)
Byron R. White (1962-1993)
Edward D. White (1894-1921)
Charles E. Whittaker (1957-1962)
James Wilson (1789-1798)
Levi Woodbury (1845-1853)
William B. Woods (1880-1888)

TIPS ON FINDING AUTOGRAPHS
by Mark Vardakis

In past articles and books that cover the subject of autograph collecting, many fine authors have suggested writing a celebrity for an in the mail response, arranging to meet your favorite celebrity in person or by buying the autographed items from a reputable dealer or auction house but, there are even more ways to find autographed material if you look a little harder.

Wile attending a flea market many years ago, I found a beautiful engraved Providence municipal bond signed by the Mayor in 1898. The dealer told me he found the piece in a trash can behind the Providence City Hall. I followed up his story by actually visiting the City archivist who confirmed that the city was cleaning out a lot of what they felt was "junk" paper and proceeded to take me to a room that still contained several more boxes of the bonds. When I suggested that I wanted to buy them he seemed shocked that I would pay real money for the bonds. After a short negotiation I purchased all of them and used them over the years as trade material with other collectors. Not only had the flea market single bond led me to five boxes more of them but as I was purchasing the bonds the city archivist told me that he heard that the City library was also disposing of some of some unwanted items. I searched therough crates of discarded library books finding many that contained excellent old engravings that I could use to matt signatures with and to top it all off I even found an old Bible signed by Daniel Webster.

While many look toward dealer auctions as I mentioned before there are other auctions to think of as well. Rhode Island, like many states, holds an annual auction of unclaimed safety box material at which over the years I have found such incredible pieces as a George Washington letter, Andrew Carnegie signed photograph, and other lesser items. These auctions are usually run by the State Treasurer and are usually advertised well in advance of the sales. Check out the Internet for some of the announcements as well as the classifieds in your local papers.

Signed books are a big collectible for many people to the point that now many modern bookstores keep separate sections of just signed books. Some decent deals have been made in these racks and even greater finds have been made by me while looking through old books from out of print bookstores and collections. Over the years many people have stuck bills (money), pressed flowers, and added slips of paper to mark places or hide in books only to come tumbling out years later into a lucky collectors hands like mine. I have even found Amelia Earhart and Charles Lindbergh autographs loosely attached to pages as reference in a couple of book son aviiation.

Advertisingg yourself in magazines and newspapers is also a good way to find new material but, is quite costly. Try first placing less expensive ads in your local classifieds looking for autographed material.

Lastly, a good source for finding autographed material is at the closing of long run establishments. I have found boxes of turn of the century stock certificates and old checks including sseveral with good signatures on them, at a train depot being cleaned out as well as an old factory closing.

Former President Jimmy Carter vacated a warehouse space that a friend of mine rented next only to find Mr. Carter had left behind a box full of signed cancelled checks.

While this is not an all inclusive list of off beat places and ways to look for autographs it is meant to be a guideline for sparking your own imagination and drive for finding material that has yet to be discovered.

Mark Vardakis' chapter comes to us courtesy of Americabilia, Inc.

KEY TO ABBREVIATIONS

Sig - A single signature in ink (Pencil is worth approx. 25% less) Uninscribed on a piece of paper or cut from a document or letter. Capable of being properly matted and not irregular, smeared or in any other way unattractive.

DS - A document signed..checks that have been found in small quantities fall into this category (see chapter on Checks for more on that).

TLS - a typed letter signed by the person. Prices run parallel with DS in this guide.

FDC - Means a First Day Cover..a special postal envelope honoring different events.

SP - Signed Photograph - For our purposes an uninscribed 8x10 portrait signed in ink with good contrast between the signature and surface of the photograph.

MQS - A musical quote signed. Often done by Composers as a souvenir for fans consisting of a few words and/or bars of music from one of their works.

Inscribed - Means that the item has been personalized i.e. : To John, etc..

LS - a letter signed by the person in question but written by someone else like a secretary. For values of an LS use the DS column .

ALS - A handwritten letter signed and entirely written in the hand of the celebrity in question.

Name	Field	SIG	DS	ALS	SP	Remarks
Aadland, Beverly	Ent	10	25		20	
Aaker, Lee	Ent	10			25	
Aames, Willie	Ent	15	25		35	Eight is Enough
Aaron, Hank	Sports	15			50	Baseball
Abba	Music	50	100		100	Signed by all Four
Abbado, Claudia	Music	20			50	Opera
Abbey, Edwin Austin	Art	20		60		
Abbot, Charles G.	Science	15			30	
Abbott and Costello	Ent	450	800		1,300	Signed by both.
Abbott, Bessie	Music	25			50	Opera
Abbott, Bud 1895-1974	Ent	250	400		450	
Abbott, George	Ent	40		80	100	Director/Producer
Abbott, Henry L.	Civil War	100				Union General/1842-1864
Abbott, Henry Larcom	Civil War	30				Union General/1831-1927
Abbott, John	Ent	10			20	
Abdul, Paula	Music	25	50	60	50	
Abdul-Jabbar, Kareem	Sports	20			50	Basketball
Abel, Walter 1898-1987	Ent	20	40		50	
Abercrombie, John J.	Civil War	50	75	125		Union General/1798-1877
Aberdeen, Fourth Earl	Political	45		85		British Prime Minister
Aberlin, Betty	Ent	15			35	
Abernathy, Ralph D.	Political	30		125	75	Civil Rights Leader
Abraham, F. Murray	Ent	15	30		35	Amadeus/AA Winner
Abrams, Creighton W.	Military	25			75	Gen. WWII Tank Cmdr.
Abruzzo, Ben A.	Aviation	35			95	
Abt, Franz	Music	90		200		Composer
Abzug, Bella	Political	10		45	20	Congresswoman
AC/DC	Music	50	100		100	Signed by Entire Group
Acheson, Dean	Military	35			90	
Acosta, Bert	Aviation	45		125	100	
Acuff, Roy	Music	20			45	Country
Adair, Allen	Military	25			75	
Adair, John	Political	50		125		Early KY Governor
Adam 12	Ent	20			40	Signed by both
Adam, Adolphe-Charles	Music	50		200	100	Opera/Composer
Adams, Abigail	First Lady	550	2,000	5,500		
Adams, Andrew	RevWar	125		350		Continental Congress
Adams, Ansel 1902-84	Art	100	200	350	200	Photographer
Adams, Brooke	Ent	5		20	15	
Adams, Bryan	Music	20			50	
Adams, Clara	Aviation	60			125	1st woman on Zeppelin
Adams, Daniel	Civil War	200		700		CSA General/1821-1872
Adams, Don	Ent	10	25		25	Get Smart

Name	Field	SIG	DS	ALS	SP	Remarks
Adams, Edie	Ent	5	20	20	15	
Adams, Edwin	Ent	15			45	1834-1877
Adams, Harriet	Author	35		75		
Adams, Henry Brooks	Author	100		300		(Am) Historian
Adams, Joey	Ent	5	15		15	
Adams, John	Civil War	275				CSA General/1825-1864
Adams, John	President	1,500	3,000	4,500		
Adams, John C.	Science	40		125		Discovered Neptune
Adams, John Quincy	President	400	800	1,700		
Adams, Julie	Ent	10	20		20	Creature/Black Lagoon
Adams, Louisa Catherine	First Lady	250	500	750		1775-1852
Adams, Maud	Ent	10			25	
Adams, Maude	Ent	40			100	1872-1953
Adams, Nick	Ent	160	300		350	TV's "Rebel"/Died Young
Adams, Samuel	RevWar	750	2,000	3,500		Signer/1722-1803
Adams, Stanley	Music	15	25		25	Composer
Adams, William Wirt	Civil War	300	550			CSA General/1819-1888
Addams, Charles	Cartoonist	50		250	250	Addam's Family
Addams, Jane	Political	75			250	Nobel Peace/Social Ref.
Addinsell, Richard	Music	15			30	Composer
Addison, Joseph	Author	100		300		
Adelaide, HRH (Queen)	Royalty	50		100		Queen of William IV
Adenhauer, Konrad	Political	50		150	150	Ist Chan. Fed Rep/Ger.
Ader, Rose	Music	35			75	Opera
Adjani, Isabelle	Music	30			75	Opera
Adler, Alfred 1870-1937	Science	125	550	750	200	Psychiatrist
Adler, Buddy	Ent	20			50	Producer
Adler, Luther	Ent	15	25	30	30	1903 - 1984
Adler, Max	Business	15			35	Pres. Sears/Roebuck
Adler, Richard	Music	20			35	
Adoree, Renee	Ent	35			75	
Adrian, Edgar Lord	Science	35			65	Nobel/Physiology
Adrian, Iris	Ent	10	20		20	
Aerosmith	Music	90	250		175	Signed by All Five
Affleck, Ben	Ent	20			50	
Aga Khan III	Royalty	125				
Aga Khan IV	Royalty	15		60	35	
Agar, John	Ent	5	15	15	15	
Agassi, Andre	Sports	20			60	Tennis
Agassiz, Jean Louis	Science	100		250	600	Zoologist
Agnew, Spiro	Vice Pres	25	120		75	
Agnus, Felix	Civil War	30				Union General/1839-1925
Aguinaldo, Emilio	Political	100			150	Phillipine Leader
Agutter, Jenny	Ent	5			15	
Aherne, Brian	Ent	15		45	50	1902 - 1986
Aiello, Danny	Ent	15	25		40	
Aiken, Conrad	Author	30			50	(Am) Pulitzer Winner
Aikman, Troy	Sports	20			60	Football
Airy, George	Science	50		200		British Astronomer

Name	Field	SIG	DS	ALS	SP	Remarks
Aitken, Robert 1734-02	Business	100				Printed Ist American Bible
Aitken, Robert Ingersoll	Art	35		150		Sculptor (Am)
Akers, Elizabeth	Author	5		20	15	
Akihito	Royalty	400		650		
Akin, Warren 1811-1877	Civil War	45		100		Confederate Congressman
Akins, Claude	Ent	10	25		35	
Akroyd, Dan	Ent	20	50		50	Blues Brothers
Aks, Frank P.	Celebrity	100				Titanic Survivor
Alabama	Music	35	75		75	Signed by All Four
Albanese, Licia	Music	35			75	Opera
Albee, Edward	Author	30			80	Pulitzer Winner
Alberghetti, Anna	Ent	30			75	Scarce
Albert I (Belgium)	Royalty	25		125	50	
Albert III (Monaco)	Royalty	100		200	150	
Albert Victor, Duke	Royalty	200			500	Oldest Son of Edward VII
Albert, Don	Music	25			50	Bandleader
Albert, Eddie	Ent	10	25	30	30	Green Acres
Albert, Herb	Music	10	20		25	Trumpet
Albert, Prince (Monaco)	Royalty	25			50	
Albert, Prince (Victoria)	Royalty	150		450		
Albertson, Jack	Ent	30	35		50	Chico & the Man
Albertson, Joseph	Business	10			20	Grocery Stores
Albright, Lola	Ent	10			20	
Albright, Madeleine	Political	15			30	Ist woman Sect State
Albury, Charles	Aviation	25		50	50	
Alcock, John William	Aviation	300	500		600	Pioneer Aviator/1892-1919
Alcorn, James Lusk	Civil War	75		225		CSA General/1816-94
Alcott, Louisa May	Author	250		450		Little Women/1832-88
Alda, Alan	Ent	20	50		55	MASH/Hawkeye Pierce
Alda, Frances	Music	30			75	Opera
Alda, Robert	Ent	10		25	25	1914-1986
Aldred, Joel	Aviation	25			50	Canadian WWII Ace
Aldrich, Bess Streeter	Author	10			35	1881-1954
Aldrich, Louis	Ent	15			35	
Aldrich, Thomas Bailey	Author	40		250	200	1836 - 1907
Aldrin, Edwin "Buzz"	Space	75	225	300	200	Second Moonwalker
Alexander I (Russian)	Royalty	300	750	900		1777 - 1825
Alexander II (Russian)	Royalty	350	750	900		Assasinated
Alexander III (Russian)	Royalty			600		
Alexander, Albert Sir	Political	25				British M.P.
Alexander, Barton S.	Civil War	50		100		Union General/1819-78
Alexander, Ben	Ent	50			125	Dragnet
Alexander, Edward (WD)	Civil War	600	1,200	2,400		CSA General
Alexander, Edward P.	Civil War	300	600	900		CSA General/1835-1910
Alexander, George	Ent	5		15	15	
Alexander, Harold	Military	75		150		Alexander of Tunis (WWII)
Alexander, Jane	Ent	10	20	20	25	
Alexander, Jason	Ent	20	45	50	50	Seinfeld/George
Alexander, John	Ent	20			40	

Name	Field	SIG	DS	ALS	SP	Remarks
Alexander, William	RevWar	300	600	1,200		Gen. in Continental Army
Alexandra (Edward VII)	Royalty	150			500	Queen of Edward VII
Alexandra (Nich II)	Royalty	125			200	Russian
Alexis, Kim	Ent	15	30	40	30	
Alfieri, Carlo	Music	10			30	Opera
Alfonso, Kristian	Ent	5			15	
Alfonso, V	Royalty					1396/1458 RARE
Alfonso, XIII	Royalty	175		550	500	
Alfred, Prince	Royalty	25		75		Son of Queen Victoria
Alfven, Hannes	Science	20		45	35	Nobel/Physics
Alger, Horatio	Author	125		250	250	1832-1899/Books for Boys
Alger, Russell Alexander	Civil War	60		100	100	Union General/1836-1907
Algren, Nelson	Author	25		100	50	
Ali Khan, Prince	Royalty	15		75		
Ali Khan, Princess	Royalty	15		60		
Ali, Muhammad	Sports	40		200	80	Boxing
Alice in Chains	Music	50			100	Signed by Entire Group
Alice, Princess	Royalty	15		60	25	
All in the Family	Ent	60			125	Signed by All Four
Allen, Andrew	Space	10			20	Astronaut
Allen, Barbara Jo	Ent	40			50	Disney Voice
Allen, Bob	Ent	25	50		60	Western Star
Allen, Debbie	Ent	5	20		15	Fame star
Allen, Elizabeth	Ent	10			20	
Allen, Ethan 1738-89	RevWar	750	1,500	3,000		Col. Green Mtn Boys
Allen, Fred	Ent	50		100	100	Radio Star
Allen, Ginger Lynn	Ent	10			35	
Allen, Gracie	Ent	100	250		175	Of Burns and Allen
Allen, Henry T.	Military	25		75	50	General WWI
Allen, Henry Watkins	Civil War	300		600		CSA General/1820-1866
Allen, Horatio	Business	75				Railroad
Allen, Ira	RevWar					Ethan's Brother/RARE
Allen, Irwin	Ent	15	40		35	Producer/Director
Allen, Joseph	Space	10			25	Astronaut
Allen, Karen	Ent	10	25		30	Indiana Jones star
Allen, Marcus	Sports	15			50	Football
Allen, Marty	Ent	5			10	Comedian
Allen, Nancy	Ent	20			50	
Allen, Peter	Music	40			75	Composer
Allen, Rex	Ent	5	20	20	15	Cowboy Star
Allen, Robert	Civil War	40		100		Union General/1811-86
Allen, Steve	Ent	10	20		20	
Allen, Tim	Ent	20			50	Home Improvement
Allen, Viola	Ent	15			30	
Allen, William Wirt	Civil War	175		550		CSA General/1835-1894
Allen, Woody	Ent	20	50		50	Director/Actor
Allenby, Edmund	Military	50		150		Br. Field Marshal/1861-36
Allende Gossens, Sal	Political	40		180	60	President of Chile
Alley, Kirstie	Ent	20	50		50	Cheers/Veronica's Closet

Name	Field	SIG	DS	ALS	SP	Remarks
Allgood, Sara	Ent	20		40	50	
Allingham, Margery	Author	45		150		Mystery Author
Allison, Bobby	SPorts	10			25	Auto Racing
Allison, Davey	Sports	50			150	Auto Racer/Killed in crash
Allison, May	Ent	20		40	50	
Allizard, Adolphe	Music	20			50	Opera
Allman Brothers	Music	40	85		100	Signed by Both
Allman, Greg	Music	20	60		50	
Allston, Washington	Art	300		700		Landscape Artist/1799-43
Allyson, June	Ent	15	20	25	20	
Alma-Tadema, Lawrence	Art	25		100		Br. Painter
Almonte, Juan N.	Military	60		250		Mexican General/1804-69
Alonso, Maria Conchita	Ent	10		25	25	
Alt, Carol	Ent	10		25	25	
Altchewsky, Ivan	Music				250	Opera - Scarce
Altman, Robert	Ent	10		30	25	
Alvarez, Luis W.	Science	15		60	30	Nobel Physics
Alvarez, Roma	Ent	5			10	
Alvary, Lorenzo	Ent	10		25	25	
Alvord, Benjamin	Civil War	30		65		Union General/1813-1884
Alyn, Kirk	Ent	15			40	First Movie Superman
Amara, Lucine	Music	20			45	Opera
Amato, Pasquale	Music	45			125	Opera
Ambler, Eric	Author	50	100	150		Br. Novelist
Ambrose, Bert	Music	15			45	Bandleader/1896-1971
Ameche, Don 1908-93	Ent	25	40	60	55	
Ames, Adelbert	Civil War	75		200		Union General/1835-1933
Ames, Ed	Ent	10			25	
Ames, Fisher 1758-1808	Political	150		450		Federalist party
Ames, Leon	Ent	15			35	
Ames, Oakes	Business	150	450	2,000		Fndr Union Pacific RR
Ames, Oliver	Business	175	1,250	2,250		Union Pacific RailRoad
Amherst, Jeffrey	RevWar	400	600	900		1717-97
Amin Dada, Idi	Political	50			80	Uganda
Amis, Kingsley	Author	25		75	50	Watership Down
Amis, Suzy	Ent	20			40	Titanic
Ammen, Daniel	Civil War	35	60	100		Union General
Ammen, Jacob	Civil War	25	50	75		Union General/1806-1894
Amos and Andy	Ent	150	250		300	Signed by Corell/Gosden
Amos, John	Ent	15			25	Good Times
Amos, Tori	Music	25			50	
Amos, Wally	Business	5		15	15	Famous Amos Cookies
Amparen, Belen	Music	15			35	Opera
Ampere, Andre Marie	Science	250		1,000		
Amsden, Ben	Aviation	10		30	30	
Amsterdam, Morey	Ent	20	30	40	50	Dick Van Dyke Show
Amundsen, Roald	Explorer	150		350	400	
Anders, Luana	Ent	10			25	
Anderson, Bill	Music	5			15	Country

Name	Field	SIG	DS	ALS	SP	Remarks
Anderson, Brad	Cartoonist	15			25	Marmaduke
Anderson, Bronco Billy	Ent	150		300	400	
Anderson, C.E. Bud	Aviation	15		45	35	Ace
Anderson, Carl	Cartoonist	25	75			Henry
Anderson, Carl David	Science	25			75	Nobel in Physics/1936
Anderson, Clifford	Civil War	70	100			CSA Congress
Anderson, Eddie	Ent	65		200	175	Rochester"/1905-77
Anderson, George B.	Civil War	225	450			CSA General/1831-1862
Anderson, George T.	Civil War	125		350	275	CSA General/1824-1901
Anderson, Gillian	Ent	25			50	X-Files
Anderson, Hans Christian	Author	450		1,250	1,650	
Anderson, Harry	Ent	20			40	Night Court
Anderson, James P.	Civil War	400		3,000		CSA General/1822-1872
Anderson, Joseph	RevWar	75	225	375		1757 - 1837
Anderson, Joseph R.	Civil War	200	450	700		CSA General/1813-92
Anderson, Judith Dame	Ent	25			50	1898 - 1992
Anderson, Loni	Ent	5	15	20	15	WKRP in Cincinatti
Anderson, Louie	Ent	10			20	Comedian
Anderson, Lynn	Music	10			20	Country and Western
Anderson, Pamela	Ent	25			50	Baywatch
Anderson, Poul	Author	15	30		45	Sci-Fi Author
Anderson, Richard Dean	Ent	20			40	MacGuyver
Anderson, Richard Heron	Civil War	60	125	250		CSA General/1821-1879
Anderson, Robert	Civil War	125	300	500	1,500	Cmdr Ft. Sumter/1805-71
Anderson, Samuel R.	Civil War	125	250	350		CSA General/1804-1883
Anderson, Willie	Aviation	10			30	WWII ACE
Andre, John	RevWar	1,200	3,000	7,000		Br.Officer/Hung as a Spy
Andress, Ursula	Ent	25			50	James Bond Girl
Andretti, Mario	Sports	15			40	Auto Racing
Andrew Sisters	Music	75			150	Signed by all Three
Andrews, Chris	Civil War	35	75	200		Union General/1829-1922
Andrews, George L.	Civil War	35	60	100		Union General/1828-99
Andrews, Julie	Ent	20	45		50	Sound of Music/Mary Popp
Andrews, Tige	Ent	15			30	
Andrews, V.C.	Author	5			10	
Andros, Edmund	RevWar	RARE	RARE	RARE	RARE	
Angel, Heather	Ent	10			30	
Angeli, Pier	Ent	50		150	100	
Angelou, Maya	Author	25		50	45	Poet
Animals, The	Music	75	200		200	Signed by entire group
Aniston, Jennifer	Ent	20			50	FRIENDS
Anka, Paul	Music	10		20	20	
Ankers, Evelyn	Ent	30			75	Horror star
Anna Ivanovna	Royalty	350	900	1,500		Empress of Russia
Annabella	Ent	15	25		40	
Annaloro, Antonio	Music	10		35	40	Opera
Anne, Princess	Royalty	100	200		150	Elizabeth II Daughter
Anne, Queen (Eng)	Royalty	500	1,500	2,000		1665 - 1714
Annseau, Fernand	Music	20			75	Opera

Name	Field	SIG	DS	ALS	SP	Remarks
Anouilh, Jean	Author	30	75	100	50	
Ansara, Michael	Ent	10	25	25	25	
Anselmi, Giuseppe	Music	50			125	Opera
Ant, Adam	Music	25			55	
Anthony, HRH	Royalty	40	100			King of Saxony
Anthony, Lysette	Ent	20			40	
Anthony, Ray	Music	5			15	Big Band Leader
Anthony, Robert N.	Science	10			20	Nobel
Anthony, Susan B.	Political	175		600	1,200	Women's Rights/1820 - 06
Antokolski, Mark M.	Art	50	75	150		Russ. Sculp. 1843-1902
Anton, Susan	Ent	5	20	20	20	
Antonelli, Laura	Ent	25		50	50	
Antonioni, Michelangelo	Ent	35			150	Director
Anwar, Gabrielle	Ent	20			50	
Aoti, Rocky	Business	5		20	15	Benihana's Restaurants
Apollinaire, Guillaume	Author	125	300			Poet and Critic/1880-18
Apollo 10	Space				300	Signed by entire crew
Apollo 11	Space				1,400	Signed by all three
Apollo 12	Space				300	Signed by entire crew
Apollo 13	Space				1,400	Signed by all three
Apollo 15	Space				500	Signed by entire crew
Apollo 16	Space				200	Signed by entire crew
Apollo 17	Space				200	Signed by entire crew
Apollo 8	Space	250			500	Signed by entire crew
Apollo 9	Space				200	Signed by all three
Apollonia	Ent	25			50	Singer/Actress w/Prince
Apollo-Soyuz	Space	200			400	Signed by entire crews
Applegate, Christina	Ent	20	50		50	Married with Children
Appleton, Daniel	Business	15				1785 - 1849
Appleton, Edward, Sir	Science	25		50	50	Nobel Physics
Apt, Jay	Space	5			15	Astronaut
Aquino, Corazon	Political	25			50	Pres. Philippines
Arafat, Yassir	Political	100			200	PLO Leader
Araisa, Francisco	Music	15			35	Opera
Araujo, Arturo	Political	15			30	Salvador
Arber, Werner	Science	20			40	Nobel Medicine
Arbuckle, Roscoe 'Fatty'	Ent	375	600	800	750	
Arcaro, Eddie	Sports	20			45	Jockey
Archer, Anne	Ent	15			30	
Archer, James J.	Civil War	200	350	600		CSA General/1817-64
Archer, Jeffrey	Author	5	15		15	
Archi, Attila	Music	20		40	40	Opera
Arden, Elizabeth	Business	30	75	150	50	Founder/Eliz. Arden Co.
Arden, Eve	Ent	20	25	40	40	1912 - 1990
Arena, Angelina	Ent	10		30	25	Opera
Argento, Dominick	Music	10		45	25	Pulitzer
Argyll, 9th Duke	Political	30	45	60		Gov Gen. Canada
Arias Sanchez, Oscar	Political	30			50	Nobel/Pres.Costa Rica
Arkin, Adam	Ent	5	15	20	15	

Name	Field	SIG	DS	ALS	SP	Remarks
Arkin, Alan	Ent	10	25		25	
Arledge, John	Ent	40			60	
Arlen, Harold	Music	200	300		350	Wizard of Oz
Arlen, Richard	Ent	25			75	1899 - 1976
Arletty	Ent	25			75	
Arliss, George 1868-46	Ent	45	50	75	100	AA Winner
Armani, Giorgio	Business	15			35	Fashion Designer
Armendariz, Pedro	Ent	35	60		75	
Armetta, Henry	Ent	25		50	65	1888 - 1945
Armistead, Lewis A.	Civil War	600				CSA General/1817-63
Armour, Philip D.	Business	200	1,250	1,750	450	Meat Packing. Armour & Co.
Armstead, Henry Hugh	Art	10		35		Br. Sculptor
Armstrong, Louis	Ent	200	450	700	450	Satchmo" 1900 - 1971
Armstrong, Bess	Ent	10			25	
Armstrong, Edw. R.	Science	50		150		Inventor Seadrome
Armstrong, Edwin H.	Science	75	200			Invented FM Broadcasting
Armstrong, Frank C.	Civil War	300				CSA General/1835-1909
Armstrong, Harry	Music	100		200		Composer
Armstrong, John	Political	75	250	450		Sect. of War/1758-1843
Armstrong, Neil A.	Space	175	550		650	First Moonwalker
Armstrong, Robert	Ent	75			250	
Armstrong, Robert	Military	175				Gen. TN Vols, Ind. Fighter
Armstrong, Samuel C.	Civil War	65	150	250		Cmdr Black Regiments
Arnaz, Desi 1917-86	Ent	55	150	200	200	
Arnaz, Lucie	Ent	5			20	
Arness, James	Ent	25	100		55	Gunsmoke
Arnett, Peter	Ent	5			10	CNN News
Arnheim, Gus	Music	15			45	Bandleader
Arno, Peter	Cartoonist	15		50	25	The New Yorker
Arno, Sig	Ent	10			25	
Arnold, Archibald	Military	20	50	75		
Arnold, Benedict 1741-01	RevWar	1,500		4,000		Am. Army Officer. Traitor
Arnold, Eddy	Music	10			30	
Arnold, Edward	Ent	30			60	
Arnold, Edwin, Sir	Author	50	100	150	100	Br. Poet/Journalist
Arnold, Fred	Aviation	20	35		50	WWII ACE
Arnold, Henry 'Hap'	Military	55	175	350	175	Air Force Gen. WWII
Arnold, Leslie P.	Aviation	10			30	'24 Round the World Flight
Arnold, Lewis Golding	Civil War	50	100	200		Union General/1817-1871
Arnold, Matthew	Author	40	75	100		British Poet
Arnold, Richard	Civil War	50				Union General/1828-82
Arnold,Tom	Ent	20	40		40	
Arntzen, Heinrich	Aviation	Scarce	Scarce	Scarce	Scarce	WWI British ACE
Arp, Jean	Art	75		225		Sculptor
Arquette, Cliff	Ent	20			40	
Arquette, David	Ent	20			40	
Arquette, Patricia	Ent	15			40	
Arquette, Roseanna	Ent	15	30		40	
Arrau, Claudio	Music				125	Pianist

Name	Field	SIG	DS	ALS	SP	Remarks
Arrhenuis, Svante A.	Science	150	300	450		Nobel Chemistry 1903
Arrington, A. H.	Civil War	75				CSA Congress
Arriola, Gus	Cartoonist	10			25	Gordo
Arrow, Kenneth J.	Science	35				Nobel Economics
Arthur, Beatrice	Ent	5	20	20	20	Maude/Golden Girls
Arthur, Chester A.	President	275	850	750	600	1830-1886
Arthur, Chester A.	President	350	700	1,500		Presidential Dated
Arthur, Duke/Connought	Political	10		25		Prime Minister
Arthur, Ellen Lewis	First Lady	600		1,200		
Arthur, George K.	Ent	5			10	
Arthur, Jean	Ent	100	150	200	200	1905 - 1991
Arthur, Julia	Ent	15			25	Pioneer Film Star
Artot, Desiree	Music	35			75	Opera
Asboth, Alexander S.	Civil War	75		150		Union General/1811-68
Asgeirsson, Asgeir	Political	25				Premier of Iceland
Ash, Roy L.	Business	10	25		35	
Ashby, Hal	Ent	10			20	
Ashby, Turner (WD)	Civil War	450		1,600		CSA General/1828-1862
Ashby, Turner 1828-62	Civil War	350		900		CSA General
Ashcroft, Dame Peggy	Ent	25			60	
Ashe, Arthur	Sports	50			100	Deceased Tennis star
Ashe, John	RevWar	100	200	350		General
Ashe, William Sheppard	Civil War	40				Blockade Runner
Ashford and Simpson	Music	15			40	
Ashley, Alfred 1835-1913	Author	20			50	British Poet Laureatte
Ashley, Elizabeth	Ent	5	20		15	
Asimov, Isaac 1920-92	Author	35	75	150	75	Sci-Fi Author
Asner, Ed	Ent	10	20	25	20	Mary Tyler Moore
Asquith, Herbert H.	Political	35	75		125	Prime Minister
Assad, Hafez	Political	15			50	
Assante, Armand	Ent	20			45	
Astaire and Rogers	Ent	175			350	Signed by Both
Astaire, Adele	Ent	35			100	Fred's Dancing Sister
Astaire, Fred 1899-1987	Ent	75	200	225	225	
Asther, Nils	Ent	25	35	65	125	
Astin, John	Ent	10	25	25	25	Addam's Family TV/Gomez
Astin, Sean	Ent	15			25	
Astley, Rick	Music	15			35	
Aston, Francis W.	Science	35		150		Nobel Chemistry 1922
Astor, John Jacob	Business	450	2,000	5,000		Fur Trader/1763-1848
Astor, John Jacob Jr.	Business	200	550	800		Union General/1822-90
Astor, John Jacob Mrs.	Business	35		75		
Astor, Mary	Ent	45			125	AA Winner
Astor, Vincent	Business	10		45	20	
Astor, John Jacob III	Business	200	550	800		Grandson of Founder
Astor, John Jacob IV	Business	400	900	1,500		Died on the Titanic
Astor, Waldorf 1879-1952	Political	15		50	45	British M.P.
Astor, Wm Backhouse 1792-1875	Business	250	800	1,200		Son of John Jacob
Astor, William Waldorf	Business	100		350		Financier

Name	Field	SIG	DS	ALS	SP	Remarks
Asturias, Miquel Angel	Author	75		225		Nobel Literature
Atchison, David Rice	President	400	800	1,000		President for One Day
Ates, Roscoe	Ent	35			65	
Atherton, Gertrude	Author	30		150	75	Am. Novelist
Athlone, Earl (Alex)	Political	15		45		Gov Gen of Canada
Atholl, Katharine, Duch.	Political	65				1874 - 1960
Atkins, Chet	Music	5			20	Country
Atkins, Christopher	Ent	10	20	25	25	Blue Lagoon
Atkinson, Brooks	Author	15	45			Theatre Critic
Atlantov, Vladimir	Music	25		75	55	Opera
Atlas, Charles	Business	15		45	35	Mail Order Muscles
Atlee, Clement 1883-1967	Political	75	150			Br. Prime Minister
Attenborough, Richard	Ent	25	40		50	AA Winner
Atterbury, William W.	Military	20	50			General WWI/1866-35
Attlee, Clement	Political	40	125		75	Prime Minister
Atwill, Lionel	Ent	100	300		250	1885 - 1946
Auber, Daniel Francois	Music	100		150		Father of Fr. Opera
Auberjonois, Rene	Ent	10	25		20	Star Trek/Benson
Aubry, Cecile	Ent	15			25	French actress
Auchincloss, Louis	Author	15	35	75	30	American novelist
Auchinleck, Claude J.E.	Military	50			100	Br Fld Mar. WWII
Auckland, Baron	Political	50		100		Gov-Gen India
Auden, Wystan Hugh	Author	200		500	550	Pulitzer
Audran, Edmond	Music	45		150		Fr. Operettas
Audran, Marius	Music	25		75		Opera
Audubon, John J.	Science	750		3,000		Ornithologist/1785-1851
Auel, Jean M.	Author	10		30	30	Clan of the Cave Bear
Auer, Leopold	Music	25			45	Violinist
Auer, Mischa	Ent	20			50	1905 - 1967
Auger, Arleen	Music	25			50	Opera
Auger, Christopher C.	Civil War	50		150		Union General/1821-98
Auger, Claudine	Ent	15			35	James Bond Girl
Auger, Claudine	Ent	20			50	James Bond babe
Augereau, P.F.C. de	Military	125	350	450		Marshal of Napoleon
Augsburg, Alex. S.	Royalty		300			Prince Bishop of Augsburg
Augusta, Queen/Prussia	Royalty		150			Empress of Germany
Augustus I, Duke of Sax	Royalty	2,000				1526-1586
Augustus III	Royalty	150		350		King Poland
Aumont, Jean Pierre	Ent	20	25	25	75	
Ausensi, Maurel	Music	20			50	Opera
Aust, Abner	Aviation	10			20	Am. ACE
Austen, Jane	Author	650	1,800			Pride & Prejudice
Austin, Bobby	Music	10			20	
Austin, Moses 1761-1821	Business	450	1,500	2,500		Texas Founder
Austin, Stephen F.	Western	800	2,000	5,000		1793 - 1836/Texas
Autry, Gene 1907 - 1998	Ent	30	100	150	75	Singing Cowboy
Avalon, Frankie	Ent	15			35	
Avebury, John Lubbock	Science	25		100		Paleontologist
Avedon, Richard	Art	50		150	125	Photographer

Name	Field	SIG	DS	ALS	SP	Remarks
Average White Band	Ent	25			45	Entire Group
Averell, William W.	Civil War	75	150	200		Union General/1832-1900
Avery, Sewell L.	Business	35	75	100		CEO Montgomery Ward
Avery, John, Jr.	RevWar	40	80			
Avery, Tex	Cartoonist	75			150	
Avery, William W.	Civil War	75	150			CSA Congress
Axelrod, Julius	Science	35		80	55	Nobel Medicine
Axtell, George	Aviation	15			35	Marine ACE
Axton, Hoyt	Music	5	20		15	Country
Aykroyd, Dan	Ent	20			45	Sat Nite Live alumni
Ayres, Agnes	Ent	60		150	125	Silent Film Star
Ayres, Lew	Ent	10	20	35	25	Dr. Kildare
Ayres, Romeyn B. (WD)	Civil War	75	100	250		Union General/1825-88
Ayres, Romeyn Beck	Civil War	50	75	125		Union General/1825-88
Ayub Khan, General	Political	30		75	100	Afghan Prince

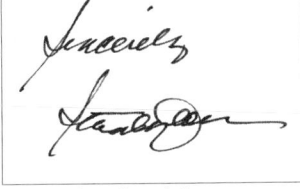

Jack Albertson

Stanley Adams

Morey Amsterdam

Adam Ant

Name	Field	SIG	DS	ALS	SP	Remarks
B 52's	Music	30			75	Entire Group
Babbage, Charles	Science	200		550		Pioneer of computers
Babbitt, Harry	Music	10			20	Vocalist
Babbitt, Milton	Music	25		65	45	
Babcock, Barbara	Ent	5			10	
Babcock, Orville E.	Civil War	30	75	150		Union General/1845-84
Babcock, Orville E. (WD)	Civil War	45	150	200		Union General
Babilee', Jean	Ent	35			70	Ballet
Baby Peggy	Ent	5			15	
Bacall, Lauren	Ent	10	35		30	
Baccaloni, Salvatore	Music	20			45	Opera
Bach, Barbara	Ent	10	25		30	James Bond Girl
Bach, Catherine	Ent	15	30		30	Dukes of Hazzard
Bach, Johann Sebastian	Music	5,000	25,000	35,000		
Bach, Richard	Author	25	75	150		Jonathan Livingston Seagull
Bacharach, Burt	Music	15	25	35	25	Composer
Bachrach, Fabian	Art	50		125	75	
Bache, Alexander D.	Science	25	50		40	lst Pres. Nat'l Acad. Science
Bacheller, Irving	Author	25			75	Am Novelist
Back, George, Sir	Explorer	25	75	125		Arctic Navigator
Backhaus, Wilhelm	Music	40			100	Ger. Concert Pianist
Backus, Jim	Ent	35	50		60	Gilligans Island/Mr.Magoo
Bacon, Francis, Sir	Author	5,500	12,000	20,000		Br. Statesman
Bacon, Kevin	Ent	15			45	
Bacon, Lloyd	Ent	15			20	Film Director
Bacon, Peggy	Art	35	65	125		
Bad Co.	Music	50			100	Signed by Entire Band
Baddeley, Hermione	Ent	15			30	
Badeau, Adam	Civil War	35	75	150		Union General/1831-95
Badeau, Adam (WD)	Civil War	75		250		Union General
Baden-Powell, Robert	Military	125	225	300	500	Br Founder of Boy Scouts
Bader, Douglas, Sir	Aviation	45	125		80	British ACE
Badger, Charles J.	Military	20	45		30	US Navy Admiral
Badger, Oscar C.	Miltary	20			50	Adm. US Navy WWII
Badham, John	Ent	20			40	Director
Badham, W.L.	Aviation	25		75	55	WWI
Badler, Jane	Ent	10		25	25	
Badoglio, Pietro	Political	30			60	Suceeded Mussolini
Badu, Erykah	Music	20			40	
Baekeland, L. H. Dr.	Science	40		125		Inventor Bakelite
Baer, Arthur "Bugs"	Cartoonist	10			35	Columnist/Cartoonist
Baer, George F.	Business	10	25		30	Pres. Reading Railroad
Baer, Max	Sports	125			300	Boxer

Name	Field	SIG	DS	ALS	SP	Remarks
Baer, Max, Jr.	Ent	35	60		60	Beverly Hillbillies/Jethro
Baez, Joan	Music	10	25		30	
Bagian, James P.	Space	5			15	
Baglioni, Bruna	Music	15		45	35	Opera
Bagnold, Enid	Author	35			70	
Bagot, Charles, Sir	Political			125		Br Diplomat/1781-1843
Bahlou, Charles	Military	30	100			WWI General
Bailey, Buster	Music	30			75	Jazz
Bailey, F. Lee	Business	15	25		25	Noted Trial Attorney
Bailey, James Anthony	Ent	400	800	RARE	RARE	Barnum & Bailey Circus
Bailey, Joseph 1825-67	Civil War	100	200			
Bailey, Mildred C.	Military	25			70	Brig General
Bailey, Pearl	Music	20	40	60	55	1918 - 1990
Bailey, Raymond	Ent	75			125	Beverly Hillbillies
Bailey, Theodorus	Civil War	35	70	145		Union Naval Officer
Baillie, Joanna 1762-51	Author	25	50	100		Scottish Poet
Bailly, Jean-Sylvain	Science	40	90	150		1736-93
Bain, Barbara	Ent	20	40		50	Mission Impossible
Bain, Conrad	Ent	5			10	Mork and Mindy
Bainbridge, William	Military	150	300	550		Officer War 1812/1774-33
Bainter, Fay	Ent	55	75	100	100	1892 - 1968
Baio, Scott	Ent	10	25		25	Happy Days/ChaChi
Bair, Hilbert L.	Aviation	10				WWI US ACE
Baird, Absalom	Civil War	35		75		Union General/1824-1905
Baird, John Logie	Science	150	300		450	
Baird, Sharon	Ent	20			40	
Baker, Alpheus	Civil War	150	275	475		CSA General/1828-1891
Baker, Anita	Music	20			45	
Baker, Art	Ent	10			20	
Baker, Benny 1907-94	Ent	10			25	
Baker, Blanche	Ent	10			20	
Baker, Bob	Ent	50	100		100	Singing Cowboy 1930's
Baker, Bonnie Wee	Music	5			15	Big Band Vocalist
Baker, Carroll	Ent	15		45	25	
Baker, Chauncey	Military	10			15	General WW I
Baker, Diane	Ent	10			20	
Baker, Edward D.	Civil War	150	450	600		Union General/1811-61
Baker, George 1915-75	Cartoonist	40			150	
Baker, Janet, Dame	Music	10	15		35	Opera
Baker, Josephine	Ent	150	400	350	400	1906 - 1975
Baker, Kathy	Ent	15			30	
Baker, Kenny	Ent	15			40	R2-D2 in Star Wars
Baker, LaFayette Curry	Civil War	100	160	200		Union General/1826-68
Baker, Laurence S.	Civil War	100	150	250		CSA General/1830-97
Baker, LaVerne	Music	30			60	Jazz Vocalist
Baker, Mark	Music	10			25	Opera
Baker, Newton D.	Political	20		75	55	Wilson Sect. of War
Baker, Royal N.	Aviation	25		75	50	Air Ace Korea, WW II
Baker, Samuel, Sir	Explorer	35	65	135		(Br)Found Source of Nile

Name	Field	SIG	DS	ALS	SP	Remarks
Bakewell, William	Ent	20			45	GWTW
Bakst, Leon 1868-1924	Art	150		600		Russian Painter
Bakula, Scott	Ent	20			50	Quantum Leap
Balanchine, George	Ent	135		250	250	Ballet/1904-83
Balbo, Italo	Aviation	125		200	200	It Air Marshall
Balck, Hermann	Military	25			75	Ger. Panzer General
Baldwin, Abraham	Political	RARE	RARE	RARE	RARE	Signer Constitution
Baldwin, Alec	Ent	20	60		50	
Baldwin, Faith	Author	35		60	45	Novelist
Baldwin, Henry	SuprCt	25	40	100		
Baldwin, James	Author	75		350	225	
Baldwin, Roger Sherman	Political	35		50		
Baldwin, Stanley	Political	50	90	125	125	British P.M./1867-57
Baldwin, Stephen	Ent	20	45		50	
Baldwin, William	Ent	20			50	
Baldwin, William E.	Civil War	350	600	1,250		CSA General/1827-64
Balewa, A. T., Sir	Political	10	35	65	25	Nigeria
Balfour, Arthur J.	Political	50	100	125	90	Br. P.M./1848-30
Balfour, Howard, Lord	Aviation	50				Br. Ace WW I
Balin, Ina	Ent	25			45	Black Orchid/Actress
Balk, Fairuza	Ent	20			45	
Ball, Albert	Aviation	125	200	250	250	Brit. RAF ACE WW I
Ball, Lucille	Ent	200	400	550	450	Full Signature/1910-1989
Ball, Lucille (Lucy)	Ent	80		225	175	Signed "Love, Lucy"
Ballard, Kaye	Ent	15	25	25	25	
Ballard, Robert, Dr.	Science	15		50	35	Found Titanic
Ballentine, Carl	Ent	10			25	
Balsam, Martin	Ent	15	30		45	
Balzac, Honore de	Author	600		1,500		Fr. Novelist/1799-50
Bampton, Rose	Music	20	35	50	50	Opera
Bananarama	Music	40	75		75	Signed by All Four
Bancroft, Anne	Ent	10			30	
Bancroft, George	Political	40	85	140		Polk Sect of Navy
Bancroft, George	Ent	20	35	50	75	1882-1956
Band, The	Music		150		100	
Bandaranike, S.W.R.D	Political	10	25	45	30	Prime Minister Sri Lanka
Banderas, Antonio	Ent	25			55	
Bangles, The	Music	40			75	Signed by All Four
Banisadr, A.	Political	15		80	40	Iran
Bankhead, Tallulah	Ent	65	125	250	175	1903 - 1968
Banks, Billy	Ent	100			250	Jazz
Banks, Ernie	Sports	15			45	Baseball
Banks, Joseph, Sir	Explorer	50	125			Sailed w/Capt. Cook
Banks, Leslie	Ent	20			35	
Banks, Nathaniel P.	Civil War	75	150	250		Union General/1816-94
Banks, Nathaniel P. (WD)	Civil War	150	450	550		Union General
Banks, Tyra	Ent	20			40	Supermodel
Banky, Vilma	Ent	50	75		150	
Banner, John 1910-73	Ent	100	150		200	Hogans Heroes/Sgt.Shultz

Name	Field	SIG	DS	ALS	SP	Remarks
Banning, Henry B.	Civil War	30	65			Union General
Banting, Frederick G.	Science	600	1,000	1,500	900	Discoverd Insulin with Best
Bara, Theda	Ent	125		200	250	
Baranski, Christine	Ent	20			45	Cybil
Barbara, Agatha	Political	10			20	Pres. of Malta
Barbarin, Paul	Music	25		65		Bandleader/Drummer
Barbeau, Adrienne	Ent	5	20		20	
Barbee, John Henry	Music	35				Blues Vocalist
Barbe-Marbois, Francois de	Political	35	75	200		Louisiana Purchase
Barber, Rex T.	Aviation	15	35	60	35	Am. ACE
Barber, Samuel 1910-81	Music	40		200	75	Opera
Barber, William	Military	25			70	
Barbera, Joe	Cartoonist	30			75	Hanna and Barbera
Barbier, George	Ent	10			25	
Barbieri, Fedora	Music	25			75	Opera
Barbour, Dave	Music	15			40	Jazz Guitar
Barbour, Philip	SuprCt	RARE	RARE	RARE	RARE	
Bardeen, John	Science	25	50	95	35	Nobel
Bardot, Brigitte	Ent	25	50	65	55	
Bardshar, F.A.	Aviation	10	30		35	Navy Ace WWII
Barere de Vieuzac, B.	Military	50		150		
Baretti, Giuseppe	Author	25		90		
Bari, Lynn	Ent	10			20	
Baring, Alexander	Business	175		600		1774-1848
Baring, Francis, Sir	Business	25		95		Dir East India Co.
Baring-Gould, Sabine	Author	20		200	60	Onward Christian Soldiers
Barishnikov, Mikhail	Ent	50			100	
Barker, Bob	Ent	5	15		10	The Price is Right
Barker, Clive	Author	15	25		30	Br. Horror Novelist
Barker, Lex 1919-1973	Ent	75	150	175	150	Tarzan
Barker, William George	Aviation	150	225	350	300	Canadian ACE, WW I
Barkhorn, Gerhard	Aviation	60			125	Ger. ACE, #2 Worldwide
Barkin, Ellen	Ent	15			45	
Barkley, Alban W.	Vice Pres	30	75	150	65	Truman VP/1877-56
Barkley, Charles	Sports	15			40	Basketball
Barks, Carl	Cartoonist	50			100	Disney Duck Artist
Barksdale, Ethelbert	Civil War	30		65		CSA Congress
Barksdale, William	Civil War	450		1,500		CSA General. KIA1821-63
Barksdale, William (WD)	Civil War	850				CSA General
Barlow, Francis C.	Civil War	75	225	235		Union General/1834-96
Barlow, Howard	Music	25			45	
Barnabee, Henry Clay	Ent	5	15	25	15	Operatic Comedian
Barnaby, Ralph S.	Aviation	25			45	
Barnard, Christian, Dr.	Science	25		75	45	Heart Specialist
Barnard, Frederick A.P.	Political	75	150	250		Educator
Barnard, John Gross	Civil War	30	60			Union General/1815-82
Barnes, Binnie	Ent	5			15	
Barnes, James	Civil War	50	125	150		Union General/1801-69
Barnes, Joanna	Ent	5			15	

Name	Field	SIG	DS	ALS	SP	Remarks
Barnes, Joseph K.	Civil War	150	400	550		Union Surg. Gen./1817-83
Barnes, Priscilla	Ent	5	15		15	
Barnet, Charlie	Music	15			30	Big Band Leader
Barnette, Vince	Ent	15	30		45	
Barney, Natalie 1876-72	Author	150	300	400		Am. Poet
Barnum, Henry A.	Civil War	45	90	145		Union General/1833-92
Barnum, Malvern H.	Military	10		35	25	General WWI
Barnum, Phineas T.	Business	200	750	550	900	1810-1891
Baronova, Irina	Ent	25			70	Rus.-Br. Ballerina
Barr, Candy	Ent	10			30	Famous Stripper
Barr, Doug	Ent	5			10	
Barr, Roseanne	Ent	25	65	125	55	Roseanne
Barrault, Jean-Louis	Ent	40			125	
Barrett, John	Military	25		50		WWI Victoria Cross
Barrett, Lawrence	Civil War	25			45	Union Officer/1838-91
Barrett, Majel	Ent	10	25	30	25	Star Trek
Barrett, Rona	Ent	5			15	Gossip
Barrett, Wilson 1846-1904	Ent	20		95	60	Br Playwright
Barrie, Barbara	Ent	5			10	
Barrie, James M, Sir	Author	85	250	250		Peter Pan/1860-1937
Barrie, Wendy	Ent	15	25	30	45	1912 - 1978
Barringer, Rufus	Civil War	135	275	400		CSA General/1821-95
Barrios, Justo R. 1835-85	Political	50	125			Pres. Guatemala
Barron, Clarence	Business	25			40	Editor/Publisher Barron's
Barrow, John, Sir	Political	75	170	325		Explorer/Author/1764-1848
Barrow, Clyde 1909-34	Criminal	1,800	4,500	RARE	RARE	Bonnie & Clyde
Barrow, Ed	Sports	200	300		475	1953 HOF
Barry, Charles, Sir	Science	25	50	125		1795-1860
Barry, Dan	Cartoonist	10			35	Flash Gordon
Barry, Dave	Author	10			20	Creator Dave's World
Barry, Don 'Red'	Ent	25			50	
Barry, Gene	Ent	10			25	
Barry, John	RevWar	1,000	2,000			Ir. Born US Naval Officer
Barry, John Decatur	Civil War	150		450		CSA General/1839-67
Barry, Thomas	Military	50		150		General WW I
Barry, Jack	Ent	10			20	
Barry, Sy	Cartoonist	20			40	Phantom
Barry, Wm. Farquhar	Civil War	75	145	190		Union General/1818-79
Barrymore, Diana	Ent	30		50	50	1921 - 1960
Barrymore, Drew	Ent	20	50		50	
Barrymore, Ethel	Ent	100	150		200	1898 - 1959
Barrymore, John	Ent	150	250	300	450	1882-1942
Barrymore, Lionel	Ent	65	150		150	1978-1954
Barrymore, Maurice	Ent	15			45	
Bartato, Elisabeth	Music	15			40	Opera
Bartel, Jean	Ent	5			15	Miss America/1943
Barth, John	Author	30	40	85	40	Am. Novelist
Barthelmess, Richard	Ent	25	40	75	65	
Bartholdi, Fred, Auguste	Art	400	750	600	900	Statue of Liberty/1834-04

Name	Field	SIG	DS	ALS	SP	Remarks
Bartholomew, Freddie	Ent	20	35	50	75	Child Star/1924 - 1992
Bartlett, Joseph Jackson	Civil War	45	110			Union General/1834-93
Bartlett, Josiah 1729-95	RevWar	250	555	750		
Bartlett, Paul Wayland	Art	15		35		Sculptor
Bartlett, Robert Abram	Explorer	50	175	125		
Bartlett, William F.	Civil War	45	80	150		Union General/1840-76
Bartok, Bela 1881-1945	Music	350	550			Pianist/Composer
Bartok, Eva	Ent	5			15	Actress
Barton, Clara 1821-1912	Political	155	450	675	800	Founder Am. Red Cross
Barton, Derek H.R, Sir	Science	20	30	40	25	Nobel Chemistry
Barton, Seth M. (WD)	Civil War	200		600		CSA General/1829-1900
Barton, Seth Maxwell	Civil War	100		300		CSA General
Bartow, Francis Stebbins 1816-61	Civil War	75		250		CSA Congress/1816-61
Barty, Billy	Ent	10	20		25	Midget Actor
Baruch, Bernard M.	Business	75	300	550	250	Financier/1870-1965
Baryshnikov, Mikail	Ent	75		150	200	Ballet
Basehart, Richard	Ent	25	45		50	Voyage to Btm of the Sea
Basie, Wm, 'Count'	Music	75	200		225	Big Band Leader
Basinger, Kim	Ent	20	45		50	
Baskett, James	Ent	200			600	Song of the South
Basov, Nickolay	Science	20	45		30	Rus. Nobel Physicist
Basquette, Lina	Ent	15			25	
Bassett, Angela	Ent	20			50	
Bassett, Charles A.	Space	40			65	Astronaut
Bassett, Leslie	Music	15	30	50		Pulitzer
Bassett, Richard	RevWar	350	700			SignerConstitution
Bassi, Amedeo	Music	40			125	Tenor
Bate, William B. (WD)	Civil War	125		450		CSA General
Bate, William Brimage	Civil War	60	125	175		CSA General/1826-05
Bateman, Jason	Ent	15	30		30	
Bateman, Justine	Ent	15	30		35	Family Ties
Bates, Alan	Ent	10			20	British Actor
Bates, Edward	Political	35	125	250	450	Lincoln Att'y Gen.
Bates, John C.	Civil War	25		110		Union General
Bates, Katharine Lee	Author	75		300		
Bates, Kathy	Ent	20	50		50	AA Winner
Bathori, Jane 1876-1970	Music	60			125	Opera
Batista, Fulgencio	Political	125	275	350	175	Cuban Dictator-Pre Castro
Batiuk, Tom	Cartoonist	5			20	Funky Winkerbean
Battaglia, Franco	Music	20			50	Opera
Battaille, Charles 1822-72	Music	15		50		Opera
Batten, Hugh	Aviation	10	25	40	30	Navy Ace WWII
Batten, Jean	Aviation	40	75			Pioneer Aviatrix
Battle, Cullen Andrews	Civil War	200	400			CSA General/1829-1905
Battu, Marie 1838-88	Music	25		75		Opera
Batz, Willhelm	Aviation	35			95	Ger. ACE, #7 Worldwide
Baudelaire, Charles-P.	Author	300	900	1,600		Poet/1821-67
Baudouin, King	Royalty	45	100	250	125	King of Belgium
Bauduc, Ray	Music	10			25	Big Band Bassist

Name	Field	SIG	DS	ALS	SP	Remarks
Bauer, Harold	Music	45	80			Pianist
Bauer, Steven	Ent	5			20	
Baulieu, Etienne	Science	20		45	40	Inventor/ Abortion Pill
Baum, Kurt	Music				40	Opera Tenor
Baum, L. Frank	Author	1,750	2,750	4,500	RARE	The Wizard of Oz books
Baum, Maud	Author	200	450	750		Wife of Frank L. Baum (Oz)
Baumer, Steven	Ent	10			25	
Baur, Hans	Aviation	25	45	90	110	Hitler's Pilot
Baur, Harry	Ent	45			150	
Bavier, Frances	Ent	100	225		175	Aunt Bee/Andy Griffith
Baxter, Anne	Ent	20	20	40	45	AA Winner
Baxter, Henry	Civil War	35	95	150		Union General/1821-1873
Baxter, Les	Music	25			50	Composer
Baxter, Warner	Ent	65	125		175	1889 - 1951
Baxter-Birney, Meredith	Ent	5			15	
Bayard, George D. (WD)	Civil War	300		900		Union General/1835-62
Bayard, George Dashiell	Civil War	150		450		Union General
Bayard, John	RevWar	50		185		Continental Congress
Bayard, William	RevWar	100	220	400		
Bayne, Beverly	Ent	10			20	
Beach Boys	Music	200	400		450	Orig five members
Beach, Amy M.	Music	75		400	225	Composer
Beach, Rex	Author	20	35	75	35	Am. Novelist
Beacham, Stephanie	Ent	5			10	
Beadle, George Wells	Science	20	30	45	40	Nobel Medicine
Beal, George Lafayette	Civil War	50	100		250	Union General/1825-96
Beal, John	Ent	15		25	25	
Beale, Richard Lee	Civil War	75	100	200		1819-93. CSA General
Beale, Richard Lee (WD)	Civil War	150		550		CSA General
Beall, William N.	Civil War	175	300	600		CSA General/1825-83
Beals, Jennifer	Ent	20			50	Flashdance
Bean, Alan L.	Space	40	150		100	Moonwalker
Bean, L.L. 1872-1967	Business	150				
Bean, Roy, Judge	Western	2,000	5,000	7,500		Western Law
Beard, "Stymie"	Ent	100			250	Our Gang
Beard, Charles A.	Author	15	30	65		Am. Historian/1874-1948
Beard, Daniel C. 1850-41	Author	125	300	200	200	Fndr Boy Scouts/America
Bearden, Romare	Art	50			200	
Beardslee, Lester A.	Military	20		100		Adm. Span -Am War
Beardsley, Aubrey	Art	175	375	475		Br Illustrator
Beastie Boys	Music	35			65	Signed by entire band
Beatles, The	Music	1,800	7,500		3,500	Four on one piece
Beaton, Cecil 1904-80	Art	65	150	200	350	
Beatrice, Princess	Royalty	25	125	115	120	Daughter Q. Victoria
Beatrix, Queen	Royalty	150		450		Netherlands
Beatty, Clyde 1903-1965	Business	50	100	150	150	
Beatty, David, Adm.	Military	35	75	100	100	
Beatty, Ned	Ent	10			20	
Beatty, Samuel	Civil War	25	50	75		Union General/1820-85

Name	Field	SIG	DS	ALS	SP	Remarks
Beatty, John	Civil War	25	50			Union General/1828-1914
Beatty, Warren	Ent	30	100		55	
Beauharnais, Eugene de	Royalty	100	350	450		Son of Josephine, Adopted
Beauharnais, Hortense	Royalty	75				Wife of Louis Bonaparte
Beaumont, Hugh	Ent	250	600		600	Leave it to Beaver/Dad
Beauregard, P.G.T.	Civil War	350	850	950	900	CSA General/1818-93
Beauregard, P.G.T.(WD)	Civil War	400	1,500	1,750	3,500	CSA General
Beauvoir, Simone de	Author	25	60	125		Fr. Novelist. Existentialist
Beaux, Cecilia 1855-1942	Art	75				Am. Portrait Painter
Beaver, James A.	Civil War	35	55	100		Union General/1837-1914
Beavers, Louise	Ent	100			250	
Bechet, Sidney 1897-59	Music	125	575		175	Jazz
Bechi, Gino	Music	25			55	Opera
Beck, Dave 1894-1993	Political	25	50	50	50	
Beck, John	Ent	5			10	
Beck, C.C	Cartoonist	20			50	Capt. Marvel
Beck, Jeff	Music	25			50	Guitarist
Becker, Boris	Sports	10			30	Tennis
Beckett, Samuel 1906-89	Author	150		400		Nobel
Beckett, Scotty	Ent	30			80	
Beckwith, Edward G.	Civil War	50				Union General/1818-81
Beckwith, Geo. Sir	RevWar		400			RevWar Br Gen/1753-23
Beckwith, J. Carroll	Art	40	80	130		
Becquerel, Edmond	Science	Scarce	Scarce	Scarce	Scarce	Fr. Physicist/1820-91
Becquerel, Henri	Science	175	400	500		Nobel Curies' Radioactivity
Bedelia, Bonnie	Ent	5			10	
Bedford, Brian	Ent	15			30	Disney Voice/Actor
Bedford, Gunning, Jr.	RevWar	350	700			Signer of Constitution
Bedford, Gunning, Sr.	RevWar	175	350			Cousin of Above
Bee Gees	Music	75	175		125	Signed by Three
Bee, Barnard E.	Civil War	300	700	1,600		CSA General/1824-61
Bee, Hamilton P.	Civil War	75		300		CSA General/1822-97
Beebe, Charles William	Explorer	25	75	100	75	1877-1962
Beebe, Marshall	Aviation	25		45	55	WWII ACE
Beech, Olive Ann	Aviation	25			50	Beechcraft Airplane Mfg.
Beecham, Thomas, Sir	Music	50				Conductor
Beecher, Henry Ward	Clergy	75		200		
Beems, Patricia	Ent	5			10	
Beene, Geoffrey	Business	10		30	25	Fashion Designer
Beerbohm, Max	Author	40		150	65	Humorist, Caricaturist
Beery, Noah 1884-1946	Ent	75			175	Scarce
Beery, Noah Jr.	Ent	20	30	35	40	
Beery, Wallace	Ent	100	150	200	225	AA Winner/1885-1949
Beeson, Jack	Music	15	35	75	30	Composer
Beethoven, Ludwig van	Music	RARE	27,500	50,000	RARE	Composer
Begin, Menachem	Political	80		250	150	Prime Minister Israel
Begley, Ed, Jr.	Ent	5			15	
Begley, Ed, Sr.	Ent	25	50		75	
Behan, Brendan F.	Author	160	400	645		Playwright/Author

Name	Field	SIG	DS	ALS	SP	Remarks
Behrman, S, N.	Author	15	25	60	25	Am. Playwright
Beichel, Rudolph	Science	25			55	Rocket Pioneer/von Braun
Beiderbecke, Bix	Music	RARE	RARE	RARE	RARE	Jazz Musician
Beinhorn, Elly	Aviation	10		40	40	Ger. Aviation Pioneer
Beith, Ian Hay	Author	10	30	30	20	Br. Novelist/Playwright
Beke, Charles Tilstone	Explorer	20	50	100		Br. Geographer, Nile
Bekhterev, Vladimir	Science			2,500		Russ. Neuropathologist
Bekins, Milo	Business	35		150	100	Bekins Van & Storage Co.
Bel Geddes, Barbara	Ent	20			25	
Bel Geddes, Norman	Art	20		100	35	Scenic Designer Theater
Belafonte, Harry	Music	20	30		40	
Belafonte, Shari	Music	5		15	20	
Belasco, David	Ent	35	50	70	75	Theatrical Producer
Belaunde, Fernando T.	Political	10	20	50	25	
Belcher, Edward, Sir	Military	15	35	60		
Belcher, Jonathan	Political	225	325	650		Colonial Gov. MA, NH, NJ
Belimer, Hans 1902-75	Art	55	160			Ger. Surrealist
Belknap, George	Civil War	15		50		Union Naval Officer
Belknap, William W.	Civil War	75		175		Union General, Sec'y War
Bell, Alexander Graham	Science	500	1,200	1,800	2,500	Telephone/1847-1922
Bell, Charles H.	Civil War	50	95	140		Union Naval Captain
Bell, Eric Temple	Author	30			55	
Bell, Henry H. 1808-1868	Civil War	60	150			Rear Adm under Farragut
Bell, Herbert A.	Business	15	20	75	50	
Bell, James	Sports	25			75	Cool Papa"/1974 HOF
Bell, John	Political	95	145			Harrison/Tyler Sect. War
Bell, Lauralee	Ent	5			15	
Bell, Rex	Ent	50			125	
Bell, Tyree Harris	Civil War	55	130	200		CSA General/1815-1902
Bellamy, Edward	Author	25	75	150		Novelist
Bellamy, Madge	Ent	10	20	35	35	
Bellamy, Ralph 1904-91	Ent	15	25	40	40	
Bellanca, Giuseppe M.	Aviation	40	85	160	125	Bellanca Aircraft
Bellaver, Henry	Ent	10			20	
Belleri, Marguerite	Music	10		30	25	Opera
Belliard, A.D. (Count)	Military	25	55	150		Fr. Gen under Napoleon
Bellincioni, Gemma	Ent	35		150	100	It. Soprano
Bellini, Vincenzo 1801-35	Music	575				It. Opera/scarce
Belloc, Hilaire 1870-1953	Author	25	55	150	50	Versatile Novelist, Poet
Belloc-Lowndes, Marie	Author	15	40	100	30	Br.Author/Historical Works
Bellon, Leoncadia	Music	15			45	Opera
Bellonte, Maurice	Aviation	75	145	270	345	
Bellow, Saul	Author	20	75	85	35	Nobel Literature, Novelist
Bellows, George	Art	100	225	375		
Bellson, Louis	Music	25		50	75	Jazz Drummer
Belmondo, Jean Paul	Ent	20			40	
Belmont, August	Business	200	750	1,200	350	Banker/Belmont Park
Belmont, August, Jr.	Business	50	124			
Belushi, James	Ent	10	30		35	

Name	Field	SIG	DS	ALS	SP	Remarks
Belushi, John	Ent	200	500		500	Sat Nite Live/Blues Bros.
Belzer, Richard	Ent	15			30	
Bemelmans, Ludwig	Author	45	105		50	
Benacerraf, Barui	Science	30	55		40	Nobel Medicine-Physiology
Benatar, Pat	Ent	20			50	
Benben, Brian	Ent	15			30	
Bench, Johnny	Sports	15			35	Baseball
Benchley, Peter	Author	15	25	50	20	Jaws
Benchley, Robert	Author	40	80	195	75	
Bendix, William 1906-64	Ent	45	125		140	
Benederet, Bea	Ent	75	125		125	Petticoat Junction
Benedict XV Pope	Clergy	125		450	550	
Benedict, Dirk	Ent	10			30	Battlestar Gallactica
Benedict, Julius, Sir	Music	15			25	Br. Pianist
Benedict, William	Ent	25			60	
Beneke, Tex	Music	30			50	Big Band/Sax for Miller
Benes, Eduard	Political	85	90	145	200	P.M. & President Czech.
Benet, Stephen Vincent	Author	80	140	175	150	Pulitzer
Ben-Gurion, David	Political	300		1,200	600	1st Prime Minister of Israel
Benham, Henry W.	Civil War	50	125	150		Union General
Benham, Henry W. (WD)	Civil War	100	225	275		Union General/1813-1884
Bening, Annette	Ent	20			50	
Benjamin, Judah P.	Civil War	300	800	1,200		CSA General/1811-84
Benjamin, Judah P.(WD)	Civil War	450	1,500	1,750		CSA General
Benjamin, William, Jr.	SuprCt	40			60	
Bennett, Arnold	Author	50	175			Br. Novelist
Bennett, Bruce	Ent	10	25	30	30	Tarzan
Bennett, Constance	Ent	30	60	120	65	
Bennett, Floyd	Aviation	300	370	750	500	Pilot with Byrd over N. P.
Bennett, James Gordon	Business	50	175			Financed Stanley-Livingstone
Bennett, Joan 1910-90	Ent	15	25	30	45	Dark Shadows
Bennett, Richard	Ent	15			35	Stage & Silent Films
Bennett, Robert Russell	Music	40			95	Great Broadway Composer
Bennett, Samuel F.	Music	30	75	150		In the Sweet Bye & Bye
Bennett, Tony	Ent	10			25	
Benning, Henry Lewis	Civil War	145	275	350		CSA General/1814-75
Benny, Jack 1894-1974	Ent	80	175		200	
Benois, Alexander	Art	45	195			Costume & Set Designer
Benson, Edward F.	Author	15	35	75		
Benson, Egbert	RevWar	35	75	150		Continental Congress
Benson, Frank Robert	Ent	15	20	35	20	British Actor
Benson, George	Music	15			25	
Benson, Jodi	Ent	10			35	Disney Voice/Ariel
Benson, Robbie	Ent	15			25	Actor/Disney Voice
Benson, William S.	Military	10	20	35	25	Adm. USN WW I
Bent, James Theodore	Explorer	5	10	25	10	Archaeologist
Benteen, Frederick W.	Civil War		3,500		2,500	Scarce
Benton, Barbi	Ent	5		15	15	
Benton, Robert	Ent	10			20	AA Winning Director

Name	Field	SIG	DS	ALS	SP	Remarks
Benton, Samuel	Civil War	345	540			CSA General/1820-64
Benton, Thomas H.	Art	100	250	600		
Benton, Thomas H.	Political	90		205		Senator
Benton, William P.	Civil War	95	130			Union General/1828-67
Benzell, Mimi	Music	15			35	Opera
Ben-Zvi, Itzhak 1884-1963	Political	75	200	275	125	2nd President Israel
Berdyaev, Nikolai	Political	75	100	130	175	
Berenger, Tom	Ent	15			45	
Berenson, Marisa	Ent	10			25	
Berenstain, Stan	Cartoonist	20			50	Bearenstein Bears
Beresford, Charles, Lord 1846-1919	Military	15	35	125	80	British Admiral
Berfson, Henri-Louis	Author	30	80	155		
Berg, Alban	Music	135	485			Composer
Berg, Gertrude	Ent	15			35	
Berg, Paul	Science	25		75	45	Nobel Chemistry
Berganza, Teresa	Music	15			35	Opera
Bergen, Candice	Ent	15	45		45	Murphy Brown
Bergen, Edgar 1903-78	Ent	50	100		150	Ventriloquist
Bergen, Frances	Ent	5			10	
Bergen, Polly	Ent	10			20	
Berger, Erna	Music	10			30	Opera
Berger, Gottlob	Military	40	120	200	75	
Berger, Senta	Ent	10	15	35	30	
Bergere, Lee	Ent	10			20	
Bergman, Ingmar	Ent	50	100		150	
Bergman, Ingrid 1915-82	Ent	125	250	300	350	AA Winner/Casablanca
Bergner, Elizabeth	Ent	15	35	60	35	1898-1968
Bergonzi, Carlo	Music	30			65	Opera
Bergson, Henri 1859-1941	Author	40	125			Nobel for Lit.. 1927
Berio, Luciano	Music	20	30	75		Composer
Berjerac, Jacques	Ent	15			30	French Actor
Berkeley, Busby 1895-76	Ent	125	250	300	300	Choreagrapher/Director
Berkley, Elizabeth	Ent	20			45	Showgirls
Berkowitz, David	Criminal	75		250		Son of Sam - Killer
Berle, Milton	Ent	10	30	35	35	Mr. Television
Berlier, Jean Baptiste	Science	15	27	45		French Engineer
Berlier, Theophile	Military	50	150	295		
Berlik, Jan	Music	25			50	Opera Tenor
Berlin, Irving 1888-1990	Music	150	750		950	Composer
Berlinger, Warren	Ent	10			20	
Berlioz, Hector 1803-69	Music	245	1,248	1,622		Composer
Berlitz, Charles	Business	15			35	
Berman, Eugene	Art	40	105	195		
Berman, Pandro S.	Ent	30			65	Producer
Berman, Shelley	Ent	5			10	
Bernadotte, Jean-Baptiste	Royalty	150	575	650		Marshal of Napolean
Bernard, Claude 1813-78	Science	145		800		
Bernard, Crystal	Ent	20			45	Wings
Bernard, Francis,1712-79	Political	175	522	750		Gov of Mass Bay Colony

Name	Field	SIG	DS	ALS	SP	Remarks
Bernard, Simon	Civil War	45	115			Engineer
Bernardi, Herschel	Ent	20			40	
Berndt, Walter	Cartoonist	10			35	Smitty
Bernhard, Sandra	Ent	5			10	
Bernhardt, Sarah d.1923	Ent	150	300	500	600	Early Stage star
Bernie, Ben	Music	20		25	25	Big Band Leader
Bernsen, Corbin	Ent	15			40	
Bernstein, Elmer	Music	20			45	Composer
Bernstein, Leonard	Music	125	450	600	250	Composer
Berosini, Josephine	Ent	10			30	
Berra, Yogi	Sports	15			30	1972 HOF/Baseball
Berringer, Tom	Ent	15			50	
Berry, Chuck	Music	35			75	
Berry, Halle	Ent	20			50	
Berry, Hiram G. 1824-63	Civil War	400	600			Union General/KIA
Berry, Ken	Ent	5	15	20	15	Mama's Family
Berry, Lucien	Military	15	50			General WW I
Berryman, Clifford	Art	55	75	95		Created the "Teddy" bear
Bertelson, Richard L.	Aviation	10		35	30	WWII Navy ACE
Berthier, L. Alexandre	Military	75	225	375		Marshal of Napoleon
Berthold, Rudolf	Aviation	200	350	650	450	WWI Ace
Berthollet, Claude-Louis	Science	60	150	330		French Chemist
Bertinelli, Valerie	Ent	5	20		20	
Bertolucci, Bernardo	Ent	15			35	Director
Berwick, Duke	Military	150	400			Gen. of Louis XIV
Berzelius, Jons Jacob	Science	75	165	475		Chemist
Besant, Walter 1836-1901	Author	35	125	190		
Beser, Jacob	Aviation	50	100		100	Enola Gay member
Bess, Gordon	Cartoonist	5			20	Redeye
Bessemer, Henry	Science	35	60	200	90	Invented Blast Furnace
Besser, Joe	Ent	45			75	Three Stooges
Bessieres, Jean-Baptiste 1766-1813	Military	175	375			Marshal of Napoleon
Best, Charles H.	Science	45	150	250	125	Co-"Discoverer of Insulin
Best, Edna	Ent	15	15	30	45	
Best, James	Ent	5		15	15	
Best, Pete	Music	25			75	Beatles Drummer/Pre-Ringo
Beatle						
Best, Willie	Ent	50			150	
Bestor, Don	Music	15				Jack Benny Bandleader
Bethe, Hans, Dr.	Science	35	55		45	Nobel Physics
Bethune, Mary McLeod	Political	125	325	500	175	Black Teacher, Activist.
Betjeman, John, Sir	Author	40	85	132	50	British Poet/1906-82
Bettelheim, Bruno	Science	35	65		150	Psychiatrist
Bettger, Lyle	Ent	10			20	
Betz, Carl	Ent	40			75	
Beugnot, J.C., Count	Military	85	160			
Beverage, John	Civil War	30	85			Union General
Bevin, Ernest	Political	25	55	125	45	(Br.) Union Leader
Bewick, Thomas	Art	100	275	625		Illustrator/Wood Engraver

Name	Field	SIG	DS	ALS	SP	Remarks
Bey, Turhan	Ent	20			35	
Bhutto, Zullikar Ali	Political	25			75	Pakistan : Pres & PM
Biasini, Piero	Music	10			35	Opera
Bickel, Theodore	Ent	10			35	
Bickford, Charles	Ent	30	45	65	100	
Biddle, Clement	RevWar	275	750	900		Rev Officer/Businessman
Biddle, Clement Carroll	Military	20	30	70		Col. of lst Inf. PA.
Biddle, George	Art	30	85	210		
Biddle, Nicholas	Business	150	600	800		Pres. U.S. Bank, Financier
Bidwell, Daniel D.	Civil War	225		600		Union General/1819-64
Bidwell, John	Western	20	100			California Pioneer
Biehn, Michael	Ent	15			40	
Bierce, Ambrose	Author	275	670	588		Short Stories
Bierstadt, Albert	Art	125	220	540		
Bigard, Barney	Music	70			150	Jazz Clarinet, Ten. Sax
Bigelow, Erastus B.	Business	100	290	595		Power Looms for Weaving
Bigelow, John 1817-1911	Business	5	10	30	15	Editor NY Evening Post
Bigelow, Poultney	Author	10		20		Journalist
Biggers, Earl Derr	Author	150		400	350	Am.Mystery Writer
Biggs, Asa	Civil War	25	60			CSA Judge
Bikel, Theodore	Ent	5			15	Actor/Singer
Bill, Tony	Ent	10			20	
Billings, Josh 1818-85	Author	25	80	165	40	American Humorist.
Billingsley, Barbara	Ent	5	15		20	Leave it to Beaver/Mom
Billo, James D.	Aviation	10		35	30	Navy ACE, WWII
Billroth, Theodor 1829-94	Science	75	225	295		Surgeon/Use of Antisepsis
Binci, Mario	Music	15			45	Opera
Bing, Herman	Ent	30			50	Disney Voice
Bing, Rudolph	Music	15	20	35	35	Metropolitan Opera Leader
Bingham, Henry	Civil War	85		160		Union General
Bingham, John A.	Political	25	35	90		Lincoln Judge Adv.
Bingham, Judson David	Civil War	45	140	185		Union General/1831-1909
Bingham, William	RevWar	120	315	340		Continental Congress
Binnig, Gerd, Dr.	Science	20	60		45	Nobel Physics
Binoche, Juliette	Ent	20			50	
Bird, Larry	Sports	20			50	Basketball HOF
Birds, The	Music	150	250		300	Signed by Entire Group
Birdseye, Clarence	Business	250	400	550	350	Birdseye Frozen Foods
Birdwood, William, Sir	Military	45	145			Br. Fid. Marshal, WW I
Birendra, Bir B.	Political	10	15		20	Prime Minister Nepal
Birney, David	Ent	5			10	
Birney, David Bell	Civil War	225	295	775		Union General/1825-64
Birney, William	Civil War	35	70	90		Union General
Bisbee, Horatio, Jr.	Civil War	25	45	100		Union Officer
Bishop, Elizabeth 1911-79	Author	35	125			Am. Poet/Pulitzer Prize '55
Bishop, J. Michael. Dr.	Science	25	40		35	Nobel Medicine
Bishop, Joey	Ent	5	20	20	20	Rat Pack member
Bishop, Julie	Ent	5			15	
Bishop, Stephen	Music	10			20	

Name	Field	SIG	DS	ALS	SP	Remarks
Bishop, Wm. 'Billy'	Aviation	150	225	300	220	ACE, WWI w/72 Kills
Bismark, Prince Otto von	Royalty	250	600	745	920	The Iron Chancellor
Bispham, David	Music	60	80	110	120	Opera
Bissell, Clayton L.	Aviation	25	40	100		
Bissell, Whit	Ent	10			20	
Bisset, Jacqueline	Ent	5			20	
Bissett, Josie	Ent	15			45	Melrose Place
Bissit, J.E.	Military	10	25		15	Comdr. HMS Queen Eliz.
Bitter, Karl Theodore	Art	25	75	155	100	Am. Sculptor
Bittrich, Wilhelm	Military	30	70	135	60	
Bixby, Bill	Ent	35	45		55	Incredible Hulk...
Bizet, Georges 1838-75	Music	350		1,200		Composer
Bjerknes, Jacob A.B.	Science	35				Discovered Origin/Cyclones
Bjoerling, Jussi 1911-69	Ent	500	650	1,000	900	
Bjork	Music	20			45	
Bjornson, Bjornstjerne	Author	50	55	140		Nobel/Literature 3x
Bjornstad, Alfred	Military	10	20	35		General WWI
Black Crowes	Music	40			80	Signed by Entire Group
Black Sabbath	Music	50			100	Signed by Entire Group
Black Sabbath	Music	50			100	Signed by Entire Band
Black, Clint	Music	20	50		50	
Black, Frank, Dr.	Music	5			30	NBC Director of Music
Black, Hugo 1886-1966	SuprCt	45	120	225	95	
Black, Jeremiah	Political	25	60	115		Att'y General (Buchanan)
Black, John Charles	Civil War	50	125	155		Union General/18399-1915
Black, Karen	Ent	5			15	
Black, Richard B.	Military	10	25	45		
Black, William	Military	20			45	General WWI
Blackburn, John T.	Aviation	15		40	30	WWII ACE
Blackett, Patrick M.	Science	20	35	50	30	Nobel Physics
Blackman, Honor	Ent	5	20		20	James Bond Girl
Blackmer, Sidney	Ent	20	35	40	40	1895 - 1973
Blackmore, Richard D.	Author	15	40	95		Br. Novelist. Lorna Doone
Blackmun, Harry A.	SuprCt	40	225	270	75	
Blackstone, Harry	Ent	120		450	250	Magician
Blackstone, Harry, Jr.	Ent	30			65	Magician
Blackwell, Mr.	Business	5			15	Fashion Critic
Blackwell, Otis	Music	25	85	175		Composer
Blaine, James G. 1830-93	Political	30	65	120	45	Sen.&Garfield's Sec'y St.
Blaine, Vivian	Ent	10		25	25	
Blair, Charles	Aviation	45			60	
Blair, Francis P. Jr.	Civil War	45	80	145		Union General/1825-1875
Blair, Janet	Ent	10			25	
Blair, John	SuprCt	150	775	1,200	48	Signer of Constitution
Blair, Linda	Ent	10	25	25	25	The Excorsist
Blair, Montgomery	Political	75	205	545		Counsel to Dred Scott
Blake, Amanda	Ent	50	60	100	85	Gunsmoke's Miss Kitty
Blake, Bud	Cartoonist	5			20	Tiger
Blake, Eubie 1883-1983	Music	45		125	90	Composer

Name	Field	SIG	DS	ALS	SP	Remarks
Blake, Madge	Ent	100	RARE	RARE	250	TV Batman's Aunt Harriet
Blake, Robert	Ent	10	20		30	Baretta
Blake, Whitney	Ent	15			35	
Blakely, Susan	Ent	10			20	
Blakeslee, Don	Aviation	10	25	35	30	WWII ACE
Blanc, Louis	Author	15		45		Fr. Socialist, Journalist
Blanc, Mel 1908-89	Ent	70	175	250	250	Man of 1,000 Voices
Blanchard, Albert G.	Civil War	100	250			CSA General/1810-91
Blanchard, Albert G.(WD)	Civil War	200	750			CSA General
Blanchard, Nina	Ent	5			15	
Blandick, Clara	Ent	650	1,200	RARE	RARE	Autnie Em/Oz
Blane, Ralph	Music	10			30	Composer
Blane, Sally	Ent	5			15	
Blasco-Ibanez, Vicente	Author	100			450	Sp. Novelist. Self Exiled
Blasiev, Lisabeth	Music	10			25	Opera
Blass, Bill	Business	10	15		25	Fashion Designer
Blatchford, Samuel	SuprCt	45	125	150		1820 - 1893
Blatty, William Peter	Author	15	45		35	The Exorcist
Bledsoe, Drew	Sports	15			45	Football
Bledsoe, Tempest	Ent	15			40	The Cosby Show
Bleeth, Yasmine	Ent	15			45	Baywatch
Blenker, Louis	Civil War	100	210			Union General/1812-63
Blennerhassett, Harman	RevWar	115	330	575		Refuge-Burr Conspiracy
Bleriot, Louis 1872-1936	Aviation	250	500	595	500	lst To Fly English Channel
Bless, Frederick	Aviation	10		35	35	ACE, Korea
Bligh, William, Capt.	Military	1,500	3,500	7,500		Br. Adm/Capt. HMS Bounty
Bliss, Arthur, Sir	Music	35		175		Br. Opera
Bliss, George Jr.	Civil War	10		25		
Bliss, Tasker H.	Military	15	25	50	25	US Gen.Cmdr. War College
Bliss, William Wallace S.	Military	130	435	500		Pvt. Sec'y Zachary Taylor
Bliss, Zenas R.	Civil War	35	110	160		Union Officer
Blitzstein, Marc	Music	80	100	250		Opera/Composer
Blixen, Karen (Isak Dinesen)	Author	110			200	Out of Africa
Bloch, Ernest 1880-1959	Music	80		300	250	Composer, Teacher
Bloch, Ernst	Author	55	140		90	Ger. Philosopher.
Bloch, Felix	Science	25	40	100	30	Nobel Physics
Bloch, Konrad, Dr.	Science	20	30	45	30	Nobel Medicine
Bloch, Raymond	Music	10	20	35	10	Composer
Bloch, Robert	Author	20	50	60	20	
Block, Henry W,	Business	20	45		30	H & R Block
Block, Richard	Business	20	35	90	25	H & R Block
Blocker, Dan	Ent	200	300		400	Bonanza's "Hoss"
Blodget, Samuel Jr.	RevWar	285	750	1,540		Inventor/Judge
Bloembergen, Nicolaas	Science	20	35	40	30	Nobel Physics
Blomberg, Werner Von	Military	30	75	165	125	Ger. Fld. Marshal WWII
Blondell, Gloria	Ent	10			25	
Blondell, Joan	Ent	35	40	65	55	
Blood, Sweat and Tears	Music	35	100		80	Signed by Entire Band
Bloom, Claire	Ent	10			20	

Name	Field	SIG	DS	ALS	SP	Remarks
Bloomer, Amelia	Political	275	350			Social Reformer
Bloomfield, Joseph	RevWar	30	95	150		
Bloomfield-Zeisler, F.	Music	25			75	Concert Pianist
Blossom Rock	Ent	100	150		200	Addam's Family Grandma
Blount, James H.	Civil War	25	40			CSA Officer
Blount, William	Political	320	900			Continental Congress
Blucher, Gebhard L. von	Military	200	550	2,200		Pruss/Fld.Marshal vs Napoleon
Blue, Ben 1901-75	Ent	25	30	60	50	
Blue, Monte 1880-1963	Ent	25		55	75	Silent Star
Blues Traveller	Music	40			80	Signed by Entire Group
Blum, Leon	Political	25	40	110	35	Pres. France during WWII
Blum, Norbert	Political	5			10	Ger. Minister/Statesman
Blumberg, Baruch S.	Science	20	30	55	25	Nobel Medicine
Blumenfeld, Felix	Music		150		300	Russ. Conductor
Blumenthal, Jacques	Music	40		350		Composer/Pianist
Blunt, Asa P.	Military	25		200		General
Blunt, James G. Dr.	Civil War	45	75			Union General/1826-81
Blyden, Larry	Ent	10			20	Whats My Line?
Blyth, Ann	Ent	10			20	
Blythe, Betty	Ent	35		50	150	Silent Star
Boardman, Eleanor	Ent	10	15	25	25	
Boardman, Russell	Aviation	25	55	95	80	
Bob & Ray	Ent	25			50	Comedy Team
Bochco, Steven	Ent	10	25		20	TV Producer
Bock, Feodor von	Military	100	295		150	Ger.Gen. WWII
Bock, Jerry	Music	30		35	80	
Bodenschatz, Karl	Aviation	30	75	150	95	
Bogart, Humphrey	Ent	850	1,400	2,200	2,550	1899 - 1957
Bogdonavich, Peter	Ent	15	30		35	Director
Boggs, Charles	Civil War	45	90	115		Union Admiral
Boggs, Wade	Sports	10			25	Baseball
Boggs, William R.	Civil War	85	195	315		CSA General/1829-1911
Boggs, William R. (WD)	Civil War	170		495		CSA General
Bohm, Karl	Music	15		75	85	Conductor
Bohr, Aage Niels 1922-	Science	25			55	Nobel Physics 1975
Bohr, Niels H.D. 1885-62	Science	200	450			Danish Physicist/Nobel '22
Boito, Arrigo	Music	45	110	325		Composer
Bok, Edward W.	Author	30	55	140	40	Editor/Curtis Pub./Pulitzer
Bokor, Margit	Music	10			30	Hungarian Soprano
Boland, Mary	Ent	20	75		70	1880 - 1965
Bolcom, William	Music	15	25	65		Composer/Pulitzer
Boles, John	Ent	30	30	45	45	1895 - 1969
Bolet, Jorge	Music	20			120	Pianist
Bolger, James	Political	10			20	P.M. New Zealand
Bolger, Ray 1904-87	Ent	65	150	350	175	Scarecrow in Wiz of Oz
Bolingbroke, Henry	Author	30	150	250		1st Viscount
Bolivar, Simon	Political	500	3,075	4,975		Statesman/RevWar Leader
Boll, Heinrich	Author	35	30	95	25	Nobel Lit./Novelist/ Poet
Bologna, Joseph	Ent	15			25	

Name	Field	SIG	DS	ALS	SP	Remarks
Bolt, John	Aviation	15	30	50	35	ACE, WWII & Korea
Bolton, Guy	Author	20	75			Playwright
Bolton, James	Science	20	70		20	Sewing Machine
Bolton, Michael	Music	25			50	
Bolton-Jones, Hugh	Art	10	25	45		Am. Landscape Painter
Bombeck, Erma	Author	20		50	45	Humorist
Bomford, George	Military	75	200			Inventor Howitzer Cannon
Bomford, James Voty	Civil War	40	80	125		
Bon Jovi, Jon	Music	25	100		50	
Bonaduce, Danny	Ent	10			25	Partridge Family
Bonaparte, Elise	Royalty	250		500		Oldest Sister of Napoeon
Bonaparte, Eugene Nap.	Royalty	75	200	375		Adopted by Napoleon
Bonaparte, Jerome	Royalty	60	135	240		Brother of Napoleon
Bonaparte, Joseph	Royalty	120	245	350		Elder Brother of Napoleon
Bonaparte, Letizia	Royalty		1,500	2,700		Mother of Napoleon
Bonaparte, Lucien	Royalty	50	100	165		Brother
Bonaparte, Marie Louise	Royalty	195	815			Wife of Napoleon
Bonaparte, Napoleon	Royalty					See Napolean
Bonci, Alessandro	Music	35			115	Opera
Bond, Carrie Jacobs	Music	35	110	170	45	Composer
Bond, Charles	Aviation	15		45	30	ACE - WWII/Flying Tigers
Bond, Ford	Ent	10			15	Radio Announcer
Bond, Johnny	Music	10			20	
Bond, Tommy Butch	Ent	10			25	Our Gang child star
Bond, Ward 1903-60	Ent	95	150		225	Western star & GWTW
Bond, William C.	Science	45	190	350		Am. Astronomer..
Bondi, Beulah	Ent	25	45		55	1904 - 1987
Bonds, Barry	Sports	15			35	Baseball
Bonerz, Peter	Ent	5			15	Bob Newhart Show
Bonesteel, Charles H.	Military	20	35	50		
Bonet, Lisa	Ent	10			25	
Bong, Richard	Aviation	500	1,200	2,000	1,800	ACE - WWII/Top U.S. Ace
Bonham, Milledge (WD)	Civil War	185	255	455		CSA General
Bonham, Milledge L.	Civil War	100	205			CSA General/1813-90
Bonheur, Rosa 1822-1899	Art	110	155	325		
Bonnard, Pierre	Art	105	280	650		Fr. Post-impressionist
Bonneville, Benj. L. E. de	Western	225	600	800		Pioneer of the NW Territory
Bonney, Barbara	Music	15			30	Opera
Bono,Sonny	Ent	40	75		75	Sonny and Cher
Bonstelle, Jessie	Ent	25		40		Actress/Producer
Bontemps, Arna	Author	30	100			(Am.) Novels/Poetry
Book, Sorrell	Ent	5			10	
Booker T and the MG's	Music	50				Signed by Entire Group
Boone, Daniel 1734-1820	Western	4,500	9,000	RARE	RARE	American Pioneer
Boone, Debbie	Music	5			20	
Boone, Pat	Music	5			10	
Boone, Richard	Ent	75	125		125	Palladin
Boone, Squire	RevWar			1,150		Father of Daniel
Boosler, Elayne	Ent	10			20	Stand Up Comedy

Name	Field	SIG	DS	ALS	SP	Remarks
Booth, Adrian	Ent	5			20	
Booth, Edwin 1833-93	Ent	115		300	250	
Booth, Evangeline	Political	35	115		90	Salvation Army
Booth, John Wilkes	Criminal	7,500	12,500	25,000	RARE	Assassin of Lincoln
Booth, Junius Brutus, Jr. 1821-83	Ent	35	85			Actor Brother of JW Booth
Booth, Maude 1865-1948	Political	45	80	225		
Booth, Shirley	Ent	30			55	TV's Hazel
Booth, William 1829-1912	Political	125	160	350	175	Founder of Salvation Army
Booth, William Bramwell	Political	40	75	100	65	Eldest Son & Organizer
Boothe, Powers	Ent	5	15		15	
Bor, Tadeusz	Military	15	45	75		
Bordaberry, Juan M	Political	10	15	25	15	Uraguay
Bordelon, Guy	Aviation	15		35	25	ACE, Korea
Borden, Lizzy	Criminal	1,800	RARE	RARE	RARE	Alleged Ax Murderess
Borden, Olive	Ent	30	35	45	150	
Bordoni, Irene	Ent	20		35	40	1895 - 1953
Borge, Victor	Ent	15			30	
Borges, Jorge Luis	Author	75	350			
Borglum, Gutzon	Art	225	375	550	800	Creator Mt. Rushmore
Borglum, Lincoln	Art	25	60	85		Son of Gutzon. Sculptor
Borgnine, Ernest	Ent	10	15	20	20	AA Winner/McHales Navy
Bori, Lucrezia 1887-1960	Music	35	95		80	Opera
Boring, Wayne	Cartoonist	30			50	Superman
Boris lll	Royalty	100			200	King & Dictator Bulgaria
Borkh, Inge	Music	10			25	Opera
Borlaug, Norman, Dr.	Science	20	35	80	30	Nobel Peace Prize
Borman, Frank	Space	30			100	Astronaut
Bormann, Martin 1900-45	Military	350	750	1,500	800	Nazi Private Sec'y to Hitler
Born, Max 1882-70	Science	175	350	575		Nobel/Physicist
Borne, Hermann von	Military	20	45	90		
Borno, Louis	Political	20	75			Pres. Haiti
Borodin, Alexander	Music	250	450	950		Russian Composer
Borowski, Felix	Music	15	40	100	50	Composer
Borso, Umberto	Music	15			45	It. Tenor
Borzage, Frank	Ent	75			150	Director-Producer
Bosanquet, Helen D.	Author	10		25		
Bose, Jagadis, Sir	Science	30	40	150		Indian Physicist
Bosley, Tom	Ent	10	20		20	Happy Days
Bostwick, Barry	Ent	15	25		35	Rocky Horror Pix Show
Bostwick, George	Aviation	10	25	40	30	WWII ACE
Boswell, Connie	Ent	5		20	10	
Boswell, James	Author	750				Biographer of Sam'l Johnson
Bosworth, Hobart	Ent	25	30	40	65	
Botha, Louis	Political	60	110	95		So.African Soldier
Bottoms, Joseph	Ent	5			15	
Bottoms, Timothy	Ent	7			15	
Boudin, Eugene-Louis	Art	105	280	475		Fr. Sea & Beach Scenes
Boudinot, Elias 1740-1821	RevWar	240		785		Washington's Att'y Gen.

Name	Field	SIG	DS	ALS	SP	Remarks
Boudinot, Elias C.	Civil War	95	250	Scarce		Cherokee Leader/1835-90
Boulanger, Nadia	Music	125			375	Composer
Boulard, Georges	Aviation	15		60	35	
Boulez, Pierre	Music	40	45	75	25	Fr. Composer-Conductor
Boulle, Pierre	Author	10	15	30	15	
Boult, Adrian, Sir	Music		45	100	75	Conductor (Br)
Bourbon-Parma, Zita	Royalty				450	Last Austrian Empress
Bourguiba, Habib	Political	15	40	100	25	Pres. Tunisia
Bourke-White, Margaret	Art	75	75	200		1904-1971
Bourmont, Louis A.V.	Military		80	160		General under Napoleon
Bourrienne, L.A.F. de	Military	45	60	120		Pvt. Sec'y to Napoleon
Bouton, Chas, Marie	Art	100	165	400		
Boutwell, George S.	Political	15	45	150	40	Grant Sec'y Treasury
Bow, Clara 1905-1965	Ent	200	350	400	450	It Girl
Bowditch, Nathaniel	Science	100	310	500		Astronomer/Mathematician
Bowen, Elizabeth	Author	25	75	150	45	
Bowen, George F., Sir	Political	10	25	35		Gov Australia, New Zealand
Bowen, Ira Sprague	Science	10	25	35	15	Dir.Wilson-Palomar Obs.
Bowen, John S.	Civil War	110	200	450		CSA General
Bowen, John S. (WD)	Civil War	175	275	750		CSA General/1830-63
Bowen, Thomas Meed	Civil War	45				Union General/1835-1906
Bowie, David	Music	30			55	
Bowie, James (Jim)	Military	RARE	15,000	RARE	RARE	Co-Cmdr. Alamo.
Bowler, Metcalf	Political	50	135	250		Opposed Stamp Act
Bowman, Lee	Ent	10	20	25	25	
Boxcar Willie	Music	5	20		15	
Boxleitner, Bruce	Ent	10			30	
Boy George	Music	25			55	
Boyd, Belle	Civil War	2,000	10,000	RARE	10,000	Confederate Spy
Boyd, Jimmy	Ent	20			55	
Boyd, William Hopalong Cassidy	Ent		200	350		375 1895 - 1972
Boyer, Charles	Ent	35	50		100	1897 - 1978
Boyer, Jean-Pierre	Political	35	125			President of Haiti
Boyington, "Pappy"	Aviation	75	150	200	175	WWII Marine ACE/Gregory
Boyle, Lara Flynn	Ent	20			50	
Boyle, Peter	Ent	20	40		35	Young Frankenstein
Boynton, Henry Van Ness	Civil War	45	80	165		Union Officer
Boys II Men	Music	50			100	Signed by all
Boze, Marie	Ent	15			50	
Brabazon-Moore, John T.	Aviation	25	60	85	50	lst Licensed. WW I Pilot
Bracco, Lorraine	Ent	20			45	
Bracken, Eddie	Ent	5			10	
Brackett, Charles	Ent	20			70	Producer/AA Screenwriter
Bradbury, Ray	Author	30	155	275	45	Am. Sci-Fi Writer
Bradford, Gamaliel	Author	10	25	35		Am. Biographer
Bradford, William	Political	125	275	450		G. Washington Att'y Gen'l
Bradlee, Ben	Author	15			40	Editor/Washington Post
Bradley, Ed	Ent	5			10	TV News
Bradley, James	Military	20	35	60		

Name	Field	SIG	DS	ALS	SP	Remarks
Bradley, John H.	Military	35	95		50	Iwo Jima Flag Raiser
Bradley, Joseph P.	SuprCt	55	100	200		
Bradley, Kathleen	Ent	5			10	Price is Right Model
Bradley, Omar N. 1893-81	Military	100	250	300	185	5 Star General WWII
Bradley, Tom	Political	6	15	30	15	Mayor Los Angeles
Bradstreet, John	Military	150	350	450		British Major General
Brady, Alice	Ent	70		125	150	1892 - 1939
Brady, James B.	Business	400	1,250	1,500	650	Diamond Jim
Brady, Mathew S.	Art	350	1,000	2,000		Photographer
Brady, Pat	Ent	100			250	1914 - 1972
Brady, Scott	Ent	15	15	25	35	
Brady, William A.	Ent	25			65	
Braga, Sonia	Ent	10	15	30	30	
Bragg, Braxton	Civil War	365	600	900	900	CSA General
Bragg, Braxton (WD)	Civil War	450		1,250		CSA General/1817-76
Bragg, Edward S.	Civil War	45	85	135		Union General
Bragg, Thomas	Civil War	135	225			CSA Att'y General/1810-72
Bragg, Wm. Henry, Sir	Science	45	95			Nobel Physics w/son Wm. L.
Bragg, Wm. Lawrence	Science	48	85			Nobel Physics w/Father Wm
Braham, John (Abraham) 1774-1856	Music	25		100		Opera
Brahms, Johannes	Music	1,000	2,000	3,500	4,500	Composer
Brailowsky, Alexander	Music	50			85	Concert Pianist
Braithwaite, Wm. Stanley	Author	35	120	235	45	
Branagh, Kenneth	Ent	20	50		50	
Branch, John 1782-1863	Political	25	75	165		Sec'y Navy
Branch, Lawrence (WD)	Civil War	450		950		CSA General/KIA
Branch, Lawrence 0.	Civil War	200	400			CSA General/KIA/1820-62
Brand, Christopher Q.	Aviation	75	150	300	200	ACE WWI/Only night Ace
Brand, Harry	Ent	10			20	Producer
Brand, Max 1892-1944	Author	50				Destry.... Dr. Kildare
Brand, Neville	Ent	75			150	
Brand, Vance D.	Space	15	40		195	Apollo Soyuz
Brandauer, Klaus Maria	Ent	15	15	30	40	
Brandegee, Augustus	Civil War	15	35	200		
Brandeis, Louis D.	SuprCt	150	400	650	1,200	lst Jewish Supr. Ct. Judge
Brando, Marlon	Ent	200	550		600	AA Winner
Brandt, Marianne	Music	25		80	75	Opera
Brandt, Willy 1913-92	Political	35	175	210	85	Ger.Chancellor
Brandy	Music	25			50	
Branigan, Laura	Music	15			35	
Branly, Edouard 1844-40	Science			635	475	Fr. Physicist/Inventor
Brant, Joseph	Western	RARE	RARE	5,000	RARE	1742-1807 Mohawk Indian Chief
Branzell, Karin	Music	40			145	Opera
Braque, Georges	Art	420	675	1,225		Developed Cubism w/ Picasso
Brattain, Walter	Science	25	50	90	45	Nobel Physics.
Bratton, John, Dr.	Civil War	95	250	375		CSA General/1831-98
Brauchitsch, Walter von	Military	75	155	210	125	Hitler Fld.Marshall
Braun, Eva	Military	1,000		2,750		Hitler's Mistress-Wife
Braun, Wernher von	Science					see Von Braun

Name	Field	SIG	DS	ALS	SP	Remarks
Brautigan, Richard	Author	45	150			Beat author
Braxton, Carter 1736-97	RevWar	275	550	1,200		Signer Decl. of Indepen.
Braxton, Toni	Music	20			40	
Brayman, Mason	Civil War	30	75			Union General/1813-95
Brayton, Charles Ray	Civil War	40	65	100		Union General/1840-1910
Brazzi, Rossano 1916-95	Ent	15			35	
Bread	Music	50			100	Signed by Entire Band
Brearley, David	RevWar	375	800			Continental Congress
Breathed, Berke	Cartoonist	25			60	Bloom County/Outland
Brecht, Bertolt	Author	400	1,500	2,500		Playwright, Poet
Breckinridge, John C.	Civil War	200	400	750		CSA General/1821-75
Breckinridge, Joseph C.	Military	25	40			
Breckinridge, Wm. C.	Civil War	110	250	275		CSA Officer
Breen, Bobby	Ent	10	15	35	25	Child Star
Breese, Lou	Music	5			15	Big Band Leader
Breese, Vance	Aviation	30	115		40	Aviator & Aircraft Designer
Brendel, El 1890-1964	Ent	15	35		60	
Breneman, Tom	Ent	15	15	30	25	
Brennan, Eileen	Ent	5			15	
Brennan, Walter 1894-74	Ent	100	150	250	175	AA Winner
Brennan, William J. Jr.	SuprCt	65	105	155	90	
Brenner, David	Ent	15			25	Comedian
Brenner, Victor D.	Art	250		675		Design Lincoln Penny/VDB
Brent, Evelyn	Ent	15	20	25	35	
Brent, George	Ent	25	30	35	60	
Brent, George Wm.	Civil War	100	210	300		
Brent, Joseph Lancaster	Civil War	90	145	345		CSA Colonel
Brent, Robert	Military	35	100	165		
Brereton, Lewis Hyde	Aviation	45	140		55	Cmdr.1st Allied Airborne
Breslau, Sophie	Music	35			90	Opera
Bresser-Gianoli, Clotilde	Music	20			55	Opera
Breton, Andre	Author	60	175	325		Poet/Essayist/Critic
Brett, George	Sports	20			45	Baseball
Brett, George H.	Military	50	125			Air Corps General WWII
Brett, Jeremy 1935-95	Ent	25			100	Played Sherlock Holmes
Brewer, David J.	SuprCt	75	95	160		
Brewer, Teresa	Music	5			15	Big Band Singer
Brewerton, Henry	Civil War			125		Union Gen. Corps of Eng.
Brewster, David, Sir	Science	30	55	180		Invented Kaleidoscope
Breyer, Stephen	SuprCt	20			40	
Brezhnev, Leonid	Political	375	975		400	Soviet Comm. Party Leader
Brian, Mary	Ent	10			25	
Brice, Benjamin W.	Civil War	15	45			Union Paymaster General
Brice, Fanny 1891-1951	Ent	100	200	300	300	
Brickell, Edie	Ent	10			30	
Brico, Antonia, Dr.	Music	15			75	Female Conductor
Bridges, Beau	Ent	15	30		35	
Bridges, Harry	Political	70	125		140	Pres. Longshoreman Union
Bridges, Jeff	Ent	15	30		35	

Name	Field	SIG	DS	ALS	SP	Remarks
Bridges, Lloyd	Ent	30	60		50	SeaHunt TV star
Bridges, Todd	Ent	15			40	
Briggs, Austin	Cartoonist	25			75	Flash Gordon
Briggs, Charles F.	Author	15	40	125		Editor NY Times
Briggs, Claire	Cartoonist	15			50	Mr. & Mrs.
Briggs, Roxanne Dawson	Ent	15			35	Star Trek Voyager
Bright, John	Political	35	50	155		
Brightman, Sarah	Music	20			50	
Brimley, Wilford	Ent	10			20	
Brinegar, Paul	Ent	10	15	20	25	
Brinkley, Christie	Ent	10	30		45	
Brinkley, David	Ent	5			15	News Anchor
Brisbane, Arthur	Author	15	35	75	30	Influential Editorial Writer
Brisson, Carl	Ent	15	15	25	25	Danish Actor
Bristol, Henry Platt	Business	250	750	900		Founder of Bristol-Myers
Bristol, Mark	Military	20	25			Admiral WWI
Bristow, Benjamin Helm	Civil War	20	65	110		Civil War Comdr of 25th KY
Britt, Maurice L.	Military	22	35			WWII Hero & Football Star
Britt, May	Ent	15			30	
Brittany, Morgan	Ent	10	15	25	30	
Britten, Benjamin	Music	115	390	512	195	Br. Conductor
Britton, Barbara	Ent	10			25	
Brix, Herman	Ent					SEE Bruce Bennett
Broadhead, James O.	Political	25		65		Att'y Friend of Lincoln
Brochier, Jan	Music	10			35	Opera
Brockett, Don	Ent	10			25	
Brocoli, Cubby	Ent	20	30		45	Producer/007 films
Broderick, Helen	Ent	25			70	
Broderick, Matthew	Ent	15	35		40	
Brodie, Benjamin C.	Science		60	90		Br. Orthopedic Surgeon
Broglie, Duke	Political	135	270	450		French Politician
Broglie, Louis Victor de	Science	20	55	105	345	Nobel Physics
Brokow, Tom	Ent	5			15	TV News Anchor
Brolin, James	Ent	15			35	
Bromberg, J. Edward	Ent	30			65	
Bromfield, John	Ent	10			20	
Bromfield, Louis	Author	35	75	150	65	Am. Novelist. Pulitzer
Bronson, Betty	Ent	35			75	
Bronson, Charles	Ent	15	40		45	Death Wish movies
Bronte, Charlotte	Author	RARE	RARE	RARE	RARE	Br. Novelist. Jane Eyre
Brook, Alexander	Art	25	40	75		
Brook, Clive 1887-1974	Ent	50		75	95	
Brooke, Alan, Fld Mar	Military	40	110	205	75	Cmdr. Br.Corps WWII,Dunkirk
Brooke, John Rutter	Civil War	45	65	193		Union General/1838-1926
Brooke, Rupert	Author	450	550	900		Br. Poet
Brooke-Popham, Robert	Military	30	65	95	50	Br, Air Chief Marshal WWII
Brooks and Dunn	Music	25			50	Country Duo
Brooks, A. Raymond	Aviation	35	60	90	75	Bi-Plane ACE, WWI
Brooks, Albert	Ent	10	20		20	

Name	Field	SIG	DS	ALS	SP	Remarks
Brooks, Avery	Ent	20			55	Star Trek Deep Space Nine
Brooks, Foster	Ent	5			10	
Brooks, Garth	Music	25	100		50	
Brooks, Geraldine	Ent	20			40	Actress
Brooks, Gwendolyn	Author	20	40		25	Poet
Brooks, James L.	Ent	10			20	
Brooks, John	Military	55	125	275		Am. Revolution General
Brooks, Leslie	Ent	10			20	
Brooks, Louise 1906-1985	Ent	150	400	450	550	
Brooks, Mel	Ent	10	30	25	25	Actor/Director AA Winner
Brooks, Phillips 1835-93	Author	50	120	130	75	0 Little Town of Bethlehem
Brooks, Rand	Ent	10	35		30	GWTW
Brooks, Randi	Ent	5			15	
Brooks, Richard	Ent	20	30		60	AA Film Director
Brooks, Wm. Thos. H.	Civil War	40	65	105		Union General/1821-70
Broom, Jacob	RevWar	350	900	2,000		Continental Congress
Brophy, Ed	Ent	25			45	
Brophy, Theodore F	Business	5			10	CEO GTE
Brosnan, Pierce	Ent	25			55	James Bond
Brothers, Joyce	Science	5			10	Early TV Psychiatrist
Brougham, Henry, Lord	Political	100		250		
Brougham, John	Ent	15			30	Actor/Playwright
Broun, Heywood 1888-39	Author	10	35	70	15	
Browder, Earl	Political	15	35	65	20	US Comm. Party Leader
Brown, A. Roy	Aviation	250				Can ACE/Downed RedBaron
Brown, Aaron V. 1795-59	Political	45	125			
Brown, Albert Gallatin	Political	45	60	90		CSA Senator
Brown, Alice	Author	15	35			Novelist/Poet
Brown, Arthur Whitten	Aviation	300	400	575	575	Alcock & Brown
Brown, Blair	Ent	5			15	
Brown, Bothwell	Ent	10	15	25	25	
Brown, Charles B.	Author	975				Father of American Novel
Brown, Clarence	Ent	10			25	
Brown, David	Ent	10			20	Producer/AA Winner
Brown, Harry Joe	Ent	25	40	65		Producer/Director
Brown, Helen Gurley	Author	5	10	20	15	Editor/Publisher
Brown, Henry B.	SuprCt	60	175	250		
Brown, Henry W.	Aviation	10		40	30	ACE, WWII
Brown, Herbert C., Dr.	Science	25	30	45	35	Nobel Chemistry
Brown, Jacob	Military	50	135			General/ War 1812
Brown, James	Ent	5			15	Actor
Brown, James	Music	25			55	
Brown, Joe E. 1892-1973	Ent	35	50	40	75	
Brown, John 1800-1859	Political	775	1,600	2,500	2,500	Abolitionist
Brown, John Calvin	Civil War	125	165	350		CSA General/1827-89
Brown, Johnny Mack	Ent	50	100		150	Cowboy Actor
Brown, Joseph Emerson	Civil War	45	60	85		Civil War Governor of GA.
Brown, Julie	Ent	5			10	
Brown, Les	Music	15			35	Big Band Leader

Name	Field	SIG	DS	ALS	SP	Remarks
Brown, Lt. John	RevWar	100	175	350		
Brown, Moses	RevWar	50		265		Naval Commander
Brown, Nicholas 1729-91	RevWar	35	50	195		
Brown, Peter	Ent	10			25	
Brown, Phyllis George	Ent	5			15	
Brown, Preston	Military	20	35		45	General VVWI/Chief of Staff
Brown, Robert	Military	25		75	125	General WWI
Brown, Robert	Science	150		600		Botanist
Brown, Ruth	Music	20			50	
Brown, Sam J.	Aviation	20	40	55	45	WWII ACE
Brown, Tom	Ent	10	15	25	25	
Browne, Chris	Cartoonist	20			35	Hagar
Browne, Dik	Cartoonist	20			65	Hagar
Browne, Hablot Knight	Art	25	90	150		Illustrator Dickens
Browne, Jackson	Music	20			50	
Browne, Leslie	Ent	5			10	
Brownell, Herbert Jr.	Political	10	25	40		Att'y Gen., Eisenhower
Browning, Eliz. Barrett	Author	500		2,500	2,500	
Browning, George	Business	200	580			Browning Arms Mfg.
Browning, John B.	Business	50	150		75	Pres. Browning Arms Co.
Browning, John Moses	Science	200		575		Inventor, Designer of Fire Arms
Browning, Ricou	Ent	10	20	25	25	Creature of Black Lagoon
Browning, Robert 1812-89	Author	240	470	900	1,150	Br. Poet
Browning, Tod	Ent	100			250	
Brownlee, John	Music	10		45	30	Opera/Baritone
Brownsville Station	Music	25			55	Signed by Entire Band
Brubeck, Dave	Music	10		25	25	Jazz
Bruce, Andrew D.	Military	50	200			Gen. 77th Infantry Div
Bruce, Blanche K.	Political	250	400			1st Afr-Am.Full Term Sen.
Bruce, Carol	Music	10			30	
Bruce, David	Ent	15			25	
Bruce, Lenny 1925-66	Ent	300	550	1,600	900	
Bruce, Nigel 1895-1953	Ent	150		300	325	Dr. Watson in films
Bruce, Thos, (7th Earl)	Political	50	190	300		
Bruce, Virginia	Ent	15			25	
Bruce, Wallace	Author	35		120		
Bruch, Max 1838-1920	Music	65	200	400	95	Opera
Bruckner, Josef Anton	Music	1,200	2,500	3,500	2,500	Composer
Brummel, Geo. B. 'Beau'	Business	100	220	600		Br. Man of Fashion
Bruna Rasa, Lina	Music	75			350	Opera
Brune, G.M.A. 1763-1815	Military	85	350	450		Marshal of Nap. Assassinated
Brunel, Marc Isambard	Science	75	150	250		French engineer
Brunet, Isambard Kingdom	Science	40	145	250		Eng. of Broad Gauge RR
Bruning, Heinrich 1885-71	Political	100			350	Ger. Chancellor. Fled to U.S.
Bruscantini, Sesto	Music	10			25	Opera
Bruson, Renato	Music	10			30	Opera
Bryan, George	RevWar	120	350	600		Jurist.Proposed Abolition 1777
Bryan, Goode	Civil War	150		440		CSA General/1812-85
Bryan, William E.	Aviation	15		45	35	ACE, WWII

Name	Field	SIG	DS	ALS	SP	Remarks
Bryan, Wm Jennings 1860-1925	Political	125		375	375	3x Pres. Nominee
Bryant, Alys McKay	Aviation	40	75	150	75	Canadian 1st Woman Flier
Bryant, Anita	Ent	5			10	
Bryant, Paul	Sports	75			175	Bear"/Coach
Bryant, William Cullen	Author	100	250	375	750	Poet/1794-78
Brynner, Yul 1915-85	Ent	50	50	70	150	AA Winner
Buchan, John, Lord	Author	50	150			
Buchanan, Edgar	Ent	45	75		75	Petticoat Junction
Buchanan, Franklin	Civil War	160		350		CSA Admiral/1800-74
Buchanan, James	President	350	750	950	750	1791 - 1868
Buchanan, James M.	Science	35	45	85	40	Nobel Economics
Buchanan, Patrick	Political	10			30	Political Commentator
Bucher, Lloyd M.	Military	35	90	150	90	Captured Capt.USS Pueblo
Buchwald, Art	Author	5	20	25	15	Syndicated Humor Column
Buck, Frank 1888-1950	Explorer	45	75	125	85	Bring'Em Back Alive
Buck, Pearl S. 1892-1973	Author	40	145	198	65	Am,Novelist/Pulitzer/Nobel
Buck, Peter	Ent	15			35	
Buckingham, Catharinus P. 1808-88	Civil War	30		95		Union General/1808-88
Buckingham, William A.	Civil War	40	65	140		Civil War Gov. CT.
Buckland, Ralph P. (WD)	Civil War	130		250		Union General/1812-92
Buckley, Betty	Ent	20			40	
Buckley, William F. Jr.	Author	10		35	20	
Buckner, Simon B.	Civil War	200		375		CSA General/1823-1914
Buckner, Simon B. (WD)	Civil War	450	1,000			CSA General
Buell, Don Carlos	Civil War	75	155	250	150	Union General/1818-98
Buffett, Jimmy	Music	20			45	
Buffington, Thomas M.	Western	350	550			Chief of Cherokee Nations
Buford, Abraham	Civil War	175		750		CSA General/1820-84
Buford, John	Civil War	300				Union General/1826-63
Buford, Napoleon B.	Civil War	65	145	375		Union General/1807-83
Buick, David D.	Business	200	600	750	350	Buick Motor Co.
Bujold, Genevieve	Ent	10			25	
Bulfinch, Charles	Science	130	375			
Bulfinch, Thomas	Author	20	45	100		Bulfinch's Mythology
Bulkley, John D.	Military	20	65		35	Adm. USN WWII
Bull, John S.	Space	15			25	Astronaut
Bull, Ole B.	Music	35		125	125	Violin Virtuoso
Bull, William	Political	75		200		Governor SC 1760
Bullard, Robert Lee	Military	20	75	130	100	General WW I
Bullard, William	Military	15	35			Admiral WW I
Buller, Redvers, Sir	Military	40	110	200	45	Cmdr-in-Chief South Africa
Bulloch, Terrence	Aviation	20			35	Br. Aviator WWII
Bullock, Jim J.	Ent	15			35	Too Close for Comfort
Bullock, Sandra	Ent	25			50	
Bulow, Bernhard H.M.K.	Political	15	35	75	40	Prussian Imperial Chancellor
Bulwer-Lytton, Edward	Author	75	200	400		
Bumbry, Grace	Music	20			55	Opera
Bunce, Francis M.	Military	25	55	125	65	Admiral Span-Am War
Bunche, Ralph J. 1904-71	Political	50	130	225	125	Nobel Peace Prize

Name	Field	SIG	DS	ALS	SP	Remarks
Bundy, McGeorge	Political	20	35	45	25	Director FBI
Bundy, Omar	Military	35	90		55	General WW I
Bunner, Henry C. 1855-96	Author	65	70	135		Editor Puck Magazine
Bunny, John	Ent	100	150	150	200	Comedian
Bunsen, Robert W.	Science	175	400	900	1,250	Ger. Chemist/Bunsen Burn
Buntline, Ned 1823-86	Author	140		250	750	
Buono, Victor	Ent	75	100		125	Character Actor
Burbank, Luther 1849-26	Science	115	275	298	165	Experimental Botanist
Burdette, Robert J.	Author	20	55	135	40	
Burger, Warren E.	SuprCt	50	175	195	75	Chief Justice
Burgess, Anthony	Author	40	55		150	Clockwork Orange
Burgess, Bobby	Ent	10			25	Mouseketeer
Burgess, Thornton W.	Author	45	150	225		Peter Rabbit
Burghoff, Gary	Ent	15			35	Radar on MASH
Burgoyne, John 1722-92	RevWar	850	1,500	2,500		Br. Gen. vs Am. Colonies
Burke, Billie 1885-1970	Ent	175	275	400	200	Glenda in Wizard of Oz
Burke, Delta	Ent	10	25		30	Designing Woman
Burke, Selma	Art	10	20	45	15	
Burke, Arleigh 1901-1996	Military	35	60	110	100	Adm. USN WWII
Burleigh, Harry Thacker	Music	25		150		
Burmester, Willy	Music	100		275		German Violinist
Burne - Jones, Edward	Art	125	235	455		Pre-Raphaelite Painter
Burnet, David G. 1788-70	Political	275	635	1,200		lst Pres. Republic TX
Burnet, William 1688-28	Political	145	465			
Burnett, Carol	Ent	10	20	35	30	
Burnett, Frances H.	Author	50	145	285		Little Lord Fauntleroy
Burnett, Peter H,	Western	200		550		California Pioneer/lst Gov.
Burnette, Johnny	Music	40				
Burnette, Smiley	Ent	40	50		75	
Burney, Cecil, Sir	Military	15	35			Br. Adm. WW I
Burnham, Hiram	Civil War	60	195			Union General
Burns & Allen	Ent	200	450		400	Both Signed
Burns, Bob	Ent	25	25	45	45	Bazooka
Burns, Edmund	Ent	30			75	Silent Screen Star
Burns, George 1896-1996	Ent	20	60		50	
Burns, James MacGregor	Author	20	30			Educator, Political Science
Burns, John 1791-1872	Civil War	350			1,250	Vet. War 1812. Vol. Gettysburg
Burns, Ken	Ent	5			15	Documentary Film Maker
Burns, Robert 1759-96	Author	500	1,450	2,750		Scottish Poet
Burns, William J.	Business	35	10	175		Chief FBI 1921-24, Det. Agency
Burns, William Wallace	Civil War	35	75	95	150	Union General/1825-92
Burnside, Ambrose (WD)	Civil War	175	375	475	725	Union General
Burnside, Ambrose E.	Civil War	125	275	350	650	Union General/1824-81
Burpee, David	Business	25	35	70	35	Burpee Seed Co.
Burpee, Jonathan	Business	10	25	50	20	Burpee Seed Co.
Burr, Aaron 1756-1836	Vice Pres	400	650	750		
Burr, Raymond 1917-93	Ent	35	50		65	Ironsides/Perry Mason
Burritt, Elihu 1810-79	Political	20		125		
Burroughs, Edgar Rice	Author	225	450	750	600	Tarzan/1875-1950

Name	Field	SIG	DS	ALS	SP	Remarks
Burroughs, John 1837-21	Author	100		200	525	Am. Naturalist
Burrows, Abe	Author	10	15	25	20	Playwright, Pulitzer
Burstyn, Ellen	Ent	10			25	
Burton, Harold H.	SuprCt	40	170		85	
Burton, Isabel, Lady	Author	25	85	180		
Burton, LeVar	Ent	25	75		50	Star Trek/Roots
Burton, Richard F.	Explorer	150	275			1821-1890
Burton, Richard Sir	Ent	110	200		200	1925 - 1984
Burton, Tim	Ent	20	60		50	Director
Buscalia, Leo	Author	10	25	40	20	Educator, Author, Lecturer
Busch, Adolphus	Business	300	2,500	3,500		Anheuser-Busch
Busch, August A.	Business	25	90	175	50	Anheuser-Busch Brewery
Busch, Fritz	Music	60		135	250	Ger. Conductor
Busch, Niven	Author	15		30		Dramatist, Screenwriter
Busch, Wilhelm 1832-08	Art	Scarce	Scarce	Scarce	Scarce	Painter & Poet.
Busell, Darcey	Music	15			40	Ballet
Busey, Gary	Ent	10			25	
Bush, Barbara	First Lady	50	145		100	
Bush, George (As Pres)	President	160	550	900	400	
Bush, George 1924-	President		275	450	200	
Bush, Owen	Ent	5			10	
Bush, Vannevar	Science	60	180	255	125	Pioneer Analog Computer
Bushman, Francis X.	Ent	45		125	100	Silent Star of Ben Hur
Bushmiller, Ernie	Cartoonist	20			50	Nancy
Bushnell, David	Science	250	750	1,250		Invented 1 st Submarine
Busoni, Ferruccio	Music	120		340	425	Pianist/1899-1924
Busse, Henry	Music	20			50	Big Band Leader
Bute, John Stuart	Royalty	85	130			Earl of Bute
Butenandt, Adolf F.J.	Science	20	30	45	25	Nobel Chemistry
Butheiezi, Gatsha M.	Political				35	Chief of Zulu Nation
Butkus, Dick	Sports	10			30	1979 HOF/Football
Butler, Benjamin F.	Civil War	125	355	229	500	Union General/1818-93
Butler, Brett	Ent	15			30	Grace Under Fire
Butler, Daws	Ent	45	75	100	75	Man of many Voices
Butler, Ellis Parker	Author	20	60	85	40	1869-1937
Butler, John	RevWar	75	185	375		Am. Loyalist.Butler's Rangers
Butler, Matthew C.	Civil War	90	170	285		CSA General/1836-1909
Butler, Matthew C. (WD)	Civil War	155	345	670		CSA General
Butler, Pierce	SuprCt	35	90	275	45	
Butler, Pierce 1744-1822	RevWar	60	180	385		Signer of Constitution
Butler, Samuel 1835-1902	Author	20	60	125		
Butler, Smedley D.	Military	15	35	75	35	
Butler, Walter 1752-81	RevWar		550	675		
Butler, William Orlando	Military	45	210			Hero Battle of New Orleans
Butler, Yancy	Ent	20			40	
Butler, Zebulon	Military	70	200			Col. Revolutionary War
Butt Rumford, Clara	Music	45			150	Opera
Butterfield, Billy	Music	25			45	Jazz Trumpet, Bandleader
Butterfield, Daniel	Civil War	75		225		Union Gen/ Composed Taps

Name	Field	SIG	DS	ALS	SP	Remarks
Butterfield, Daniel (WD)	Civil War	150	250	350	450	Union Gen/Composed TAPS
Buttons, Red	Ent	5			20	
Buttram, Pat	Ent	35	45		60	Gene Autry's Sidekick
Butts, Alfred M.	Science	40				Inventor of Scrabble game
Buzzi, Ruth	Ent	5			15	Laugh In
Byers, Samuel Hawkins	Author	25	40	60		Union Soldier-Author
Byington, Spring	Ent	20			55	
Byner, John	Ent	5			10	
Byng, Geo. Viscount	Military	25	75			Br. Adm.Destroyed Sp.Fleet 1719
Byrd, Charlie	Music	15			25	Jazz Guitar
Byrd, Ralph	Ent	100	150		350	
Byrd, Richard E. 1888-57	Aviation	75	275	450	325	Adm. USN, Polar Expl.
Byrds, The	Music	100	250		200	Entire Group Signed
Byrne, Gabriel	Ent	25			50	
Byrnes, James F.	SuprCt	30	125	235	55	
Byron, Arthur	Ent	15		20	35	
Byron, Geo, G. Lord	Author	1,600		2,750		Scarce

Ethel Barrymore

Johannes Brahms

Robert Browning

Name	Field	SIG	DS	ALS	SP	Remarks
Caan, James	Ent	10	30		30	
Cabal, Bob	Ent	10			25	
Cabell, Earle	Political	10				Dallas Mayor/JFK Assas.
Cabell, James B.	Author	30	120	165		
Cabell, William L.	Civil War	175	405			CSA General/1827-1911
Cable, Geo. Washington	Author	35	50	75	45	CSA Soldier/Writer
Cabot, Bruce 1904-72	Ent	60		100	150	King Kong
Cabot, George 1751-1823	Political		50	100		
Cabot, Sebastian	Ent	40	60		75	Disney Voice/Family Affair
Caceres, Andreas A.	Political	10	25	65	20	Peru
Cadbury, George	Business	35		170	50	Cadbury Chocolate Mfg.
Cadbury, Richard	Business	30	45	160	50	Cadbury Chocolate Mfg.
Cade, Robert, Dr.	Business	15			25	Inventor of Gatorade
Cadman, Chas. W.	Music	60	215	360	100	Composer
Cadmus, Paul	Art	36	85	120		
Cadwalader, George	Civil War	50	110	160		Union General/1830-79
Cadwalader, Lambert	RevWar	55	140	335		Continental Congress
Cady, Frank	Ent	40			75	Green Acres
Caesar, Irving	Music	25	55	125	45	Lyricist (Tea for Two)
Caesar, Sid	Ent	5	20		20	
Cage, John M. 1912-92	Music	95	95	200	55	Composer
Cage, Nicholas	Ent	20	60		50	AA Winner
Cagney and Lacy	Ent	20			40	Signed by both stars
Cagney, James 1899-86	Ent	70	200	250	275	AA Winner
Cahier, Madame Charles	Music	25			90	Opera
Cahn, Sammy 1913-93	Music	20	80	125	50	Composer
Cain, Dean	Ent	20			45	TV's Superman
Cain, James	Author	40	55	90		
Caine, Michael	Ent	20			50	
Caine, Thos. Hall	Author	15	45	85	25	Br. Novelist
Calamity Jane	Western	RARE	20,000	35,000	RARE	
Calder, Alexander	Art	125	225		150	Sculptor/1898-1976
Caldwell, Erskine	Author	35	150	210	75	Tobacco Road
Caldwell, John Curtis	Civil War	35	75		95	Union General
Caldwell, Sarah	Music	15			20	1 st Woman Conductor NY Met.
Caldwell, Taylor	Author	35	150	225	50	
Caldwell, Zoe	Ent	5	25	15	15	
Calhern, Louis	Ent	30		45	45	1895 - 1956
Calhoun, John C.	Vice Pres	145	350	475	375	Andrew Jackson VP
Calhoun, Rory	Ent	10	40		20	
Callaghan, James	Political	40	75	140	45	Br. Prime Minister
Callahan, Laurence K.	Aviation	10	20	45	30	
Callas, Charlie	Ent	10			20	

Name	Field	SIG	DS	ALS	SP	Remarks
Callas, Maria 1923-77	Music	300	850	875	1,000	Opera
Calleia, Frank	Ent	20	25	45	45	
Calleia, Joseph	Ent	25			55	
Calley, William	Military	20	35	45	40	My Lai, Viet Nam
Calloway, Cab 1907-95	Music	30	45	50	150	Big Band Leader
Calve, Emma	Music	55	90	120	450	Opera
Calvert, Louis	Ent	5		15	15	
Calvert, Phyllis	Ent	5	15		15	
Calvet, Corinne	Ent	10			20	
Calvin, John	Clergy	7,500	15,000	30,000		RARE
Calvin, Melvin, Dr.	Science	25	35	55	20	Nobel Chemistry
Camacho, Manuel Avila	Political	35		80	20	Pres. Mexico
Camargo, Alberto	Political	10		35	20	Columbia
Cambern, Donn	Ent	10			20	
Cambon, Jules	Political	20	25	35		Fr. Ambassador to US
Cambridge, Godfrey	Ent	35			80	
Cameron, George	Military	20		45		General WWI
Cameron, James	Political	30		45		Senator PA. Sec'y War
Cameron, Kirk	Ent	15	30		35	Growing Pains
Cameron, Robert	Civil War	35	75			Union General/1828-94
Cameron, Rod	Ent	10			25	
Cameron, Simon (WD)	Civil War	125	200	275	375	
Cameron, Simon 1800-89	Civil War	75	125	175	300	Lincoln Sec'y War
Cammaerts, Emile	Author	10	20	40	15	Poet/Writer
Camp, Colleen	Ent	10			25	
Campanella, Roy	Sports	200			350	1969 HOF/Baseball
Campanini, Italo	Ent	65	80	175		
Campbell, Archibald	RevWar	95	275			Br. General.
Campbell, Archie	Music	10			25	
Campbell, Beatrice	Ent	20	35	45	45	1865-1940
Campbell, Bruce	Ent	20			40	
Campbell, Chas Thomas	Civil War	35	80	110		Union General/1823-95
Campbell, Colin	Military	16	45	75		Br. Gen during War of 1812
Campbell, Douglas	Aviation	45	65	80	95	WWI Bi-Plane ACE
Campbell, Glen	Music	5			20	
Campbell, John	RevWar	65	175	290		Br. General
Campbell, John A.	SuprCt	100	150	200		1811 - 18889
Campbell, Mary	Ent			50		Miss America 1922-23
Campbell, Naomi	Ent	20			50	SuperModel
Campbell, Neve	Ent	25			50	
Campbell, Patrick, Mrs.	Ent	35	60		80	
Campbell, William (Bill)	Ent	20			45	Rocketeer
Campbell, William B.	Civil War	40	55	95		Union General/1807-67
Campbell-Bannerman, H.	Political	20	45	100		Prime Minister
Campora, Giuseppe	Music	10			40	Tenor - Opera
Camus, Albert 1913-1960	Author	75	250	600		Nobel
Canary, David	Ent	10			20	
Canby, Edward R.	Civil War	65	250	370		Union General/1817-73
Cander, John	Music	40				Composer

Name	Field	SIG	DS	ALS	SP	Remarks
Candler, Asa Griggs	Business	600	1,750	2,500		Founder of Coca Cola
Candy, John	Ent	60			125	Died Young
Canetti, Elia	Author	65	225	350		
Canfield, Dorothy (Fisher)	Author	50	65	300		1879 - 1958
Canham, Erwin	Author	10	20			Christian Science Monitor
Caniff, Milton 1907-88	Cartoonist	25	82	100	150	Terry & Steve Canyon
Caniglia, Maria	Music	15			75	Opera
Canned Heat	Music	35			75	Signed by Entire Band
Cannell, Stephen J.	Ent	5			10	TV Producer
Canning, Charles John	Political	15		65	45	lst Viceroy of India
Canning, Effie	Author	75		300		
Canning, George	Political	50	90	150		Prime Minister
Cannon, Dyan	Ent	10	20	25	20	
Cannon, George Q.	Political	50	140	200		Utah's lst Congressman
Cannon, Jos. G.	Political	20	40	95	40	Speaker of the House
Cannon, Martha H., Dr.	Science	25	30	60	30	
Canova, Antonio 1757-22	Art	100	250	550		Italian Sculptor
Canova, Diana	Ent	10			20	
Canova, Judy	Ent	10	15	20	25	
Canseco, Jose	Sports	10			25	Baseball
Cantinflas	Ent	35			90	
Cantor, Eddie 1892-1964	Ent	85	150		125	
Canutt, Yakima	Ent	20		60	65	AA Winner
Capers, Ellison	Civil War	75				CSA General
Capers, Ellison (WD)	Civil War	125		550		CSA General/1837-1903
Caperton, William	Military	20			50	WWI Admiral
Capone, Al	Criminal	3,000	8,000	RARE	RARE	Gangster
Capote, Truman 1924-84	Author	125	225		250	In Cold Blood"
Capp, Al	Cartoonist	55			125	Lil Abner
Capra, Frank 1897-1991	Ent	30	150		85	AA Winning Director
Capshaw, Kate	Ent	15			35	
Captain & Tennile	Music	20			40	Signed by Both
Capucine	Ent	25	30	70	65	
Cara, Irene	Music	15			30	
Caraway, Hattie 1878-50	Political	25	55	35	40	1st Woman US Senator
Cardigan, 7th Earl	Military	75	175	250	130	Br.Gen. Charge of Lt Brigade
Cardinale, Claudia	Ent	15			40	James Bond Girl
Cardozo, Benjamin N.	SuprCt	160	350	600	650	
Carere, Christine	Ent	10			20	
Carerre, Tia	Ent	20			50	
Carey, Drew	Ent	20			40	Drew Carey Show
Carey, Harry Jr.	Ent	10	20		20	
Carey, Harry Sr.	Ent	100	110	175	250	
Carey, Macdonald	Ent	10			30	
Carey, Mariah	Music	25			55	
Carey, Michele	Ent	5	6	15	25	
Carey, Ron	Ent	5	6	10	10	
Carias, Andino, Tiburcio	Political	40	125		45	Pres. Honduras
Carl XIV Johan 1763-1844	Royalty	150	580			King Sweden

Name	Field	SIG	DS	ALS	SP	Remarks
Carl XV 1826-72	Royalty	125	425			King of Sweden & Nor. from 1859
Carl XVI Gustaf	Royalty	55	150			King Sweden
Carl, Marion	Aviation	15	35	55	40	WWI 1st Marine ACE
Carle, Frankie	Music	15			35	Big Band Leader
Carleton, Guy 1724-1808	Military	250	645	800		Br. Commander-in-Chief
Carleton, James H.	Civil War	30		110		Union General/1814-73
Carleton, Will 1845-1912	Author	15	50	150	25	Ir. Novelist
Carlin, George	Ent	10	25		25	
Carlisle, 7th Earl	Author	20	45	115		Poet/Orator
Carlisle, Belinda	Music	20			50	Go-Go's Lead Singer
Carlisle, Kitty	Music	5			15	
Carlisle, Mary	Ent	10	20	25	20	
Carlo Alberto 1798-1849	Royalty	75	150	375		King of Sardinia
Carlotta (Marie-Charlotte-Amalie)	Royalty	340	770	1,700		Empress of Mex. Became Insane
Carlson, Richard	Ent	20			40	
Carlton, Guy 1724-1808	RevWar	Scarce	Scarce	Scarce	Scarce	British General
Carlton, Steve	Sports	10			25	1994 HOF/Baseball
Carlyle, Russ	Music	5			15	Bandleader
Carlyle, Thomas	Author	90	225	450	85	Br. Philosopher, Social Critic
Carmen, Jean	Ent	5			10	
Carmer, Carl	Author	20	45	175		
Carmichael, Hoagy	Music	45	200		200	Composer/1899-1991
Carnarvon, Henry IV Earl	Political	15	35	80		Created Fed. Dom/Canada
Carne, Judy	Ent	5			10	Laugh In
Carne, Judy	Ent	10			20	Laugh In
Carnegie, Andrew	Business	275	1,250	1,250	1,100	Carnegie Steel
Carnegie, Dale 1888-1955	Author	50			75	How to Win Friends and...
Carnera, Primo	Sports	200			450	Boxer
Carnes, Kim	Music	10			30	
Carney, Art	Ent	10	30	35	25	Honeymooners
Carney, Robert B.	Military	10	20	25		
Carnot, Lazare N.M.	Military	85	235	350		Min. of War. Exiled
Carnot, Marie Francois S	Political			165		Pres. France/Assasinated
Carnovsky, Morris	Ent	15		40	45	
Caroline (Geo. IV-Eng)	Royalty	95	150	210		Estranged Queen
Caroline (Monaco)	Royalty	25			80	Princess/Graces Daughter
Caroline 1768-1821	Royalty			450		Estranged Queen George IV
Caroline 1776-1841	Royalty		90	170		2nd Queen of Maximilian I
Caroline of Anspach	Royalty	335	450	1,000		Queen of George II (Eng)
Caron, George R.	Aviation	35		100	90	Enola Gay Tail gunner
Caron, Leslie	Ent	20	30		50	
Carpenter, John	Ent	10			25	Director/Writer
Carpenter, Karen	Music	150	300		300	
Carpenter, Mary-Chapin	Music	15			40	
Carpenter, Richard	Music	15	25		35	
Carpenter, Scott	Space	25	75	125	100	Mercury 7 Astronaut
Carpenter, William B.	Explorer	10	35	60		Br. Physiologist
Carpenter, William S.	Military	10	15	45	20	
Carpenters, The	Music	250	400		375	Signed by Both

Name	Field	SIG	DS	ALS	SP	Remarks
Carr, Eugene Asa	Civil War	35	80		220	Union General/1820-1910
Carr, Gerald P.	Space	5			15	Astronaut
Carr, Jane	Ent	5			15	
Carr, Tommy	Ent	15			35	
Carr, Vicki	Music	5			15	
Carradine, David	Ent	20			50	Kung Fu
Carradine, John	Ent	75	100		125	Dracula
Carradine, Keith	Ent	10			25	
Carradine, Robert	Ent	10			25	
Carranza, Venustiano	Political	50	205	400		Murdered Mexican Pres.
Carrel, Dr. Alexis	Science	75	220	300	85	Nobel Medicine
Carreno, Terresa	Music	20		135	90	Pianist
Carrera, Barbara	Ent	10			30	
Carrera, Tia	Ent	20			40	
Carrere, Christine	Ent	5			15	French Actress
Carrey, Jim	Ent	30	100		65	
Carrillo, Leo 1880-1961	Ent	55	75		125	
Carroll, Charlesl 1737-32	RevWar	275	679	765		Signer
Carroll, Daniel	RevWar	175	685	710		Continental Congress
Carroll, Diahann	Ent	10			20	
Carroll, John	Ent	10	15	20	20	
Carroll, Leo G. 1892 - 72	Ent	65			100	Man from UNCLE
Carroll, Lewis	Author					See C.L. Dodgson
Carroll, Madeleine	Ent	25			55	1906 - 1987
Carroll, Mickey	Ent	10	30		30	Wizard of Oz Munchkin
Carroll, Nancy	Ent	10	15	20	35	
Carroll, William	Military	25		90		Gen. TN Militia
Carroll, William H.	Civil War	60	145			CSA General/1810-68
Cars, The	Music	50			85	
Carson, Christopher "Kit"	Western	6,000 RARE	40,000	15,000		Scout/Indian Trader/Fur
Carson, Jack	Ent	15			50	
Carson, John	Military	10			35	General WW I
Carson, Johnny	Ent	15	30		50	Tonight Show Host
Carson, Leonard Kit	Aviation	15		45	30	WWII ACE
Carson, Rachel 1907-1964	Science	70	205	285	275	
Carson, Sunset	Ent	25		65	55	Western Star
Carter, Ann S.	Aviation	25	40		45	1st Woman Helicopter Pilot
Carter, Ben	Ent	100			250	
Carter, Benny	Music	40	60	100	90	Jazz
Carter, Betty	Music	15			35	Lionel Hampton Vocalist
Carter, Carlene	Ent	10			25	
Carter, Dixie	Ent	10			35	Designing Women
Carter, Elliot	Music	20		125		Pulitzer/Composer
Carter, Helen	Music	10			20	
Carter, Helena Bonham	Ent	20	30		40	
Carter, Howard	Science	1,500 RARE		2,500 RARE		Found King Tut's Tomb
Carter, Jack	Ent	10			20	
Carter, Jimmy	President	40	275	575	160	
Carter, Leslie, Mrs.	Ent	20	75	90	70	

Name	Field	SIG	DS	ALS	SP	Remarks
Carter, Lynda	Ent	10	20	25	25	Wonder Woman
Carter, Mother Maybelle	Music	40			80	Country
Carter, Nell	Ent	10	20		20	Gimme a Break
Carter, Rosalynn	First Lady	25	75	100	50	
Carter, Terry	Ent	10			20	
Carteret, George 1610-80	Military	Scarce	Scarce	Scarce	Scarce	Br. Naval Off/Fndr NJ
Cartland, Barbara	Author	15	35	70	75	Romance Novelist
Cartwright, Angela	Ent	5			15	Lost in Space TV series
Cartwright, Nancy	Ent	15			35	Voice of Bart Simpson
Carty, John J.	Science	60	150	275	150	Telephone Pioneer. AT&T
Caruso, Anthony	Ent	25			50	
Caruso, David	Ent	15			40	NYPD Blues
Caruso, Enrico 1873-1921	Music	240	550	675	850	
Carver, Geo. Washington 1864-1943	Science	200		700	1,750	Botanist/1864-43
Carvey, Dana	Ent	20			45	Sat Nite Live alumni
Casadesus, Robert, Dr.	Music	45		100	100	Pianist/Composer
Casals, Pablo 1876-1973	Music	100	150	383	427	Spanish Cellist
Casanovo, Giacomo	Author	150	580	915		
Case, Allen	Ent	10			20	
Case, Jerome	Business	30	60	155		Case Tractors & Farm Implements
Caselia, Alfredo	Music	35	130	250		Composer/Pianist
Casellato, Renzo	Music	10			20	Opera
Caselotti, Adriana	Ent	20		65	60	Voice of Snow White
Casement, Jack	Civil War	45	170			Union General
Casey, Silas 1807-82	Civil War	50	105	165		Union General/1807-82
Cash, Johnny	Music	20	60		50	
Cash, June Carter	Music	5			15	
Cash, Rosanne	Ent	5			20	
Casimir-Perier, Jean P.	Political			150		Pres. France 1894-95
Caspar, Billy	Sports	10			25	1978 HOF/Golf
Cass, Lewis 1782-1866	Political	50	110	150		Jackson Sec'y War
Cass, Peggy	Ent	10			20	
Cassatt, Mary	Art	225	475	750		
Cassavetes, John	Ent	20	15	20	45	Actor/Director
Cassidy, David	Ent	15	45		45	Partridge Family
Cassidy, Jack	Ent	25			55	
Cassidy, Joanna	Ent	5			15	
Cassidy, Shaun	Ent	15			35	Hardy Boys/Singer
Cassidy, Ted	Ent	175	300		450	Addams Family/Lurch
Cassin, Jimmy	Music	10	30			Composer
Cassin, Rene	Political	30	75	175	45	Founder UNESCO/Nobel
Cassini, Oleg	Business	15			35	Fashion Designer
Casson, Mel	Cartoonist	10			20	Redeye
Castagna, Bruna	Music	20			100	Opera
Castanzo, Jack	Music	10			30	Jazz
Castelnuovo-Tedesco, M.	Music	65		300	125	Composer
Castle, Irene	Ent	50		75	75	
Castle, Peggy	Ent	10			25	
Castle, Vernon	Ent	50			150	

Name	Field	SIG	DS	ALS	SP	Remarks
Castle, William	Ent	40			100	
Castro, Fidel	Political	675	750		950	Cuban Premier
Cates, Clifton B.	Military	10	25	50	18	
Cates, Phoebe	Ent	15			45	
Cather, Willa 1873-1947	Author	200	400	550		
Catherine I (Rus)	Royalty	520	2,000	4,500		
Catherine II (The Great)	Royalty	600	1,200	2,400		Empress of Russia
Catkin, Dick	Cartoonist	75				Buck Rogers
Catlett, Walter	Ent	30			60	
Catlin, George 1796-1872	Art	100	310			Indian Scenes
Catlin, Isaac	Civil War	50	95	330		Union General
Catt, Carrie Chapman	Political	60	120	250		Suffragette Leader
Catton, Bruce	Author	30	150	125	30	Historian/Pulitzer
Caulfield, Joan	Ent	20			30	1922 - 1991
Caulfield, Maxwell	Ent	15			30	
Cavalieri Muratore, Lina	Music	75			200	Opera
Cavallaro, Carmen	Music	15			35	Big Band Leader
Cavanagh, Paul	Ent	10			20	
Cavell, Edith 1865-1915	Science	225	375	750		
Cavett, Dick	Ent	5			15	
Cavour, Camillo, Count	Political		425			Architect of It. Unification
Cayce, Edgar	Author	70	225			Psychic?
CCR	Music	50	150		100	Signed by All
Ceausecu, Nicolae	Political	40	335		120	Romanian Pres/Assas.
Cech, Thomas R., Dr.	Science	20	35		25	Nobel Chemistry
Celi, Adolfo	Ent	25			65	Largo" in James Bond film
Cellini, Benvenuto	Art	1,000	4,800	RARE	RARE	Goldsmith and Sculptor
Cello, Aldo	Business	5			15	
Cerf, Bennett	Author	15	20	30	10	Random House Editor
Cermak, Anton J.	Political	25	40	75	100	Assas. Mayor of Chicago
Cernan, Eugene A.	Space	35			100	Moonwalker Astronaut
Cervantes, Miguel de	Author	7,500	10,000	RARE	RARE	Don Quioxte
Cesky, Charles J.	Aviation	10		35	30	WWII ACE
Cezanne, Paul	Art	1,100	2,300	RARE	RARE	Fr Impressionist
Chabas, Paul Emile	Art	35	60	135		
Chabert, Lacey	Ent	20			50	Child Actress
Chabot, Phillipe de Brion	Military	Scarce	Scarce	Scarce	Scarce	Fr.Cmdr.In Chief
Chabrier, Alexis E.	Music	70	255	400		Opera/Composer
Chadwick, James, Sir	Science	80	215	450		Discovered Neutron/Nobel
Chaffee, Adna R.	Civil War	35	80	115		
Chaffee, Roger	Space	200			400	Died in Apollo Fire (1-27-67)
Chagall, Marc 1887-1985	Art	185	350	Scarce	350	
Chaka Kahn	Music	15			35	
Chakiris, George	Ent	10	15	25	25	
Chaliapin, Feodor	Music	200	260	500	550	Opera
Chalker, Jack	Author	10	20	40	20	
Chalmers, James (WD)	Civil War	250				CSA General
Chalmers, James R.	Civil War	130	350			CSA General/1831-98
Chamberlain, Austen	Political	20	85	100	100	Nobel Peace Prize

Name	Field	SIG	DS	ALS	SP	Remarks
Chamberlain, Joseph A.	Political	58	85	85	90	Statesman/Nobel
Chamberlain, Joshua L.	Civil War	700	1,255	1,800		Union General/1828-1914
Chamberlain, Neville	Political	75	400	400	165	Prime Minister
Chamberlain, Owen, Dr	Science	25	35	75	30	Nobel Physics
Chamberlain, Richard	Ent	15	15	30	35	
Chamberlain, Wilt	Sports	50			150	1978 HOF/Basketball
Chamberlaine, William	Military	10		35	20	General WW I
Chamberlin, Clarence	Aviation	50	250	375	250	Record Non-Stop Flight NY-Ger.
Chambers, Marilyn	Ent	15			35	
Chambers, Robert Wm.	Author	10	15	20		Life Mag Illustrator
Chambers, Whittaker	Author	15	50	150	25	Journalist
Chaminade, Cecile	Music	85	195	300	225	Composer/1857-1944
Champion, Gower	Ent	25	30	50	65	Dancer
Champion, Marge	Ent	15		30	35	Dancer
Chan, Jackie	Ent	25			50	Martial Arts Film Star
Chancellor, John	Ent	15			30	News Anchor
Chandler, A.B.	Sports	15			45	Happy"/1982 HOF
Chandler, Jeff	Ent	60	75	150	125	1918 - 1961
Chandler, Lane	Ent	20			40	
Chandler, Norman	Business	15	35	75	30	L.A. Times
Chandler, Otis	Business	20	45	95	40	Founder L.A. Times
Chandler, Raymond	Author	500	1,200	RARE	RARE	Detective Novelist
Chandler, William E.	Political	20	40	65		Sect. Navy
Chandler, Zachariah	Political	25	35	50		Sec'y Int./Att'y Gen'l
Chanel, Coco	Business	50	110	235	85	Fashion Designer
Chaney, Lon, Jr. 1906-73	Ent	350	650	Scarce	575	Wolfman ...
Chaney, Lon, Sr.	Ent	1,000	2,500	Scarce	1,650	Man of a 1000 Faces
Chang	Ent	25			65	Chinese Giant
Channing, Carol	Ent	5	20		10	Hello Dolly/Broadway
Channing, Stockard	Ent	5			10	
Channing, William Ellery	Author	40	70	120		Clergy
Chapin, Harry	Music	100			295	
Chapin, Lawrence	Ent	15			35	
Chaplin, Charles	Ent	330	600	Scarce	700	1889 - 1977
Chaplin, Geraldine	Ent	10		30	30	
Chaplin, Lita Grey	Ent	20	25	45	25	
Chaplin, Sydney	Ent	15	15	35	30	
Chapman, Graham	Ent	15	20	25	30	
Chapman, Leonard, Jr.	Military	15	30		55	USMC General, WWII
Chapman, Marguerite	Ent	10			20	
Chapman, Mark David	Criminal	75		200		Murdered John Lennon
Chapman, Oscar L.	Political	15	20	30	35	Sec'y Interior 1849
Chappell, William	Business	20	45	110	35	Music Publisher
Chaptal, Jean Antoine	Political	135	200			Min Agriculture/Interior
Charcot, Jean Martin	Science	90	225	575		Fr. Neurologist
Charisse, Cyd	Ent	10			30	
Charlemagne	Royalty	75,000	RARE	RARE	RARE	Institutionalized
Charles & Diana	Royalty				3,500	Prince and Princess
Charles Albert (Sardinia)	Royalty			225		Count of Savoy

Name	Field	SIG	DS	ALS	SP	Remarks
Charles Edw, Stuart	Royalty	110	350	815		Bonnie Prince Charlie
Charles Emmanuel I	Royalty	595	900			1562-1630
Charles Emmanuel I	Royalty		400			King of Sardinia
Charles I (Eng) 1600-49	Royalty	625	1,750	4,000		
Charles II (Eng) 1630-85	Royalty	900	2,000	2,500		
Charles II (SP)	Royalty	275	395			
Charles IV (Eng)	Royalty	245	1,100			
Charles IV (Sp)	Royalty	185		600		
Charles IX (Fr) 1560-74	Royalty	292	1,283	1,700		
Charles V (Charles II)	Royalty	580	2,100	4,000		
Charles VI (Charles III)	Royalty	375	1,200			
Charles X (Fr)	Royalty	150	450	725		
Charles XIV John (Swe)	Royalty	145	675	880		
Charles XV (Swe-Nor)	Royalty	45	140	320		
Charles, Prince of Wales 1948-	Royalty	400		1,500	600	Philip Arthur George
Charles, Ray	Music	200	250		Scarce	Blind
Charles, Suzette	Ent	10			20	Miss American 1984
Charlie's Angels	Ent	50			100	Signed by all three orig. stars
Charlotte, Grand Duchess	Royalty	20	75	180	50	Luxembourg
Charlotte, Sophia	Royalty	145	275	450		Queen of George III (Eng)
Charo	Music	5			10	
Charpentier, Gustave	Music	100	250	300	300	1880-1956
Charteris, Leslie	Author	40	75	125	125	The Saint
Chartoff, Melanie	Ent	10			25	
Charvet, David	Ent	20			45	Baywatch
Chase, Charley	Ent	30			100	
Chase, Chevy	Ent	10			35	Sat Nite Live
Chase, Ilka	Ent	12	15	20	25	Author
Chase, Mary	Author	35	75	150		Harvey" and others...
Chase, Salmon P.	SuprCt	90	150	352	300	Chief Justice
Chase, Samuel	RevWar	275	775	1,550		Signer
Chase, William C.	Military	10	20	35		
Chase, William Merritt	Art	100				US Painter/Western Scenes
Chateaubriand, Francois	Author	120	250	550		Fr. Novelist
Chatterton, Ruth	Ent	20			55	
Chauncey, Isaac	Military	20	95	90		Am. Naval - War 1812
Chausson, Ernest	Music	50	145	345		Opera
Chauvel, Henry, Sir	Military	25	75			Aussie General WW I
Chavez, Carlos	Music	15	35	70	40	Conductor/Composer
Chavez, Cesar E. 1927-93	Political	40			110	Migrant Labor Organizer
Chavez, George A.	Aviation	45	65	175	65	
Chayefsky, Paddy	Author	75	150	250	125	
Cheap Trick	Music	35			60	Signed by Entire Band
Cheatham, Benj. F. (WD)	Civil War	390		652		CSA General
Cheatham, Benj. F.	Civil War	225	400			CSA General/1820-86
Checker, Chubby	Music	15	50		40	The Twist
Cheech n' Chong	Ent	25			55	Signed by both
Cheers	Ent				350	Signed Cast/All Six
Cheever, Charles A, Dr.	Science	40	100		75	

Name	Field	SIG	DS	ALS	SP	Remarks
Cheever, John	Author	45	125	250	100	Novelist/Pulitzer
Chekhov, Anton 1860-04	Author	560	1,815	5,500	8,000	Russian Novelist
Chen, Joan	Ent	15			45	
Cheney, Sherwood	Military	5		25		General WW I
Chennault, Claire L.	Aviation	500		660	525	Flying Tigers. USAAF Gen.
Cher	Music	20	65		55	Sonny and Cher
Cherkassky, Shura	Music	20			60	Opera
Chernov, Vladimir	Music	15			30	Opera
Cherubini, Luigi	Music	175	250	500		Opera Composer
Chesebrough, Robert	Business	15	30	50		Vaseline Products
Cheshire, Leonard	Military	15	50	65	40	Br. RAF
Chester, Bob	Music	20			40	Big Band Leader
Chester, Colby M.	Business	10			55	CEO General Foods
Chester, John	RevWar	35	80			Continental Army. Judge
Chesterton, Gilbert Keith	Author	50	390	325	190	Father Brown, Detective
Chestnut, James	Civil War	250				CSA General/1815-85
Chestnutt, Mark	Music	15			30	
Chevalier, Albert	Music	6	25	40	25	Composer
Chevalier, Maurice	Ent	35		150	125	
Chevrolet, Louis 1879-41	Business	800	4,500	RARE	RARE	Chevrolet Auto Mfg
Chicago	Music	40			100	Signed by Entire Band
Chichester, Francis, Sir	Aviation	35	100	165	75	Aviator, Sailed Gypsy Moth IV
Chickering, Thos.E.	Civil War	70	90	175		Union General/1824-71
Chiklis, Michael	Ent	10			25	
Child, Julia	Author	5		15	15	TV Chef. Cookbook Author
Child, Lydia Maria	Author	30	75	150		Abolitionist/Reformer
Childress, Alvin	Ent	50			125	
Childs, George Wm.	Author	10	15	25		Publisher
Chiles, Lois	Ent	10			25	James Bond Girl
Chilton, Robert H.	Civil War	185				CSA General/1816-79
Chilton, Robert Hall (WD)	Civil War	390				CSA General
Chirac, Jacques	Political	25	75	150	35	French Prime Minister
Chirico, Giorgio de	Art			780		Major Italian Surrealist
Cho, Margaret	Ent	10			20	Comedian
Choate, Joseph H.	Political	15	60	95	25	Prosecuted Tweed Ring
Chong, Rae Dawn	Ent	10			20	
Chopin, Frederic	Music	1,500	3,500	8,000		Composer
Chou En-Lai	Political	1,250	RARE	RARE	2,500	Chinese Premier
Chouteau, Auguste	RevWar	300	600	900		Am. Fur Trader/Pioneer
Christian IX (Den)	Royalty	90	250			1818-1906
Christian VII (Den & Nor) 1749-1808	Royalty	125	325	625		King of Denmark
Christian, Claudia	Ent	10			25	
Christianson, Helena	Ent	15			30	
Christie, Agatha	Author	150	400	Scarce	Scarce	1891 - 1976
Christie, Julie	Ent	10	15	28	55	
Christina, Queen (Swe)	Royalty	250	1,675	2,300		
Christo	Art	25			75	
Christophe, Henry	Political	1,200				Haitian Revolution/1767-20
Christopher, William	Ent	5	20		20	MASH

Name	Field	SIG	DS	ALS	SP	Remarks
Christy, Eileen	Ent	5			25	Vintage Actress
Christy, Howard Chandler	Art	65	125	220	400	Book Illustrator/1873-52
Christy, June	Music	10			20	Stan Kenton Vocalist
Chrysler, Walter P.	Business	400	1,000	1,500	900	Chrysler Motors/1879-40
Chung, Connie	Ent	5		20	15	TV News Anchor
Church, Benjamin	RevWar	200	500	900		Am. Physician & Spy
Church, Frederick E.	Art	150	375	750		Am. Landscapes/1826-00
Church, Frederick S.	Art	40	75	125		
Church, Thomas Hayden	Ent	15			35	Wings
Churchill, Clementine	First Lady	75	150	200	150	Wife of Winston
Churchill, John 1650-1722	Military	1,100				1st Duke of Marlborough
Churchill, Randolph	Political	45	95	285		Father of Winston S.
Churchill, Sarah	Ent	20	35	30	35	Daughter of Winston S.
Churchill, Thomas (WD)	Civil War	192				CSA General
Churchill, Thomas J.	Civil War	75	80	200		CSA General/1824-1905
Churchill, Winston	Author	15	35	50	35	
Churchill, Winston S.	Political	800	1,600	2,750	2,750	PM During WWII/1874-65
Ciano, Galeazzo, Conte	Royalty	65	295			Son-in-Law of Mussolini
Cigna, Gina	Music	55	70			Opera
Cimaro, Pietro	Music	10	25	50		It. Conductor
Cimino, Michael	Ent	10		20	20	Director
Citroen, Andre 1878-1935	Business	75	350		700	Citroen Auto Mfg.
Clair, Rene 1898-1981	Ent	100		300		Fr. Filmaker
Clairborne, Liz	Business	10			20	Clothing Designer
Claire, Ina	Ent	15	15	35	25	
Claire, Marion	Music	10			25	Am. Soprano
Clamorgan, Jacques	Western		750			Missouri Co. 1795
Clampett, Bob	Cartoonist	100	200		300	Beany & Cecil/Warner Bros
Clancey, Tom	Author	10	15		10	Am. Novelist
Clanton, Jimmy	Music	20			25	Rock
Clapton, Eric	Music	30		175	60	
Clark, Abraham 1726-94	RevWar	320	800			Signer Decl. of Indepen.
Clark, Bruce C.	Military	5	20	35	15	
Clark, Buddy	Music	10			25	40's Singer
Clark, Candy	Ent	5			15	
Clark, Carol Higgins	Author	5	15		20	
Clark, Charles	Civil War	110	275	350		CSA General/1811-77
Clark, Cottonseed	Music	15			30	
Clark, Dick	Ent	10	20		25	
Clark, Edward	Civil War		195			CSA General/1815-80
Clark, Fred	Ent	25			50	
Clark, George Rogers	RevWar	675	2,900	3,750		General, Frontier Leader
Clark, James B. Champ	Political	60	40	145	95	Speaker of the House
Clark, James, Sir	Science	15	35	85		Dr. to King and Queen
Clark, John Bullock,Sr.	Civil War	100				CSA General/1831-1903
Clark, L. Gaylord	Author	20	35	95		Editor Knickerbocker Mag
Clark, Marcia	Celebrity	15			35	OJ Simpson Trial
Clark, Marguerite	Ent	20			50	Stage
Clark, Mark W. 1896-1984	Military	35	190	275	100	Gen. WWII 5th Army.

Name	Field	SIG	DS	ALS	SP	Remarks
Clark, Mary	Military	5		15	15	
Clark, Mary Higgins	Author	15	25		25	Suspense Novels
Clark, Petula	Music	10			25	
Clark, Roy	Music	5			15	
Clark, Susan	Ent	5	10		15	
Clark, Tom C.	SuprCt	40	100	125	125	
Clark, Walter J.	Aviation	10		35	30	WWII ACE
Clark, William 1770-1838	Western	400	1,500	2,000		Lewis & Clark Expedition
Clark, William A.	Business	35	135	195		Railroad & Mining Magnate
Clarke, Arthur C.	Author	15	35	75	40	Sci-Fi Author
Clarke, Charles M.	Science	20	65	140		Br. Obstetrician
Clarke, Henri J.G. Duc	Military	75	250	350		Marshal of Napoleon
Clarke, Ken	Ent	10			25	
Clarke, Mae	Ent	35		60	65	Frankenstein
Clarke, Thomas	RevWar	150	450			
Clarkson, Mathew	RevWar	50	100	175		
Clary, Robert	Ent	10	25		25	Hogans Heroes
Clavell, James	Author	10	25	55	20	
Clay, Andrew Dice	Ent	15			35	
Clay, Cassius	Sports	125			300	Muhammad Ali
Clay, Cassius Marcellus	Civil War	80	220	450		Union General/1810-1903
Clay, Henry 1777-1852	Political	125	300	950		Sec'y State
Clay, Lucius D. 1897-1978	Military	30	125	145	100	Gen.WWII
Clayburgh, Jill	Ent	5			20	
Clayton, Jan	Ent	5			15	
Clayton, John M.	Political	35	75	150		Taylor Sec'y State
Clayton, Joshua	RevWar	220	425			First DE Governor
Clear Sky, Chief	Western	20			50	Iroquois Chief
Cleaveland, Moses	RevWar	170				Cleveland, Ohio Namesake
Cleburne, Patrick R.	Civil War	1,050	1,650			CSA General/1828-64
Cleese, John	Ent	15	25		35	Monty Python member
Clem, John L.	Civil War	150	250	350 RARE		Union Drummer
Clemenceau, Georges	Political	100	150	175		Prime Minister France
Clemens & Twain	Author	1,200			RARE	Dual Signed
Clemens, Orion	Western	125		200		Sect of Nevada Territory
Clemens, Roger	Sports	25			75	Baseball
Clemens, Samuel L.	Author	750	1,500	2,000		Mark Twain/1835-1910
Clement VI II, Pope	Political	550	1,300			
Clemente, Roberto	Sports	250			500	1973 Baseball HOF
Clements, John	Ent	20			40	Br. Director/Actor
Cleveland, Frances F.	First Lady	52	80	216	225	1864-1957
Cleveland, Grover	President	225	550	750	800	As President
Cleveland, Grover	President	200	375	600	500	1837-1905
Clewes, Henry	Business	25	45			Banker
Cliburn, Van	Music	25		50	75	Pianist
Clifford, Nathan 1803-81	SuprCt	75	175	200	150	Att'y Gen., Ambassador
Clift, Montgomery	Ent	225	355	600	750	1920 - 1966
Clifton, Joseph C.	Aviation	15	35	60	40	
Cline, Patsy	Music	500		1,500	1,500	Scarce in All Forms

Name	Field	SIG	DS	ALS	SP	Remarks
Clingman, Thomas Lanier	Civil War	95	295	440		CSA General/1812-97
Clinton, De Witt 1769-28	Political	100	300	500		Mayor NYC
Clinton, George1739-1812	Vice Pres	135		385		
Clinton, Henry, Sir	RevWar	425	925	2,200		Br. Soldier
Clinton, Hillary Rodham	First Lady	200	450	Scarce	450	
Clinton, James	RevWar	200	490			General Revolutionary War
Clinton, William J. "Bill"	President	350	750	900	450	42nd U.S. President
Clive, Colin	Ent	225			400	
Clive, E.E.	Ent	20			50	
Clive, Robert	Military	250	600	1,200		Baron Clive of Plassey
Cloggers, Stoney Mtn.	Music	30			60	
Clokey, Art	Cartoonist	20			45	Gumby
Clooney, George	Ent	20			45	ER/Batman
Clooney, Rosemary	Ent	20			45	
Close, Glenn	Ent	15			45	
Clostermann, Pierre	Military	50	100	125	75	
Clover, Richardson	Military	35	125			USN Admiral
Clovio, Giorgio Guilio	Art	650	1,400	2,000		It. Miniaturist/1498-1578
Clyde, Andy	Ent	60			150	
Clymer, George 1739-13	RevWar	125	505	900		Signer Decl. of Indepen.
Coates, Eric	Music	25	55	85	130	Composer
Coates, Phyllis	Ent	10			20	
Coats, Bob	Aviation	10	22	38	30	WWII ACE
Cobain, Kurt	Music	125			250	Nirvana/Suicide
Cobb, Calvin H.	Military	15	40	75		
Cobb, Howell	Civil War	100	200	400		CSA General/1815-68
Cobb, Howell (WD)	Civil War	225			950	CSA General
Cobb, Irvin S. 1876-1944	Author	25	45	150	95	
Cobb, Jerrie	Aviation	10			25	
Cobb, Lee J.	Ent	75	50	75	85	1911 - 1976
Cobb, Sylvanus 1823-87	Author	15			40	
Cobb, Thos. Reade (WD)	Civil War	1,200		2,000		CSA General/KIA
Cobb, Thos. Reade R.	Civil War	500	1,950	1,910		CSA General/KIA/1823-62
Cobb, Ty	Sports	500	1,000	1,500	1,500	1936 HOF Baseball
Cobham, Alan J., Sir	Aviation	25	65	85	45	Br. Aviation Pioneer
Coburn, Charles 1877-61	Ent	45	90	155	125	AA
Coburn, James	Ent	10	15	25	25	
Coca, Imogene	Ent	15			25	
Cochran, Eddie 1938-60	Music	220	650		575	Dead at age 22
Cochran, Jacqueline	Aviation	45	175		150	Record Speed Holder
Cochran, Johnnie	Celebrity	15			35	OJ Simpson Trial
Cochran, Steve	Ent	15	15	30	30	
Cochrane, Basil, Sir	Military	15	25	30		
Cochrane, John	Civil War	30	45	100		Union General/1813-98
Cockburn, George, Sir	Military	40	100	140		Br. Admiral War 1812
Cockcroft, John Douglas	Science	60	110	245	75	Nobel Physics
Cocke, Philip St. George	Civil War	Scarce	Scarce	Scarce	Scarce	CSA General/1809-61
Cocker, Joe	Music	20	50		50	
Cockrell, Francis Marion	Civil War	70	110	200		CSA General/1834-1915

Name	Field	SIG	DS	ALS	SP	Remarks
Coco, James	Ent	15	20	25	35	
Cocteau, Jean	Author	125		600	600	
Coda, Eraldo	Music	10			25	Opera
Cody, Iron Eyes	Ent	15			50	Cherokee Indian Actor
Cody, Lew	Ent	15	20	25	35	
Cody, William F.	Western	750	1,500	2,000	4,500	Buffallo Bill
Coffin, Charles C.	Civil War	100				
Coffin, Isaac, Sir 1759-39	Military	20		75		Boston Born Br. Naval Officer
Coffin, John 1756-1838	RevWar	175	500			Loyalist General
Coffin, Tris	Ent	20			35	
Coffyn, Frank	Aviation	40	65		95	
Coghlan, Frank, Jr.	Ent	10	25		25	GWTW
Coghlan, Joseph B.	Military	25			60	Adm USN-Spanish American War
Cogswell, William	Civil War	15	35	75		
Cohan, George M.	Music	100	175	200	200	Composer/1878-1942
Cohen, Octavus Roy	Author	15	30	45	25	Novels and Screenplays
Cohen, Stanley, Dr.	Science	20	35		25	Nobel Medicine
Cohn, Harry	Business	35	85	165	65	Co-Founder Columbia Pix
Cohn, Jack	Business	25	70	140	55	Co-Founder Columbia Pix
Coit, James Brolles	Civil War	25		125		Union General
Coke, Edward, Sir	Political		2,000	3,500		Jurist/Lord Chief Justice
Colbert, Claudette	Ent	40	125		85	1905 - 1997
Colby, Leonard	Military	40	90			General. Indian Fighter
Colden, Cadwallader	RevWar	100	240			Am. Colonialist
Cole, Nat King 1919-65	Music	175	300		350	
Cole, Natalie	Music	15			45	
Cole, Tommy	Ent	20			45	
Coleman, Dabney	Ent	10	20		25	Nine to Five
Coleman, Gary	Ent	10	25		35	
Coleman, George	Music	20			40	Jazz Sax
Coleridge, Samuel T.	Author	325	575	1,250		Br. Poet and Critic
Coleridge-Taylor, S.	Music	30	70	150	45	Composer/1875-1912
Colette, Sidonie-Gabrielle	Author	100	250	350	600	French Novelist
Colfax, Schuyler	Vice Pres	75	125		250	Grants VP
Colgate, James C.	Business	10	25	50	40	Colgate University. Donor
Colgrass, Michael	Music	20	35	85		Composer/Pulitzer
Collective Soul	Music	25			45	Signed by all
Collier, Constance	Ent	25			75	British Actress
Collier, Peter F.	Business	15	35	70		
Collins, J. Lawton	Military	15	50	75	35	General WWII
Collins, Jackie	Author	10	15	20	15	
Collins, Joan	Ent	5	25	35	25	
Collins, Judy	Music	10			20	
Collins, Michael	Space	100	150	250	150	Astronaut
Collins, Phil	Music	30			55	
Collins, Ray	Ent	50	60	150	175	
Collins, Wilkie	Author	100	309	530	1,380	Br. Novelist
Collis, Charles	Civil War	25		60		Union General
Collishaw, Raymond	Aviation	75	175	375	225	Brit. ACE, WW I

Name	Field	SIG	DS	ALS	SP	Remarks
Collyer, June	Ent	15			35	
Colman, Ronald	Ent	65	125		175	AA Winner/1891-1958
Colman, Samuel	Art	20		95		
Colombo, Scipio	Music	10			30	Opera
Colonna, Jerry 1903 - 86	Ent	20			35	Comedian/Disney Voice
Color Me Badd	Music	25			55	Entire Group
Colquitt, Alfred H.	Civil War	85	165	275	250	CSA General/1824-94
Colston, Raleigh E.	Civil War	70	425			CSA General/1825-96
Colt, Samuel 1814-1862	Business	500	2,000	2,750		Founder Colt Firearms
Coltrane, John	Music	RARE	RARE	RARE	RARE	Jazz
Colum, Padraic	Author	30	150		40	Irish Poet & Playwright
Columbo, Russ	Ent	50	90	200	165	
Comaneci, Nadia	Sports	20			45	Olympic Gymnast
Combs, Sean "Puffy"	Music	20			40	
Comden, Betty & Green, A.	Music	10	45		30	Composers on broadway
Comiskey, Charles	Sports	600			1,500	1939 Baseball HOF
Commager, Henry S.	Civil War	25	60	105		Union General/1825-67
Commodores	Music	25			60	Entire Group
Como, Perry	Music	10			35	
Compson, Betty	Ent	15	30	60	70	
Compton, Arthur H.	Science	90	205	275	100	Nobel Physics. Atom Bomb
Compton, Fay	Ent	5			15	
Compton, Joyce	Ent	10			20	
Compton, Karl T.	Science	90	200		110	Physicist, Pres. M.I.T.
Conant, A. Roger	Aviation	10		35	30	ACE/WWII/Marine Ace
Conati, Lorenzo	Music	25			65	Opera
Conaway, Jeff	Ent	15			30	Taxi/Grease
Conchita, Maria	Ent	5			10	
Conde', Louis II 1621-86	Military		750			French General
Condon, Eddie	Music	40			60	Composer
Condon, Richard	Author	5	15	35	10	
Cone, Fairfax M.	Business	10	35	45	20	Foote,Cone & Belding, Adv.
Cone, Hutchinson	Military	25	35			Admiral WW I
Congreve, William	Author	200	550	750		1670-1729
Coningham, Sir Arthur	Aviation	35	60			Cmdr. RAF lst Tactical
Conklin, Chester	Ent	100	115	220		
Conklin, Hal	Ent	10			25	
Conlee, John	Ent	5			10	
Conley, Eugene	Music	20	30		50	Opera
Conley, Joe	Ent	5			10	
Connally, John B.	Political	25	60	95	45	Gov. TX, Sec'y Treasury
Connelly, Christopher	Ent	10			25	
Connelly, Jennifer	Ent	20			50	
Connelly, Marc 1890-1980	Author	20	75	75	35	Am. Dramatist. Pulitzer
Connelly, Matthew J.	Political	10	25	35	15	Pres. Truman Aide
Conner, James	Civil War	100	210	270		CSA General. lst Bull Run
Conner, Nadine	Music	10			35	Opera/Radio
Connery, Sean	Ent	50	125		125	James Bond
Connick, Harry, Jr.	Music	25			45	

Name	Field	SIG	DS	ALS	SP	Remarks
Connick, Harry, Jr.	Music	25			45	
Conniff, Ray	Ent	25	35	65	45	
Connolly, Walter	Ent	50		100	65	
Connor, Harry P.	Aviation	15	30	45	50	
Connor, James	Civil War	95	205	260		CSA General/18829-83
Connor, Patrick Edward	Civil War	35	65			Union General/1820-91
Connors, Chuck	Ent	30	75	75	70	The Rifleman
Connors, Mike	Ent	10	20		20	Mannix
Conquest, Ida	Ent	15	15	25	30	
Conrad, Charles Jr.	Space	35			100	3rd Moonwalker.
Conrad, Charles Magill	Political	45	55	190		Sec'y War/1804-1878
Conrad, Joseph 1857-24	Author	230	1,125	1,450	1,250	Br. Novelist. Lord Jim etc.
Conrad, Michael	Ent	15	20	40	35	
Conrad, Robert	Ent	20	50		40	Wild, Wild, West
Conrad, William	Ent	30	45		55	Cannon
Conried, Hans	Ent	25	45		40	Disney Voice/Actor
Conroy, Kevin	Ent	10			20	Voice of Animated Batman
Conroy, Pat	Author	20			45	Great Santini, Prince of Tides
Constable, John 1776-37	Art	258	610	2,400		Br. Landscapes, Rural Life
Constantine I, 1868-1923	Royalty	90				King of Greece. Resigned
Constantino, Florencio	Music	75			365	Opera
Conte, John	Ent	5			15	
Conte, Richard	Ent	15			25	1911 - 1975
Conti, Bill	Music	60	85	100	40	Composer
Convy, Bert	Ent	20			25	
Conway, Henry Seymour	Military	25	60	135		Br. Fld. Marshal. /1721-95
Conway, Pat	Ent	10			25	
Conway, Shirl	Ent	10			25	
Conway, Thomas	RevWar	65	105	250		Maj. Gen. Rev, War
Conway, Tim	Ent	5		15	20	Carol Burnett Show
Conway, Tom	Ent	50			125	The Saint
Coogan, Jackie 1914-84	Ent	30	50		60	Fester/Addams Family
Coogan, Richard	Ent	5		15	15	
Cook, Ann T.	Ent	10			25	Model For Gerber Baby Products
Cook, Elisha Jr. 1902-95	Ent	75			100	Character Actor
Cook, Eliza	Author			75		Poet
Cook, Everett R.	Aviation	10	30		50	ACE WW I
Cook, Francis Augustus	Military	75		55	30	Spanish American War
Cook, Frederick Albert	Explorer	75	145	175	150	Claimed lst at North Pole
Cook, James, Capt.	Military	3,800	8,850	RARE	RARE	Captain Cook
Cook, Philip	Civil War	150	300	395		CSA General/1817-94
Cook, Robin	Author	10			25	Coma, Sphinx...
Cook, Thomas	Business	35	110			Fndr Br Tourist Comm.
Cook, Tommy	Ent	20			45	Child Actor
Cook, Walter V.	Aviation	15		45	30	ACE/WWII
Cooke, Alistair, Sir	Ent	20	95	140	75	TV Host. Masterpiece Theatre
Cooke, Jack Kent	Business	10	22		15	
Cooke, Jay 1821-1905	Business	300	1,250	2,250		Banker, Financier
Cooke, Nicholas	RevWar	Scarce	700	1,000	Scarce	Rev-War Gov. RI

Name	Field	SIG	DS	ALS	SP	Remarks
Cooley, Denton A., Dr.	Science	15		75	45	Heart Transplant Surgeon
Cooley, Lyman E.	Science	10		35		Civil Engineer
Cooley, Spade	Music	15			35	King of Western Swing
Coolidge, Calvin	President	150	400	900	450	
Coolidge, Calvin (AS)	President	200	550	Scarce	550	
Coolidge, Grace	First Lady	80	240	150	165	
Coolidge, Rita	Music	10			25	
Coolidge, William David	Science	45	85	165	125	GE Researcher/Inventor
Coolio	Music	20			50	
Coombs, Patricia	Art	10	20	35	15	
Cooper, Alice	Music	20			55	
Cooper, Emil	Music	30	180	80	72	Russian Composer
Cooper, Gary 1901-61	Ent	170	360	500	450	
Cooper, Gladys, Dame	Ent	35	35	65	55	1888 - 1971
Cooper, Gordon	Space	30	75		85	Mercury 7 Astronaut
Cooper, Jackie	Ent	20	25	35	55	Child Actor
Cooper, James Fenn	Author	90	180			Am. Novelist/1789-1851
Cooper, Leon N., Dr.	Science	20	35	60	30	Nobel Physics
Cooper, Leroy, Jr.	Space	40				Apollo VII (Early Sig.)
Cooper, Merian C.	Ent	150	300		250	King Kong
Cooper, Miriam	Ent	35			75	
Cooper, Peter 1791-1883	Business	150	500	750		Am. Inventor, Philanthropist
Cooper, Samuel	Civil War	120	230	445		CSA General/1798-1876
Cooper, Samuel (WD)	Civil War	175		750		CSA General
Cooper, Thos. Sidney	Art	10	20	35		
Coors, W. K.	Business	20	60	95	50	Coors Brewery
Coots, J. Fred	Music	35	45	100	40	Composer
Copage, Marc	Ent	10			25	
Copas, Cowboy	Music	100			225	
Copeland, L. du Pont	Business	20		50		
Copland, Aaron 1900-90	Music	65	165	300	150	Composer
Copley, John Singleton	Art	350	710	RARE		1738-1815
Copley, Teri	Ent	5			15	
Coppens, Willy (Baron)	Aviation	20	40	125	50	
Copperfield, David	Ent	15	45		45	Magician
Coppola, Francis Ford	Ent	30	75		60	AA Film Director
Coquelin, Benoit-Const	Ent	25	50	60		
Corbett, Boston	Assasin	965	RARE	1,800	RARE	Shot John Wilkes Booth
Corbin, Bary	Ent	10			25	
Corbin, Henry Clarke	Civil War	50		115		Union General
Corbusier, Le 1887-1965	Science	85	575		575	Jeanneret, Charles Edouard
Corby, Ellen	Ent	25	45		45	The Waltons
Corcoran, Michael (WD)	Civil War			1,723		Union General/1827-63
Corcoran, William W.	Business	150	600	1,200		Banker, Philanthropist
Cord, Alex	Ent	10			15	
Corden, Henry	Ent	15			35	2nd Voice/Fred Flintstone
Corea, Chick	Ent	15			35	
Corelli, Franco	Music	25		100	100	Opera
Corelli, Marie 1855-1924	Author	40	60	75	75	English Novelist

Name	Field	SIG	DS	ALS	SP	Remarks
Corena, Fernando	Music	20			45	Opera
Corey, Elias	Science	20	35		30	Nobel Chemistry
Corey, Jeff	Ent	5			15	
Corey, Wendell	Ent	35	45	80	75	
Cori, Carl F.	Science	15	25	47	20	Nobel Medicine
Corio, Ann	Ent	15	15	20	30	
Corlett, Irene	Ent	5			10	
Cormack, Allan M.	Science	20	35	50	25	Nobel Medicine
Corman, Roger	Ent	10			30	
Cornbury, Edward Hyde	Political	200	450			lst Colonial Gov. NJ
Cornelius, Don	Ent	10			20	
Cornelius, Peter	Music	100		250		Opera
Cornell, Ezekiel	Military	60	200			Brig. Gen. American Rev.
Cornell, Ezra	Business	30	80	165	75	Western Union Financier
Cornell, Joseph 1903-72	Art	135	1,200	700		Am. Surrealist Sculptor
Cornell, Katharine	Ent	20	35	75	75	1898-1974
Cornell, Lydia	Ent	5			15	
Corner, George W.	Science	75	150		100	
Cornfeld, Bernard	Business	10	20	55	35	
Cornforth, John W., Sir	Science	15	35	45	20	Nobel Laureate/Chemistry
Corning, Erastus 1794-72	Business	70	175	295		Pres. NY Central RR
Cornwallis, Charles E.	RevWar	175	650	1,200		Br. General RevWar
Corot, J.B. Camille	Art	250	500	900	2,000	Impressionist
Corrigan, Douglas	Aviation	65	80	200	100	Wrong Way
Corrigan, Mairead	Political	35	40	100	50	Nobel Peace Prize 1976
Corrigan, Ray Crash	Ent	50			150	
Corsaut, Aneta	Ent	40	75	75	75	Andy Griffith Show
Corse, John Murray	Civil War	35	245	80		Union General/1835-93
Corse, Montgomery D.	Civil War	120		325		CSA General/1816-95
Cortez, Hernando	Explorer	6,000	20,000	RARE	RARE	Sp. Conqueror of Mex.
Cortez, Ricardo	Ent	25			40	
Cortina, Juan	Military	Scarce	Scarce	Scarce	Scarce	Mexican General
Corwin, Thomas	Political	35	60	100		Fillmore Sec'y Treasury
Cosby, Bill	Ent	10	30		30	
Cosby, George B.	Civil War	60	130	200		CSA General/1831-1909
Cosell, Howard	Ent	20			55	Radio-TV Sports News
Cosgrave, William T.	Political	70	150	275		Sinn Fe'in Easter Uprising.
Coslow, Sam	Music	75	200	300	350	AA Winning Composer
Cossotto, Fioranza	Music	10			30	Opera
Cossutta, Carlos	Music	5			25	Opera
Costa Lo Giudice, Silvio	Music	40			100	Opera
Costa, Michael, Sir	Music	15	40	95	25	Br. Conductor.Opera
Costas, Bob	Ent	5			10	TV Host & Sports Commentator
Coste, Dieudonne	Aviation	125	235	385	275	
Costello, Delores	Ent	30	45	75	60	
Costello, Elvis	Music	15			40	
Costello, Lou 1906-59	Ent	175	250	400	400	Abott and Costello
Costner, Kevin	Ent	25			50	AA Winner
Coswell, Henry T.	Aviation	55	105	150		lst Balloon ascent 1844

Name	Field	SIG	DS	ALS	SP	Remarks
Cotten, Joseph 1905-94	Ent	20	25		35	
Cotton, Carolina	Music	15			30	
Coty, Frangois	Business	100	400	475		Coty Perfume & Cosmetics
Couch, Darius Nash	Civil War	50	75	150		Union General/1822-97
Coulouris, George	Ent	10			25	Character Actor
Coulter, Jessie	Music	5			15	
Coulter, Richard	Civil War	40	75	95		Union Bvt. General
Couples, Fred	Sports	15			30	Golfer
Courbet, Jean D. Gustave	Art	225	600	900		Leader of Realist School
Couric, Katie	Ent	5			15	TV Host of Today Show
Court, Hazel	Ent	10			35	
Courtney, Inez	Ent	15			35	
Cousins, Norman	Author	10	25	40	15	Saturday Review Editor
Cousteau, Jacques	Science	60		175	150	Underwater Explorer, Films
Cousteau, Jim (Son)	Science	25			75	Underwater Explorer
Couter, John B.	Military	15	45			
Coward, Noel, Sir	Author	100	200	340	275	1899-1973
Cowl, Jane	Ent	20		35	45	
Cowles, Gardner	Business	10		25	15	Publisher
Cox, George H.	Author	5	15	30		Br. Historical Writer
Cox, Jacob D.	Civil War	25		95		Union General/1828-1900
Cox, Samuel S. 1824-89	Political	25		125		Civil War Repr. OH
Cox, Wally	Ent	25	30		45	
Cox, William R.	Civil War	60	85	105		CSA General/1832-1919
Cox, Archibald	Political	15	185	55	20	Att'y Gen/Watergate
Cox, Courtney	Ent	20			50	Friends
Cox, Nikki	Ent	20			40	
Cox, Palmer	Cartoonist	50	140	275	225	Brownies
Coxe, Tenche	RevWar	40	100	170		Continental Congress
Coyote, Peter	Ent	15			35	
Crabbe, Buster 1909-83	Ent	35			65	Flash Gordon/Tarzan
Crabbe, Cullen	Ent	15			35	
Crabtree, Lotta	Ent	25	75	100	100	
Craddock, "Crash" Billy	Music	10			25	
Craig, Edward Gordon	Ent	15	40	155	190	
Craig, James	Civil War	45	75	95		Union General/1820-88
Craig, Jenny	Business	5			10	Diet Guru
Craig, Yvonne	Ent	10	20		20	TV's Batgirl
Crain, Jeanne	Ent	15	20	40	45	
Cram, Donald J., Dr.	Science	20	35		30	Nobel Chemistry
Cramer, Floyd	Music	5			15	
Crampton, Barbara	Ent	15			25	
Cranch, Christopher P.	Art	5		25	35	1813-1892
Crane, Bob	Ent	150	250		250	Hogan of Hogans Heroes
Crane, Charles Henry	Civil War	25	175	210		Union General.Surgeon
Crane, Fred	Ent	35			75	GWTW
Crane, Hart	Author	130	600	1,500	350	Am. Poet, The Bridge
Crane, John	Military	100	250			RevWar General
Crane, Richard	Ent	20			45	

Name	Field	SIG	DS	ALS	SP	Remarks
Crane, Roy	Cartoonist	30			75	Wash Tubbs, B. Sawyer
Crane, Stephen	Author	1,500 RARE		4,500 RARE		Red Badge of Courage
Crane, Walter 1845-1915	Art	75	150	250		Br. Painter-Illustrator.
Crane, William H	Ent	30	45	75	50	1845-1928
Crass, Franz	Music	10			25	Opera
Craven, Frank	Ent	20			55	
Craven, John	Ent	10			25	
Craven, Wes	Ent	10			25	Director
Cravens, Jordan E.	Civil War	25		80		CSA Officer
Crawford, Broderick	Ent	35	75		100	
Crawford, Christina	Ent	5		30	15	Daughter of Joan Crawford
Crawford, Cindy	Ent	25			50	Model
Crawford, Francis M.	Author	12	15	25		Am. Novelist/1854-1909
Crawford, J. W. Capt.	Military	35		250		Indian Wars Scout
Crawford, Joan 1904-77	Ent	75	175	250	225	
Crawford, Johnny	Ent	10			25	The Rifleman
Crawford, Michael	Ent	25			55	Phantom of the Opera
Crawford, Samuel W.	Civil War	48	85	210		Union General/1829-92
Crawford, William H.	Political	40	155	150		Madison Sect of War
Crawford-Frost, Wm. A.	Business	15	25	70	20	
Cream	Music	75			150	Signed by All Three
Creeley, Robert	Author	5			10	
Cregar, Laird 1916-44	Ent	100		200	300	Character Actor/Dead at 28
Creighton, Johnston	Civil War	100	350			Union Admiral
Cremer, Peter Erich	Military	75		125		
Crenna, Richard	Ent	10	25		25	Rambo
Cresap, Mark	Business	5			10	
Creston, Paul	Music	25			125	Composer
Crews, Laura Hope	Ent	200			350	Aunt Pittypat-GWTW
Crichton, Michael	Author	15	100		75	Jurassic Park. etc.
Crick, Francis, Dr.	Science	50	75			Nobel in Medicine, DNA
Crier, Katherine	Ent	5			10	TV Commentary
Crippen, Robert L.	Space	10			115	Shuttle Orbiter 102 Crew
Cripps, Richard Stafford	Political	30	90	210		Br.Economist
Crisp, Donald	Ent	50	60	90	150	
Cristal, Linda	Ent	10	15	30	20	
Crittenden, John J.	Political	25	60	125		Attorney General/Senator
Crittenden, Thomas (WD)	Civil War	85				Union General
Crittenden, Thomas L.	Civil War	50	135	285	250	Union General/1819-93
Croce, Benedetto	Author	25	35	80		
Croce, Jim	Music	160	300		450	Died Young
Crocker, Charles	Business	500	2,000	3,000		Am. Financier/RARE
Crockett, David 1786-36	Military	6,000	9,000	20,000		Died at Alamo
Crockett, Samuel R.	Author	7	15	35		
Croft, Dwayne	Music	10			25	Opera
Croghan, George	Business	200	400	800		Indian Treaty Maker/Trader
Croker, Richard Boss	Political	20	45	80		Tammany Hall Leader
Crompton, Richmal	Author	15	40	80	30	
Cromwell, James	Ent	15			40	

Name	Field	SIG	DS	ALS	SP	Remarks
Cromwell, Oliver 1599-58	Political	1,200	RARE	RARE		Named Lord Protector Eng.
Cromwell, Richard	Ent	5			15	
Cronenberg, David	Ent	10			25	Film Director
Cronin, A. J.	Author	25	85	170	30	Br. Physician-Novelist.
Cronin, Hume	Ent	15	25	30	35	1911 - 1997
Cronin, James VV.	Science	15	25	35	20	Nobel Physics
Cronkite, Walter	Ent	10	20	35	20	TV News Anchor
Crook and Chase	Ent	15			25	Lorianne & Charlie
Crook, George	Civil War	150	438	375	400	Union General/1818-90
Crookes, William, Sir	Science	130		180		Nobel Chemistry/1832-19
Crooks, Richard	Music	20		45	50	Opera
Crosby, Bing 1901-77	Ent	65	200	300	200	
Crosby, Bob	Music	15			25	Big Band Leader
Crosby, Cathy Lee	Ent	10			25	
Crosby, Denise	Ent	15			35	
Crosby, Gary	Ent	5			10	
Crosby, J.T.	Aviation	10		40	30	ACE/WWII/Navy Ace
Crosby, Kathryn	Ent	10	15	25	25	
Crosby, Mary	Ent	5		10	15	
Crosby, Norm	Ent	5		15	10	
Crosby, Percy	Cartoonist	40			85	Skippy
Crosby, Stills & Nash	Music	60	125		125	
Crosley, Powel Jr.	Business	20	75	95	35	Crosley Radio Corp.
Crosman, George H.	Civil War	20		80	48	Union General/1798-1882
Crosman, Henrietta	Ent	10			25	
Cross, Christopher	Music	10			20	
Cross, Marcia	Ent	15			50	Melrose Place
Crosse, Andrew 1784-55	Science			165		Br. Electrical Pioneer
Crossfield, A. Scott	Aviation	15	30	45	55	lst U.S. Test Pilot of X-15
Crothers, Rachel	Author	5	30	40	15	Am. Playwright.
Crothers, Scatman	Ent	30	40		65	Disney Voice/Actor
Crouse, Russell	Author	10	15	45	60	Playwright. Life With Father
Croves, H. (B.Traven)	Author	250	600			Ger. Novelist
Crow, Sheryl	Music	20			50	
Crowe, Russell	Ent	20			45	
Crowe, William	Military	15	45		25	Admiral U.S. Navy
Crowell, Rodney	Ent	15			30	
Crowley, Pat	Ent	5		15	15	
Crowninshield, Benj. W.	Political	30	85	185		Sec'y Navy 1814
Crozier, William	Military	35			60	General WWI, Inventor
Cruger, Henry	Business	250	900			1739-1827 Amer. Merchant
Cruikshank, George	Art	160	115	345	375	Illustrator,Caricaturist
Cruise, Tom	Ent	35	200	Scarce	75	
Crumb, George	Music	25			45	Composer/Pulitzer
Crumb, Robert	Cartoonist	25			75	Underground Comic Books
Cruz, Brandon	Ent	15			35	Courtship of Eddie's Father
Cruzen, Richard H.	Explorer	20		50	75	Adm. Arctic-Antarctic/Byrd
Cruz-Romo, Gilda	Music	15			30	Opera
Cryer, Jon	Ent	20			40	Breakfast Club

Name	Field	SIG	DS	ALS	SP	Remarks
Crystal, Billy	Ent	20			45	
Cudahy, Michael F.	Business	25	65	135	50	Meat Packer. Refrigeration
Cugat, Xavier	Music	20	30	35	100	Big Band Rhumba King
Cui, Cesar 1835-1918	Music	100	200	450		Composer
Cukor, George	Ent	40	100		100	Stage and Screen Director
Culbertson, Ely 1891-55	Author	25	80		150	Championship Bridge.
Culkin, Macaulay	Ent	25			50	Home Alone
Cullen, Bill	Ent	10			20	
Cullen, Countee 103-46	Author	200	410	400		Am. Black Poet
Cullum, George W.	Civil War	25		70		Union General/1809-92
Culp, Julia	Music	35			150	Opera
Culp, Robert	Ent	10	25		25	I Spy
Cumming, Alfred	Civil War	100	295	330		CSA General/1829-1910
Cummings, E.E.	Author	200	350	500	690	Am. Poet, Painter
Cummings, Homer	Political	25	40	75	125	FDR Att'y Gen./1870-56
Cummings, Robert	Ent	15			35	1908 - 1990
Cunard, Samuel, Sir	Business	90	130	210		Br. Shipowner.Cunard Line
Cunningham, Andrew B. 1883-1963	Military		100	200		Br. Adm. S. Afr, & WW I
Cunningham, E.V.	Author	20			35	Howard Fast
Cunningham, Merce	Ent	40		150	75	Dancer/Choreographer
Cunningham, R. Walter	Space	10	20	30	25	Astronaut
Cunningham, Randy D	Aviation	15	25	45	35	ACE, Nam, Only Navy Ace
Cuomo, Mario	Political	15	35		50	Governor NY
Curbs, Samuel Ryan	Civil War	50	60	235		Union General/1817-66
Curie, Marie 1867-1934	Science	1,050	1,550	2,600	Scarce	
Curie, Pierre 1859-1906	Science	440	895	RARE		
Currie, Donald, Sir	Business	10	20	40		Scot. Shipowner
Currier, Nathaniel	Art	225	800			Currier & Ives, Lithographers
Curry, B.	Civil War	30	70			CSA Officer
Curry, George	Military	30	90			lst Territorial Gov. NM
Curry, Jabez L.M.	Civil War			40		CSA Congress/1825-1903
Curry, John Stewart	Art	75		300		
Curry, Tim	Ent	20			50	Rocky Horror Show
Curtin, Jane	Ent	10	15	20	25	Sat Nite Live
Curtis, Alan	Ent	10	15	35	25	
Curtis, Benjamin R.	SuprCt	35	150	200		Resigned in Protest
Curtis, Charles	Vice Pres	55	125	175	90	
Curtis, Cyrus H. K.	Business	35	55	140	95	Curtis Publishing Co.
Curtis, Edward Sheriff	Art		500		1,300	Photographer/1868-52
Curtis, George Wm.	Author	60	130	55		Editor Harper's Weekly
Curtis, Jamie Lee	Ent	25	100		50	
Curtis, Ken 1916-91	Ent	35		100	75	Festus on Gunsmoke
Curtis, Newton M.	Civil War	30	85			Union General/1835-1910
Curtis, Robin	Ent	10		25	20	Star Trek movie
Curtis, Tony	Ent	10	25	25	20	
Curtis, Verna Maria	Music	10			30	Am. Soprano
Curtis, Wilfred A.	Aviation	10	25	40	25	
Curtiss, Glenn	Aviation	300	500	650	850	Pioneer Aircraft
Curtiz, Michael	Ent	30	75		100	Director

Name	Field	SIG	DS	ALS	SP	Remarks
Cusack, Joan	Ent	20			40	
Cusack, John	Ent	20			45	
Cushing, Caleb 1800-79	Political	25	55	100		Pierce Att'y Gen., Diplomat
Cushing, Harvey, Dr.	Science	165	475	675		Specialist in Neurosurgery
Cushing, Peter	Ent	40		80	75	Horror star
Cushing, Thomas	Military	450	900			Patriot/1725-88
Cushman, Charlotte S.	Ent	20		45	60	
Custer, Elizabeth	Author	100	200	Scarce	375	Wife of George A. Custer
Custer, George A.	Civil War	3,500	7,500	10,000	15,000	Union General/1839-76
Custine, Adam Philippe	RevWar	100	350			Fr.Gen.in RevWar
Cutler, Lysander	Civil War	90	185	260		Union General/1806-66
Cutler, Manasseh 1742-23	RevWar	425	550			Am.Clergyman
Cuvier, Georges, Baron	Science	70	350	365		Fr. Comparative Anatomy
Cuyler, Theodore L.	Author	10	15	35		
Cyrus, Billy Ray	Music	20			40	
Czerny, Carl	Music	100	200	400		Composer
Czerny, Vincenz	Science	125				Pioneer/Abdominal Surgery

Charles Chaplin

Agatha Christie

Noel Coward

Name	Field	SIG	DS	ALS	SP	Remarks
D'Abo, Maryan	Ent	10			30	
D'Abo, Olivia	Ent	20			40	
Dache, Lilly	Business	55	70	130	150	Coutourier.Specialty-Hats
Dafoe, Allan Roy, Dr.	Science	75	60	135	225	Delivered Dionne Quintuplets
Dafoe, Willem	Ent	15		40	40	
Dagmar	Ent	20			35	
Dagover, Lil	Ent	75			200	
Daguerre, Louis	Science	250	490	1,250		Fr. Inventor Daguerreotype
Dahl, Arlene	Ent	10		15	20	
Dahl, Perry	Aviation	10	22	38	28	ACE/WWII
Dahl, Roald	Author	50	150		100	Childrens Books
Dahlberg, Edward	Author	15	25	35	20	Am. Writer & Critic
Dahlberg, Ken	Aviation	15	30	50	40	WWII ACE
Dahlgren, John A.	Civil War	100	300	400		Adm. Union Navy/1809-70
Dahlgren, Ulric	Civil War	270		1,250		Planned Jeff Davis Capture
Dailey, Dan	Ent	15	25	45	40	1914 - 1978
Dailey, Janet	Author	5	10		10	
Daily, Bill	Ent	10			20	
Dal Monte, Toti	Music	35			100	Opera
Daladier, Edouard	Political	30	75	150	50	
Dalai Lama XIV	Political	75	160	200	100	Tibetan Religious Leader
D'Albert, Eugene	Music	100	200		200	Opera
Daley, Cass	Ent	5		20	15	
Daley, Richard J.	Political	20	40	85	40	Mayor Chicago
Daley, Richard M.	Political	5			10	Mayor Chicago
Dali, Salvador 1904-89	Art	200	450	650	850	Sp. Surrealist Painter
Dallapozza, Adolf	Music	10			25	Vienna Operettas
Dallas, Alexander J.	Political	42	150	190		Madison Sec'y Treasury
Dallas, George M.	Vice Pres	75	200	300		Dallas Named for Him
Dalmores, Charles	Music	25			85	Opera
Dalton, Dorothy	Ent	20	25	65	60	
Dalton, Lacy J.	Music	5			15	
Dalton, Emmett 1871-37	Western	800	1,600	3,500	Scarce	Western Train Robber
Dalton, Frank	Western	850	2,500			U.S.Marshal-Old West
Dalton, John	Science	150	400	750		Br. Chemist & Philosopner
Dalton, Tristan	Military	500		2,500		Am. Patriot/1738-1817
Dalton,Timothy	Ent	20			50	James Bond
Daltry, Roger	Music	30			60	Lead singer of the Who
Daly, James	Ent	5		15	15	
Daly, James	Ent	10			20	
Daly, John Charles	Ent	5			10	Broadcaster
Daly, Timothy	Ent	20			40	Wings
Daly, Tyne	Ent	10			20	Cagney and Lacey

Name	Field	SIG	DS	ALS	SP	Remarks
Damita, Lili	Ent	30	80	95	85	
Damon, Cathryn	Ent	10			20	
Damon, Les	Ent	15			45	The Thin Man
Damon, Matt	Ent	25			50	
Damone, Vic	Music	5			10	Singer
Damrosch, Walter	Music	50	195	115	200	Composer/1862-1950
Dana, Charles A. 1819-97	Business	20	35	70	35	Owner & Editor NY Sun
Dana, James D.	Science	15		45		
Dana, James Jackson	Civil War	40	140			Union General
Dana, Napoleon J.T.	Civil War	30	55			Union General/1822-05
Dana, Richard Henry, Jr.	Author	50	200	215		1815-1882
Dandridge, Dorothy	Ent	75			300	1923-1965
Dandridge, Ruby	Ent	35			90	
Dandy, George B.	Civil War	50	100			Union General/1830-1911
Dane, Nathan	RevWar	25	75	125		Continental Congress
Dane, Taylor	Music	20			40	
Dane, Karl	Ent	10			15	
Danes, Claire	Ent	25			50	
Danforth, Thomas	Political	300	500			Deputy Governor MA
D'Angelo, Beverly	Ent	15			30	
Dangerfield, Rodney	Ent	10	15	25	20	
Danges, Henry 1870-1948	Music	35				Opera
Daniel, Peter Vivian	SuprCt	40	125	230		
Daniell, Henry	Ent	50			150	Character Actor
Daniels, Babe	Ent	20	25	65	75	
Daniels, Billy	Music	10			20	
Daniels, Charlie	Music	10			20	
Daniels, Jeff	Ent	15			40	
Daniels, Josephus	Political	25	50	150	125	Sec'y Navy WWI
Daniels, William	Ent	10			20	
Danilova, Alexandra	Music	20	35	60	75	Rus-Am Ballerina, Teacher
Dannay, Frederick	Author	75	200	300	Scarce	Ellery Queen
Dannay, Frederick	Author	75	150	300		ELLERY QUEEN
Dannenberg, Konrad	Science	20			55	Rocket Pioneer/von Braun
Danner, Blythe	Ent	10			25	
Danning, Sybil	Ent	10			25	
D'Annunzio, Gabriele	Author	75	175	150	375	It Writer/1863-1938
Dano, Royal	Ent	15		45	45	Hawaii 5-0
Danson, Ted	Ent	20			45	Cheers
Dantine, Helmut	Ent	15	15		40	
Danton, Georges-Jacques	Military	1,000	2,500			Guillotined Leader of Rev.
Danton, Ray	Ent	10			15	
Danza, Tony	Ent	10	15	30	30	Taxi and Who's the Boss
Darby, Kim	Ent	15			35	
Darcel, Denise	Ent	25			50	Actress
Darcy, Emery	Music	15			45	Met Tenor
Darin, Bobby	Music	100		250	300	1936 - 1973
Darion, Joe	Music	10			30	Composer
Darlan, Francois 1881-42	Military			450		Fr. Adm. Vichy. Assassinated

Name	Field	SIG	DS	ALS	SP	Remarks
Darling, J.N. "Ding"	Cartoonist	25			75	Political Cartoonist
Darlington, William	Science	35		125		Naturalist/1782-1863
Darnell, Linda 1923-65	Ent	50	150		200	Died Tragically in Fire
Darrah, Thomas	Military	35	50			General WW I
Darrall, Chester B.	Civil War	15	45	60		Union Surgeon CW
Darrell, Johnny	Music	10			20	
Darren, James	Ent	10			20	
Darro, Frankle	Ent	75			150	Disney Voice/Child actor
Darrow, Charles B.	Business	350				Inventor of Monopoly
Darrow, Clarence	Political	450	1,600	2,200	1,300	Scopes Trial Lawyer
Dart, Justin	Business	50	100	250	75	
D'Artagnan, Comte de	Military			6,500		Capt.Louis XIV Musketeers
Darwell, Jane 1880-1967	Ent	100	200		200	GWTW
Darwin, Charles 1809-92	Science	750	1,600	1,750	RARE	Theory of Evolution
Dassin, Jules	Ent	20			45	Director
Daubigny, Charles F.	Art	95	280	410		Fr. Landscape Painter
Daudet, Alphonse	Author	35	75	175		
Daugherty, Harry M.	Political	25	55	125	50	Attorney General
Daumier, Honore	Art	250	500	1,000		Fr. Caricaturist
Dauphin, Claude	Ent	35			75	
Dausset, Jean, Prof.	Science	20	45		30	Nobel Medicine
Dave Clarke Five	Music	100	150		200	Signed by Entire Band
Davenport, Addington	RevWar	140	250	500		Am. Colonial Jurist1670-36
Davenport, Fanny	Ent	20			50	
Davenport, Harry	Ent	150			225	1866 - 1949
Davenport, Homer C.	Cartoonist	30	60	125		Uncle Sam cartoonist
David, Felicien-Cesar	Music	100	300			Composer/1810-76
David, Ferdinand	Music	50		175		Ger. Violinist
David, Hal	Music	20	30	65	35	Composer
David, Jacques Louis	Art	175	350	500		Fr. Classical Painter
David, Mack	Music	20			40	Lyricist
Davidson, Allen Turner	Civil War	25	80	125		CSA Congress
Davidson, Arthur d.1950	Business		2,000			RARE/Harley Davidson
Davidson, Gordon	Business	Scarce	2,750			One of Harley-Davidson Founders
Davidson, Jo	Art	35	75	135		Am. Sculptor
Davidson, John	Ent	5			10	
Davidson, William H.	Business	Scarce	3,000	4,000		Harley-Davidson Pres./Scarce
Davies, Gail	Music	5			10	
Davies, Marion	Ent	30	50	150	125	
Davies, Peter Maxwell	Music	30			100	Opera
Davies, Rhys	Author	5	20	30	15	
Davies, William	RevWar	35		170		VA Sec'y War
Davis, Ann B.	Ent	10	20		25	Brady Bunch
Davis, Benjamin 0. Jr	Aviation	20	35	75	40	WWII ACE
Davis, Bette 1908-89	Ent	80	200	350	200	
Davis, Brad	Ent	30			45	
Davis, Charles Henry	Civil War	30	65	105		Union Admiral/1807-77
Davis, Clifton	Ent	5			15	
Davis, David/1815-1886	SuprCt	75	200	225		Sen. IL. Pres Pro Tem

Name	Field	SIG	DS	ALS	SP	Remarks
Davis, Dwight F.	Political	25	80	170	65	Sec'y War
Davis, Fay	Ent	5			10	
Davis, Gail	Ent	15	20	25	35	
Davis, Geena	Ent	20	50		50	AA Winner
Davis, Henry Greene	Civil War	55	130			Union General
Davis, James J.	Political	20	50	95	75	Sec'y Labor
Davis, Jefferson (WD)	Civil War	700	2,400	3,750		President CSA
Davis, Jefferson 1808-89	Civil War	500	1,500	1,750	2,500	President of the CSA
Davis, Jefferson C.	Civil War	50	80	110		Union General/1828-79
Davis, Jim	Cartoonist	35	75	225	175	Garfield
Davis, Jim	Ent	45	50	70	85	
Davis, Jimmie	Political	30	45		60	Gov. LA
Davis, Joan	Ent	25			55	
Davis, John 1761-1847	Author	30	175	290		US Treasury Comptroller
Davis, John 1787-1854	Political	25	50	70		Gov. MA
Davis, John William	Political	20	35	70	40	Dem. Presidential Candidate
Davis, Mack	Music	10			20	
Davis, Meyer	Music	15			35	
Davis, Miles	Music	125			300	Jazz Trumpet
Davis, Nancy (Reagan)	First Lady	100			225	Scarce as Davis
Davis, Nelson H.	Civil War	25	50	75		Union General/1821-90
Davis, Ossie	Ent	10			25	
Davis, Patti (Reagan)	Ent	10			25	
Davis, Phil	Cartoonist	30			75	Mandrake the Magician
Davis, Phyllis	Ent	10	15	20	25	
Davis, Reuben	Civil War	50		270		CSA General/1813-90
Davis, Rich'd Harding	Author	10	25	40	20	
Davis, Robert	Military	10		25		General WW I
Davis, Rufe	Ent	25			55	
Davis, Sammy, Jr.	Ent	45	75	150	150	
Davis, Varina	First lady	150	250	500	750	Mrs. Jefferson Davis
Davison, Bruce	Ent	5			10	
Davison, Wild Bill	Music	30			75	Jazz Cornet-Bandleader
Davisson, Clinton Joseph	Science	25	75			Nobel Physics
Davout, Louis Nicolas	Military	45	210	250		Marshal of Napoleon
Davy, Humphry Sir	Science	100	270	500		
Dawber, Pam	Ent	10	20		25	Mork and Mindy
Dawes, Charles G.	Vice Pres	30	150	295	275	Nobel Peace Prize
Dawes, William 1745-99	RevWar	Scarce	20,000	3,000	RARE	Rode w/ Revere
Dawson-Briggs, Roxanne	Ent	15			35	Star Trek Voyager
Day, Chon	Cartoonist	10	30		50	Brother Sebastian
Day, Dennis	Music	10		25	30	
Day, Doris	Ent	10			35	
Day, Laraine	Ent	10			40	
Day, Linda (George)	Ent	5		15	15	
Day, William R. d.1923	SuprCt	40	90	135	65	Sec'y State
Dayan, Moshe 1915-1981	Military	125	235	275	250	Israeli Soldier, Politician
Dayan, Yael	Author	5			25	
Day-Lewis, Daniel	Ent	30			60	AA Winner

Name	Field	SIG	DS	ALS	SP	Remarks
Daymond, Gus	Aviation	15	25	55	40	ACE/WWII Eagle Squadron
Dayne, Taylor	Music	15			45	
Dayton, Elias	RevWar	100	200	350		Gen. Continental Congress
Dayton, Jonathan	RevWar	175	450	657		Continental Congress
Dayton, William L.1807-67	Political	25	40	110		
De Luca, Giuseppe	Music	25	50	100	175	Opera
De Palma, Brian	Ent	15		30	30	Film Director
De Quincey, Thomas	Author	150	300			
De Reszke, Edouard	Music	75			150	Opera/1853-1917
De Reszke, Jean 1850-25	Music	100	150		300	Opera
De Rita, Joe Curly	Ent	35	65		75	Three Stooges
De Almeida, Antonio	Music	10			45	
De Beauvoir, Simone	Author	35	95	200		
De Bono, Emilio	Military	75	225		375	
De Bray, Xavier B.	Civil War	125				CSA General/1818-95
De Corsia, Ted	Ent	20	25		40	
De Duve, Christian R.	Science	10			40	Nobel
De Falla, Manuel 1876-46	Music	425	1,200			Composer
De Forest, Lee, Dr.	Science	350	900	1,200	1,500	1873-1961
De Gaulle, Charles	Political	375	1,000	1,500	2,500	1890-1969
De Havilland, Geoffrey	Aviation	75	150	200	125	De Havilland Aircraft Co.
De Kooning, Elaine	Art	75			275	
De Kooning, Willem	Art	100	250	450	150	
De La Cierva, Juan	Aviation	100		250	350	Inventor Autogyro
De La Mare, Walter	Author	20	50	75	30	
De La Renta, Oscar	Business	10	15	35	20	Fashion Designer
De Lancey, Stephen	RevWar	75	150	225		
De Leo, Sarafina	Music	15			40	Opera
De Mornay, Rebecca	Ent	10	25		35	
De Peyster, John W. Jr.	Civil War	10	25	45		Aide to Gen.Kearny
De Ridder, Anton	Music	10		45	35	Opera
De Russy, Gustavus	Civil War	50	250	233		Union General/1818-91
De Seversky, Alex.	Aviation	100	200	200	225	1894-1973
De Toth, Andre'	Ent	10			20	Film Director
De Trobriand, P. R.	Civil War	75	325	395		Union General/1816-97
De Valera, Eamon	Political	50	125	200	100	Pres.PM/1882-1975
De Vere, Aubrey T.	Author	20	50	125		
De Wilde, Brandon	Ent	100			300	Child Actor
De Windt, Harry 1856-33	Explorer	30		75	50	Br. Explorer
Deacon, Richard	Ent	40	60		65	Dick van Dyke Show
Dean, Billy	Music	10			20	
Dean, Dizzy	Sports	100			300	1953 Baseball HOF
Dean, Donald J.	Military	15	45			WW I Victoria Cross
Dean, Eddie	Music	10		20	25	
Dean, James 1931-55	Ent	1,750	6,000	RARE	6,500	
Dean, Jimmy	Music	5			10	
Dean, John W.	Political	5	15	25	95	Legal Counsel to Nixon
Dean, William F.	Military	15	35	45	35	Gen.WWII
Deane, Silas	RevWar	230	550	1,050		

Name	Field	SIG	DS	ALS	SP	Remarks
Dearborn, Henry	Political	100	400	550		RevWar/Jeffersons Sect
Dearborn, Henry A.S.	Political	55	175	250		1783-1851
Debakey, Michael, Dr.	Science	20	35		35	1st Coronary Artery Bypass Op.
Debeck, Billy	Cartoonist	35			75	Barney Google & Snuffy Smith
DeBlanc, Jeff	Aviation	15		45	40	WWII ACE
DeBray, Xavier B.	Civil War	95		248		CSA General/1818-95
Debs, Eugene	Political	75	225	250	150	U.S. Socialist Leader.
Debussy, Claude 1862-18	Music	400		1,200		
DeButts, John D.	Business	10	35	45	20	
Debye, Peter J.W.	Science	50	100	175		Nobel/Discovered Rayon
Decamp, Rosemary	Ent	10			40	Am.Radio & Film Star
DeCarlo, Yvonne	Ent	10	30		30	Munsters/Lily
Decatur, Stephen	Military	1,000	2,700	4,500		American Naval Hero, War 1812
DeCisneros, Eleanora	Music	50			175	Opera
DeCordova, Fred	Ent	5			15	
Dee, Francis	Ent	5			25	
Dee, Ruby	Ent	5			20	
Dee, Sandra	Ent	10			35	
Deems, 'Cousin'	Music	5			15	
Deep Purple	Music	75			125	Signed by Entire Group
Deere, Allan Christopher	Aviation	15	40	50		Nazi Ace WWII, 22 Kills
Deere, John 1804-86	Business	500	1,500	1,500		
Deering, James	Business	10	25	45	25	.
Deering, Olive	Ent	15			35	
Dees, Rick	Music	5		20	10	
Defoe, Daniel 1660-1731	Author	1,500	Scarce	Scarce	Scarce	
DeFore, Don	Ent	10			15	
DeFranco, Buddy	Music	15			25	Bandleader
Degas, Edgar 1831 - 17	Art	650		2,000		Fr.Impressionist
DeGeneres, Ellen	Ent	20			40	
DeHart, John	RevWar	30	65	140		
DeHaven, Gloria	Ent	5		15	20	
DeHaven, Robert	Aviation	10	20	40	30	WWII ACE
DeHavilland, Olivia	Ent	30	60	30	55	GWTW
Dehmelt, Hans G., Dr.	Science	20	35		30	Nobel Physics
Deisenhofer, Johann	Science	25			35	Nobel
Dekker, Albert	Ent	5			10	
DeKlerk, F.W.	Political	75	150		150	Nobel Peace/Pr.Minister
DeKoven, Reginald	Music	25	45	150	100	Composer/1859-1920
Del Monaco, Mario	Music	50	75	125	175	Opera
Del Rio, Delores	Ent	30	35	55	65	
Del Tredici, David	Music	15	35	80		Composer/Pulitzer
Delacroix, F.V. Eugene	Art	200	375	550		Murals/1798-1886
Delafield, Richard	Civil War	40	75	100		Union General. Engineer
DeLagnel, Julius A.	Civil War	100		200		CSA General/1827-1912
DeLaHoya, Oscar	Sports	20			50	Boxer
DeLancie, John	Ent	15			40	Star Trek's "Q"
DeLand, Margaret	Author	15	25	75	25	Am. Novelist
Delaney, Dana	Ent	10			35	China Beach

Name	Field	SIG	DS	ALS	SP	Remarks
Delaney, Kim	Ent	5			15	
Delany, Dana	Ent	10			35	China Beach
Deledda, Grazia	Author	50	100	250		Nobel Literature 1926
Delibes, Leo	Music	100	200	300		Opera
Delius, Frederick 1862-34	Music	300	450	650		Composer
Dell, Gabriel	Ent	15	20	25	35	
Dell, Myrna	Ent	5		10	10	
Della Casa, Lisa	Music	10			25	Opera
Della Chiesa, Vivian	Music	5		15	15	Soprano
Della Joio, Norman	Music	35	115	240	55	Pulitzer/Composer
Delna, Marie	Music	35			100	Opera
DeLong, Phillip C.	Aviation	10	25	40	30	WWII ACE
Deluise, Dom	Ent	10			25	
DeMarco, Antonio	Ent	10	25			Producer
DeMarco, Tony	Ent		25			Dancer
Demarest, William	Ent	20		30	45	My Three Sons/1881-59
DeMille, Agnes	Ent	75	150		150	Dancer/Choreographer
DeMille, Cecil B. 1881-59	Ent	100	250	450	300	Director/Producer
DeMille, Katherine	Ent	10		15	25	
DeMille, William C.	Ent	25	50		50	Director/Producer
Demme, Jonathan	Ent	20			40	
DeMornay, Rebecca	Ent	15			30	
Dempsey, Jack	Sports	75			175	Boxer
Dempsey, Patrick	Ent	10			15	
Dench, Dame Judi	Ent	15			35	James Bond's "M"
Deneuve, Catherine	Ent	10	15	25	35	
Denfeld, Louis E.	Military	10	25	40	25	Adm.Chief Naval Operations WWII
DeNiro, Robert	Ent	25			60	
Denman, G. Tony	Aviation	10	20	35	25	ACE, WWII, Navy Ace
Denman, Thomas, 3rd Baron	Political	10	15	35		Gov. General Australia
Dennehy, Brian	Ent	15	35		25	
Denning, Richard	Ent	5		15	15	
Dennis, Sandy	Ent	38	45		85	
Dennison, Anthony	Ent	10			25	
Dennison, Jo Carroll	Ent	5			10	
Dennison, William	Political	150		450		Lincoln P.M.
Denny, Reginald	Ent	35			65	Mary Poppins
Denslow, W.W.	Cartoonist	75			175	Illustrator Of Wizard Of Oz
Dent, Elliott	Aviation	10		35	30	WWII ACE
Dent, Frederick T.	Civil War	35	90	185		Union General/1821-92
Denton, Jeremiah A., Jr.	Military	10	20	30	20	WWII Admiral
Denver, Bob	Ent	10	25		25	Gilligans Island
Denver, James W.	Civil War	100	210	450		Union General/1817-92
Denver, John	Music	35	75		75	Died in Plane Crash
Depardieu, Gerard	Ent	15			45	
Depeche Mode	Music	50			100	Signed by Entire Band
Depew, Chauncey M.	Business	150	450	900	500	NY Central Railroad
Depp, Johnny	Ent	25			50	
Derain, Andre'	Art	125	200	400		

Name	Field	SIG	DS	ALS	SP	Remarks
Derby,14th Earl	Political	50	35	95		Br. Prime Minister
Derek & the Dominoes	Music	50			150	All have signed
Derek, Bo	Ent	20			50	
Derek, John	Ent	25	50		50	
Deringer, Henry 1786-68	Business	2,000	RARE	6,500	RARE	Invented Derringer Pistol
Derleth, August	Author	25	75			
Dern, Bruce	Ent	15			30	
Dern, Laura	Ent	10			35	Jurassic Park...
Dershowitz, Alan M.	Political	15	20		30	Trial Attorney
Desai, M.R.	Political	5	15	25		Prime Minister India
Descartes, Rene	Science	RARE	17,500	20,000	RARE	Mathematician
Deschanel, Paul Eugene	Political			100		President France
Descher, Sandy	Ent				30	Child Actress
DeSilva, Howard	Ent	10	12	20	25	
Desmond, Johnny	Music	5			10	
Desmond, Shaw 1877-60	Author	25	75			Irish Playwright
Desmond, William	Ent	40			85	
Despretz, Cesar	Science	10		30		Inventor Electric Arc Furnace
D'Estaing,V. Gistard	Political	15	40	100	60	Pres. France
Destinn, Emmy 1878-1930	Music	100		225	200	Czech Soprano
Detaille, Edwouard	Art	125		325		Fr. Military & Portr. Painter
DeTreville, Yvonne	Music	35			85	Opera
Deutekom, Cristina	Music	15			35	Soprano
Deutsch, Patti	Ent	5			10	
DeVane, William	Ent	10		10		
Devens, Charles, Jr.	Military	30	50	150	150	Union Gen.-Att'y Gen.
Devereux, James P.S.	Military	35	75	100	150	WWII General
Devers, Jacob L.	Military	10	25	35	35	WWII General
Devine, Andy 1905-77	Ent	60	125		150	Roy Rogers Sidekick
DeVito, Danny	Ent	20	50		50	Taxi...
Devo	Music	35			60	Signed by all five
DeVos, Rich	Business	15			25	Founder Amway
DeVries, William, Dr.	Science	15	25	35	25	
Dewey, George	Military	100	150	200	300	Span-Am Admiral
Dewey, John	Author	50	125	250	75	Philosopher
Dewey, Thomas E.	Political	40	75	150	100	Presidential Candidate
Dewhurst, Colleen	Ent	20		40	45	1926 - 1991
DeWitt, Joyce	Ent	15	30		30	Three's Company
DeWolf, H.G.	Military	10	25		20	Canadian Adm. WWII
DeWolfe, Billy 1907-74	Ent	25	50	50	45	
Dey, Susan	Ent	10	20	35	25	Partridge Family
Di Stefano, Giuseppe	Music	25		65	75	It. Opera
Diaghilev, Sergei 1872-29	Music	600		2,250		Ballet Impresario
Diamond Rio	Music	15			35	
Diamond, Bobby	Ent	15			30	
Diamond, David	Music	25		45		Composer
Diamond, Neil	Music	25			50	
Diamond, Selma	Ent	30	40	55	75	
Diana, Princess (Eng)	Royalty	1,100	RARE	4,000	2,500	Princess Di

Name	Field	SIG	DS	ALS	SP	Remarks
Diaz, Armando Vittorio	Military	35	100	175	125	It. General WWI
Diaz, Cameron	Ent	25			50	
Diaz, Porfirio	Political	100	200	250	225	Dictatorial Pres. of Mexico
Dibrell, George G. (WD)	Civil War	300				CSA General
Dibrell, George Gibbs	Civil War	150	300	300		CSA General/1822-88
Dicaprio, Leonardo	Ent	30			60	Titanic
Dick, Douglas	Ent	10			25	
Dick, Fred	Aviation	15		40	30	ACE, WWII
Dick, Samuel	RevWar	50	150	225		Continental Congress NJ
Dickens, Charles 1812-70	Author	500	1,200	1,400	Scarce	Christmas Carol ...
Dickens, Jimmy	Music	5	20		10	
Dickenson, Don M.	Political	15	20	45	20	P.M. General 1888
Dickerson, Mahlon	Political	25	75	150		Jackson Sec'y Navy
Dickey, James	Author	15	35	55	45	Am.Poet
Dickinson, Angie	Ent	5	20		20	Police Woman
Dickinson, Anna Eliz.	Author	25	75	150		Abolitionist-Lecturer
Dickinson, Emily	Author	850	2,500	RARE	RARE	
Dickinson, Jacob M.	Political	25	50	125		Taft Sec'y of War
Dickinson, James S.	Civil War	25	40	75		CSA Congressman
Dickinson, John P.	RevWar	200	575			Continental Congress
Dickison, J. J.	Civil War	75	150	200		CSA Cav'ry Off.
Diddley, Bo	Music	25	50		50	
Diefenbaker, John	Political	15	35		20	Prime Minister Canada
Diem, Ngo Dinh	Political	50				Pres. So. Viet Nam
Diemer, Walter E.	Business	30		75	90	Inventor Dubble Bubble Gum
Diesel, Rudolf	Science	900		2,500		Ger. Mech. Engineer
Diesenhofer, Johann, Dr.	Science	20	25		40	Nobel Chemistry
Dieterle, William	Ent	30			75	Director
Dietl, Eduard	Military	75			150	German Military
Dietrich, Marlene 1901-92	Ent	60	150	300	175	
Dilke, Charles W.	Author	15	25	45		Br. Travel Books, Politician
Diller, Phyllis	Ent	5			15	
Dillinger, John	Criminal	5,000		15,000		1902-1934
Dillman, Bradford	Ent	5		20	15	
Dillon, Kevin	Ent	15			30	
Dillon, Matt	Ent	10	25		35	
DiMaggio, Joe	Sports	100			200	1955 Baseball HOF
Dimitrova, Ghana	Music	15			35	Opera
D'Indy, Vincent 1851-1931	Music	40	125			Composer
Dinesen, Isak	Author	150	500		500	Out of Africa/1885-1962
Dion	Music	15			25	
Dion, Celine	Music	25			50	
Dior, Christian	Business	125	350		225	Fashion Designer
Dippel, Andreas	Music	35			125	Opera
Dire Straits	Music	35	100		75	Entire Band
Dirks, Rudolph 1877-1968	Cartoonist	75		175	150	Katzenjammer Kids
Disney, Roy E.	Business	20	75		35	Brother of Walt
Disney, Walter E.	Cartoonist	1,200	2,500	RARE	3,750	Mickey Mouse/1901-66
Disraeli, Benjamin	Political	175	350	900		Prime Minister

Name	Field	SIG	DS	ALS	SP	Remarks
Disraeli, Isaac	Author	25	80	150		
Ditka, Mike	Sports	10			25	Football
Divine	Ent	50	100		100	Drag Queen
Divine, M.J. 'Father'	Clergy	125	350	500	200	Fndr. Communal Society
Dix, Dorothy	Author	15	30	45	25	Am. Journalist
Dix, Dorothea L. 1802-87	Civil War	75	200	350		
Dix, John Adams	Civil War	65	295	150	450	Union General/1798-1879
Dix, John Adams (WD)	Civil War	115		370		Union General
Dix, Richard	Ent	20	40	65	65	1894 - 1949
Dix, Robert	Ent	10			25	
Dixey, Henry E. 1859-43	Ent	10	20	30	25	lst Success as Adonis
Dixon, Donna	Ent	10	20		25	
Dixon, Jeane	Ent	10			15	Syndicated Columnist
Dixon, Thomas	Author	150		450		Birth of a Nation
Dixon, Willie	Music	50			100	Blues
Dmytryk, Edward	Ent	20			40	Film Director
Dobbin, James C.1814-57	Political	30	75	150		Pierce Sec'y Navy
Dobbin, John F.	Aviation	20	40	65	45	ACE, WWII, Marine Ace
Dobehoff, F.L.	Aviation	25			75	
Dobie, J. Frank	Author	25	50	125	75	Western Author
Dobrinyin, Anatole	Political	40	130	375	75	U.S.S.R. Political Power
Dobson, Kevin	Ent	5		15	15	
Dockery, Thomas P.	Civil War	100		300		CSA General/1833-98
Dockery, Thomas P.(WD)	Civil War	275	350			CSA General
Doctorow, E. L.	Author	15	35	75	30	Am. Novelist. Ragtime
Dodd, Jimmie	Ent	30	75		75	Mouseketeer
Dodd, William E.	Political	15	60	75	25	Ambassador to Nazi Germany
Dodge, Charles C.	Civil War	40				Union General/1841-1910
Dodge, Grenville M.	Civil War	200	500	750	375	Union General/1831-1916
Dodge, Grenville M.	Civil War	300	900	1,200		Union General/War Dated
Dodge, Joseph M.	Business	10	25	50		Banker, Built Jap. Economy
Dodge, Mary Abigail	Author	10	20			
Dodge, Mary Mapes	Author	15	40	75	30	Children's Books.
Dodge, William Earl	Business	150	500	900		
Dodge, William G.	Civil War	25	50	75		
Dodgson, Charles L.	Author	400	900	1,500		Alice in Wonderland
Dodson, Jack	Ent	20	40		40	Andy Grifith Show
Doefflinger, Joseph	Aviation	15		50	45	
Doenitz, Karl 1891-1980	Military	75	200	250	175	Ger. Adm/WWII
Doering, Arnold	Aviation	10		35	25	
Doherty, Shannen	Ent	20			50	Beverly Hills 90210
Dohnanyi, Erno von	Music	50	125	225		Composer/Conductor
Doisy, Edward A.	Science	20	45	165	30	Nobel Medicine. Vitamin K
Dolby, Ray	Science	20	35		45	Inventor Dolby Sound
Dolby, Thomas	Music	20			40	
Dole, Elizabeth	Political	10			25	
Dole, James D.	Business	50	150	225	75	Fdr.Hawaiian Pineapple Industry
Dole, Robert "Bob"	Political	30			55	
Dole, Sanford B. 1844-26	Business	50	250	350	100	Pres. Repub. HI.

Name	Field	SIG	DS	ALS	SP	Remarks
Dolenz, Mickey	Music	10		25	35	Monkees
Dolin, Anton	Music	25	40	100	75	Ballet
Dollar, Robert	Business	25	50	100	50	Dollar Steamship Line.
Domingo, Placido	Music	20		40	50	Opera
Domino, Fats	Music	10	50		25	
Donahue, Al	Music	15			40	Big Band Leader
Donahue, Archie	Aviation	15	25	50	35	WWII ACE in one Day
Donahue, Elinor	Ent	5		15	15	
Donahue, Phil	Ent	15			30	TV Talk Show Host
Donahue, Troy	Ent	5	20		25	
Donaldson, Jesse M.	Political	10	15	35	15	1st Postman Becomes P.M. Gen.
Donaldson, Sam	Ent	5			15	TV News Anchor
Donat, Robert 1905-1958	Ent	55	75	100	200	
Doniphan, Alexander W.	Military	120	250	475		
Donizetti, Gaetano	Music	500	800	1,500		Composer/1797-1848
Donlevy, Brian	Ent	25			60	1899 - 1972
Donnell, Jeff	Ent	5			10	
Donnelly, Ruth	Ent	10		25	25	
Donner, Clive	Ent	10			25	Film Director
Donner, Richard	Ent	10			20	
Donohue, Amanda	Ent	10			25	
Donovan, King	Ent	15			35	
Donovan, Tate	Ent	10			25	Voice of Disney's Hercules
Donovan, Wm. J.	Military	50	200	300	100	Fighting 69th,OSS-CIA
Doobie Brothers	Music	40			80	Signed by entire band
Doohan, James	Ent	15		45	45	Star Trek
Dooley, Paul	Ent	5			15	
Dooley, Thomas A., Dr.	Science	125	200	300	125	1927-1961
Doolittle, Hilda	Author	75	205	475		1886-1961
Doolittle, James H.	Aviation	50	150	200	75	Gen. WWII/Bombed Tokyo
Doors & Jim Morrison	Music	1,500	2,500		2,500	
Doors, The w/o Morrison	Music	60	150		100	
Dor, Karin	Ent	25			60	James Bond babe
Doraine, Lucy	Ent	20			40	Actress
Doran, Ann	Ent	15	15	25	20	
Dorati, Antal	Music	25			75	Conductor
Dore, Paul Gustave	Art	50	150	550		
Dorff, Stephen	Ent	20			45	
Dornberger, Walter R.	Military	40	100	125	75	Rocket Engineer
Dors, Diana	Ent	35			150	
D'Orsay, Alfred, Count	Political	25	65	175		Fr. Artist
D'Orsay, Fifi	Ent	15	20	25	35	
Dorsey, Jimmie	Music	50	150		250	Big Band/1904 - 1957
Dorsey, Tommy 1905-56	Music	75	150		200	Big Band
Dortch, William T.	Civil War	25	40	75		CSA Senator NC
Dostoevsky, Fyodor	Author	1,500	5,700	RARE	RARE	Crime & Punishment
Doubleday, Abner	Civil War	500	2,200	1,450		Union General/1819-93
Doubleday, Frank N.	Business	65	185	375		Book Publisher
Douglas, Beverly B.	Civil War	30	40	55		CSA Officer

Name	Field	SIG	DS	ALS	SP	Remarks
Douglas, Chas. W.H.	Military	25	70	195		Br. Gen./1850-1914
Douglas, Donald W. Jr.	Business	25	60		45	Douglas Aircraft
Douglas, Donald W. Sr.	Aviation	150	295	450	360	Pioneer Aircraft Mfg.
Douglas, Donna	Ent	5	15	20	20	Beverly Hillbillies
Douglas, Eric	Ent	10			20	Son of Kirk Douglas
Douglas, Kirk	Ent	25	75	75	50	
Douglas, Lloyd C.	Author	25	45	75	45	
Douglas, Melvyn	Ent	30			60	1901 - 1981
Douglas, Michael	Ent	20	50		45	Son of Kirk
Douglas, Mike	Ent	5			15	Singer. Early TV Host
Douglas, Paul	Ent	10			35	
Douglas, Paul P.	Aviation	10		40	35	WWII ACE
Douglas, Robert	Ent	10			25	
Douglas, Stephen A.	Political	100	225	450	270	Pres. Candidate/1813-61
Douglas, William 0.	SuprCt	75	175	150	200	1898 - 1980
Douglass, Frederick	Political	250	450	RARE	RARE	Author/Educator/1817-95
Doulton, Henry, Sir	Business	20	35	70		Royal Doulton China
Doumer, Paul 1857-1932	Political	60		100		Pres. France 1931-32. Assassinated
Doumergue, Gaston	Political			195		Pres. France. P.M. France
Dove, Billie	Ent	15		45	60	
Dow, Neal	Civil War	50		300		Union General/1804-97
Dow, Tony	Ent	15			40	Leave it to Beaver
Dowden, Edward	Author	10		25		Ir. Critic, Editor, Professor
Dowling, Eddie	Ent	20		50	45	1895-1975
Down, Lesley-Anne	Ent	10			20	
Downey, Morton	Ent	10	15	20	25	
Downey, Robert, Jr.	Ent	20			50	Actor
Downey, Roma	Ent	25			50	Touched by an Angel
Downing, Big Al	Ent	5			10	
Downing, George, Sir	Political	Scarce	Scarce	Scarce	Scarce	1623-84
Downs, Hugh	Ent	10		25	22	TV Co-Host 20/20
Downs, Johnny	Ent	55			100	Our Gang
Doyle, Arthur Conan, Sir	Author	400	750	1,250	1,750	Sherlock Holmes/1859-30
Doyle, David	Ent	15			40	Charlie's Angels
Dr. Seuss	Cartoonist	75		400	250	Cat in the Hat etc...
Dragonette, Jessica	Music	18	20		45	Soprano
Dragoni, Maria	Music	10			30	Opera
Drake, Alfred	Music	10			20	
Drake, Frances	Ent	10			25	
Drake, Michele	Ent	5			15	
Drake, Samuel Adams	Civil War	45		75		Union General
Drake, Stan	Cartoonist	20			45	Blondie
Draper, Polly	Ent	10			25	
Draper, Ruth	Ent	20	45	70	50	Am. Monologuist
Draper, William F.	Civil War	25	75			Union General/1842-1910
Drayton, Gracie	Cartoonist	25			75	Campbell Soup Kids
Drayton, Thomas F.	Civil War			230		CSA General/1808-91
Drees, Willem	Political	25	50	100		Survivor Buchenwald
Dreiser, Theodore	Author	75	200	300	300	1871-1945

Name	Field	SIG	DS	ALS	SP	Remarks
Drescher, Fran	Ent	20			50	The Nanny
Dresser, Louise	Ent	30			55	
Dressler , Marie	Ent	125			250	AA Winner/1869 - 1934
Drew, Ellen	Ent	5			10	
Drew, John 1853-1927	Ent	60	75	185	100	
Drexel, Anthony	Business	45	65	145		Philanthropist
Drexel, J. A.	Aviation	43	60	100	65	
Dreyfus, Alfred 1859-1935	Military	140	310	800		
Dreyfus, Julia Louis	Ent	25			50	Seinfeld
Dreyfuss, Henry	Business	10	15	25		
Dreyfuss, Richard	Ent	20			50	AA Winner
Dribrell, George G.	Civil War	100	250	300		
Drinkwater, John	Author	20	50	125	25	Poet/1882-1937
Driscoll, Bobby	Ent	150			450	Child star/Disney Voice
Driver, Minnie	Ent	25			50	Good Will Hunting
Dru, Joanne	Ent	10			25	
Druckman, Jacob	Music	25	50	100		Pulitzer/Composer
Drum, Hugh A. Lt.Gen	Military	25	50	100	50	General WW 1, WW II
Drum, Richard C.	Civil War	30	50	80		
Drury, Allen	Author	10	30	65	35	
Drury, Frank	Aviation	10	25	40	30	ACE, WWII Marine Ace
Drury, James	Ent	15			35	The Virginian
Dryer, Fred	Ent	10		25	25	Hunter
Drysdale, Don	Sports	25			60	1984 Baseball HOF
Du Barry, Jeanne, C.	Political	300	900	1,200		Arrested/Guillotined
Du Chaillu, Paul B.	Explorer	35	80	65	75	1831-1903
Du Maurier, Daphne	Author	50	150	150	50	Rebecca
Du Maurier, George	Author	15	45	125		And Illustrator of Punch
Du Pont, Henry A.	Business	150	400	750		1838-1926
Du Pont, Lammot	Business	20			50	CEO Du Pont Chemical
Du Pont, Pierre S.	Business	400	1,250	2,000		Du Pont Chemical
Du Pont, Pierre-Samuel	Business	45	110	240		Progenitor of Du Pont's
Du Pont, R.	Aviation	40	110			Am Aviation Exec
Du Pont, Samuel F.	Civil War	150	215	450		Union Admiral
Du Vigneaud, Vincent	Science	25	55	145	45	Nobel/Synthz.Penicillin
Duane, James 1733-1797	RevWar	110	325	750		1st Continental Congress
Dubcek, Alexander	Political	80	130			Czech. Reformer
DuBois, W. E. B.	Author	300	750		425	Black Rights
Dubose, Dudley	Civil War	95	275			CSA General/1834-83
DuBridge, Lee, Dr	Science	30	100	145	50	Pres. Cal-Tech
Dubuffet, Jean 1931-85	Art	150	400	950		Swiss proponent of raw art
Duchamp, Marcel 1887-68	Art	125	350	575		Fr. Avante Garde Artist
Duchin, Eddie	Music	25	40		120	Big Band Leader, Pianist
Duchin, Peter	Music	5		20	15	Pianist, Band Leader
Duchovny, David	Ent	30			60	X-Files
Duckworth, John T.Sir	Military	55	180			Br. Admiral
Ducos, Jean Francois	Military	36	100	205	45	Pres.Chechen Republic
Dudley, Joseph 1647-1720	Political	400	800	1,000		Col,Gov.MA
Duesenberg, Frederick	Business	500	1,250			

Name	Field	SIG	DS	ALS	SP	Remarks
Duff, Arthur, Sir	Military	15	45	70		Br. Admiral
Duff, Howard	Ent	15		25	35	
Duffer, Candy	Music	20			45	
Duffie, Alfred Napoleon	Civil War	35	72	85		Union Calv. Gen./1835-80
Duffy, Julia	Ent	10			20	Newhart
Duffy, Patrick	Ent	10			20	Step by Step/Dallas
Dufy, Raoul 1877-1953	Art	300	450	750	500	Fr. Impressionist, Fauvism
Duggan, Andrew	Ent	15			25	
Dukakis, Olympia	Ent	15	25	35	30	
Dukas, Paul 1865-1935	Music	55	160	355		Composer
Duke, Basil Wilson	Civil War	80	170	500		CSA General/1838-1916
Duke, Basil Wilson (WD)	Civil War	Scarce	Scarce	RARE	Scarce	CSA General
Duke, Charles M., Jr.	Space	30	150		75	Moonwalker
Duke, Patty	Ent	20		35	30	
Duke, Vernon 1903-69	Music	25	50	150		Composer
Dulbecco, Renato	Science	25	45	60		Nobel Physiology-Medicine
Dulles, Allen W.	Political	30	165	225	75	Stae Department
Dulles, John Foster	Political	30	120	150	75	Sec'y State, Diplomat, UN
Dumas, Alexandre (Pere)	Author	110	225	550	750	Fr.Novelist/3 Musketeers
Duna, Steffi	Ent	10		15	25	
Dunagin, Ralph	Cartoonist	5			20	The Middletons
Dunaway, Faye	Ent	15	30		30	
Dunbar, Bonnie J.	Space	5			15	Astronaut
Dunbar, Dixie	Ent	5		15	15	
Dunbar, Paul Lawrence	Author	750				Afro-Am. Poet, Novelist etc.
Duncan, James 1811-49	Military	75				Mexican War Hero
Duncan, Johnny	Music	10			20	
Duncan, Isadora 1878-27	Ent	400		1,000	1,000	Am. Interpretive Dancer
Duncan, Sandy	Ent	10	20		20	
Duncan, Thomas	Civil War	20	50	80		Union General
Duncan, Todd	Music	35			100	First Porgy
Dunlap, John	Business	150	450			1st to Print Decl of Indep.
Dunn, Artie	Music	15			40	The Three Sons
Dunn, Emma	Ent	20			35	
Dunn, Holly	Music	10			25	
Dunn, James	Ent	45			125	1905 - 1967
Dunn, William McKee	Civil War	25	40	70		Union General
Dunne, Dominick	Author		30		35	
Dunne, Griffin	Ent	15			30	
Dunne, Irene	Ent	15	25	35	50	1901 - 1990
Dunne, Phillip	Author	5	20	35	15	
Dunnock, Mildred	Ent	15			25	1904 - 1991
Dunsany, Edw.J.Plunkett	Author	50		225	120	
Dunst, Kirsten	Ent	25			50	
DuPonceau, Pierre	Military	25	50	125		
Dupre, Marel	Music	45			125	Organist
Duran Duran	Music	50			100	Entire Band Signed
Durand, Asher Brown	Art	100	175	200		Hudson River School
Durant, Don	Ent	10			25	

Name	Field	SIG	DS	ALS	SP	Remarks
Durant, William C.	Business	250	850	1,075		Durant Motor Car. GM, Chevrolet
Durante, Jimmy 1893-80	Ent	35	100		90	
Durbin, Deanna	Ent	20			45	
Durer, Albrecht	Art	3,000	RARE	RARE	RARE	Foremost Ger. Renaissance Artist
Durham, Bobby	Music	10			20	
Durning, Charles	Ent	10			25	
Duroc, Geraud C.M.	Military	25	65	185		Napol. Grand Marshal
Durocher, Leo	Sports	30			60	1994 Baseball HOF
Durrell, Lawrence	Author	25	70	190	40	Br-ir Poet, Playwright, Travel
Duryea, Charles E.	Science	150	450	Scarce	RARE	Built lst Am. Gas Motor Car
Duryea, Dan	Ent	15	15	30	35	
Duryea, Hiram	Civil War					Union General
Duse, Eleanore 1859-1924	Ent	200	400	795	575	
Dussault, Nancy	Ent	5			10	
Dussek, Jan L 1760-1812	Music	30	90	145		
Dustinn, Emmy	Music	35			125	Opera
Dutra, Enrico Gaspar	Political	10	20	50	35	Pres. Brazil
Dutton, Charles	Ent	15			30	Roc
Duv, Christian de, Dr.	Science	20	35		30	Nobel Medicine
Duval, Gabriel	SuprCt	45	115	245		
Duvalier, Francois	Political	75			150	Papa Doc. Haitian President
Duvall, Robert	Ent	20	15	25	35	
Duvall, Shelley	Ent	10			20	
Dvorak, Antonin	Music	475	900	1,500		Composer
Dwight, Theodore	Author	35	50	150		1764 - 1846
Dwight, Timothy 1752-17	Author	20	55			Yale President
Dyer, Edward 1543-1607	Author	Scarce	Scarce	Scarce	Scarce	Br Poet
Dyer, George C.	Military	15	40	60		Admiral USN
Dyer, Nehemiah 1839-10	Military	25				Admiral
Dyke, Leroy Van	Music	5			15	
Dylan, Bob	Music	175	350	550	450	
Dylan, Jakob	Music	20			45	

Matt Damon

Johnny Downs

Jack Dempsey

Clifton Davis

Kirsten Dunst

Edgar Degas

Name	Field	SIG	DS	ALS	SP	Remarks
Eads, James Buchanan	Civil War	100	300	450		Shipbuilder for the Union
Eagles	Music	100			250	All signed
Eagleston, Glenn	Aviation	25	45	75	50	WWII ACE
Eaker, Ira	Aviation	35	75	100	150	WW II Air Force Cmdr
Earhart, Amelia	Aviation	400	1,750	RARE	1,500	1897 - 1937 ?
Early, Jubal A.	Civil War	500	800	1,000		CSA General/1816-94
Early, Jubal A. (WD)	Civil War	700		2,000		CSA General
Earp, Virgil	Western	2,000	4,500	7,500		US Marshal
Earp, Wyatt	Western	5,000	15,000	30,000		Gunfighter/All pieces Rare
East, James	Western	250	750			Cowboy
Eastlake, Charles L., Sir	Art	75	150	350		Pres. of Royal Academy
Eastman, George	Business	350	1,200	3,000	1,500	Fndr Eastman Kodak.
Eastman, John	Art	50		150		American Artist
Eastman, Max	Author	35	75	100		Editor-Fdr. The Masses
Easton, Florence	Music	50			150	Opera
Easton, Sheena	Music	20			45	
Eastwood, Clint	Ent	30	150		65	AA Winner
Eaton, Amos Beebe	Civil War	25	50	90		Union General/1806-77
Eaton, Dorman 1823-99	Political	10	25	55		Nat'l Civil Service Act
Eaton, John Henry	Political	25	50	100		Sect War
Eaton, Shirley	Ent	10			25	Golden girl in "Goldfinger"
Eaton, William 1764-1811	Military	35		75		
Eban, Abba	Political	25	75	75	65	
Ebb, Fred	Music	10		35	20	Composer/"NY,NY"
Ebbets, Charles H.	Business	150			175	Brooklyn Dodgers Field
Eberhart, Richard	Author	10	20	45	15	Poet/Pulitzer
Eberly, Bob	Music	20		40		
Eberly, Ray	Music	20		60		
Ebert, Roger	Ent	10			35	Movie critic
Ebsen, Buddy	Ent	10	30		35	Beverly Hillbillies
Eccles, John C.	Science	20	30	40	30	Nobel Medicine
Echols, John	Civil War	95	195	300		CSA General
Echols, John (WD)	Civil War	190	550			CSA General/1823-96
Eckener, Hugo von	Aviation	200	400	550	550	Built Graf Zeppelin
Eckert, Thomas T.	Civil War	475				Union Gen.Telegraph Giant
Eckstine, Billy	Music	25			50	Bandleader
Eddington, Arthur	Science	25	125	150		Mathemetician
Eddy, Duane	Music	35			75	
Eddy, Mary Baker	Clergy	1,250	2,500	Scarce	Scarce	
Eddy, Nelson	Ent	45	75		100	1901 - 1967
Edelman, Herb	Ent	10			20	
Eden, Anthony, Sir	Political	50	150	200	90	Prime Minister
Eden, Barbara	Ent	10	30		30	I Dream of Jeannie

Name	Field	SIG	DS	ALS	SP	Remarks
Ederle, Gertrude Trudy	Ent	25			60	
Edeson, Robert	Ent	20			45	Silent Star
Edison, Thomas Alva	Science	475	800	1,500	2,000	Am. Inventor/1847-31
Edmonds, Walter D.	Author	10	25	40	20	
Edmundson, Henry A.	Civil War	40	65	80		CSA Officer
Edward III (Reign of ...)	Royalty	RARE	RARE	RARE	RARE	
Edward IV (England)	Royalty	25,000	RARE	RARE	RARE	1442-83
Edward VI (Reign of ...)	Royalty	RARE	RARE	RARE	RARE	
Edward VII (Eng) (As King)	Royalty		200			King From 1901-10
Edward VIII 1894-1972	Royalty	300	900	650	750	
Edward VIII, as Prince	Royalty	150	475	660	675	
Edward VII (England)	Royalty	110	275	300	600	Queen Victoria's Eldest Son
Edward, Duke of Kent	Royalty	50	135	350		Father of Queen Victoria
Edward, Duke Windsor	Royalty	200	600		655	1894-1972
Edwards, Anthony	Ent	20			50	ER
Edwards, Blake	Ent	20	45		45	Producer/Director
Edwards, Clarence	Military	35				General WW I
Edwards, Cliff	Ent	65			100	Voice of Jimminy Cricket
Edwards, Douglas	Ent	5			15	Radio-TV News
Edwards, Joan	Ent	5			10	
Edwards, Oliver	Civil War	25	60	100		Union General/1835-1904
Edwards, Ralph	Ent	5	15		15	This Is Your Life
Edwards, Tommy	Music	25	75			
Edwards, Vince	Ent	10			25	Dr. Ben Casey
Egan, Richard	Ent	5		15	15	
Eggar, Samantha	Ent	10			20	
Eggert, Nicole	Ent	20			50	Baywatch
Eggerth, Marta	Music	15			45	Opera
Eggleston, Edward	Author	5		30		Am Novelist/1837-02
Eggleston, Geo. C.	Author	15	25			1839-1911
Eglevsky, Andre	Music	40	55	110	75	Ballett Teacher
Ehrlich, Paul, Dr.	Science		1,250	1,850	1,380	Nobel. Diphteria, Syphillis
Eichelberger, Robert L.	Military	20	45	70	40	WWII General
Eichelbrenner, E. A.	Science	50	100	200		
Eichmann, Adolf	Military	275	500	1,250	750	
Eiffel, Gustave 1832-23	Science	300	600	900	1,250	Architect/Eiffel Tower
Eigar, Edward, Sir	Music	100	350	767	525	Composer/1867-1934
Eigen, Manfred	Science	20	35	80	40	Nobel Chemistry
Eilers, Sally	Ent	15	15	30	45	
Einstein, Albert 1879-55	Science	900	1,800	3,500	2,750	
Eisele, Donn F.	Space	50			85	Astronaut
Eisenberg, Maurice	Music	10	15		20	Cellist
Eisenhower, Arthur B.	Business	5	15		10	Brother to Ike. Banker
Eisenhower, Barbara	Political	5	15		10	Daughter-in Law to Ike
Eisenhower, Dwight (AS)	President	400	900	Scarce	650	
Eisenhower, Dwight D.	President	200	550	Scarce	450	1890-1969
Eisenhower, Edgar N.	Political	5	20		15	Brother & Lawyer to Ike
Eisenhower, John S. D.	Military	10	20	35	15	General & Only Son of Ike
Eisenhower, Julie Nixon	Political	5	10	25	25	Daughter & Inlaw To Ike

Name	Field	SIG	DS	ALS	SP	Remarks
Eisenhower, Mamie	First Lady	58	122	165	50	
Eisenhower, Milton	Political	10	30		20	Brother. Pres. Penn. State U.
Eisenstaedt, Alfred	Art	15	40		125	
Eisley, Anthony	Ent	10			15	
Eisner, Michael O.	Business	25	75		50	CEO Walt Disney Co.
Eizey, Arnold	Civil War	350		1,400		CSA General
Ekberg, Anita	Ent	10			20	
Ekland, Britt	Ent	10		25	30	
El Fadil, Siddig	Ent	20			50	Star Trek Deep Space Nine
Elam, Jack	Ent	5		15	15	
Elbert, Samuel 1743-1788	RevWar		110	170		
Elder, Ruth	Aviation	100	190	310	350	Pioneer Aviatrix
Elder, Will	Cartoonist	30			65	Lil Annie Fanny
Eldridge, Florence	Ent	10			35	
Eldridge, Roy	Music	30			65	Jazz Trumpet
Electra, Carmen	Ent	20			50	
Electric Light Orchestra	Music	50			100	Signed by entire band
Eleniak, Erika	Ent	20			50	Baywatch
Elfman, Jenna	Ent	20			45	Dharma and Greg
Elg, Taina	Ent	10			30	Ballet-Actress/Gene Kelly
Elgart, Les	Music	30			75	Bandleader
Elijah, Muhammad	Political	175	275		425	Religious Activist
Elion, Gertrude, Dr.	Science	20	65		35	Nobel Medicine
Eliot, George (Pseud.)	Author	160	595	1,250		British Novelist
Eliot, T(homas) S.	Author	175	400	Scarce	750	British Poet/1888-1965
Elizabeth 1 1533-1603	Royalty	5,500	12,000	30,000	RARE	
Elizabeth II & Philip	Royalty		750		925	
Elizabeth, II	Royalty	350	775	800	775	
Elizabeth, Queen Mother	Royalty	100	390	425	500	Queen of George VI
Elizondo, Hector	Ent	15			30	
Ellerbee, Linda	Ent	10	25		15	TV News, Commentator
Ellery, William 1727-1820	RevWar	175	360	785		Signer Decl. of Indepen.
Ellicott, Andrew	RevWar	60	185	320		Surveyor, Mathematician
Ellington, Duke 1899-74	Music	200	500		450	Composer
Elliott, Bill	Sports	10			25	Auto Racing
Elliott, Bob	Ent	5			10	
Elliott, Carter	Music	40	125	280		Composer
Elliott, Cass (Mama)	Music	200	400		450	Mamas and Papas
Elliott, Denholm	Ent	30			60	Indiana Jones
Elliott, Maxine	Ent	30	40	75	70	
Elliott, Sam	Ent	20			50	
Elliott, Washington L.	Civil War	35				Union General/1825-88
Elliott, Wild Bill	Ent	65			150	
Ellis, F. H.	Aviation	15	35		30	
Ellis, Havelock 1859-1939	Science	35		155	275	Br. Pioneer in Sex Ed.
Ellis, Robert H.	Military	10	25	45		
Ellison, James	Ent	10		15	30	
Ellison, Ralph W. 1914-94	Author	45	150			Invisible Man
Ellsberg, Daniel	Political	20	35	50	25	Leaked Pentagon Papers

Name	Field	SIG	DS	ALS	SP	Remarks
Ellsworth, Ephraim (WD)	Civil War	RARE	RARE	RARE	RARE	(War Dated Material)
Ellsworth, Ephriam E.	Civil War	595	1,550	2,500		Union Zouave Col./1837-61
Ellsworth, Oliver 1745-07	SuprCt	100	275	575		Chief Justice
Elman, Mischa 1891-1967	Music	35	175		80	Russian/American Violinist
Elman, Ziggy	Music	25			75	Trumpet
Elmore, E.C.	Civil War	55	105			CSA Treasurer
Eluard, Paul	Author	110	225	375		Fr Poet
Elvira	Ent	15			45	
Elwes, Cary	Ent	15			30	
Ely, Paul, General	Military	65		140	90	Fr. Cmdr. Indochina
Ely, Ron	Ent	20			45	Tv's Tarzan
Emberg, Kelly	Ent	10			25	Model
Embry, Joan	Ent	5			24	Zoologist
Emerson, Faye	Ent	5			30	
Emerson, George	Ent	10			30	
Emerson, Lake & Palmer	Music	35	125		100	Signed by All Three
Emerson, Ralph Waldo	Author	200	300	450	Scarce	1803-1882
Emery, Ralph	Ent	5			10	TV Host
Emma, Queen	Royalty	100				Wife of King Kamehameha IV
Emmett, Daniel D.	Music	300	425	600		lst Minstral Show. Dixie
Emmons, Ebenezer	Science	25	40	70		Natural History Proff.
Emory, William H.	Civil War	75	150	300		Union General/1811-87
Empey, James W.	Aviation	15	25			WWII ACE
Enders, John Franklin	Science	25	60	110	45	Nobel Medicine.
Endicott, William C.	Political	25	30	55	40	Sec'y War/1826-1900
Enesco, Georges	Music	125	275	550	550	Composer
Engel, Georgia	Ent	10	15		20	Mary Tyler Moore Show
Engel, Samuel G.	Ent	10			15	Producer
Engle, Frederick	Civil War	45				Union Commodore
Engle, Joe Henry	Space	15			45	Astronaut
Engler, Irvin	Author	10	25	30		Poet
English, Thos. Dunn	Author	25	30	45		Poet/Lawyer/1819-1902
Englund, Robert	Ent	10			30	Freddy
Ennis, Skinnay	Music	25			65	Bandleader
Enos, Roger 1729-1808	Military	55	175	295		General
Enriquez, Rene	Ent	15			35	
Ensor, James Sydney	Art	50	160	390		Belgian Painter
Ephron, Nora	Author	15			35	
Ephron, Phoebe	Author	15			25	Playwright Mother of Nora
Epp, Franz Xaver von	Military	15	40		75	WWI General
Epstein, Brian	Music	350	600	750		Beatles Manager
Epstein, Jacob, Sir	Art	150	210	392		Br/Am Sculptor
ER (Cast)	Ent	100			225	All Six Signed
Erdrich, Louise	Author	5			10	Novelist. The Bingo Palace
Erhard, Ludwig	Political	20	70	160	50	Chancellor W. Germany
Erickson, Leif 1911-86	Ent	20			50	
Ericsdotter, Siw	Music	25			60	Opera
Ericson, B.A.	Aviation	10	25			Piloted XC-99
Ericsson, John 1803-89	Civil War	75	195	400		Designed & Built Monitor

Name	Field	SIG	DS	ALS	SP	Remarks
Ernest Augustus	Royalty	100		300		1st Hanover King
Erni, Hans	Art	65		225		
Ernouf, Manuel L.J	Military	35	85	160		
Ernst, Max 1891-1976	Art	200	300	575		Surrealist-Dada Movement
Errol, Leon	Ent	35			65	
Erskine, Graves B.	Military	15	35	65	40	Led Marines at Iwo Jima
Erskine, John 1879-1951	Author	35	125	175		Novelist
Erte	Art	125	275	450		
Erwin, James	Military	45				General WW I
Erwin, Sam J.	Political	20	80			Watergate Investigation
Erwin, Stuart	Ent	20			45	1903 - 1967
Esaki, Leo	Science	20	35	50	45	Nobel Physics
Escobedo, Mariano	Military	50	225			Captured Maximillian
Eshkol, Levi 1895-1969	Political	295	250	560		PM of Israel
Esnault-Pelterie, Robert	Aviation	75	250			Pioneer Aviator
Esperian, Kalen	Music	10			30	Opera
Estaing, Charles Hector	RevWar	175	500	750		Fr.Gen-Adm. Pro American Hero
Este, Isabella	Royalty	RARE	4,000	RARE	RARE	Art Patron
Estefan, Gloria	Music	20			50	
Esterhasy, Gunt A.	Political	20	70			Austria
Esterhazy, Prince Pal A.	Political	25		70		Austro-Hung. Diplomat
Estevez, Emilio	Ent	15	35		40	
Estrada, Erik	Ent	10	25		25	CHIPS
Etheridge, Melissa	Music	20			45	
Etter, Philippe	Political	15	50			Switzerland
Etting, Ruth	Ent	25			60	
Eubanks, Bob	Ent	5			15	Game Show Host
Eubanks, Kevin	Music	15			30	Jay Leno's Tonight Show
Eugenie, Empress	Royalty	195	305	375		
Eurythmics	Music	35			75	Signed by both
Eustis, Abraham	Military	40		350		War 1812. Br. Gen.
Eustis, William 1753-1825	Political	35	125	185		Sect War
Evangelista, Linda	Ent	10			25	
Evans, Clement A.	Civil War	90		300		CSA General/1833-1911
Evans, Clement A. (WD)	Civil War	175	750	900		CSA General/1833-1911
Evans, Dale	Ent	25		65	55	
Evans, De Lacy	Military	150	220			Br. Col./Burned White House
Evans, Edith, Dame	Ent	15	30		35	1888-1976
Evans, Edw. R.G.	Explorer	35			75	Admiral, Arctic Explorer
Evans, Gene	Ent	5		15	30	
Evans, Geraint, Sir	Music	10			35	Opera
Evans, Joan	Ent	5	10	15	10	
Evans, Linda	Ent	5			25	
Evans, Lt. Col. D. M	Civil War	15	25	40		
Evans, Madge	Ent	15	15	35	30	1909 - 1981
Evans, Maurice	Ent	55		90	75	Bewitched
Evans, Nathan G.	Civil War	175		575		CSA General/1824-68
Evans, Ray	Music	15	35	45	40	Composer
Evans, Robley D.	Civil War	30	65	110	150	Capt. USN, Fight'n Bob

Name	Field	SIG	DS	ALS	SP	Remarks
Evans, Ronald E.	Space	50			100	Astronaut
Evans, William M.	Political	30	90	150	50	Attorney General/1818-01
Everest, F.K. 'Pete'	Aviation	15	30	45	35	
Everett, Chad	Ent	5		15	20	
Everett, Edward 1794-65	Political	75	165	175	100	Fillmore Sec'y State
Everett, Rupert	Ent	25			50	My Best Friends Wedding
Everhart, Angie	Ent	15			35	
Everly Brothers	Music	30			75	
Evers, Medgar 1925-63	Political	RARE	RARE	RARE	RARE	Civil Rights
Evigan, Greg	Ent	10			25	My Two Dads/TekWar
Ewell, I.R.L.	Civil War	190	395			
Ewell, Rich'd S. (WD)	Civil War	650		1,500		CSA General
Ewell, Rich'd Stoddert	Civil War	375	550	900		CSA General/1817-72
Ewell, Tom	Ent	10			25	
Ewing, James	Military	45	125			Officer Am. Revolution
Ewing, Patrick	Sports	15			45	Basketball
Ewing, Thomas 1789-71	Political	40	110	245		
Exelmans, Rene' J.	Military	20	35	135		Marshal of France
Exile	Music	25			50	All Four Signed
Extreme	Music	40			75	Signed by Entire Band
Eyre, Edward John	Explorer	50		150		Gov. Australia. Eyre Rock
Eytinge, Rose 1838-1911	Ent	25		50	45	

Amilia Earhart

Walter Edmonds

Dwight D. Eisenhower

Denholm Elliott

Erika Eleniak

Name	Field	SIG	DS	ALS	SP	Remarks

Name	Field	SIG	DS	ALS	SP	Remarks
Fabares, Shelley	Ent	5	20		20	Coach
Faber, John Eberhard	Business	150	500	725		Eberhard Faber Pencil Co.
Fabian	Music	10			20	
Fabio	Ent	15			35	Male Model
Fabray, Nanette	Ent	5		15	25	
Factor, Max	Business	25	125	175	60	Cosmetic Mfg.
Factor, Max Jr.	Business	10	30	55	45	Cosmetic Mfg.
Fagan, James F.	Civil War	Scarce	Scarce	Scarce	Scarce	CSA Gen.& U.S.Marshal
Fagerbakke, Bill	Ent	15			35	Coach
Fagoaga, Isidodo	Music	15			50	Opera
Fahey, Jeff	Ent	10			25	The Marshal
Faick, Wolfgang	Aviation	20	45	60	40	
Fair, James G.	Political	30	145	110		Mining/CA Developer
Fairbank, Calvin	Political	40	85	150		Freed Fugitive Slaves
Fairbanks, Charles W.	Vice Pres	50	100	275	150	T. Roosevelt VP
Fairbanks, Douglas, Jr.	Ent	20	40		45	
Fairbanks, Douglas, Sr.	Ent	150			300	Silent Film Swashbuckler
Fairchild, David G.	Science	5	10	20	10	Am Botanist
Fairchild, Lucius	Civil War	20	45	65		Union General/1831-96
Fairchild, Morgan	Ent	10	20	25	25	
Fairchild, Sherman	Business	25	60	115	40	Fairchild Camera & Equipment Co
Fairfax, George Wm.	Political	75	200	300		
Fairless, Benjamin F.	Business	35	100	200	75	CEO US Steel
Faisal, King	Royalty	25	50	95	125	King Saudi Arabia
Faith, Percy	Music	15			150	Conductor-Arranger
Faithfull, Emily	Business	25	45	55		Br Painter
Falana, Lola	Ent	10			20	
Falconer, William	Author	45	350			Br Poet/1732-69
Falk, Peter	Ent	10	25		25	Columbo
Falkenburg, Jinx	Ent	5	6	10	25	
Fall, Albert B.	Political	40	85	150	60	Sec'y Interior.Teapot Dome
Fall, Leo 1873-1925	Music	35			105	Composer
Falla, Manuel de 1876-46	Music	175	510		900	Composer
Falstaff, John, Sir	Military	RARE	RARE	RARE	RARE	
Faneuil, Peter	RevWar	125	225	555		Faneuil Hall, Boston
Fantin-Latour, Henri	Art	35	90	175		Fr. Illustrator, Lithographer
Faraday, Michael 1791-67	Science	175		450	650	Br Chemist
Farentino, James	Ent	15			30	
Fargo, Donna	Music	10			20	
Fargo, James C.	Business	450	1,200			Founder Wells Fargp
Fargo, William G. 1818-81	Business	450	900			Wells-Fargo, Am. Expr
Farina, Dennis	Ent	15	35		25	
Farley, Chris	Ent	50			90	Died Young/Sat Nite Live

Name	Field	SIG	DS	ALS	SP	Remarks
Farley, James A.	Political	15	40	70	25	FDR P.M. General
Farman, Henri	Aviation	60	110	175	165	Pioneer Aviator/Manftg
Farman, Maurice	Aviation	75		190		Pioneer Aviator
Farmer, Art	Music	10			25	Jazz Fluegelhorn-Trumpet
Farmer, Fannie Merritt	Author	190			250	
Farmer, Frances	Ent	150	200	300	500	1914 - 1970
Farnsworth, Charles	Military	25			65	General WW I
Farnsworth, John F.	Civil War	45	110			Union General
Farnsworth, Philo T.	Science	RARE	RARE	RARE	RARE	Invented first TV camera
Farnsworth, Richard	Ent	10		15	20	
Farnum, Dustin	Ent	50	45	90	130	The Virginian
Farnum, William	Ent	50			175	
Farr, Jamie	Ent	5	20		20	MASH/Klinger
Farragut, David G.	Civil War	170	450	875		Union Admiral/1801-70
Farrakhan, Louis	Political	70			150	Leads Nation of Islam
Farrar, Geraldine 1882-67	Music	65		120	110	Opera, Concert
Farrell, Charles	Ent	15	20	30	45	
Farrell, Eileen	Music	25			95	Opera
Farrell, Glenda	Ent	25	35		75	1904 - 1971
Farrell, Mike	Ent	5			20	MASH
Farrentino, Deborah	Ent	10			25	
Farrow, Mia	Ent	10	30		30	
Fassbaender, Brigitte	Music	10			25	Ger. Mezzo Soprano,Opera
Fast, Howard	Author	15	125		20	
Faulkner, William	Author	350	1,500	2,500	Scarce	Nobel Lit/Pulitzer Fiction
Fauquier, Francis	Political	200	575			Colonial Administrator
Faure, Felix 1841-99	Political	30		125		Pres. France 1895-99
Faure, Gabriel 1845-1924	Music	100	220	192	550	Composer. French
Fausto, Cleva	Music	30			65	Opera
Faversham, William	Ent	25			40	1868-1940
Fawcett, Edgar	Author	45	105	225		
Fawcett, Farrah	Ent	15			45	Sig in full/Charlies Angels
Fawcett, Millicent, Dame	Political	35	35	100		Womens Suffrage
Fay, Frank	Ent	15	25	45	45	
Faye, Alice	Ent	20			45	1912 - 1998
Faye, Julia	Ent	5			15	
Faylon, Frank	Ent	45			75	
Fazenda, Louise	Ent	25			75	
Fazio,Tom	Sports	100			200	Golfer
Featherston, Winfield S.	Civil War	85	225	215		CSA General/1819-91
Fegelein, Hermann Otto	Military	500				Ger. SS Gen. WWII
Feinhals, Fritz	Music	30			50	Ger. Baritone, Opera
Feld, Fritz	Ent	10			20	
Feldany, Eric	Ent	5			10	
Feldman, Charles K.	Business	10	20	40	15	Fndr. Famous Artists Corp.
Feldman, Marty	Ent	50			100	
Feldon, Barbara	Ent	5	20		20	Get Smart
Feliciano, Jose	Music	10			20	Guitar-Vocalist
Felix, Maria	Ent	10			30	

Name	Field	SIG	DS	ALS	SP	Remarks
Feller, Bob	Sports	10			25	1962 HOF Baseball
Fellini, Frederico 1920-93	Ent	50	200		100	AA Film Director-Producer
Fellows, Edith	Ent	10			20	
Fels, Joseph	Business	100	200	400		Fels Naptha Soap
Felt, Harry, Adm.	Military	10	30	50	25	
Fenn, Sherilyn	Ent	10			40	
Fenneman, George	Ent	15			35	Announcer/You Bet Your Life
Fenton, Ruben E.	Civil War	30	50	80		Civil War Gov. NY
Feoktistov, Konstantin	Space	25			75	Pioneer Russian Cosmonaut
Ferber, Edna 1887-1968	Author	110	350	450		Novelist/Pulitzer
Ferdinand I 1503-1564	Royalty	400	1,235			Holy Roman Emperor
Ferdinand I 1793-1875	Royalty	70	245			Emperor of Austria
Ferdinand I 1865-1927	Royalty				580	King of Roumania
Ferdinand I, III, IV	Royalty	RARE	3,500	RARE	RARE	King of Naples
Ferdinand II 1578-1637	Royalty	100	460			Holy Roman Emperor
Ferdinand II, The Catholic	Royalty	450	1,700	4,385		Spain
Ferdinand V 1452-1516	Royalty		2,750			King of Spain
Ferdinand VII (Sp)	Royalty	125	475			
Ferebee, Thomas	Aviation	50	125	250	100	Bombadier of Enola Gay
Ferenczi, Sandor	Science	70	180	350		
Ferguson, Maynard	Music	10			30	Trumpet Player
Ferguson, Miriam A. 'Ma'	Political	60	150			Governor TX
Ferguson, Samuel (WD)	Civil War	270		700		CSA General
Ferguson, Samuel W.	Civil War	180	350	550		CSA General/1834-1917
Ferguson, William J.	Ent	175	225	425		
Ferlinghetti, Lawrence	Author	20	75	90	25	Poet/Beat Movement
Fermi, Enrico 1901-1954	Science	500	1,500	2,000		
Ferrar, Geraldine	Music	35			130	Opera
Ferrara, Franco	Music	45			250	Conductor
Ferrare, Cristina	Ent	5		15	15	Model
Ferrari, Enzo 1898-1988	Business	300	550		550	Auto Mfg. Race Car Driver
Ferrer, Jose	Ent	20	25	40	55	AA Actor
Ferrer, Miguel	Ent	5			15	
Ferrero, Edward	Civil War	45	145	235		Union General
Ferrero, Edward (WD)	Civil War	75	245			Union General/1831-99
Ferrigno, Lou	Ent	10			25	Incredible Hulk
Ferry, Orris S.	Civil War	50	75	150	300	Union General/1823-75
Fesch, Cardinal	Political		220	450		Married Napoleon & Josephine
Fessenden, Francis	Civil War	50	90	200		Union General/1839-1906
Fessenden, Francis (WD)	Civil War	75	175			Union General
Fessenden, James	Civil War	20	50	70		Union General/1833-82
Fessenden, William P.	Political	40	65	175		Lincoln Sec'y Treasury
Fetchit, Stepin	Ent	45			150	
Few, William	RevWar	200	450	750		Continental Congress
Feynman, Richard P.	Science	25	40	85	30	Nobel Physics
Fidler, Jimmy	Ent	5		15	15	Gossip Columnist
Fiedler, Arthur	Music	30			50	Conductor Boston Pops
Fiedler, John	Ent	5			15	Voice of Disney's Piglet
Field, Cyrus W. 1819-92	Business	125	550	1,500		Atlantic Cable, Financier

Name	Field	SIG	DS	ALS	SP	Remarks
Field, Eugene 1850-95	Author	110	230	400	200	Children's Poet, Journalist
Field, Marshall, III	Business	95	160	350		Communications Empire
Field, Marshall, Jr.	Business	30	110	170	75	1916-1965
Field, Marshall, Sr.	Business	400	1,000	1,500	650	Marshall Field & Co.
Field, Rachel	Author	20	100			Am Novelist
Field, Sally	Ent	10	25		25	AA Winner
Field, Stephen J.	SuprCt	75	150	250	225	
Field, Virginia	Ent	5		15	15	
Fields, Debbi	Ent	5			10	
Fields, Gracie	Music	20	35	55	75	1898 - 1979
Fields, James T. 1817-81	Author		20	35		Publisher
Fields, Shep	Music	15			40	Big Band Leader
Fields, Stanley	Ent	15	15	35	40	
Fields, W. C. 1879-1946	Ent	275	550	775	1,500	
Fiennes, Ralph	Ent	25			50	
Fieseler, Gerhard	Aviation	25	50	75	75	
Figueres, Jose	Political	15	45	110	20	
Filacuridi, Nicola	Music	15			45	Opera
Filippeschi, Mario	Music	25			85	Opera
Fillmore, Caroline	First Lady	600	950	800		
Fillmore, Millard	President	400	800	2,500	RARE	As President
Fillmore, Millard 1800-74	President	250	900	1,200	RARE	
Finch, Peter	Ent	75		150	150	AA Winner
Findlay, William 1768-46	Political	45	60	115		Gov PA
Fine, Larry	Ent	100			350	Three Stooges
Finegan, Bill (William J.)	Music	20			40	Big Band Leader
Finkel, Fyvush	Ent	10			20	Picket Fences
Finlay, Frank	Ent	5	15		15	
Finley, Jesse J.	Civil War	75	125	200		CSA General/1812-1904
Finney, Albert	Ent	9	10	20	25	
Finnie, Linda	Music	10			30	Opera
Finston, Nat W.	Music	10			20	Conductor-Violinist
Fiorentino, Linda	Ent	20			45	
Fio-Rito, Ted	Music	15			35	Big Band Leader
Firestone, Harvey S.	Business	450	1,500	2,000	650	Founder Firestone Tire
Firestone, Jr., Harvey S.	Business	25	50	85	35	Pres. CEO Firestone Tire....
Firestone, Leonard K.	Business	15	40	70	25	
Fischer, Edmond H., Dr.	Science	20	45		30	Nobel Medicine
Fischer, Harold E.	Aviation	10	25	45	35	ACE, Korea, Double Ace
Fischer, Siegfried	Aviation	10	15	25	15	
Fish, Hamilton 1808-1893	Political	20	95	100		Gov/Senator
Fish, Nicholas	RevWar	40	120	245		Aide-de-Camp Gen. Scott
Fishburne, Lawrence	Ent	20			45	
Fishel, Danielle	Ent	20			45	Boy Meets World
Fisher, Bud (Harry C.)	Cartoonist	75	95		150	Mutt & Jeff
Fisher, Carrie	Ent	20	50		50	Star Wars
Fisher, Eddie	Ent	5	10	20	25	
Fisher, Frances	Ent	20			45	Titanic
Fisher, Fred J.	Business	90				Mfg, Auto Body. Gen'l Motors

Name	Field	SIG	DS	ALS	SP	Remarks
Fisher, Gail	Ent	10			25	
Fisher, Ham	Cartoonist	100		225	150	Joe Palooka
Fisher, Harrison	Art	40				
Fisher, Joely	Ent	20			40	
Fisher, John, Lord	Military	15	25			Brit, Adm. of the Fleet 1905
Fisher, Lawrence P.	Business	90	150	410		Co-Founder Fisher Body
Fisk, Clinton B.	Civil War	55	70	95		Union General/1828-90
Fisk, James 1834-1872	Business	1,000	RARE	RARE	2,500	Robber Baron/RARE
Fiske, Bradley	Military	15		35		Admiral WW I
Fitch, Val L., Dr.	Science	20	35		30	Nobel Physics
Fitz, Reginald H. 1843-13	Science			300		Physician.Disc Apendicitus
FitzGeraid, Edward	Author	90	250	600		Poet.Translator Rubaiyat....
Fitzgerald, Barry	Ent	125	135	195	250	
Fitzgerald, Ella	Music	30	35	80	85	
Fitzgerald, F. Scott	Author	450	1,500	Scarce	Scarce	1896-1940
Fitzgerald, Geraldine	Ent	15	35		50	1912 - 1992
Fitzgerald, John	RevWar	35	90	190		
Fitzsimmons, Thomas	RevWar	200	315	400		Continental Congress
Five Presidents	President	1,500			4,500	5 Presidents on One Piece
Fix, Paul	Ent	25			80	
Fixx, Jim	Author	15	35			
Flack, Roberta	Music	20			45	
Flagg, Fannie	Ent	5	10	20	15	Author/Actress
Flagg, James Montgomery	Art	60	190	250	300	
Flagler, D. W.	Military	15	20	25	20	
Flagler, Henry M.	Business	Scarce	2,500	6,500	2,000	Standard Oil Pioneer
Flagstad, Kirsten	Music	100			263	Nor. Soprano/1895-62
Flammarion, Nicolas-C..	Science	40	65	165		Fr. Astronomer
Flamsteed, John 1646-19	Science	800	975			Br. Ist Astronomer Royal
Flanagan, Edward, Fr.	Political	45	125		250	Boy's Town Founder
Flannery, Sean Patrick	Ent	20			50	Young Indiana Jones
Flatt and Scruggs	Music	50			125	Earl and Lester
Flaubert, Gustave	Author	175	635	1,500		Fr. Novelist. Realist School
Fleetwood Mac	Music	125	250		275	Signed by All 6
Fleetwood, Mick	Music	30			50	Fleetwood Mac
Fleischer, Charles	Ent	10			25	Voice of Roger Rabbitt
Fleischer, Leonora	Author	15		40	30	Shadowlands
Fleischer, Max 1883-1972	Cartoonist	250			400	Created Betty Boop
Fleischer, Richard	Ent	10			20	Film Director
Fleischmann, Charles L.	Business	100	300			Fleischmann's Yeast
Fleming, Alexander, Sir	Science	225	600	750	900	Nobel for Penicillin
Fleming, Art	Ent	10			25	
Fleming, Eric	Ent	225	250		350	Original Rawhide
Fleming, Francis	Aviation	10		40	30	ACE/WWII
Fleming, Ian	Author	575	1,500	Scarce	1,800	Creator of James Bond
Fleming, John Ambrose	Science	25	65	145		Br. Electrical Engineer
Fleming, Rhonda	Ent	10	25	25	45	
Fleming, Victor	Ent	450	900		900	Director GWTW and OZ
Fleming-Sandes, Alfred	Military	10	50			WW I Victoria Cross

Name	Field	SIG	DS	ALS	SP	Remarks
Fleta, Miguel	Music	45			250	Opera
Fletcher, Bramwell	Ent	45			75	1904 - 1988
Fletcher, Frank Jack	Military	25	60	120	60	
Fletcher, Harvey 1884-81	Science	225				Stereo Sound 1934
Fletcher, John Gould	Author	15	30	100		Pulitzer Poet
Fletcher, Louise	Ent	10			25	AA Winner
Flint, Austin 1812-86	Science	75	225	400		Eminent Physician-Teacher
Flint, Lawrence	Aviation	10		35	25	
Flippen, Jay C.	Ent	25			60	
Flockhart, Calista	Ent	25			50	Ally McBeal
Floege, Ernest	Military	25	45		70	
Floren, Myron	Music	5			10	Accordian. Lawrence Welk
Florence, William J.	Ent	15	25	40	75	Actor/Playwright
Florey, Howard Walter	Science	25	40	75	35	Nobel Medicine, Penicillin
Florey, Robert	Ent	15			35	
Flory, Paul J., Dr.	Science	20	35	70	30	Nobel Chemistry
Flotow, Frederich von	Music	75	220	450		Composer
Flower, Wm.Henry, Sir	Science	10	25	50		Br.Zoologist
Flowers, Bess	Ent	5			15	
Flowers, Wayland	Ent	25			50	Marionette Artist/Madame
Floyd, John Buch. (WD)	Civil War	Scarce	Scarce	Scarce	Scarce	CSA General
Floyd, John Buchanan	Civil War	175	320	400		CSA General/1806-63
Floyd, William 1734-21	RevWar	450	1,250	1,600		Signer Decl. of lndepen.
Fluckey, Gene	Military	45		110	90	Top US Submarine Cmdr.
Flynn, Errol 1909-59	Ent	250	500	750	550	
Flynn, Joe	Ent	50	60	110	125	
Flynt, Larry	Business	5			15	Hustler Magazine
Foch, Ferdinand	Military	50	125	280	235	Fr. General WWI, Marshal
Foch, Nina	Ent	10			20	
Fogelberg, Dan	Music	15			35	
Fogerty, John	Music	20			45	CCR
Fokker, Anthony	Aviation	200	295	530	500	Am Aircraft Designer
Foley, Red	Music	30			85	
Follett, Ken	Author	5	10		15	Br. Mystery Novelist
Folsom, Nathaniel	RevWar	125		450		Am General
Foltz, Frederick	Military			45	100	General WW I
Fonck, Paul-Rene'	Aviation	1,000	1,900			WWI Top Allied ACE/Fr
Fonda, Bridget	Ent	20			50	
Fonda, Henry 1905-1982	Ent	60	150		150	AA Winner
Fonda, Jane	Ent	15	40		40	
Fonda, Jelles	RevWar	50	155	225		RevWar Officer
Fonda, Peter	Ent	10	30		35	Easy Rider
Fonda, Ten Eyck H.	Civil War	50		95		Military Telegrapher Hero
Fong, Benson	Ent	25			40	
Fontaine, Frank	Ent	10			20	
Fontaine, Joan	Ent	15			35	
Fontanne, Lynn	Ent	15			40	
Fonteyn, Margot 1919-91	Music	40	55	135	194	Premier Ballerina
Foo Fighters	Music				75	Signed by Entire Group

Name	Field	SIG	DS	ALS	SP	Remarks
Foote, Andrew Hull	Civil War	45	110	300		Union Admiral/1806-63
Foote, Arthur	Music	30	85	195		Composer
Foote, Henry S.	Civil War	25	40	70		Senator
Foote, Horton	Author	5		20	15	Playwright, Scriptwriter
Foote, Shelby	Author	15	35			
Foran, Dick	Ent	15	20	35	45	
Foray, June	Ent	5	20		20	Voice of Rocky & Bullwinkle
Forbes, Bertie Chas.	Business	35	225	175	65	Founder Forbes Magazine
Forbes, M. Steve	Business	5			15	Presidential Candidate
Forbes, Malcolm S.	Business	35	75	150	75	Publisher
Forbes, Ralph	Ent	15	15	30	25	
Forbes, Scott	Ent	10			25	
Forbes-Robertson, John	Ent	25		150	50	1853-1957
Force, Manning F.	Civil War			100		Union General/1824-99
Ford, Benson	Business	5	15	30	15	Ford Motor Car
Ford, Betty	First Lady	35	90		55	
Ford, Edsel 1893-1943	Business	250	550		500	Ford Motor Co.
Ford, Edsel II	Business	5	10	20	10	Ford Motor Co.
Ford, Eileen	Business	5	30		10	Ford Modelling Agency
Ford, Elaine	Business	20			30	
Ford, Gerald R.	President	50	225	400	75	
Ford, Gerald R. (AS)	President	125	600	1,300	250	Served Only 2 Years
Ford, Glenn	Ent	30			75	
Ford, Harrison	Ent	50	100		100	Indiana Jones/Star Wars
Ford, Henry 1863-1947	Business	900	3,500	5,000	2,550	Pioneer Auto Mfg.Important DS $28500
Ford, Henry II	Business	10	15	30	55	Ford Motor Co.
Ford, John	Ent	150			300	Western Film Director
Ford, John Thompson	Ent	475	600	750		Ford's Theater, Wash. D.C.
Ford, Lita	Music	15			45	Singer
Ford, Paul	Ent	15			35	
Ford, Ross	Ent	10			20	
Ford, Sewell 1868-1946	Author		15	35		Short Story Writer
Ford, Tennessee Ernie	Music	15			40	
Ford, Wallace	Ent	20			50	
Foreignor	Music	50	150		100	Signed by Entire Band
Foreman, George	Sports	15			45	Boxer
Forepaugh, Adam	Business	50				Early Circus Owner
Forester, C[ecil] S[cottl	Author	75		90	95	Novelist
Forman, Milos	Ent	25			75	AA Winning Director
Forman, Thomas M.	RevWar	45	100			
Formica, Fern	Ent	15	25		30	Munchkin, Wizard of Oz
Forney, John H.	Civil War	Scarce	Scarce	Scarce	Scarce	CSA General/1829-1902
Forney, William H.	Civil War	90	135	300		CSA General/1823-94
Forrest, Edwin 1806-1972	Ent	30	80	125	150	Early Great Am. Actor
Forrest, Frederick	Ent	5			15	Actor
Forrest, French (WD)	Civil War	165	658			CSA Naval Commander
Forrest, French 1796-66	Civil War	95	140	175		CSA Naval Commander
Forrest, Hal	Cartoonist	25			80	Tailspin Tommy/Tarzan
Forrest, Nathan B.	Civil War	575	Scarce	Scarce	RARE	CSA General/1821-1877

Name	Field	SIG	DS	ALS	SP	Remarks
Forrest, Nathan B. (WD)	Civil War	750	Scarce	RARE	RARE	CSA General
Forrest, Sally	Ent	5			15	
Forrest, Steve	Ent	5			15	
Forrestal, James 1892-49	Political	45	100		25	Sec'y Navy. 1st Sec'y Defense. Suicide
Forster, Edw. Morgan	Author	65	240	338		Br. Novelist. Howard's End
Forster, John 1812-76	Author	20	25	50		Br. Historian, Biographer
Forster, Robert	Ent	5			15	
Forsyth, Frederick	Author	10	40	80	20	Spy Novelist. Br.
Forsyth, James W.(WD)	Civil War	40	120	185		Union General
Forsyth, James William	Civil War	35	105	175		Union General/1835-1906
Forsyth, John 1780-1841	Political	25	55	150		Sec'y of State (Jackson)
Forsythe, John	Ent	15			30	Dallas
Fort, Luigi	Music	20			45	Opera
Fortas, Abe	SuprCt	25	150	200		Resigned from Court
Forte, Fabian (Fabian)	Ent	5		25	20	
Forti, Carmen Fiorella	Music	25			60	Opera
Forward, Walter 1786-52	Political	20	50	80		Sec'y Treasury 1841
Foss, Joe	Aviation	30	75	85	55	WWII ACE
Foss, Sam Walter	Author	5	10	20	10	
Fosse, Bob 1927-1987	Ent	35	120	90	60	AA Winning Choreagrapher
Foster, Abiel 1735-1806	Political	120	345			Cont. Congress
Foster, Charles 1828-04	Political	35	55	100		Gov Ohio
Foster, Dianne	Ent	10			20	
Foster, Jodie	Ent	35			75	AA Winner
Foster, John Gray	Civil War	35	40	65		Union General/1823-74
Foster, John Gray (WD)	Civil War	45	90	200		Union General
Foster, John W. 1836-17	Political	25		65	140	Sect State/1892
Foster, Lafayette S.	Political	25	60	95		Civil War Senator CT
Foster, Myles B.	Art	20	40	70		
Foster, Norman	Ent	15	15	35	45	Director
Foster, Preston	Ent	20	85		65	1901 - 1970
Foster, Stephen	Music	1,000	3,500	RARE	RARE	Composer/Scarce
Foster, Susanna	Ent	15			35	
Fountain, Pete	Music	5	10	20	25	Jazz-Dixieland Clarinetist
Four Non Blondes	Music	35			75	Signed by Entire Band
Four Presidents	President	1,000			2,500	Four Signed on One Piece
Four Seasons, The	Music		150		125	Signed by all four
Four Tops	Music	40			95	Signed by entire group
Fournier, G.	Military	55	85			
Fowler, Gene	Author	20	90		30	
Fowler, William, Dr.	Science	20	30	45	30	Nobel Physics
Fowles, John	Author	30	70	150	35	Br Novelist
Fowley, Douglas	Ent	10			30	
Fox, Charles 1749-1806	Political	30	65	175		Br Reformer
Fox, Edward	Ent	5			15	
Fox, Fontaine T.	Cartoonist	35	50		150	Toonerville Trolley
Fox, Fred S.	Ent	10		45		
Fox, Michael J.	Ent	20	45		40	Spin City/Family Ties
Fox, Samantha	Music	15			45	

Name	Field	SIG	DS	ALS	SP	Remarks
Fox, Vivica	Ent	20			50	
Fox, William	Business	200	550		400	Founder Fox Film Corp.
Foxworth, Robert	Ent	5			10	
Foxworthy, Jeff	Ent	10			35	
Foxx, Jimmie	Sports	250			1,000	1951 Baseball HOF
Foxx, Redd	Ent	25	45		60	Sanford and Son
Foy, Eddie, Jr.	Ent	20	25	40	45	
Foy, Eddie, Sr.	Ent	25			60	
Foy, Maximilian S.	Military	15	35	80		General at Waterloo
Fradona, Ramone	Cartoonist	15			50	Brenda Starr
Frakes, Jonathan	Ent	15			45	Star Trek Next Generation
Frampton, George	Art	15		35		Br Sculptor/1860-28
Frampton, Peter	Music	25			50	
France, Anatole	Author	50	130	235	300	Novelist
Franchetti, Alberto	Music	35		130	90	Wrote 9 Operas
Franchi, Sergio	Ent	15			40	
Franciosa, Anthony	Ent	5			15	
Francis I (1494-1547)	Royalty	500	750			France
Francis I (1777-1830)	Royalty		200			King Two Sicilies
Francis II (1768-1835)	Royalty	100	300	425		Last Hooly Roman Emperor
Francis V (1819-75)	Royalty	40	100			Duke of Modena
Francis, Anne	Ent	5	20		20	
Francis, Arlene	Ent	5		15	10	
Francis, Connie	Music	5			15	
Francis, Dick	Author	25	70	80	40	Mystery Writer
Francis, Genie	Ent	5		15	15	General Hospital
Francis, Kay	Ent	25	30	70	95	
Franciscus, James	Ent	10		15	20	
Franck, Cesar 1822-1920	Music	340	1,100	700		Composer
Franco, Francisco	Political	175	750	1,300	275	Sp. Soldier & Dictator
Frank, August	Military	10	30	45		
Frank, Hans	Military	275	500			Nazi Lawyer
Frank, Otto	Military	300	550			Ann Franks father
Franken, Rose	Author	10	25	40		Playwright
Frankenheimer, John	Ent	10		30	25	Film Director
Frankfurter, Felix	SuprCt	145	1,250	1,195	750	Founder Am. Civil Liberties Un,
Franklin, Aretha	Music	20			40	
Franklin, Benjamin	Revolutionary War	4300			11404	21450 Rev.
War Dte. DS $25,000	RevWar	4,500	9,000	16,000	RARE	1706 - 1790
Franklin, Bonnie	Ent	5			20	One Day at a Time
Franklin, Herbert H, 1867-1956	Business		35	125		Pioneer Auto Manufacturer
Franklin, Jane 1792-1875	Author	65		395		Wife of John Franklin, Traveller
Franklin, John, Sir	Political	125	320	610		Proved NW Passage
Franklin, William	Political	145	475	865		Brit. Gov. NJ, Son of Benj.
Franklin, Wm. Buell	Civil War	75	130	175	200	Union General
Franklin, Wm. Buell (WD)	Civil War	125		250		Union General/1823-1903
Frann, Mary	Ent	15			45	Newhart
Frantz, Charton C.	Business	10	35	45	20	
Franz Josef II	Royalty	40	75	140	45	Liechtenstein

Name	Field	SIG	DS	ALS	SP	Remarks
Franz Joseph I 1830-16	Royalty	155	540	875		Emperor of Austria
Franz, Arthur	Ent	10			20	
Franz, Dennis	Ent	15			45	NYPD Blue
Fraser, Brendan	Ent	20			50	
Fraser, Elizabeth	Ent	10			20	
Fraser, James Earle	Art	500	650			Sculptor/Buffalo Nickel
Fraser, Malcolm	Political	10			30	P.M. Australia
Fraser, Peter	Political	10	25		20	Prime Minister New Zealand
Frasier	Ent	100			200	Signed by All Five
Frawley, William	Ent	250	400	550	450	I Love Lucy
Frazer, John Wesley	Civil War	165	255			
Frazer, Joseph W.	Business	275	600			Kaiser-Frazer Auto Mfg.
Frazetta, Frank	Cartoonist	50			85	Johnny Comet
Freddy & The Dreamers	Music	100	150			Signed by Entire Group
Frederic, Harold	Author	10	35	70		Novelist
Frederic, Prince	Royalty	10	25			The Just Saxony
Frederick Augustus I	Royalty		275			1750-1827
Frederick Augustus II	Royalty		175			King Saxony/1797-1854
Frederick I	Royalty	25	95			Wurtemburg
Frederick II, The Great	Royalty	400	1,200	2,000		1712-86
Frederick III 1831-1888	Royalty	65	260	550	500	Prussia
Frederick IV 1671-1730	Royalty		320	750		Denmark
Frederick IX 1899-1972	Royalty	50	175	350		Denmark
Frederick V 1723-66	Royalty	90	270	500		Denmark
Frederick VI 1768-1839	Royalty	80	225			Denmark
Frederick VII 1808-63	Royalty	45	150			Denmark
Frederick Wm. I 1688-40	Royalty	145	420			Prussia
Frederick Wm. II	Royalty	65	450	475		Prussia/1770 - 1840
Frederick Wm. IV	Royalty	100	425	750		Prussia. Insane/1795 - 61
Frederick, Pauline	Ent	15	30		80	Silent Cinema Star
Fredericks, Fred	Cartoonist	20		60	40	Mandrake The Magician
Frederique	Ent	20			40	
Freeland, Paul van	Political	10		40	20	Prime Minister
Freeman, Kathleen	Ent	5			15	
Freeman, Mona	Ent	5			15	
Freeman, Morgan	Ent	20	55		50	
Freeman, Samuel	RevWar	15	45	100		Rev. War Patriot
Freleng, Friz 1906 - 95	Cartoonist	40			65	Looney Tunes/Pink Panther
Fremont, Jessie Benton	Author	35	80	270		Wife of John C.
Fremont, John C.	Civil War	200	600	900		Union General/1813-80
Fremont, John C. (WD)	Civil War	275	750	1,250		Union General
Fremstad, Olive	Music	125			375	Opera
French, Daniel Chester	Art	75	175	225	125	Sculptor, Lincoln Memorial
French, Samuel Gibbs	Civil War	155	285	309		CSA General/1818-1910
French, Victor	Ent	15			40	
French, William H.	Civil War	40	125	250		
Freni, Mirelia	Music	10			40	Opera
Freron, Louis M.S.	RevWar	20	45	90		
Fresnay, Pierre	Ent	10			45	Fr. Actor/Director

Name	Field	SIG	DS	ALS	SP	Remarks
Freud, Anna 1895-1982	Science		570	350		Daughter of Sigmund Freud
Freud, Sigmund 1856-39	Science	1,650	3,500	4,500	6,000	
Frey, Richard	Aviation	25	50	100	65	
Friant, Louis, Count	RevWar	30	75	150		
Frick, Henry Clay	Business	200	Scarce	900		Carnegie Steel
Fricke, Janie	Music	5			10	
Fricker, Brenda	Ent	20		35	65	
Friedman, Jerome I.	Science	20	35		30	Nobel Physics
Friends (Cast)	Ent	100			200	Cast of 6
Friml, Rudolf 1879-1972	Music	100	275	325	242	Composer
Frisch, Karl von	Science	15	30	40	25	Nobel Medicine
Fritchle, Barbara	Civil War	RARE	RARE	RARE	RARE	PatrioticHeroine
Frith, William P.1819-09	Art	25	45	110		
Fritsch, Werner von	Military	55	150	210	175	
Frizzell, Lefty	Music	25			65	
Frobe, Gert	Ent	60			100	Goldfinger
Frohman, Daniel	Ent	15	50		55	Dean/Am Theatre Producers
Froman, Jane 1907-80	Music	15	15	20	45	
Fromm, Erich	Science	45	150		75	Psychoanylyst/Philosopher
Fromme, Lynette	Political	50	100	150		Charles Manson Follower
Frondizi, Arturo	Political	15	35	75	55	PresidentArgentina
Frontiersmen, The	Music	25			50	
Frost, A.B.	Cartoonist	50			125	Illustrator
Frost, Daniel Marsh	Civil War	170	245	450		CSA General/1823-1900
Frost, David	Ent	5			15	
Frost, Edwin B.	Science	10	25	45		Am. Astronomer
Frost, Lindsay	Ent	15			25	
Frost, Robert 1874-1963	Author	150	600	1,000	750	Pulitzer in Poetry 4x
Fry, Christopher	Author	20	95	150		
Fry, James Barnet	Civil War	30	50	100		Union General/1827-94
Frye, Dwight	Ent	1,200		1,800	2,000	Character Actor/RARE
Fuchida, Mitsuo	Aviation	300	350	500		Led Attack on Pearl Harbor
Fuchs, Rutger	Military	50	125	200	100	
Fuchs, Vivian E. Sir	Explorer	25	75	150		Br. Antarctic Expl.
Fuentes, Daisey	Ent	20			50	
Fukuda, Takeo	Political	15		50	30	Prime Minister Japan
Fukui, Kenichi	Science	20	30	45	25	Nobel Chemistry
Fulbright, James W.	Political	20	45	100	55	AR Senator
Fulgham, Robert	Author	5			15	
Fuller, Alfred C.	Business	125		195	150	Founder Fuller Brush Co.
Fuller, Buckminster R.	Science	30	85	150	175	Architectural Engineer
Fuller, Delores	Ent	20			50	
Fuller, Margaret 1810-50	Political	140	250	450		Feminist
Fuller, Melville W.	SuprCt	50	150	275	175	1839 - 1910
Fuller, Robert	Ent	5			10	
Fuller, Sam	Ent	35			80	Film Director
Fulton, Robert 1765-1815	Science	325	1,300	2,500	RARE	Submarine, Steamboat
Funicello, Annette	Ent	40	100		80	Full Signature/Less if not
Funk, Isaac K.	Author	25	80	135		Funk & Wagnalls Dictionary

Name	Field	SIG	DS	ALS	SP	Remarks
Funk, Larry	Music	15			30	Bandleader
Funston, Frederick	Military	75	195	300		Span Am War
Funt, Alan	Ent	15	50		45	Candid Camera
Furlong, Edward	Ent	25			50	T2
Furness, Betty	Ent	15		25	25	1916 - 1994
Furrer, Reinhard	Space	25			75	German Astronaut
Furstenberg, Betsy von	Business	5			10	Fashion Designer
Furtwangler, Wilhelm	Music	400	500	800	775	German Conductor
Fuseli, Henry 1741-1825	Art	200	525			Br/Swiss Painter

William Faulkner

Henry Ford

Yuri Gagarin

Chief Geronimo

Name	Field	SIG	DS	ALS	SP	Remarks
Gable, Clark 1901-60	Ent	350	450	Scarce	900	
Gable, Kay	Ent	10			25	Wife of Clark
Gabor, Eva	Ent	30	50		60	Green Acres
Gabor, Zsa Zsa	Ent	5	20		15	
Gabreski, Frances	Aviation	35	95	125	72	ACE, WW 11, #3 US
Gabriel, Peter	Music	25			50	
Gabrielle, Monique	Ent	20			40	
Gabrilowitsch, Ossip	Music	75	125	200	125	Pianist, Conductor
Gacy, John Wayne	Criminal	60	125	150	175	Serial Killer
Gadsden, James	Political	175	350	550		Gadsden Purchase
Gadski-Tauscher, Johan	Music	50		75	100	
Gagarin, Yuri 1934-68	Space	400			1,500	First Man in Space
Gage, Thomas	RevWar	225	885	950		British General
Gagnon, Ren, A.	Military	25	30		40	Iwo Jima Flag Raising
Gail, Max	Ent	10			20	Barney Miller
Gailand, Adolf	Aviation	40	75	150	135	German WWII ACE
Gainsborough, Thomas	Art	270	760	1,600		Br, Portraitist. Landscapes
Gajdusek, D. Carleton	Science	20	35		30	Nobel Medicine
Galbraith, John Ken	Author	15	35		20	Author Books Economics
Gale, Zona 1874-1938	Author	10	55	75	15	Am. Novelist
Galer, Robert E., Jr.	Aviation				50	WWII General
Galileo 1564-1642	Science	RARE	25,000	50,000	RARE	It. Astronomer
Gallagher, Megan	Ent	15			40	
Gallagher, Peter	Ent	15			35	
Gallatin, Albert 1761- 49	Political	75	275	390		
Galle, Emile 1846-1904	Art	100	325	600		Fr. Artist in Glass
Gallico, Paul W.	Author	15	110		35	Am.Novelist
Galli-Curci, Amelita	Music	75	150	250	200	Opera/1889-1963
Gallo, Ernest & Julio	Business	40			65	Gallo Winery, Sonoma, CA
Gallo, Gustavo	Music	25			50	Opera
Gallo, Robert, Dr.	Science	20	40		45	Co-Discoverer HIV Virus
Galloway, Don	Ent	10			25	
Galloway, Joseph	RevWar	Scarce	3,500	Scarce	Scarce	Continental Congr.& Army
Gallup, Benadam	Military	25	75	100		French and Indian War
Gallup, George, Jr.	Business	10	20		25	Gallup Poll
Galsworthy, John	Author	30	75	175	325	Br. Novelist, Playwright
Gamble, Hamilton R.	Civil War	25		190		Civil War Governor
Gance, Abel 1889-1981	Ent		190	500		Director. Fr.
Gandhi, Indira 1917-84	Political	150	350	350	Scarce	Assassinated P.M. India.
Gandhi, Mohandas K.	Political	550	1,200	1,500	Scarce	Spiritual Leader India
Gandhi, Rajiv	Political	40		85	150	P.M. of India, Assasinated
Gann, Ernest K.	Author	10	20	35		
Gannett, Frank E.	Business	20	45		35	Newspapers

Name	Field	SIG	DS	ALS	SP	Remarks
Ganz, Rudolph	Music	15			45	Conductor
Garat, Pierre (Pere)	Music	125		300		French Tenor
Garber, Jan	Music	15			35	Big Band Leader
Garbo, Greta 1905-91	Ent	1,350	2,200	6,000	12,000	RARE in Authentic SP
Garcia, Andy	Ent	20			50	
Garcia, Jerry	Music	150	300		300	Grateful Dead
Garcia-Robles, Alfonso	Political	35		130	60	Nobel Peace Prize
Gardanne, Gaspard A.	Military	40	115	250		
Garden, Mary 1874-1967	Music	25	35	60	125	Opera
Gardiner, Reginald	Ent	20			35	1903 - 1980
Gardner, Ava 1922-90	Ent	50	80		125	
Gardner, Erle Stanley	Author	75	200	300	200	1889-1970
Gardner, Franklin	Civil War	225	215	850		CSA General/1823-73
Gardner, Franklin (WD)	Civil War	375	500	1,400		CSA General
Gardner, John L.	Civil War	25		125		Union General/1813-69
Garfield, James A.	President	250	600	1,300	2,000	Union General/1831-81
Garfield, James A.	President	3,000	Scarce	Scarce	Scarce	Assassinated/As President
Garfield, James R.	Political	20	35	70	35	Sec'y Interior 1907
Garfield, John 1913-1952	Ent	75	90		395	
Garfield, Lucretia R.	First Lady	95	180	135		1832-1918
Garfunkel, Art	Music	10			25	Simon and Garfunkel
Gargan, William	Ent	15		35	50	1905 - 1979
Garibaldi, Giuseppe	Political	155	370		650	1807-1882
Garland, Augustus H.	Political	75	150	200		Att'y Gen. & CSA Congress
Garland, Beverly	Ent	10			20	
Garland, Hamlin	Author	20	35	50	85	Pulitzer. Novelist, Essayist
Garland, Judy 1922-69	Ent	395	750	950	775	
Garner, Erroll	Music	75			150	Jazz Pianist
Garner, James	Ent	5	20		20	Rockford Files/Maverick
Garner, John Nance	Vice Pres	55	195	225	175	FDR VP
Garner, Peggy Ann	Ent	30			75	
Garnett, Francis H.	Author	20	60	125		
Garnett, Richard Brooke	Civil War	650	535	615		1817-1863
Garnett, Tay	Ent	10	25		30	Director-Producer
Garofalo, Janeane	Ent	20			50	
Garr, Teri	Ent	5			20	
Garrard, Kenner	Civil War	45	75	160		Union General/1828-79
Garrett, Patrick R. (Pat)	Western	Scarce	2,500	3,000		Killed Billy the Kid
Garrett, Thomas	Political	100	250	395		Chief Engineer Underground RR
Garrison, Lindley M.	Political	35	85	140	50	Sec'y War 1913
Garrison, Vermont	Aviation	15	25	45	35	ACE, WWII & Korea
Garrison, Wm. Lloyd	Political	80	120	250	200	1805-1879
Garros, Roland	Aviation	125			425	French ACE
Garroway, Dave	Ent	10			25	
Garson, Greer 1908 - 96	Ent	35	60	100	75	AAWinner
Garth, Jennie	Ent	20			50	
Gartrell, Lucius J.	Civil War	95	250	300		CSA General/1821-91
Gary, Elbert Henry	Business	125	450	650	250	U.S.Steel, Gary, Ind.
Gasser, Heber S.	Science	20	35	60	50	Nobel Medicine

Name	Field	SIG	DS	ALS	SP	Remarks
Gassman, Vittorio	Ent	25			85	
Gately, George	Cartoonist	5			20	Heathcliff
Gates, Bill	Business	25			50	Microsoft
Gates, Daryl	Political	15			30	Chief Police of L.A.
Gates, Horatio 1727 - 06	RevWar	275	600	1,250		General, Continental Army
Gates, John W.	Business	500	1,000			Bet a Million Gates
Gates, Larry	Ent	10			20	
Gates, Seth 1800-77	Political	25	40	80		Anti-Slavery Repr. from NY
Gatlin, Larry & Brothers	Music	10			20	
Gatlin, Richard C.	Civil War	90	248			CSA General/1809-96
Gatling, Richard J.	Science	400	1,200	2,500		Inventor of Gatling Gun
Gatti-Casazza, Giulio	Music	50	150	250		Opera
Gatty, Harold	Aviation	75	275	450	175	Australian, Wiley Post Navigator
Gaugin, Paul	Art	585	1,250	3,600		Fr. Post-impressionist
Gautier, Dick	Ent	5			15	Get Smart
Gavarni, Paul	Art	85		300		
Gavaudan, Pierre	Music			135		Opera. Tenor/1772-1840
Gavin, James M. 1907-93	Military	45	100	275	125	WWII General
Gavin, John	Ent	20			55	Actor
Gaxton, William	Ent	10	15	25	25	
Gay, George A.	Civil War	15	25	45		
Gaye, Marvin	Music	115	200		200	Killed by His Father
Gayle, Crystal	Music	5			15	
Gaynor, Janet	Ent	25	35	55	85	1906 - 1984
Gaynor, Mitzi	Ent	20			45	
Gazzara, Ben	Ent	5			15	
Geary, Anthony	Ent	5			15	General Hospital
Geary, Cynthia	Ent	15			35	
Geary, John W.	Civil War	55	125	275	250	Union General/1819-73
Gedda, Nicolai	Music	15		35	35	Opera
Geer, Will	Ent	30			60	Waltons
Geffrard, Nicholas Fabre	Political	35	125			Pres. Haiti
Gehlen, Reinhard	Military	15	40	45		
Gehrig, Lou	Sports	1,000			4,000	1939 Baseball HOF
Geiger, Johannes H.	Science	125	350	750		Geiger Counter
Geisel, Theodore	Cartoonist					SEE Dr. Seuss
Gell, William, Dr.	Science	25	40			Br. Archaeologist
Geller, Sarah Michelle	Ent	20			50	
Gelston, David	RevWar	85	170			
Genesis	Music	60	175		100	Entire Band
Genet, Edmond Citizen	Military	55	150	850		lst Fr. Minister to U.S.
Gentilini, Amerigo	Music	15			45	Opera
Gentry, Bobbie	Music	5			15	
George (Pr. Denmark)	Royalty		275			Consort of Queen Anne
George I (Eng) 1660-1727	Royalty	225	1,000	2,500		
George I (Gr) 1845-1913	Royalty	45	85	130		
George II (Eng) 1683-60	Royalty	400	550	1,200		
George II (Greece)	Royalty	50	100	200	400	
George III (Eng) 1738-20	Royalty	200	400	Scarce		

Name	Field	SIG	DS	ALS	SP	Remarks
George IV (Eng) 1762-30	Royalty	125	275	550		
George V (Eng) 1865-36	Royalty	125	475	750	600	
George V And Queen	Royalty	250			800	Queen Mary of Tack
George VI (Eng) 1895-52	Royalty	200	400	300	450	
George VI and Queen E.	Royalty	275	550		1,200	Queen Elizabeth
George, Alexander	Ent	10			20	
George, Boy	Music	25			50	Culture Club
George, Christopher	Ent	20	25	65	75	
George, Gladys	Ent	65	90		85	1900 - 1954
George, Grace	Ent	25			60	
George, Harold L.	Military	35	90	170	75	
George, Henry	Author	30	100	200	35	Author, Reformer, Editor
George, Phyllis	Ent	5			10	Miss America
George, Susan	Ent	5		15	15	
Gerard, Francis R.	Aviation	10	22	38	28	Ace/WWII
Gerard, Gil	Ent	15			30	Buck Rogers in 25th Century
Gerard, Richard	Music	50	95	165		Composer
Gerardo	Ent	15			35	
Gerardy, Jean	Music	125			190	Belg. Violin-Cellist
Gere, Richard	Ent	35	125		75	
Gerlache de Gomery, A.	Explorer	85	180	300		Belg. Naval Offr., Antarctic
Gerland, Alfred	Aviation	15	35	55	40	
German, Edward, Sir	Music	35	100	175	85	Operettas/1862-36
Gernreich, Rudi	Business	10	15	40	25	Fashion Designer
Geronimo	Western	5,500	RARE	RARE	RARE	1829 - 1909
Gerry, Elbridge 1744-14	RevWar	265	675	2,880		Signer Decl. of Indep.
Gersel Cemal	Political	20	65	170	35	Turkey
Gershon, Gina	Ent	20			40	Showgirls
Gershwin, George	Music	675	1,200	RARE	2,750	Composer/1898 - 1937
Gershwin, Ira 1896-1983	Music	75	150	250	200	Composer
Gerson, Betty Lou	Ent	25			55	Voice of Cruella DeVil
Gertz, Jamie	Ent	15			30	
Gervais, John L. 1753-98	RevWar	25		100		Continental Congress
Gerville-Reache, Jeanne	Music	100			275	Opera
Gessendorf, Mechthild	Music	10			25	Opera
Get Smart	Ent	20			50	Signed by Feldon and Adams
Getty, Estelle	Ent	10			25	Golden Girls
Getty, George W.	Civil War	30	50			Union General/1819-1901
Getty, George W. (WD)	Civil War	40	95			Union General
Getty, J. Paul 1892-1976	Business	185	750	1,500	375	Billionaire Oil Mogul.
Getz, Stan	Music	85			225	Am. Jazz Saxophonist
Ghali, Boutros Boutros	Political	10			30	Pres. U.N.
Gholson, Samuel J.	Civil War	150	350	575		CSA General/1808-83
Ghostley, Alice	Ent	5			15	Bewitched
Giannini, A. P.	Business	150	290	500		Bank of America Founder
Gibb, Andy	Music	75			150	Overdosed young
Gibb, Cynthia	Ent	5		15	35	
Gibbon, Edward	Author	300	885	1,800		Decline/Fall Roman Empire
Gibbon, John	Civil War	150		750		Union General/1827-96

Name	Field	SIG	DS	ALS	SP	Remarks
Gibbons, Barry	Business	5			20	Founder Burger King
Gibbons, Cedric	Ent	100	225	450		AA Winning Director
Gibbons, Floyd 1887-39	Aviation	55	175	320	155	Pioneer Aviator
Gibbons, Leeza	Ent	5			15	
Gibbs, Alfred	Civil War	30	80	95		Union General/1823-68
Gibbs, Georgia	Music	15			35	Big Band Vocalist
Gibbs, Marla	Ent	10	20		25	Jeffersons/227
Gibran, Kahlil	Author	125	325	750	150	Syrian Poet
Gibson, Charles Dana	Art	80	200	200	300	Illustrator-Gibson Girl
Gibson, Debbie	Music	20			40	
Gibson, Hoot 1892 - 62	Ent	150	200		225	Film Cowboy
Gibson, Horatio G.	Civil War	50				Union General/1828-1924
Gibson, James	Military	75	230	425		Officer War 1812. Wounded, Died
Gibson, Mel	Ent	35			75	
Gibson, Randall L. (WD)	Civil War	200		1,600		CSA General
Gibson, Randall Lee	Civil War	100	300	600		CSA General/1832-1892
Gide, Andre	Author	175	350	600		Nobel/Literature
Gielgud, John, Sir	Ent	25	45		50	
Gieseking, Walter	Music	35			135	Concert Pianist
Gifford, Francis	Ent	5			10	
Gifford, Kathie Lee	Ent	5			20	
Gifford, Walter S.	Business	5	15	25	10	Pres. AT&T 1925-48
Gigli, Benjamino 1890-57	Music	100	200	300	300	Opera
Gilbert, A. C.	Business	60	95	175		Inventor Erector Set.
Gilbert, Billy	Ent	20	25	45	45	Disney Voice
Gilbert, Cass	Science	20	60		35	Architect/Supreme Court...
Gilbert, John	Ent	125		250	250	
Gilbert, L. Woolfe	Music	15	50	75	35	Composer
Gilbert, Melissa	Ent	10			35	
Gilbert, Sara	Ent	16			25	Roseanne
Gilbert, William S.	Music	165	365	700	700	Gilbert & Sullivan
Gill, Eric	Art	35	75	150		Br. Sculptor
Gill, Vince	Music	20			45	
Gillespie, Darlene	Ent	15			35	Mouseketeer
Gillespie, Dizzy 1917-93	Music	50			70	Jazz. Trumpet
Gillette, Anita	Ent	5			10	
Gillette, King Camp	Business	250	750	2,500	500	Gillette Co. (Safety Razor)
Gillette, William 1855-37	Ent	55	175	215	150	Portrayed Sherlock Holmes Originally
Gilley, Mickey	Music	5			15	Country
Gillmore, Quincy A.	Civil War	30	95	175		Union General/1825-88
Gillmore, Quincy A. (WD)	Civil War	55	140	225		Union General
Gilman, John T. 1753-28	RevWar		100	140		Cont. Congr.Gov. NH
Gilman, Nicholas	RevWar	100	300	500		Continental Congress
Gilmer, Jeremy F.	Civil War	125		400		CSA General/1818-83
Gilmer, John H.	Civil War	35		85		CSA Congress from NC
Gilmer, Thomas W.	Political		95	145		Tyler Sec'y Navy
Gilmore, James R.	Author	20	60	150		Merchant/1822-1903
Gilmore, Joseph A.	Civil War	35	135			Gov. NH
Gilmore, P.S.	Music	35	80	180		Composer

Name	Field	SIG	DS	ALS	SP	Remarks
Gilmore, Virginia	Ent	10	15	30	30	
Gilpin, Peri	Ent	20			45	Frasier
Gimbel, Bernard F.	Business	60	175	375	90	Gimbel Bros, Dept. Stores
Giminez, Eduardo	Music	10			30	Opera
Gingold, Hermione	Ent	10			25	1897-1987
Gingrich, Newt	Political	10	45		40	Congressman
Ginsberg, Allen	Author	35	200	225	75	Beat Poet
Ginsberg, Ruth Bader	SuprCt	30	40		40	
Giordano, Umberto	Music	250	400	475	700	Opera Composer
Girard, Stephen 1750-31	RevWar	125	350	325		Merchant
Gish, Annabeth	Ent	20			40	
Gish, Dorothy 1898 - 1968	Ent	55			125	Lillians acting sister
Gish, Lillian 1896-1993	Ent	30	75	75	85	Silent Star
Gissing, George Robert	Author	50	175	345		Br, Novelist./1857-03
Gist, States Rights	Civil War	450	900	1,250		CSA General/1831-64
Given, Robin	Ent	15			35	Head of the Class
Givenchy, Hubert de	Business	35	70	95		Fashion Designer
Gladden, Adley H.	Civil War	450	900			CSA General/1810-62
Gladstone, William E.	Political	70	95		100	Prime Minister/1809-98
Glaser, Donald A.	Science	20	35	70	30	Nobel Physics
Glaser, Paul Michael	Ent	15			30	Miami Vice
Glasgow, Ellen	Author	50	150			Novelist. Pulitzer. VA Life
Glashow, Sheldon Lee	Science	15	35		30	Nobel Physics
Glaspell, Susan	Author	25	65	100		Am. Playwright. Pulitzer
Glass, Philip	Music	30			150	Opera
Glass, Ron	Ent	10	25		25	Barney Miller
Glassman, Alan	Music	10			25	Opera
Glazer, Tom Paul	Music	15			30	
Glazunov, Alexander	Music	225	365	675	250	Russian Composer
Gleason, Jackie 1916-87	Ent	75	175	250	150	The Honeymooners
Glenn, John	Space	40	150	Scarce	65	1st To Orbit Earth
Glenn, Scott	Ent	10			30	
Gless, Sharon	Ent	10	25		25	Cagney and Lacey
Glossop, Peter	Music	10			30	Opera
Gloucester, Henry Wm.	Royalty	10	20	50	30	
Glover, Danny	Ent	15			35	Lethal Weapon films
Glover, John	RevWar	240	610	1,250		Gen. Continental Army
Glubb, John, Sir Pasha	Military	20	45	55	30	Br. General
Gluck, Alma	Music	20	35	45	100	Opera
Glyn, Elinor	Author	20	70	165	45	Br. Novelist, Film Scenarios
Gnys, Wladek	Aviation	50			150	Shot Dwn 1st Plane/WWII
Gobbi, Tito	Music	25			85	It. Baritone, Opera
Gobel, George 1918-91	Ent	10			25	
Godard, Benjamin	Music	75	120	225	150	Opera
Godard, Louis	Aviation	200	575			
Goddard, Paulette	Ent	30			100	1911 - 1990
Goddard, Robert H.	Science	450	1,750	1,425	Scarce	Am. Rocket Pioneer
Goderich, Fred. John R.	Political	15	40	95		Br PM
Godey, Louis A. 1804-78	Author	40	85	150		Godey's Ladies Book

Name	Field	SIG	DS	ALS	SP	Remarks
Godfrey, A. Earl	Aviation	30	60	100	75	
Godfrey, Arthur	Ent	15	50	55	25	
Godfrey, Capt. Johnny	Aviation	50			150	Ace/29 Victories
Godolphin, Sidney	Political	75	200			P.M. Eng.Queen Anne
Godoy, Manuel de	Political	300				Prime Minister
Godt, Eberhard	Military	25		70		
Godunov, Alexander	Music	33			60	Ballet/Defected
Goebbels, Joseph	Military	350	1,025	1,250	1,250	Nazi Minister of Propaganda
Goebel, Arthur	Aviation	40			110	Pioneer Aviator
Goering, Hermann W.	Military	450	2,044	2,425	1,475	Marshal of the Reich
Goethals, George W.	Military	175	585			Panama Canal
Goethe, Johann W. von	Author	1,200	2,550	Scarce		German Novelist/Poet
Gogh, Vincent van	Art	4,000	RARE	RARE	RARE	
Gogol, Nicholai	Author	750	3,350	6,500		Father of Rus. Realistic Lit.
Go-Go's	Music	35			75	Signed by all four
Going, Joanna	Ent	20			40	
Golan, Menahem	Ent	5			15	Film Producer
Gold, Missy	Ent	10			20	Benson
Gold, Tracy	Ent	10	20		30	Growing Pains
Goldberg, Arthur J.	SuprCt	50	145		115	Resigned
Goldberg, Reiner	Music	15			30	Opera
Goldberg, Rube 1883-70	Cartoonist	50	95		150	Ike & Mike, Boob McNutt
Goldberg, Stan	Cartoonist	10			30	Archie
Goldberg, Whoopi	Ent	20			45	
Goldblum, Jeff	Ent	20			50	
Golden Girls, The	Ent	40			75	Signed by All Four
Goldenson, Leonard H.	Business	10	20	30	15	TV Broadcasting Exec.
Golding, Louis	Author	55	85	125	50	Br. Verse, Stories, Novels
Golding, William 1911-94	Author	55	225	585	65	Nobel Lit.,Lord of the Flies
Goldman, Edwin Franco	Music	25	50	75		Bandmaster
Goldman, Emma	Author	60	240	550	75	Deported. Author-Editor
Goldman, William	Author	45		125		Princess Bride etc..
Goldmark, Peter C.	Science	25		40		Inventor. LP Records
Goldowsky, Boris	Music	15			35	Opera Coach
Goldsboro, Bobby	Music	5			10	Singer
Goldsborough, Louis M.	Civil War	75	125	200		Rear Admiral USN
Goldschmidt, Berthold	Music	65			175	His work Banned by Nazis
Goldschmidt, Richard	Science	20		40		World Famous Geneticist
Goldsmith, Jerry	Ent	5			10	
Goldwater, Barry	Political	10			30	Presidential Candidate
Goldwyn, Sam	Ent	100	150	250	200	Goldwyn Studios
Goldwyn, Sam, Jr.	Ent	5			15	Producer
Goldwyn, Tony	Ent	10			25	
Golino, Valerie	Ent	15			45	
Gollob, Gordon	Aviation	75	150		200	WWII German ACE
Gombell, Minna	Ent	25	30	50	50	
Gomes, Carlos 1836-96	Music	25		150		Brazilian. Opera
Gomes, Francisco	Political	15	55	135	25	
Gomez, Aurea	Music	10			20	Opera, Brazilian Soprano

Name	Field	SIG	DS	ALS	SP	Remarks
Gomez, Thomas	Ent	30			50	1905 - 1971
Gompers, Samuel	Political	150	225	450		Fndr Pres AFL-CIO
Goodacre, Jill	Ent	20			40	Victoria's Secret model
Gooden, Dwight	Sports	10			20	Baseball
Gooding, Cuba Jr.	Ent	25			50	Jerry McGuire
Goodman, Al	Music				45	Bandleader
Goodman, Benny 1909-86	Music	50	150		150	Big Band Leader-Clarinetist
Goodman, Dody	Ent	5			10	
Goodman, John	Ent	20	45		45	Roseanne
Goodpaster, Andrew	Military	15	35	50	25	Gen.WWII
Goodson, Mark	Ent	10			30	Producer TV
Goodwin, Hugh H.	Military	25	65	125	50	
Goodwin, Nat C.	Ent	20			30	
Goodyear, Charles	Science	400	2,000	RARE	RARE	Rubber Vulcanization
Goodyear, Charles Jr.	Business	20	60	150	30	Goodyear Tire & Rubber
Goosens, Eugene, Sir	Music	15	45	90	65	Conductor/Composer
Gorbachev, Mikhail	Political	300		900	575	Russian President
Gorcey, Leo	Ent	125			175	1915 - 1969
Gordon, Alex., 4th Duke	RevWar	20		35		
Gordon, Anita	Ent	10			25	
Gordon, Bruce	Ent	10			20	
Gordon, Charles G.	Military	110	350	1,217	600	
Gordon, Gale	Ent	25			60	Lucy Show
Gordon, Gavin 1901-83	Ent	40				
Gordon, George H.	Civil War	35	65	95		Union General/1823-86
Gordon, George W.	Civil War	225	350	475		CSA General/1836-11
Gordon, Huntley 1897-56	Ent	15	30		45	
Gordon, John B. (WD)	Civil War	200	900	Scarce		CSA General
Gordon, John Brown	Civil War	150	200	400		CSA General/1832-1904
Gordon, Mack	Music	30	60	130	40	Lyricist
Gordon, Ruth 1896 - 85	Ent	20	25	40	35	AA Winner
Gore, Albert A., Jr.	Vice Pres	25			80	Vice President
Gorgas, Josiah	Civil War	200	400			CSA General/1813-83
Gorgas, Josiah (WD)	Civil War	350		750		CSA General
Gorgas, William C., Dr.	Science	125	225	325		Eradicated Yellow Fever
Gorham, Nathaniel	RevWar	375	425	1,200		Pres. Continental Congress
Goritz, Otto 1873-1929	Music	30			75	Operatic Baritone
Gorky, Maxim 1868-1936	Author	400	900	1,200	1,200	Russian/Novelist
Gorman, Margaret	Ent	40				lst Miss America 1921
Gorshin, Frank	Ent	10	20		35	
Gosfield, Maurice	Ent	15			30	
Gosse, Edmund, Sir	Author	20	35	50	30	Br. Poet, Man of Letters
Gossett, Louis, Jr.	Ent	20			50	
Gottfrederson, Floyd	Cartoonist	100			200	Mickey Mouse Strip Art
Gotti, John	Criminal	125			200	Mafia Boss
Gottschalk, Louis M.	Music	500	1,200	1,600	Scarce	Composer
Goudal, Jetta	Ent	15		30	40	
Goudsmit, Samuel A.	Science	15	25	40	20	Atomic Physicist
Gould, Chester	Cartoonist	50			150	Dick Tracy

Name	Field	SIG	DS	ALS	SP	Remarks
Gould, Elliott	Ent	10			20	
Gould, George	Business	100	150	250	175	Son of Jay Gould
Gould, Gordon	Science	15	40			Commercial Laser Inventor
Gould, Harold	Ent	5		15	15	
Gould, Jay 1836-92	Business	250	550	1,500	1,200	Financier, Pres. Erie RR
Gould, John 1804-81	Science	150		450		Br. Ornithologist
Gould, Morton	Music	20	45	70	40	Composer
Gould, Robert Simonton	Civil War	25	75	100		CSA Commander
Goulet, Robert	Music	10			20	Handsome Baritone Broadway, Concert Star
Gounod, Charles 1818-93	Music	150	365	500	550	Composer
Gouraud, Henri-Joseph	Military	40	150		75	Fr. Gen. WW I
Govan, Daniel C.	Civil War	100		400		CSA General/1829-1911
Goya, Francisco	Art	2,500	RARE	RARE	RARE	Painter
Grabe, Ronald J.	Space	5			20	Astronaut
Grable, Betty 1916-73	Ent	100	150	200	200	WWII Pin Up Girl
Grace de Monaco	Royalty	165	300	450	300	Signed as Princess
Grace, Eugene G.	Business	25	65	140	40	
Grace, William R.	Business	15	30	45	30	Mayor NYC
Grace/Prince Rainier	Royalty	175	300		350	
Gracen, Elizabeth Ward	Ent	5			10	Miss America '82
Grady, Don	Ent	5			15	
Graf, Herman	Aviation	35			85	Ger. ACE. #9 Worldwide
Graf, Steffi	Sports	15			45	Tennis
Graham, Billy	Clergy	20	75		60	Evangelist
Graham, Donald	Business	10	25	40	15	
Graham, George 1772-30	Military	20	50	85		Monroe Sec. War
Graham, Heather	Ent	20			50	Lost in Space movie
Graham, John 1774-1820	Political	65	215	430		Aided Jefferson, Madison,Monroe
Graham, Katherine	Author	15	30	60	20	Chm. CEO Washington Post
Graham, M. Gordon	Aviaton	25			50	WWII ACE
Graham, Martha 1895-86	Music	100	300	400	300	Dancer/Teacher
Graham, Sheila	Author	25		40	35	Journalist, Gossip Columnist
Graham, Virgnia	Ent	5			10	TV Host, Commentator
Graham, William A.	Political	20	40	65		Fillmore Sec. Navy 1850
Grahame, Gloria	Ent	50	100		150	AA Winner
Grahame, Kenneth	Author	75	125	200		Wind in the Willows
Grahame-White, Claude	Aviation	75	100	250	125	lst Br. School of Aviation
Grainger, Percy	Music	40	110	215	125	Composer
Gramegna, Anna	Music	45			100	Opera
Grammer, Kelsey	Ent	20			50	Cheers/Frasier
Grandi, Dino, Count	Political	25	45	90	40	Mussolini Cabinet
Grandval, Marie F.C.	Music	10		95		Fr. Woman Composer
Grandy, Fred	Ent	15			30	Love Boat
Grange, E. R.	Aviation	10	25	45	35	
Grange, Red	Sports	75			150	1963 HOF Football
Granger, Farley	Ent	15			35	
Granger, Gideon	Political	75	100	250		P.M. General 1801
Granger, Gordon	Civil War	50	100	150		Union General/1822-76
Granger, Robert S.	Civil War	30		65		Union General/Captured

Name	Field	SIG	DS	ALS	SP	Remarks
Granger, Stewart	Ent	20			50	
Granit, Ragnar	Science	20	45	110	35	Nobel Medicine
Granlund, Nils T.	Ent	20			40	Producer
Grant, Amy	Music	10			20	
Grant, Cary 1904-86	Ent	200	450		400	AA Winner
Grant, Duncan 1885-1978	Art	70		300		Impressionist
Grant, Frederick Dent	Military	20				Son Of U.S. Grant
Grant, Hugh	Ent	20			50	
Grant, Julia Dent 1826-02	First Lady	140	375	750		
Grant, Kirby	Ent	15		30	35	Western star
Grant, Lee	Ent	10	30		30	
Grant, U.S. III	Military	10	30	50		
Grant, Ulysses S. (WD)	President	750	1,500	Scarce	3,500	
Grant, Ulysses S. 1822-85	President	500	1,100	1,500	2,500	
Grant, William T.1876-72	Business	50	125	350	275	WT Grant Dept Stores
Granville, Bonita	Ent	15	15	20	35	1923 - 1988
Grapewin, Charles	Ent	350	800		600	Uncle in "Wizard of Oz"
Grass Roots, The	Music	125	200		200	All Five Signed
Grass, Gunter	Author	40	135	260	130	Ger. Novelist. Nazi Era
Grasser, Hartmann	Aviation	15	25	50	30	
Grassi, Rinaldo	Music	35		100		Opera
Grateful Dead	Music	200	450		450	Entire Band signed
Gratiot, Charles	Military	150	205			War 1812/General
Gratz, Barnard	RevWar	75	200	400		
Graue, Dave	Cartoonist	20			60	Alley Oop
Grauman, Sid	Ent	40	75	100	75	Owner of Opulent Theaters
Graveline, Duane E.M.D.	Space	5			20	Astronaut
Graves, Peter	Ent	15	30		35	Mission Impossible
Graves, Robert	Author	60	175	250	100	Br. Poet, Novelist, Critic
Graves, Teresa	Ent	10			20	
Graves, William	Military	50				General WW I
Gray, Asa 1810-88	Science	35	60	175		Am Botanist
Gray, Billy	Ent	10			20	
Gray, Charles	Ent	20			60	Blofeld/James Bond film
Gray, Colin	Aviation	35		90		Top New Zealand ACE
Gray, Colleen	Ent	15	25	45	30	
Gray, Delores	Music	40			85	Am. Singer, Dancer
Gray, Elisha 1835-1901	Science	250	1,500	3,000		Telephone Pioneer
Gray, Erin	Ent	10			20	Buck Rogers/25th Century
Gray, Gilda 1901-59	Ent	50			120	Popularized the Shimmy
Gray, Glen	Music	15			35	Big Band Leader
Gray, Harold	Cartoonist	100			200	Little Orphan Annie
Gray, Horace	SuprCt	50	150	250	100	1828 - 19022
Gray, Jack Stearns	Aviation	150				
Gray, Linda	Ent	10	20		20	Dallas
Gray, Thomas 1716-71	Author	950	2,100	Scarce		Br. Poet
Grayco, Helen	Music	5			15	Vocalist & Wife Spike Jones
Grayson, Kathryn	Ent	15			30	
Graziano, Rocky	Sports	45			100	Boxer

Name	Field	SIG	DS	ALS	SP	Remarks
Greco, Jose	Ent	10	15		40	Dance
Greeley, Horace 1811-72	Western	65	275	300	750	Go West, Young Man...
Greely, Adolphus W.	Explorer	85	200	200	150	Union General/Explorer
Green, Adolph	Music	10	15		20	Collaborated/Betty Comden
Green, Al	Music	10			20	
Green, Anna Katherine	Author	50	75			1846-1935
Green, Charles 1785-1870	Aviation	50	100	250		Br. Balloonist
Green, Dorothy	Ent	5			15	
Green, Herschel	Aviation	15	30	50	35	ACE/WWII/Triple Ace
Green, John(ny)	Music	25	80	145	35	Composer
Green, Mitzi 1920-69	Ent	20	35		40	
Green, Richard	Ent	30			75	
Green, Thomas (WD)	Civil War	175	600	Scarce		CSA General/KIA
Green, Thomas 1814-64	Civil War	100	200			CSA General/KIA
Green, William F.	Political	50	95	195	125	Pres AFL/Labor Leader
Greenaway, Kate	Art	1,000	1,500			1846 - 1901
Greene, George S.	Civil War	30	70			Union General/1801-99
Greene, Graham 1904-91	Author	95	342	615	385	Br Novelist
Greene, Lorne 1915-87	Ent	40	75		75	Bonanza
Greene, Michele	Ent	5		25	20	
Greene, Nathaniel	RevWar	900	2,400	3,000		Am RevWar/1742-86
Greene, Richard	Ent	20			40	1914 - 1985
Greene, Sarah Pratt	Author	20				
Greene, Shecky	Ent	5		15	15	
Greenspan, Alan	Business	15	30		35	Chairman Fed. Reserve Bd.
Greenstreet, Sidney	Ent	225	400		500	Casablanca/1879-1954
Greenwood, Charlotte	Ent	20			40	1893-1978
Greenwood, Edward D.	Science	10	15	35		
Greenwood, Lee	Music	5			10	
Greer, Jane	Ent	5		15	15	
Gregg, David M.	Civil War	40	75	170	125	Union General/1933-1916
Gregg, David M. (WD)	Civil War	100	175	400		Union General/1833-1916
Gregg, John 1828-64	Civil War	RARE	RARE	RARE	RARE	CSA General/KIA
Gregg, John R.	Business	65	85	150	90	Inventor Gregg Shorthand
Gregg, Maxcy (WD)	Civil War	600	RARE	RARE	RARE	CSA General/KIA
Gregg, Maxcy 1814-62	Civil War	400	600			CSA General/KIA
Gregg, Virginia	Ent	10		20	25	
Gregor XVI, Pope	Clergy		1,200			Catholic Pope 1831-46
Gregory, Dick	Ent	20			40	
Gregory, F. H. (WD)	Civil War	60	95	115		Union Naval Captain
Gregory, F.H.	Civil War	20		75		Union General
Gregory, James	Ent	5		15	15	
Gregory, Thomas W.	Political	20			45	Attorney General/Wilson
Greico, Richard	Ent	20			45	
Grenfell, Wilfred T.	Author	35	75	75	130	Medical Missionary
Grenville, George	Political	200	750			Br PM/Stamp Act
Grenville, Wm. W.	Political	95	285	650		Br. Pro Rom.Cath. Emancipation
Gresham, Walter Q.	Civil War	45	70	100		Union General/1832-95
Gretchaninoff, Alex	Music	75	150	300		Composer

Name	Field	SIG	DS	ALS	SP	Remarks
Gretzky, Wayne	Sports	20			50	Hockey
Grevy, Jules 1807-91	Political	40				Pres. France 1879-87
Grew, Joseph C.	Political	10	25		35	Ambassador Japan 1931-41
Grey, Chas. 2nd Earl of	Political	50	75	160		Prime Minister
Grey, George Sir 1799-82	Political	5	25	55		Br. Statesman
Grey, Jennifer	Ent	25			50	Dirty Dancing
Grey, Joel	Ent	10			20	Cabaret
Grey, Virginia	Ent	10	15	15	20	
Grey, Zane 1875-1939	Author	75	200	400	400	
Gridley, Chas. V.	Military	250	410	895		Cmdr. of Adm. Dewey Flagship
Gridley, Richard 1711-96	RevWar	170	450	790		Gen.Continental Army, Artillery
Grieco, Richard	Ent	20			40	
Grieg, Edvard 1843-1907	Music	350	600	1,125	1,095	Composer
Grier, Pam	Ent	10			25	
Grier, Robert C. 1794-70	SuprCt	80	175	250		
Grierson, Benjamin H.	Civil War	55		235		Union General/1825-1911
Grierson, Benjamin(WD)	Civil War	120	235	545		Union General
Griesbach, Franz	Military	25			50	Ger. Infantry General
Griffes, Charles T.	Music	175	350			Composer
Griffin, Charles 1826-67	Civil War	40	125			Union General
Griffin, Chris	Music	10			25	Jazz Trumpet
Griffin, Cyrus	RevWar	360	765			Continental Congress
Griffin, Merv	Ent	5			15	
Griffin, W.E.B.	Author	5			10	Fiction
Griffith, Andy	Ent	20	45	75	45	Andy Griffith Show
Griffith, Corinne	Ent	35	45	90	100	
Griffith, D.W 1874-1948	Ent	350	550	Scarce	1,100	Producer/Director
Griffith, Hugh 1912-80	Ent	190	275		450	Scarce
Griffith, Melanie	Ent	20	50		50	
Griffith-Joyner, Florence	Sports	25			60	Track Star
Griggs, John W.	Political	15	45	110		Politician-Jurist, Gov. NJ
Griggs, S. David	Space	60	150		140	Astronaut
Grimes, Tammy	Ent	5			15	
Grimm, Jacob	Author	565	1,840	3,760		Grimm's Fairy Tales
Grimm, Wilhelm	Author	500	1,425	3,150		Grimm's Fairy Tales
Grinnell, Henry 1799-74	Business	45	160			Financed Arctic Expeditions
Grinnell, Moses H.	Business	25	60	120		Merchant
Gris, Juan 1887-1927	Art	200		Scarce		Cubist Painter
Grisham, John	Author	40	150		75	The Firm/Pelican Brief...
Grisi, Giulia	Ent	250		300	195	It. Ballerina
Grissom, Virgil l.'Gus'	Space	275	725		900	Astronaut/1922-67
Griswald, O.W.	Military	15	35			
Griswold, Putnam	Music	20			50	Opera
Grizzard, George	Ent	5		15	15	
Grizzard, Lewis	Author	20			45	Southern humorist
Grodin, Charles	Ent	5		20	15	
Groener, Harry	Ent	10			30	
Groening, Matt	Cartoonist	35			90	Simpsons
Grofe, Ferde	Music	100	200	245	125	Composer

Name	Field	SIG	DS	ALS	SP	Remarks
Gromyko, Andrei A.	Political	125	160	295	150	Russ Ambass to US
Gronau, Wolfgang von	Aviation	75	135	235	195	
Groom, Victor	Aviation	20	45	75	55	
Groom, Winston	Author	20			55	Forrest Gump
Gropius, Walter 1883-69	Science	125	150	450	400	
Gropper, William	Art	40	80	200		Am. Social Protest Artist
Gross, Arye	Ent	20			40	Ellen
Gross, Chaim	Art	50	85	165		
Gross, Clayton K.	Aviation	10		30	25	WWII ACE
Gross, Courtlandt	Business	5		15	10	
Gross, Milt	Cartoonist	20			60	Nize Baby
Grosser, Heinz	Science	15			45	Rocket Pioneer/von Braun
Grossinger, Jennie	Business	23	60	135	35	Grossinger's Hotel,Catskill Mts
Grossmith, George	Ent	10			25	1874-1935
Grosvenor, Charles H.	Civil War	25	40	55		Union General/1833-1917
Grosvenor, Gilbert H.	Business	135	100	195	95	Pres.National Geographic
Grosz, George 1893-1959	Art	55	250	250		
Grouchy, Marquis E. de	Military	100	250			Marshal of Napoleon, Exiled
Grover, Cuvier	Civil War	30	65	85		Union General/1828-85
Groves, Leslie R.	Military	55	145	220	85	General WWII
Grow, Galusha A.	Political	10	175	145	35	Speaker of the House
Gruberova, Edita	Music	15			40	Opera
Gruelle, Johnny	Cartoonist	35			100	Raggedy Ann & Andy
Gruen, George John	Business	30	80	150	55	Chm. Gruen Watch Co
Gruenther, Alfred M.	Military	15		30	25	WWII General
Grumman, Leroy R.	Business	50	145		70	Grumman Aircraft
Guden,Hllde	Music	25		75	50	Opera
Guderian, Heinz	Military	50	175	285	500	WWII German Panzer
Gudunov, Alexander	Ent	15		40	35	Rus. Ballet
Guelfi, Piero	Music	10			25	Opera
Guerin, Jules	Art	10		35		Muralist
Guest, Edgar A.	Author	25	75	165	50	Am Journalist
Guest, Winston Mrs.	Business	5		15	10	
Guevaro, Ernesto Che	Military	340	600			Aide to Castro in Cuba
Gueymard-Lautiers, P.	Music	30		120		Opera
Guggenheim, Daniel	Business	20	125	85	35	Guggenheim Foundation
Guggenheim, Harry F.	Aviation		75			
Guggenheim, Peggy	Business	15	25	70	20	Patron of Arts/Collector
Guggenheim, William	Business	55	125		75	Industrialist/Philanthropist
Guilbert, Yvette	Ent	50	80	125	150	
Guillaume, Robert	Ent	10	20	20	25	Benson/Disney Voice
Guillemin, Roger C.L.	Science	20	55	110	35	Nobel Medicine
Guillotin, Joseph-Ignace	Science	275	Scarce	Scarce	Scarce	Fr Dr./Supported Guillotine
Guiney, Louise Imogene	Author	50		300		Poet
Guingand, Francis	Military	15	35	50		Fr. General
Guinness, Alec, Sir	Ent	20	40	40	40	AA Winner/Star Wars
Guinness, Benjamin L.	Business	30	50	110		Guinness Brewing Co.
Guinness, Edward C.	Business	15	25	45	20	Guinness Brewing Co.
Guisewite, Cathy	Cartoonist	25			45	Cathy

Name	Field	SIG	DS	ALS	SP	Remarks
Guiteau, Charles 1842-82	Criminal	400	900	2,500	Scarce	Shot Pres. Garfield
Gumbel, Bryant	Ent	5			10	
Guns 'N Roses	Music	75			150	Signed by entire Band
Gunsche, Otto	Military	50		85	55	
Gur, Mordechai	Military	25	75			Israeli Gen. 6 Day War
Gurie, Sigrid	Ent	20	25	60	45	
Gusmeroli, Giovanni	Music	5			15	Opera
Gustavus III (Swe)	Royalty	115	700	985		
Gustavus IV Adolphus	Royalty	150				
Gustavus V (Swe)	Royalty				275	
Gustavus, Adolphus	Military	350	2,250	2,300		Saved Protestantism/Ger.
Guston, Philip 1913-80	Art			175		Canadian-born Am. Painter
Guthrie, Arlo	Music	5		15	15	
Guthrie, James 1792-69	Political	25	45	80		Pierce Sec'y Treas.
Guthrie, Woody	Ent	300				Folksinger/Songwriter
Guttenberg, Steve	Ent	10			35	
Guy, Buddy	Ent	25			55	
Guy, Jasmine	Ent	15			35	Different World
Guynemer, Georges	Aviation	225	400	650	500	WWI ACE
Guyot, Arnold 1807-1884	Science	25	45	195		Geographer, Mapmaker
Guyot, Pierre	Military	25	55	125		French Revolution
Guyton-Morveau, L.B.	Science	20	50	95		Fr. Chemist
Gwenn, Edmund 1875-59	Ent	80	125		175	Miracle 34th Street
Gwinnett, Button	RevWar	85,000	150,000	RARE	RARE	Signer/RARE
Gwynn, Tony	Sports	10			30	Baseball
Gwynne, Anne	Ent	5			15	
Gwynne, Fred	Ent	75	150		150	Munsters/Herman

Zane Grey

Joseph Ignace Guillotin

Button Gwinnett

Name	Field	SIG	DS	ALS	SP	Remarks
Haab, Robert	Political	25	70			Switzerland
Haag, Carl 1820-1915	Art		30	80		Ger.-Born Br. Court Painter to Victoria
Haakon VII (Nor)	Royalty	120	205			1st Indep King of Sweden
Haakon VII and Maud	Royalty	200			450	King & Queen of Norway
Habberton, John	Author	10	15	25		
Habersham, Joseph	RevWar	95	260	540		Continental Congress
Hack, Shelley	Ent	5			15	
Hackett, Bobby	Music	20			45	
Hackett, Buddy	Ent	5	15		20	
Hackett, Joan	Ent	10	15	25	25	
Hackman, Gene	Ent	20	60		50	
Hadley, Jerry	Music	10			35	Opera
Hadley, Reed	Ent	15			30	
Haenschen, Gus	Music	15		25	30	Big Band
Hagar, Sammy	Music	20			50	
Hagegard,Hakan	Music	15			30	Opera
Hagen, Jean	Ent	5			10	
Hagen, Johannes 1847-30	Science	15	40	100		
Hagen, Uta	Ent	10		20	20	
Hagen, Walter	Sports	400			1,250	1974 Golf HOF
Haggard, Henry Rider	Author	100	125	275	270	King Solomon's Mines
Haggard, Merle	Music	10			30	
Haggerty, Dan	Ent	5		15	15	
Hagman, Larry	Ent	15	30		30	I Dream of Jeannie/Dallas
Hagood, Johnson	Civil War	100	200	300		CSA General/1829-98
Hahn, Jessica	Ent	10			20	Playboy
Hahn, Otto 1879-1968	Science	150	300	Scarce	350	German Nobel Chemistry
Hahn, Reynaldo	Music	75	150			Opera/Composer
Haider, Michael	Business	15			40	Pres. Standard Oil NJ
Haig, Alexander M.	Military	20	45	50	45	Gen. WWII/Sec'y State
Haig, Douglas. lst Earl	Military	25	75	135	60	Br General
Haim, Corey	Ent	15			35	
Haines, Connie	Music	20			50	Big Band Vocalist
Haines, Daniel 1801-1877	Political	30	45	90		
Haines, William 1900-73	Ent	15	15	35	40	
Hairston, Jester	Ent	15			30	
Haise, Fred W. Jr.	Space	10			95	Astronaut
Halban, H.H., Dr.	Science	30	65			Fr. Pioneer Of Uranium Fission
Haldane, John B.S.	Science		125	195		Br. Geneticist & Author
Haldeman, George W.	Aviation	30	55	105	75	
Haldeman, H. R	Political	10	20	45	15	Nixon-Watergate
Halder, Franz	Military	50	100	150	125	
Hale, Alan Jr.	Ent	80	125		125	Gilligans Island

Name	Field	SIG	DS	ALS	SP	Remarks
Hale, Alan Sr.	Ent	50	75	100	100	
Hale, Barbara	Ent	10	15	25	30	Perry Mason
Hale, Edward Everett	Author	75	200	250	225	Author Man Without a Country
Hale, George E.	Science	25	100			Invented Spectroheliograph
Hale, John Parker	Political	15	45	100		Abolitionist/1806-73
Hale, Monte	Ent	5		20	25	Big Time Cowboy Star
Hale, Nathan	Political	15,000	RARE	RARE	RARE	
Hale, Richard	Ent	5		15	15	
Hale, Robert	Music	15			30	Opera
Hale, Sarah J. B.	Author		150	225		Mary Had a Little Lamb
Halevy, Jacques 1799-62	Music	45	80	125		Opera
Halevy, Ludovic	Author	25	70	120		Novels, Libretti For Operas
Haley, Alex 1922-92	Author	40	125	150	140	Am Novelist/Roots, Hotel...
Haley, Bill	Music	225	550		450	Rock Around the Clock
Haley, Jack 1899-1979	Ent	100	150		200	Wiz of Oz/Tin Man
Hall and Oates	Music	25			45	
Hall, Arsenio	Ent	15			30	TV Talk Show Host
Hall, Deidre	Ent	10			30	
Hall, Fawn	Ent	10			25	
Hall, Gus	Political	30	55	150	30	US Communist Party Leader
Hall, Harry	Ent	5			10	
Hall, Huntz	Ent	10	15	25	40	
Hall, Jerry	Ent	10			30	
Hall, Jon	Ent	30	45	85	50	1913 - 1979
Hall, Josephine	Ent	5		15	15	
Hall, Joyce C.	Business	100	450		200	Hallmark Greeting Cards
Hall, Juanita	Ent	75			100	1901 - 1968
Hall, Lyman 1724-90	RevWar	2,200	2,950	3,500		Signer Decl. of Indepen.
Hall, Monty	Ent	5			15	
Hall, Nathan	Political	20	35	75		Fillmore P.M. General
Hall, Pauline	Ent	10			30	Vintage Actress
Hall, Radclyffe	Author		45	135		Well of Loneliness
Hall, Thurston	Ent	10			25	
Hall, Tom T.	Music	5			15	
Hall, William	Civil War	50		100		Union General
Hallam, Henry 1777-1859	Author	35	115	175		Br. Historian
Halleck, Fitz-Greene	Author	25	80			Poet/1790-1867
Halleck, Henry W. (WD)	Civil War	200	800	900	200	Union General
Halleck, Henry Wager	Civil War	125	250	670		Union General/1815-1872
Hallett, Mal	Music	20			35	Big Band Leader
Halliburton, Richard	Author	30			50	World Traveller, Lecturer
Halop, Billy	Ent	75	75	120	150	Dead End Kids
Halop, Florence	Ent	15			25	
Halpin, Luke	Ent	15			35	
Halpine, Charles G.	Author	20	35	90		
Halsey, Wm. F. 'Bull'	Military	75	175	225	200	WWII Admiral/1882-1959
Halstead, Murat	Author	10	20	35		Journalist
Halston	Business	15	20	40	30	Designer
Halstrom, Holly	Ent	5			10	Price is Right Model

Name	Field	SIG	DS	ALS	SP	Remarks
Hamblen, Stewart	Music	15			30	
Hamel, Veronica	Ent	5	10	20	20	
Hamer, Frank	Military	110				
Hamer, Rusty	Ent	35		55	75	
Hamil, Veronica	Ent	15			35	
Hamill, Mark	Ent	20	50		50	Star Wars
Hamilton, Alex. Jr.	Military	15	40	150		Officer War 1812
Hamilton, Alexander	Political	800	3,000	3,500		Washington Sect Treasury
Hamilton, Andrew J.	Civil War					Union General/1815-75
Hamilton, Charles Smith	Civil War	30	65	110		Union General/1822-91
Hamilton, Donald	Author	10			20	
Hamilton, Gail	Author					See Dodge, Mary A.
Hamilton, George	Ent	10	25		30	
Hamilton, Ian, Sir	Military	50				Br. General VVW I
Hamilton, Ian, Sir	Military	15				Brit. General
Hamilton, James	Political	65	160			Colonial Gov. PA
Hamilton, John	Ent	400				Superman
Hamilton, Linda	Ent	20			50	Terminator
Hamilton, Margaret	Ent	100	250	350	200	Wiz of Oz/Wicked Witch
Hamilton, Neil	Ent	50	90	125	100	Batmans Comm Gordon
Hamlin, Hannibal	Vice Pres	85	250	300		Lincoln VP
Hamlin, Harry	Ent			15	30	
Hamlin, V.T.	Cartoonist	50			325	Alley Oop
Hamlisch, Marvin	Music	10		65	35	Composer
Hammarskjold, Dag	Political	125	550	750		Sec'y Gen. United Nations
Hammer, Armand	Business	50	535	275	150	Occidental Petroleum
Hammer, MC	Music	25			50	
Hammerstein, Oscar II	Music	125	250		250	Composer/1895 - 1960
Hammett, Dashiell	Author	550	1,500	RARE	Scarce	Hardboiled Mystery Genre
Hammond, James B.	Science	25	100			Typewriter
Hammond, James H.	Political		45	115		US Senator/1807-1867
Hammond, William A.	Civil War	50	120	300		Union General/1828-1900
Hampden, Walter	Ent	20		45	45	
Hampson, Thomas	Music	15			40	Opera
Hampton, Hope	Ent	40			75	
Hampton, Lionel	Music	40			65	Big Band Leader-Vibes
Hampton, Wade	Civil War	270	550	900		CSA General/1818-02
Hampton, Wade (WD)	Civil War	400	1,500	Scarce		CSA General
Hamsun, Knut	Author	40	80	125	75	Nobel/Literature
Hanami, Kohei	Military	100	250			
Hancock, Herbie	Music	20			45	
Hancock, John 1737-93	RevWar	2,200	4,500	6,000		First Signer
Hancock, W. Scott (WD)	Civil War	200	450	750	675	Union General/1824-86
Hancock, Winfield Scott	Civil War	110	200	300	675	Union General
Hand, Edward	RevWar	185	475	900		
Handel, George F.	Music	1,000	5,800	RARE	RARE	Composer
Handelman, Stanley M.	Ent	5			10	
Handler, Ruth	Business	40			60	Creator/Barbie
Handy, W. C. 1873-1958	Music	275	475	Scarce	450	Composer

Name	Field	SIG	DS	ALS	SP	Remarks
Hanks, Tom	Ent	30			60	AA Winner
Hanna & Barbera	Cartoonist	50	250		100	Jetsons,Flinstones etc..
Hanna, Bill	Cartoonist	35	150		75	Jetsons, Flinstones etc..
Hanna, Marcus A.	Business	25			45	1837 - 1904
Hannah, Daryl	Ent	20	50		50	
Hansen, William	Ent	5		15	15	
Hanson	Music	75			125	Signed by All Three
Hanson, Howard	Music	15	35	80		Pulitzer. Dir.Eastman Sch.
Hanson, John	RevWar	2,250	Scarce	Scarce	Scarce	Pres. Continental Congress
Harbach, Otto 1873-1963	Music	125	100		175	Playwright
Harbison, John	Music	20		75		Pulitzer/Composer
Harbord, James G.	Military	60	145	185	125	WWI Chief of Staff
Harburg, E. Y. 'Yip'	Music	200	400			Composer/Over the Rainbow
Hardaway, Tim	Sports	10			30	Basketball
Hardee, William J. (WD)	Civil War	300	875	1,110	950	CSA General/1815-73
Hardenberg, K.A. von	Political	20	60	125		Prussian Politician
Hardie, James Allen	Civil War	45	205	245		Union General/1823-1876
Hardie, James Allen	Civil War	55	155			Union General
Hardie, Russell	Ent	10		25	25	
Hardin, Gus	Music	5			10	
Hardin, John Wesley	Western	1,800	3,750	9,000	RARE	Gunslinger/1853 - 1895
Hardin, Ty	Ent	10			20	
Harding, Ann	Ent	15	15	35	30	
Harding, Florence Kling	First Lady	60	180		75	
Harding, Tonya	Sports	15			35	Ice Skater
Harding, Warren G.	President	125	250	750	450	1865-1923
Harding, Warren G. (AS)	President	250	400	950	600	
Hardinge, Chas., lst Bar	Political	10	750	35	25	Br.Viceroy India
Hardinge, Henry, Sir	Military			585		Br. Field Marshal/1785-56
Hardwicke, Cedric, Sir	Ent	75			150	1893 - 1964
Hardy, Oliver 1892-1957	Ent	250	300	500	550	
Hardy, Thomas 1840-28	Author	275	1,000	1,425	1,400	Br. Novelist, Poet, Dramatist
Hardy, Thomas M.	Military	75	250			1769-1839 Br. Adm./Nelson
Hare, John, Sir	Ent	20	30		50	
Haring, Keith	Art	25	40	95	200	Pop Artist
Harkins, Paul	Military	15	30	50	30	
Harlan, John Marshall	SuprCt	55	95	175		1833-1911
Harland, Marion	Author	10	15	20		
Harley, William S.	Business	1,000	3,500	RARE	RARE	Co-Fndr, Harley-Davidson
Harlin, Renny	Ent	20			40	Director
Harlow, Jean	Ent	1,100	2,500	2,700	3,000	1911 - 1937
Harman, Fred	Cartoonist	40			125	Red Ryder
Harmon, Mark	Ent	15			30	
Harmonica Rascals	Music	10			25	
Harned, Virginia	Ent	15			35	
Harney, William (WD)	Civil War	50		330		Union General
Harper, Robert G.	RevWar	75		150		General RevWar
Harper, Tess	Ent	10	10	20	25	
Harper, Valerie	Ent	5			20	Rhoda, MTM Show

Name	Field	SIG	DS	ALS	SP	Remarks
Harrel, Scotty	Music	5			15	
Harrelson, Woody	Ent	20			50	Cheers
Harridge, Will 1883-1971	Business		125			Pres. Org. Known as American League
Harries, George	Military	20	35	80		General WW I
Harriman, Edw. Henry	Business	200	750			US RR Magnate
Harriman, Edward R.	Business	20	55	120	35	CEO Union Pacific RR
Harriman, W. Averell	Political	25	70	100	50	1891-1986
Harrington, Pat	Ent	5			15	One Day at a Time
Harris, Arthur T, Sir	Military	30	85	110	150	Cmdr.-in-Chief RAF WWII
Harris, Barbara	Ent	5			15	
Harris, Cecil	Aviation	14	25	50	40	WWII ACE
Harris, Ed	Ent	10		25	25	
Harris, EmmyLou	Music	10			35	Country
Harris, Isham 1818-97	Civil War	45	65			Governor Tennessee
Harris, Jean	Criminal	40	70			Killed/Dr. Herman Tarnower
Harris, Joel Chandler	Author	250	450	750		Uncle Remus
Harris, John 1726-91	Western	125	265	700		Founder Harrisburg, PA
Harris, Jonathan	Ent	10	25		20	Lost in Space/Doctor
Harris, Julie	Ent	20			35	
Harris, Mel	Ent	10			40	
Harris, Neil Patrick	Ent	15			40	Doogie Howser
Harris, Paul Percy	Business	20	45		25	Fndr. & Pres. Emeritus Rotary
Harris, Phil	Ent	40			75	Disney Voice/BandLeader
Harris, Richard	Ent	20			40	
Harris, Robert	Author		50			
Harris, Thomas	Author	30	50			Silence of the Lambs
Harris, Thomas S.	Aviation	15	45			WWII ACE & Test Pilot
Harrison, Anna Symmes	First Lady	675	975	2,500		
Harrison, Benjamin	President	200	300	700		1833-1901
Harrison, Benjamin	RevWar	450	675	1,800		Signer Decl. of Indepen.
Harrison, Benjamin (AS)	President	275	550	1,900		
Harrison, Caroline Scott	First Lady	160	250	1,150	750	1832-1892
Harrison, Carter H.	Political	15	35	45		Mayor Chicago 1897
Harrison, George	Music	200	450	575	300	Beatle
Harrison, George	Civil War	90		275		CSA General/1841-1922
Harrison, George (WD)	Civil War		220			CSA General
Harrison, Gregory	Ent	5		20	15	
Harrison, Helen	Aviation	50	125			Am Aviatrix
Harrison, Jenilee	Ent	5			15	Three's Company
Harrison, Linda	Ent	15			35	Planet of the Apes
Harrison, Mary Lord	First Lady	70	130	175	120	1858-1948
Harrison, Noel	Ent	5			15	
Harrison, Rex 1908-90	Ent	35	75		75	Br. My Fair Lady
Harrison, Richard B.	Ent	25	85		150	1865-1935
Harrison, Robert Hanson	RevWar	210	400	750		Sec'y to G. Washington
Harrison, William Henry	President	550	950	1,500		President Only 1 Month
Harrold, Kathryn	Ent	10			20	
Harrold, Kathryn	Ent	15			30	
Harry, Debbie	Music	25			50	Blondie

Name	Field	SIG	DS	ALS	SP	Remarks
Harry, Jackee	Ent	10			30	
Harryhausen, Ray	Ent	10			35	Film Director
Harshaw, Margaret	Music	10		40	65	Opera
Hart, Corey	Music	15			35	
Hart, Dolores	Ent	10			20	
Hart, Dorothy	Ent	15		25	35	
Hart, John	Ent	10			20	Lone Ranger
Hart, John 1711-1879	RevWar	320	644	1,300		Signer Decl. of Indepen.
Hart, Johnny	Cartoonist	30			75	B.C. & Wizard Of Id
Hart, Lorenz	Music	500	RARE	RARE	RARE	Composer w/Rogers
Hart, Mary	Ent	5			15	Entertainment Tonite host
Hart, Melissa Joan	Ent	20			50	TV's Sabrina
Hart, Moss	Author	20	55	105	30	1904 - 1961
Hart, Paul	Ent	5		15	15	
Hart, Thomas C.	Military	40			65	WWII Admiral
Hart, Veronica	Ent	10	15	35	35	
Hart, William S.	Ent	130	180	235	425	1870 - 1946
Harte, Francis Brett	Author	90	185	150		Frontier Life/1836-1902
Hartford, George L.	Business	40	295	280		Great Atlantic & Pacific Tea Co
Hartford, Huntington	Business	15	30	45	20	Patron of the Arts
Hartford, John	Music	15	45	70		Composer
Hartley, Mariette	Ent	5		15	15	
Hartley,Nina	Ent	20			45	
Hartline, Haldan K.	Science	25	80	140	35	Nobel Medicine
Hartman, David	Ent	5			10	Good Morning America host
Hartman, Don	Ent	10			35	Producer
Hartman, Lisa (Black)	Ent	5			20	
Hartman, Paul	Ent	10			20	
Hartman, Phil	Ent	40			75	Sat Nitle Live alumni/
Murdered						
Hartmann, Erich	Aviation	125			300	WWII German ACE
Hartranft, John F.	Civil War	80	125	150		Union General/1830-89
Harts, William	Military	10		35		General WWI
Hartsuff, George L.	Civil War	45	75	95		Union General/1830-74
Hartwell, Alfred S.	Civil War	24	80	105		Union General
Harvey, George B. M.	Author	25	75		100	Fostered W. Wilson Nomination
Harvey, Lawrence	Ent	100			150	
Harvey, Lilian	Ent	10			25	
Harvey, Paul	Author	10	25		20	
Harvey, Steve	Ent	15			30	
Harvey, William 1578-57	Science	750	3,750	Scarce	Scarce	lst Theory Blood Circulation
Hasbrouck, Robert W.	Military	50	165		75	Am. Gen. WWII
Hasen, Irwin	Cartoonist	10			20	Dondi
Haskell, James K.	Ent	10	15	30	25	
Haskell, Peter	Ent	5			10	Actor
Haskin, Joseph Abel	Civil War	50				Union General/1817-74
Hassam, Childe 1859-35	Art	150	350	500		Foremost in Am. Impressionism
Hassam, Crown Prince	Royalty	15	35	80	50	Morocco
Hasselhoff, David	Ent	20			50	Baywatch

Name	Field	SIG	DS	ALS	SP	Remarks
Hasso, Signe	Ent	10			20	
Hastings, Bob	Ent	10			20	
Hastings, Warren 1732-18	Political	75	150	225		Gov Gen India
Haswell, Charles H.	Civil War	25	35	50		Union Naval Architect
Hatch, John Porter	Civil War	30	50	80	75	Union General/1822-1901
Hatcher, Richard G.	Political	5			15	African American Mayor
Hatcher, Teri	Ent	20			50	Lois & Clark/James Bond
Hatfield, Hurd	Ent	15	20	30	35	
Hatfield, Lansing	Music	25			85	Opera
Hathaway, Henry	Ent	40			95	
Hatlo, Jimmy 1898-1963	Cartoonist	25	50		80	Little Iodine
Hatton, Raymond	Ent	50			125	
Hatton, Robert	Civil War	125	250	350		RARE
Hauer, Rutger	Ent	20	50		45	LadyHawke
Haught, Helmut	Aviation	10		30	20	
Haupt, Herman 1817- 05	Civil War	35				Union General
Hauptman, Herbert A.	Science	20	35		30	Nobel Chemistry
Hauptmann, Bruno R.	Criminal	450	Scarce	Scarce	Scarce	Lindbergh Baby Kidnapper
Hauptmann, Gerhart	Author	100	295	575	375	Nobel Prize Literature 1912
Havel, Vaclav	Political	20			45	Czech.
Haven, Annette	Ent	10		20	25	
Havens, Beckwith	Aviation	20	40	55	50	
Havoc, June	Ent	5			15	
Hawes, Elizabeth	Art	10	25	35		
Hawke, Ethan	Ent	20			50	
Hawke, Robert	Political	15	40	100	25	Prime Minister Australia
Hawkins, Anthony Hope	Author	30		100		Prisoner of Zenda...
Hawkins, Coleman	Music	130			250	Jazz Tenor Sax
Hawkins, Jack	Ent	45			100	
Hawkins, John	Civil War	35		125		Union General/1830-1914
Hawkins, William	Political	35	85			Governor NC. War 1812
Hawks, Frank Monroe	Aviation	80	135	325	250	Pioneer Aviator/1897-38
Hawks, Howard	Ent	100	200		250	Director
Hawley, Joseph R.	Civil War	45	90	120		Union General/1826-1905
Hawn, Goldie	Ent	20	50		50	Laugh In
Haworth, Jill	Ent	5			10	
Hawthorn, Alex. Travis	Civil War	155	295	445		CSA General/1835-99
Hawthorne, Julian	Author	30		225		Son of Nathaniel Hawthorne
Hawthorne, Nathaniel	Author	400	950	1,750		Novelist/1804-65
Hay, John H.	Military	5		15		
Hay, John Milton	Political	50	150	225	135	1838-1905
Hay, William Henry	Military	5	15	30		
Hayakawa, Sessue	Ent	120			250	
Hayden, Charles 1870-37	Business	20	45			
Hayden, Russell	Ent	25			75	
Hayden, Sterling	Ent	25			50	1916 - 1986
Haydn, Joseph Franz	Music	3,500	RARE	RARE	RARE	Composer
Haydon, Benj. R. 1786-46	Art			200		Br Painter
Hayek, Salma	Ent	20			45	

Name	Field	SIG	DS	ALS	SP	Remarks
Hayes, George 'Gabby'	Ent	145	250		450	1885 - 1969
Hayes, Helen 1900-94	Ent	20	40	45	65	
Hayes, Ira H., Corporal	Military	400				Iwo Jima Flag Raising
Hayes, Isaac Israel	Civil War	95	190	275		
Hayes, Joseph	Civil War	55	95	170	150	
Hayes, Lucy Webb	First Lady	230		400	700	
Hayes, Margaret	Ent	10			15	
Hayes, Roland	Music	100			250	Am Tenor
Hayes, Rutherford B.	President	200	500	600	1,250	Union General/1822-93
Hayes, Rutherford B.	President	225	800	900	2,400	As President
Haynes, Linda	Ent	5			10	
Hays, Frank A.	Aviation	35	55	95	65	German SS ACE
Hays, Harry Thompson	Civil War	185	450			CSA General/1820-76
Hays, Harry Thos. (WD)	Civil War	300	900			CSA General
Hays, Robert	Ent	5			15	
Hays, Will H. 1879-1859	Ent	30	45		50	
Hays, William	Civil War	35	85	145		Union General/1819-75
Hayward, George	Science	10	20	35	15	
Hayward, Louis	Ent	10	15	25	50	
Hayward, Susan 1918-75	Ent	135	200	450	375	
Haywood, Thomas	Military	5		15	10	
Hayworth, Rita 1918-87	Ent	150	250	Scarce	475	
Hazelwood, John	RevWar	75	190	370		1726 - 1800
Hazen, Wm. Babcock	Civil War	25	45	95		Union General/1830-87
Head, Edith	Ent	35			125	Costumer/AA Winner 8x
Headle, Marshall	Aviation	25	70		85	Lockheed Chief Test Pilot
Healey, George	Art	125	250	450		19th Century Portrait Artist
Healey, Robert C.	Author	10		25		
Healy, Ted	Ent	50				
Hearst, George 1820-91	Business	300		1,200		Newspaper Dynasty
Hearst, Patricia	Political	325				
Hearst, Phoebe A.	Business	20	40	75		
Hearst, Wm. Randolph	Business	150	600	950	695	Publisher/1863-1951
Hearst, Wm. Randolph Jr	Business	10	20	45	20	
Heart	Music	40			75	Signed by both
Heath, Edward	Political	40	90	115	45	Br.Prime Minister
Heath, William 1737-1814	RevWar	160	742	1,500		General Continental Army
Heatherton, Joey	Ent	10	10	20	25	
Hebert, Louis	Civil War	100	250			CSA General
Hebert, Louis (WD)	Civil War	200	500			CSA General/1820-1901
Hebert, Paul 0.	Civil War	100	175	250		CSA General/1818-80
Hecht, Ben 1894-1964	Author	15	45		45	AA.Playwright, Novelist, Newsman
Heckart, Eileen	Ent	15		15	15	
Heckerling, Amy	Ent	5		15	15	
Heckman, Charles A.	Civil War	30	75			Union General/1826-96
Hedi, Walter	Music	15	45	90		Composer
Hedin, Sven	Explorer	65		150	125	Swe. Asian Explorer
Hedison, David	Ent	5	15		15	Voyage to the Btm of Sea
Hedman, Robert Duke	Aviation	20	45	75	45	WWII ACE Flying Tigers

Name	Field	SIG	DS	ALS	SP	Remarks
Hedren, Tippi	Ent	10	20		20	The Birds
Hedrick, Roger	Aviation	15	25	40	35	WWII ACE
Heflin, Van 1910-71	Ent	30	75	90	90	
Hefner, Christie	Business	10		30	20	Publisher/Playboy
Hefner, Hugh	Business	15			35	Founder Playboy
Heft, Bob	Art	20				Designed US 50 Star Flag
Hefti, Neal	Music	20	35	50	40	Composer
Hegel, Geo. Wilhelm F.	Political	850	1,500	2,050		Ger. Idealist Philosopher
Heggie, O.P.	Ent	400			750	Character Actor
Heidt, Horace	Music	20			40	Big Band Leader
Heifetz, Jascha 1901-87	Music	130			585	Violin Virtuoso
Heimlich, Henry Jay, Dr.	Science	20		45	40	Created Heimlich Maneuver
Heine, Heinrich 1797-56	Author	Scarce	Scarce	6,500	Scarce	German Poet/Critic
Heinlein, Robert A.	Author	50	165	350		Sci-Fi Fiction
Heinrich, Albert H.	Aviation	35		120		
Heintzelman, Samuel P.	Civil War	50	125	200		Union General/1805-80
Heinz, Henry John	Business	150		550	350	A Founder H.J. Heinz Co.
Heinz, Henry John II	Business	35				Food Manufacturer
Heisenberg, Werner, Dr.	Science	75	225	650		Nobel Physics
Helbig, Joachim	Aviation	10	20	35	25	
Held, Anna	Ent	45	75	125	85	Mrs. Florenz Ziegfield
Held, John, Jr. 1889-1958	Cartoonist	150			250	Created the Flapper
Heldy, Fanny	Music	45			125	Opera
Helena, Princess	Royalty	10	20	50	30	Third Daughter Queen Victoria
Helgenberger, Marg	Ent	15			35	
Heller, John R., Dr.	Science	10	20		20	
Heller, Joseph	Author	20	30	45	40	Catch 22
Helletsgruber, Luise	Music	25			75	Opera
Hellinger, Mark	Author	35	105	200	40	Columnist, Playwright
Hellman, Lillian 1905-84	Author	50	145		100	Am Dramatisit
Helm, Benj. Hardin	Civil War	195	250			CSA General/1830-63
Helm, Fay	Ent	25			50	Actress
Helmond, Katherine	Ent	10	20		20	Soap
Helmsley, Leona	Business	10			35	Hotel Magnate
Helnwein, Gottfried	Art	20			50	
Heloise	Author	5			10	Columnist.
Helps, Arthur, Sir	Author	10	15	40		1817 - 1875
Helton, Percy	Ent	20			65	
Hemingway, Ernest	Author	1,000	2,000	3,000	2,500	Nobel Literature/1899-61
Hemingway, Margaux	Ent	40			80	Daughter E. Hemingway
Hemingway, Mariel	Ent	10			50	Daughter E. Hemingway
Hempel, Frieda	Music	20			70	German Soprano/Opera
Hemsley, Sherman	Ent	5	20		20	Jeffersons
Hench, Philip S.	Science	20	45	90	25	Nobel Medicine
Henderson, Archibald	Military	65	195			Marine General War 1812
Henderson, Fletcher	Music	15			35	Bandleader
Henderson, Florence	Ent	5	20		15	Brady Bunch
Henderson, J. Pinckney	Political	300	500			Gen. TX Army, Gov. Texas
Henderson, Marcia	Ent	10			20	

Name	Field	SIG	DS	ALS	SP	Remarks
Henderson, Skitch	Music	15			35	Composer
Hendricks, Barbara	Music	10			30	Opera
Hendricks, Thos. A.	Vice Pres	50	200	200	75	Cleveland VP/1819-95
Hendrix, Jimi 1942-1970	Music	775	1,750	Scarce	1,800	
Hendrix, Wanda	Ent	10	15		35	
Hendry, Gloria	Ent	10			20	Bond girl
Heney, Hugh	Western	325	750			Scout for Lewis & Clark
Henie, Sonja 1910 - 1969	Ent	70	100		175	Olympic Gold Medal
Henley, Don	Music	25			50	The Eagles
Henner, Marilu	Ent	10	25		25	Taxi
Henning, Paul	Ent	20			45	TV Producer
Henreid, Paul	Ent	40	100		100	Casablanca
Henri, Robert	Art	80	175	215		Portrait Painter
Henrikson, Lance	Ent	15			30	
Henry II	Royalty	300	1,050	2,400		France
Henry III	Royalty	250	675	1,250		France
Henry IV (Fr) 1553-1610	Royalty	200	700	Scarce		And Navarre. Assassinated
Henry IV (Sp)	Royalty		1,750			King of CastileThe Impotent
Henry V (Fr)	Royalty	40	65	150		Pretender to Throne
Henry VI	Royalty	200	525	1,200		England
Henry VII (Eng)	Royalty	1,200	RARE	RARE		
Henry VIII 1491-1547	Royalty	3,500	15,000	RARE	RARE	
Henry, Bill	Aviation	10	25	40	30	WWII ACE
Henry, Bill	Ent	15		35	30	
Henry, Buck	Ent	10		10	20	
Henry, Gloria	Ent	5		10	15	
Henry, John 1750-1798	RevWar	35	135	220		Continental Congress.
Henry, Joseph 1797-1878	Science	55	200	250		First Electric Motor
Henry, O.	Author					SEE W.S. Porter
Henry, Patrick 1736-99	RevWar	1,000	1,500	1,800		
Henschel, George, Sir	Music	75			150	Composer/Conductor
Henshaw, David	Political	20	60	105		Tyler Sec'y Navy
Henson, Jim 1936-90	Ent	75	150		225	Created the Muppets
Henson, Matthew A.	Explorer	130	350			Afro-Am. Arctic Explorer
Henstridge, Natasha	Ent	20			50	
Henze, Hans Werner	Music	45			150	Ger. Opera, Theater Works
Henze, Karl	Aviation	15	40	70	45	
Hepburn, Audrey 1929-93	Ent	125	400	500	275	AA Winner/My Fair Lady
Hepburn, Katharine	Ent	125	250	450	600	AA Winner
Hepworth, Barbara	Art	75	150		125	Br Sculpture
Herbeck, Ray	Music	5			15	Big Band Leader-Sax
Herbert, Don	Ent	10			25	
Herbert, F. Hugh	Author	10	20	30	20	Am. Playwright, Producer
Herbert, Frank	Author	15	20	35	20	Am. Sci-Fi. Dune Trilogy
Herbert, Geo.E.	Science	25	50	100		With Carter, King Tut Tomb
Herbert, Hugh	Ent	30	45	70	75	
Herbert, P.O.	Civil War	100		375		
Herbert, Sidney	Ent	15	25	30	25	
Herbert, Victor 1859-1924	Music	100	200	375	350	Composer

Name	Field	SIG	DS	ALS	SP	Remarks
Herdman, George	Cartoonist	100			250	Krazy Kat
Hergesheimer, Joseph	Author	25	65	145	30	Am. Psychological Novels
Herget, Wilhelm	Aviation	20		50		
Hering, Constantine	Science	15	25	50		lst Homeopathic School
Herkimer, Nicholas	RevWar	RARE	3,700	RARE	RARE	General of Militia.
Herkomer, Hubert von	Art	30	85	130		Br. Portrait Painter
Herman, Jerry	Music	15	40	65	30	Composer/Hello Dolly
Herman, Pee Wee	Ent	20			45	
Herman, Woody	Music	25	90		65	Big Band Leader-Clarinetist
Hermann, Bernard	Music	Scarce	550	Scarce	Scarce	Composer/1911-1975
Hermann, Hajo	Aviation	25	50		60	
Herndon, William	Political	200	450	900		Lincolns Law Partner
Herring, John F. 1795-65	Art	75		275		Br.Race Horses
Herriot, Edouard 1872-57	Political	35	80	175		Premier of Fr., Nazi Prisoner
Herriot, James (Wight)	Author	15	40	75	25	
Herrmann, Adelaide	Ent	50			75	Magicians/and Al
Herrmann, Bernard	Music	Scarce	875	Scarce	Scarce	Film Composer
Herron, Francis J.	Civil War	45	80	125		Union General/1837-1902
Herschbach, Dudley, Dr.	Science	25	35		40	Nobel Chemistry
Herschel, John Fred. Wm.	Science	82	170	275	1,265	Br Astronomer
Herschel, William, Sir	Science	150	475	675		Discovered Uranus
Hersey, John 1914-93	Author	20	75	125	25	Bell for Adano Pulitzer
Hershey, Alfred D., Dr.	Science	20	30	45	30	Nobel Medicine
Hershey, Barbara	Ent	20			40	
Hershey, Lewis B.	Military	15			25	General
Hersholt, Jean 1886-1956	Ent	25		95	65	
Hertz, Alfred	Music	45			125	Conductor
Hervey, Irene	Ent	15			35	
Herzberg, Gerhard, Dr.	Science	25	65		30	Nobel Chemistry
Herzner, Hans-Albrecht	Military	700	Scarce	Scarce	Scarce	1st Ger engaged in WWII
Herzog, Chaim	Political	30	65	175	60	Pres. Israel
Hess, Myra, Dame	Music	20	40	65	35	Br. Pianist
Hess, Rudolf	Military	155	450	750	750	Nazi WWII 2nd to Hitler
Hess, Victor F.	Science	20	30	55	25	Nobel Physics
Hess, Walter R.	Science	20	30	50	25	Nobel Medicine
Hesse, Hermann 1877-62	Author	100	500	550	400	German Artist/Author
Hesseman, Howard	Ent	5	15	20	15	WKRP in Cincinatti
Heston, Charlton	Ent	10			35	
Heth, Henry	Civil War	1,500	450	600		CSA General
Heth, Henry (WD)	Civil War	750	3,000	3,500		CSA General/1825-99
Hewes, Joseph 1730-80	RevWar	2,500	7,250	8,500		Signer Decl. of Indepen.
Hewish, Anthony	Science	20	40	85	30	Nobel Physics. Pulsars
Hewitt, Abram S.	Business	35	60	85		Iron Manafacturing
Hewitt, H.K.	Military	20	50	85		
Hewitt, Jennifer Love	Ent	20			50	
Hewlett, William R.	Business	25	70	145	30	Hewlett-Packard
Hexum, Jon-Erik	Ent	60			125	
Heydrich, Reinhard	Military	200		1,350	600	Specialist in Nazi Terror
Heydt, Louis Jean	Ent	45			80	

Name	Field	SIG	DS	ALS	SP	Remarks
Heyerdahl, Thor	Explorer	30	50	95	35	
Heyse, Paul	Author	45	135	350		German Novelist/Nobel
Heyward, Dorothy	Author	55	200			Co-writer of Porgy & Bess
Heyward, DuBose	Author	140	300	450		Co-Writer of Porgy & Bess
Heyward, Thomas Jr.	RevWar	600	1,300	1,800		Signer Decl. of Indepen.
Heywood, Anne	Ent	10			20	
Heywood, Eddie	Music	35			100	Big Band Leader-Piano
Hichens, Robert S.	Author	15	45			Br. Novelist.Garden of Allah
Hickenlooper, Andrew	Civil War	30	55	80		Union General/1837-1900
Hickman, Dwayne	Ent	5			15	
Hickman, Ron	Science	20	50			Black & Decker Workmate
Hicks, Catherine	Ent	10		25	20	
Hidalgo, Miguel C.	Military	1,500	Scarce	Scarce	Scarce	Mex Revolutionary
Higgins, Andrew Jackson	Business	25		50		
Higgins, Charles	Science	15	35			
Higginson, Henry L,	Business	10	20	35		
Higginson, Thos. W.	Civil War	100		200		Antislavery Writer
Hildebrand, Samuel	Civil War	Scarce	1,750	Scarce	Scarce	Quantrill Raider-Murderer
Hildegarde	Ent	5			10	
Hill, Ambrose P. (WD)	Civil War	2,500	5,500	Scarce	Scarce	CSA General/KIA
Hill, Ambrose Powell	Civil War	2,000	3,000	Scarce	Scarce	CSA General KIA/1825-65
Hill, Archibald V.	Science	25	45		35	Nobel Medicine 1922
Hill, Arthur	Ent	5			15	
Hill, Benjamin H. 1823-82	Civil War	65	165	230		Signed CSA Constitution
Hill, Benjamin J. 1825-80	Civil War	110	200	335		CSA General
Hill, Benny	Ent	25			30	
Hill, Dana	Ent	5		15	15	
Hill, Daniel H. (WD)	Civil War	600		1,550		CSA General
Hill, Daniel Harvey	Civil War	320	500	600		CSA General/1821-89
Hill, David Lee Tex	Aviation	15	30	45	35	WWII Flying Tigers ACE
Hill, Faith	Music	15			40	
Hill, George Roy	Ent	10			25	AA
Hill, George Washington	Business	80	220			American Tobacco Co.,Pres.
Hill, Grace Livingston	Author	25	40	75		Am. Novelist
Hill, James J.	Business	400	1,500	2,000	950	RR Executive/Financier
Hill, Napoleon	Author	75	300			Think & Grow Rich
Hill, Rowland, Sir	Science	150	300	600		Originator of Penny Postage
Hill, Teresa	Ent	15			40	
Hill, Tiny	Ent	5			15	
Hill, Walter	Ent	10	20		20	Director
Hill, William	Ent	5			10	
Hillary, Edmund, Sir	Explorer	70	150	275	125	lst To Climb Mt.Everest
Hillegas, Michael	RevWar	225	645			U.S. Treasurer 1777
Hillegess, C.K. Cliff	Author	10			20	Cliff's Notes
Hiller, Arthur	Ent	5			15	Film Director
Hiller, Ferdinand	Music	40	75	125		Conductor, Pianist
Hiller, Frank, Jr,	Aviation	75	150	250	150	
Hiller, Wendy	Ent	20		35	30	AA
Hillerman, John	Ent	10	25		30	Magnum PI

Name	Field	SIG	DS	ALS	SP	Remarks
Hilliard, Harriet	Ent	20			35	Harriet Nelson/Maiden Nm
Hilliard, Henry W.	Civil War	35	80	100		Conf. Commissioner to TN
Hilliard, Robert	Ent	20			40	
Hillig, Otto	Aviation	40	85	150	115	
Hillis, Marjorie	Author	5	20	15		
Hilton, Barron	Business	10		25	25	
Hilton, Conrad	Business	60	90	190	110	Fndr. Hilton Hotel Dynasty
Hilton, James, Sir	Author	35	120	205	35	Lost Horizon
Himmler, Heinrich	Military	250	750	1,500	750	Nazi Head of the Gestapo
Hinckley, John, Jr.	Criminal	35	150	200		Attempt on Pres. Reagan
Hindemith, Paul	Music	100	295	425		German Teacher/Theorist
Hindenburg, Paul von	Political	160	380	400	575	1847-1934
Hindman, Thomas C.	Civil War	320				CSA General/1818-68
Hines, Duncan	Business	75	250		150	Duncan Hines
Hines, Earl K. Fatha	Music	125			250	Pianist/Composer
Hines, Gregory	Ent	15			30	
Hines, Herm	Music	10			25	Jazz Sax
Hines, Jerome	Music	20			40	Opera
Hingle, Pat	Ent	5		15	15	
Hinks, Edward W.	Civil War	50	185			Union General/1830-94
Hinshelwood, Cyril N.	Science	20	45		35	Nobel Chemistry
Hinton, Walter	Aviation	40	85	130	90	NC-4 Pilot
Hippel, Hans Joachim	Aviation	10			35	WWI and II Fighter Pilot
Hirohito	Political	2,000	RARE	RARE	12,000	RARE
Hirsch, Judd	Ent	10	25		25	Taxi
Hirschfeld, Al	Art	45			125	
Hirshfield, Harry	Cartoonist	20			75	Able The Agent
Hirt, Al	Music	10			25	Trumpet
Hiss, Alger	Political	40	65	200		Spy
Hitchcock, Alfred	Ent	200	400	575	700	1899-1980
Hitchcock, Ethan Allen	Civil War	50	150	200		Union General/1798-1870
Hitchcock, Raymond	Ent	20			35	
Hitchings, George, Dr.	Science	20	30	70	30	Nobel Medicine
Hite, Les	Music	100			275	Saxophone
Hitler, Adolf 1889-1945	Political	1,500	2,250	RARE	2,500	
Hittorff, Jacques 1792-67	Science	5	20	30		Fr. Architect
Hitzfeld, Otto Maximilian	Military	20			50	Ger, Infantry General
Hix, John	Author	15	50			Strange as it Seems
Ho Chi Minh	Political	600	1,225	2,000	2,600	Vietnam
Ho, Don	Music	5		10	15	
Hoagland, Everett	Ent	20			57	Jazz Clarinetist. Bandleaer
Hoban, James	RevWar	250	550			Architect White House
Hobart, Garret A.	Vice Pres	75	200	300	200	
Hobart, Rose	Ent	10			25	
Hobbes, Halliwell	Ent	25			45	
Hobson, Richard P.	Military	95	250			Span Am War/1870-37
Hobson, Richmond P.	Military	75	260	385	150	Admiral/Blew up Merrimac
Hobson, Valerie	Ent	25			60	
Hoche, Lazare	Military	200	450			General French Republic

Name	Field	SIG	DS	ALS	SP	Remarks
Hockney, David	Art	60		75		
Hodes, Art	Music	10			25	Pianist-Bandleader
Hodge, Al	Ent	25			100	
Hodges, Courtney	Military	15	150		25	WWII General
Hodgkin, Dorothy C.	Science	25		35		Nobel Chemistry
Hodiak, John	Ent	20	25	45	45	
Hoe, Richard M.	Business	100	300	500		Invented Rotary Press
Hoest, Bill	Cartoonist	10		35	40	The Lockhorns
Hoey, Dennis	Ent	75			200	1893 - 1960
Hofer, Andreas	Military		3,000			Tyrolean Patriot,executed
Hoffa, James R.	Political	275			400	Teamsters Union (disappeared)
Hoffman, Dustin	Ent	20			50	AA Winner
Hoffman, Gaby	Ent	15			30	Blossom
Hoffman, Kurt-Caesar	Military	25			65	
Hoffman, Paul G.	Business	10	20	35	20	Auto Mfg.-Studebaker Cars
Hoffmann, Peter	Music	25			55	Opera
Hoffmann, Roald, Dr.	Science	20	30	45	25	Nobel Chemistry
Hofmann, Josef 1876-57	Music	40	100	140	150	Composer/Pianist
Hofstadter, Robert	Science	20	30	45	25	Nobel Physics
Hogan, Ben	Sports	125		350	275	1974 Golf HOF
Hogan, Paul	Ent	10	15	20	25	Dundee
Hogarth, Burne	Cartoonist	25			75	Tarzan-2nd Artist
Hogarth, Wm. 1697-1764	Art	450	1,665	3,500		Br. Painter-Engraver.
Hogeback, Hermann	Aviation	10			40	Ger. Bomber Pilot.
Hoimquest, Donald L.	Space	10	15		20	Astronaut
Hoiris, Holger	Aviation	40	85	155	95	
Hoistrom, E.W. 'Brick'	Military	15	35	70	25	
Hoke, Robert Frederick	Civil War	100		300		CSA General/1837-1912
Hokinson, Helen	Cartoonist	20			75	Magazine Cartoonist
Holbrook, Hal	Ent	10	20		20	Barney Miller
Holden, Fay	Ent	20			50	
Holden, William 1918-81	Ent	75			200	
Holder, Geoffrey	Ent	20			50	James Bond villain
Holiday, Billie 1915-59	Music	450	800	Scarce	1,500	Jazz Singer
Holladay, Ben	Business	125	250	450		Indian Trade
Holland, Edmund M.	Ent	15			45	
Holland, John Philip	Science	75	150	250		Internal Combustion Engine
Holland, Josiah Gilbert	Author	25	65	75		Co-Founder Scribners
Hollen, Andrea Lee	Military	10	20	35	15	
Holley, Marietta 1836-26	Author	10	15	35		Am. Humorist
Holley, Robert, Dr.	Science	15	20	35	20	Nobel Chemistry
Holliday, Judy	Music	125			300	
Holliday, Polly	Ent	10	20		20	Alice/Flo
Holliman, Earl	Ent	5		10	15	
Holliman, John	Ent	5			15	TV News Commentator
Hollins, Geo. Nichols	Civil War	275	450			Commodore CSA Navy
Holloway, Stanley	Ent	20			60	
Holloway, Sterling	Ent	40	60		55	Voice of Winnie the Pooh
Hollowell, George	Aviation	10	25	35	30	ACE/WWII/Marine Ace

Name	Field	SIG	DS	ALS	SP	Remarks
Holly, Buddy 1936-1959	Music	750	900	RARE	2,000	
Holly, Lauren	Ent	20			45	
Holm, Celeste	Ent	5		15	15	
Holm, Eleanor	Ent	10			30	
Holman, Libby	Music	10	35		75	Vintage Torch Singer
Holmes, Augusta 1847-03	Music	10		85		Composer
Holmes, Burton 1870-58	Author	15	20	45	25	
Holmes, Christopher	Space	15	25		25	Astronaut
Holmes, Larry	Sports	15			35	Golf
Holmes, Oliver W., Jr.	SuprCt	250	300	550	600	1841 - 1935
Holmes, Oliver W., Sr.	Author	75	200	350		1809 - 94
Holmes, Theophilus H.	Civil War	205	245			CSA General/1804-1880
Holst, Gustav	Music	50	100	300		Composer
Holt, Jack	Ent	40	75		100	
Holt, Jennifer	Ent	5			10	
Holt, Joseph (WD)	Civil War	75		400		Union General
Holt, Joseph 1807-94	Civil War	55		250		Union General
Holt, Tim	Ent	50			125	
Holt, Victoria	Author	5			15	
Holten, Samuel 1738-16	RevWar	90	195			Patriot/Statesman
Holyoake, Keith, Sir	Political	45	95	125	50	NZ Prime Minister
Holzer, Helmut	Science	20			40	Rocket Pioneer/von Braun
Home, A. Douglas	Political	45	70	150	135	Br. Prime Minister
Homer, Louise	Music	35			85	Opera. Am Mezzo
Homer, Winslow 1836-10	Art	350	500	850		Seascapes/Landscapes
Homesteaders, The	Music	25			50	
Homma, Masaharu	Military	75	205	340	180	Jap.Gen,Invasion of Philippines
Honda, Soichiro 1904-94	Business	Scarce	Scarce	Scarce	Scarce	Founder Honda Motor
Honeymooners, The	Ent	150			275	Signed by all four
Honnegger, Arthur	Music	45	130	290	50	Composer
Hood, Alexander Sir	Military	55	135	245		Accompanied Capt. Cook
Hood, Arthur Wm.	Military	20				Admiral, lst Baron
Hood, Darla	Ent	150		200	350	Our Gang member
Hood, John Bell	Civil War	800	1,500	1,600	1,000	CSA General/1831-79
Hood, Samuel, Sir	Military	35	80	135		Br. Adm. with Lord Nelson
Hood, Sir Arthur W.	Military	20				lst Baron, Admiral
Hood, Thomas	Author	50	150	275		Br. Humorist, Poet
Hook, James Clarke	Art	25		85		Brit. Royal Academy
Hooker, John Lee	Music	40	100		100	Jazz
Hooker, Joseph (WD)	Civil War	275	600	900		Union General
Hooker, Joseph M.	Civil War	200	450	600		Union General/1814-79
Hooks, Jan	Ent	10			25	Sat Nite Live alumni
Hooks, Kevin	Ent	10			20	
Hooper, William 1742-90	RevWar	Scarce	3,000	Scarce	Scarce	Signer Decl of Indep
Hooten, Ernest A.	Science	25	65	140		Anthropologist
Hootie and the BlowFish	Music	65			110	Signed by Entire Group
Hoover, Herbert	President	200	275	850	450	As President
Hoover, Herbert 1874-64	President	125	175	500	325	
Hoover, J. Edgar 1895-72	Political	60	160	220	145	FBI Director for 48 Years

Name	Field	SIG	DS	ALS	SP	Remarks
Hoover, Lou Henry	First Lady	50	100	200		
Hope, Bob	Ent	35	100		75	
Hopf, Hans	Music	25			65	Opera
Hopkins, Anthony	Ent	20			50	AA Winner
Hopkins, Bo	Ent	10			20	
Hopkins, Claude	Music	30			60	Composer
Hopkins, Esek 1718-1802	Military	180				Cont Navy
Hopkins, Frederick G.	Science	45	120	200		Nobel Medicine 1929
Hopkins, Johns 1795-73	Business	175	500			Financier, Phiianthropist
Hopkins, Miriam	Ent	35	50		75	1902 - 1972
Hopkins, Samuel 1721-03	RevWar	100	280	375		Cont Army Officer
Hopkins, Stephen	RevWar	250	600	900		Signer/1707-85
Hopkinson, Francis	RevWar	250	450	900		Signer, Author, Composer
Hopkinson, Joseph	Author	100	200			1770-1842
Hopper, Bill	Ent	10			20	
Hopper, Dennis	Ent	15			45	
Hopper, DeWolfe	Ent	20	40	50	85	1858 - 1935
Hopper, Hedda	Ent	20	20		30	1890 - 1966
Hordern, Michael, Sir	Ent	10		20	35	
Horenstein, Jascha	Music	75				Conductor
Horina, Louise	Music	15			45	Opera
Hormel, Jay C.	Business	50	100	150	100	
Hornberger, H. Richard	Author	20		30	45	
Horne, L. Donald	Business	5			10	CEO Mennen Co.
Horne, Lena	Ent	15	25		35	Singer/Actress
Horne, Marilyn	Music	15			35	Opera
Horner, H. Mansfield	Business	5			10	Aircraft Exec.
Hornsby, Bruce	Music	20			40	and the Range
Hornsby, Roger	Sports	250			500	1942 Baseball HOF
Horowitz, Vladimir	Music	150			175	Piano Virtuoso/1903-89
Horrocks, Gen. Sir Brian	Military	15	25	40	25	Cmdr. XIII Corps WWII
Horsford, Eben N. 1818-74	Science	15	25	70		Am. Analytical Chemist
Horsley, John Calcott	Art	40				Brit. Royal Academy
Horsley, Lee	Ent	10			25	Matt Houston
Horthy, Miklos, Adm.	Political	75	190	485	150	Hungarian Admiral
Horton, Edw. Everett	Ent	30	45		45	1886-1970
Horton, Peter	Ent	20			40	
Horton, Robert	Ent	5			15	
Horwich, Frances	Ent	10			25	
Hoskins, Bob	Ent	15			30	Roger Rabbit
Hosmer, Titus 1736-80	RevWar	35	95	200		Continental Congress
Hotchkiss, Benjamin J.	Civil War			900		Union Arms Supplier
Hotchkiss, Charles T.	Civil War	40		100		
Houdini, Harry	Ent	800	2,000	Scarce	2,500	Magician / 1874 - 1926
Houghton, Katharine	Ent	35				
Hounsfield, Godfrey	Science	20	30	40	25	Nobel Medicine
House, Edw. M.'Colonel'	Political	35	100	310	45	Confidant of Pres.Wilson
Houseman, John	Ent	20			55	Actor/Director
Housman, Alfred Edward	Author	75	225	600		Br. Poet, Scholar

Name	Field	SIG	DS	ALS	SP	Remarks
Houssay, Bernando A.	Science	65	135	250	100	Nobel in Medicine/1947
Houston, David	Music	5			10	Country
Houston, Sam 1793-1863	Military	600	1,500	2,200		Pres. Repub. Texas
Houston, Temple	Western	375		1,667	750	Son of Sam Houston
Houston, Whitney	Music	25			50	
Houston, William C.	RevWar	35		125		Continental Congress, etc.
Hovey, Alvin	Civil War	25	50	75		Union General/1821-91
Hovis, Larry	Ent	20			45	Hogans Heroes
Howard, James H.	Aviation	15	30	55	45	WWII Flying Tigers ACE
Howard, John	Ent	15	25		40	
Howard, Ken	Ent	5			15	
Howard, Clint	Ent	10			25	
Howard, Curly	Ent	450	900	Scarce	900	Three Stooges
Howard, Leslie	Ent	250	275	Scarce	400	GWTW/1890-1943
Howard, Moe 1895-1975	Ent	200	275	600	450	Three Stooges
Howard, Oliver Otis	Civil War	100	200	250		Union General/1830-1909
Howard, Oliver Otis (WD)	Civil War	150		400		Union General
Howard, Robert, Sir	Author	100	300			1626-1698
Howard, Ron	Ent	25	50		50	Actor/Director
Howard, Shemp 1891-55	Ent	450	600	Scarce	575	Three Stooges
Howard, Sidney	Author	100	175	375	150	Am. Playwright. Pulitzer
Howard, Trevor	Ent	10			35	
Howard, Willie	Ent	10		20	20	
Howe, Albion P. (WD)	Civil War	35	100	450		Union General/1818-97
Howe, Elias 1819-67	Science	400	Scarce	Scarce	Scarce	Invented Sewing Machine
Howe, James Wong	Ent	40			65	Director
Howe, Julia Ward	Author	100	150	300		Battle Hymn of Republic
Howe, Richard	RevWar	150	675	775		Br. Adm.Rev. War.
Howe, William, Sir	RevWar	200	850			Cmdr-in-Chief Br. Forces in Am.
Howell, C.Thomas	Ent	10	30	25	25	
Howells, William Dean	Author	75	195			Novelist, Critic, Editor
Howes, Barbara	Author	5			10	
Howland, Beth	Ent	10			20	Alice/Vera
Howlin, Olin	Ent	100			125	GWTW star
Hoyle, Edmond 1671-69	Author	150	675	750		Established Card Rules
Hoyt, John W.	Political	50	85			Governor Wy Territory
Hubbard, Elbert	Author	50	160	275	145	'
Hubbard, L. Ron 1911-86	Author	200	900	Scarce	Scarce	Religious Activist
Hubbard, Thomas H.	Civil War	15	35			Union General/1838-1915
Hubble, Edwin P.	Science	20	60			Am. Astronomer.
Hubel, David H., Dr.	Science	20	30	45	25	Nobel Medicine
Hubley, Adam	RevWar	75	300			Officer Cont. Army
Hudson, George	Business	10	20	35		Controlled 1,000 Miles Railrd
Hudson, Rochelle	Ent	35		45	45	1914 - 1972
Hudson, Rock 1925-85	Ent	45	60		125	
Hudson, W.H.	Author		135	495		Green Mansions
Huemer, Dick	Cartoonist	15			45	Disney Artist
Huerta, Victoriano	RevWar	75	250	500	120	Mex. General/Exiled
Huger, Benjamin (WD)	Civil War	175	550			CSA General

Name	Field	SIG	DS	ALS	SP	Remarks
Huger, Benjamin 1805-77	Civil War	90	250	300		CSA General
Huger, Isaac 1742-97	RevWar	100	215	450		General Continental Army
Huggins, Charles, Dr.	Science	25			35	Nobel Medicine
Huggins, Roy	Ent	15			25	TV Producer
Huggins, William, Sir	Science	35	100	200	45	Br.Astron, Stellar Spectroscope
Hughes, Barnard	Ent	15			30	
Hughes, Charles E.	SuprCt	45	150		250	Chief Justice, Sec'y of State
Hughes, Howard	Business	1,250	2,000	3,500	2,750	1905 - 1976
Hughes, Langston	Author	200	350	750	575	Afro-Am.Poet/1902-67
Hughes, Mary Beth	Ent	10		20	15	
Hughes, Richard	RevWar	25	50			Br. Adm. during Rev. War
Hughes, Rupert	Author	15	50	75		Poet, Author, Historian
Hughes, Sarah T.	Political	45	100			Judge/Swore In L.BJ in '63
Hughes, Thomas	Author	40		125		Tom Brown's School Days
Hughs, Finola	Ent	15			35	
Hugo, Victor 1802-85	Author	200	375	650	975	Novelist-Politician-Poet
Hulce,Tom	Ent	20			40	Disney Voice
Hull, Cordell 1871-1955	Political	50	135		125	Nobel, Father Fed.Income Tax
Hull, Henry	Ent	45	45		95	1890 - 1977
Hull, Isaac 1773-1843	Military	190	570	565		Cmdr. War of 1812
Hull, Josphine 1884-1957	Ent	150		300	300	
Hull, Warren	Ent	30			50	1903 - 1974
Hull, William	Military	145	370	700		Revolutionary War Gen.
Humble Pie	Music	60			175	Signed by all
Humboldt, Alexander	Science	70	125	300		German Naturalist
Hume, Joseph 1777-1855	Political	10	30	80		Br.Physician
Humes, William Y.	Civil War	140	235	435		CSA General
Hummel, Johann N.	Music	150	190	400		Piano Virtuoso
Humperdinck, Engelbert	'Music	100	225	375	250	Composer
Humphrey, Hubert H.	Vice Pres	40	160		65	1911-1978
Humphreys, Andrew A.	Civil War	65	180	250		Union General/1810-1883
Humphreys, David	RevWar	55	150	200		
Hunt, Bonnie	Ent	15			30	
Hunt, E. Howard	Political	15	25	90	25	CIA/Watergate
Hunt, H. L.	Business	90	485	580	175	Texas Oil King
Hunt, Helen	Ent	25			50	AA Winner/Mad About You
Hunt, Henry J. (WD)	Civil War	70	145			Union General
Hunt, Henry J. 1819-89	Civil War	50	75	125		Union General
Hunt, James Bunker	Business	5		35	15	
Hunt, Leigh 1784-1859	Author	30				Br. Essayist, Poet
Hunt, Linda	Ent	15			65	AA Winner
Hunt, Marsha	Ent	10			20	
Hunt, Nelson Bunker	Business	10	20	40	15	
Hunt, Pee Wee	Music	15			45	Trombone-Vocalist
Hunt, Ward	SuprCt	65	80	175		
Hunt, William Holman	Art	75	165	330		Br. Pre-Raphaelite Painter
Hunt, WIlliam Morris	Art	50	215	500		American Portraitist
Hunter, David 0. (WD)	Civil War	85	220	375		Union General
Hunter, David 1802-86	Civil War	65	150	175	250	Union General

Name	Field	SIG	DS	ALS	SP	Remarks
Hunter, Holly	Ent	25			50	AA Winner
Hunter, Ian	Music	10			30	
Hunter, Jeffrey	Ent	100	150		100	Brief Star Trek Captain
Hunter, Jim	Sports	10			25	Catfish"/Baseball
Hunter, Kim	Ent	5	15	15	15	AA Winner/Planet of Apes
Hunter, R. M. T. 1809-87	Civil War	95	170	190		CSA Sec'y State, US Sen. ALS '63$360
Hunter, Rachel	Ent	10			25	Model
Hunter, Robert	RevWar	220	500	900		Br. Gen. Colonial Gov.
Hunter, Tab	Ent	20			45	
Hunter, William 1774-49	Political	55	80	125		Statesman, Senator RI
Huntington, Agnes	Music	35			125	Opera
Huntington, Benjamin	RevWar	60	175	275		Continental Congress
Huntington, Collis P.	Business	125	450	Scarce	750	Pioneer Am. Railroad Builder
Huntington, Daniel	Art	75	150	250		PortraitPainter
Huntington, Ebenezer	RevWar	125	250	300		Statesman, Army General
Huntington, Henry E.	Business	75	125	200		Railroad Magnate
Huntington, Jabez W.	Political	25	30	45		Senator CT 1840
Huntington, Jedediah	Military	75	125	230		Gen. Revolutionary War
Huntington, Samuel	RevWar	250	750	1,200		Signer Decl. of Indepen.
Hunton, Eppa	Civil War	125	250			CSA General/1823-1908
Huppert, Isabelle	Ent	15			35	
Hurd, Peter	Art	100	200	300		
Hurlbut, Stephen A.	Civil War	60	125	300		Union General/1815-82
Hurley, Elizabeth	Ent	25			50	Austin Powers
Hurst, Fannie 1889-1968	Author	25	45	150	85	Novelist
Hurt, John	Ent	10	20		30	
Hurt, Mary Beth	Ent	5			15	
Hurt, William	Ent	20	25	50	50	
Husa, Karel	Music	15	30	50		Composer/Pulitzer
Hussein, King	Royalty	75	135	300	75	King of Jordan
Hussey, Olivia	Ent	10			20	
Hussey, Ruth	Ent	15			25	
Huston, Anjelica	Ent	10			30	AA Winner
Huston, John 1906-87	Ent	30	100	50	75	AA Film Director-Actor
Huston, Walter 1884-1950	Ent	85		150	175	AA Winner
Hutchence, Michael	Ent	20			50	
Hutchins, Will	Ent	10	15		15	
Hutchinson, Frederick S.	Civil War	35		130		Union Officer
Hutchinson, John W.	Music	15		50		Composer
Hutchinson, Josephine	Ent	10	15	25	25	
Hutchinson, Thomas	Political	185	450			Royal Gov. MA. Exiled
Hutton, Betty	Ent	10			25	
Hutton, Gunilla	Music	5			10	
Hutton, Jim	Ent	40	70	110	100	
Hutton, Lauren	Ent	10	20	25	25	Model/Actress
Hutton, Robert	Ent	25	40	110	100	
Hutton, Timothy	Ent	20			45	AA Winner
Huxley, Aldous 1894-63	Author	75	300	350	350	Br. Novelist.
Huxley, Julian Sorell	Science	40	148	175		Br Biologist/1887-1975

Name	Field	SIG	DS	ALS	SP	Remarks
Huxley, Thomas Henry	Science	65	150	235		Br. Biologist/1825-1895
Hyams, Leila	Ent	20	25	50	40	
Hyde-White, Wilfrid	Ent	15		35	35	
Hyer, Martha	Ent	5		15	25	
Hylton, Jack 1892-1965	Music	25			70	Br. Bandleader
Hynde, Chrissie	Music	25			45	The Pretenders
Hyndman, Henry M.	Political	75		350		Br. Marxist-Socialist

John Hancock

Matta Hari

Nathaniel Hawthorne

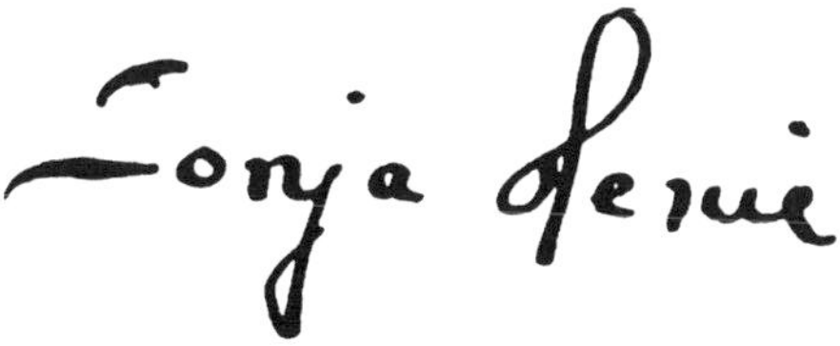

Sonja Henie

Paul von Hindenburg

Name	Field	SIG	DS	ALS	SP	Remarks
Iacocca, Lee A.	Business	15	50		35	CEO Chrysler Motors
Ian, Janis	Music	10	40		20	
Ibert, Jacques-Francois	Music	75		325		Composer
Ibsen, Henrik 1828-1906	Author	200	600	1,500	1,325	
Icart, Louis 1888-1950	Artist	250		875		FR. Art Deco
Ice Cube	Music	20			45	
Ice T	Music	20			50	
Ickes, Harold L.	Political	20	35	60	25	Roosevelt Sec'y Interior
Idol, Billy	Music	20			45	
Iglesias, Julio	Music	20			50	
Ikeda, Hayato	Political	15		65		Japan
Iman	Ent	25			50	Super Model
Imboden, John Dan'l	Civil War	165	400			CSA General/1823-1895
Imboden, John Dan'l	Civil War	450	750			CSA General/War Dated
Imbruglia, Natalie	Music	25			50	
Immelmann, Max	Aviation	200	425	700	500	1st German ACE in WWII
Ince, Thomas H.	Ent	50			125	Film Dir. Civil War Epics
Indiana, Robert	Art	45	100	150	125	
Indigo Girls	Music	30			65	Signed by all
Ingalls, Laura	Aviation		295			1st Non-Stop Trans. Flight
Ingalls, Rufus (WD)	Civil War	55		450		Union General
Ingalls, Rufus 1818-93	Civil War	35	75	125		Union General
Inge, William	Author	50	125	175		Am. Playwright. Pulitzer
Ingels, Marty	Ent	10			15	Comedian
Ingersoll, Jared 1749-22	RevWar	100	250	400		Signer Constitution
Ingersoll, Robert Green	Civil War	30	60	85	40	
Ingersoll, Robert H.	Business	80	175	300	225	Ingersoll Watch Co.
Ingham, Samuel D.	Political	35	120	145	80	Sec'y Treasury 1829
Ingle, Red	Business	10			20	Ingles Grocery Chain
Ingle, Robert P	Business	5	15	25		
Ingraham, Duncan N.	Civil War	150				Capt.CSA Navy
Ingram, Rex	Ent	125			300	1895 - 1969
Ingres, Jean-Auguste-D.	Art	205		1,050		
Ingrid, Victoria (Fred. IX)	Royalty	15	40			
Ink Spots, The	Music	150			250	SIgned by all four
Inman, Henry	Art	125	250	450		American Portraitist
Inman, Jerry	Music	10			20	
Inness, George 1824-94	Art	75	225	425		Am. PainterCont.
Inskeep, Jonathan	RevWar	80	175			Pvt. Sec'y Edison.
Insull, Samuel 1859-1938	Business	150	750	1,200		Financier
INXS	Music	35			75	Signed by all
Ionesco, Eugene	Author	40	125	195		
Ireland, Jill	Ent	25	50		65	

Name	Field	SIG	DS	ALS	SP	Remarks
Ireland, Kathy	Ent	15			35	Super Model
Irish, James M.	Military	10	30	50		
Irons, Jeremy	Ent	20			50	
Irvin, James B. "Jim"	Space	55	175	250	125	Moonwalker/1930-1991
Irvine, James 1735-1819	Military	55	130	250		Gen. Militia. Cmdr. Fort Pitt
Irvine, William 1741-1804	RevWar	150	500	600		Gen./Continental Congress
Irving, Amy	Ent	10			25	
Irving, Clifford	Author	15	60	100	25	
Irving, Henry, Sir	Ent	30	60	90	70	1838 - 1905
Irving, John	Author	20			65	World According to Garp
Irving, Margaret	Ent	10			20	
Irving, Washington	Author	150	385	550		Rip Van Winkle
Irwin, May	Ent	25		35	45	First Film Kiss
Irwin, Will 1873-1948	Author	20		40		War Correspondent
Isabella I, Of Castile	Royalty	850	2,500	5,000		Sp Queen/Columbus
Isabella II 1830-1904	Royalty	175	400	600		Spain.Abdicated
Isabey, Jean-Baptiste	Art		115	350		Court Painter to Napoleon
Ish Kabibble	Music	15			25	Kay Kyser Novelty Singer
Isherwood, Christopher	Author	50	140	225	300	Br. Novelist, Playwright
Ishiguro, Kazuo	Author	25			50	Remains of the Day
Ismay, Hastings Lionel	Military	20	35	60		Churchill Chief-of-Staff WWII
Israels, Jozef	Art	75	150	300		
Ito, Hirobumi (Prince)	Political	65	125			Japan/Prime Minister 1886
Ito, Lance	Political	50			75	O.J. Trial Judge
Ito, Robert	Ent	10			25	Quincy
Iturbi, Jose	Music	20			50	Classical Pianist
Iturbide, Augustin de	Political		875			Emperor of Mexico
Ivan IV, The Terrible	Royalty	35,000	75,000	RARE	RARE	
Iverson, Alfred, Jr.	Civil War	150	300	500		CSA General/1829-1911
Ives, Burl 1909 - 1997	Ent	25	40		45	AA Winner
Ives, Charles E. 1874-54	Music	250	750	1,500	500	Tonal Experimentation
Ivey, Judith	Ent	15			35	
Ivogun, Maria	Music	45			175	Opera
Izak, Edouard	Military	20	45			

Ice T

Marty Ingels

Billy Idol

Amy Irving

Jeremy Irons

Name	Field	SIG	DS	ALS	SP	Remarks
Jabotinsky, Vladimir	Political	45	120	310	60	Zionist Leader WW I
Jack, Thomas M. 1831-80	Civil War	45				CSA Colonel
Jackson, Alan	Music	20			50	Country
Jackson, Alfred Eugene	Civil War	Scarce	Scarce	950	Scarce	CSA General
Jackson, Andrew	President	550	1,200	2,500		1767-1845
Jackson, Andrew	President	750	1,550	3,900		As President
Jackson, Anne	Ent	5			15	
Jackson, Charles T.	Science	200				Co-Discoverer of Ether
Jackson, Clairborne F.	Civil War		175	200		CSA General
Jackson, Eugene P.	Ent	10			20	Our Gang
Jackson, Glenda	Ent	15			35	AA Winner
Jackson, Gordon	Ent	15		50	55	Upstairs, Downstairs
Jackson, Helen Hunt	Author	15	35	50	25	Am.Novelist, Poet. Ramona
Jackson, Henry R.	Civil War	90	195	300		CSA General/1820-98
Jackson, Howell E.	SuprCt	50			110	
Jackson, James S.	Civil War	200	Scarce	Scarce	Scarce	Union General/KIA
Jackson, James S. (WD)	Civil War	RARE	RARE	RARE	RARE	Union General/KIA/1823-62
Jackson, James, Dr.	Science	10	100		25	1st Am. to Perform Vaccinations
Jackson, Janet	Music	35	100		75	
Jackson, Jesse	Political	15		45	35	
Jackson, Joe	Music	20			45	
Jackson, Joe	Sports	20,000	RARE	RARE	RARE	Shoeless Joe" Baseball
Jackson, Kate	Ent	20	45		45	Charlie's Angels
Jackson, LaToya	Ent	20		45	45	
Jackson, Mahalia	Music	75			150	Gospel Singer
Jackson, Maynard	Music	5		20	15	Trumpet
Jackson, Michael	Music	125	450	Scarce	250	
Jackson, Rachel	First Lady	575	Scarce	Scarce	Scarce	
Jackson, Reggie	Sports	20			40	Baseball
Jackson, Robert H.	SuprCt	50	295		125	Chief Prosec/Nuremberg
Jackson, Samuel L.	Ent	20			50	
Jackson, Samuel M.	Civil War	Scarce	Scarce	600	Scarce	Union General
Jackson, Sherry	Ent	10			20	
Jackson, Stonewall	Civil War	4,000	10,000	20,000	RARE	CSA General/1824-1863
Jackson, Stonewall	Civil War	5,500	12,000	24,000	RARE	CSA General/War Dated
Jackson, Victoria	Ent	10			25	Sat Night Live
Jackson, Wanda	Music	10			20	
Jackson, William 1759-28	RevWar	120	350	750		Gen. Washington Aide
Jackson, William Henry	Art	40	110			Photographer/1843-1944
Jackson, Wm. Hicks	Civil War	90	185	240		CSA General/1835-1903
Jacob, Francois	Science	20	30	55	30	Nobel Medicine 1965
Jacob, Irene	Ent	15			25	
Jacobi, Derek	Ent	5			15	

Name	Field	SIG	DS	ALS	SP	Remarks
Jacobs, Josef	Aviation	30	40	80	55	
Jacobs, Lou	Ent	50	100		100	Clown
Jacobs, William W.	Author	10		50		Br. Monkey's Paw
Jacobsen, Fritz	Aviation	10	20	35	40	Ace WW I
Jacquet, Illinois Jean	Music	35			75	Jazz Sax, Bandleader
Jadlowker, Hermann	Music	100			250	Opera
Jaeckel, Richard	Ent	10			20	
Jaeger, James A.	Aviation	10		30		
Jaehnert, Erhard	Aviation	5		20	15	
Jaffe, Sam 1893-1984	Ent	25			45	Gunga Din
Jagger, Bianca	Music	10			25	
Jagger, Dean	Ent	15	25		35	1903 - 1991/AA Winner
Jagger, Mick	Music	60	Scarce	Scarce	125	
Jakes, John	Author	15	50	75	50	Holiday for Havoc
James I & VI (Eng)	Royalty	800	1,200	RARE	RARE	
James II (Eng) 1633-1701	Royalty	530	1,200	1,700		
James, Daniel, Jr.	Military	20	35	85	45	1st Black 4 Star General.
James, Etta	Music	20			40	Rock
James, Frank 1844-1915	Western	975	1,600	2,750		
James, Harry	Music	20			40	55	Big Band Leader-Trumpet
James, Henry 1811-82	Author	75		200		
James, Henry 1843-1916	Author	110	360	675		
James, Manley	Military	10		45		WW I Victoria Cross
James, P.D.	Author	20	65			Br. Mystery Author
James, Rick	Music	20			40	
James, Sheila	Ent	10			20	
James, Sonny	Music	15			30	
James, Will	Author	75	250	400	600	Illustrated Western Novels
James, William 1842-10	Science	90	350	495	125	Psychologist
Jameson, House	Ent	10			20	
Jan & Dean	Music	20			45	
Janes Addiction	Music	25			50	Signed by all
Janis, Conrad	Ent	5			15	Mork and Mindy
Janis, Elsie	Ent	25	50		50	
Janney, Leon	Ent	35			75	Our Gang
Janowitz, Gundula	Music	25			50	Opera
Jansen, Marie	Music	15			40	Opera
Janssen, David	Ent	80	100		150	TV's "The Fugitive
Janssen, Famke	Ent	20			45	James Bond babe
January, Lois	Ent	5			15	
Jardine, William	Political	10	25	55	20	Sec'y Agriculture 1925
Jarman, Claude, Jr.	Ent	10			35	
Jarman, Maxie	Business	15			45	Jarman Shoes
Jaroff, Serge	Ent	15			35	Jaroff Ballet
Jarreau, Al	Music	20			40	
Jarrett, Art	Music	15			30	Bandleader
Jarriel, Tom	Ent	5			10	TV News
Jarvik, Robert, Dr.	Science	15	35	60	35	Inventor Artificial Heart
Jarvis, Anna M.	Political	65	175			Mothers Day Sponsor

Name	Field	SIG	DS	ALS	SP	Remarks
Jarvis, Gregory B.	Space	100			275	Astronaut
Jarvis, Howard	Political	5		30	15	Sponsor Proposition 13
Jason, Rick	Ent	5			15	
Jason, Sybil	Ent	5		15	15	
Jawlensky, Aleksey von	Art	Scarce	Scarce	600	Scarce	Russian Painter
Jaworski, Leon	Political	10	20	45	15	Dir. Watergate Prosecution Force
Jay, James, Sir 1732-15	Science	100	275	400		Phys. to G. Washington
Jay, John 1745-1829	SuprCt	550	1,750	2,250		
Jay, John (Grandson)	Political	15	25	40		Opposed Slavery
Jean, Gloria	Ent	5		20		
Jean, Norma	Music	10			20	
Jeans, James, Sir	Science	10	30	65	20	Br. Physicist
Jedlichka, Ernest	Music	50			200	Rus-Pol Pianist
Jeffers, Robinson 1887-62	Author	65	350	450	90	Prize Winning Poet
Jeffers, William M.	Business	25	70	135	50	Union Pacific RR
Jefferson Airplane	Ent	100			300	Signed by Entire Band
Jefferson, Joe 1829-1905	Ent	30	70	125	65	
Jefferson, Martha W.	First Lady	RARE	RARE	RARE	RARE	
Jefferson, Thomas	Ent	45			125	Silent Film Star
Jefferson, Thomas	President	2,500	3,500	7,500		1743-1826
Jefferson, Thomas	President	3,500	4,500	12,000		As President
Jeffreys, Anne	Ent	10		15	25	
Jellicoe, John R.	Military	20	65	120	50	WWI Br Admiral
Jenckes, Joseph	Political	90	250			Colonial Governor RI
Jeni, Richard	Ent	10			25	Comedian
Jenkins, Allen	Ent	25			45	
Jenkins, Butch	Ent	10			25	
Jenkins, Thornton Alex.	Military	10	25	35		Chief-of Staff Farragut Squad.
Jenner, Bruce	Sports	10			25	Olympic Star
Jenner, Edward, Dr.	Science	450	850	Scarce	Scarce	Smallpox Vaccination
Jenner, William, Sir	Science	35	110	295		Phys. to Queen Victoria
Jennings, Emil	Ent	200			350	lst Academy Award Winner
Jennings, Peter	Ent	5	15	25	15	TV News Anchorman
Jennings, Waylon	Music	10	20		20	
Jennison, Ralph D.	Business	10	35	45	20	
Jensen, Karen	Ent	5			10	
Jensen, Maren	Ent	10			25	
Jepson, Helen	Music	15			40	Opera
Jeritza, Maria 1887-1984	Music	30			90	Opera
Jernstedt, Ken	Aviation	10	25	40	30	WWII Flying Tigers ACE
Jerome, Jerome K.	Author	35	70	95		Humorist, Playwright
Jerusalem, Siegfried	Music	15			45	Opera
Jessel, George	Ent	30	80		90	1898 - 1981
Jesup, Thomas S.	Military	45	125	190		General/1788-1860
Jesup, William H.	Military	5	15	25		
Jeter, Michael	Ent	10			25	Evening Shade
Jethro Tull	Music	30			75	By Entire Band
Jett, Joan	Music	20			45	and the Blackhearts
Jewel	Music	20			50	

Name	Field	SIG	DS	ALS	SP	Remarks
Jewell, Marshall	Political	40	75	195		Governor/Cabinet Member
Jewett, Sarah Orne	Author	45	200	300		1849-1909
Jewison, Norman	Ent	10			20	Director
Jillian, Ann	Ent	10			25	
Jimenez, Enrique A.	Political	10		25	20	Panama
Jimenez, Marcos P.	Political	10	25	50	20	Venezuela
Joachim, Joseph 1831-07	Music	95	150	337	220	Violinist/Composer
Jodl, Alfred	Military	150	500	550	250	Chief-of-Staff To Keitel
Joel, Billy	Music	25			55	
Joffre, Joseph Jacques C.	Military	75	155	250	225	Marshal of France WW I
Johann, Zita	Ent	25			50	The Mummy
John II (King Castile)	Royalty	RARE	RARE	RARE	RARE	Patron of Literature &Arts
John of Austria	Royalty	150				1629-1679
John XXIII, Pope	Clergy	500			650	Angelo Giuseppe Roncalli
John, Augustus	Art	50	135	330		Welch. Portraits, Landscapes
John, Elton	Music	30	100		60	
Johns, Glynis	Ent	15		30	30	
Johns, Jasper	Art	20	60		30	Am. Pop Artist
Johnson, Amy (Mollison)	Aviation	75	85	135	200	Br, Aviation Pioneer
Johnson, Andrew	President	400	1,200	Scarce	2,500	1808-1875
Johnson, Andrew	President	600	1,500	Scarce	Scarce	As President
Johnson, Art	Aviation	10	20	40	30	USAF WWII ACE
Johnson, Arte	Ent	5			15	Laugh In
Johnson, Ben	Ent	30	75		60	Western star
Johnson, Ben 1572-1637	Author	450	1,500			Br. Poet, Playwright
Johnson, Betty	Ent	5			10	
Johnson, Brad	Ent	10			20	
Johnson, Bradley T.	Civil War	90	370	272		CSA General/1829-1903
Johnson, Bradley T.(WD)	Civil War	300	1,425	970		CSA General
Johnson, Bunk	Music	200			550	Jazz Trumpet
Johnson, Bushrod Rust	Civil War	115	300			CSA General/1817-1880
Johnson, Cave 1793-1866	Political	50	110	195		PM General
Johnson, Chic	Ent	45			75	(Olsen & Johnson)
Johnson, Crockett	Cartoonist	50			150	Barnaby
Johnson, Don	Ent	20			50	Miami Vice
Johnson, Eastman	Art	75		185	300	Am. Portrait & Genre Artist
Johnson, Edward	Music				75	Canadian Tenor
Johnson, Eliza M.	First Lady	750	1,500			
Johnson, Ervin	Sports	25			65	Magic"/Basketball
Johnson, Fred	Cartoonist	15			35	Moon Mullins
Johnson, Gerald	Aviation	15	30	50	40	WWII ACE
Johnson, Gorgean	Ent	10			20	
Johnson, H. Hank	Business	5			15	Pres. Spiegel
Johnson, Harold K.	Military	15	35	50	30	WWII Four Star General
Johnson, Henry A.	Business	5			15	CEO Spiegel Inc.
Johnson, Herschel	Civil War	40	110			Gov. GA, CSA Senator
Johnson, Hiram W.	Political	25	60			Senator CA/1866-1945
Johnson, Howard S.	Business	15	30		35	
Johnson, Hugh S.	Political	15	90	150	25	

Name	Field	SIG	DS	ALS	SP	Remarks
Johnson, Jack	Sports	600			1,500	Boxer
Johnson, James Johnnie	Aviation	30	65	120	95	WWII Br RAF Top ACE
Johnson, James K.	Aviation	10	25	38	32	ACE, Korea, Double Ace
Johnson, James Weldon	Author	30	100	225		
Johnson, Jesse G.	Military	35	85	170		WWII Admiral
Johnson, John H.	Business		50		65	Ebony/Jet...
Johnson, Jonathan E.	Art	25	150			Am. Portrait Painter
Johnson, June	Ent	10			20	
Johnson, Lady Bird	First Lady	40	100		95	
Johnson, Leon W.	Military	10	20	35		
Johnson, Lyndon B.	President	300	900	RARE	650	As President
Johnson, Lyndon B.	President	200	450	RARE	500	1908-1973
Johnson, Lynn	Cartoonist	10			25	For Better Or Worse
Johnson, Lynn-Holly	Ent	10			25	
Johnson, Martin 1884-37	Art	15	40			Wildlife Photographer
Johnson, Nunnally	Author	20	60		40	Am Playwright
Johnson, Osa	Explorer	15		35	30	Wild Animal Films
Johnson, Philip	Science	25			125	Early Skyscrapers
Johnson, Reverdy	Political	25	95	95		Statesman, Att'y Gen
Johnson, Richard L.	Aviation	15	20	30	20	
Johnson, Richard M.	Vice Pres	100	200	350	400	Van Buren Vice Pres.
Johnson, Robert S.	Aviation	25		45	80	ACE, WWII #5 US
Johnson, Russ	Ent	5			10	
Johnson, Samuel C.	Business	5			10	Pres. Johnson's Wax
Johnson, Samuel, Dr.	Author	1,750	Scarce	Scarce	Scarce	Lexicographer, Critic
Johnson, Van	Ent	15	35		35	
Johnson, William B.	Business	5			10	CEO Railway Express
Johnson, William Cost	Political	10	20	35		MOC MD 1833
Johnson, William Sam'l	RevWar	130	375	675		Continental Congress
Johnston, Albert Sidney	Civil War	290	1,500	2,000		CSA General/1803-1862
Johnston, Frances	Art	10	25			Photographer/1864-1952
Johnston, George D.	Civil War	95	250	300		CSA General/1832-1910
Johnston, Harriet Lane	First Lady	200		600		Buchanan's Niece
Johnston, J. Lawson	Business	15	35	60		
Johnston, Johnny	Aviation	20	45		55	
Johnston, Joseph E.	Civil War	300	600	750	1,600	CSA General/1807-91
Johnston, Joseph E. (WD)	Civil War	450	900	1,500	Scarce	CSA General
Johnston, Richard M.	Author	5	10	20		
Jolie, Angelina	Ent	20			50	
Joliot-Curie, Frederic	Science			500		Fr. Chem.Nobel '35.
Joliot-Curie, Irene	Science	50		200		1897-1956
Jolson, Al 1886-1950	Ent	150	250		275	Star of 1st Talkie Film
Jones, Allan 1908 - 1992	Music	15		35	30	Film & Concert Singer
Jones, Anne	Music	10			20	
Jones, Annisa	Ent	200			350	Buffy on "Family Affair"
Jones, Anson	Political	350		1,200		President of Texas Republic
Jones, Anthony A.	Music	10			20	
Jones, Barry	Ent	20			40	Br. Actor
Jones, Buck 1889-1942	Ent	175	250	Scarce	350	Vintage Film Cowboy

Name	Field	SIG	DS	ALS	SP	Remarks
Jones, Carolyn	Ent	100	200		300	TV Addams Family/Morticia
Jones, Casey	Aviation	45	90	175	150	
Jones, Catherine-Zeta	Ent	25			50	
Jones, Chuck	Cartoonist	35			75	Warner Bros. Animator
Jones, Claude A.	Military	40	65			
Jones, David (Davy)	Music	20			45	The Monkees
Jones, David R. (WD)	Civil War	370	RARE	RARE	RARE	CSA General
Jones, David R. 1825-63	Civil War	300	800	RARE	RARE	CSA General
Jones, Dean	Ent	10		20	20	
Jones, Dick	Ent	10			35	
Jones, Edward F.	Civil War	50	110	155	150	Union Officer
Jones, George	Music	10			25	
Jones, Gordon	Ent	10			20	
Jones, Grace	Ent	20			40	
Jones, Grandpa	Music	25			45	Country
Jones, Gwyneth	Music	15			40	Opera
Jones, Henry	Ent	5			15	
Jones, Howard	Ent	10			20	
Jones, Isham	Music	15			40	Vintage Big Band
Jones, J. Carey	Military	20	45			Admiral WWII
Jones, Jack	Ent	10			25	
Jones, James	Author	50	150			From Here to Eternity
Jones, James Earl	ENt	10			30	Voice of Darth Vader/CNN
Jones, Janet	Ent	10		30	30	
Jones, Jeffrey	Ent	20			40	
Jones, Jennifer	Ent	125	175		250	AA Winner
Jones, Jenny	Ent	10			20	Talk Show Host
Jones, Jim	Clergy	250	375	650	850	
Jones, John Marshall	Civil War	225	650			CSA General/1821-64
Jones, John Paul	RevWar	8,000	25,000	65,000	RARE	Naval Hero
Jones, Louis R.	Military	10	30			
Jones, Mary H. 'Mother'	Political	75	150	300		Labor Organizer
Jones, Quincy	Music	15		35	30	Composer
Jones, Rickie Lee	Music	20			45	
Jones, Robert T.	Sports	1,250			2,500	Bobby" Legendary Golfer
Jones, Samuel (WD)	Civil War	180	580	765		CSA General
Jones, Samuel 1819-87	Civil War	95	300			CSA General
Jones, Shirley	Ent	10	25		25	Partridge Family
Jones, Spike 1911 - 1965	Music	25			65	Big Band Leader
Jones, Thomas V.	Business	15	30		25	
Jones, Tom	Music	10			20	
Jones, Tommy Lee	Ent	25	75		50	
Jones, William E. (WD)	Civil War	275	Scarce	Scarce	Scarce	CSA General/KIA
Jones, William E.1824-64	Civil War	140	250	600		CSA General/KIA
Jong, Erica	Author	10		20	15	Fear of Flying Novel
Jongkind, Johan	Art	200	450	750		1819-1891
Jope, Bernhard	Aviation	15	25	45	30	
Joplin, Janis 1943-70	Music	750	1,500	2,500	1,750	
Joplin, Scott	Music	750	1,200	2,000		Rag Time Composer

Name	Field	SIG	DS	ALS	SP	Remarks
Jordan, Dorothy	Ent	15		35	30	
Jordan, Hamilton	Political	5	15	20	15	Chief of Staff Carter Admin.
Jordan, Jim (Fibber)	Ent	15	20	35	25	
Jordan, Louis	Music	25			65	Big Band Leader
Jordan, Michael	Sports	35			90	Basketball
Jordan, Thomas (WD)	Civil War	135	380	900		CSA General
Jordan, Thomas 1819-95	Civil War	80	255	350		CSA General
Jordanaires, The	Music	30			75	All Four
Jordon, Richard	Ent	15		25	30	
Jorn, Carl	Music	30			85	Opera
Jory, Victor 1902-82	Ent	45	65		100	
Jose, Richard J.	Music	10			15	
Joseffy, Raphael	Music	25			125	Pianist, Pupil of Llszt
Joseph II 1741-1790	Royalty	125	350	875		German King
Josephine, Empress	Royalty	750	1,500	2,500		Fr. Wife of Napoleon
Joslyn, Allyn	Ent	25			55	
Joswig, Wilhelm	Aviation	10			30	
Jouett, James	Civil War	25	55	125		Union Naval Officer
Jouhaux, Benjamin	Political	25	60	140	50	Nobel Peace Prize 1951
Jourdan, Jean B., Count	Military	55	260	290		Marshal of Napoleon
Jourdan, Louis	Ent	15			25	1919 - 1993
Journey	Music	45			85	By Entire Band
Jovavich, Milla	Ent	25			50	Fifth Element
Joy, Leatrice	Ent	15			30	
Joyce, Alice 1890-1955	Ent	15	25		60	Silent Star
Joyce, Elaine	Ent	5			15	
Joyce, James 1882-1941	Author	400	590	2,500	RARE	Ir. Novelist/Poet/Playwright
Joyce, Richard	Military	40	100	175		
Juan Carlos, King	Royalty	55	120	245	150	Spain
Juarez, Benito 1806-1872	Political	425	1,200	1,500	1,500	Pres. Mexico
Judas Preist	Music	35			75	Signed by all
Judd, Ashley	Ent	20			45	
Judd, Naomi & Wynona	Music	35			65	
Judd, Wynonna	Music	20			50	
Judge, Arline	Ent	15		35	30	
Julia, Raul	Ent	35			75	Addams Family Gomez
Julian, George W.	Political	15	30	75		Co-Founder Free Soil Party, Repr. IN
Juliana, Queen	Royalty	100	250	710	150	Netherlands
Jump, Gordon	Ent	10			20	WKRP in Cincinatti
Jung, Carl Gustav	Science	600	1,500	3,500		Swiss Psychiatrist
Junkers, Hugo	Science	50		300		Ger. Airplane Designer
Junot, Andache, Duc A.	Military	70	235			Fr. Gen., Sec'y to Napoleon
Junot, Jean Androche	Military	30	90	185		French Revolution
Jurgens, Curt	Ent	15			40	
Jurgens, Dick	Music	20			45	Big Band Leader
Jusserand, Jean Jules	Author	20		45		Pulitzer Prize/1855-32
Justice, Bill	Cartoonist	35			75	The Chipmunks
Justice, Dave	Sports	15			45	Baseball

Name	Field	SIG	DS	ALS	SP	Remarks
Kabaiwanska, Raina	Music	15			35	Opera
Kabalevsky, Dmitri	Music	75	300	250		Composer
Kabasta, Oswald	Music	125				Conductor/Suicide
Kadar, Janos	Political	50	125			
Kaelin, Kato	Ent	35		75	55	Houseguest 0 J. Simpson
Kafka, Franz	Author	1,000	RARE	RARE	RARE	German Novelist
Kahn, Madeline	Ent	10	20		25	
Kahn, Otto H. 1867-1934	Business	30		100	60	Banker, Patron of the Arts
Kahn, Yahya	Political	30			50	Pakistan
Kahoutek, Lubos	Science	5		30	15	Am. Astronomer
Kaiser, Henry J.	Business	200	900		375	
Kai-Shek, Chiang	Political	100	220	450	700	Republic of China
Kai-Shek, Mayling S.	Author	50	120		100	Madame Chiang
Kalakaua, David 1836-91	Royalty	100	425	850	1,500	King Hawaii
Kallen, Kitty	Music		20		25	Big Band Vocalist
Kaltenborn, H. V.	Ent	5	15	30	15	Radio Commentator
Kaltenbrunner, Ernst	Military	150	500		175	Guilty of Nazi Atrocities
Kamburg, Arthur, Dr.	Science	10	20			Nobel
Kamehameha IV 1824-63	Royalty		2,500			King of Hawaii
Kamehameha, Liholiho	Royalty	1,000	RARE	RARE	RARE	King Hawaii/1797-1824
KamehamehaI, K.	Royalty	750	1,500			King Hawaii
Kamen, Milt	Ent	15			35	
Kaminsky, Max	Music	10			30	Dixieland Jazz Bandleader
Kamio, Mitsuomi	Military	110		225		
Kammhuber, Josef	Aviation	20	30	65	35	Ger. Air Defense Gen. WW 11. RK
Kanaly, Steve	Ent	10			20	
Kander, John	Music	5	20	35	10	Composer
Kandinski, Vasili 1866-44	Art	200	500			Russian Painter
Kane, Bob	Cartoonist	75			150	Batman Creator
Kane, Carol	Ent	10		20	25	Taxi
Kane, Elisha Kent	Explorer	95	200	450		Grinnell Arctic Expedition
Kane, Helen 1904-1966	Ent	35			75	Boop Boop a Doop Girl
Kane, Richard	Military	25			75	
Kane, Thomas L.	Civil War	50	100			Union General/1822-83
Kanin, Garson	Author	25			45	
Kansas	Music	30			60	Signed by Entire Group
Kant, Immanuel 1724-04	Author	1,000				German Philosopher
Kantor, MacKinlay	Author	15			25	Pulitzer
Kaper, Bronislaw	Music	10			15	Composer
Kaplan, Gabe	Ent	20			50	Welcome Back Kotter
Kaplan, Gilbert	Music	5			15	Conductor
Kaplioani 1834-1899	Royalty	Scarce	Scarce	Scarce	1,200	Queen of Hawaii
Karas, Alex	Ent	5			15	

Name	Field	SIG	DS	ALS	SP	Remarks
Karas, Anton	Music	25			100	Composer
Karloff, Boris 1887-1969	Ent	275	450	750	550	Frankenstein
Karman, Theodore von	Business	25			50	Designed Karman Ghia
Karns, Roscoe	Ent	35			75	
Karpis, Alvin	Criminal	75			100	Public Enemy Number One
Karsavina, Tamara	Ent	100			300	Russian Dancer
Karsh, Yousuf	Art	35			75	Photographer
Kasavubu, Joseph	Political	20			45	Rep of Congo
Kaschmann, Guiseppe	Music	75			300	Baritone
Kasem, Casey	Ent	15			25	Radio/Voice of Shaggy
Kasem, Jean	Ent	10			25	
Kasha, Al	Music	15			45	Composer
Kashfi, Anna	Ent	10			35	
Kassell, Art	Music	20			50	Bandleader
Kastler, Alfred	Science	15			45	Nobel
Kasznar, Kurt	Ent	25			50	Land of the Giants
Katchinsky, Victorin	Aviation	20			45	
Katt, William	Ent	10			25	
Katz, Bernard	Science	15			35	Nobel/Medicine
Katzenberg, Jeffrey	Business	15	45		35	Dreamworks Executive
Katzir, Ephraim	Political	10			45	Pres of Israel
Kaufman, Andy	Ent	75	150		200	Taxi/Died young
Kaufman, George S.	Author	35			55	1889 - 1961
Kaunda, Kenneth	Political	40			70	First Pres. of Zambia
Kavner, Julie	Ent	20			45	Voice of Marge Simpson
Kawato, Masajiro	Aviation	50			150	WWII Ace/Shot Boyington
Kay, Beatrice	Ent	10			25	
Kay, Diane	Ent	5			15	
Kay, Herbie	Music	10			30	Bandleader
Kay, Mary	Business	5			15	Cosmetics Empire
Kaye, Danny	Ent	65	100		100	1913 - 1987
Kaye, Sammy	Music	15			45	Big Band Leader
Kaye, Stubby	Ent	10			25	
Kazan, Elia	Ent	15	45		35	Director/Producer
Keach, Stacey	Ent	10			20	
Keane, Bill	Cartoonist	10			25	The Family Circus
Keane, Edward	Ent	10			25	
Keane, Jane	Ent	5			15	
Kearny, Philip	Civil War	350	650	850		Union General/KIA
Kearny, Stephen	Military	85	225	350		War of 1812/First Gov. CA.
Keaton, Buster	Ent	250	400	Scarce	675	1895 - 1966
Keaton, Diane	Ent	20	50		50	
Keaton, Michael	Ent	20			50	Batman in Movies
Kedrova, Lila	Ent	10			40	
Keel, Howard	Ent	5			15	
Keeler, Ruby	Ent	35			55	
Keene, Carolyn	Author	50		100	100	Nancy Drew Mysteries
Keene, Charles	Ent	10			25	
Keene, Tom	Ent	25			50	

Name	Field	SIG	DS	ALS	SP	Remarks
Keeshan, Bob	Ent	10			25	Capt. Kangaroo
Keitel, Harvey	Ent	20			50	
Keitel, Wilhelm (d.1946)	Military	350	575		650	WWII Ger. Field Marshal
Keith, Brian	Ent	25	55		55	Family Affair
Keith, David	Ent	10			20	
Keith, David	Ent	15			30	
Keith, George Keith	Military	45	135	155		British Admiral 1746-1823
Keith, Ian	Ent	15				
Keith, William	RevWar	135		700		Colonial Lt. Gov of PA/DE
Kelland, Clarence B.	Author	20			30	Am. Novelist
Kellar, Harry	Ent	Scarce	Scarce		250 Scarce	Magician
Kellard, Ralph	Ent	10			25	
Kellaway, Cecil	Ent	25			75	
Keller, Helen 1880-1968	Author	200	400	Scarce	875	Blind, Deaf, Mute
Kellerman, Annette	Ent	45			175	Dancer and Swimming Star
Kellerman, Sally	Ent	10			25	
Kelley, Deforest	Ent	35			75	Star Trek
Kelley, Kitty	Author	10			20	Celebrity Biographer
Kellogg, Charlotte	Business	5			15	Mrs. Vernon Kellogg
Kellogg, Frank 1856-1937	Political	35			35	Nobel Peace Prize
Kellogg, John Harvey	Business	25	150			Cereal/Health Reformer
Kellogg, Ray	Ent	5			15	
Kellogg, W.K.	Business	125	250	400	250	Founder WK Kellogg Co.
Kelly, Brian	Ent	10			25	
Kelly, Emmett Sr.	Ent	65	150		275	Famous Clown
Kelly, Gene	Ent	25	100	150	65	AA Winner/1912-1996
Kelly, Grace 1928-1982	Ent	250		750	525	Signed "Grace Kelly"
Kelly, Jack	Ent	15			45	
Kelly, John 1840-64	Civil War	475	Scarce	Scarce	Scarce	CSA Gen./Youngest Killed
Kelly, Moira	Ent	20			50	
Kelly, Nancy	Ent	10			25	
Kelly, Patsy	Ent	30			60	
Kelly, Paul	Ent	25			50	
Kelly, Paula	Ent	5			15	
Kelly, Sheila	Ent	10			25	
Kelly, Thomas	Military	10			15	Gen. During Desert Storm
Kelly, Walt	Cartoonist	75	175			Pogo
Kelsey, Linda	Ent	5			15	
Kelton, Pert	Ent	15			45	
Kelvin, William T.	Science	100			175	Kelvin Scale
Kemble, Edward W.	Art	50			175	Am. Illustrator (1861-1933)
Kemmer, Ed	Ent	10			20	
Kemp, Hal	Music	15			45	Big Band Leader
Kemper, James L.	Civil War	200				CSA General/1823-95
Kendall, Cy	Ent	25			50	
Kendall, Edward	Science	30			35	Nobel Medicine 1950
Kendall, Henry	Science	20			30	Nobel Physics 1990
Kendren, John	Science	15			20	
Keneally, Thomas	Author	10			20	Schindlers List

Name	Field	SIG	DS	ALS	SP	Remarks
Kennedy, Adam	Ent	10			20	
Kennedy, Anthony	SuprCt	30			50	
Kennedy, Arthur	Ent	35			75	1914 - 1990
Kennedy, Caroline	Political	25		75		JFK's Daughter
Kennedy, Douglas	Music	5			15	AKA Keith Douglas
Kennedy, Edgar	ENt	125			250	
Kennedy, Edward (Ted)	Political	15	25		25	
Kennedy, Ethel	Political	15	45		35	Mrs. Robert Kennedy
Kennedy, George	Ent	15			45	AA Winner
Kennedy, George C.	Aviation	40			200	
Kennedy, Jacqueline	First Lady	400	1,200	1,500	900	Value Higher if As 1st Lady
Kennedy, Jayne	Ent	5			15	
Kennedy, John F.	President	1,150	1,700	4,500	2,500	1917-1963
Kennedy, John F. Jr.	Political	25			50	Publisher of "George"
Kennedy, Joseph P.	Political	75			150	Kennedy Family Father
Kennedy, Madge	Ent	15			30	
Kennedy, Robert F.	Political	200	800		675	
Kennedy, Rose F.	Political	100	150		100	Kennedy Family Mother
Kennedy, Tom	Ent	50			100	
Kenney, George	Military	25			50	WWII General USAF
Kenny G.	Music	20			45	
Kenny, Bill	Music	25			50	Ink Spots Lead Singer
Kenny, Elizabeth	Science	175			275	Polio Treatments
Kenny, Nick	Music	20			40	Ink Spots Singer
Kensit, Patsy	Ent	20			50	
Kent, Atwater	Business	50	175	Scarce	Scarce	Radio Manafacturer
Kent, Edward Augustus	Royalty	50				Son of George III
Kent, Ford J.	Military	100				Gen. Took San Juan Hill
Kent, Jack	Cartoonist	10			30	King Aroo
Kent, James	RevWar	100		250		
Kent, Rockwell	Art	40			75	1882-1971
Kent, Walter	Music	40			65	Composer
Kenton, Simon	Western	400				Spy/General/Trapper
Kenton, Stan	Music	35			100	Big Band Leader
Kenyatta, Jomo	Political	125			150	PM of Kenya
Kenyon, Doris	Ent	15			45	
Kepford, Ira	Aviation	15			45	WWII Ace
Kepner, William	Military	15			25	
Kerbs, Edwin	Science	20			40	Nobel Medicine
Kercheval, Ken	Ent	10			20	
Kercheval, Ralph	Sports	15			45	Football
Kerensky, Alexander	Political	200			450	Russ.Politican
Kern, Jerome	Music	250	650	Scarce	2,000	Composer. (1885-1945)
Kerns, Joanna	Ent	10			30	Growing Pains
Keroauc, Jack	Author	400	1,500	RARE	RARE	Beat Generation Poet
Kerr, Deborah	Ent	10			30	
Kerr, Ruth	Business	25			75	Kerr Glass Co.
Kerrigan, Nancy	Sports	15			45	Olympic Figure Skater
Kerrigan, Warren	Ent	25			60	

Name	Field	SIG	DS	ALS	SP	Remarks
Kershaw, Joseph B.	Civil War	200		900		CSA General/1822-94
Kesey, Ken	Author	20	40		50	One Flew Over the Cukoo's Nest
Kesselring, Albrecht	Military	100			175	WWII Ger Field Marshal
Kestnbaum, Meyer	Business	20	30		25	
Ketcham, Hank	Cartoonist	25	75		75	Dennis the Menace
Ketcham, John H.	Civil War	65				Union General/1832-1906
Ketcham, John H. (WD)	Civil War	150		300		Union General
Ketelby, Albert W.	Music	15		75		Composer
Kettering, Charles F.	Science	100	160	325	125	
Kevorkian, Jack, Dr.	Science	25			75	Dr. assists in suicides
Key, David M. 1824-1900	Civil War	30	45	90		P.M. General. CSA Officer
Key, Francis Scott	Author	450	650	950		1779-1843
Key, Ted	Cartoonist	20		60	60	Hazel
Keyes, Erasmus D.	Civil War	50	120	300		Union General/1810-95
Keyes, Erasmus. D. (WD)	Civil War	70	250	400		Union General
Keyes, Evelyn	Ent	15		45	35	GWTW star
Keyes, Roger J.B.	Military	15	30	55	25	Boxer Rebellion
Keynes, John Maynard	Science	75		585	230	Br. Economist
Keys, Ancel	Science	5		25	15	
Khachaturian, Aram	Music	150		675	650	Composer
Khalid, King	Royalty	20	65	135	60	Saudi Arabia
Khambatta, Persis	Ent	25			60	Star Trek:Motion Picture
Khan, Chaka	Music	25			50	
Khan, Mohammad Ayub	Political	30	95			
Khanh, Nguyen, Gen.	Political	20	60	175	35	
Khomeini, Ruhollah	Political	500	RARE	RARE	RARE	Iranian Moslem Leader
Khorana, Har G., Dr.	Science	15	25	45	20	Nobel Medicine 1968
Khruschchev, Nikita	Political	300	400	550	1,200	Premier Soviet Union
Kiam, Victor	Business	10	25		15	Remington Razor Co.
Kibbee, Guy	Ent	20			40	
Kidder, Margot	Ent	20			40	Movie "Lois Lane"
Kidman, Nicole	Ent	35			65	
Kiel, Richard	Ent	10	25		25	Jaws" in Bond films
Kielmansegg, Graf J.A.	Military	15			35	Gen. German Army
Kienzl, Wilhelm 1857-41	Music	15		50		Composer
Kiepura, Jan	Music	45			125	Opera
Kilban, B.	Cartoonist	10	25		100	New Yorker Cartoonist
Kilbride, Percy 1888 - 64	Ent	175			350	Ma and Pa Kettle films
Kilby, J. S. Jack	Science	15	35	60	30	Inventor of Micro Chip
Kiley, Richard	Ent	10		15	25	
Kilgallen, Dorothy	Ent	15			25	
Kilgore, Merle	Music	10			20	
Kilian, Victor	Ent	10		20	25	
Kilmer, Joanne Whalley	Ent	20			40	
Kilmer, Joyce	Author	200	550			Poet
Kilmer, Val	Ent	25			50	Batman
Kilpatrick, Hugh J.	Civil War	120	225	400	415	Union General/1836-1881
Kilpatrick, Hugh J. (WD)	Civil War	195	500	600		Union General
Kimball, J. Golden	Political	25	150			Pioneer Mormon Leader

Name	Field	SIG	DS	ALS	SP	Remarks
Kimball, John W.	Civil War	45		200		Union Officer
Kimball, Spencer W.	Political	25		35	30	Morman Leader
Kimball, Ward	Cartoonist	30	75		75	Disney Cartoonist
Kimberly, John W.	Political	20	30	90		
Kimberly, R. Lewis	Civil War	25	40	50		Union General
Kimbrough, Charles	Ent	20			40	Murphy Brown
Kimbrough, Emily	Author	10	20	45	15	
Kimmel, Husband E.	Military	400	RARE	RARE	650	US Cmdr at Pearl Harbour
Kindelberger, James H.	Business	45			75	
Kindermann, K. B.	Aviation	5		15	10	
Kindler, Hans	Music	15			45	Conductor
King, Alan	Ent	5		15	15	
King, Andrea	Ent	10			20	
King, B.B.	Music	25	55		55	
King, Ben E.	Music	20			50	Stand by Me
King, Billie Jean	Sports	10			35	Tennis
King, Cammie	Ent	10			30	GWTW Star
King, Carole	Music	15			25	
King, Charles	Author	50		150		During Civil War
King, Coretta Scott	Political	20	75		30	Mrs. Martin Luther King, Jr.
King, Ernest J. 1878-1956	Military	30	100		125	Adm Comdr US Fleet
King, Frank	Cartoonist	35			80	Gasoline Alley
King, Henry	Ent	30			75	Director
King, Horatio 1811-1897	Political	50	175			P.M. General 1861
King, John 'Dusty'	Ent	25	35	45	50	
King, Larry	Ent	10	20	35	15	Talk Show Host
King, MacKenzie	Political	60	55	90	55	Prime Minister Canada
King, Martin Luther, Jr.	Clergy	1,500	2,750	3,500	3,000	Assasinated
King, Martin Luther, Sr.	Clergy	35	45	60	65	
King, Pee Wee	Music	5			15	Bandleader/Composer
King, Perry	Ent	10	20		20	
King, Rufus 1755-1827	RevWar	250	475	450		Continental Congress
King, Rufus 1814-76	Civil War	35	100			Union General
King, Stephen	Author	60	150	400	100	Horror Author
King, Walter Woolf	Music	20			50	Broadway Star
King, Wayne	Music	15			20	Big Band Leader
King, William R.	Vice-Pres	200	340			Pierces VP
King, Wm. L. Mackenzie 1874-1950	Political	40	300			Prime Minster/Canada
Kingman, Dong	Art	25	50	100		
Kingsford-Smith, Charles	Aviation	45	250		200	
Kingsley, Ben	Ent	10		20	35	AA Winner
Kingsley, Charles 1819-75	Author	45	95	160		British Novelist
Kingston, William H.	Author	25		100		
Kinks	Music	40			85	Five current Lineup
Kinnear, Greg	Ent	20			50	As Good as it Gets
Kinsey, Alfred, Dr.	Science	150	225	350	250	1894-1956
Kinskey, Leonid	Ent	10			25	
Kinski, Klaus	Ent	20		35	45	
Kinski, Natassia	Ent	15	45		35	

Name	Field	SIG	DS	ALS	SP	Remarks
Kipling, Rudyard 1865-36	Author	200	550	700	900	Nobel Prize in Literature
Kiplinger, Austin	Business	10	20	45	15	
Kipnis, Alexander	Music	35	75		85	Opera
Kirby, Durwood	Ent	10			20	
Kirby, George	Ent	5			15	
Kirby, Jack	Cartoonist	25			65	Comic Book Artist/Creator
Kirby, Rollin	Cartoonist	25			75	
Kirby-Smith, Edmund	Military	75	150	250		CSA General
Kirk, Florence	Music	10			30	Opera
Kirk, George	Aviation	10		35	30	WWII ACE
Kirk, Norman T.	Military	40				U.S. Gen. WWII
Kirk, Phyllis	Ent	20			45	
Kirk, Tommy	Ent	15	35		25	Child Star
Kirkby-Lunn, Louise	Music	30			95	Opera
Kirkconnell, Clare	Ent	5			10	
Kirkham, Ralph W.	Civil War	30	55	75		Union General/1821-93
Kirkland, Sally	Ent	10			20	
Kirkwood, Joe, Jr.	Ent	45	75	150	100	
Kirsten, Dorothy	Music	20			50	Soprano/Opera
Kiss	Music	55			125	Signed by All Four
Kissinger, Henry A.	Political	35	125		60	Sec'y State
Kistiakowsky, G.B., Dr.	Science	40	135			Nobel Chemistry
Kitchener, Horatio H.	Military	85	200	335	200	Ir.-born Br. Field Marshal
Kitt, Eartha	Ent	10			30	TV's Catwoman
Kittinger, Joe	Aviation	25	45			
Kittredge, Walter	Music	30				Composer
Kleber, Jean-Baptiste	Military	145	400	750		French General
Klee, Paul	Art	205	600	1,500		Swiss Surrealist Painter
Klein, Calvin	Business	10	15	35	25	Fashion Designer
Klein, Robert	Ent	5			15	
Klemperer, Otto	Music	50			170	German Conductor
Klemperer, Werner	Ent	10	25		25	Col. Klink/Hogan's Heroes
Klimt, Gustav 1862-1918	Art	165	575	950		Murals
Kline, Kevin	Ent	20			50	AA Winner
Klose, Margarete	Music	20			65	Opera/1902 - 1968
Kluge, Hans Gunther von	Military	75		250		Ger.Gen.WWII (Suicide)
Klugman, Jack	Ent	10	25		25	Odd Couple
Knern, H.H.	Cartoonist	35			75	Katzenjammer Kids
Knievel, Evel	Ent	10	25	40	45	Daredevil Motorcycle Rider
Knight, Fuzzy	Ent	50			150	
Knight, Gladys	Music	15	45	60	45	
Knight, Jordan	Ent	15			45	
Knight, June	Ent	10		20	25	
Knight, Laura, Dame	Art	60	100	175		British/1877-1970
Knight, Phil	Business	20	35	45	25	Nike Athletic Shoes Etc.
Knight, Shirley	Ent	10	10	20	25	
Knight, Ted	Ent	30	50		60	Mary Tyler Moore Show
Knight, Wayne	Ent	20			45	Seinfeld/Third Rock...
Knopf, Alfred A.	Business	10		35		Knopf Publishing

Name	Field	SIG	DS	ALS	SP	Remarks
Knopfler, Mark	Music	20			40	Dire Straits
Knote, Heinrich	Music	25			50	Opera
Knott, Walter	Business	150			475	Founder Knott's Berry Farm
Knotts, Don	Ent	10	25	30	25	Barney Fife
Knowles, James S.	Author	15	25	45		
Knowles, Patrick	Ent	10			25	
Knox, Alexander	Ent	20		30	35	
Knox, Elyse	Ent	10	20	35	25	
Knox, Frank 1874-1944	Political	50	100	95	100	Sec'y Navy
Knox, Henry 1750-1806	RevWar	150	300	650		
Knudsen, William S.	Business	20	35	85	45	Pres. GM During WWII
Koch, Edward	Political	10	20	35	15	Mayor NYC
Koch, Heinrich H. Robert	Science		1,200	2,200	1,500	Nobel Medicine/1905
Koch, Howard W.	Ent	10			25	
Koch, Robert, Dr. 1843-10	Science			1,367	2,300	Fndr. Modern Bacteriology
Kodaly, Zoltan	Music	125	250	450	450	Composer/1882 - 1967
Koehl, Herman	Aviation	75			250	
Koehler, Armin	Aviation	10	20	35	25	
Koening, Walter	Ent	15	40	45	35	Star Trek
Kohl, Helmut	Political	15	30	65	25	Chancellor Germany
Kohler, Walter J.	Business	10	30			Founder Kohler Corp.
Kohner, Susan	Ent	10			20	
Kokoschka, Oskar	Art	100		350	275	1886-1980
Kolff, Willem J., Dr.	Science	15	55		40	Created Artificial Kidney
Kolker, Henry	Ent	10			20	
Kolleck, Teddy	Political	15	25		35	Mayor of Jerusalem
Kollo, Rene	Music	10		35	25	Opera
Kollwitz, Kathe	Art	75		300		Ger. Sculptor/1867 - 1945
Komarov, Vladimir	Space	125			200	Cosmonaut
Konetzni, Anny	Music	35			65	Opera
Konya, Sandor	Music	15			40	Opera/Tenor
Koontz, Dean	Author	25	65		70	Horror
Koop, C. Everett, Dr.	Military	10	20	50	30	Adm/US Surgeon General
Kopell, Bernie	Ent	5			15	Love Boat Doctor
Koppel, Ted	Ent	10	15	30	20	TV News
Korbut, Olga	Sports	15			45	Olympic Gymnast
Korda, Alexander	Ent	55		90	85	1893 - 1956
Koren, Edward	Cartoonist	25			50	New Yorker Cartoonist
Korman, Harvey	Ent	10	20	20	20	Carol Burnett Show
Kornberg, Arthur	Science	20	30	45	25	Nobel Medicine
Kornby, Arthur	Science	15		20		
Korngold, Erich W.	Music	75	200	350	100	Opera/Composer
Korolyov, Sergei	Science		1,500	2,200		1906 - 1966
Korvin, Charles	Ent	5			10	
Kosciusko, Thaddeus	RevWar	300	750	2,000		Patriot
Kosleck, Martin	Ent	15			35	
Kossa, Frank R.	Military	10			10	
Kossuth, Lajos 1802-94	Political	120	825	475	90	Hungarian Patriot
Kostal, Irwin	Music	5		20	10	Composer

Name	Field	SIG	DS	ALS	SP	Remarks
Kostelanetz, Andre	Music	15	25	45	25	Conductor/1901-1980
Koster, Henry	Ent	15	35		40	Director
Kosygin, Aleksei	Political	275		875	480	Premier of Soviet Union
Kotto, Yaphet	Ent	30			65	James Bond Villain
Koufax, Sandy	Sports	25			65	Baseball
Kovack, Nancy (Mehta)	Ent	5			10	
Kovacs, Ernie	Ent	200	400		400	Scarce
Kovansky, Anatol	Art	15		40	25	
Kove, Martin	Ent	5			15	
Kowarski, L.	Science	10	25	60		
Kozky, Alex	Cartoonist	10			20	
Kozlovsky, Ivan	Music	RARE	RARE	RARE	1,500	Tenor
Kraft, James L.	Business	30	95	175	50	Founder Kraft Foods Co.
Kramer, Stanley	Ent	15	35		35	Director/Producer
Kramer, Stephanie	Ent	10			30	
Krantz, Judith	Author	25		40	35	Novelist
Krasner, Milton	Ent	20			45	AA Winning Director
Kraus, Alfredo	Music	15			35	Opera
Kraus, Clemens	Music	75			220	Austrian Conductor
Kraus, Robert	Art	10	25	50	25	
Kravitz, Lenny	Music	25			50	
Krebs, Hans Adolf, Sir	Science	15		40	20	Nobel Medicine
Kreisler, Fritz 1875-1962	Music	100	160	300	225	Violinist
Kremer, Andrea	Ent	5			15	ESPN News
Krenek, Ernst	Music	15	35	90	55	Composer
Krenn, Fritz	Music	15			35	Opera
Kresge, S. S.	Business	150	250	300	200	Kresge Stores
Kretschmer, Otto	Military	45	140		185	U-Boat Commander
Kreutzer, Conradin	Music	125	300	650		Ger. Composer/Conductor
Krige, Alice	Ent	15			35	
Kristel, Sylvia	Ent	20			45	
Kristofferson, Kris	Ent	10		35	30	Actor/Singer
Kroc, Ray A.	Business	40		150	100	McDonalds
Krock, Arthur	Author	10	20	40	15	Bureau Chief,Columnist NY Times
Kroesen, Fred J.	Military	5	15	20	10	
Kroft, Steve	Ent	5			15	60 Minutes
Kroll, Gustov	Science	10			30	Rocket Pioneer/von Braun
Kropotkin, PeterA.	Political	30	75			Russian Prince
Kruger, Kurt	Ent	10		15	35	
Kruger, Otto 1885-1974	Ent	30			75	
Kruger, Paul	Political	75	350		175	
Kruger, Stephanus J.P.	Political	125	450		650	Krugerrand Named For Him
Krupa, Gene 1909-73	Music	40	195		95	Big Band Leader-Drums
Krupinski, Walter	Aviation	15	30	55	60	WWII German ACE
Krupp, Alfred	Business	180	450	500		Founder Krupp Works
Krupp, Friedrich Alfred	Business	125	350			Arms Manufacturer
Krylov, Ivan A.	Author	15	40	75	20	Russian Fables
Kschessinska, Matilda	Music	150		400		Prima Ballerina
Kubelik, Jan	Music	45	125	225	225	Violinist

Name	Field	SIG	DS	ALS	SP	Remarks
Kubelik, Rafael	Music	20	50		50	Conductor
Kubitschek, Juscelino	Political	10	35	75	25	Brazilian Head of State
Kubrick, Stanley	Ent	50	100		100	Director
Kuchta, Gladys	Music	10			30	Opera
Kudrow, Lisa	Ent	20			50	FRIENDS
Kulp, Nancy	Ent	40			75	Miss Jane/Beverly Hillbillies
Kuncewiczowa, Maria	Author	150		300		Escaped Nazi German
Kunstler, William	Political	20	35	75	25	
Kupka, Frantisek 1871-57	Art	110	225	350		Czech Abstract Artist
Kuralt, Charles	Ent	10	20	35	15	TV News Commentator
Kurtz, Swoosie	Ent	10			30	
Kusch, Polykarp, Dr.	Science	20	50		25	Nobel Physics
Kwan, Michelle	Sports	15			45	Figure Skater
Kwan, Nancy	Ent	20			45	
Ky, Nguyen Cao	Political	30	100		75	
Kyne, Peter B.	Author	5	15	30	10	
Kyser, Kay	Music	15			30	Big Band Leader

John Keats

Joanne Kerns

Nicole Kidman

Cammie King

Name	Field	SIG	DS	ALS	SP	Remarks
L A Law	Ent				250	Cast signed by Ten
La Belle, Patti	Music	15			35	
La Cava, Gregory	Ent	20			45	Director
La Forge, Frank	Music	15			45	
La Revelliere-Lepaux,L.	Political	25	70	145		French Revolution
La Rocque, Rod	Ent	20		45	55	
La Rue, Jack	Ent	10			25	Western Star
La Verne, Lucille	Ent	75			150	Disney Voice
LaBeauf, Sabrina	Ent	15			25	Cosby Show
Labouisse, Eve Curie	Science	15	45	75	35	
Lacepede, Bernhard de	Science	35	75	150		Fr. Naturalist
Lachaise, Gaston	Art	75	125	250		Sculptor/1882 - 1935
Laciura, Anthony	Music	10			25	Opera
Ladd, Alan 1913-64	Ent	50	100		175	
Ladd, Cheryl	Ent	10	20		25	Charlie's Angels
Ladd, David	Ent	10			25	Producer
Ladd, Diane	Ent	5		15	15	
Ladd, Sue Carol	Ent	5		15	15	
Laemmle, Carl	Business	100	250	600	700	Founder Universal Studios
Laennec, Rene T.H.	Science	3,500	3,500	6,500		Invented Stethoscope
LaFarge, John 1835-1910	Art	40	95	175		Am Landscape Painter
Lafayette, Marquis de	RevWar	400	850	1,600		
Lagerkvist, P.	Author	30	70	175	100	Nobel Literature 1951
Lagerlof, Selma 1858-40	Author	95	250		125	Nobel Literature 1909
LaGuardia, Fiorello	Political	35	100	125	150	Reform Mayor NYC
Lahm, Frank	Aviation	35	75	140	90	
Lahr, Bert 1895-1967	Ent	275	450		550	Wiz of Oz/Cowardly Lion
Lahti, Christine	Ent	5			15	
Laine, Frankie	Ent	5			15	
Laine, J.L.J.Viscount	Military	30	85	175		French Revolution
Lake, Arthur	Ent	50			60	Dagwood (Blondie)
Lake, Ricki	Ent	20			40	TV Talk Show Hostess
Lake, Simon 1866-1945	Science	60	150	450		Submarine
Lake, Veronica 1919-73	Ent	125	225	275	400	Scarce
Lakes, Gary	Music	15			30	Opera
LaLanne, Jack	Ent	10		30	25	TV Body Builder
Lalique, Rene 1860-1929	Art	200		600		Glass Artist
Lamar, Joseph R.	SuprCt	45	100	200		
Lamar, Lucius Q.C.	SuprCt	75		200		CSA Officer/1825-1893
Lamar, Mirabeau B.	Political	100	300			1789-1859
LaMarck, Jean Baptiste	Science	400	950	1,000		Forerunner of Darwin
LaMarr, Hedy	Ent	35	100		75	
LaMartine, Alphonse de	Author	100	200	225		Fr Poet/Statesman

Name	Field	SIG	DS	ALS	SP	Remarks
Lamas, Fernando	Ent	20	25	45	45	
Lamas, Lorenzo	Ent	10		20	25	
Lamb, Charles	Author	125	399	550		Br. Essayist, Critic
Lamb, Gil	Ent	10			20	Dancer/Comic
Lambert, Christopher	Ent	25			50	Highlander
Lambert, William C.	Aviation	75	135	175	150	WWI ACE
Lammers, Hans	Military	150	500			Hitlers Legal Advisor
Lamond, Frederic	Music	20		75	100	Pianist/Composer
Lamont, Forrest	Music	25			65	Opera
Lamont, Thomas	Political	15	30	45		Lincoln Pvt. Sec'y
Lamotta, Jake	Sports	15			35	Boxer
LaMotta, Vikki	Ent	5		10	5	
Lamour, Dorothy	Ent	20	50		50	
L'Amour, Louis 1908-88	Author	90	200	RARE	200	Old West Novelist
Lancaster, Burt	Ent	45	150		75	1913 - 1996
Lanchester, Elsa 1902-86	Ent	50	100		100	Bride of Frankenstein
Land, E. S.	Military	25	65		35	WWII Admiral
Land, Edwin H. 1909-92	Science	100	225		175	Polaroid Camera Inventor
Landau, Martin	Ent	20	50		50	AA Winner
Lander, Frederick West	Civil War	150	225	375		Union General/1821-62
Landers, Ann	Author	10	20	30	20	Advice Columnist
Landers, Audrey	Ent	5	20	20	15	
Landers, Harry	Ent	10			20	
Landers, Judy	Ent	5	20	20	15	
Landesberg, Steve	Ent	15			25	Barney Miller
Landi, Bruno	Music	25			60	Opera
Landi, Elissa	Ent	45	30	60	70	
Landis, Carole 1919-48	Ent	75			175	Suicide at 29
Landis, Jessie Royce	Ent	30			75	1904 - 1972
Landis, John	Ent	15			25	Director
Lando, Joe	Ent	15			35	Dr. Quinn
Landon, Alfred M.	Political	25	95	110	50	1887-1987
Landon, Michael	Ent	100	125		200	
Landseer, Charles	Art	30		75		Keeper of Royal Academy
Landseer, Edwin H., Sir	Art	30	65	250		Landscape Painter
Landseer, John	Art	25		125		Father of Edwin H.
Landseer, Thomas	Art	25	40	75		Brother of E. H.
Landsteiner, Karl, Dr.	Science	50	90	175		Nobel Medicine
Lane, Abbe	Music	15			20	Vocalist
Lane, Allan Rocky	Ent	100			250	Voice of Mr. Ed
Lane, Christy	Music	5		15	15	Gospel Singer
Lane, Diane	Ent	10	20		15	
Lane, Evelyn	Ent	10			25	Brit. Actress. Vintage
Lane, Harriet	First Lady	100	250	375		Actg. lst Lady, Buchanan
Lane, James H. (WD)	Civil War	175	350	550		Union General
Lane, James H. 1814-66	Civil War	85	135	300		Union General/Suicide
Lane, James Henry	Civil War	100	200	335	950	CSA General/1833-1907
Lane, Joseph	Political	40	75	130		First US Senator
Lane, Nathan	Ent	25	50		50	Actor/Disney Voice

Name	Field	SIG	DS	ALS	SP	Remarks
Lane, Priscilla	Ent	10	20	25	25	
Lane, Rosemary	Ent	15	25	35	35	
Lang, Anton	Ent	25	25	45	40	
Lang, Fritz	Ent	100	375		175	Director/Metroplis...
Lang, K. D.	Music	20	20		50	
Lang, Rosa	Ent	5			10	
Lang, Sebastian	Ent	20	25	45	45	
Lang, Walter	Ent	20			45	Director
Langan, Glenn	Ent	10	15	35	25	
Langdon, Harry	Ent	100			225	
Langdon, John	RevWar	210	400	1,200		Signer Constitution
Langdon, Sue Anne	Ent	10			20	
Lange, David	Political	5	15	30	15	New Zealand
Lange, Hope	Ent	10			30	
Lange, Jessica	Ent	15			45	AA Winner
Lange, Ted	Ent	10			20	Love Boat Bartender
Langella, Frank	Ent	20	50		50	Dracula
Langford, Frances	Music	10			20	Big Band
Langley, Samuel P.	Aviation	250		600		Aeronautical Pioneer
Langmuir, Irving	Science	35	75	125		Nobel Chemistry 1932
Langtry, Lillie 1852-1929	Ent	350		550		Actress/Mistress/Edw VII
Lanier, Sidney	Author	300	590	900		Poet
Lanphier, Thomas G., Jr.	Aviation	40	70	120	85	WWII ACE
Lansbury, Angela	Ent	10	20	30	25	Murder She Wrote
Lansing, Robert	Political	40	125			Sec'y State
Lansky, Meyer 1902-83	Criminal	300	1,000			Mafia Boss
Lantieri, Rita	Music	10			20	Opera
Lantz, Walter 1900-94	Cartoonist	60	100	100	100	Woody Woodpecker
Lanza, Mario 1921-1959	Music	145			650	Tenor/Died Young
LaPaglia, Anthony	Ent	15			30	
LaPlace, P.M.,Marquis	Science	500				Fr. Astronomer
Lapoype, J.F.C., Baron	Military	20		125		French Revolution
Lara, Joe	Ent	20			40	Tarzan
Lardner, Dionysius	Author	45	175			
Lardner, James L.	Civil War	35	85	125		Union Naval Commodore
Lardner, Ring 1885-1933	Author	65	195	300	75	Am Humorist
Lardner, Ring Jr.	Author	10	20	35	15	
Laredo, Ruth	Ent	15	20	30	35	
LaRocca, D.J. Nick	Music	75			200	Composer
Larrey, Dominick Baron	Military	60	150	250		French Revolution
Larroquette, John	Ent	15	25		35	Night Court
Larsen-Todsen, Nanny	Music	20			50	Opera
Larson, Gary	Cartoonist	20			55	Far Side
Larson, Leonard, Dr	Science	5		25	10	
LaRue, Lash	Ent	20		65	50	
Lasker, Mary	Business	5		15	10	
Lasky, Jesse L.	Ent	40	85	150	75	Pioneer Film Producer
LaSorda, Tommy	Sports	10			20	Baseball
Lasser, Louise	Ent	10			25	

Name	Field	SIG	DS	ALS	SP	Remarks
Laswell, Fred	Cartoonist	25			50	B.Google & Snuffy Smith
Latham, Hubert	Aviation	25	35	90	75	
Latham, Louise	Ent	10			20	
Lathrop, George P.	Author	25	50	150		Am. Journalist, Writer
Latifah, Queen	Music	20			45	
Latour-Maubourg, M.	Military	20		75		Cavalry Gen.
Latrobe, Benjamin H.	Art	RARE	500	RARE	RARE	Architect of White House
Lattimore, Richard	Author	10	20	25	15	
Lauck, Chet	Ent	25	75			Radio. Lum & Abner
Lauder, Estee	Business	10			30	Cosmetics
Lauder, Harry, Sir	Ent	55	90	145	70	
Lauer, Matt	Ent	15			25	
Laughton, Charles	Ent	75	125		275	AA Winner/1899-1962
Lauper, Cyndi	Music	25	35	60	50	
Laurants, Arthur	Author	5			20	Playwright
Laurel, Stan 1890-1965	Ent	150	400	525	375	
Laurel,Stan/Hardy,Oliver	Ent	575			1,200	Signed by Both
Lauren, Ralph	Business	10	20	40	25	Fashion Designer.
Laurencin, Marie	Art	125		590		Fr. Painter & Printmaker
Laurens, Henry 1724-92	RevWar	800	1,200	1,600		Pres. Continental Congress
Laurie, Piper	Ent	5		15	20	
Lauter, Harry	Ent	5			15	
Lauterbach, Johann C.	Music	35	100	200		Ger. Violinist
Lavin, Linda	Ent	20	45		45	Alice
Lavoisier, Antoine L. de	Science	750	RARE	RARE	RARE	Fr. Fndr Modern Chemistry
Law, Andrew Bonar	Political	35	75	125		Br. Prime Minister
Law, Evander McIvor	Civil War	100	250	500		CSA General/1836-1920
Law, John 1671-1729	Political	150				Economist
Law, John Phillip	Ent	10			25	Barbarella
Law, Ruth	Aviation	35			100	
Lawford, Peter 1923 - 84	Ent	45	125		125	Rat Pack member
Lawler, Michael K.	Civil War	35	100			Union General/1814-1882
Lawless, Lucy	Ent	25			50	Xena, Warrior Princess
Lawrence, Barbara	Ent	10			20	
Lawrence, Carol	Ent	5	15		15	
Lawrence, D. H.	Author	300	590	2,500		Lady Chatterly's Lover
Lawrence, Elliot	Music	20			40	Big Band Leader
Lawrence, Ernest	Science	100	275	400	200	Nobel Physics
Lawrence, Gertrude	Ent	20	50		45	1902-1952
Lawrence, Herbert A.	Military	10	30	50	25	
Lawrence, Ist Baron	Political	10	30	75		India
Lawrence, Jacob	Art	15	25			
Lawrence, Joey	Ent	15			30	Brotherly Love
Lawrence, John	RevWar	35	95	175		Ct Statesman
Lawrence, Marc	Ent	10		25	25	
Lawrence, Marjorie	Music	10			125	Opera
Lawrence, Sharon	Ent	25			50	NYPD Blue
Lawrence, Steve	Ent	5			15	
Lawrence, Thomas	Art	150	225	200		Br. Portrait Painter

Name	Field	SIG	DS	ALS	SP	Remarks
Lawrence, Thos-E.	Author	650	1,250	RARE	RARE	Lawrence of Arabia
Lawrence, Tracy	Music	15			30	
Lawrence, Vicki	Ent	5	15		15	Carol Burnett Show
Lawson, Ted	Aviation	15	30		40	
Lawton, Alexander (WD)	Civil War		650	775		CSA General
Lawton, Alexander R.	Civil War	125	300	350		CSA General/1818-96
Lay, Herman W.	Business	10	25	50	30	Lay's Potato Chips
Lazarev, Alexander	Music				65	Conductor
Lazarus, Emma 1849-87	Author	RARE	2,000	RARE	RARE	Poem on Statue of Liberty
Lazarus, Mel	Cartoonist	5			20	Miss Peach/Momma
Lazarus, S. Ralph	Business	5		10	5	Pres.Benrus Watch
Lazenby, George	Ent	25	65		55	James Bond
Lazzari, Virgillo	Ent	15			45	
Lea, Homer	Military	50	150			
Leachman, Cloris	Ent	10	25		20	AA Winner
Leadbetter, Danville	Civil War	150	450			CSA General/1811-66
Leahy, William Daniel	Military	35		100	175	
Leake, J. B.	Civil War	20	55	75		
Leakey, Louis B.	Science	45	125	225	75	Anthropologist, Archaeologist
Leakey, Mary D.	Science	15	25	60	30	Anthropologist, Archaeologist
Leakey, Meave, Dr.	Science	20	60			
Leakey, Richard, Dr.	Science	125				Br. Anthropologist
Lean, David, Sir	Ent	45			70	Director
Lear, Edward	Art	150		450		Br. Painter/Poet
Lear, Norman	Ent	10		45	20	TV Producer
Lear, Tobias	RevWar	75	240	325		Pvt Sect to Washington
Lear, William P. Sr.	Business	30	100	150	100	Lear Jet Aircraft
Learned, Michael	Ent	10		20	25	
Leary, Timothy, Dr.	Political	35	65		75	
Leavenworth, Henry	Military	250		750		Frontier Soldier, General
LeBlanc, Matt	Ent	20			45	Friends
LeBrock, Kelly	Ent	10	20		25	
Lebrun, Albert 1871-1950	Political	30	50	125	35	
Lebrun, Chas. F. Duc de	Military	50	100	150		3rd Consul/Bonaparte
LeCarre, John	Author	20	45	75	30	Br. Realistic Spy Novels
Lecuona, Ernesto	Music	150			300	Composer
Led Zeppelin	Music	200	400		450	Signed by Entire Band
Ledbetter, Huddie	Music	RARE	RARE	4,000	RARE	RARE/"Leadbelly"/Jazz
Lederer, Francis	Ent	10			25	
Lederman, Leon M., Dr.	Science	15	25	50		Nobel in Physics
Ledoux, Harold	Cartoonist	10			25	Judge Parker
Ledyard, John 1751-89	Explorer		475			Accompanied Capt.Cook
Lee, Anna	Ent	5			15	
Lee, Bernard	Ent	75			100	Bond films as M
Lee, Brandon 1964-93	Ent	200	550	RARE	550	Bruce Lee's Son
Lee, Brenda	Music	5			15	
Lee, Bruce	Ent	600	800	1,250	950	Photo/Letters are Scarce
Lee, Canada	Ent	55			125	
Lee, Charles (1731-82)	Military	RARE	RARE	2,000	RARE	Turncoat Gen. Rev. War

Name	Field	SIG	DS	ALS	SP	Remarks
Lee, Charles (1758-1815)	Political	125	250	550		Washington's Att'y Gen.
Lee, Christopher	Ent	30			60	Dracula
Lee, Dr. Tsung-Dao	Science	20		45	25	Nobel Physics
Lee, E. Hamilton	Aviation	15	25	50	35	
Lee, Edwin G.	Civil War	125	250	400		CSA General/1835-70
Lee, Fitzhugh (WD)	Civil War	250		600		CSA General
Lee, Fitzhugh 1835-1905	Civil War	150	200	300	500	CSA General
Lee, Francis Lightfoot	RevWar	660	1,050	3,000		Signer Decl. of Indepen.
Lee, Geo. Wash. Custis	Civil War	155		410		CSA General/1832-1913
Lee, Geo. Wash.C.	Civil War	300				CSA General/War Dated
Lee, Gypsy Rose 1913-70	Ent	75	125		350	Burlesque Queen
Lee, Harper	Author	100	250		250	To Kill a Mocking Bird
Lee, Henry 1756-1818	RevWar	200	600	625		Light-Horse Harry
Lee, Jason Scott	Ent	15			35	The Bruce Lee Story
Lee, Manfred	Author	100	300	450	RARE	Ellery Queen
Lee, Mary Custis	Civil War	150		690	475	Mrs. Robert E. Lee
Lee, Michelle	Ent	5		15	15	
Lee, Peggy	Music	10			30	
Lee, Pinkie	Ent	15			35	
Lee, Richard Henry	RevWar	400	1,600	2,250		Signer Decl. of Indepen.
Lee, Robert E.	Civil War	2,000	3,500		6,500	CSA General/1807-1870
Lee, Robert E.	Military	3,000	7,500	12,500	7,500	CSA General/War Dated
Lee, Ruta	Ent	5			10	
Lee, Samuel P.	Civil War	60	210	275		Union Admiral
Lee, Sheryl	Ent	10			25	
Lee, Spike	Ent	10	25		25	Director
Lee, Stephen Dill	Civil War	125	325	400		CSA General/1833 - 1908
Lee, Stephen Dill (WD)	Civil War	250	RARE	RARE	RARE	CSA General
Lee, Tommy	Music	25			50	
Lee, William H. 1837-91	Civil War	200		550		CSA General
Lee, William Raymond	Civil War	15	45	70		Union General/1804-91
Lee, Yuan T., Dr.	Science	20	35	45	30	Nobel Chemistry
Leech, Richard	Music	15			35	Opera
Leeds, Andrea	Ent	10			25	
Leese, Oliver, Sir	Military	20	50		35	WWII Br. General
Leeves, Jane	Ent	20			50	Frasier
Lefebvre, F.J., Duke	Military	160	300			Marshal of Napoleon
LeGallienne, Eva	Ent	10	25	50	35	
LeGallienne, Richard	Author	25	50	65		Brit. Man of Letters
Leger, Fernand	Art	100	240	500		Fr. Abstract Painter
Leggett, Mortimer D.	Civil War	20	40	65		Union General/1821-96
Legrand, Michel	Music	10	45	25	20	Composer
Leguizamo, John	Ent	20			40	
LeHand, M. A. (Missy)	Political	20	80	130	40	FDR's Personal Sect.
Lehar, Franz 1870-1948	Music	85	200	550	350	Composer/Merry Widow
Lehmann, Ernst August	Aviation	100		365		Ger. Aeronautical Engineer
Lehmann, Lilli 1848-1929	Music	150				German Soprano
Lehmann, Lotte	Music	50	75	150	120	Opera
Lehmann, Marie	Music	50			175	

Name	Field	SIG	DS	ALS	SP	Remarks
Lehr, Lew	Ent	15	25	35	30	
Leibman, Ron	Ent	10	20	20	20	
Leider, Frida	Music	45			150	Opera
Leiferkus, Sergei	Music	10			25	Opera
Leigh, Janet	Ent	5	20	20	20	Psycho Star
Leigh, Jennifer Jason	Ent	25			50	
Leigh, Vivien 1913-67	Ent	350	550	650	750	Gone with the Wind
Leighton, Frederic	Art	50		150		Pres. Br.Royal Academy
Leighton, Laura	Ent	25			50	Melrose Place
Leinsdorf, Erich	Music	25			75	Austro-Amer Conductor
Leisure, David	Ent	10		20	20	Empty Nest
Lejeune, John Archer	Military	35	75	150	75	Us Marine Corps Cmndr
Leland, Henry M. 1843-32	Business	900	2,500	RARE	RARE	Lincoln Motor Co.
Leland, W. C.	Business	20	55	140	45	
Leloir, Luis Frederico	Science	20	40	45	25	Nobel Chemistry
LeMaire, Charles	Ent	15			25	Director
Lemass, Sean	Political	10	25	60	30	Prime Minister Ireland
LeMay, Curtis S.	Military	30	75		75	AF Gen./WWII/SAC
Lemeshev, Sergei	Music	Scarce	Scarce	Scarce	500	Opera/Russian Tenor
Lemmon, Jack	Ent	10	20	25	25	AA Winner
Lemnitz, Tiana	Music	45			125	Opera
Lemnitzer, Lyman L.	Military	30	40	90	35	WWII Supreme Allied Cmdr
Lemon, Mark 1809-70	Author	15		35		Br Playwright
Lemonheads	Music	25			50	Signed by all
L'Enfant, Pierre Charles	Aviation	400	850	1,200		
Lenin, Vladimir Ilyich	Political	RARE	RARE	RARE	RARE	
Lennon Sisters, The	Music	20			45	
Lennon, Janet	Ent	15			30	
Lennon, John 1940-1980	Music	500	2,000	1,600	900	Assasinated Beatle
Lennon, Julian	Music	20			40	Johns singing son
Lennon, Kathleen	Ent	10			25	
Lennon, Peggy	Ent	10			25	
Lennox, Annie	Music	25			50	Eurythmics
Lennox, Vera	Ent	10			20	
Leno, Jay	Ent	10			35	Tonite Show Host
Lenoir, William B.	Space	10			20	Astronaut
Lenormand, Rene	Music	50			175	Composer
Lenox, Lucie	Ent	15			40	
Lenske, Rule	Ent	5			15	
Lenya, Lotte	Ent	75	100		125	James Bond Villainess
Leonard, Elmore	Author	15			25	Get Shorty,...
Leonard, Gloria	Ent	5		15	15	
Leonard, Sheldon	Ent	5		15	15	
Leoncavallo, Ruggiero	Music	175	500	500	675	Composer
Leone, Sergio	Ent	100	200	RARE	400	Director of Westerns
Leoni, Tia	Ent	20			50	
Leonov, Aleksei	Space	130	155		275	Cosmonaut/1st Space Walk
Leontif, Wassily, Dr.	Science	20	35		40	Nobel Economics
Leontovich, Eugenie	Ent	15		30	45	

Name	Field	SIG	DS	ALS	SP	Remarks
Leopardi, Giacomo	Author	100	300	450		
Leopold I	Royalty	105	475			Belgium
Leopold I	Royalty	100	375	625		Hungary
Leopold II	Royalty	65	325	540		Belgium
Lermontov, Mikhail	Author	750 RARE	RARE	RARE		Novelist/Poet-Killed in Duel
Lerner, Alan Jay 1918-96	Music	50	95		125	Composer
Lerner, Max	Author	10	30	40	20	
LeRoy, Hal	Ent	10			15	Director
LeRoy, Mervyn	Ent	35	50		75	Director
Leslie, Frank 1821-80	Business	100				Fndr Illustrated Newspaper
Leslie, Frank, Mrs.	Business	20		75	75	Leslie's Magazine
Leslie, Joan	Ent	10	20	20	20	
Leslie, Thomas J.	Civil War	10		35		Union General
Lesseps, Ferdinand, de	Political	150	225	475	600	Engineer/Suez Canal
Lester, Buddy	Ent	5	15		15	
Lester, Jerry	Ent	15			25	
Lester, Tom	Ent	15			25	
Lesters, The	Music	10			25	
Leszczynski, Stanislaus	Royalty	575				Stanislaw 1, King of Poland
Letcher, John 1813-84	Civil War	80	200	240		CW Gov. VA
Letterman, David	Ent	25			50	Late Nite Show Host
Letterman, Jonathan	Civil War	100	175			Medical Services
Leutze, Emanuel	Art	75		275		Washington Crossing DE
Levant, Oscar	Ent	20			45	
Levenson, Sam	Ent	10	35		15	Radio, TV Comic
Leventhrope, Collett	Civil War	90	165			CSA General/1815-89
Lever, Lord	Business	30	100	175	60	Br. Soap/Lever Brothers
Levi-Montalcini, Rita, Dr.	Science	20	65			Nobel Medicine
Levin, Ira	Author	25	35		30	Rosemary's Baby
Levine, David	Cartoonist	15			45	Caricaturist
Levine, Irving R.	Ent	5	10		5	TV News Commentator
Levine, James	Music	15		35	25	Conductor
Levinson, Barry	Ent	10	20		20	
Levy, David H.	Science	15			20	Discovered Meteor Crater
Lewes, Lauren	Ent	5			15	Love Boat
Lewinsky, Monica	Celebrity	35			75	Mistress Clinton
Lewis, Al	Ent	10	20		20	GrandPa Munster
Lewis, C(live) S(taples)	Author	300	550	1,500		Br Medievelist
Lewis, Cathy	Ent	10			25	
Lewis, Daniel Day	Ent	25			50	
Lewis, David 'Duffy'	Aviation	15	30	50	40	
Lewis, Emmanuele	Ent	10	25		20	Webster
Lewis, Francis	RevWar	400	1,250	2,500		Signer Decl. of Indepen.
Lewis, Geoffrey	Ent	5			10	
Lewis, George	Ent	10			20	
Lewis, Huey	Music	25			50	And the News
Lewis, J. C.	Music	10			25	Blues Drummer
Lewis, James	Ent	15		30	25	
Lewis, Jerry	Ent	15	25		30	

Name	Field	SIG	DS	ALS	SP	Remarks
Lewis, Jerry Lee	Music	30	100	RARE	65	
Lewis, Joe E.	Ent	20	30	45	40	
Lewis, John	Political	5	15			Civil Rights Leader
Lewis, John L. 1880-1969	Political	40	60	195	105	AFL-CIO Labor Leader
Lewis, Juliette	Ent	25			50	
Lewis, Meriwether	Explorer	RARE	6,000	11,500	RARE	Lewis & Clark Expedition
Lewis, Morgan	RevWar	50	70	110		
Lewis, Ramsey	Music	25			50	Pianist-Composer
Lewis, Richard	Ent	10			20	
Lewis, Shari	Ent	20	40		40	Puppet/Vetriloquist
Lewis, Sinclair 1885-1951	Author	100	325	550	300	First Nobel for Literature
Lewis, Ted	Ent	20	25		75	
Lewis, William Arthur	Science	20	25	40	25	Nobel Economics
Lewis, William H.	Aviation	10	20	40	30	WWII ACE
Lewishon, Ludwig	Author	20		25		German Author
Lewisohn, Adolph	Business	20	45	65	25	Mining
Lewitt, Sal	Art	25			50	
Ley, Bob	Ent	5			10	ESPN News
Ley, Willy	Science	25	75	145	35	Rocker Expert
Libby, Willard F.	Science	20	35	55	25	Nobel Chemistry
Liberace	Ent	70	150		145	
Liberace, George	Ent	10	20		20	Liberaces Brother
Lichtenstein, Roy	Art	30	65	140	50	
Liddy, G. Gordon	Political	5	20	50	30	Watergate/Convicted
Lie, Jonas	Author	15	40	60		
Lie, Trygve 1896-1968	Political	50	150	250	175	1st Sect Gen/UN
Lieber, Fritz	Ent	45		100		
Liebermann, Max	Art	125		250		Ger. Impressionist/1847-35
Liebig, Justus von	Science	200				German Chemist
Liggett, Hunter	Military	15	45	60	35	Gen. WW I
Liggett, Louis Kroh	Business	90	170	350		Liggett's Drug Store Chain
Light, Judith	Ent	15	20	25	30	
Lightner, Winnie	Ent	20	25	45	45	
Ligi, Josella	Music	10			25	Opera
Liles, Brooks	Aviation	10	20	35	25	USAF WWII ACE
Lilienthal, David E.	Business	15	30		20	
Lilienthal, Otto 1848-96	Science	RARE	RARE	2,500	RARE	Aeronautical Engineer
Liliuokalani, Lydia K.	Royalty	150	400	750	475	Queen Hawaii
Lillie, Beatrice 1894-1989	Ent	20		60	35	
Lillie, Gordon W.	Western	275	550	750	500	Buffalo Bill's Partner
Limbaugh, Rush	Ent	20			50	Radio/TV Commentator
Lin, Y. S. Maya	Art	25	75			Designed Viet Nam Wall
Lincke, Paul	Music	70	185	325		Composer
Lincoln, Abraham	President	3,000	5,000	9,500	RARE	1809-1865
Lincoln, Abraham	President	3,500	9,000	12,500	RARE	As President
Lincoln, Benjamin	Military	100	175	500		RevWar General
Lincoln, Benjamin	Political	45	160			Father of Gen. Lincoln
Lincoln, Elmo	Ent	500	RARE	RARE	1,500	First to Play Tarzan
Lincoln, Evelyn	Political	15	25	45	35	JFK Presidential Sec'y

Name	Field	SIG	DS	ALS	SP	Remarks
Lincoln, Joseph	Author	15	20	30		
Lincoln, Levi	Political	35	85	130		Memb. Continental Congr
Lincoln, Mary Todd	First Lady	350	900	1,500	RARE	
Lincoln, Robert Todd	Political	100	200	325		Capt. CW.
Lincoln, Rufus	RevWar	RARE	1,650	RARE	RARE	
Lind, Jenny	Ent	65	125	250	775	Opera/1820-87
Lindberg, Charles W.	Military	25	65		40	Iwo Jima Flag Raiser
Lindbergh, Anne Morrow	Author	15	45	100	30	Am. Writer-Poet.
Lindbergh, Charles A.	Aviation	575	1,250	2,400	2,500	1902-1974
Linden, Hal	Ent	10	20		20	Barney Miller
Lindfors, Viveca	Ent	15			45	
Lindholm, Bent	Music	10			25	Opera
Lindley, Audra	Ent	20			40	Three's Company
Lindsay, E. Lin	Aviation	10	20	35	30	ACE, WWII USAAF Ace
Lindsay, Howard	Ent	10		25	25	Theatrical Producer
Lindsay, John	Political	5			10	Mayor NYC
Lindsay, Margaret	Ent	15	25	45	50	
Lindsay, Vachel	Author	50	185	450	125	Poet/Artist
Lindsey, George	Ent	10		15	20	
Lindstrom, Pia	Ent	5			15	TV News
Linkletter, Art	Ent	10	25		15	Radio-TV MC,
Linnaeus, Carolus von	Science	925	RARE	RARE	RARE	Botanist
Linn-Baker, Mark	Ent	10	25		20	Perfect Strangers
Linville, Larry	Ent	20	40		40	MASH
Liotta, Ray	Ent	25			50	
Lipchitz, Jacques	Art	125	200	225		Cubist Sculptor
Lipfert, Helmut	Aviation	35			70	German ACE
Lipkovska, Lydia	Music	100			325	Rus. Soprano
Lipman, Clara	Ent	10			20	Stage Actress
Lipmann, Fritz A.	Science	25	45	70	30	Nobel Medicine 1953
Lippman, Walter	Author	25	75		30	Journalist, Editor, Pulitzer
Lipscomb, William N.	Science	20	35		30	Nobel Chemistry
Lipsner, B.B.	Aviation	30	65		90	Pioneer Air Mail Pilot
Lipton, Peggy	Ent	15	40		25	Mod Squad
Lipton, Peggy	Ent	15	45		45	Mod Squad
Lipton, Thomas, Sir	Business	125	550	900	400	Br. Tea Merchant
List, Emanuel	Ent	35			75	
Lister, Joseph, Lord	Science	225	400	600		1827-1912
Liston, Robert 1794-1847	Science	15	30	50		Skilled Scottish Surgeon
Liston, Sonny	Sports	200			450	Boxer
Liszt, Franz 1811-86	Music	450	650	950	1,600	Composer
Litchfield, Grace D.	Author	10		25		1849-1944
Litel, John 1892-1964	Ent	15	15	35	35	
Lithgow, John	Ent	20			50	Third Rock from the Sun
Little Richard	Music	35	125		75	Penniman
Little River Band	Music	35			60	Signed by Entire Band
Little, Cleavon	Ent	35			75	Blazing Saddles
Little, Little Jack	Music	15			35	Big Band Leader
Little, Rich	Ent	5			10	

Name	Field	SIG	DS	ALS	SP	Remarks
Littlejohn, Dewitt C.	Civil War	40	85	120		Union Officer/1818-1892
Litvinov, Maksim M.	Political	50		95	65	Soviet Foreign Minister
Livermore, Mary A.	Political	60	75	125		Womans Suffrage
Liverpool, 2nd Earl	Political	120	135	200		
Livingston, Alan	Music	15	55			Composer
Livingston, Edward	Political	30	85	150		Sec'y of State 1831
Livingston, Henry B.	SuprCt	100	300	600		1757 - 1823
Livingston, Jay	Music	15	40	85	40	Composer
Livingston, Margaret	Ent	10			25	
Livingston, Mary	Ent	15	25	45	40	
Livingston, Philip	RevWar	288	1,080	1,175		Signer Decl. of Indepen.
Livingston, Robert	Ent	35			85	
Livingston, Robert	RevWar	175	350	400		1742-94
Livingston, Robert R.	RevWar	200	400	900		Continental Congress
Livingston, Stanley	Ent	15			35	
Livingston, William	RevWar	300	900	1,600		Continental Congr.
Livingstone, David	Explorer	225	750	1,600		1813-187
LL Cool J	Music	25			50	
Llewelyn, Desmond	Ent	10			25	Q" in James Bond films
Lloyd, Christopher	Ent	20	45		50	Taxi
Lloyd, Emily	Ent	15			40	
Lloyd, Frank	Ent	35	75			AA Winning Director
Lloyd, Harold 1894-1971	Ent	200	275		400	
Lloyd, Jake	Ent	25			55	Star Wars/Anakin
Lloyd-George, David	Political	100	250	425	250	Br. Prime Minister, lst Earl
Lo Giudici, Franco	Music	50			150	Opera
Loan, Nguyen Ngoc	Military	150			375	Gen. Viet Nam
Loasby, Arthur W.	Business	5	20			Wall Street Banker
Locane, Amy	Ent	25			50	Melrose Place
Locke, John 1632-1704	Author	700	1,950	RARE	RARE	
Locke, Sandra	Ent	10		20	25	
Locke, William John	Author	20	35	75	30	Br. Novelist
Lockhart, Gene	Ent	20			50	
Lockhart, June	Ent	10	25		25	Lost in Space/Lassie
Lockheed, Alan	Aviation	75	150	250	150	Aviator/Plane Designer
Locklear, Heather	Ent	10	20	25	35	
Lockwood, Belva A.	Political	225	325	700		
Lockwood, Gary	Ent	10			25	
Lockwood, Margaret	Ent	15	20	40	55	1916-1990
Lodge, Henry Cabot	Political	45	160	200	95	
Lodge, Henry Cabot, Jr.	Political	20	60	95	25	Ambassador UN, Diplomat
Lodge, Oliver J., Sir	Science	90	130	225	250	Br. Physicist, Spiritualist
Loeb, William	Business	15	30	55	35	
Loesser, Frank	Music	125				Broadway Composer
Loew, Marcus	Business	30	40	65	45	
Loewe, Frederick	Music	35	65	145	50	Composer/1901-1988
Loewy, Raymond	Business	35	90	140	75	Designer
Lofting, Hugh 1886-1947	Author	95				
Logan, Benjamin 1752-02	Military	350	560	675		Pioneer Hero

Name	Field	SIG	DS	ALS	SP	Remarks
Logan, Ella	Ent	5		20	15	
Logan, John A. (WD)	Civil War	95				Union General
Logan, John A. 1826-86	Civil War	65	200	250		Union General
Logan, Josh(ua) 1908-88	Ent	30	40		45	Producer/Director
Logan, Olive	Author	25	35			
Logan, Thomas M.	Civil War	100	225	400		CSA General/1840-1919
Loggia, Robert	Ent	5	20		20	
Loggins and Messina	Music	25	50		50	
Loggins, Kenny	Music	20			40	
Lolobrigida, Gina	Ent	10		25	35	
Lom, Herbert	Ent	25			45	
Lomax, Lunsford Lindsey	Civil War	100	270	370		CSA General/1835-1913
Lombard, Carole	Ent	275	750	RARE	750	1908 - 1942
Lombardi, Vince	Sports	200	300		450	1971 HOF/Coach
Lombardo, Guy 1902-77	Music	25	75	120	100	Big Band Leader
London, George	Music	35			70	Opera
London, Jack 1876-1916	Author	400	750	RARE	RARE	Novelist (Am)
London, Julie	Ent	5			15	
London, Tom	Ent	50			100	
Long, Armistead L.	Civil War	85	100	350		CSA General/1825-91
Long, Huey P.	Political	75	175			Sen/Gov LA
Long, Johnny	Music	25			50	Big Band. Violinist
Long, Lotus	Ent	10			30	
Long, Pierse 1739-89	RevWar	30	75	160		Continental Congress
Long, Richard	Ent	25			65	
Long, Shelley	Ent	15	40		45	Cheers
Longacre, James B.	Political	150		400		Chief Engr. of US Mint
Longfellow, Henry W.	Author	175		600	950	Poet/1807-1882
Longstreet, James	Civil War	400	900	1,200	900	CSA General/1821-1904
Longstreet, James (WD)	Civil War	800	1,250	RARE	RARE	CSA General
Loo, Richard	Ent	25			50	
Loomis, Gustavus	Civil War	30	75	100		Union General/1789-1872
Loos, Anita	Author	15	35	70	30	Am Novelist
Loos, Walter	Aviation	10	20	35	25	
Loper, Don	Business	5	15	35	10	Fashion Designer
Lopez, Jennifer	Ent	20			50	Selena
Lopez, Vincent	Music	20			50	Big Band Leader
Loraine, Robert	Aviation	20		50		
Lorca, Frederico Garcia	Author	400	1,200	RARE	RARE	Poet
Lord, Jack	Ent	30	60	60	60	Hawaii 5-0
Lord, Marjorie	Ent	10			25	Danny Thomas Show
Lord, Walter	Author	5			10	
Lords, Traci	Ent	15	40	40	40	
Loren, Sophia	Ent	10	30		30	
Lorengar, Pilar	Music	20			40	Opera
Lorillard, Peter	Business	125	250	450		Tobacco Industry
Loring, Gloria	Ent	5	15		15	
Loring, William W. (WD)	Civil War	180		600		CSA General
Loring, Wm. Wing	Civil War	120	240	300	425	CSA General/1818-86

Name	Field	SIG	DS	ALS	SP	Remarks
Lorne, Marion	Ent	100	150		200	Bewitched's Aunt Clara
Lorre, Peter	Ent	150	250		300	1904 - 1964
Losey, Joseph	Ent	15			60	Director
Lott, Felicity	Music	15			35	Opera
Loubet, Emile Frangois	Political			125		Pres. France 1899-1906
Loughlin, Lori	Ent	20			45	
Louis Philippe (Fr)	Royalty	75	215	375		Citizen King Duc D'Orleans
Louis XII (Fr)	Royalty	800	1,750	RARE		King of France
Louis XIII (Fr)	Royalty	500	900	RARE		King of France
Louis XIV (Fr)	Royalty	450	1,000	RARE		The Sun King
Louis XV	Royalty	750	900	RARE		King of France
Louis XVI	Royalty	375	600			King of France. Guillotined
Louis XVIII (Fr) 1755-1824	Royalty	200	400	1,250		Louis Stanislas Xavier
Louise Caroline Alberta	Royalty	25		65	175	4th Daugfhter of Queen
Louise, Anita	Ent	25			45	1915 - 1970
Louise, Tina	Ent	10	20		25	Gilligans Island/Ginger
Louise, Victor	Royalty	15		105	195	Princess Royal
Love, Bessie	Ent	25	50		60	
Love, Courtney	Music	25			50	
Love, Montagu	Ent	20			50	
Love, Mother	Ent	5			15	
Lovecraft, H. P.	Author	400 RARE		1,000 RARE		Horror Writer
Lovejoy, Frank	Ent	25			55	
Loveless, Patty	Music	15			35	
Lovell, Bernard Dr.	Science	15	25	40	20	
Lovell, James	RevWar	75	195	450		Continental Congress
Lovell, James A. Jr.	Space	40	125		125	
Lovell, Mansfield (WD)	Civil War	185	560	800		CSA General
Lovell, Mansfield 1822-84	Civil War	100	250	300		CSA General
Loverboy	Music	25			50	
Lovett, Lyle	Music	25			50	
Low, David, Sir	Cartoonist	15	45	110	140	
Low, Nicholas	RevWar	100	245	450		Backed Revolution
Low, Seth 1819-1916	Political	15	35	45		Mayor NYC
Lowe, Ed	Science	20			45	Kitty Litter Inventor
Lowe, Edmund	Ent	25		60	50	1890 - 1971
Lowe, Hudson, Sir	Military	200		500		Last custodian of Napoleon
Lowe, Rob	Ent	20			45	
Lowe, Thaddeus S.	Civil War	200	325	500		Aeronaut/Ballonist
Lowell, Amy	Author	45	125	250		Poet/Critic
Lowell, Carey	Ent	10	20		20	
Lowell, James Russell	Author	75	145	225	350	Poet
Lowell, John H.	Aviation	15	25	40	35	WWII ACE
Lowell, Percival	Science	20	40	65		Am. Astronomer, Author
Lowell, Robert	Author	50	150			Pulitzer Poetry
Lowery, Robert	Ent	85	150		125	Serial Batman
Loy, Myrna 1905-93	Ent	25	40	50	55	
Lubbock, Francis R.	Civil War	150	185	295	350	CSA Governor TX
Lubin, Arthur	Ent	25			65	Director

Name	Field	SIG	DS	ALS	SP	Remarks
Lubin, Germaine	Music				275	Opera
Lubitsch, Ernst	Ent	55			120	Director
Lubke, Heinrich	Political	10		25		Pres. Ger. Fed. Repub.
Lucas, George	Ent	35	150		75	Director/Star Wars...
Lucca, Pauline	Music	30	70	102		Opera
Lucci, Susan	Ent	5	20	20	20	Soap Star
Luce, Clare Boothe	Author	30	100	175	40	Ambassador, Playwright
Luce, Henry R.	Business	40	115	2,000	50	Time, Life, Fortune, Sports
Luce, Stephen Bleecker	Military	10	35	95	30	
Luckinbill, Laurence	Ent	20			50	Star Trek Movies
Luckner, Felix, von	Military	75	200	200	100	The Sea Devil WWII
Luckner, Nicholas	Military	225	550			
Ludden, Allen	Ent	10			25	
Ludde-Neurath, Walter	Military	15			45	Aide-de-camp to Donitz
Ludendorff, Erich von	Military	100	225	350	275	WWI German General
Ludin, Hanns	Military	130	350			WWII Germ Storm Trooper
Ludlington, Marshall	Civil War	65	135	195		Union Officer
Ludlum, Robert	Author	10	20	35	20	Super Spy novels
Ludwig I 1786-1868	Royalty	65	338	450		King of Bavaria
Ludwig II	Royalty	55	255	470		King of Bavaria
Ludwig, Emil	Author	50	120	200		
Lufbery, Raoul	Aviation	125	350	550	400	WWI ACE
Luft, Lorna	Ent	10			20	Judy Garlands Daughter
Lugosi, Bela 1882-1956	Ent	325	1,500	RARE	975	SP as Dracula - 2500
Lukas, Foss	Music	25			75	Composer
Lukas, Paul	Ent	50			100	AA Winner/1887-1971
Luke, Frank	Aviation	150	400	600	500	WWI ACE
Luke, Keye	Ent	25	50		50	Charlie Chan films/Kung Fu
Luks, George Benjamin	Art	20	50	200		1867-1933
Lum & Abner	Ent	40	90		75	Both
Lumet, Sidney	Ent	20			40	TV Director
Lumiere, Louis 162-1954	Science	175		500	375	Cinematographe Projector
Lumley, Joanna	Ent	5	20		15	
Luna, Barbara	Ent	5			10	
Lunceford, Jimmie	Music	50			125	Big Band Leader
Lund, John	Ent	5	15		15	
Lunden, Joan	Ent	10			20	TV Host
Lundgren, Dolph	Ent	20			40	
Lundigan, William	Ent	15			30	
Lunney, G.	Space	5			15	Astronaut
Lunt, Alfred & Fontaine	Ent	45			90	Joan
Lupino, Ida	Ent	25	75	75	70	1914 - 1995
Lupino, Stanley 1893-42	Ent	15			35	
Lupton, John	Ent	10			20	
Lupus, Peter	Ent	10			25	TV's Mission Impossible
Luria, Salvador F.	Science	20	35	55	25	Nobel Medicine
Lurie, Bob	Business	10	25	45	15	
Luse, Harley	Music	10			20	
Luther, Hans	Political	40	55	85		Chancellor Ger., Ambass

Name	Field	SIG	DS	ALS	SP	Remarks
Luther, Martin	Clergy	15,000	40,000	55,000	RARE	
Lutzow, Gunther	Aviation	175		445	450	
Lvov, Alexis	Music	75		200		Russian Composer
Lyautey, Louis	Military	15	50	75	35	Marshal of France
Lyell, Charles, Sir	Science	95		425		Br Fndr Modern Geology
Lyman, Abe	Music	15			45	Big Band Leader
Lynch, David	Ent	25			50	TV Director
Lynch, John R.	Political		250			
Lynch, Kelly	Ent	20			50	
Lynch, Thomas Jr.	RevWar	20,000	35,000	RARE	RARE	Signer
Lynde, Paul	Ent	35	50		65	Bewitched's Uncle Arthur
Lynen, Feodor	Science	20	40		25	Nobel Medicine
Lynley, Carol	Ent	15		35	35	
Lynn, Diana 1926-1971	Ent	45			65	Bedtime for Bonzo
Lynn, Jeffrey	Ent	10		20	20	
Lynn, Loretta	Music	5			15	Country
Lynn, Vera Dame	Music	25			75	Br. WW II Singing Star
Lyon, Ben	Ent	15			35	
Lyon, Nathaniel 1818-61	Civil War	350	RARE	RARE	RARE	Union General. KIA
Lyon, Sue	Ent	10		20	25	
Lyons, Lord Admiral	Military	25		130		
Lyons, Richard B.P.	Royalty	20		100		1st Earl
Lytell, Bert	Ent	30	45	90	60	
Lytton, E. George B.	Author	40	100	200		

Sir Laurence Olivier

Abraham Lincoln

Tsar Nicholas II

Eugene O'Neill

M

Name	Field	SIG	DS	ALS	SP	Remarks
Ma, Yo Yo	Music	30			60	Cellist
Mabley, Jackie Moms	Ent	75			200	
MacArthur, Arthur	Military	45	90	125	70	Span - Am War General
MacArthur, Charles	Author	15	30		25	Playwright
MacArthur, Douglas	Military	225	600	750	500	Five Star General/WWII
MacArthur, James	Ent	15			35	
MacArthur, Jean	Military	15	20	25	20	Mrs. Douglas MacArthur
MaCartney, George	Political	10	35	85		
MaCaulay, (Emilie) Rose	Author	10	20	35		Br. Novelist and Critic
MaCaulay, Thos. B. Lord	Author	45	65	115		Historian/Poet
Macbeth, Florence	Music	20			50	Am. Soprano
Macchio, Ralph	Ent	20			50	Karate Kid
MacDonald, Charles H.	Aviation	15	30	50	45	WWII ACE
MacDonald, J. Farrell	Ent	25			50	
MacDonald, J. Ramsey	Political	45	130	170	255	British Prime Minister
MacDonald, Jacques E.J.	Military	75	100	250		Marshal of Napoleon
MacDonald, Jeanette	Ent	60	175	275	175	
MacDonald, John A.	Political	35	90			Ist Prime Minister/Canada
MacDonald, Ross	Author	50	150	250		Mystery Writer
MacDonogh, P. M. W.	Military	10		25		
MacDonough, Thomas	Military	100	300	600		
MacDowell, Andie	Ent	20	45		45	
MacDowell, Edward	Music	140	290	600	400	Composer
MacDowell, Melbourne	Ent	15			40	
MacFadden, Bernarr	Business	15	45	75	35	Publisher
MacGraw, Ali	Ent	15	30		25	
Machado, Anesia P.	Aviation	35	50	75	65	
Machiavelli, Niccolo	Author	500	1,250	RARE	RARE	1469-1527
Mack, Connie	Sports	175			400	1937 HOF Baseball
Mack, Helen	Ent	10			30	
Mack, Marion	Ent	10		45	35	
Mack, Ted	Ent	10			15	Amateur Hour
Mackaill, Dorothy	Ent	20	30	70	65	
MacKall, William	Civil War	250		1,250		CSA General/War Dated
MacKall, William W.	Civil War	125	250			CSA General/1816-91
Mackay, John William	Business	50	100	200		Founder Postal Telegraph
MacKaye, Percy 1875-56	Author	40	90	150		Am. Poet
Mackensen, August von	Military	20		40	85	WWI Ger Field Marshal
Mackenzie, Morell, Sir	Science	75	175	350		
Mackie, Bob	Business	5		25	15	Fashion Designer
MacLachlan, Kyle	Ent	10			30	
MacLaine, Shirley	Ent	15	25	35	50	
MacLane, Barton	Ent	50			125	Maltese Falcon...

Name	Field	SIG	DS	ALS	SP	Remarks
MacLaren, Donald M.	Military	25	40	95	75	
MacLeish, Archibald	Author	30	115	135	40	Am Poet
MacLeod, Gavin	Ent	5	20	20	20	Love Boat Captain
MacInnes, Helen	Author	10		20		Novelist
MacMahon, Aline	Ent	25			60	
MacMahon, Marie E.P.	Political	35	110	225		Fr.Soldier, Marshal
MacMillan, Donald B.	Explorer	40	75	150		Am. w/Peary /North Pole
MacMillan, Harold	Political	25	85	150	50	British Prime Minister
MacMurray, Fred	Ent	25	65		50	1907 - 1991
MacNee, Patrick	Ent	15			35	The Avengers
MacNelly, Jeff	Cartoonist	25			50	Shoe
MacPherson, Elle	Ent	20			40	Super Model
MacRae, Gordon	Ent	20			35	1921 - 1986
MacRae, Meredith	Ent	5			15	
MacRae, Sheila	Ent	5			15	
MacReady, George	Ent	20			40	
MacReady, William C.	Ent	15		122		
MacVeagh, Franklin	Political	10	25	50	25	Sec'y Treasury
MacVeagh, Wayne	Political	60		100		Attorney General
Macy, Bill	Ent	5	20		15	Maude
Madden, Charles Edw.	Military	45	100	200	100	British Admiral
Madden, John	Sports	10			20	Football
Madeira, Jean	Music	15			40	Am. Contralto
Madigan, Amy	Ent	15			40	
Madison, Dolley Payne	First Lady	RARE	RARE	12,000	RARE	1768-1849
Madison, Guy	Ent	10			25	
Madison, James	President	550	1,100	3,000	2,500	1751-1836
Madonna	Music	125	900	900	250	
Madriguera, Enric	Music	15			30	Big Band Leader
Madsen, Chris	Western	RARE	RARE	RARE	RARE	Outlaw & Indian Fighter
Madsen, Michael	Ent	15			30	
Madsen, Virginia	Ent	10			25	
Maeterlinck, Maurice	Author	35	115	205	425	Nobel in Literature
Magnani, Anna	Ent	275			450	1908 - 1973
Magrath, Andrew G.	Civil War	35	60	80		CSA Governor of SC
Magritte, Renb 1898-1967	Art	200	350	900		Surrealist Painter
Magruder, John B.	Civil War	275	525	475		CSA General/1807-71
Magsaysay, Ramon	Political	25	50	150	35	Pres. Philippines
Maguire, W.A Cpt.	Military	25	50	75	60	
Mahan, Alfred Thayer	Military	50	75	100		US Naval Officer
Maharis, George	Ent	10		25	20	
Mahen, Robert A.	Business	15	30	70	40	
Mahendra Bir Bikram	Royalty	35	50	125	50	King, Leader Nepal
Mahler, Alma	Author	30		125		
Mahler, Gustav 1860-1911	Music	550	1,200	3,500	RARE	Austrian Composer
Mahone, William	Civil War	120	252	365		CSA General/1826-95
Mahoney, Jock	Ent	25	50	60	55	
Mahoney, John	Ent	20			40	Frasier
Mahurin, Walker M.	Aviation	20	35	50	40	WWII ACE

Name	Field	SIG	DS	ALS	SP	Remarks
Maiakovski, Vladimir V.	Author	300	795	RARE	RARE	
Mailer, Norman	Author	35	125	175	75	
Maillol, Aristide	Art	200	460	800		Fr Sculptor
Main, Marjorie	Ent	105			250	
Maintenon, Francoise	Royalty			975		2nd Wife Louis XIV
Maison, Nicholas J.	Military	45	150	175		General under Napoleon
Maison, Rene	Music	30			65	Opera
Maitland, Lester J.	Aviation	20		40		
Major, John	Political	10			30	Br. Prime Minister
Majors, Lee	Ent	10	25		30	Six Million Dollar Man
Makarios III, Mikhail	Political	50	65	140	75	Cyprus
Makarova, Natalia	Music	10			15	Ballet
Malamud, Bernard	Author	25	40	105	30	Am. Novelist, Pulitzer
Malcolm X 1925 - 1965	Political	1,250	4,000	14,000	RARE	Playboy Interview - 3000
Malden, Karl	Ent	10	20		25	
Malenkov, Georgi M.	Political	175	350		250	Union Sov. Russia
Malet, C. Francois de	Military	120	240			Gen/Court martial/Shot
Malher, J.P.F.	Military	25	80			French Revolution
Malis, David	Music	10			25	Opera
Malko, Nlcolai	Music	75			225	Russian Conductor
Malkovich, John	Ent	20			50	
Mallarme, Stephane	Author	150				French Poet
Malle, Louis	Ent	20		30	45	Director
Mallory, Charles M.	Aviation	10	25	35	30	WWII ACE
Mallory, Stephen R.	Civil War	125	225	240		CSA Sec'y of Navy.
Malmesbury, Ist Earl	Political	15	30	45		
Malone, Dorothy	Ent	35	60		65	
Malten, Therese	Music	35			125	Opera
Malthus, Thomas Robert	Author	300	900			Educator, Author
Mamas and the Papas	Music	350	750		775	Signed by all four members
Mamet, David	Ent	10			25	DIrector
Mamoulian, Rouben	Ent	10	35		35	Director
Mana-Zucca	Music	30			100	Composer/Singer
Manchester, Melissa	Music	20			40	
Manchester, William	Author	5		20	15	
Mancini, Henry	Music	30	60		75	Composer/Conductor
Mandel, Howie	Ent	10			20	
Mandela, Nelson	Political	200	RARE	RARE	375	
Manderson, Charles	Civil War	70	105	150		Union General/1837-1911
Mandrell, Barbara	Music	10			25	
Mandylor, Costas	Ent	20			40	
Manet, Edouard 1832-83	Art	RARE	2,000	RARE	RARE	Impressionist School Fndr
Maney, George E.	Civil War	150				CSA General/1826-1901
Manfrini, Luigi	Music	45			125	Opera
Mangano, Silvana	Ent	25	35	60	50	
Mangione, Chuck	Music	5	20		15	
Manhattan Transfer	Music	35			75	Signed by Entire Band
Manigault, Arthur M.	Civil War	125	250			CSA General/1824-86
Manilow, Barry	Music	25	50		50	

Name	Field	SIG	DS	ALS	SP	Remarks
Mankiewicz, Joseph L.	Ent	20		55	55	AA Winning Director
Mankiller, Wilma	Author	5			20	
Manley, N. W.	Political	10		25	20	Prime Minister Jamaica
Mann, Delbert	Ent	20			45	Director
Mann, Hank	Ent	100				Keystone Kop
Mann, Heinrich	Author	35	145	275		German Novelist
Mann, Horace 1796-1859	Political	35	135	250		Education Reformer
Mann, Iria	Ent	10		20		
Mann, Manfred	Music	90			175	Signed by entire group
Mann, Orrin L.	Civil War	20	35	60		Union Officer
Mann, Thomas	Aviation	15	25	45	35	WWII Double ACE
Mann, Thomas 1875-1955	Author	200	450	900	1,100	Ger, Novelist, Nobel Prize
Manne, Shelly	Music	15			45	Drummer
Mannerheim,C. Gustave	Political		290	850	775	Pres. Finland
Mannering, Mary	Ent	15		25		
Manners, David	Ent	40	75		75	
Manning, Irene	Ent	5		10		
Manning, Stephen H.	Civil War	30	50	100		Union Officer
Manoff, Dinah	Ent	10	20		20	Empty Nest
Manone, Wingy	Music	20			50	Jazz Trumpet
Mansfield, Joseph K.F.	Civil War	150	300	400		Union General/1803-62
Mansfield, Jayne	Ent	175	350		400	1933 - 1967
Mansfield, Joseph K.	Civil War	275	RARE	RARE	RARE	Union Gen.KIA 1862
Mansfield, Richard	Ent	50		150		
Manship, Paul Howard	Art	75	275	450		Am Sculptor
Manson, Charles	Criminal	75	250	350	200	Murderer, Cult Figure
Manson, Marilyn	Music	40			80	Signed by Entire Group
Manson, Marilyn	Music	25			50	
Manstein, Erich von	Military	25	75	100	75	Planned Assault vs France WWII
Mantegna, Joe	Ent	15			35	
Mantell, Gideon A .	Science	10	25	40		Paleontologist
Mantelli, Eugenia	Music	25			65	Opera
Manteuffel, Edwin F.	Military	150	400	400		WWII Pruss Field Marshal
Manteuffel, Hasso von	Military	50	150	200	100	Ger. Tank Commander
Mantle, Mickey	Sports	75			150	Baseball/1974 HOF
Mantovani	Music	10			20	Conductor-Arranger
Manuel, Lisa	Business	100	350			Fur Trader
Mao, Tse Tung	Political	3,000	RARE	RARE	RARE	Chinese Communist Leader
Maples, Marla	Ent	10		25		
Mapleson, James H.	Music	75				Opera
Marat, Jean-Paul	Military	RARE	RARE	4,500	RARE	
Marbot, J.B.A.M.	Military	25	70	125		Napoleonic General
Marceau, Marcel	Ent	25	70		95	Mime
March, Fredric 1897-1975	Ent	35	75	100	100	AA Winner
Marchesi, Mathilde	Music	50		160	175	Ger. Mezzo-Sopr. Teacher
Marciano, Rocky	Sports	250			600	Boxer
Marconi, Guglielmo	Science	300	750	1,400	650	Inventor/Nobel 1874-1937
Marcos, Ferdinand E.	Political	50	125		125	Pres. Philippines
Marcos, Imelda	Political	15	35		25	Phillipines

Name	Field	SIG	DS	ALS	SP	Remarks
Marcus, Rudolph A.	Science	20	35		30	Nobel Chemistry
Marcus, Stanley	Business	25	75	150	50	Merchant. Nieman-Marcus
Marcy, Randolph B.	Civil War	60		150		Union General/1812-87
Marcy, Randolph B.	Civil War	75		600		Union General/War Dated
Marcy, William L.	Political	50	150	225		Sec'y War, State
Maren, Jerry	Ent	15			35	Oz Munchkin
Marescot, Armand S.	Military	45		150		French Revolution
Maressyev, Alexei	Aviation	125				Russian ACE
Maret, Hugues B.	Military	75	150	300		Napoleans Advisor
Maret, Hugues B.	Military	100	200			PM/Napolean Advisor
Margie	Cartoonist	20			75	Little Lulu
Margret, Ann	Ent	15			35	
Marguerite De Valois	Royalty		1,750			Queen of France
Maria (Castile)	Royalty		2,500			Queen of Alfonso V
Maria Theresa 1717-80	Royalty	200	680	900		
Mariborough,John C.	Military	220	700			British General
Marie Amelie	Royalty	170	240	500		Queen of Louis Phillippe I
Marie Antoinette (Fr)	Royalty	1,200	4,850	RARE	RARE	Queen of Louis XVI France
Marie of Modena	Royalty	335	530			Queen of James II
Marie of Naples	Royalty	20		85		Queen of King Louis-Phillipe I
Marie of Romania	Royalty	85	115	240	100	
Marin, John	Art	100	225	450		Am. Watercolorist
Marinaro, Ed	Ent	5			15	
Marino, Dan	Sports	20			50	Football
Marion, Francis 1732-95	RevWar	4,000	7,500	12,500	RARE	The Swamp Fox
Maris, Roger	Sports	150			300	Baseball
Mariscal, Don Ignacio	Political	20	35	55		VP/Mexico
Markey, Enid 1890 - 1981	Ent	150	Scarce	Scarce	Scarce	First Jane/Tarzan
Markham, Edwin	Author	35	125	140	65	The Man With The Hoe
Markham, William	Political	150	400			Colonial Gov. PA
Markova, Alicia	Music	20			50	Ballet
Markowitz, Harry M., Dr.	Science	20	35	45		Nobel Economics
Marks, Johnny	Music	35	75	125	50	Composer
Marks, William, Jr.	Political	35	140			PA Senator
Marley, Bob	Music	600	RARE	RARE	RARE	Rock HOF
Marlin, Mahlon F.	Business	45	125	200		Pres/Marlin Firearms
Marlow, Lucy	Ent	5	15		15	
Marlowe, Hugh	Ent	25			50	
Marlowe, Julia	Ent	25	35	70	60	
Marmaduke, John (WD)	Civil War			2,400		CSA General
Marmaduke, John S.	Civil War	100	300			CSA General/1833-87
Marmont, A.F.L.V. Duke	Military	45	90			Marshal of France
Marquand, John P.	Author	40	120	165	45	Am. Novelist. Pulitzer
Marques, Antonio	Music	35			85	Opera
Marquez, Gabriel	Author	100			245	Nobel Prize Winner
Marriott, J.	Business	20	35	70	30	Marriott Hotel Chain
Marryat, Frederick	Military	30	100	225		Br. Naval Cmmdr. Novelist
Marsala, Joe	Music	30			65	Composer
Marsalis, Branford	Music	10			25	Conductor

Name	Field	SIG	DS	ALS	SP	Remarks
Marsalis, Wynton	Music	15			30	Trumpet
Marsh, Jean	Ent	10			20	
Marsh, Joan	Ent	15	20	40	35	
Marsh, Mae	Ent	30	40	75	40	
Marsh, Marion	Ent	15			40	
Marsh, Ngaio, Dame	Author	20	35	50	40	
Marshall, Catherine	Author	75	100	150	125	
Marshall, E. G.	Ent	10			25	
Marshall, George C.	Military	200	300	550	400	WWII Chief of Staff
Marshall, George E.	Ent	35			75	Director
Marshall, Herbert	Ent	20	75		65	1890 - 1966
Marshall, Humphrey	Civil War	200	300			CSA General/1812-72
Marshall, Humphrey (WD)	Civil War	250	450			CSA General
Marshall, John	SuprCt	600	1,200	2,500		Chief Justice
Marshall, John, Sir	Political	10	20	35	20	Prime Minister/New Zealand
Marshall, Margaret	Music	10			25	Opera
Marshall, Penny	Ent	20	45		50	Actress/Director
Marshall, Peter	Ent	20			40	Hollywood Squares
Marshall, Thomas R.	Vice Pres	75	175	400	175	Wilson VP
Marshall, Thurgood	SuprCt	115	200		175	lst Afro-Am. Justice
Marshall, William	Civil War	25	40	75		Union General/1825-96
Marshall, William	Ent	15			25	Director
Marston, Gilman 1811-90	Civil War	30	80			Union General
Marterie, Ralph	Music	10			20	Big Band Leader
Martin & Lewis	Ent	150	500		250	Both Signed
Martin, Andrea	Ent	10			20	
Martin, Billy	Sports	75			150	Baseball
Martin, Chris Pin	Ent	50		100		
Martin, Dean 1917-95	Ent	35	110		90	
Martin, Dean Vincent	Ent	5	15		15	
Martin, Dewey	Ent	10			25	
Martin, Dick	Ent	5			20	Laugh In
Martin, Frank 1890-1974	Music	20			90	Swiss Composer
Martin, Freddie	Music	35			65	Big Band Leader-Pianist
Martin, George	Music	25			60	Beatle's Producer
Martin, Glenn L.	Aviation	75	170	265	250	Aeronautical Pioneer
Martin, James G. (WD)	Civil War	182	663			CSA General
Martin, James Green	Civil War	95	225			CSA General/1819-78
Martin, Kellie	Ent	10			25	
Martin, Luther	RevWar	70	175	360		Continental Congress
Martin, Mary 1913-1990	Ent	35	45		50	Peter Pan on Broadway
Martin, Pamela Sue	Ent	10			20	Nancy Drew
Martin, Ricardo	Music	15			45	Opera
Martin, Ricky	Music	25			50	
Martin, Ross	Ent	45	65		100	Wild,Wild West
Martin, Steve	Ent	15	45		40	
Martin, Struther	Ent	35			80	
Martin, Theodore, Sir	Author	5		25	10	
Martin, Tony	Ent	10			25	

Name	Field	SIG	DS	ALS	SP	Remarks
Martin, William T.	Civil War	100	250	400		CSA General/1823-1910
Martin, William T. (WD)	Civil War	170	400	500		CSA General
Martinelli, Giovanni	Music	30	50		65	Opera/Tenor
Martini, Nino	Music	15			45	Opera/Tenor
Martini, Steve	Author	5	10		10	
Martino, Al	Ent	5			10	
Martino, Donald	Music	20	35	75		Pulitzer
Marton, Eva	Music	20			50	Opera
Marvin, Lee	Ent	100	150		200	
Marx Brothers	Ent	1,200			2,550	Four Brothers
Marx Brothers	Ent	900			1,750	Chico,Groucho,Harpo (3)
Marx, Chico	Ent	125	170	325	325	
Marx, Groucho	Ent	200	400		350	1890 - 1977/Full Signature
Marx, Harpo	Ent	400			750	Scarcest Brother
Marx, Karl 1818-83	Author	750	1,500	RARE	RARE	Ger. Political Philosopher
Marx, Richard	Music	20			50	
Marx, Zeppo 1901-79	Ent	75	125		125	Fifth Marx Brother
Mary (of Teck) 1867-1953	Royalty	125	200	200	300	Queen of George V (Eng.)
Mary Adalaide	Royalty	25	70	150		Duchess of Teck
Mary I 1516-58	Royalty	1,000	3,000	RARE		
Mary II (Eng)	Royalty	400	1,200	RARE	RARE	
Masaryk, Jan	Political	75	155	275	450	Pres. Czechoslavakia
Masaryk, Thomas G.	Political	100	250	500	600	Czech First President
Mascagni, Pietro 1863-45	Music	165	375	500	600	Composer
Mascherini, Enzo	Music	20			50	Opera
Masefield, John 1878-67	Author	35	70	212	75	Br. Poet Laureate
MASH (Cast)	Ent				550	Eight Main Characters
Maskelyne, Nevil	Science	85	250	405		Br. Astronomer
Mason, George	RevWar	RARE	4,500	RARE	RARE	
Mason, Jackie	Ent	10	20		20	
Mason, James	Ent	40	65	75	90	1909 - 1984
Mason, James M.	Civil War	50	100	150		CSA Diplomat
Mason, LeRoy	Ent	50			150	
Mason, Marsha	Ent	10			25	
Massena, Andre Duke	Military	100	300	400		Napolean General
Massenet, Jules 1842-12	Music	65	145	255	295	Composer
Massey, Daniel	Ent	10			20	
Massey, Gerald 1828-1907	Author	25	70	95		Poet
Massey, Illona	Ent	20		30	40	1912 - 1974
Massey, Louise & Curt	Music	25			45	Country Western
Massey, Raymond	Ent	30			55	1896 - 1983
Massie, Paul	Ent	5	15		10	
Massine, Leonide	Music	25			75	Dancer/Choreagrapher
Masson, Andre	Art	40	55	95		
Masters and Johnson	Science	20			40	Sex Researchers
Masters, Edgar Lee	Author	50	150	250	65	Poet/1869-1950
Masters, Frankie	Music	10			25	Big Band Leader
Masterson, Mary Stuart	Ent	20			50	
Masterson, Wm. "Bat"	Western	5,000	RARE	RARE	RARE	Sheriff/Gambler

Name	Field	SIG	DS	ALS	SP	Remarks
Mastroantonio, Mary E.	Ent	15	20		45	
Mastroianni, Marcello	Ent	20			45	
Mata Hari (M.G. Zelle)	Military	450	1,100	RARE	RARE	WWI/Spy/Executed
Mather, Cotton	RevWar	900	1,750	2,500		Author
Mathers, Jerry 'Beaver'	Ent	20	45		45	Leave it to Beaver/Beaver
Matheson, Tim	Ent	15			40	
Mathews, George	RevWar	90	175			General/1739-1812
Mathews, Larry	Ent	10			20	
Mathewson, Christy	Sports	1,200			3,500	1936 Baseball HOF
Mathis, Johnny	Music	15	35		30	
Mathis, Samantha	Ent	30			75	
Matisse, Henri 1869-1954	Art	550	750	1,200	RARE	Dr Painter and Sculptor
Matlack, Timothy	RevWar	100	275	400		Continental Congress
Matlin, Marlee	Ent	20	40	50	40	AA Winner
Matoni, Walter	Aviation	10			35	WWII German ACE
Matsushita, Konosuke	Business	25	65	145	40	Japanese Electronic Giant
Mattea, Kathy	Music	5			15	Country
Mattern, Jimmie	Aviation	15	25	50	35	
Matthau, Walter	Ent	10	25	30	25	AA Winner
Matthews, DeLane	Ent	10			30	Dave's World
Matthews, Jessie	Ent	15			30	
Matthews, Stanley	SuprCt	50	150	275		
Mattingly, Thos. Ken	Space	35			90	Astronaut
Mattson, Conrad	Aviation	10		30	25	WWII ACE
Mature, Victor	Ent	20			40	
Matzky, Gerhard	Military	20	60			WWII Nazi General
Maugham, W. Somerset	Author	85	250	350	400	Br. Novelist and Playwright
Mauldin, Bill	Cartoonist	25			60	Willie & Joe
Maupassant, Guy de	Author	275	700	900		French Short Story Writer
Maura, Antonio	Political	100	175			
Mauro, Ermanno	Music	15			40	Opera
Maurois, Andre	Author	35	75	125		Fr. Biographer, Novelist
Maury, Dabney H.	Civil War	100		350		CSA General/1822-1900
Maury, Dabney H. (WD)	Civil War	140	280		560	CSA General
Maury, Matthew F.	Civil War	100		672	1,550	CSA Naval Cmdr/1806-73
Mawson, Douglas, Sir	Explorer	75	150	300		Australian Polar Explorer
Max, Peter	Art	125	350			Am. Contemporary Art.
Maxey, Samuel B. (WD)	Civil War	250		RARE		CSA General
Maxey, Samuel Bell	Civil War	125	225	250		CSA General/1825-95
Maxey, Virginia	Ent	5			10	
Maxim, Hiram Percy	Science	40	265			Inventor Maxim Gun Silencer
Maxim, Hiram Stevens	Science	95	190	375	300	Inventor Maxim Machine Gun
Maxim, Hudson 1853-27	Science	60	150	175	175	Inventor Smokeless Powder
Maximilian II	Royalty	110	415	770		Holy Roman Emperor
Maximilian, Ferdinand	Royalty	400	675	1,250		Emperor Mexico
Maxon, R.	Cartoonist	20			50	Tarzan
Maxwell, Lois	Ent	10			25	
Maxwell, Marilyn	Ent	10			35	1921 - 1972
Maxwell, Robert	Aviation	10	25	30	25	WWII ACE

Name	Field	SIG	DS	ALS	SP	Remarks
Maxwell, Robert	Business	50			125	Publisher/Died Mysteriously
May, Edna	Ent	20		30	30	
May, Marty	Ent	10			20	
Mayall, John	Ent	10			30	
Mayer, Louis B.	Ent	75	175	275	225	MGM Film Studio
Mayer, Maria, Dr.	Science	30	85		50	Nobel Physics
Maynard, Ken 1895-1973	Ent	100		150	175	Cowboy Star
Maynor, Dorothy	Ent				275	
Mayo, 6th Earl	Political	10		30		
Mayo, Charles H., Dr.	Science	140	290	380	475	Co-Founder Mayo Clinic
Mayo, Charles W., Dr.	Science	65	140	235	350	Surgeon Mayo Clinic
Mayo, Henry Thomas	Military	15	40	75	40	
Mayo, Virginia	Ent	10			25	
Mayo, William J., Dr.	Science	105	290	380	475	Co-Founder Mayo Foundation
Mayron, Melanie	Ent	15			40	
Maytag, Frederick L.	Business	100	275	600	200	Maytag Appliances
Mazurski, Paul	Ent	20	45		40	Director
Mazzini, Joseph	RevWar	50	150	450		Italian Patriot
Mazzoleni, Ester	Music	75			200	Opera
McAdam, John	Science	RARE	850	RARE	RARE	
McAdoo, William G.	Political	25	75	150	50	Wilson Sec'y Treasury
McAllister, Lon	Ent	15			30	
McArdle, Andrea	Ent	5		15	15	
McArthur, John 1826-06	Civil War	40				Union General
McAuliffe, Anthony A.	Military	85	175	175	350	WWII General
McAuliffe, Christa	Space	450	1,000	1,250	800	Died in Challenger Disaster
McAvoy, May	Ent	10			25	
McBain, Diane	Ent	5		15	10	
McBain, Ed	Author	10	20	50	15	
McBride, Martina	Ent	15			30	
McCaffrey, Anne	Author	5			10	Novelist
McCain, John N.	Military	15	35			WWII Admiral
McCalla, Irish	Ent	10		25	25	Sheena of the Jungle
McCallister, Lon	Ent	10			30	
McCallum, David	Ent	15	40	40	35	Man from UNCLE
McCambridge, Mercedes	Ent	40			75	
McCampbell, David S.	Aviation	15	25	45	75	WWII Top Navy ACE
McCann, Chuck	Business	5		30	10	
McCarey, Leo	Ent	35			65	Director/Producer
McCarthy, Andrew	Ent	20			40	
McCarthy, Jenny	Ent	25			50	
McCarthy, Joe 1908-1957	Political	35	150		95	Senator WI. McCarthyism
McCarthy, Kevin	Ent	10			30	
McCarthy, Mary	Author	45	100		50	Novelist
McCarthy, Michael W.	Business	5			10	
McCartney, Paul	Music	150	400	RARE	300	Beatle
McCauley, Rose, Dame	Author	20			45	
McCay, Peggy	Ent	10			35	
McCay, Winsor	Cartoonist				250	Little Nemo

Name	Field	SIG	DS	ALS	SP	Remarks
McClanahan, Rue	Ent	10			25	Golden Girls
McClellan, George (WD)	Civil War	350	500	750		Union General
McClellan, George B.	Civil War	200	250	500		Union General/1826-85
McClernand, John (WD)	Civil War	70	160	225		Union General
McClernand, John A.	Civil War	45	110	175		Union General/1812-1900
McClintock, Francis Leopold	Explorer	45	115	200		Br. Adm., Arctic Navigator
McClintock, John	Space	5	15		20	Astronaut
McClinton, Delbert	Music	10			25	
McCloskey, Lee	Ent	5	15		15	
McClure, Doug	Ent	10			30	
McClurg, Alexander C.	Civil War	50	85			Union Officer/1832-1901
McColpin, Carroll W.	Military	25	45	75	50	WWII ACE
McComb, Wm. 1828-18	Civil War	95	235	350		CSA General
McConaughey, Matthew	Ent	20			50	
McConnell, Joseph, Jr.	Aviation	75	140	175	150	Top Korean ACE
McCoo, Marilyn	Music	5		15	15	Fifth Dimension
McCook, Alex. M.	Civil War	45		195		Union General/War Dated
McCook, Alex. M. D.	Civil War	35	70	115		Union General/1831-1903
McCook, Anson	Civil War	30	55			Union Officer/1835-1917
McCord, Kent	Ent	10			20	Adam 12
McCormack, John	Music	45	150	300	125	Tenor
McCormack, John W.	Political	10	30	75		Speaker of the House
McCormack, Patty	Ent	5		20	15	
McCormic, Mary	Music	20			45	Opera
McCormick, Anne O'Hare	Author	30	45	100	35	1st Pulitzer Woman Journalist
McCormick, Cyrus H.	Science	350	850	2,000		Invented the Reaper
McCormick, Myron	Ent	20	25	45	40	1907 - 1962
McCormick, Nettie F.	Business	25		90		Mrs. Cyrus McCormick
McCormick, Robert R.	Business	35	140	165	60	Editor Chicago Tribune
McCown, John P.	Civil War	245	750	RARE	RARE	CSA General/War Date
McCown, John Porter	Civil War	95	310			CSA General/1815-79
McCoy, Charles B.	Business	25		75	45	Pres. DuPont Co.
McCoy, Clyde	Ent	5	20		15	
McCoy, Tim	Ent	65	100		150	1891-1978
McCoy, Wilson	Cartoonist	15			50	Phantom
McCrea, Joel	Ent	15	45		40	
McCreary, Richard L.	Military	30	75		40	WWII British General
McCudden, James T.B.	Aviation	125	225	350	300	WWI ACE
McCullers, Carson	Author	50	150	350	85	Am. Novelist/1917-67
McCulloch, Ben 1811-62	Civil War	155	470	565		CSA General
McCulloch, Henry E.	Civil War	145	350			CSA General
McCulloch, Hugh 1808-95	Political	45	140	135		
McCullough, Colleen	Author	35	105	225	45	Novelist/The Thorn Birds
McCullough, John	Ent	10			35	1832-1885
McCullough, Julie	Ent	10			20	Growning Pains/Playboy
McCutcheon, John T.	Cartoonist	10			30	Pulitzer Political Cartoonist
McDaniel, Hattie	Ent	600	1,450	RARE	1,800	AA Winner/GWTW
McDermott, Dylan	Ent	15			35	
McDevitt, Ruth	Ent	10			20	

Name	Field	SIG	DS	ALS	SP	Remarks
McDivitt, James A.	Space	30			35	Astronaut
McDonald, John D.	Author	100	600	Scarce	Scarce	Travis McGee novels
McDonald, M. Nick	Political	15	40		25	Captured LHarvey Oswald
McDonald, Marie	Ent	45	60	90	85	1923-1965
McDonald, Richard J.	Business	75	275		250	McDonalds
McDonald, Skeets	Music	10			20	
McDonnell, James S.	Business	20	45	95	35	Fndr. McDonnell Aircraft
McDonnell, Mary	Ent	20			50	
McDougall, Alexander	RevWar	90	200	400		Gen Continental Army
McDougall, Clinton	Civil War	35	60			Union General
McDowell, Andre	Ent	10			30	
McDowell, Irvin	Civil War	120	235	525	950	Union General/War Date
McDowell, Irvin 1818-85	Civil War	75		250		Union General
McDowell, Malcolm	Ent	20			50	
McDowell, Roddy	Ent	25	50		50	Planet of the Apes
McEntire, Reba	Music	20			50	
McFadden, Gates	Ent	15			40	Star Trek:Next Generation
McFarland, Spanky	Ent	35			75	Little Rascals/Our Gang
McGarru, William D.	Aviation	15	30	45	40	WWII Flying Tigers ACE
McGavin, Darren	Ent	25			50	The Night Stalker
McGee,Don	Aviation	25				WWII ACE
McGillis, Kelly	Ent	15			45	Top Gun
McGinley, Phyllis	Author	10	30	45	20	Poet/Pulitzer Prize Winner
McGoohan, Patrick	Ent	20			45	TV's The Prisoner
McGovern, Elizabeth	Ent	10	20		20	
McGovern, George	Political	10	45		25	
McGovern, John	Author	25	40			
McGregor, Ewan	Ent	30			60	Star Wars
McGuire, Barry	Music	10			25	New Christy Minstrels
McGuire, Dorothy	Ent	15			30	
McGuire, Phyllis	Music	5			10	McGuire Sisters
McGuire, Thomas B.	Aviation	150	300	650	450	WWII/ACE #2 in US
McGwire, Mark	Sports	100			250	Baseball
McHenry, James	Military	200	275	RARE		Signer Constitution
McHugh, Frank	Ent	20	25	65	60	
McHugh, Jimmy	Music	25	75			Composer
McIntire, John	Ent	20			50	
McIntosh, Lachlan	RevWar	550	750	1,375		Killed Button Gwinett/Duel
McKay, Gardner	Ent	5		15	20	
McKean, Thomas	RevWar	250	475	800		Signer/1734-1817
McKeever, Chauncey	Civil War	40		175		
McKellan, Ian	Ent	15			30	
McKenna, Joseph	SuprCt	35	50	80	40	Att'y General
McKenna, Siobhan	Ent	15			35	
McKenzie, Fay	Ent	5			15	
McKeon, Nancy	Ent	10			30	Facts of Life
McKeon, Phillip	ENt	15			35	Alice
McKern, Leo	Ent	15			40	
McKinley, Ida S.	First Lady	400	625	975	550	

Name	Field	SIG	DS	ALS	SP	Remarks
McKinley, Ray	Music	25			65	Bandleader, Drummer
McKinley, William	President	240	375	750	900	Assassinated by Anarchist
McKinley, William	President	340	500	2,400	1,200	As President
McKinly, John	RevWar	75	175			First Gov. DE
McKone, John R,	Military	10		40	30	
McKuen, Rod	Author	20	25	35	50	Poet
McLaglin, Andrew V.	Ent	10		25		
McLaglin, Victor	Ent	125			275	AA Winner/1886-1959
McLain, Raymond S.	Military	30			45	WWII General
McLane, Louis	Business	35	150			Pres. Wells Fargo & Co.
McLane, Louis 1786-1857	Political	15	45	60		Jackson Sec'y Treasury
McLane, Robert	Political	35	80	135		US Minister to Japan
McLaughlin, E.A.	Business	10	35	45	20	
McLaughlin, Kyle	Ent	25			75	
McLaws, Lafayette	Civil War	175	300	400		CSA General/1821-97
McLean, Don	Music	20			45	American Pie
McLean, John 1785-1861	SuprCt	55	200	285		
McLean, Nathaniel C.	Civil War	60	80	170		Union General/1815-1905
McLeod, Archibald N.	Business	RARE	2,500	RARE	RARE	Hudson's Bay Co.
McLeod, Catherine	Ent	5			15	
McMahon, Ed	Ent	10			25	The Tonight Show
McMahon, Horace	Ent	20			50	
McManus, George	Cartoonist	50			125	Bringing Up Father
McMichael, Morton	Author	50	100			1st Ed. Sat Eve Post
McMillan, Edwin M.	Science	20	35	60	30	Nobel Chemistry 1952
McMillan, James W.	Civil War	40				Union General/1825-1903
McMillan, Terry	Ent	5			10	
McMullen, Clements	Military	50	175			WWII General
McNair, Howard	Ent	500	RARE	RARE	RARE	Andy Griffith Show
McNair, Leslie J.	Military	35	100	150	100	WWI General
McNair, Ronald E.	Space	100			275	Died in Challenger Crash
McNally, Stephen	Ent	10			20	
McNamara, Robert S.	Political	15	45		30	
McNamara, William	Ent	10		25	25	
McNarney, Joseph T.	Military	20	50			WWII General
McNaughton, Kenneth	Military	5			10	
McNeill, Don	Ent	10			20	
McNichol, Kristy	Ent	15	25		30	Family/Empty Nest
McPartland, Jimmy	Music	30	50		75	Jazz Trumpet
McPhatter, Clyde	Music	400		800		Scarce
McPhearson, Elle	Ent	15			35	
McPherson, Aimee S.	Clergy	100	300	400	350	
McPherson, James B.	Civil War	125	225	300		Union General/1828-64
McQuade, James	Civil War	25	70	175		Union General/1829-85
McQuade, James	Civil War	45	85			Union General/War Date
McQueen, Butterfly	Ent	55	85	100	75	GWTW "Prissy"/1911-97
McQueen, Steve 1930-80	Ent	200	325	400	325	
McRaney, Gerald	Ent	15			45	Major Dad
McReynolds, James C.	SuprCt	30	125	145	100	Wilson Att'y Gen.

Name	Field	SIG	DS	ALS	SP	Remarks
McShane, Ian	Ent	10		20	25	
McShann, Jay	Music	50			125	Jazz Pianist
McVey, Patrick	Ent	10			20	
McWethy, John	Ent	5			20	ABC News
McWhorter, Hamilton	Aviation	15	25	45	35	WWII ACE
McWilliams, Caroline	Ent	5			10	
Mead, Margaret 1901-78	Science	70	125	170	225	
Meade, George G.	Civil War	300	400		450	Union General/1815-72
Meade, George G.	Civil War	650	900	RARE	RARE	Union General War Dated
Meadows, Audrey	Ent	25	55		55	HoneyMooners
Meadows, Jayne	Ent	10			20	
Meagher, Thomas	Civil War	150	600	950		Union General/War Dated
Meagher, Thomas F.	Civil War	75	175	250		Union General/1823-67
Meaney, Colm	Ent	15			35	Star Trek : Next Generation
Meany, George	Political	15	30		90	Pres. AFL-CIO
Meara, Anne	Ent	5			15	
Meat Loaf	Music	20			45	
Medawar, Peter B., Sir	Science	20	30	60	25	Nobel Medicine 1960
Medici, Cosimo I. de	Royalty	375	1,200			Duke of Florence
Medici, Fernando de	Royalty	370	1,250	RARE		Great Duke
Medicis, Catherine de	Royalty	270	800	RARE		Queen of Henry II of France
Medicis, Francesco de	Royalty	100	200	500		
Medicis, Marie de	Royalty	350	950	RARE		Queen of Henry IV (Fr)
Medill, Joseph	Author	125		250		A founder Repub. Party
Medina, Patricia	Ent	5			15	
Medley, Bill	Music	10			20	
Meeker, Ralph	Ent	25			40	
Meese, Edwin III	Political	10	20	35	25	Att'y General
Mehta, Zubin	Music	20			50	Conductor
Meier, Waltraud	Music	15			35	Opera
Meighan, Tom	Ent	35			75	
Meigs, Montgomery	Civil War	45	250	255		Union General/War Dated
Meigs, Montgomery C.	Civil War	45	120	150	200	Union General/1816-92
Meigs, Return J., Jr.	Military	80	200	325		Monroe P.M. General
Meinl, Tanaka	Music	35			75	Opera
Meir, Golda 1898-1979	Political	125	250	550	300	
Melba, Nellie 1859-1931	Music	75	135	250	450	Opera/Soprano
Melbourne, Wm. Lamb	Political	40	75	150		
Melchior, Lauritz	Music	35	75		150	Opera/Tenor
Melis, Carmen	Music	35			75	Opera
Mellencamp, John C.	Music	25			50	
Mellnik, Steve	Military	10	25	35		
Mellon, Andrew 1855-37	Business	250	900	1,200	400	
Melton, James	Music	20			55	Opera Tenor
Melvill, Thomas	RevWar	90	250	550		Memb. Boston Tea Party
Melville, George W.	Military	40	105	170		Union Admiral
Melville, Herman	Author	750	2,000	RARE	RARE	Moby Dick/1819-91
Melville, Sam	Ent	10			25	
Memminger, Christopher	Civil War	165	480	550		CSA Sec'y of Treasury

Name	Field	SIG	DS	ALS	SP	Remarks
Mencken, Henry L.	Author	100	225	350	450	1880-1956
Mendel, Gregor Johann	Science	400	850	2,000		
Mendeleyev, Dmitry	Science	RARE	RARE	1,650	RARE	
Mendelssohn-Bartholdy	Music	600	1,375	3,000	RARE	Composer
Mendes, Abraham C.	Author	15	35	100		Fr. Poet
Mengelberg, Willem	Music	75			200	Dutch Conductor
Menjou, Adolphe	Ent	20	25		75	1890-1963
Menkes, Sara	Music	25			50	Opera
Mennin, Peter	Music	20		65		Composer
Menninger, Karl	Science	30	65	75	60	Menninger Clinic
Menninger, Roy	Science	10	25	40	30	
Menninger, William C.	Science	15	40	70	35	Psychiatrist
Menocal, Mario G.	Political	25			40	Pres. Cuba 1913-21
Menon, V. Krisna	Political	20		25		Ambassador Gr. Britain
Menotti, Gian Carlo	Music	150	250	495	350	Composer
Menuhin, Yehudi	Music	40	55		134	Concert Violinist
Menzies, Robert, Sir	Political	15	50	75	30	Australian Prime Minister
Mercadante, Saverio	Music	150		450		Composer
Mercer, Frances	Ent	5			15	
Mercer, Hugh W.	Civil War	90	170			CSA General/1808-77
Mercer, Marian	Ent	10			35	
Mercer, John Francis	Military	70		125		Aide-de-Camp Gen Lee
Mercer, Johnny	Music	50			135	Vocalist. Pianist
Merchant, Natalie	Music	20			40	
Mercouri, Melina	Ent	25	30	45	65	
Mercury, Freddie	Music	150			300	Lead singer of Queen
Meredith, Burgess	Ent	20	30	45	40	Batman/Penguin 1908-98
Meredith, Samuel	Political	100	200	300		RevWar General
Meredith, Solomon	Civil War	150		450		Union General/1810-75
Merivale, Philip	Ent	10		25	25	
Meriwether, Lee	Ent	5		20	15	Catwoman/Barnaby Jones
Merkel, Una	Ent	15			25	1903-1986
Merli, Francesco	Music	25			75	Opera/Tenor
Merli, Gino J.	Military	10	25			WWII
Merlin de Douai, P.A.	Military	50		150		French Revolution
Merlin, Jan	Ent	10			20	
Merman, Ethel	Ent	25	50		50	1909-1984
Merrick, David	Ent	60			100	Theatrical Producer/Scarce
Merrick, Samuel V.	Business	40	175			Financier
Merrill, Dina	Ent	5	15		15	
Merrill, Frank D.	Military	225		325		General WWII/1903-55
Merrill, Gary 1914-90	Ent	15	20	45	35	
Merrill, Henry T.	Aviation	30	45	100	100	
Merrill, Lewis	Civil War	60	175			Union Officer/1834-96
Merrill, Richard Dick	Aviation	35	55	105	75	
Merrill, Robert	Music	30			50	
Merrill, Stuart	Author	30		125		American Poet
Merriman, Nan	Music				60	Opera
Merritt, Chris	Music	10			30	Opera

Name	Field	SIG	DS	ALS	SP	Remarks
Merritt, Wesley 1834-10	Civil War	85	300	200		Union General
Merton, Thomas	Author	375	900			Priest/Poet
Mesmer, F. Anton, Dr.	Science	115	285	535		1734-1815
Messerschmitt, Wilhelm	Aviation	125	275		395	Ger. Aircraft Designer-Mfg.
Messiaen, Olivier	Music	70	200			Composer
Messick, Dale	Cartoonist	15			60	Brenda Starr
Messick, Don	Ent	30			60	Many Cartoon Voices
Messing, Debra	Ent	10			25	
Messmer, Otto	Cartoonist	75			200	Felix The Cat
Mesta, Perie	Business	25	30	70	35	Washington Hostess
Metallica	Music	55			90	Signed by Entire Band
Metcalf, Laurie	Ent	20			50	Roseanne
Metcalf, Victor H.	Political	20	50	100		Sect Navy
Metchnikoff, Elie	Science	60	100		150	Nobel Physiology 1908
Metternich, Prince	Political	75	250	400		
Meusel, Lucille	Music	10			25	Soprano
Mewman, Larry	Aviation	25			75	
Meyer, E. C.	Military	10		30	20	
Meyerbeer, Giacomo	Music	175	250	400	300	German Composer
Miaskovsky, Nikolai	Music	125				
Michael, George	Music	30			60	Wham/Later Solo Artist
Michaels, Barbara	Author	5	20		15	
Michaels, Bret	Ent	10	20	50	45	
Michaels, Lorraine	Ent	5			10	Playboy Model
Michaels, Marilyn	Ent	5		25	20	
Michelangelo	Art	RARE	RARE	RARE	RARE	
Michele, Denise	Ent	5			10	
Michelet, Jules	Author	40		75		1798-1874
Michelson, Albert A.	Science	120		450		Nobel Physics 1907
Michelson, Charles	Political	15				Speech Writer New Deal
Michener, James A.	Author	40	265	340	115	Am. Novelist. Pulitzer
Middleton, Arthur	RevWar	5,000	12,000	25,000	RARE	Signer Decl. of Indepen.
Middleton, Charles	Ent	125	RARE	RARE	250	Ming the Merciless
Middleton, Henry	RevWar	RARE	4,500	RARE	RARE	President of Congress
Middleton, Robert	Ent	50			150	
Middleton, Velma	Music	30			70	Jazz Vocalist
Midler, Bette	Ent	30			50	
Mielziner, Jo	Ent	15		40	35	Director
Mifflin, Thomas	RevWar	150	450	600		General/1744-1800
Mifune, Toshiro	Ent	15	25	65	40	
Migenes, Julia	Music	15			35	Opera
Mihalovivi, Marcel	Music	30			150	Rumanian
Miklas, Wilhelm 1872-56	Political	35				Pres. Austria
Milano, Alyssa	Ent	20	50		50	Who's the Boss
Milanov, Zinka	Music	20			120	Metropolitan Opera
Milch, Erhard	Aviation	80	250	400	175	
Miles, Josephine	Author	10		25	10	
Miles, Nelson A. 1839-25	Civil War	130	285	350		Union General
Miles, Sarah	Ent	10		25	25	

Name	Field	SIG	DS	ALS	SP	Remarks
Miles, Sylvia	Ent	10	20	35	35	
Miles, Vera	Ent	10		15	20	
Milestone, Lewis	Ent	45			85	Director
Milhaud, Darius 1892-74	Music	150	250	300	450	Composer
Mill, James	Author	75	250	450		Scot.Philosopher,Historian
Mill, John Stuart	Author	150	400	850		Br. Economist, Philosopher
Millais, John Everett, Sir	Art	50	75	250		Pre-RaphaelitePainter
Milland, Ray	Ent	30	50		75	1905-1986
Millay,Edna St. Vincent	Author	140	325	800	1,265	American Poet/1892-1950
Miller, Alice Duer	Author	15	25	45		Novelist, Poet
Miller, Ann	Ent	10			30	
Miller, Arthur	Author	50	100	200	100	Pulitzer/Am. Playwright
Miller, Caroline	Author	10	20			Pulitzer
Miller, Charles Henry	Art	25			100	Landscape Painter
Miller, Denny	Ent	5		20	20	Tarzan
Miller, Eddie	Music	20			45	Big Band Tenor
Miller, Frederick C.	Business	15	35	55	25	Miller Beer
Miller, Glenn 1904-44	Music	200	400	600	450	Big Band Tenor
Miller, Henry	Ent	35	40	75	70	
Miller, Henry V. 1891-80	Author	85	160	350	150	Tropic of Cancer
Miller, Jason	Ent	10			25	
Miller, Joaquin	Author	50		125		American Poet
Miller, John	Civil War	35	50	60		Union General/1831-86
Miller, Ken	Ent	10			20	Child Actor
Miller, Marilyn	Ent	75		240	215	Ziegfield Dancing Star
Miller, Marvin	Ent	10			25	
Miller, Mitch	Music	5			15	Conductor, Arranger
Miller, Patsy Ruth	Ent	25	35	55	45	
Miller, Penelope Ann	Ent	20			50	
Miller, Roger	Music	35			50	
Miller, Samuel F.	SuprCt	95	185	250		1816-1890
Miller, Stanley	Science	15	35	65	20	
Miller, Stephen	Civil War	95	195	295		Union General/1816-81
Millerande, Alexandre	Political	40	45	60	35	Pres of France 1920-24
Milles, Carl	Art	30	55	90		Am, Sculptor
Millet, Jean Frangois	Art	200	450	RARE	RARE	Fr Classical/Religious
Millikan, Robert A., Dr.	Science	100	200	400	200	Nobel Physics
Millinder, Lucky	Music	40			125	Bandleader
Millo, Aprile	Music	15			35	Opera
Mills Brothers	Music	100			200	Signed by All Four
Mills, Darius Ogden	Business	250	750	2,000		Merchant,Banker, Philan.
Mills, Donna	Ent	10			30	Producer
Mills, Earle W.	Military	10	30			
Mills, John, Sir	Ent	20			35	
Mills, Juliette	Ent	10			20	
Mills, Roger Q.	Civil War	25	35	50		CSA Colonel
Mills,Hayley	Ent	15			30	The Parent Trap
Milne, A. A. 1882-1956	Author	225	450	750	550	Winnie the Pooh Creator
Milner, Martin	Ent	5			15	

Name	Field	SIG	DS	ALS	SP	Remarks
Milnes, Sherrill	Music	10			25	Opera
Milosz, Czeslaw, Dr.	Author	45	85		50	Nobel Literature
Milroy, Robert H. 1816-90	Civil War	25	80			Union General
Milsap, Ronnie	Music	5			15	
Milstein, Nathan	Music	35			75	Rus. Violinist
Miltonberger, Butler	Military	35	60			
Mimieux, Yvette	Ent	5			20	
Mincus, Leon	Music	100			375	Composer
Mindil, George W.	Civil War	50		200		Union Officer
Minelli, Liza	Ent	15			30	
Mineo, Sal 1939-76	Ent	200	250		300	Murdered at 37
Mingus, Charlie	Music	RARE	RARE	RARE	RARE	Jazz Musician
Minh, Duong Van Gen.	Military	15	40	75	40	
Minh, Ho Chi	Political	500	1,500	RARE	1,500	Pres. & Fndr N. Vietnam
Minich, Peter	Music	10			20	Opera
Minnelli, Vincente	Ent	30			75	AA Film Director
Minor, Mike	Ent	10			20	
Minter, Mary Miles	Ent	100	150	175	200	1902-1984
Minton, Sherman	SuprCt	50	150	250	100	
Minton, Yvonne	Music	10			25	Opera
Minvielle, Gabriel	Military	850	RARE	RARE	RARE	French Revolution
Miollis, S.A.F.	Military	100	215			French Revolution
Mirabeau, Gabriel H.R	Military	95	275	475		Diplomat/Statesman
Miramon, Miguel (Mex)	Military	25	85	140		Cmdr. Army vs Juarez.
Miranda, Carmen	Ent	100	200		350	1913-1955
Miranda, Isa	Ent	35			85	
Miro, Juan 1893-1983	Art	200	575	700	310	
Mister Mister	Music	25			55	
Mistral, Frederic	Author	30	75	130	50	Nobel Literature 1904
Mistral, Gabriela	Author	20	35	60	25	Nobel Literature in 1943
Mitchel, Ormsby M.	Science	125		475		Union General
Mitchell, Billy (William)	Aviation	200	900	975	1,495	WWI General
Mitchell, Cameron	Ent	15			40	
Mitchell, Charles E.	Business	20	35	65	25	Chmn. National City Bank
Mitchell, Don	Ent	10			20	
Mitchell, Edgar D.	Space	20		150	85	Moonwalker. Apollo 14
Mitchell, Grant	Ent	35			75	
Mitchell, John Grant	Civil War	30	50	125		Union General/1838-94
Mitchell, John N. 1913-88	Political				275	Attorney General
Mitchell, John W.	Aviation	15	25	40	35	WWII ACE
Mitchell, Joni	Music	10			25	
Mitchell, Maggi 1832-18	Ent	25			50	
Mitchell, Margaret	Author	750	1,750	2,500	RARE	Pulitzer/1900-1949
Mitchell, Maria	Science	75	175	275		Astronomer
Mitchell, Ormsby M.	Civil War	RARE	RARE	1,000	RARE	Union General
Mitchell, Silas Weir	Science	35	75			Civil War Surgeon
Mitchell, Stephen Mix	RevWar	75	200			
Mitchell, Thomas	Ent	250			550	GWTW/Scarce
Mitchum, Robert	Ent	10	20		30	

Name	Field	SIG	DS	ALS	SP	Remarks
Mitford, Jessica	Author	20	25	20	20	
Mitropoulous, Dimitri	Music	35	50	95	135	Greek Conductor
Mitscher, Marc A.	Military	375			550	WWII Admiral/RARE
Mitterand, Francois	Political	15	25	40	25	Pres. France
Mittford, Mary Russell	Author	15	20	40		Br. Poet. Historical Drama
Mix, Tom 1880-1940	Ent	150			400	
Mobley, Mary Ann	Ent	5			15	
Modesti, Giuseppe	Music	15			35	Opera
Modigliani, Amedeo	Art	275	840	1,400		
Modine, Matthew	Ent	10			20	
Moessbauer, Rudolf, Dr.	Science	25			55	Nobel
Moffett, W.A., Adm.	Military	15		50	55	
Moffo, Anna	Music	15			35	Opera
Mohler, A. L.	Business	10	20	40	15	
Mohnke,Wllhelm	Military	55			150	German General SS
Moholy-Nagy, Laszlo	Art	80	255			Painter/Photographer
Mohr, Gerald	Ent	35			75	
Mojica, Jose	Music	75			225	Opera
Molders, Werner	Aviation	175	275	400	325	WWII ACE
Molinari, Al	Ent	15			30	Happy Days
Molitor, Gabriel J.J.	Military	75	175	250		Napolean Gen/Fr Marshal
Moll, Kurt	Music	15			35	Opera
Moll, Richard	Ent	10			20	Night Court
Mollet, Guy	Political	20	40	65		Socialist Premier France
Molnar, Ferenc 1878-52	Author	75	160	275		Playwright,Novelist
Moltke, H. Johann L.	Military	15	30	60	30	Nephew Helmuth
Moltke, Helmuth von	Military	100	220	400	295	Prussian Field Marshal
Momaday, N. Scott	Author	10		25	15	
Momo, Giuseppe	Music	15			35	Opera
Monaghan, Tom	Business	10			20	Domino's Pizza
Moncada, Rivera y	Military	RARE	4,500	RARE	RARE	
Moncey, Bon-Adrien J.	Military	50	135	160		Marshal of France
Monck, George 1608-70	Military	95				
Mondale, Walter	Vice Pres	25	40		45	
Mondrian, Piet	Art	225	675	1,600		Dutch.Traditional-Cubism
Monet, Claude 1840-1926	Art	450	1,200	1,500	RARE	Fr. Impressionist
Monk, Thelonious	Music	50			150	Jazz Musician
Monkees	Music	75			150	Signed by all four
Monroe, Bill	Music	50		150		Father of Blue Grass Music
Monroe, Elizabeth	First Lady	RARE	RARE	RARE	RARE	
Monroe, James	President	450	900	2,000		1758-1831
Monroe, Marilyn	Ent	RARE	RARE	15,000	RARE	Signed Norma Jean
Monroe, Marilyn 1926-62	Ent	1,800	2,250	7,500	6,000	
Monroe, Vaughn	Ent	15	25		30	
Montagu, Edwin Samuel	Political	15	50	75	35	Br. Statesman
Montagu, John	Political	75	200	400		Earl of Sandwich
Montalban, Ricardo	Ent	10	15	25	25	Fantasy Island
Montalivet, J.P.B. Count	Military	35	100	225		
Montana, Ashley	Ent	15			35	

Name	Field	SIG	DS	ALS	SP	Remarks
Montana, Bob	Cartoonist	40			175	Archie
Montana, Bull	Ent	25			50	
Montana, Joe	Sports	25			65	Football
Montana, Patsy	Music	15			35	
Montand, Yves	Ent	10			35	
Montcalm, Louis J.	Military	575	1,500	2,500		Marquis
Montefiore, Moses, Sir	Political	45		275		
Montenegro, Conchita	Ent	10			20	
Montessori, Maria	Science	295		900		1st Italian Woman Doctor
Monteux, Pierre	Music	25	50		35	Conductor
Monteverde, Alfred de	Aviation	25	50	85	55	
Monteverde, George de	Aviation	25	50	85	55	
Montez, Lola	Explorer	200		500		
Montez, Maria	Ent	50			100	1920-1951
Montgolfier, Jacques-E.	Aviation	RARE	RARE	1,800	RARE	1st Hot Air Balloonist
Montgolfier, Joseph	Aviation	RARE	RARE	RARE	RARE	
Montgomery, Bernard L.	Military	75	225		350	Br. WWII General
Montgomery, Douglass	Ent	10	15	25	25	
Montgomery, Elizabeth	Ent	60	60		100	Bewitched/Samantha
Montgomery, George	Ent	10			25	
Montgomery, James	Music	15				Composer/1771-1854
Montgomery, John M.	Ent	15			25	
Montgomery, Melba	Music	10			20	
Montgomery, Ray	Ent	10			25	
Montgomery, Robert	Ent	20	30	50	35	1904-1981
Monti, Carlotta	Ent	15	40		40	W.C. Fields Mistress
Monti, Nicola	Music	35			85	Opera
Montoya, Carlos	Music	10		25	25	Classical Guitarist
Moody Blues	Music	150			275	Signed by All Five
Moody, Dwight L.	Clergy	50	100	200	125	Evangelist
Moody, William H.	SuprCt	50	125	175	100	
Moody, William V.	Author	30	85	125		Poet. Playwright
Moog, Bob	Science	50	70	110	65	Inventor. Synthesizer
Moon, Keith	Music	175	250	RARE	350	Deceased Who member
Mooney, Art	Music	10			20	Big Band Leader
Moore, Alfred	SuprCt	3,000	RARE	RARE	RARE	
Moore, Alvy	Ent	10			20	Green Acres
Moore, Andrew B.	Civil War	45	105			CSA Governor/1806-73
Moore, Clayton	Ent	10		40	30	The Lone Ranger
Moore, Clement C.	Author	160	460	RARE	RARE	'Twas the Night Before ....
Moore, Colleen 1900-88	Ent	10	25		35	Silent Screen Major Star
Moore, Constance	Ent	10			20	
Moore, Demi	Ent	35	150		75	
Moore, Dick	Ent	10			15	
Moore, Dudley	Ent	10			35	
Moore, Foster	Cartoonist	15			50	Napoleon
Moore, Francis D., Dr.	Science	10	30	55	20	
Moore, Gary	Ent	10			25	
Moore, George	Author	45	150	125		Irish Novelist

Name	Field	SIG	DS	ALS	SP	Remarks
Moore, Grace 1901-47	Music	65	90		150	Opera/Deceased
Moore, Henry	Art	50	200	450	100	Br. Sculptor. The Thinker
Moore, Jeremy, Sir	Military	5		25	15	General
Moore, Joanna	Ent	10			25	
Moore, John Bassett	Political	75		200		International Lawyer
Moore, John, Sir 1761-09	Military	75		300		
Moore, Julianne	Ent	15			30	
Moore, Marianne C,	Author	75	150		75	Am. Poet. Pulitzer
Moore, Mary Tyler	Ent	10			30	
Moore, Mary Tyler Show	Ent				300	Six Main Characters
Moore, Ray	Cartoonist	25			60	Phantom
Moore, Roger	Ent	25	60		55	James Bond
Moore, Roy D.	Business	10	25		20	
Moore, Samuel P.	Civil War	595	725	800		Surgeon General CSA
Moore, Sara Jane	Criminal	30	80	200		Attempted Ford Assasinat
Moore, Sydenham	Civil War	40	55	90		CSA Officer
Moore, Terry	Ent	5		15	45	
Moore, Thomas	Civil War		440			CSA Gov. of LA/1803-76
Moore, Thomas 1779-52	Author	45	105	475		Irish Poet
Moore, Victor	Ent	25			50	
Moore, William	Political	90	225			
Moorehead, Agnes	Ent	55	75		90	Endora on Bewitched
Moorer, Thomas	Military	70	145		100	Admiral
Moores, Dick	Cartoonist	10			30	Gasoline Alley
Morales, Ramon V.	Political	15	30			Ecuador
Moran, Erin	Ent	40	75		75	Happy Days
Moran, Lois	Ent	5	15		15	
Moran, Thomas	Art	100	225	350		American Western
Moranis, Rick	Ent	10			30	
Moranville, H. Blake	Aviation	10	20	40	30	WWII Naval ACE
More, Thomas, Sir	Author	25,000	RARE	RARE	RARE	
Moreau, Jean-Victor	Military	100	275	300		Fr. General/Napoleon
Morehead, James B.	Aviation	10		35	25	USAF WWII ACE
Moreland, Mantan	Ent	100	125		200	
Morell, George W.	Civil War	45	95	300		Union General/War Dated
Morell, George W.	Civil War	30		100		Union General/1815-89
Moreno, Anthony	Ent	5			10	
Moreno, Bertha	Music	35			100	Opera
Moreno, Buddy	Music	15			45	Bandleader
Moreno, Rita	Ent	10		25	20	
Morgan, Charles L.	Author	25	50	75		British Novelist
Morgan, Dennis	Ent	10		15	15	
Morgan, Edward J.	Ent	10			25	
Morgan, Edwin Denison	Civil War	40	65	95		Union General/1811-83
Morgan, Frank 1890-1949	Ent	375	575	RARE	600	Wizard of OZ
Morgan, George	RevWar	125	425	675		Indian Agent
Morgan, George W.	Civil War	RARE	RARE	RARE	RARE	Union General/1820-93
Morgan, Harry	Ent	5	20	20	15	MASH's Col. Potter
Morgan, Helen 1900-1941	Ent	50	175		200	

Name	Field	SIG	DS	ALS	SP	Remarks
Morgan, Henry	Ent	10			20	
Morgan, Jane	Ent	10			20	
Morgan, Jaye P.	Ent	5			15	
Morgan, John Hunt	Civil War	800	995	1,750		CSA General/1825-64
Morgan, John P. II	Business	275				Financier, Banker
Morgan, John Pierpont	Business	300	900	2,500	1,200	Banker,Financier/1837-13
Morgan, John Tyler	Civil War	125	200	350		CSA General/1824-1907
Morgan, John Tyler	Civil War	200		1,200		CSA General/War Dated
Morgan, Lorrie	Ent	10			25	
Morgan, Michele	Ent	10			25	
Morgan, Ralph	Ent	35			65	1882-1956
Morgan, Russ	Music	20			65	Big Band
Morgan, Sydney, Lady	Author	15	35	60		Ir.Author.The Wild Irish Girl
Morgan, Thomas H.	Science	95	200	425	125	Nobel Medicine 1933
Morgan, Thos. Jeff.	Civil War	70	90	125		Union General/1839-1902
Morgan, Wm. H.	Civil War	25	55	75		Union Officer
Morganna	Ent	5		20	15	The Kissing Bandit
Morgenthau, Henry Jr.	Political	35	75	145	60	FDR Sec'y Treasury
Moriarty, Cathy	Ent	20			40	
Moriarty, Michael	Ent	20			40	Law and Order
Morini, Erica	Music	20			50	Austrian-born Violinist
Morisette, Alanis	Music	25			50	
Morison, Patricia	Ent	15	15	30	25	
Morita, Pat	Ent	10		25	25	Karate Kid
Mork and Mindy	Ent	25			50	Signed by Dawber/Williams
Morley, Christopher	Author	45	90	145		Am. Writer, Editor
Morley, Robert 1908-92	Ent	25	50		65	Noted Br. Actor
Morrill, Justin Smith	Political	45	60	110		1810-98
Morris, Anita	Ent	10			20	
Morris, Charles	Military	20	60			Commodore USN
Morris, Chester	Ent	25	40		60	1901-1970
Morris, Felix J.	Ent	15			40	
Morris, Garrett	Ent	15			30	Sat Nit Live alumni
Morris, Gouverneur	RevWar	190	585	625		Continental Congress
Morris, Greg	Ent	25			50	Mission Impossible
Morris, Howard	Ent	10			20	Andy Griffith Show
Morris, James	Music	10			25	Opera
Morris, Lewis 1726-98	RevWar	675	950	1,500		Signer Decl, of Indepen.
Morris, Lewis, Sir	Author	5		20		
Morris, Robert 1734-1806	RevWar	325	750	750		Signer
Morris, Thomas A.	Civil War	RARE	RARE	3,520	RARE	Union General/1811-1904
Morris, Wayne	Ent	25			60	
Morris, William 1834-96	Art	125	275	550		British Poet
Morris, William Walton	Civil War	25	55	80		Union General/1801-65
Morrison, Herb	Aviation	40	85	160	100	Reporter/Hindenburg Crash
Morrison, Jim 1943-71	Music	650	1,500	RARE	1,550	Lead Singer/The Doors
Morrison, Toni	Author	35	35	90	25	Nobel/Literature
Morrison, Van	Music	15			45	
Morrison, William Ralls	Civil War	25		80		Union Officer

Name	Field	SIG	DS	ALS	SP	Remarks
Morrow, Dwight W.	Political	10	35			Ambass to Mexico
Morrow, Jeff	Ent	5		15	15	
Morrow, Pat	Ent	10			20	
Morrow, Rob	Ent	15			40	
Morrow, Vic 1932-82	Ent	100	150		200	Died Filming Movie
Morse, Barry	Ent	10			20	
Morse, Carleton E.	Author	20	25		30	Radio Writer/Producer
Morse, Jedediah	Science		75	125		Father Modern Geography
Morse, Samuel F. B.	Science	550		1,250	RARE	Telegraph/1791-1872
Mortier, Edouard A.C.J.	Military	35	100	200		French Revolution
Morton, J. Sterling	Political	25	50	145	75	Father Arbor Day
Morton, John 1724-77	RevWar	500	1,200	1,400		Signer Decl. of Indepen.
Morton, Levi 1824-1920	Vice Pres	60	85	240	240	
Morton, Wm. Thos.	Science	170	450	825		1st to use Ether
Mosby, John S.	Civil War	450	900	2,000	2,750	Mosbys Rangers/1833-16
Mosby, John S.	Civil War	350	RARE	4,000	RARE	War Dated
Moscona, Nicola	Music	30			45	Opera
Mosconi, Willie	Sports	30			75	Billiard Legend/Deceased
Moseley, George Van H.	Military		100			MacArthur's Chief of Staff
Moser, Edda	Music	10			25	Opera
Moses, Anna Mary R.	Art	175	500	860	600	GrandMa
Moses, Robert 1888-1981	Political	15	35	65		Dominated NY Politics
Mosley, Jack	Cartoonist	25			65	Smilin' Jack
Mosley, Oswald, Sir	Political	25	65	180	140	
Moss, Kate	Ent	20			50	Super-Model
Mossadegh, Muhammad	Political	45	75	150		Iranian Premier
Mossbauer, Rudolf L.	Science	25	50	75	45	Nobel Physics
Mossman, Doug	Ent	10			20	
Mostel, Zero 1915-77	Ent	50	125		160	Stage, Film Comedy Star
Moszkowski, Moritz	Music	50		150		Ger. Pianist
Motherwell, Robert	Art	75	225	300		Am. Abstract Expressionist
Motley Crue	Music	45			100	
Motley, John Lothrop	Author	30	50	125		Historian,Diplomat
Mott, Charles S.	Business	25				Pioneer Auto. Exec.
Mott, Frank L.	Author	10		35	20	Educator, Pulitzer
Mott, Gershom	Civil War	50	125			Union General/War Dated
Mott, Gershom 1822-84	Civil War	25		50		Union General
Mott, John R.	Clergy	30	45	75	100	Nobel Peace Prize
Mott, Lucretia	Political	70	150	375	250	Reformer, Abolitionist
Mott, Neville F. Dr.	Science	20	35	50	25	Nobel Physics
Moulton, Louise C.	Author	25	70	125		1835-1908
Moulton, William	RevWar	25	125			
Moultrie, William 1730-05	RevWar	160	300			Revolutionary War Gen.
Mountbatten, Louis, Lord	Military	100	175	250	200	Admiral of Fleet/1900-79
Mountevens, Baron	Military	20	60		335	Br. WW I Naval Hero
Moutrie, Alexander	RevWar	35		200		
Mowbray, Alan	Ent	45			75	
Mowbray, H. Siddons	Art	25	40	70		Muralist
Mower, Joseph A.	Civil War	35	100	125		Union General

Name	Field	SIG	DS	ALS	SP	Remarks
Moyers, Bill	Author	5	20	25	15	TV Host
Mozart, Wolfgang A.	Music	RARE	RARE	75,000	RARE	Composer
Mubarak, M. Hosni	Political	60	110	275	80	President Egypt
Mucha, Alphonse	Art	100	RARE	400	RARE	Czech Painter & Illustrator
Muck, Karl, Dr.	Music	20			50	Conductor
Mudd, Roger	Ent	5	10	30	15	Radio-TV News
Muhammed, Elijah	Political	100	250			
Muhlenberg, John Peter	RevWar	150	250	RARE	RARE	General Continental Army
Muir, Jean	Ent	10			20	
Muir, John 1838-1914	Science	600	1,450	1,950		Scot.-Am. Naturalist
Muldaur, Diana	Ent	20			40	
Muldoon, Robert	Political	10	20	30	20	Prime Minister New Zealand
Mulgrew, Kate	Ent	20			45	Star Trek : Voyager
Mulhare, Edward	Ent	15			40	
Mulheen, R.J.	Business	5			10	CEO Boston & Maine RR
Mull, Martin	Ent	10	20		20	Roseanne
Muller, Herman J.	Science	20	35	75	25	Nobel Medicine 1946
Muller, Hermann	Political	50		200		1876-1931
Mulligan, Gerry	Music	10			25	
Mulligan, James A.	Civil War	225				Union Col. KIA Irish Brig
Mulligan, Richard	Ent	10	20		30	Empty Nest/Soap
Mulliken, Robert S., Dr.	Science	30	185	65	35	Nobel Chemistry
Mullowney, Deborah	Ent	5			15	
Mulrooney, Dermot	Ent	20			40	
Mumy, Bill	Ent	10	25		25	Lost in Space
Munch, Charles	Music	10			35	Ger. Conductor
Munch, Edvard 1863-44	Art	75	250			Nor.Painter-Printmaker
Mundelein, George Wm.	Clergy	50	100	200	90	Cardinal
Munford, Thomas T.	Civil War	125		225		CSA General/1831-1918
Muni, Paul 1895-1967	Ent	90	100	125	175	AA Winner
Munro, Caroline	Ent	10	20		25	Bond Girl
Munro, Peter Jay	Political	30	75	150		Nephew of John Jay.
Munsel, Patrice	Ent	20	35	50	50	
Munson, Ona	Ent	125		250	200	GWTW/1906-1955
Munster, Earl of	Military	10	25	40		
Munteanu, Petre	Music	40	110	165		Opera
Muntz, Earl 'Madman'	Business	10		25	20	Pioneer TV Advertiser
Murat, Joachim 1767-15	Military	135	675	590		Napolean Marshall
Murchison, Clint	Business	10		25	20	TX Oil Entrepreneur
Murchison, Clint, Jr.	Business	5		20	15	
Murdoch, Rupert	Business	10	35	55	40	
Murphy Brown	Ent				225	Seven Main Characters
Murphy, Audie 1924-71	Military	125	175	300	350	
Murphy, Ben	Ent	5		15	15	
Murphy, Eddie	Ent	25			50	
Murphy, Frank 1890-1949	SuprCt	65	195	250	150	
Murphy, George L.	Ent	15	20	25	25	1902-1992
Murphy, John Cullen	Cartoonist	20			35	Prince Valiant
Murphy, Turk	Music	20	40		50	Composer/BandLeader

Name	Field	SIG	DS	ALS	SP	Remarks
Murphy, William P., Dr.	Science	30	75	120	35	Nobel Medicine 1934
Murray, Anne	Music	10			30	
Murray, Arthur	Business	10		30	15	Ballroom Dance Studios
Murray, Bill	Ent	25			50	Sat Night Live
Murray, Bob	Aviation	15	25	40	30	WWII ACE
Murray, Don	Ent	5			15	
Murray, Eli	Civil War	30	65			Union General/1844-96
Murray, Jan	Ent	5			10	
Murray, Joseph E., Dr.	Science	20	30		25	Nobel Medicine
Murray, Ken	Ent	15		20	15	1903-1988
Murray, Mae	Ent	30	35	70	60	
Murray, Philip	Political	35	45	70	50	
Murray, Stuart S.	Military	25	75		45	
Murray, William Vans	RevWar	25	40	90		Diplomat
Murrow, Edward R.	Ent	30			75	News Anchor
Murrow, Edward R.	Author	130	300		250	You Can Hear(See) It Now
Musial, Stan	Sports	20			50	1969 Baseball HOF
Mussolini, Benito 1883-45	Political	300	450	RARE	1,200	Fascist Italian Dictator
Muybridge, Eadward	Ent	300		900		RARE
Myers, Mike	Ent	20			50	Sat Nite Live
Myers, Russell	Cartoonist	10		25	35	Broom Hilda
Myerson, Bess	Ent	10		30	25	Miss America

Van Johnson

Louis Jourdan

Juan Carlos I

Sir Isaac Newton

Sir William Osler

Name	Field	SIG	DS	ALS	SP	Remarks
Nabokov, Vladimir	Author	325			900	Novelist
Nabors, Jim	Ent	10	25	25	20	Gomer Pyle
Nache, Maria Luise	Music	20			45	Opera
Nadar (F. Tournachon)	Art	100	175	300		Caricaturist
Nader, George	Ent	15		45	45	
Nadir Shah, Mohammed	Royalty	65				King Afghanistan. Assass.
Nafta, Giulio	Science	25	35	75		Nobel Chemistry 1963
Nagaoka, Guishi	Military	RARE	RARE	RARE	RARE	Father/Japanese Aviation
Nagel, Anne 1912-66	Ent	25			50	
Nagel, Conrad	Ent	20	25	45	70	1897 - 1970/AA Winner
Naglee, Henry M.	Civil War	30	65			Union General/1815-1886
Nagy, lmre	Political	50	150			Hungarian Prem./Executed
Naish, J. Carrol	Ent	50			100	
Najimy, Kathy	Ent	25			50	Veronica's Closet
Nakasone, Y.	Political	25	35	85	35	Japan
Naldi, Nita	Ent	40			65	1899 - 1961
Nansen, Fridtjof 1861-30	Explorer	85	475	375	450	Nor. Zoologist, Statesman
Napavilova, Zofie	Music	25			65	Opera
Napier, Alan	Ent	45	75	150	65	Alfred on TV's Batman
Napier, Chas, James, Sir	Military	15	30	75		Br. Gen. vs U.S. War 1812
Napier, Robert C.	Military	45	35	125		Field Marshal/1810-90
Napier, Sir Wm. F.P.	Military	20	40	70		British General
Napoleon I	Royalty	700	2,200	RARE	RARE	
Napoleon II	Royalty	300	700	2,000		
Napoleon III, Emperor of	Royalty	150	400	500		Nephew of Napolean
Napoleon, Eugene L.	Military				575	
Narz, Jack	Ent	10			20	
Nash, Clarence	Ent	125			175	Voice of Donald Duck
Nash, Graham	Music	15			35	
Nash, Johnny	Music	25			50	
Nash, Ogden	Author	45	65	100	65	Poet
Nash, Walter	Political	15	40	65	25	P.M. New Zealand
Nasir-edun Shah Qajar	Royalty	750		3,500		King (Shah) Persia
Nasmyth, James 1808-90	Science	100				Steam Hammer
Nasser, Garnet Abdel	Political	75	400	350	275	President Egypt
Nast, Thomas 1840-1902	Cartoonist	125	350	300	RARE	Political Cartoonist.
Nathan, George Jean	Author	10		35	15	Drama Critic
Nathans, Daniel, Dr.	Science	25	35	45	35	Nobel Medicine
Nation, Carry 1846-1911	Clergy	75	185	200	RARE	Temperance Agitator
Natividad, Kitten	Ent	10			20	Model
Natwick, Mildred	Ent	25	35		30	1908 - 1998
Navon, Yitzhak	Political	20			50	Israel
Nazimova, Alla	Ent	75			100	1879 - 1945

Name	Field	SIG	DS	ALS	SP	Remarks
Neagle, Anna, Dame	Ent	10	25		30	1904-1986
Neal, Bob	Aviation	15	35	45	40	WWII ACE/Flying Tigers
Neal, Patricia	Ent	5	20	25	20	AA Winner
Neal, Sam	Ent	15			45	Jurassic Park
Neal, Tom	Ent	10			20	
Neale, Bob	Aviation	25			70	WWII Flying Tiger
Nebel, Rudolf	Science	40	100			
Neblett, Carol	Music	15			35	Opera
Necker, Jacques	Military	125	350			Fr. Financier & Statesman
Needham, Hal	Ent	10			20	Director
Neel, Louis Eugene F.	Science	20	30	40	25	Nobel Physics
Neeson, Liam	Ent	25			60	Darkman/Star Wars
Negley, James S.	Civil War	40	75	100		Union General/1826-1901
Negri, Joe	Ent	10			20	
Negri, Pola	Ent	35	75		125	
Nehru, B.K.	Political	10			20	Ambassador
Nehru, Jawaharlal	Political	130	350	700	400	Assasinated PM/1889-64
Neidlinger, Gustav	Music	15			40	Opera
Neil, Vince	Music	20			50	
Neill, James	Ent	15			35	
Neill, Noel	Ent	10	25		20	TV's first Lois Lane
Neiman, LeRoy	Art	40	150	150	75	Sports Artwork
Nelligan, Kate	Ent	10		25	20	
Nelson, Barry	Ent	15			25	
Nelson, Craig T.	Ent	15			40	Coach
Nelson, David	Ent	15	40		55	Ozzie & Harriett
Nelson, Ed	Ent	10			15	
Nelson, Gene 1920-96	Ent	20			60	
Nelson, Harriet Hilliard	Music	25			50	Singer/TV star
Nelson, Horatio 1758-05	Military	800	1,900	3,000		Br. Admiral
Nelson, John	Political	20	50	100		Tyler Att'y General
Nelson, Lori	Ent	5		15	15	
Nelson, Ozzie	Ent	35			75	Ozzie and Harriet Fame
Nelson, Ozzie & Harriet	Ent	100	200			Signed by Both
Nelson, Rick	Music	100	300	RARE	275	
Nelson, Samuel	SuprCt	50	150	200		1792 - 1873
Nelson, Thomas Jr.	RevWar	550	1,400	2,500		Signer
Nelson, Willie	Music	15			40	Country
Nemerov, Howard	Author	10		35	25	3rd Poet Laureate US
Nemeth, Maria	Music	20			60	Opera
Nero, Peter	Music	5		15	15	Jazz Pianist
Nesbit, Wilbur	Author	10	20	30		
Nesbitt, Cathleen	Ent	15			30	
Nesmith, Michael	Music	25			50	The Monkees
Ness, Eliot	Political	375	800	RARE	RARE	
Nethersole, Olga	Ent	15	40		45	
Nettleton, Lois	Ent	5		15	15	
Neubert, Frank	Aviation	25	75			
Neurath, Constantin von	Political	45	80	150	100	

Name	Field	SIG	DS	ALS	SP	Remarks
Nevelson, Louise	Art	50	80	150	90	Am Sculptor/Large Pieces
Neville, Aaron	Music	10			25	
Neville, Henry	Music	10			25	
Nevin, Ethelbert	Music	75	150	300	100	Composer
New Kids on the Block	Music	50			150	Signed by All in the Group
Newcomb, Simon	Science	75	200	300		Am. Astronomer
Newell, David	Ent	10			20	
Newhart, Bob	Ent	5	20	25	20	Newhart
Newhouse, Samuel	Business	15	25	45	25	Newspaper-Radio-TV
Newley, Anthony	Music	5			15	
Newman, Barry	Ent	5			10	
Newman, Paul	Ent	100	200	RARE	250	
Newman, Randy	Music	10	25		25	
Newmar, Julie	Ent	10	25	35	25	Catwoman on TV's Batman
Newsom, Tommy	Music	10	20		20	Bandleader/Tonite Show
Newton - John, Olivia	Ent	25	60		50	Singer-Actress
Newton, Huey P.	Political	100			350	Afro-Am. Activist
Newton, Isaac, Sir	Science	4,000	12,000	25,000	RARE	
Newton, John 1823-95	Civil War	60		300		Union General
Newton, Juice	Music	10	30		20	
Newton, Robert	Ent	50	75	100	75	
Newton, Wayne	Ent	10			35	
Ney, Michael	Military	125	250	500		Marshal of France
Ney, Richard	Ent	15			35	
Ngo, Dinn Diem	Political	100				South Vietnamese Pres.
Niarchos, Stavro	Business	45	125	150	75	
Nicholas I 1796-1855	Royalty		1,200			Czar of Russia
Nicholas II 1868-1918	Royalty		2,500	RARE		Last Czar of Russia
Nicholas, Denise	Ent	5			15	
Nicholas, Prince & King	Royalty	25	60	150		Greece
Nicholls, Francis R. T.	Civil War	75	125	175		CSA General/1834-1912
Nichols, Barbara	Ent	20			45	
Nichols, Ebenezer B.	Business	50	150			Early TX Banker
Nichols, Mike	Ent	35			100	Film Director
Nichols, Nichelle	Ent	15			35	Star Trek
Nichols, Red	Music	35			75	Jazz Instrumentalist
Nichols, Ruth Roland	Aviation	125	250		250	
Nichols, William A.	Civil War	25	75			Union Officer/1818-69
Nicholson, Jack	Ent	25	100	RARE	50	Joker in Batman Movie
Nicholson, John 1783-46	Military	30	75	175		Commodore U.S. Navy
Nicholson, Meredith	Author	20	50	125	30	
Nickerson, Franklin S.	Civil War	25	50	65		Union General
Nicklaus, Jack	Sports	50			150	1974 Golf HOF
Nicks, Stevie	Music	25		75	50	Fleetwood Mac
Nicol, Alex	Ent	10			25	
Nicolai, Elena	Music	30			65	Opera
Nicolay, John G.	Civil War	35	150	250		Lincoln Personal Sec'y.
Nicollet, Joseph N.	Explorer	100	225	300		
Nielsen, Alice 1876-1943	Music	45			150	Opera

Name	Field	SIG	DS	ALS	SP	Remarks
Nielsen, Asta	Music	20			50	Opera
Nielsen, Brigitte	Ent	10	30		25	
Nielsen, Carl	Music	200	450	750		Danish Composer
Nielsen, Gertrude	Ent	10			25	
Nielson, Leslie	Ent	10			20	
Niemack, Horst	Military	20			50	Ger. General Major
Niesen, Gertrude	Music	10			15	
Nietzsche, Friedrich	Author	475		775	RARE RARE	German Poet
Nigh, William	Ent	15			30	
Nightingale, Florence	Science	450	750	750		1820-1910
Nijinsky, Vaslav 1890-50	Music	500		RARE RARE		Ballet
Nikisch, Artur	Music	35	65	85		Hungarian Conductor
Nikolayev, Andryan G.	Space	150			200	Russian Cosmonaut
Niles, Wendell	Ent	10			20	
Nillson, Christine	Music	45		175		Opera
Nilssen, Anna Q.	Ent	15	25		45	
Nilsson, Birgit	Music	15			35	Swe. Soprano, Opera
Nilsson, Harry	Music	50	100		100	
Nimersheim, Jack	Author	5		20	20	Campbell Award nominee
Nimitz, Chester W.	Military	125	300	350	400	1885-1966
Nimoy, Leonard	Ent	35	75		75	Spock on Star Trek
Nin, Anais	Author	60	125	200	100	
Nirenberg, Marshall W.	Science	15	25	45	25	Nobel Medicine 1968
Nirvana	Music	160	400		350	Signed by All Three
Nissen, Greta	Ent	10			25	
Nitty Gritty Dirt Band	Music	35			65	Signed by all
Niven, David 1909-83	Ent	40	75	125	75	AA Winner
Nixon, John 1733-1808	RevWar	125	275			
Nixon, Marni	Ent	10			20	
Nixon, Patricia 1912-92	First Lady	40	75	250	175	
Nixon, Richard M.	President	200	600	3,500	300	1913-1994
Nixon, Richard M.	President	250	1,500	RARE	650	As President
No Doubt	Music	50			90	Signed by Entire Group
Nobel, Alfred	Science	250	400		450	
Nobile, Umberto 1885-78	Aviation	65	200	300	175	
Noble, Chelsea	Ent	15			30	
Noble, James	Ent	5		15	15	
Noble, John W. 1831-12	Civil War	35	50	120	90	Union General
Noel-Baker, Philip	Political	30	40	90	25	Nobel Peace Prize
Noguchi, Isamu	Art	25		65		Am. Sculptor
Noir, Haing S.	Ent	45	75		100	Murdered AA winner
Nolan, Kathleen	Ent	5			15	
Nolan, Lloyd 1902-85	Ent	20	65		55	
Nolin, Gene Lee	Ent	20			50	Baywatch
Nolte, Nick	Ent	20			50	
Nono, Luigi 1924-90	Music	100			175	Composer/Opera
Noonan, Fred J. 1893-37	Aviation	RARE	RARE	RARE RARE		
Noone, Peter	Music	20			50	Lead/Hermans Hermits
Noor, Queen	Political	25		100	75	Queen of Hussein (Jordan)

Name	Field	SIG	DS	ALS	SP	Remarks
Nordau, Simon Max	Science	50	100		75	1849-1923
Nordenskjoid, Nils Adolf	Explorer	200			350	
Nordenskjoid, Nils Otto	Explorer	200			300	Led Antarctic Expedition
Nordhoff, Charles	Author	25	35	60		Mutiny on Bounty w/
Nordhoff, Heinz, Dr.	Business	25			50	Auto Mfg.-VW
Nordica, Lillian 1859-14	Music	75			250	Am. Soprano
Noriega, Manuel A.	Political	75	100		100	
Norman, Greg	Sports	20			45	Golfer
Norman, Jessye	Music	30			45	Opera
Normand, Mabel	Ent	150			400	Scarce
Norris, Chuck	Ent	15			40	Walker, Texas Ranger
Norris, Frank 1870-1902	Author	125	275	450		War Correspondent
Norris, Kathleen	Author	20	40	60	25	Prolific Am. Novelist
Norstad, Lauris	Military	20	50		40	Gen.WWII
North, Frederick, Lord	Political	95	385	595		1732-1792
North, Jay	Ent	10	25		25	Denace the Menace
North, John Ringling	Business	45	90		85	Ringling Brothers Circus
North, Oliver L.	Military	35	100	175	65	Marine Colonel
North, Sheree	Ent	5			15	
North, William 1755-1836	Military	75	185		400	Gen. Cont. Army
Northbrook, Lord	Political	15	25	50		
Northrop, John H.	Science	50	150		100	Nobel Chemistry 1946
Northrop, John K.	Business	45	125	250	100	Founder Northrop Aircraft
Northumberland, 2nd Dk	RevWar	50	150	225		
Norton, Edward	Ent	25			50	
Norton, Oliver P.	Civil War	20	30	45		Civil War Governor
Norton-Taylor, Judy	Ent	10	20		20	
Norville, Deborah	Ent	5			15	TV News Anchor
Norvo, Red	Music	15			40	Bandleader
Norworth, Jack	Music	130		250		Take Me Out to BallGame
Nourse, Joseph	Military	500	950	RARE		1754-1841
Novak, Kim	Ent	25	55		60	
Novak, Vitezslav	Music	50			150	Czech. Composer
Novarro, Ramon	Ent	40			100	Mexican Actor/1899-1968
Novatna, Jarmila	Music	15	45		35	Czech. Soprano
Novello, Ivor	Music	25		75	75	Composer
Nowak, Max	Science	15			45	Rocket Pioneer/von Braun
Noyce, Phillip	Ent	10		25	20	Director
Noyes, Alfred	Author	15	40	55	30	British Poet
Nucci, Danny	Ent	25			50	Titanic
Nugent, Elliott	Ent	5			15	
Nugent, Ted	Music	15		50	45	
Nungesser, Charles	Aviation	135	225	300	300	
Nureyev, Rudolf 1938-93	Music	80	125	200	160	Dancer/Choreagrapher
Nurmella, Kari	Music	15			30	Opera
Nuyen, France	Ent	10	20		15	
Nye, Bill (Edgar Wilson)	Author	20		75		Humorist
Nye, James W.	Political	75	125	175		
Nyerere, Julius	Political	10	25	50	30	Tanzania

Name	Field	SIG	DS	ALS	SP	Remarks
Oak Ridge Boys, The	Music	10			25	
Oakes, Randi	Ent	5			15	
Oakie, Jack	Ent	20	75		50	
Oakley, Annie 1860-1926	Western	2,500	6,000	9,000	7,500	Am. Markswoman
Oakley, Violet	Art	35	75			
Oates, Joyce Carol	Author	20	30	60	30	American Novelist
Oates, Warren	Ent	25			50	
Ober, W.O. 'Willy'	Aviation	25		55		
Oberhardt, William	Art	30	65	135		
Oberon, Merle	Ent	40			80	1911 - 1979
Oberth, Hermann, Dr.	Science	72	200		250	Early Rocket Pioneer
Oboler, Arch	Ent	10		35	25	Writer-Producer
Obratszova, Elena	Music	15			45	Opera
O'Brien, Conan	Ent	10			25	Late Night TV Host
O'Brien, Cubby	Ent	5	20		15	Mickey Mouse Club
O'Brien, Edmond	Ent	20	40		50	AA
O'Brien, George	Ent	20			40	
O'Brien, Hugh	Ent	25	50		55	TV Wyatt Earp
O'Brien, James	Business	5		20	15	
O'Brien, Lawrence F.	Political	10		40	20	JFK Adviser-Strategist.P.M.
O'Brien, Margaret	Ent	15			35	
O'Brien, Pat	Ent	45	100		100	
O'Brien, Virginia	Ent	5			10	
Ocasek, Ric	Music	25			50	The Cars
O'Casey, Sean l880-1964	Author	100	275	400	300	Irish Playwright
Ochoa, Severo, Dr.	Science	20	35	75	30	Nobel Physiology
Ochs, Adolph S. 1858-35	Business	150	165			Founder NY Times
O'Connell, Arthur	Ent	35			65	
O'Connell, Charles	Business	10		30	15	
O'Connell, Daniel	Political	75	250			Irish Nationalist Leader
O'Connell, Helen	Ent	15			25	
O'Conner, Flannery	Author	300	750			Am Author/Died Young
O'Connor, Carroll	Ent	10	25		25	All in the Family
O'Connor, Donald	Ent	10	20	30	20	Singing in the Rain
O'Connor, Glynnis	Ent	5			15	
O'Connor, Rene	Ent	25			55	Xena : Warrior Princess
O'Connor, Sandra Day	SuprCt	25	125	200	45	
O'Connor, Una	Ent	40			85	
O'Connor,Thos. P.	Author	60	100			Irish Journalist
Odd Couple (Movie)	Ent	25			50	Sgnd by Mathau/Lemmon
Odd Couple (TV)	Ent	25			50	Sgnd by Klugman/Randall
Odell, George C.D.	Author	5		30		Educator, Theatre Arts
Odets, Clifford	Author	55	90	175	150	Playwright.Golden Boy, etc.

Name	Field	SIG	DS	ALS	SP	Remarks
O'Donald, Emmett	Aviation	15	30	50	35	
O'Donnell, Chris	Ent	25			50	'Robin' in Batman
O'Donnell, Rosie	Ent	25	50		50	
O'Driscoll, Martha	Ent	5			10	
Oersted, Hans Christian	Science	2,500	RARE	RARE	RARE	Electromagnatism
Oesau, Walter 'Gulle'	Aviation	150		400	275	
Offenbach, Jacques	Music	145	250	450	275	1819-1880
Offenhauser, Fred	Science	130	395			Automobile/Racing Engine
O'Flaherty, Liam	Author	100	275			Ir. Novelist
O'Flynn, Damien	Ent	10			20	
Ogden, Aaron	RevWar	45	110	225		Rev War Soldier
Ogden, Francis B.1783-57	Military	15	45	80		Steam Engine Pioneer
Ogden, Thomas L.	Political	20		45		
Oglesby, Richard J.	Civil War	40	80	100	150	Union General/1824-99
O'Grady, Gail	Ent	10			25	NYPD Blue
O'Hara, Geoffrey	Music	20	45		25	Composer
O'Hara, John	Author	150	450	600		Am. Novelist, Short Stories
O'Hara, Mary (Alsop)	Author	20	50	75		Novelist/My Friend Flicka
O'Hara, Maureen	Ent	15	20		20	
O'Higgins, Harvey	Author	10	20	50	15	Am. Journalist, Novelist
Ohms, Elizabeth	Music	45			150	Opera
O'Keefe, Dennis	Ent	5	20		15	
O'Keefe, Georgia	Art	350		950		Scarce
O'Keeffe, Adrian	Business	5			10	CEO First National Stores
Oland, Warner 1880-1938	Ent	150	200		250	Charlie Chan
O'Laughlin, Gerald S.	Ent	10			20	
Olcott, Chauncey	Music	65	90	150	90	My Wild Irish rose...
Oldenburg, Claes Thure	Art	15	35	75	35	Swe Sculptor
Older, Charles H.	Aviation	15	30	45	35	WWII ACE/Flying Tigers
Older, Charles S.	Civil War	25	40	55		
Oldman, Gary	Ent	25			50	Dracula
Olds, Ransom E. 1864-50	Business	300	1,200			Oldsmobile Motors
Olds, Robin	Aviation	15	30	45	35	WWII ACE/Korea/Vietnam
Olin, Ken	Ent	5			10	
Olin, Lena	Ent	20			50	
Oliphant, Laurence	Author	10	25	60		Br Writer/Cape Town
Oliphant, Pat	Cartoonist	10			25	Political Cartoonist
Olitzka, Rosa	Music	40			125	Pol./Ger. Mezzo
Oliver, Andrew	RevWar	75	150	225		Am, Colonial Politician
Oliver, Edna May	Ent	45			120	
Oliver, Henry W., Jr.	Business	45	60			Iron & Steel Tycoon
Oliver, Jane	Ent	5			15	
Oliver, Paul A.	Civil War	25	50	75		Union Off/Inv. of Dynamite
Oliver, Sy	Music	35			75	Trumpet/Composer
Olivero, Magda	Music	25			60	Opera
Olivier, Laurence, Sir	Ent	75	125		175	1907-1969
Olmos, Edward James	Ent	10	25		25	
Olmstead, Frederick L.	Science	100	175	300		Landscape architect
Olsen & Johnson	Ent	35			75	Hellzapoppin

Name	Field	SIG	DS	ALS	SP	Remarks
Olsen, Merlin	Ent	10		20	25	
Olsen, Ole	Ent	25			50	
Olson, Nancy	Ent	5	15		15	
O'Malley, J. Pat	Ent	25			50	
Onassis, Aristotle	Business	175	300		225	Shipping Magnate
Onassis, Jacq. Kennedy	Political	375	800	1,400	900	
O'Neal, Ralph A.	Military	25	40	85	70	
O'Neal, Ryan	Ent	10	30		35	
O'Neal, Tatum	Ent	15	35		40	AA Winner
O'Neil, Barbara	Ent	150	RARE	RARE	275	GWTW star/1908-1980
O'Neill, Charles	Military	10	25	45		Adm. USN
O'Neill, Eugene 1888-53	Author	200	350		RARE	Playwright/Nobel/Pulitzer
O'Neill, Henry 1891-1964	Ent	20			50	
O'Neill, James	Ent	20	25	45	45	
O'Neill, Jennifer	Ent	5			15	
O'Neill, Peggy	Ent	5	20		15	
O'Neill, Thomas 'Tip'	Political	15	30		45	Speaker of the House. MA
Ono, Yoko	Music	40		75	75	
Ontkean, Michael	Ent	5		15	15	
Opatoshu, David	Ent	15			25	
Opp, Julie	Music	10			25	Opera
Oppenheimer, Rob't, Dr.	Science	450	RARE	RARE	RARE	Dir. Manhatten Project
Opper, Frederick Burr	Cartoonist	25		75	125	Happy Hooligan
Orbach, Jerry	Ent	10	25		20	Law and Order
Orbison, Roy	Music	125	200		200	
Orczy, Emmuska	Author	35	55	100	145	Br. Novelist
Ord, E.O.C. 1818-83	Civil War	100	150	400		Union Gen-Indian Fighter
Orff, Carl 1895-1982	Music	45			150	Ger. Carmina Burana
Orgonotzova, Ludmilia	Music	10			25	Opera
Orita, Zenji	Military	50	150		100	
Orlando, Vittorio E.	Political	65	135	250		It Prime Minister
Ormandy, Eugene	Music	25	45	90	80	Hungarian Conductor
Ormond, Julia	Ent	25			50	
Orpen, William, Sir	Art	45	125		350	
Orr, William T.	Ent	25	50			Film Director-Producer
Ory, Edward Kid	Music	100			200	Bandleader
Osborn, Joan	Music	15			40	
Osborn, Super Dave	Ent	10			20	
Osborne, Baby Marie	Ent	10			20	
Osborne, John 1929-94	Author	10	20	40	20	Br. Playwright, Screenwriter
Osborne, Ozzy	Music	20			45	
Oscar I, Joseph-Francois	Royalty	100	215	425		King Sweden & Norway
Oscar II	Royalty	35	70	145		King Sweden & Norway
Osgood, Charles	Ent	5			15	TV News, Host
Osgood, Samuel	RevWar	125	300	500		
O'Shea, Michael	Ent	10			25	
Oslin, K.T.	Music	5	15		20	
Osmena, Sergio	Political	75	150			Pres. Philippines 1944-46
Osmond Brothers	Music	45	100		55	Signed by all Five

Name	Field	SIG	DS	ALS	SP	Remarks
Osmond, Donny	Music	15	30		30	
Osmond, Ken	Ent	10			20	
Osmond, Marie	Music	10		25	20	
Osten, Hans Georg von	Aviation	30			60	German WWI ACE
Ostenso, Martha	Author	25	45	70		Am. Novelist, Poet
Oster, William, Dr.	Science	350	500	1,500		Medical Historian
Osterhaus, Peter J.	Civil War	35	70	100		Union General/1823-1917
Osterkamp, Theo	Aviation	35	60	130	70	
Osterman, Kathryn	Ent	20			50	
O'Sullivan, Gilbert	Music	25	75			
O'Sullivan, Maureen	Ent	20	35		45	Tarzan's Jane
Osvoth, Julia	Music	25			45	Opera
Oswald, Lee Harvey	Criminal	RARE	7,500	12,000	RARE	Murdered John F. Kennedy
Oswald, Mark	Music	10			25	Opera
Otis, Elita Proctor	Ent	10	25		25	
Otis, Elwell S.	Civil War	25	40	65		Union General/1838-1909
Otis, James 1725-83	RevWar	250	475	650		
Otis, Johnny	Ent	25			40	Director/Producer
O'Toole, Annette	Ent	10			30	
O'Toole, Peter	Ent	25	60		50	Lawrence of Arabia
Ott, Mel	Sports	300			650	Baseball
Otto I (Othon I) 1815-67	Royalty	100	300	250		Greece
Otto I (The Great)	Royalty	2,000	RARE	RARE	RARE	King of Germany
Oudinot, Charles N. Duc	Military	75	150			Marshal of Napoleon
Ouida (Louise dela Ram)	Author	25	60	100		Br Novelist
Ould, Robert 1820-82	Civil War	60	135			CSA Colonel
Ouspenskaya, Maria	Ent	225	400	RARE	400	1876 - 1949
Outcault, Richard	Cartoonist	125			275	Yellow Kid, Buster Brown
Outlaw, Edward C.	Aviation	15	25	40	35	WWII ACE in One Day
Overall, Park	Ent	10	20		20	Empty Nest
Overman, Lynn	Ent	15			45	Character Actor
Overmyer, Robert	Space	20			65	2nd Space Shuttle Flight
Ovington, Earle	Aviation	45		200	200	Pilot 1st Air Mail Plane
Owen, Joshua T.	Civil War	75		225		Union General/War Dated
Owen, Joshua T. 1821-87	Civil War	35	125			Union General
Owen, Reginald	Ent	25			50	
Owen, Robert 1771-1858	Political			250		Br. Utopian Socialist
Owen, Robert Dale	Political	25		125		1801-1877
Owen, Ruth Bryan	Political	25			45	
Owens, Buck	Aviation	15	35		30	Marine WWII ACE
Owens, Buck	Music	5			15	
Owens, Jesse	Sports	100			250	Olympic Star
Owens, Tex	Music	10			20	
Oxenberg, Catherine	Ent	25			40	
Oxnam, G. Bromley	Clergy	35	50	95	45	Bishop
Oz, Frank	Ent	15	35		45	Voice of Miss Piggy/Yoda
Ozbourne, Ozzy	Music	20			50	

Name	Field	SIG	DS	ALS	SP	Remarks
Paar, Jack	Ent	20	50		60	
Pabst, Fred	Business	150	450		400	Pabst Brewing Co.
Paca, William 1740-99	RevWar	750	1,500	2,500		Signer
Pacetti, Iva	Music	25			75	Opera
Pache, Jean Nicholas	Military	25		150		French Revolution
Pacino, Al	Ent	25	100		50	Godfather
Pack, Denis, Sir	Military	25	75	125		
Packard, David	Business	20		65	30	Co-Fndr Hewlett-Packard
Packard, James Ward	Business	RARE	RARE	5,000	RARE	Fndr. Packard Automobile
Packard, Kelly	Ent	15			30	
Packard, Vance	Author	10		40	20	Am. Nonfiction Writer
Packwood, Bob	Political	10	25		35	Senator OR
Paderewski, Ignace J.	Music	175		550	450	Composer
Paduca, Duke of	Music	20			40	
Paer, Ferdinando	Music	50	100	200		Composer
Pafti, Amalia	Ent	50		125	150	Opera
Paganini, Nicolo	Music	450	RARE	RARE	RARE	1782-1840
Page, Anita	Ent	10			15	
Page, Bettie	Ent	25			65	Model
Page, Geraldine	Ent	20			45	AA Winner/1924-1987
Page, Lawanda	Ent	10			20	Sanford and Son
Page, Patti	Ent	5			15	
Page, Richard Lucian	Civil War	100	175	450		
Page, Thomas Nelson	Author	10		40		Am Novelist
Page, William 1811-85	Art	150		350		Am. Portrait Painter
Paget, Debra	Ent	25			50	
Pagliughi, Lina	Music	45			125	Opera
Pahlavi, Mohammed R.	Political	125	200	300	300	Shah of Iran/1919-80
Paige, Janis	Ent	10	15		15	
Paige, Mabel	Ent	10			25	Vintage Radio
Paine, John Knowles	Music	15	40	50		Composer
Paine, Robert Treat	RevWar	250	450	900		Signer/1731-1814
Paine, Thomas	RevWar	3,500	RARE	RARE	RARE	Am. Philosopher-Author
Pakula, Alan J.	Ent	5			15	Director
Pal, George	Ent	50			125	
Palacio, Ernesto	Music	15			30	Opera
Palade, George E., Dr.	Science	20	35		25	Nobel Medicine 1974
Palance, Jack	Ent	30	75		75	AA Winner/Scarce
Palet, Jose	Music	75			175	Opera
Paley, William S.	Business	15	35	60	35	Founded CBS in 1928
Palfrey, F.W.	Civil War	25		75		Union General/1834-1906
Pallette, Eugene	Ent	60			85	
Palma, Tomas Estrada	Political	20	35	45		1st President Cuba

Name	Field	SIG	DS	ALS	SP	Remarks
Palmenteri, Chaz	Ent	20			50	
Palmer, Arnold	Sports	25			65	1974 Golf HOF
Palmer, Gregg	Ent	15			35	
Palmer, Innis N.	Civil War	75				Union General/War Dated
Palmer, Innis N. 1824-00	Civil War	45				Union General
Palmer, Jimmy	Music	15			40	Bandleader
Palmer, John McCauley	Civil War	80	125	175		Union General/1817-1900
Palmer, Lilli	Ent	15	35		65	1911 - 1986
Palmer, Potter	Business	225	750	1,250	450	Palmer House Hotel
Palmer, Robert	Music	25			50	
Palmerston, Henry J.T.	Political	50	100	150		Prime Minister Eng.
Paltrow, Gwyneth	Ent	25			50	
Pan, Hermes	Music	35	60		65	Choreographer
Panerai, Rolando	Music	10			25	Opera
Pangborn, Clyde	Aviation	75	150		250	Aviation Pioneer
Pangborn, Franklin	Ent	40			65	Comedic Character Actor
Pankhurst, Christabel	Political	25	75	150		
Pankhurst, E. Sylvia	Political	75	150	250		1882-1960
Pankhurst, Emmeline	Political	50	125	200		
Pantoliano, Joe	Ent	10			20	
Papen, Franz von	Military	50	150	200	150	Hitlers Vice-Chancellor
Papp, Joseph	Ent	30	40		55	Theatre Producer
Paquin, Anna	Ent	35			75	AA Winning child actress
Paris, Joel B., III	Aviation	15		40	35	WWII ACE
Park, Ray	Ent	20			50	Star Wars/Dart Maul
Parke, John Grubb	Civil War	50	150	150		Union General/1827-1900
Parker, Charlie 1920-55	Music	400	800	RARE	RARE	Alto Sax Jazz Musician
Parker, David	Military	15	35	50		
Parker, Dorothy	Author	30		75	45	Poet/1893-1967
Parker, Edward P.	Business	65	150			Parker Bros. Pen Co.
Parker, Eleanor	Ent	5			15	
Parker, Ely Samuel	Civil War	300				Union General/Seneca Chf.
Parker, Fess	Ent	10	25	35	25	Davy Crockett
Parker, Frank	Music	15			35	Jack Benny's Ist Vocalist
Parker, Gilbert 1861-1921	Author	15				
Parker, Graham	Ent	20			35	
Parker, Isaac 1768-1830	Political	25		100		
Parker, Isaac C. 1838-96	Western	500	1,500			The Hanging Judge
Parker, Jameson	Ent	10	20		20	
Parker, Jean	Ent	15	30		30	
Parker, Joel 1816-1888	Civil War	15	30	75		Civil War Gov. NJ
Parker, John	Civil War		750			Captured by Commanches
Parker, Mary Louise	Ent	20			40	
Parker, Roy, Jr.	Music	5			15	
Parker, Sarah Jessica	Ent	20			40	
Parker, Suzy	Ent	5	15		15	
Parker, Thomas	RevWar	50	100	150		Continental Army General
Parker, Tom, Colonel	Ent	25	50		50	Elvis' Manager
Parker, Trey	Cartoonist	20			50	Co-Creator of South Park

Name	Field	SIG	DS	ALS	SP	Remarks
Parker, Willard	Ent	10			25	
Parkins, Barbara	Ent	10	20		20	
Parkinson, Dian	Ent	5			15	Price is Right Model
Parkman, Francis	Author	25	75	150		Historian. The Oregon Trail
Parks, Bert	Ent	10			30	
Parks, Gordon	Author	20	50	60	40	Photographer
Parks, Larry	Ent	30			50	1914-1975
Parks, Rosa L.	Political	40	100		100	Civil Rights, Bus Boycott
Parks, Trina	Ent	25			50	James Bond babe
Parr, Ralph	Aviation	15	30	40	30	Korean Double ACE
Parrish, Anne 1888-1957	Author	15	30			Am. Novelist
Parrish, Helen	Ent	10			20	
Parrish, Julie	Ent	5			10	
Parrish, Maxfield 1870-66	Art	175	500	800		Checks - 250
Parry, Charles Hubert H.	Music	15		50		Historian
Parseval, August von	Aviation	100				Ger. Aeronautical Engineer
Parsons, Albert Ross	Music	5			10	
Parsons, Estelle	Ent	10			20	
Parsons, Louella	Ent	20	40	75	50	1893 - 1972
Parsons, Mosby M.	Civil War	200				CSA General/1819-65
Parsons, Samuel H.	RevWar		300	450		Continental General
Parton, Dolly	Music	15	45		45	Country
Parton, Stella	Music	5			10	
Partridge, Bernard, Sir	Art	25		40		Brit. Punch Cartoonist
Partridge, Wm. Ordway	Art	10		35	30	Am. Sculptor
Parvis, Taurino	Music	40			100	Opera
Pasero, Tancredi	Music	35			75	Opera
Paskalis, Kostas	Music	15			45	Opera
Pasternak, Boris 1890-60	Author	400	750	1,600		Dr. Zhivago
Pasternak, Joe	Ent	35	75	100	75	Director
Pasteur, Louis 1822-1895	Science	500	900	1,750	RARE	Pasteurization, Vaccines
Pastor, Tony	Music	10			35	Big Bandleader
Pastorelli, Robert	Ent	15			30	Murphy Brown
Patch, Alexander M.	Military	75	150	300	200	Am. General WWII
Pate, Michael	Ent	5			15	
Paterson, John	RevWar	75	200	300		1744 - 1808
Paterson, William	SuprCt	RARE	RARE	RARE	RARE	
Patinkin, Mandy	ENt	20			40	
Paton, Alan	Author	40	100	200		South African Author
Patric, Jason	Ent	15			35	
Patrick, Butch	Ent	5	25	25	20	Eddie Munster
Patrick, Dennis	Ent	5			10	
Patrick, Gail	Ent	10	20		15	
Patrick, Marsena R.	Civil War	35	50	90		Union General/1811-88
Patrick, Marsena R.	Civil War	45	85	125		Union General/War Dated
Patten, Gilbert	Author	30	70	150	50	
Patten, Luana	Ent	35			55	
Patterson, Daniel Tod	Military	50	150	200		
Patterson, Floyd	Sports	15			35	Boxer

Name	Field	SIG	DS	ALS	SP	Remarks
Patterson, Robert	Civil War	25	60	75		Union General/1792-1881
Patti, Adelina (Niccolini)	Music	150	200	350	375	Opera
Patton, George S. III	Military	10	20	35	20	Son of WWII General
Patton, George S. Jr.	Military	950	2,000	3,500	5,000	1885-1945/General
Paul I & Frederica	Royalty	150			250	King & Queen of Greece
Paul I, Pavel Petrovich	Royalty	225	600	1,500		Emperor Russ.Son of Cath. Great
Paul II, Pope	Clergy		400			
Paul III, Pope	Clergy		1,200			
Paul VI, Pope	Clergy	300	475	900	600	Giovanni Battista Montini
Paul VI, Pope 1897-1978	Clergy		500		900	
Paul, Adrian	Ent	25			50	TV's Highlander
Paul, Alexandra	Ent	20			45	Baywatch
Paul, Les	Music	25	35		60	
Paul, Wolfgang	Science	10			30	Nobel Physics 1989
Paulding, Hiram	Civil War	25	50	70		Commanded Navy Yard NY
Paulding, James Kirke	Author	40	85	150		Van Buren Sec'y Navy
Pauley, Jane	Ent	5	15		15	
Paulham, Louis	Aviation	40	75	125	80	
Pauling, Linus 1901-94	Science	60	250	400	125	Nobel in Chemistry
Paulsen, Valademar	Science	40	120			
Paulson, Pat	Ent	15			35	
Paulton, Harry	Ent	5			10	
Paulucci, Jeno F.	Business	15	25	35	30	
Pauly, Rose	Music	25			60	Opera
Pavarotti, Luciano	Music	35		100	65	Opera
Pavie, Auguste-Jean-Ma	Political	50	125	200		French Explorer
Pavlov, Ivan 1849-1936	Science	RARE	RARE	3,500	RARE	Rus. Physiologist
Pavlova, Anna 1882-1931	Music	350		450	550	Russian Ballerina
Pawnee Bill (Lillie,G.A.)	Western					See Lillie, Gordon A.
Paxinou, Katina	Ent	150		300	250	
Paxton, Bill	Ent	20			45	
Paxton, Elisha F. (WD)	Civil War	750	RARE	RARE	RARE	CSA General/1828-63
Paycheck, Johnny	Music	10			25	Country
Payer, Julius von	Explorer	100	200		275	North Polar Expedition
Payne, Eugene B.	Civil War	25	45	65		Union Officer
Payne, Freda	Music	10			20	
Payne, Henry C.	Political	15		35		P.M. General 1902
Payne, John 1912-89	Ent	20	30	55	55	
Payne, John Howard	Music	90	250	400		
Payne, William H.	Civil War	85	200	300		CSA General/1830-1904
Payne, William H. (WD)	Civil War	160	390			CSA General
Pays, Amanda	Ent	15			40	
Peabody, Charles, Dr.	Science	10	20	25		
Peabody, Eddie	Ent	15	15	35	30	
Peabody, George	Business	50	150	400		Merchant/1795-1869
Peabody, George F.	Business	35	100	300		Merchant/1852-1938
Peale, Chas. Wilson	Art	250	450	750		Portrait Painter
Peale, Norman Vincent	Author	20	50	100	40	Clergy
Peale, Rembrandt	Art	250	475	1,200		Am. Portrait Artist

Name	Field	SIG	DS	ALS	SP	Remarks
Peale, Titian 1799-1885	Art		225	750		
Pearce, Alice	Ent	100			250	Bewitched
Pearce, Richard	Ent	10	15		20	Director
Pearl Jam	Music	45			125	Entire Group
Pearl, Minnie	Music	20			45	Country
Pearson, Lester B.	Political	35	75	150	45	Nobel Peace Prize
Peary, Harold	Ent	20			45	
Peary, Robert E. 1856-20	Explorer	150		450	600	Adm. Arctic Explorer
Peck, Gregory	Ent	25	75		50	AA Winner
Peck, Robert Newton	Author	10		25		Am. Novelist
Peckham, Rufus W.	SuprCt	65	125	250	125	1838 - 1909
Peckinpah, Sam	Ent	100	200		200	Director
Peddie, G.	Military	15		45		Gen.WWII
Pederson, Monte	Music	15			30	Opera
Pederzini, Gianna	Music	25			75	Opera
Pedro II	Royalty	80	200	300		Emperor Brazil
Peel, Robert, Sir	Political	50	100	150		Prime Minister/1788-1850
Peeples, Nia	Ent	15			25	
Peerce, Jan 1904-84	Music	30			75	Opera
Pegler, Westbrook	Author	15		35	30	Journalist
Pegram, John	Civil War	900	1,800	RARE	RARE	CSA General/War Dated
Pegram, John 1832-65	Civil War	600	800	800		CSA General
Pei, I.M.	Science	35	75	140		Architect
Peirce, Benjamin	Science	20	30	60		Astronomer/1809-1880
Pele	Sports	25			65	Soccer Star
Pelham, Henry	Political	50	150	250		Prime Minister/1696-1754
Pelham-Holies, Thomas	Political	50	100	175		Prime Minister
Pellegrini, Margaret	Ent	15	30		35	Munchkin, Wizard of Oz
Pelletier, St. Marie E.	Clergy			2,500		Saint Canonized 1940
Pelouze, Louis H.	Civil War	75	175	200		Union General/1831-78
Pemberton, John C.	Civil War	150	350	400	500	CSA General/1814-81
Pemberton, John C.	Civil War	250	500	800		CSA General/War Dated
Pemsel, Max	Military	20			45	Nazi General
Pena, Elizabeth	Ent	10			20	
Pender, William Dorsey	Civil War	400				CSA General/1834-63
Penderecki, Krzysztof	Music	25		75		Opera
Pendergast, Thomas J.	Political	20	50	75	35	
Pendleton, Alex	Civil War	200	400	475		CSA Star Officer
Pendleton, Edmund	RevWar	350	600	900		Continental Congress
Pendleton, George Hunt	Political	20	40	75		Presidential Candidate
Pendleton, Karen	Ent	10			20	
Pendleton, Nat	Ent	30	45	60	45	
Pendleton, William N.	Civil War	300		500	900	CSA General/1809-83
Penn & Teller	Ent	20			45	Magicians/Signed by Both
Penn, Arthur	Ent	10			20	
Penn, John 1741-88	RevWar	750	1,500	RARE	RARE	Signer
Penn, Sean	Ent	20			50	
Penn, William 1644-1718	Political	1,500	3,500	7,500	RARE	Founder PA
Pennell, Joseph	Art	50	150	250		Am. Artist/Printmaker

Name	Field	SIG	DS	ALS	SP	Remarks
Penner, Joe	Ent	20	45		45	Comedian
Penney, J. C. 1875-1971	Business	100	300	400	300	Founder of J.C. Penney
Pennington, Ann	Ent	25	35	50	60	Ziegfield Star
Penny, Joe	Ent	10	25		25	Jake and the Fat Man
Pennypacker, Galusha	Civil War	75	160	225		Union General/1844-1916
Penske, Thomas H.	Business	10	30		20	
Penzias, Arno, Dr.	Science	15	35	50	25	Nobel Physics
Peppard, George	Ent	30	50		60	A-Team/1929 - 1994
Pepper, Art	Music	30			75	Bandleader
Pepper, Claude 1900-89	Political	15	35		20	
Pepperell, William, Sir	Military	125	250	400		American General
Pepys, Samuel	Author	550				Br. Sec'y of the Navy
Pequet, Henri	Aviation	15		35		
Perceval, Spencer	Political	125	250			Br. P.M. Assasinated
Percival, John	Military	50	100	150		Am. Navy 1812
Percy, Walker	Author	75		200		Am. Novelist
Perelman, S.J.	Author	50		150		Humorist
Peres, Shimon	Political	25	100		75	Israeli Statesman
Perez, Mariano	Political	15		50	20	President Colombia
Perez, Rosie	Ent	20		60	50	
Perez, Vincent	Ent	25			50	The Crow II
Perier, Jean	Music	25			75	French Baritone
Perignon, D.C. Marquis	Military	75	200	375		Marshal of Napoleon
Perkins, Anthony	Ent	75	100		100	Psycho/1932-1992
Perkins, Carl	Music	25	50	75	50	Blue Suede Shoes...
Perkins, Elizabeth	Ent	10			25	
Perkins, Frances	Political	25	75		60	
Perkins, Millie	Ent	10			30	
Perkins, Osgood	Ent	35			75	
Perlman, Itzhak	Music	20	45	60	45	Am. Violinist
Perlman, Rhea	Ent	15			40	Cheers
Perlman, Ron	Ent	20			45	Beauty and the Beast
Peron, Eva (Evita)	Political	400		600		Argentina
Peron, Juan & Eva	Political	600	800			
Peron, Juan Domingo	Political	125	300	500	600	President Argentina
Perot, H. Ross	Business	30	60		100	Presidential Candidate
Perrault, Charies	Author	RARE	RARE	RARE	RARE	Fr Poet/1628-1703
Perrin, Jean 1870-1942	Science	75				Nobel Prize '26 Physics.
Perrine, Valerie	Ent	10	25		25	
Perris, Adriana	Music	10			30	Opera
Perry, Alexander J.	Civil War	25				Union Officer/1829-1913
Perry, Lucas	Ent	20			45	
Perry, Matthew	Ent	20			50	Friends
Perry, Matthew C.	Military	450	775	1,400		Opened Japan/Trade
Perry, Nora	Author	5		20		Novelist
Perry, Oliver H.	Military	675		950		
Perry, Ralph Barton	Author	10		35		Philosopher, Pulitzer Prize
Pershing, John J. 1860-48	Military	100		300	400	Comm-in-Chief AEF WWI
Persichetti, Vincent	Music	10	25	45	25	Composer

Name	Field	SIG	DS	ALS	SP	Remarks
Pertile, Aureliano	Music	40			125	Opera
Perulli, Franco	Music	20			50	Opera
Perutz, Max	Science	20	40	60	30	Nobel Chemistry 1962
Pesci, Joe	Ent	20			50	AA Winner
Petain, Henri-Phillippe	Political	35	90		50	Hero WWI/Treason WWII
Peter & Gordon	Music	75			125	Signed by Both
Peter I	Royalty	90	225	400		King of Serbs, Croats
Peter I, The Great	Royalty	RARE	5,500	7,500	RARE	Czar of Russia
Peter, Paul & Mary	Music	20	45		35	Signed by All Three
Peters, Bernadette	Ent	5	20		20	
Peters, Brock	Ent	5			15	
Peters, Jean	Ent	50			85	
Peters, Mike	Cartoonist	10			25	Mother Grimm
Peters, Richard Jr.	RevWar	40	95	150		Soldier
Peters, Roberta	Music	10			25	Opera
Peters, Susan	Ent	75		95	100	
Petersen, Paul	Ent	5			15	
Peterson, Chesley	Aviation	15	30	55	40	WWII ACE
Peterson, Oscar	Music	25			45	Jazz Pianist
Peterson, Paul	Ent	10			20	
Peterson, Roger Tory	Author	20	35		25	
Petiet, Claude	Military	125	240			French Revolution
Petion, Alexandre	Political	275	400			Haitian General, President
Petrella, Clara	Music	20			50	Opera
Petrie, Wm. Matthew F.	Science	100	200			Egyptologist
Petrillo, James C.	Political	25	50			Czar of Musician's Union
Petroff, Paul	Music	30			90	Am. Ballet Dancer-Teacher
Petrova, Olga	Ent	35			75	Silent Films
Pettigrew, James	Civil War	375	RARE	RARE	RARE	CSA General/War Dated
Pettigrew, James J.	Civil War	150	500			CSA General/1828-63
Pettit, Charles	RevWar	75	185	300		Continental Congress
Pettus, Edmund W.	Civil War	85	170	300		CSA General/1821-1907
Petty, Lori	Ent	20			40	
Petty, Richard	Sports	10			25	Auto Racing
Petty, Tom	Music	25			50	
Peugeot, Eugene	Business	75	125	250		Fndr. Peugeot Automobile
Pfeiffer, Michelle	Ent	35	100		75	
Pflug, Jo Ann	Ent	5			15	
Phelps, John Smith	Civil War	25	65	100		Union General/1814-86
Phelps, John Wolcott	Civil War	45	135	200		Raised lst Negro Troops
Phelps, Noah 1740-1809	Military	50	150			Soldier, Patriot, Spy
Philbin, Mary	Ent	25			50	
Philbin, Regis	Ent	5			10	TV Host
Philip (Duke Edinburgh)	Royalty	125	200	300	350	Prince Consort ElizabethII
Philip II (Sp)	Royalty	250				
Philip III (Sp) Philip II	Royalty	250	750			
Philip IV (Sp),III (Port)	Royalty	250	550	900		
Philip V (Sp)	Royalty	150	350			Founder Bourbon Dynasty
Philippe II	Royalty		500			Regent of Fr. for Louis XV

Name	Field	SIG	DS	ALS	SP	Remarks
Philippi, Alfred	Military	15				German Gen WWII
Phillip, Jack W.	Military	25	75			Captain USN
Phillips, Chynna	Music	25			50	Wilson Phillips
Phillips, John	Music	15			35	Mamas and Papas
Phillips, Julianne	Ent	25			45	
Phillips, Lee	Ent	10			20	
Phillips, Lou Diamond	Ent	15			40	
Phillips, Mackenzie	Ent	10	25		35	One Day at a Time
Phillips, Michelle	Music	10			35	
Phillips, Phil	Music	15			35	
Phillips, Wendell	Political	35	50	100	50	Abolitionist/1811-84
Phillips, William	RevWar	200	500	700		Br. Major General
Phillpotts, Eden	Author	15	35	55		Br Novelist
Phipps, Spencer	Political	200	800	1,000		Br. Colonial Gov. MA
Phoenix, Joaquin	Ent	20			50	Rivers Younger Brother
Phoenix, River	Ent	175	450		300	Died Young
Piaf, Edith	Ent	150	300		250	
Piaget, Jean 1896-1980	Science		400			Swiss Psychologist
Piatigorsky, Gregor	Music	125	200	300	300	Rus./Am. Cellist
Piazza, Marguerite	Music	10			30	American Soprano
Picard, Emile	Science	75	200	400		Fr. Mathematician
Picasso, Pablo 1881-1973	Art	750	1,500		1,500	
Picasso, Paloma	Art	25			50	Daughter of Pablo/Designer
Piccaluga, Nino	Music	35			75	Opera
Piccard, Auguste	Science	35	100	150	100	Physicist. Bathyscaphe
Piccard, Jacques	Science	15	40	50	25	
Piccard, Jean-Felix	Science	65	150		125	Chemist, Aeronautical Eng.
Piccaver, Alfred	Music	75			200	Opera
Piccolomini, Marietta	Music	100	250		275	It. Soprano
Pichegru, Charles	Military	35	100	150		Fr Gen/Killed in Prison
Pick, Lewis A.	Military	35	100		50	Gen.WWII
Pickens, Francis W.	Civil War	35	75	150		CSA Gov SC/1805-69
Pickens, Jane	Ent	25			50	
Pickens, Slim	Ent	100			200	Scarce
Pickens, T. Boone	Business	20	50		50	
Pickering, John 1737-05	Political	175	250			
Pickering, Thomas	Political	10			20	Ambassador to Russia
Pickering, Timothy	Political	250	750	1,500		1745-1829
Pickering, William, Dr.	Science	15	35	50	25	Astronomer
Pickett, Cindy	Ent	5			10	
Pickett, George Edward	Civil War	600	1,200	2,000		CSA General/1825-75
Pickford, Jack	Ent	50			150	
Pickford, Mary 1893-1979	Ent	40	150	200	150	Co-Fndr United Artists
Picon, Molly 1898-1992	Ent	15	35		45	Yiddish Stage & Film Star
Pidgeon, Walter	Ent	25	75		75	1897-1984
Pied Pipers, The	Music	20			45	Big Band Singing Group
Pierce, Benjamin	RevWar	75	125	200		Gov. NH
Pierce, Benjamin 1809-80	Science	35		75		Am. Math.& Astronomy
Pierce, David Hyde	Ent	20			45	Frasier/Niles Crane

Name	Field	SIG	DS	ALS	SP	Remarks
Pierce, Franklin 1804-69	President	400	700	950		
Pierce, James	Ent	45	125		75	Early Tarzan
Pierce, Jan	Music	20			50	Opera
Pierce, Jane M.	First Lady	200	500	900		
Pierce, N. B.	Civil War	30	60	90		
Pierce, Web	Music	5			10	
Pierne, H.C. Gabriel	Music	15	50	100	200	Conductor
Pierrepont, Edwards	Political	15	45	75		Att'y General 1875
Pierson, Roland	Aviation	10	25	35	30	
Pigni, Renzo	Music	15			35	Opera
Pike, Albert 1809-91	Civil War	100	175	250		CSA General/1809-91
Pike, Christopher	Author	5			10	Novelist
Pike, James A.	Clergy	75	150	275	125	Bishop
Pike, Zebulon 1751-1834	RevWar	40	75	135		Officer Revolutionary Army
Pike, Zebulon M.1779-13	Military	225	600	950		Discovered Pike's Peak
Pilatre De Rozier, Jean	Aviation	125		500		Pioneer Balloonist
Pillow, Gideon J.	Civil War	100		350		CSA General/1806-78
Pillow, Gideon J.	Civil War	160	400	500		CSA General/War Dated
Pillsbury, George A.	Business	Scarce	1,250	2,000		Founder of Flour Co.
Pillsbury, John S.	Business	100	400			Pillsbury Flour
Pilsudski, Joseph K.	Military	125	300	450	275	
Pinay, Antoine (Fr)	Political	15	35	50		France
Pinchback, Pinckney	Political	125	350	450		
Pinchot, Bronson	Ent	20	45		45	Perfect Strangers
Pinchot, Gifford	Political	35	95	120		Governor PA, Forester
Pinckney, Charles	RevWar	450		1,200		Continental Congress
Pinckney, Charles C.	RevWar	175		600		Diplomat/XYZ Affair
Pinckney, Thomas	RevWar	200	450			Continental Army
Pincus, Harry	Art	15		50		
Pine, Phillip	Ent	5			15	
Pinero, Arthur Wing, Sir	Author	15	35		55	British Actor
Ping, Deng Xiao	Political	200	RARE	RARE	RARE	China
Pingel, Rolf	Aviation	10		30	25	
Pink Floyd	Music	75	250		150	Signed by Five
Pinkerton, Allan 1819-84	Business	300	750	1,200	RARE	Pinkerton Detective Agency
Pinkerton, Robert A.	Business	35	100	200	75	CEO Pinkerton's Inc.
Pinkerton, William A.	Civil War	100	200			US Secret Service
Pinkett, Jada	Ent	20			40	
Pinkney, William	Political	100	100	200		Attorney General
Pinochet, Augusto	Political	30	100	200	50	Chilean Mil. Leader
Pinza, Ezio	Music	50			125	Opera/1893 - 1957
Pioneers, Sons of the	Music	150			300	Five Signatures
Piper, William Thomas.	Aviation	175	350			Founder Piper Aircraft Corp.
Pippen, Scottie	Sports	15			45	Basketball
Pirandello, Luigi 1867-36	Author	75	175	300	375	Nobel/Literature
Pirchoff, Nelly	Music	10			30	Opera
Piscopo, Joe	Ent	10			35	Sat Nite Live
Pissarro, Camile 1830-03	Art	250		1,200		Fr. Impressionist
Piston, Walter	Music	75	200	400	100	Pulitzer/Music

Name	Field	SIG	DS	ALS	SP	Remarks
Pitney, Gene	Ent	10			25	
Pitney, Mahlon	SuprCt	20	50	145	30	
Pitt William (Elder)	Political	150	300			The Great Commoner
Pitt, Brad	Ent	25			55	
Pitt, Ingrid	Ent	10	25		20	Hammer Horror Star
Pitt, John, Sir 1756-1835	Military	45		95		
Pitts, Zazu	Ent	35			75	1890 - 1963
Pius IX, G.M. Mastori	Clergy	175	250	400		G. M. Mastori
Pius IX, Pope	Clergy	50	150	250		
Pius VII, Pope	Clergy		1,500			
Pius X, Pope 1835-1914	Clergy		700		RARE	Giuseppe MelchiorreSarto
Pius XI, Pope	Clergy	450	950	RARE		A.D. Achille Ratti
Pius XII, Pope	Clergy		1,500			Eugenio Pacelli
Plainsmen, The	Music	25			50	Signed by Entire Group
Planck, Max 1858-1947	Science	200	400	750	RARE	Nobel Physics 1918
Plancon, Pol	Music	150			400	Opera
Plant & Page	Music	65			125	Both Signed/Led Zeppelin
Plant, Robert	Music	30			60	
Plato, Dana	Ent	20	45		45	Different Strokes
Platt, Ed	Ent	75	100		150	Chief/Get Smart
Platters, The	Music	125	250		250	Signed by all Five
Playfair, Lyon, lst Baron	Science	10	25	40		Modern Sanitation
Pleasanton, Alfred	Civil War	35		100		Union General/1824-97
Pleasanton, Alfred	Civil War	125	200	600		Union General/War Dated
Pleasence, Donald	Ent	35	50		60	
Pleshette, Suzanne	Ent	10	20		20	Bob Newhart Show
Plimpton, George	Author	10	25		20	
Plimpton, Martha	Ent	20			40	
Plishka, Paul	Music	10			25	Opera
Plitsetskaya, Maya	Music	15			40	Ballet
Plowright, Joan	Ent	10	25		25	
Plummer, Amanda	Ent	15			35	
Plummer, Christopher	Ent	10			25	
Poe, Edgar Allan	Author	RARE	15,000	RARE	RARE	1809-1849
Pogany, Willy	Art	75	150			Muralist/Illustrator
Poggi, Gianni	Music	10			25	Opera
Poindexter, John	Military	40			150	US Adm. Iran-Contra
Poinsett, Joel R.	Political	70	250	250		1779-1851
Pointer Sisters	Music	30	65		60	Signed by All Three
Poitier, Sidney	Ent	25	55		60	AA Winner
Polando, John	Aviation	30	60	90	75	
Polanski, Roman	Ent	30			75	Director
Polaski, Deborah	Music	10			25	Opera
Police, The	Music	70			125	Signed by entire group
Polk, James K.	President	350	1,500	3,000		1795-1849
Polk, James K.	President	475	1,750	4,000		As President
Polk, Leonidas	Civil War	500	650	RARE	RARE	CSA General/War Dated
Polk, Leonidas 1806-64	Civil War	300				CSA General KIA
Polk, Sarah Childress	First Lady	400	600	900	1,200	

Name	Field	SIG	DS	ALS	SP	Remarks
Poll, Afro	Music	15			45	Opera
Pollack, Sidney	Ent	10	30		25	AA Director-Actor
Pollard, Snub	Ent	75			200	Keystone Cop
Pollen, Tracy	Ent	10			35	
Pollock, Channing	Author	30	55		45	Am. Playwright
Pollock, Kevin	Ent	15			30	
Pompadour, Mme	Royalty	150	400	900		Louis VI Mistress
Pompidou, Georges	Political	10	25		20	Premier, President France
Ponce, Poncie	Ent	10			20	
Ponchielli, Amilcare	Music	250				Opera/Ballets
Pond, Julian	Science	100		300		
Poniatowski, Jozef A.	Military	500	RARE	RARE	RARE	Napolean Marshal
Pons, Juan	Music	10			25	Opera
Pons, Lily	Music	50			125	Soprano
Ponselle, Carmela	Music	25				Opera
Ponselle, Rosa	Music	25		75		Opera
Ponti, Carlo	Ent	15	30		30	It. Film Producer
Ponty, Jean-Luc	Ent	5			15	
Pool, Tilaman E.	Aviation	10		35	30	WWII Navy ACE
Poor, Enoch	RevWar	175	550	875		General. Patriot, Hero
Pope Pius X	Clergy	500			1,500	Giuseppe Melchiorre Sarto
Pope, A.J.	Aviation	20	35			American WWII ACE
Pope, Alexander	Author	600	RARE	RARE	RARE	Br. Poet
Pope, Alexander	Art	150	300	600		
Pope, John	Civil War		450	RARE	RARE	Union General/War Dated
Pope, John 1822-92	Civil War	80	125	300	450	Union General
Popham, William	RevWar	175		350		1752-1847
Popovich, Pavel	Space	50			175	Rus. Cosmonaut
Popp, Lucia	Music	20			50	Opera
Porizkova, Paulina	Ent	25			50	Model/Actress
Porsche, Ferdinand, Dr.	Business	225	450		550	Designer VW & Porsche
Portal, Charles	Aviation	25	45	75	50	
Porter, Cole 1891-1964	Music	225	450		650	Composer
Porter, David 1780-1843	Military	50	145	250		Am. Naval Officer
Porter, David Dixon	Civil War	150		450		Union Admiral/1813-91
Porter, Don	Ent	5			15	
Porter, Fitz-John	Civil War	50	100	400	RARE	Union General/1822-1901
Porter, Gene Stratton	Author	50	150	250	100	Am. Novelist
Porter, George, Sir	Science	15	35	60	30	Nobel Chemistry 1967
Porter, Horace 1837-1921	Civil War	50	175	300		Union General
Porter, James M.	Political	25	75	125		Sec'y War 1843
Porter, Jane 1776-1850	Author	100		300		Br. Novelist
Porter, Katherine Anne	Author	75	125	300	150	Pulitzer/Amercian Author
Porter, Peter 1773-1844	Political	75	150	175		Sec'y War J.Q.Adams
Porter, William Sidney	Author	350	850	1,717		
Portes-Gil, Emilio	Political	40		85		President Mexico
Portland, 3rd Duke	Political	50	200			Prime Minister
Portman, Eric	Ent	35			75	
Portman, Natalie	Ent	25			50	The Professional

Name	Field	SIG	DS	ALS	SP	Remarks
Portsmouth, Duchess	Royalty	75	200	450		Louise-Renee' Keroualle
Posey, Parker	Ent	20			50	
Poshetko, Joseph	Aviation	10		25	30	WWII Flying Tiger Ace
Possart, Ernst	Music	20		55	50	Classical Musician
Post, Augustus	Aviation	25	45	55	50	Pioneer Aviator, Balloonist
Post, Emily 1873-1960	Author	65		125		US Ettiquette
Post, Marjorie M.	Business	15		50	25	Postum Cereal
Post, Markie	Ent	15	30		35	Night Court
Post, Wiley 1900-35	Aviation	350		650	750	I st Solo Around the World
Poston, Tom	Ent	10			30	Newhart
Potter, Beatrix	Author	250		750		Childrens Author
Potter, Cora	Ent	10		30	25	
Potts, Annie	Ent	10	25		30	Designing Women
Poulenc, Francis-Jean	Music	125	275	450		
Poulter, Thomas C.	Explorer	20	40			2nd Arctic Expedition
Pound, Ezra 1885-1972	Author	250	675	900		Poet
Poundstone, Paula	Ent	5			15	Standup Comedienne
Povey, Len	Aviation	10		25	20	
Povich, Maury	Ent	10			20	TV Host
Powderly, Terence V.	Political	30	75		50	Am. Labor Leader
Powell, Adam Clayton	Political	30	40	50	35	
Powell, Colin L.	Military	35	100		100	Chmn. Joint Chiefs of Staff
Powell, Dick	Ent	35	45	60	65	1904-1963
Powell, Eleanor	Ent	20	35		60	Film Dancer/1910-1982
Powell, Jane	Ent	10	20		25	
Powell, Lewis F. Jr.	SuprCt	30	100			
Powell, Maud	Music	30			90	Violinist
Powell, Max	Music	10			20	
Powell, Robert	Ent	5			10	
Powell, Ross E.	Military	10		30		
Powell, Talmage	Author	10	20	40	20	Am. Novelist Mysteries
Powell, William	Ent	40	65		90	
Power, Tyrone	Ent	75	100		200	1913 - 1958
Powers, Francis Gary	Aviation	50			100	U2 Pilot/Shot Down/USSR
Powers, Hiram	Art	50	150	250	150	19th Cent. Major Sculptor
Powers, Preston	Art	25	75	150		
Powers, Stephanie	Ent	15			35	Hart to Hart
Pownall, Thomas	Political	250	600	900		Colonial Gov. MA
Powter, Susan	Author	5			10	Excercise and Diet
Powys, Llewelyn	Author	30	65	90	45	Essayist, Novelist
Powys, Theodore F.	Author	100		300		Br. Allegorical Novels
Poynter, Edward John	Art	25		75		Pres. Royal Academy
Pozzo de Borgo, Chas.	Political	50		200		Opponent of Napoleon
Prado, Perez	Music	25			75	Bandleader
Pratt, Francis & Whitney	Science		450			Pratt & Whitney Engine
Preble, George H.	Civil War	25	50	75		
Preddy, George E.	Aviation	15	30	45	30	
Preger, Kurt	Music	10			20	Opera
Prelog, Vladimir	Science	20	30	45	25	Nobel Chemistry 1975

Name	Field	SIG	DS	ALS	SP	Remarks
Preminger, Otto 1906-86	Ent	40	65		80	Director
Prentice, John	Cartoonist	15			40	Rip Kirby
Prentiss, Paula	Ent	10			20	
Prescott, Oliver	RevWar	75	175	400		Shays Rebellion
Prescott, Wm. Hickling	Author	30	60			
Presley, Elvis 1935-77	Music	575	1,400	RARE	900	
Presley, Priscilla	Ent	10	35	30	25	
Preston, Kelly	Ent	25			50	
Preston, Robert	Ent	40			90	1918 - 1987
Preston, William	Civil War	150	600			CSA General/War Dated
Preston, William 1816-87	Civil War	100	400			CSA General
Preston, William Ballard	Civil War	25	50	110		CSA Governor
Pretenders	Music	35			65	Signed by Entire Group
Pretty Things, The	Music	45			80	Signed by all Five
Preuss, Georg	Military	20		40		
Previn, Andre	Music	20	40	80	75	Conductor
Previn, Dorey	Music	5	10	20	10	Composer
Prevost, Eugene-Marcel	Author	10	25	45		Fr. Moralist, Feminist Fiction
Prey, Hermann	Music	10			30	Opera
Price, Leontyne	Music	25		50	55	Am. Soprano, Opera
Price, Margaret	Music	15			45	Opera
Price, Nick	Sports	15			35	Golf
Price, Ray	Music	5			15	Country
Price, Sterling	Civil War	380		RARE	RARE	CSA General/War Dated
Price, Sterling 1809-67	Civil War	200	350			CSA General
Price, Vincent 1911-93	ENt	50	100	150	100	
Pride, Charley	Music	5			15	
Prien, Guenther	Military	300			750	
Priest, Pat	Ent	10			20	Munsters
Priest, Royce W.	Aviation	10	25	35	30	USAF WWII ACE
Priestley, J. B. 1894-1984	Author	40	85	175	125	Playwright, Novelist
Priestley, William O. Sir	Science	50	100	200		Obstetric Physician
Priestly, Jason	Ent	20	50		50	
Priestly, Joseph	Science	350	900	1,400		Br. Chemist
Prieur-Duvernois, Claude	Military	35	125			Fr. Revolutionary
Prigogine, Ilya	Science	20		45	25	Nobel Chemistry 1977
Prima, Louis	Ent	35			65	BandLeader/Disney Voice
Primrose, William	Music	75			225	Violinist
Prince	Music	75	200		200	Scarce
Prince, Harold 'Hal'	Ent	15	30		30	
Prince, Henry	Civil War	35	75	80		
Principal, Victoria	Ent	15		25	35	
Pringle, Aileen	Ent	15		35	30	
Prinz, Rosemary	Ent	5			10	
Prinze, Freddie	Ent	50	75		90	Suicide Young
Pritchard, John, Sir	Music	15			45	Opera
Procol Harum	Music	35			65	Signed by Entire Group
Proctor, Edna Dean	Author	35		75		Am. Poet
Proctor, Redfield	Political	10	25	50	30	1831-1908

Name	Field	SIG	DS	ALS	SP	Remarks
Proctor, Richard Anthony	Science	10		35		Br. Astonomer
Profumo, John	Political	40	65		100	
Profumo, Valerie	Ent	10	25		25	British film star
Prokofieff, Serge	Music	400	750	1,200	950	1891-1953
Prosky, Robert	Ent	5			15	
Protti, Aldo	Music	10			20	Opera
Prouse, Juliet	Ent	10			40	
Proust, Marcel 1871-1922	Author	500	875	1,600	RARE	
Provost, Jon	Ent	10	25		25	Timmy in "Lassie"
Prowse, Dave	Ent	15			30	Darth Vader in Star Wars
Prowse, Juliet	Ent	10			20	
Pryce, Jonathan	Ent	10			25	
Pryor, Richard	Ent	30	60		75	Scarce
Pryor, Roger	Ent	15	25		45	
Pryor, Roger A.	Civil War	175		650		CSA General/War Dated
Pryor, Roger A. 1828-19	Civil War	100	250	300		CSA General
Pucci, Emilio	Business	10	25	40	25	It. Fashion Designer
Puccini, Giacomo	Music	500	750	1,250	950	Composer
Puck, Wolfgang	Business	5			15	Owner of Spago
Puente, Tito	Music	15			45	Bandleader
Pulitzer, Joseph 1847-11	Business	125	350	500		Pulitzer Pr. Editor
Pulitzer, Joseph, Jr.	Business	15	25		20	Editor-Publisher
Pulitzer, Ralph 1879-1939	Business	75		250		Journalist/Publisher
Pulitzer, Roxanne	Ent	5		35	20	
Pullman, Bill	Ent	20			45	
Pullman, George M.	Business	225	450	500		Pullman RR Cars
Puma, Salvatore	Music	10			20	Opera
Pupin, Michael, Dr.	Science	100	300	300	225	Physicist-Inventor-Author
Purcell, Edward M., Dr.	Science	20	30	45	25	Nobel Physics 1952
Purcell, Lee	Ent	5			10	
Purcell, Sarah	Ent	5	15	20	10	
Purdy, James	Author	20	50			
Purl, Linda	Ent	10			20	
Purvis, Melvin	Western	25	100	150	100	
Purvis, Robert	Political	25	45	85		Underground Railroad
Pushkin, Alexander	Author	825	2,600	RARE	RARE	Russ. Poet/Author
Pusser, Buford	Political	125	250			Tennessee Sheriff/Slain
Putnam, George Palmer	Business	15	50	75	35	Book Publisher, Author
Putnam, Israel 1718-90	RevWar	200		750		Dont Fire Until You See....
Putnam, Rufus	RevWar	175	400	650		General. Ohio Pioneer
Puzo, Mario	Author	25	75		55	Novelist/Godfather
Py, Gilbert	Music	10			25	Opera
Pyle, Denver	Ent	10			20	
Pyle, Ernie	Author	200	300	450	350	WWII Correspondent
Pyle, Howard 1853 - 1911	Art	175	300		600	Am.Art Nouveau Illustrator
Pynchon, John 1621-1703	Military	RARE	RARE	3,750	RARE	Stateman/Soldier

George S. Patton

Name	Field	SIG	DS	ALS	SP	Remarks

Name	Field	SIG	DS	ALS	SP	Remarks
Qaddafi, Muammar	Political	100		500	200	Libyan-Arab Republic
Quackenbush, Stephen	Civil War	45		175		Union Admiral
Quaid, Dennis	Ent	20			50	
Quaid, Randy	Ent	15	40		35	
Quale, Anthony	Ent	20	25		45	
Quang, Thich Tri	Political	30		125		
Quantrill, Wm. C.	Military	900		3,500		CSA Army Guerilla Leader
Quarles, William A.	Civil War	75	225			CSA General
Quarry, Robert	Ent	10			25	
Quasimodo, Salvatore	Author	25	40	50	35	Nobel Literature 1959
Quayle, Dan	Vice Pres	35			45	
Quayle, Marilyn	Political	20			50	
Queen	Music	175	400		450	Signed by Entire Group
Quesada, E,R, 'Pete'	Military	15		50	25	
Quesada, Elwood R.	Aviation	15	30	45	30	
Questel, Mae	Ent	75	150	150		Voice Betty Boop/Olive Oyl
Quincy, Josiah	Political	125		200		1772 - 1864
Quine, Richard	Ent	10			20	Actor/Director
Quinn, Anthony	Ent	15	40		45	AA Winner
Quinn, Martha	Music	5			10	MTV V-Jay
Quinn, Aida	Ent	15			25	
Quintard, Charles Todd	Civil War	75	100	150		
Quirk, Michael J.	Aviation	15	25	40	30	WWII ACE
Quiros, Jean B.	Political	45	75			
Quisling, Vidkun	Military	125	200	350	450	
Quitman, John A.	Military	25				General/1799-1858

Name	Field	SIG	DS	ALS	SP	Remarks
Raab, Julius	Political	5		30	15	Chancellor Austria
Raabe, Meinhardt	Ent	15	35		35	Munchkin in Wiz of Oz
Rabaud, Henri	Music	50			150	Composer/1873 - 1949
Rabi, Isador	Science	25	50	75	40	Nobel Physics 1944
Rabin, Yitzhak	Political	150	250	350	450	PM Israel/Assasinated
Raboy, Mac	Cartoonist	20			45	Flash Gordon
Rachmaninoff, Sergei	Music	225	600	775	475	Composer/1873-1943
Racine, Jean 1639-99	Author	4,500	RARE	RARE	RARE	
Rackham, Arthur	Art	100	200	400		Illustrator Children's Books
Radford, William	Military	125		350		Naval Officer/1808-1890
Radhakrishnan, Sarvepa	Political	45	150	300	75	Pres. India

Name	Field	SIG	DS	ALS	SP	Remarks
Radner, Gilda	Ent	75	150		150	Sat Nite Live
Rae, Cassidy	Ent	10			30	
Rae, Charlotte	Ent	5			15	
Raeder, Erich	Military	65	175	400	125	German Naval Commdr
Raff, Joseph Joachim	Music	45		150		Composer
Rafferty, Frances	Ent	5			10	
Raffin, Deborah	Ent	5			15	
Rafko, Kaye Lani	Ent	10			15	Miss America 1988
Raft, George	Ent	45	100	125	125	1895 - 1980
Ragsland, Rags	Ent	40			75	
Rahman, Abdul	Political	10		40	25	Ambassador
Raimondi, Ruggero	Music	20			50	Opera
Rainer, Luise	Ent	15		40	45	
Raines, Ella	Ent	10			20	
Rainey, Ford	Ent	5			10	
Rainger, Ralph	Music	20			40	Composer
Rainier, Prince	Royalty	75		200	125	Monaco
Rain-in-the-Face	Western	13,000	RARE	RARE	RARE	Indian Chief
Rains, Claude	Ent	125	250		275	1889 - 1967
Rainwater, Leo James	Science	20		45	30	Nobel Physics 1975
Rainwater, Marvin	Music	15			30	
Raisa, Rosa 1893-1963	Music	30			60	Opera
Raisch, Bill	Ent	10			20	
Raitt, Bonnie	Music	15			45	
Raitt, John	Ent	5			15	
Rall, Guenther	Military	40	65	125	90	WWII German ACE
Ralston, Esther	Ent	10	25	35	30	
Ralston, Vera H.	Ent	10			25	
Ralston, William	Business	50	100	150		Founder Bank of California
Rama VI	Royalty	150				King Siam (Thailand)
Rambeau, Marjorie	Ent	25		45	45	
Rambo, Dirk	Ent	20			40	
Ramey, Samuel	Music	15			35	Opera
Ramirez, Carlos	Music	10			25	Baritone
Ramos, Mel	Art	20			40	
Rampling, Charlotte	Ent	10			20	
Ramsay, William, Sir	Science	150	300	450		Nobel Chemistry 1904
Ramseur, Stephen	Civil War	RARE	RARE	RARE	RARE	CSA General
Ramsey, Norman F., Dr.	Science	10			20	Nobel Physics 1989
Rand, Ayn 1905-82	Author	500			750	Objectivist Novels
Rand, Sally	Ent	25			60	
Randall, James R.	Music	75				Composer
Randall, Tony	Ent	10	20	25	20	Odd Couple
Randolph, Beverly	Revwar	100	250			Virginia Governor
Randolph, Boots	Music	5			15	
Randolph, Charles D.	Western	100	200	300		
Randolph, Edmund J.	RevWar	200	450	550		Secretary of State
Randolph, George W.	Civil War	250	400	550		CSA General/1818-67
Randolph, John	RevWar	100	225	375		Senator VA

Name	Field	SIG	DS	ALS	SP	Remarks
Randolph, Joyce	Ent	10	25	30	20	Honeymooners
Randolph, Lillian	Ent	100			250	
Randolph, Peyton	RevWar	400				1st Pres Cont Congress
Randolph, Thos. Mann	Political	75	225			
Rank, J. Arthur, lst Baron	Business	25		75	50	Br. Film Magnate
Rank, Otto	Science	200		400		Austrian Psychoanalyst
Rankin, Jeannette	Political	100	200			1880-1973
Rankin, Nell	Music	15			25	Am. Contralto
Rankin, Robert J.	Aviation	15	30	40	35	WWII ACE in one day
Ransom, John Crowe	Author	45	90	200		Am Poet
Ransom, Matt W.	Civil War	100	275			CSA General/1826-1904
Ransom, Robert, Jr.	Civil War	250				CSA General/1828-92
Rapaport, Lester	Art	10		30	15	
Rapee, Erno	Music	15			45	
Raphael	Art	3,500	9,000	RARE	RARE	
Raphael, Sally Jessy	Ent	5			20	TV Talk Show Hostess
Rapper, Irving	Ent	15			35	40's Film Director
Rappold, Marie	Music	30			75	Opera, Concert
Rashad, Phylicia	Ent	15			35	Cosby Show
Raskob, John J.	Business	10			15	CEO General Motors
Rasmussen, Knud J.V.	Explorer	150		300	250	Danish Arctic Explorer
Rasputin, Gregori E.	Clergy	2,000	4,500	6,000		Rus. Mystic. Assassinated
Rathbone, Basil	Ent	200	450	450	500	Sherlock Holmes/1872-16
Ratoff, Gregory	Ent	20	60		60	Film Director
Ratzenberger, John	Ent	15			35	Cheers
Raum, Green B.	Civil War	30	65			Union General/1829-1909
Ravel, Maurice	Music	450		1,400	1,600	Composer/1875-1937
Rawdon, Francis l732-97	RevWar	150		450		Br. Gen'l Rev. War.
Rawdon-Hastings, F.	RevWar	25	60	100		Br. Off'r. Bunker Hill
Rawlings, Edward V.	Military	10				
Rawlings, Marjorie K.	Author	50		150		Am. Pulitzer. The Yearling
Rawlins, John A.	Civil War	75	145	225		Union General/1831-69
Rawlinson, Herbert	Ent	15		45	50	1886-1953
Rawls, Lou	Music	15	45		35	
Rawson, Edward	Political	125	250	450		1615-93
Ray, Aldo	Ent	5			15	
Ray, James Earl	Criminal	75		200		Shot Martin Luther King, Jr.
Ray, Johnny	Ent	15			40	
Ray, Leah	Ent	10			15	
Ray, Man (Rudnitsky)	Art	250	450			Painter/Photographer
Raye, Collin	Music	10			25	
Raye, Martha	Ent	20	40		45	
Raymond, Alex	Cartoonist	50			100	Flash Gordon/Rip Kirby...
Raymond, Gene	Ent	10		25	25	
Raymond, Henry J.	Business	45		150		Fndr./New York Times
Raymond, Jim	Cartoonist	15			35	Blondie
Raymond, Paula	Ent	5			15	
Razaf, Andy	Music	50		175		Lyricist Ain't Misbehavin'
Rea, Steven	Ent	20			40	

Name	Field	SIG	DS	ALS	SP	Remarks
Read, Albert Cushing	Aviation	50		150	125	
Read, George 1733-98	RevWar	350	450	1,250		Signer Decl. of Indepen.
Read, T. Buchanan	Art	20		40		
Reade, Charles	Author	50	75	125		Br. Novelist, Dramatist
Reagan, John H.	Civil War	150	450	600		CSA Postmaster General
Reagan, Maureen	Political	5		25	15	Daughter of President
Reagan, Nancy	First Lady	35		100	75	
Reagan, Ron, Jr.	Ent	10			30	Dancer
Reagan, Ronald	President	225	600	RARE	400	As President
Reagan, Ronald 1911-	President	200	450	850	300	
Real, Pierre F., Count	Military	20		50		French Revolution
Reale, Antenore	Music	25			50	Opera
Ream, Vinnie	Art	200		400		Am. Sculptor/Scarce
Reason, Rex	Ent	10			20	
Reasoner, Harry	Ent	15			40	60 Minutes
Rector, Henry M.	Civil War	200	450			CSA Governor
Red Hot Chili Peppers	Music	35			75	Signed by all four
Reddy, Helen	Music	10	25	25	25	
Redenbacker, Orville	Business	10	30	30	30	Popcorn King/1907-95
Redford, Robert	Ent	60	150		100	The Sting/Butch Cassidy
Redgrave, Lynn	Ent	10			25	
Redgrave, Michael, Sir	Ent	20			40	
Redgrave, Vanessa	Ent	20	30		45	
Redman, Don	Music	20			45	Jazz Musician
Redmond, John E.	Political	5		30	15	
Redon, Odilon	Art	75		275		Lithographer & Engraver
Redout, Pierre Joseph	Art	250	600	900		Fr. Painter/Lithographer
Reed, Alan	Ent	60	100		80	Orig. Voice/Fred Flinstone
Reed, Carol, Sir 1906-76	Ent	50			150	Br. Director
Reed, Donna 1921-86	Ent	90	125		175	Its a Wonderful Life
Reed, Jerry	Music	5	20		15	Singer/Actor
Reed, John	Author	200			300	Radical Am. Journalist
Reed, Joseph 1741-85	RevWar	75	200	350		
Reed, Lou	Music	20			50	
Reed, Oliver	Ent	15			30	
Reed, Phillip	Ent	15	25		30	
Reed, Rex	ENt	5			15	
Reed, Robert	Ent	55	75		100	Brady Bunch/Dad
Reed, Roland	Ent	15			35	
Reed, Shanna	Ent	15			25	
Reed, Stanley 1884-1980	SuprCt	50	90	150		
Reed, Thomas Brackett	Political	15	35	45		Speaker of the House
Reed, Walter	Ent	10			25	
Reed, Walter 1851-1902	Science	400	750	RARE	675	Yellow Fever
Rees, Roger	Ent	10			20	
Rees, Thomas	Business	10	25	40	25	
Reese, Della	Ent	15	40		40	Touched by an Angel
Reese, Pee Wee	Sports	15			30	Baseball
Reeve, Christopher	Ent	65	150		150	Superman/Paralyzed

Name	Field	SIG	DS	ALS	SP	Remarks
Reeves, George	Ent	850	1,500	RARE	1,500	50's Superman TV Star
Reeves, Keanu	Ent	25	60		50	Speed
Reeves, Martha	Music	5			20	Composer
Reeves, Ronna	Music	5			10	
Reeves, Steve	Ent	15			35	
Reeves-Smith, Olive	Ent	5			15	
Regan, Donald	Political	10			30	Sec'y Treasury
Regan, Phil	Ent	10	45		25	
Reger, Max	Music	75	200	450		German Composer
Reginald, Lionel	Ent	10			20	
Regnaud de Saint-Jean	Military	30		90		French Revolution
Rehan, Ada	Ent	20			40	
Rehm, Dan	Aviation	15	25	45	30	WWII ACE
Rehnquist, William H.	SuprCt	50	150	175	100	Chief Justice
Reich, Wilhelm	Science	125	300	550		Austr. Psychoanalyst
Reichers, Lou	Aviation	35	45	60	65	
Reid, Tim	Ent	5			15	
Reid, Wallace	Ent	200			550	
Reid, Whitelaw	Author	30	75		50	
Reik, Theodor 1888-1969	Science	100	250	450		Austrian Psychoanalyst
Reilly, Charles Nelson	Ent	5			10	
Reinburg, J. Hunter	Aviation	15	35	50	40	WWII Marine ACE
Reinecke, Karl	Music	75	150	225	250	
Reiner, Carl	Ent	10	30	30	25	
Reiner, Fritz	Music	75	150		200	Hungarian Conductor
Reiner, Rob	Ent	10	25		25	Director
Reinert, Ernst Wilhelm	Aviation	25			50	German ACE
Reinhardt, Max 1873-43	Ent	100	175	400	275	Austrian Director
Reinhold, Judge	Ent	15			30	
Reinking, Ann	Ent	5		20	15	
Reisch, Walter	Ent	10			20	Director
Reiser, Paul	Ent	25			55	Mad About You
Reiserer, Russell	Aviation	15		40		WWII ACE
Reitsch, Hanna	Aviation	75	150	250	150	Flew lst Practical H'Copter.
Reitz, Francis W.	Political	50	125			South Africa
Remarque, Erich Maria	Author	40	125	250	65	All Quiet on Western Front
Rembrandt van Rijn	Art	3,000				Dutch Painter-Etcher
Remer, Otto	Military	25			65	WWII SS General
Remick, Lee	Ent	30			65	1935 - 1991
Remington, Eliphalet Jr.	Business	250	550			Remington Guns Co.
Remington, Frederic	Art	575	800	1,750	1,750	Sculptor/Writer/1861-1909
Remington, Samuel	Business	Scarce	1,250			Fndr Remington Gun CO.
Renaldo, Duncan	Ent	40		100	120	Cisco Kid/1904-1980
Renaud, Maurice	Music	50			175	Opera
Renaud, Paul	Political	50			100	Premier France
Renault, Louis	Political	35	75	125		Nobel Peace Prize 1907
Renner, Karl, Dr.	Political	25	50	100	50	
Rennie, John 1761-1821	Science			600		Eng. Built Waterloo Bridge
Rennie, Michael	Ent	100			200	1909 - 1971

Name	Field	SIG	DS	ALS	SP	Remarks
Reno, Jean	Ent	20			40	
Reno, Marcus A.	Military	1,000	2,750			Battle of Little Big Horn
Renoir, Jean	Ent	125	275			French Filmaker
Renoir, Pierre-Auguste	Art	300	700	2,100	RARE	
Renquist, William	SuprCt	75			150	Chief Justice
Renwick, Edward S.	Science	25	45	75		Father Modern Poultry Ind.
REO Speedwagon	Music	35			65	Signed by Entire Group
Resnick, Mike	Author	10	20	30	20	
Resnick, Regina	Music	25			60	Opera
Resnik, Judith	Space	100	250		200	Astronaut
Respighi, Oftorino	Music	100	200	450		Italian Opera
Reston, John 'Scotty'	Author	10	20	35	15	Journalist
Rethberg, Elisabeth	Music	45			125	Opera
Rethy, Ester	Music	10	20	35	30	Opera
Rettig, Tommy	Ent	10			25	Lassie
Reuther, Walter P.	Political	25	40	75	35	
Revelle, Hamilton	Ent	5			10	
Revels, Hiram Rhoades	Political	500				1st Black U.S. Senator
Revere, Anne	Ent	25			60	AA Winner/1903 - 1990
Revere, Paul 1735-1818	RevWar	2,500	5,500	9,400	RARE	
Rey, Alvino	Music	10			25	Big Band Leader
Reybold, E.	Military	15	35	45		Gen. WWII Engineer Corps
Reymann, Hellmuth	Aviation	30		75		
Reynolds, A.W.	Civil War	65	145	175		CSA General/1817-76
Reynolds, Albert	Political	15			25	P.M. Ireland
Reynolds, Burt	Ent	10			20	Smokey and the Bandit
Reynolds, Craig	Ent	10			25	
Reynolds, Daniel H.	Civil War	100		350		CSA General/1832-1902
Reynolds, Debbie	Ent	10	20	25	20	
Reynolds, Donn	Music	10			20	
Reynolds, Gene	Ent	5			15	
Reynolds, John Fulton	Civil War	350	RARE	RARE	RARE	Union General/KIA
Reynolds, Joseph Jones	Civil War	45	125	175		Union General/1822-99
Reynolds, Joshua, Sir	Art	200	300	550		Br Portrait
Reynolds, Marjorie	Ent	20	45		40	GWTW
Reynolds, R.J.	Business	250	600			Founder Tobacco Empire
Reynolds, Richard S.	Business	40	125	225	65	Reynolds Aluminum Co.
Reynolds, William	Ent	5			15	
Rhames, Ving	Ent	25			50	
Rhee, Syngman 1875-65	Political	175	200	955	250	1st Pres. So. Korea
Rheims, Bettina	Art	35			100	
Rhett, Alicia	Ent	200	RARE	RARE	RARE	RARE GWTW Star
Rhett, Robert Barnwell	Civil War	150	300	550		CSA General/1800-76
Rhodes, Billie	Ent	15			35	
Rhodes, Cecil John	Political	125	250	400	600	1853-1902
Rhys-Davies, John	Ent	15			35	Indiana Jones Films
Ribbentrop, Joachim von	Military	200	450	550	325	Hitlers Foreign Affairs Adv.
Ribbentrop, Rudolf von	Military	65	100	150		
Ricci, Christina	Ent	20	50		50	Addams Family movies...

Name	Field	SIG	DS	ALS	SP	Remarks
Ricciarelli, Katia	Music	10			25	Opera
Rice, Alice C.	Author	75		225		
Rice, Anne	Author	25			45	Novelist
Rice, Dan	Business	50	100	300		Circus Clown & Owner
Rice, Donna	Ent	15			30	
Rice, Elmer 1882-1967	Author	100	250		150	Pulitzer Prize. Playwright
Rice, Grantland	Author	25			75	Sportswriter
Rice, Jerry	Sports	20			50	Football
Rice, Tim	Music	10	30	65	30	Composer/Disney
Rich, Buddy 1917-87	Music	35			125	Big Bandleader-Drummer
Rich, Irene	Ent	5		20	15	
Richards, Ann	Political	10			20	Governor TX
Richards, Cliff	Music	15			40	
Richards, Denise	Ent	20			45	
Richards, Dickinson W.	Science	25	35	55	35	Nobel Medicine 1956
Richards, Jeff	Ent	10			20	Child Star
Richards, Keith	Music	50	175		100	Rolling Stones Guitarist
Richards, Michael	Ent	25	50		50	Kramer on "Seinfeld"
Richardson, Dorothy	Author	50	125	250		
Richardson, Elliot	Political	10	25	35	20	Attorney General
Richardson, Ian	Ent	5			15	
Richardson, John, Sir	Science	20	60	125		Surgeon
Richardson, Michael	Ent	25			50	Sieinfeld/Kramer
Richardson, Miranda	Ent	25			55	Br. Actress
Richardson, Natasha	Ent	20			50	
Richardson, Patricia	Ent	25			50	Home Improvement
Richardson, Ralph, Sir	Ent	20		50	45	
Richardson, Robert V.	Civil War	450	750			CSA General
Richardson, Tony	Ent	15			25	Director
Richardson, William A.	Political	25	45	75		Sec'y Treas.1873
Richelieu, Armand E. du	Political	100	225	300		Prime Minister France
Richelieu, Armand-Jean	Political	300	750	1,600		
Richey, Helen	Aviation	25	50		50	
Richie, Lionel	Music	20	60		45	Composer-Singer-Arranger
Richman, Harry	Aviation	15			35	
Richter, Burton, Dr.	Science	20	45	60	35	Nobel Physics 1976
Richter, Charles, Dr.	Science	25			65	Devised Richter Scale
Richter, Hans	Music	150		450		German Conductor
Richters, Christine	Ent	5			15	Playboy Pin-Up
Richthofen, Manfred von	Aviation	2,000	RARE	RARE	6,500	WWI ACE/Red Baron
Rickenbacker, Edw V.	Aviation	100	200	450	275	WWI ACE
Rickles, Don	Ent	5	20	15	15	
Rickover, Hyman G.	Military	100	200	350	250	Father of Atomic Sub
Riddle, George	Music	10			20	
Ride, Sally K.	Space	15	45		35	lst US Woman in Space
Ridgway, Matthew B.	Military	90	195	175	125	Supreme Allied Cmdr. WWII
Riefenstahl, Leni	Art	30	45	75	65	Hitler's Photographer
Rieger, Vince	Aviation	10	25	35	30	WWII Navy ACE
Riegger, Wallingford	Music	20	65	125	35	Composer

Name	Field	SIG	DS	ALS	SP	Remarks
Rigal, Delia	Music	15			45	Opera
Rigg, Diana	Ent	20	45		45	Avengers TV Series
Riggs, Clinton E.	Science	20			40	Created Yield Sign
Riggs, Tommy	Ent	5			15	
Righteous Brothers	Music	45			90	Signed by Both
Riis, Jacob A. 1849-1914	Author	20	50	75		Journalist
Riley, James Whitcomb	Author	85	150	450	225	Poet/1849-1916
Riley, Jeannie C.	Music	5		20	15	Harper Valley PTA
Riley, Larry	Ent	5			10	
Rilke, Rainer Maria	Author	150	345			German Poet
Rimes, Lee Ann	Music	25			50	
Rimsky-Korsakov, N.	Music	600	1,500	2,500	1,500	Russian Composer
Rinehart, Mary Roberts	Author	25		75	55	Mystery Writer
Ringling, Albert C.	Business	150	400			Ringling Bros/Barnum...
Ringling, Chas. 1863-26	Business	125	300			Ringling Bros/Barnum..
Ringling, Henry	Business	125	350			Ringling Bros/Barnum...
Ringling, John 1866-1936	Business	125	600			Ringling Bros/Barnum...
Ringling, Otto 1858-1911	Business	250	550			Ringling Bros/Barnum ...
Ringo, John	Western	2,000	RARE	RARE	RARE	Cowboy Gunslinger
Ringwald, Molly	Ent	20	45	60	50	
Ripken, Cal	Sports	20			50	Baseball
Ripley, Eleazar W.	Military	75		225		General War 1812
Ripley, George	Political	150	325	575		
Ripley, James Wolfe	Civil War	65	185	200		Union General/1794-1870
Ripley, Robert 1893-1949	Cartoonist	100		225	250	Believe It Or Not
Ripley, Roswell 1823-87	Civil War	175		400		CSA General
Ripley, Roswell S. (WD)	Civil War	225		900		CSA General
Ritchard, Cyril 1896-1977	Ent	20			50	Br. Dancer & Comedian
Ritchie, Adele	Ent	15		50	40	
Ritchie, Neil, Sir	Military	15	35	50	30	General
Ritchie, Steve	Aviation	15	35	45	40	
Ritt, Martin	Ent	35			65	Director
Rittenhouse, David	Science	850	1,100	RARE	RARE	Am Astronomer
Ritter, John	Ent	10	25		25	Three Company
Ritter, Tex	Music	75			225	1907 - 1974
Ritter, Thelma	Ent	50			150	
Ritterscheim, Karl	Music	10			20	Opera
Ritz Brothers, The	Music	85			150	Jimmy, Al, Harry
Ritz, Jimmy	Music	15			40	
Rivera, Diego	Art	300	550	800	1,200	Political-Social Muralist
Rivera, Geraido	Ent	15	45		30	TV Host
Rivers, Joan	Ent	5			15	
Rivers, Larry	Art	45	75	150		Pop Art Movement
Rivington, James 1724-02	RevWar	100	200			Journalist-Publisher-Spy
Rizutto, Phil	Sports	10			25	1994 Baseball HOF
Roach, Hal, Jr.	Ent	5			15	
Roach, Hal, Sr.1892-1992	Ent	100	300		175	AA Film Pioneer. Our Gang
Roarke, Hayden	Ent	60			75	Dr. Bellows/Jeannie
Robards, Jason	Ent	15	25		30	AA Winner

Name	Field	SIG	DS	ALS	SP	Remarks
Robbins, Frederick C.	Science	20	30	45	25	Nobel Medicine 1954
Robbins, Gale	Ent	15		35	30	
Robbins, Harold	Author	20	75	100	35	The Carpetbaggers
Robbins, Jay T.	Aviation	15	25	40	35	WWII ACE
Robbins, Jerome	Music	40	75	90	75	Ballet Dancer
Robbins, Marty	Music	25			50	Country
Robbins, Reg. L.	Aviation	25			55	Pioneer Aviator
Robbins, Tim	Ent	25			50	
Roberti, Margherita	Music	15			30	Am. Soprano
Roberts, Cokie	Ent	5			15	TV-Radio Journalist
Roberts, David	Art	40	90	175		Scottish Painter
Roberts, Doris	Ent	5			15	
Roberts, Eric	Ent	10			25	
Roberts, Frederick S.	Military	50			100	Field Marshal
Roberts, Jack	Music	10			20	
Roberts, Jonathan	Political	75		250		1771-1854
Roberts, Julia	Ent	35	150		65	
Roberts, Kenneth	Author	40	80	150		Am. Historical Novels
Roberts, Lee S.	Music	35	75	Scarce	Scarce	Composer
Roberts, Oral	Clergy	20		50	25	Am. Evangelist
Roberts, Owen J.	SuprCt	50	150	200	100	
Roberts, Pernell	Ent	65	100		100	Bonanza
Roberts, Ray	Ent	10			20	
Roberts, Tanya	Ent	15	25		25	Charlie Angels
Roberts, Tony	Ent	5			15	
Roberts, William P.	Civil War	125				Youngest in CSA/1841-10
Roberts, Xavier	Business	15	25	35	25	
Robertson, Beverly H.	Civil War	65	140			CSA General/1826-1910
Robertson, Cliff	Ent	20			40	AA Winner
Robertson, Dale	Ent	15			35	
Robertson, James	RevWar			975		Br Gen in RevWar
Robertson, Morgan	Author	25		60		Sea Stories
Robertson, Pat, Rev.	Clergy	15	25	40	20	
Robeson, George M.	Political	25	50	75		Sec'y Navy 1869
Robeson, Paul 1898-1976	Ent	125	200	250	500	Singer/Actor
Robespierre, Maximilien	Military	1,250	2,500	RARE	RARE	French Revolution
Robin, Mado	Music	50			175	Opera
Robinson, Bill Bojangles	Ent	100	250	450	400	Dancer in Films
Robinson, Dwight P.	Business	5	15	20	15	
Robinson, Edward	Science		200	400		Archaeologist
Robinson, Edward G.	Ent	60	125		200	1893-1973
Robinson, Holly	Ent	10			20	
Robinson, Jackie	Sports	400	600		900	Baseball
Robinson, John 1761-28	RevWar	65	150	275		Soldier/Merchant
Robinson, John C.	Civil War	75	150	200		Union General/1817-97
Robinson, Smokey	Music	25	50		45	of the Miracles
Robinson, Sugar Ray	Sports	100			200	Boxer
Robson, Flora, Dame	Ent	30			75	1902 - 1984
Robson, May	Ent	40			75	1858 - 1942

Name	Field	SIG	DS	ALS	SP	Remarks
Robson, Stuart	Ent	20	30		45	
Rocco, Alex	Ent	10			20	
Rochambeau, Count de	RevWar	300		750		Fr. Gen. in Am. Revolution
Roche, James M.	Business	10		30	20	Pres. Ford Motor Co.
Rochefort, Henri	Author	20		50		Fr. Journalist
Rochford, Leonard	Aviation	20	40			WWI Br. ACE
Rock, Blossom	Ent	150	200	RARE	300	Addams Family
Rockefeller, Abby A.	Business	15	30	45	25	
Rockefeller, David	Business	15	35	45	25	Banker
Rockefeller, Happy	Business	5	15	20	10	Wife of Nelson Rockefeller
Rockefeller, John D.	Business	500	1,650	2,250	1,500	Standard Oil. Philantropist
Rockefeller, John D., Jr.	Business	35	125	175	75	Rockefeller Ctr
Rockefeller, Laurance	Business	5		25	10	Philanthropist
Rockefeller, Nelson A.	Vice Pres	30	75		45	Governor NY
Rockne, Knute	Sports	600	1,800		2,500	Football Legend
Rockwell, George L.	Political	50	100	200	100	Am. Nazi Party
Rockwell, Norman	Art	150	250	475	400	Am. Illustrator-Artist
Rockwell, Robert	Ent	10	25		25	
Roddenberry, Gene	Ent	100	175	RARE	200	Creator of Star Trek
Roddey, Philip D.	Civil War	100	300	400		CSA General/1826-97
Roddey, Philip D. (WD)	Civil War	200	750	1,500		CSA General
Roden, George	Civil War	30	45	75		
Rodenburg, Carl	Military	15			40	Ger General
Roderick, Milton David	Business	5			10	CEO U.S. Steel
Rodes, Robert E.	Civil War	1,000	RARE	RARE	RARE	CSA General
Rodes, Robert Emmett	Civil War	400		950		CSA General/Scarce
Rodgers & Hammerstein	Music	500				Signed together
Rodgers and Hart	Music	650	1,250			Signed by Both
Rodgers, Geo. W.	Military	50	100	200		Naval Officer War of 1812
Rodgers, John	Aviation	65	125	225	135	
Rodgers, John 1771-1838	Military	80	425	100		
Rodgers, John 1812-82	Civil War	125	300	450		
Rodgers, Richard 1902-79	Music	75	250		225	Composer/Pulitzer
Rodin, Auguste	Art	250	450	475	RARE	1840 - 1917
Rodney, Caesar 1728-84	RevWar	500	900	2,000		Signer Decl. of Indepen.
Rodriguez, Chi Chi	Sports	10			25	1992 Golf HOF
Rodzinski, Artur	Music	35	75		75	Polish Conductor
Roe, Edward Payson	Author	15	25	35		Novelist
Roe, Tommy	Music	25	45		45	
Roebling, John A.	Science	75	175	275		Designer/Brooklyn Bridge
Roebling, Washington A.	Science	100	225	400		Builder of Brooklyn Bridge
Roebuck, Alva Curtis	Business	150	1,500		375	Co-Fndr. Sears & Roebuck
Roederer, Pierre C.	Military	25	50	75		French Revolution
Roell, Werner	Aviation	10			20	
Roentgen, Wilhelm	Science	650	1,300	2,400		lst Nobel in Physics
Roethke, Theodore	Author	35	135	275	40	Am. Poet. Pulitzer
Rogatchewsky, Joseph	Music	25			75	
Rogers, Bernard W.	Military	10	25	45	40	
Rogers, Buddy	Ent	10	20	30	30	

Name	Field	SIG	DS	ALS	SP	Remarks
Rogers, Fred	Ent	5	15		15	Mr. Rogers
Rogers, Ginger 1911-95	Ent	50	150		150	AA Winner
Rogers, Jean	Ent	25			55	
Rogers, Jimmy	Music	75			165	
Rogers, John	Military	150	350	350		
Rogers, Joseph W.	Aviation	15	35	55	35	
Rogers, Kenny	Music	20	45		45	
Rogers, Mimi	Ent	20			40	
Rogers, Randolph	Art	20		35		Sculptor/1825-1892
Rogers, Robert	RevWar	400	900	RARE	RARE	Frontier Soldier
Rogers, Roy	Ent	50	200		100	
Rogers, Samuel	Author	15	30	60		Br. Poet
Rogers, Wayne	Ent	10	25		25	MASH
Rogers, Will 1879-1935	Ent	250			800	
Rogers, William F.	Civil War	15	25	35		Union Officer
Roget, Peter M., Dr.	Author	30	65	125		Rogets Thesaurus
Rohmer, Eric	Ent	50	175			Fr. Director
Rohmer, Sax (A.S.Ward)	Author	75	225	250	100	Fu Manchu
Roland de La Platiere	Military	30	75	150		Fr. Statesman/Suicide
Roland, Gilbert 1909-94	Ent	20			45	
Roland, Ruth	Ent	25	35		45	
Roldan, Salv. C.	Political	10	20	35	20	Columbia
Rolland, Romain	Author	30	75	100	45	Nobel/Literature in 1915
Rolle, Esther	Ent	10	25		20	Good Times
Rolling Stones	Music	275			600	Signed by all Five
Rollins, Sonny	Music	30			50	Jazz Tenor Sax
Rolls, Charles S.	Business	300		600		Roll-Royce Motors
Roman, Ruth	Ent	10			25	
Romanoff, Michael	Business	30	65	125	55	Romanoffs Restaurant
Romanov, Stephanie	Ent	15			40	
Rombauer, Irma S.	Author	5		30	10	The Joy of Cooking
Romberg, Sigmund	Music	75	200	300	225	Composer/1887-1951
Rome, Harold	Music	15	50	75	30	Composer
Romero, Cesar 1907- 93	Ent	35			65	TV's Batman/Joker
Romijn, Rebecca	Ent	20			40	
Rommel, Erwin 1891- 44	Military	750	1,150	RARE	1,500	Ger. Field Marshal WWII
Romney, George 1734-02	Art	150	375	450		
Romney, George W.	Business	15	30	50	25	Pres. American Motors.
Romulo, Carlos P.	Political	25	60	75	50	
Ronne, Finn	Explorer	20		70		Proved Antarctic/Continent
Ronstadt, Linda	Music	20	40		45	
Rooney, Mickey	Ent	10	30	35	25	
Roosa, Stuart R.	Space	15			150	Astronaut
Roosevelt, Alice	Political	40				Presidents Daughter
Roosevelt, Edith Kermit	First Lady	75	200	250	350	1861-1948
Roosevelt, Eleanor	First Lady	75	200	400	250	1884-1962
Roosevelt, Franklin D.	President	300	900	1,400	900	1882-1945
Roosevelt, Franklin D.	President	400	1,250	RARE	1,200	As President
Roosevelt, Franklin Jr.	Political	10			20	

Name	Field	SIG	DS	ALS	SP	Remarks
Roosevelt, James	Political	10	25	45	15	
Roosevelt, John A.	Political	20	35			FDR's Son
Roosevelt, Nicholas J.	RevWar	25	60	125		Inventor
Roosevelt, Sarah D.	Political	40	100	75	50	FDR's Mother
Roosevelt, Theodore	President	250	600	1,200	1,200	1858-1919
Roosevelt, Theodore	President	400	1,200	2,000	2,750	As President
Roosevelt, Theodore, Jr.	Military	20	50	75	40	Gov of Puerto Rico in WWI and WWII
Root, Elihu 1845-1937	Political	65			140	Secretary of War
Root, George F.	Music	50	125	150		Composer
Root, Jesse	RevWar	25	60	100		Continental Congress
Rops, Felicien 1833-98	Art	55	165	350		
Rorem, Ned	Music	25	45	90		Composer/Pulitzer
Rosas, Juan M.	Political	15	25	40		Argentina
Rose Marie	Ent	10	20		20	Dick VanDyke Show
Rose, Axl	Music	25			50	Guns and Roses
Rose, Billy	Ent	25	60	65	55	Producer
Rose, David	Music	10	20	35	20	Composer
Rose, Fred	Music	30			60	
Rosebery, Archibald P.	Political	35	75	125		Prime Minister
Rosecrans, William S.	Civil War	75	175	250		Union General/1819-98
Rosecrans, William S.	Civil War	145	375	900		Union General/War Dated
Rosenberg, Alfred	Military	175	350		450	Nazi Head of Foreign Policy
Rosenbloom, Maxie	Sports	60			125	Slapsy
Rosendahl, Charles E.	Aviation	75	160	200	200	
Rosenquist, James	Art	25	50	100		Am Pop Art
Rosenthal, Joe	Art	75	200	250	250	
Rosenthal, Laurence	Music	5		20	10	Composer
Rosenwald, Julius	Business	400	1,200			1862-1932
Ross, David 1755-1800	RevWar			400		Cont'l Army & Congress
Ross, Diana	Music	25	75		60	of the Supremes
Ross, Edmund G.	Political	35	100			KS Sen/Impeachment Trial
Ross, George 1730-79	RevWar	250	450	950		Signer Decl. of Independ.
Ross, Joe E.	Ent	100			250	
Ross, John	Western	350	600	1,000		Chief Cherokee Nation
Ross, John, Sir 1777-1856	Explorer	65	150	250		Arctic Expeditions
Ross, Katharine	Ent	20			40	
Ross, Lawrence Sullivan	Civil War	175	550			CSA General/Texas Gov.
Ross, Marion	Ent	15	25	25	25	Happy Days / Mom
Ross, Nellie Tayloe	Political	35	75	125		1st US Woman Governor
Ross, Ronald 1857-1932	Science	65	125	250		
Rosselini, Isabella	Ent	20			45	
Rosser, Thomas L.	Civil War	125	250	350	350	CSA General/1836-1910
Rossetti, Christina	Author	50	125	245		Br Poet. Sister of Dante
Rossetti, Dante Gabriel	Art	150	225	550		Br. Poet & Painter
Rossetti, Wm. M, 1829-19	Author	75		350		Pre-Raphaelite Art Critic
Rossi, Dick	Aviation	10	25	45	30	WWII Flying Tigers ACE
Rossini, Gioacchino	Music	RARE	1,000	1,750	RARE	Composer
Rossmann, Edmund	Aviation	20			50	Ger. Ace WWII
Rostand, Edmond	Author	75	200	400	775	Fr. Playwright. Cyrano de....

Name	Field	SIG	DS	ALS	SP	Remarks
Rostropovich, Mstislav	Music	25	75	100	75	Cello Virtuoso, Conductor
Roth, David Lee	Music	25	75		50	Formerly w/ Van Halen
Roth, Lillian 1910-1980	Music	40	60	75	75	
Roth, Philip	Author	15	35	45	25	Portnoys Complaint
Roth, Tim	Ent	20			45	
Rothafell, S. L. 'Roxy'	Business	15	25	40	45	Theatre Owner
Rothenstein, William	Art	25	45	75		WWI and II Artist
Rothschild, Alix de	Business	100	200	375		Banker
Rothschild, Amschel M.	Business	RARE	1,000	RARE	RARE	1733-1855
Rothschild, Guy de	Business	25	45	75	60	
Rothschild, Jakob	Business	125	600			1792 - 1868
Rothschild, Leopold	Business	35	75	125		Grandson of Nathan Mayer
Rothschild, Lionel N.	Business	25	75	125	45	Son of Nathan Mayer
Rothschild, Mayer A.	Business	150	350	550		Fndr House of Rothschild
Rothschild, Nathan	Business	50	150			Eldest son of Lionel
Rothschild, Nathan M.	Business	275	850			Founder London Bank
Rouault, Georges	Art	200	475	750	900	Landscapes,Clowns.
Rouget de Lisle, Claude	Military	125	275	775		Composed La Marseillaise
Roundtree, Richard	Music	10			25	Opera
Rourke, Mickey	Ent	20			50	
Rous, F. Peyton, Dr.	Science	20		45	30	Nobel Medicine 1966
Rousseau, Jean-Jacques	Author	300		RARE	RARE	Fr. Philosopher
Rousseau, Lovell H.	Civil War	45	80			Union General/1818-69
Rousseau, Theodore	Art	75	175	475		Fr. Leader of Barbizon
Roux, Pierre Paul Emile	Science	20	45	60	40	French Bacteriologist
Rovero, Ornella	Music	20			45	Opera
Rowan, Andrew S.	Military	35	75	150	75	
Rowan, Dan	Ent	25	50	50	40	Laugh In
Rowan, John 1773-1853	Political	100	250			
Rowan, Stephen C.	Civil War	35		150		Union Naval Commodore
Rowe, Misty	Ent	10			20	
Rowland, David	Political	50	150			
Rowland, Gena	Ent	10			25	
Rowlandson, Thomas	Art	250	500	800		Br. Caricaturist, Illustrator
Rowling, William E.	Political	10	15		20	New Zealand
Roxas, Manuel	Political	35		100	75	lst Pres. Philippines
Roxette	Music	25			50	Signed by leads
Royce, F. Henry, Sir	Business	600		1,200		Founder Rolls-Royce, Ltd.
Roze, Marie	Music	50			145	Opera
Rubattel, Rudolph	Political	30	55			Switzerland
Rubens, Alma 1899-1931	Ent	65	85	150	150	Actress
Rubens, Peter Paul	Art	2,000	RARE	RARE	RARE	Flem.Baroque Landscapes
Rubik, Erno	Science	35	75	75	50	Rubik's Cube/Hungarian
Rubinoff, David	Music	20			40	Rubinoff & His Violin
Rubinstein, Anton	Music	75	200	300	400	Composer/1829-1894
Rubinstein, Artur 1887-83	Music	40	125	235	175	Pianist
Rubinstein, Helena	Business	75	145	225	350	Cosmetics
Rubinstein, Ida	Ent	150			500	Russian Ballerina
Rubio, P. Ortiz	Political	40				Pres. Mex. 1930-32

Name	Field	SIG	DS	ALS	SP	Remarks
Ruby, Harry	Music	30	90	125	50	Composer
Ruby, Jack 1911-67	Criminal	200	400	RARE	RARE	Killed Lee Harvey Oswald
Rucker, Daniel H.	Civil War	25	65	75	100	Union Col/Brvt. General
Rudel, Hans-Ulrich	Aviation	150	300	RARE	350	German ACE
Rudner, Rita	Ent	5			15	Stand-Up Comedian
Rudolf I (Hapsburg)	Royalty			750		(Aus)
Rudorffer, Erich	Aviation	40			75	German ACE (#7)
Ruehl, Mercedes	Ent	30			60	AA Winner
Ruff, Charles F.	Civil War	25	50	60		Union General/1817-85
Ruffo, Titta 1887-1953	Music	100	RARE	RARE	400	Italian Baritone
Ruge, Friedrich	Military	65			175	German Vice Admiral
Ruger, Thomas H.	Civil War	30		75		Union General/1833-1907
Ruggles, Charles	Ent	35			70	
Ruggles, Daniel	Civil War	150	600	950		CSA General/War Dated
Ruggles, Daniel 1810-97	Civil War	90	300	600		CSA General
Ruggles, Wesley	Ent	20		45	45	Director
Rulter, John	SuprCt	RARE	RARE	RARE	RARE	
Rumpler, Edward	Aviation	25	40	75	50	
Rumsfeld, Donald	Political	10	20	45	20	Sec'y Defense
Rundstedt, Karl R. Gerd	Military	200		350	275	Ger Field Marshal
Runyon, Damon 1884-46	Author	125	275	350	225	Sports Writer
Rush	Music	75			125	Signed by Entire Group
Rush, Barbara	Ent	5			15	
Rush, Benjamin	RevWar	750		2,250		Signer Decl. of Indepen
Rush, Isadore	Ent	10			30	
Rush, Richard 1780-1859	Political	75	150	275		Attorney General
Rusk, Dean	Political	25	60		50	Sec'y State
Rusk, Jeremiah M.	Civil War	25	50	90		Union General/1830-93
Rusk, Thos. Jefferson	Military	350		700		TX Provisional Governor
Ruskin, John 1819-1900	Art	75	125	275		British Painter
Rusling, James F.	Civil War	15	30	40		Union Officer
Russell, Bertrand	Author	85	275	450	250	Math/Nobel/1872-1970
Russell, Bruce	Cartoonist	25			50	Political Cartoonist
Russell, Charles M.	Art	250	750	1,500		Western Artist
Russell, George W.	Author	35	100		75	
Russell, Harold	Ent	10		30	25	Military Hero/AA
Russell, Jane	Ent	15	40	40	35	The Outlaw
Russell, John	Ent	20			45	
Russell, John, Lord	Political	35	75	125		Br. Prime Minister, 1864-65
Russell, Johnny	Music	5			15	
Russell, Jonathan	Political	400	750			1771-1832
Russell, Keri	Ent	25			50	TV's "Felicity"
Russell, Kurt	Ent	25			50	Tombstone
Russell, Lillian 1861-1922	Music	100	150	275	400	Operetta Star
Russell, Mark	Ent	5			10	
Russell, Nipsey	Ent	10			20	
Russell, Rosalind	Ent	35	45		80	MAME/1908-1976
Russell, Theresa	Ent	10	15	30	25	
Russo, Rene	Ent	20			45	

Name	Field	SIG	DS	ALS	SP	Remarks
Rust, Albert 1818-70	Civil War	75	150			CSA General
Rustin, Bayard	Political	15	35	55	25	
Rutan, Dick	Aviation	15			30	
Rutgers, Henry	RevWar	100	250	325		1745 - 1830
Ruth, Babe	Sports	900	1,400		2,750	1936 Baseball HOF
Rutherford, Ann	Ent	10	20	25	20	
Rutherford, Ernest	Science	150	350	RARE	225	Physicist/Nobel
Rutherford, Kelly	Ent	15			30	
Rutherford, Margaret	Ent	75		150	175	Dame
Rutledge, Edward	RevWar	200	500	750		Signer
Rutledge, John	SuprCt	200	600	1,200		Continental Congress
Rutledge, Wiley B.	SuprCt	30	100	250	50	
Ruttan, Susan	Ent	5			15	
Ryan, Irene	Ent	100	150		200	Granny/Bev Hillbillies
Ryan, Jeri	Ent	20			40	Star Trek : Voyager
Ryan, Meg	Ent	30			60	Scarce Signer
Ryan, Peggy	Ent	10	15	35	30	
Ryan, Robert	Ent	15	30		50	
Ryan, Sheila	Ent	5	15		15	
Ryan, T. Claude	Aviation	100			225	Ryan Aircraft Mfg
Rydell, Bobby	Music	15			30	
Ryder, Albert P. 1847-17	Art	100	250	450		Am. Landscapes,Marine,Portraits
Ryder, Winona	Ent	35			55	
Ryle, Martin, Sir	Science	30	100	150	45	Nobel Physics 1974

Esther Ralston

Luise Rainer

Paul Robeson

William Penn Adair Rogers

Erwin Rommel

Theodore Roosevelt

Baron Nathan Mayer Rothschild

Name	Field	SIG	DS	ALS	SP	Remarks
Saarinen, G. Eliel	Science	20	75	100	40	Am. Architect
Sabatier, Paul	Science	75		150		Fr. Chem. Nobel 1912
Sabatini, Rafael	Author	25	50	75		
Sabato, Antonio Jr.	Ent	15			30	
Sabin, Albert Bruce, Dr.	Science	35		150	150	Polio Vaccine
Sabin, Florence R.,Dr.	Science	25		125		1871-1953
Sabine, Edward, Sir	Military	50		175		Br. General/1788-1833
Sablon, Jean	Music	20	25	40	45	French Singer
Sabu 1924-63	Ent	50			150	Child Star
Sacco, Nicola	Criminal	RARE	RARE	3,700	RARE	With Vanzetti
Sacher-Masoch, Leopold	Author	150	275	400		
Sacks, Oliver, Dr.	Science	15			30	Awakenings"/ Neurologist
Sadat, Anwar 1918-81	Political	100		300	500	Assassinated Pres/ Egypt
Sade	Music	25			45	
Sade, Marquis de	Author	250	750	1,500		
Safer, Morley	Ent	5	20	25	15	60 Minutes
Sagan, Carl, Dr.	Science	15	30	45	30	Am. Astronomer/Pulitzer
Sage, Russell 1816-1906	Business	200	750	1,500		Financier/Jay Gould
Sagendorf, Bud 1915-94	Cartoonist	35			75	Popeye (After Segar)
Sager, Carole Bayer	Music	10	25		25	
Saget, Bob	Ent	10	20		20	Full House
Sahl, Mort	Ent	5			15	Political Humorist
Said, Nuri	Political	5		35	10	Pr. Minister Iraq
Saint Hilaire, L.V, Jos.	Military	30	75	155		French Revolution
Saint James, Susan	Ent	15			35	
Saint Laurent, Yves	Business	25	35	50	45	Fashion Designer
Saint, Eva Marie	Ent	15	25		30	AA Winner
Saint-Cyr, Gouvion	Military	50	150	175		Fr. Minister of War
Saint-Exupery, Antoine	Aviation	50	125	175	125	Fr. Aviator and Author
Saint-Gaudens, Augustus	Art	200		900	1,200	Monuments...
Saint-Just, Louis	Military	375	750			French Revolution
Saint-Saens, Camille	Music	150	300	400	400	Opera/1835-1921
Saito, Makoto, Baron	Political	100	200	300		Prime Minister Japan
Sakai, Saburo	Aviation	50			100	3rd Highest Japanese Ace
Sakharov, Andrei	Science	300		RARE		Nobel Physics
Salalm, Abdus	Science	20	30	45	25	Nobel Physics 1979
Salan, Raoul	Military	20	50	75	50	
Sale, Chic 1885-1937	Ent	25	35	60	75	Comedian-Actor
Sales, Soupy	Ent	5	15	20	15	
Saleza, Albert	Music	15			45	Opera
Salinger, J[erome] D.	Author	RARE	3,000	4,500	RARE	Catcher in the Rye
Salinger, Pierre	Political	20		40	40	Press Sec'y Pres. JFK
Salisbury, 3rd Marquis	Political	40		75		Prime Minister

Name	Field	SIG	DS	ALS	SP	Remarks
Salisbury, Frank	Art	25	75	100		Br. Portrait Painter
Salk, Jonas, Dr. 1914-93	Science	45	150	250	200	Polio Vaccine
Salling, John	Civil War	15	25	50		
Salt, Titus, Sir 1803-76	Business	10	25	40		Pioneer Wool Industry
Salten, Felix 1870-1946	Author	75	100	200		Bambi
Sam the Sham	Music	25	45		45	and the Pharoahs
Samaroff-Stokowski	Music	25			75	Pianist/Teacher
Sambora, Richie	Music	20			40	
Samms, Emma	Ent	15	25	30	30	
Samples, Candy	Ent	25			55	
Samples, Junior	Ent	10			20	
Sampras, Pete	Sports	20			50	Tennis
Sampson, Will	Ent	75		150	200	Scarce/Cukoos Nest...
Sampson, William T.	Military	30	75	125	75	Adm. Sp.- Am. War
Samuelson, Paul A., Dr.	Science	25	40		35	Nobel Economics
San Giacomo, Laura	Ent	20	40		45	Just Shoot Me
San Juan, Olga	Ent	5			10	
San Martin, Jose de	Political	500	750	RARE	RARE	Soldier Hero of Argentina
Sand, George 1804-76	Author	100	200	400		
Sandburg, Carl	Author	100	225	300	400	1878 - 1967
Sanders, Deion	Sports	10			35	Football
Sanders, George	Ent	80			150	AA Winner
Sanders, Harland	Business	45		150	125	KFC Colonel Sanders
Sanders, Horace T.	Civil War	20	40	55		Union Officer
Sanderson, Julia	Ent	15		35	30	Radio
Sandoz, Marie	Author	25	50	100	50	
Sands, Julia	Ent	10			25	
Sands, Tommy	Ent	10			15	
Sandwich, 4thEarl	Political	125	300	400		
Sanford, Edw. Terry	SuprCt	75	150			
Sanford, Isabel	Ent	10	20		20	Weezy on the "Jeffersons"
Sanger, Frederick	Science	20	35	60	35	Nobel Chemistry 1958
Sanger, Margaret	Political	50	200	250	100	Birth Control Advocate
Sangster, Margaret E.	Author	30	55	125		Journalist, Poet, Editor
Santa Anna, Antonio L.	Political	400	1,100	1,400	675	Pres of Mexico
Santa Cruz, Andres	Political	100	225			Pres. Bolivia/Exiled
Santa Rosa, Annibale S.	Military	25		125		
Santana, Carlos	Music	20			50	
Santayana, George	Author	75	175	275		Poet, Philosopher, Critic
Santley, Charles, Sir	Music	50			150	Baritone
Santos-Dumont, A.	Aviation	300		600	750	Brazil/Pioneer Aeronaut
Santunione, Orianna	Music	10			20	Opera
Saperstein, Abe	Business	RARE	RARE	RARE	175	Coach/Harlem Globetrotters
Sara, Mia	Ent	20			50	
Sarandon, Susan	Ent	25	50		50	
Sarasate, Pablo de	Music	100		250		Violin Virtuoso
Sarazan, Gene	Sports	15			45	1974 Golf HOF
Sardi, Vincent	Business	5		20	10	Fndr. Sardi's Restaurant
Sardou, Victorien	Author	25	45	100	125	Playwright/1831-1908

Name	Field	SIG	DS	ALS	SP	Remarks
Sarett, Lew	Author	75	100			
Sarfatti, Margherita	Author	10	30	50		
Sarg, Tony 1882-1942	Art	25			75	
Sargent, Dick	Ent	35	50		65	Darren/Bewitched
Sargent, John G.	Political	15	30	50	25	Att'y General 1925
Sargent, John Singer	Art	100	250	350		1856-1925/Am. Portraitist
Sargent, Kenny	Music	20			45	Big Band Singer
Sargent, Winthrop	RevWar	30	100	240		1st Gov Miss.Territory
Sarnoff, David 1891-1971	Business	75	400	750	150	Broadcasting Pioneer
Sarocco, Suzanne	Music	10			25	Opera
Saroyan, William	Author	50	150	200	100	Pulitzer
Sartain, John 1808-97	Art	25		100		
Sartre, Jean-Paul	Author	100	300	400		1905 - 1980
Sassoon, Beverly	Ent	5			15	
Sassoon, Siegfried	Author	75	150	300		Br. Poet.Anti-War Verse
Sassoon, Vidal	Business	15	20	25	25	Hair Design & Products
Satie, Erik	Music	300	700	1,250		
Sato, Eisaku	Political	20	50	100	35	Premier Japan
Sauckel, Fritz	Military	75	200			Nazi War Criminal. Hanged
Sauer, Emil	Ent	15	25	60	30	
Sauguet, Henri	Music	75		250		Opera/Ballet
Saumarez, James, Sir	Military	100	250	450		Br. Adm./Battle of the Nile
Saunders, Alvin	Political	15	35	60		
Saunders, Hugh W.	Aviation	5		20	15	
Saunders, Lori	Ent	5			15	
Savage, Fred	Ent	20			45	Wonder Years/Working
Saval, Dany	Ent	10		25	20	French Actress
Savalas, Telly	Ent	25	45		45	Kojak
Savannah	Ent	75			150	Deceased porn star
Savitch, Jessica	Author	75			150	TV News
Savitt, Jan	Music	15			45	Bandleader
Savoia, Attilio	Art	15	35	60		
Sawyer, Diane	Ent	10	20		25	TV Broadcast Journalist
Sawyer, Joe	Ent	75			200	
Sax, Adolphe	Science	75	150	300		Inventor of the Saxophone
Saxbe, William B.	Political	5		20	15	Att'y General 1974
Saxe, John G.	Author	10	30	45	30	
Saxon, John	Ent	5			15	
Saxon, Rufus, Jr.	Civil War	25	45	65		
Sayao, Bidu	Music	25			75	Opera Soprano
Sayers, Dorothy 1893-57	Author	200	350	475		Br. Mystery Novelist
Scacchi, Greta	Ent	15			40	
Scacchi, Greta	Ent	15			30	
Scaggs, Boz	Music	15			35	
Scagliarini, Eleanora	Music	15			40	Opera
Scales, Alfred M.	Civil War	175		350		CSA General/1827-92
Scalia, Antonin	SuprCt	30	75		55	
Scalia, Jack	Ent	10			25	
Scammell, Alexander	RevWar	350		1,200		1746-81

Name	Field	SIG	DS	ALS	SP	Remarks
Scancarelli, Jim	Cartoonist	10			30	Gasoline Alley
Scarlatti, Alessandro	Music	RARE	RARE	20,000	RARE	Opera/1660-1725
Schacht, Hjalmar	Military	75	150	300		Nazi Minister WWII
Schaeffer, Rebecca	Ent	75			150	Murdered by fan
Schafer, Natalie	Ent	35	40		60	Mrs Howell/Gilligans Island
Schaffner, Franklin J.	Ent	30			75	
Schaffner, Hans	Political	10			20	Pres. Austria
Schally, Andrew V., Dr.	Science	20	30	45	30	Nobel Medicine 1977
Schanberg, Sydney, H.	Author	10	30	50	15	
Scharwenka, Franz X.	Music	25		75	150	Pianist
Schary, Dore 1905 - 1980	Ent	15		25	35	Producer, Director, Writer
Schawlow, Arthur L., Dr.	Science	20	30	35	35	Nobel Physics 1981
Scheer, Reinhard	Military	20	45	95	40	Ger. Admiral/1863-1928
Scheff, Fritzi 1882-1954	Ent	20		30	25	Silent Films
Scheider, Roy	Ent	25	50		50	Jaws/SeaQuest DSV
Schell, Maria	Ent	5		20	15	
Schell, Maximillian	Ent	10		35	30	AA Winner
Schenck, Robert C.	Civil War	35	45	70		Union General/1809-90
Schick, Bela, Dr.	Science	50	100	200	75	Schick Test for TB
Schiffer, Claudia	Ent	25			50	SuperModel
Schifrin, Lalo	Music	10		25	25	Composer
Schildkraut, Joseph	Ent	75	150		150	1895 - 1964
Schiller, Hans von	Aviation	20		45		
Schilling, David	Aviation	20		50	45	WWII ACE
Schipa, Tito	Music	45			125	Opera
Schirra, Walter M.	Space	25	75	150	75	Mercury 7 Astronaut
Schlafly, Phyllis	Political	10		35	25	Activist, Feminist
Schlesinger, Arthur Jr.	Author	10	30	50	20	
Schlesinger, John	Ent	20			50	Director
Schley, Winfield Scott	Military	100	200	300	350	Arctic rescue of Greely
Schliemann, Heinrich	Science	250		RARE	RARE	Archaeology
Schmalz, Wilhelm	Military	15	40	60	30	
Schmidt, Helmut	Political	15	25	40	20	
Schmidt, Joseph	Music	150			400	Opera Singer/RARE
Schmidt, Maarten, Dr.	Science	10	25	30	20	
Schmidt, Mike	Sports	15			45	1995 Baseball HOF
Schmidtmer, Christiane	Ent	5			15	German Actress
Schmitt, Harrison H.	Space	20	125		75	Apollo 17 Moonwalker
Schmitt-Walter, Karl	Music	10			35	Opera
Schnabel, Artur	Music	50	125	200		Austrian Pianist
Schnaut, Gabriella	Music	10			25	Opera
Schneider, John	Ent	15			35	Dukes of Hazzard
Schneider, Romy	Ent	75			125	
Schoenberg, Arnold	Music	300			600	Composer/1874-1951
Schoene, Heinrich	Military	125	250		200	Ger. Gen. Storm Trooper
Schoenebeck, Karl	Aviation	30	65		75	
Schoenert, Rudolf	Aviation	10	25	40	25	
Schoepfel, Gerhard	Aviation	5		25	15	
Schofield, John M.	Civil War	50	75	150		Union General/1831-1906

Name	Field	SIG	DS	ALS	SP	Remarks
Schofield, John M. (WD)	Civil War	125	175	300		Union General/War Dated
Schopenhauer, Arthur	Author	1,500	RARE	RARE	RARE	Ger. Philosopher
Schorner, Ferdinand	Military	50		125		
Schrader, Paul	Ent	10			20	Director
Schramm, Margit	Music	5			15	Opera
Schreiber, Avery	Ent	5			15	Comedian
Schrieffer, John R.	Science	10		35	15	Nobel Physics 1972
Schriver, Edmund	Civil War	50	100	125		Union General/1812-99
Schroder, Ricky	Ent	20			45	Child Star/Silver Spoon
Schroeder-Feinen, U.	Music	10			30	Opera
Schroer, Werner	Aviation	30			65	WWII German ACE
Schubert, Franz	Music	2,500	5,000	RARE	RARE	Composer
Schuk, Walter	Aviation	25	45		75	German ACE
Schulberg, Budd	Author	5	35		15	Novelist
Schulz, Charles	Cartoonist	100	225	RARE	250	PEANUTS
Schulze, William	Science	15			45	Rocket Pioneer/von Braun
Schuman, William	Music	20	35	60	60	Composer
Schumann, Clara	Music	75	150	300	650	Pianist/Composer
Schumann, Elizabeth	Music	40			125	Opera
Schumann, Robert	Music	1,000	RARE	RARE	RARE	Composer/1810-56
Schumann-Heink, E.	Music	50			150	Opera
Schurz, Carl 1829-1906	Civil War	45	100	150		Union General
Schuschnigg, Kurt von	Political	50	85	150	75	
Schuyler, Philip J.	RevWar	200	450	750		Soldier, Statesman
Schwab, Charles M.	Business	125	350	750	250	Pres Carnegie/US Steel
Schwab, Frank X.	Political	5	20			Mayor Buffalo, NY
Schwantner, Joseph	Music	15		50	40	Pulitzer
Schwartz, Melvin, Dr.	Science	25			30	Nobel Physics 1988
Schwarzenegger, Arnold	Ent	40	200		75	
Schwarzkopf, Elizabeth	Music	20			50	Opera
Schwarzkopf, Norman	Military	35		125	75	Gen. Desert Storm
Schweickart, Russell L.	Space	10			25	
Schweitzer, Albert, Dr.	Science	150		550	750	Nobel/1875-1965
Schwimmer, David	Ent	25			50	Friends
Schwinger, Julian, Dr.	Science	15	30	45	25	Nobel Physics 1965
Sciorra, Annabella	Ent	15			30	
Sciorra, Annabelle	Ent	10			30	
Scobee, Dick	Space	50			175	Challenger Victim
Scofield, Paul	Ent	20	40		35	AA Winner
Scoggins, Tracy	Ent	10		25	20	
Scolari, Peter	Ent	10			20	Newhart
Scopes, John T. 1900-70	Political	300		RARE	1,500	Defendant In Monkey Trial
Scorpions, The	Music	25			50	Signed by all
Scorsese, Martin	Ent	25			50	Director
Scorupco, Izabella	Ent	20			40	
Scott, Campbell	Ent	15			30	
Scott, Charles	RevWar	100	200	300		General/Indian Fighter
Scott, Charles Wm. A.	Aviation	25	50	75	50	Br. Won Harmon Trophy
Scott, David R.	Space	50			200	Moonwalker

Name	Field	SIG	DS	ALS	SP	Remarks
Scott, Eric	Ent	5			10	
Scott, Fred	Ent	25	55	75	50	Western Star
Scott, George C.	Ent	25	55		50	AA Winner
Scott, Gordon	Ent	15			30	Tarzan actor
Scott, Gustavus	RevWar	35	75			Lawyer, Patriot (MD)
Scott, Hazel	Ent	35			125	
Scott, Jerry	Cartoonist	10			30	Nancy
Scott, John Morin	RevWar	35	65	150		General and Patriot
Scott, Lizabeth	Ent	10	20		20	
Scott, Martha	Ent	10			20	
Scott, Randolph	Ent	40	100		100	1898-1987
Scott, Raymond	Music	25	40	65	50	Composer/Big Bandleader
Scott, Robert Falcon	Explorer	100	250	500	200	Br. Arctic Expeditions
Scott, Robert Kingston	Civil War	50				Union General/1826-1900
Scott, Robert L., Jr.	Aviation	15		60	35	WWII Flying Tiger ACE
Scott, Walter, Sir 1771-32	Author	150	500	900		Poet/Novelist
Scott, Willard	Ent	5			10	
Scott, Winfield (WD)	Civil War	175	400	675		Union General/War Date
Scott, Winfield 1786-1866	Civil War	125	300	550	450	Union General
Scott, Zachary	Ent	25			50	
Scotto, Renata	Music	25			50	Opera
Scowcroft, Brent	Military	10			20	
Scriabin, Alexander	Music	1,000	3,500	RARE	RARE	Composer/1872-1915
Scribe, Eugene 1791-61	Author	20		60		
Scribner, Charles	Business	200	900			Fndr Publishing Co.
Scripps, William E.	Aviation	15	50		40	
Scuderi, Sara	Music	35			85	Opera
Scullin, James H.	Political	40				P.M. Australia
Scully, Thomas	Art	200	375	550		
Seaborg, Glenn	Science	40	75	150	75	Chm. AEC. Nobel Chemistry 1951
Seaforth, Susan	Ent	10			20	
Seagal, Steven	Ent	20			50	Action/Martial Arts Star
Seal	Music	25			50	
Seals, Dan	Music	5			15	
Sears, Richard Warren	Business	RARE	RARE	6,000	RARE	Founder of Sears/Roebuck
Seaton, George	Ent	35			75	Director
Seaver, Tom	Sports	15			35	1992 Baseball HOF
Seawell, Molly Elliot	Author	5	15	30	10	
Sebastini, H.F.B.	Military	75		150		Gen Under Napolean
Seberg, Jean	Ent	75			150	Suicide
Sechelles, Marie - Jean	Military			900		Att'y to Louis XVI
Sedaka, Neil	Music	10	20		20	
Seddon, James A.	Civil War	250	500	RARE	RARE	CSA Sect of War//1815-80
Seddon, Margaret R.	Space	10			20	
Sedgewick, John	Civil War	125	350			Union General (Uncle John)
Sedgwick, Catherine M.	Author	10		45		Am. Novelist
Sedgwick, John 1813-64	Civil War	250	750			Union General/KIA
Sedgwick, Kyra	Ent	20			50	
See, Elliot M. Jr.	Space	175			250	Astronaut

Name	Field	SIG	DS	ALS	SP	Remarks
Seeburg, Justus Percival	Business	50	125	200		
Seeger, Pete	Music	20	50	75	40	
Seeley, Jeannie	Music	10			20	
Segal, Erich	Author	20				Love Story
Segal, George	Ent	10			35	Just Shoot Me
Seger, Bob	Music	30			60	and Silver Bullit Band
Seger, Elzie C.	Cartoonist	125			275	Popeye
Segovia, Andres	Music	100		300	150	Classical Guitar Virtuoso
Segre, Emilio, Dr.	Science	20	35	50	30	Nobel Physics 1959
Segura, Wiltz	Aviation	15	25	40	30	USAF WWII ACE
Segurola, Andres de	Music	50			150	
Seidel, Toscha	Music	25			75	Russian/American Violinist
Seidelman, Susan	Ent	5	15		10	Director
Seignolle, Claude	Author	100	175	200		
Seinfeld	Ent	150			300	Signed by Four
Seinfeld, Jerry	Ent	25			55	Scarce Signer
Seipel, Ignas Dr.	Political	15	30	60	40	
Selassie, Haile 1891-1975	Political	200	300	550	750	Emperor of Ethiopia
Selena	Music	200			400	Murdered pop star
Selfridge, Thos.	Civil War	40	75	125		Union Naval Commander
Sellecca, Connie	Ent	10	20		30	
Selleck, Tom	Ent	25			50	Magnum PI
Sellers, David Foote	Military	20	50	75	50	
Sellers, Peter 1925-80	Ent	100	150	250	175	Pink Panther Movies
Sellers, Winfield S.	Military	15	40	65	40	
Selman, John	Western	1,200	2,500			
Selznick, David O.	Ent	125	350		275	Film Producer (GWTW)
Selznick, Irene	Ent	10	15		20	Film Executive
Sembrich, Marcella	Music	100		200	200	Opera
Semenov, Nikolai	Science	35	100		75	Rus.Chem/Physicist/Nobel
Semmelwels, Ignaz	Science	500	900	RARE	RARE	Obstetrician/Antisepsis
Semmes, Paul J. 1815-63	Civil War	700	900	900		CSA General
Semmes, Raphael	Civil War	300	750	1,400	1,500	CSA Admiral/1809-77
Sen Young, Victor	Ent	75			200	Hop Sing on "Bonanza"
Senechal, Michel	Music	10			25	Opera
Senn, Nicholas	Civil War	35		125		Union Surgeon
Sennett, Mack 1880-1960	Ent	300	550		750	
Sergievsky, Boris	Aviation	75			150	
Serkin, Rudolf	Music	40		150	125	Piano
Serling, Rod	Ent	125	200		450	Outer Limits/Night Gallery
Serurier, Jean M.P.	Military	50	125	200		Marshal of Napoleon
Service, Robert VV.	Author	75		200	400	Canadian Poet
Sessions, Roger	Music	15		90		Composer/Pulitzer
Seton, Ernest Thompson	Author	50	100	175	90	Co-Fndr Boy Scouts
Seuss, Dr.	Author	75			250	Theodore Gieisel
Severance, Joan	Ent	10			25	
Severeid, Eric	Ent	10			25	
Severeid, Susanne	Ent	5			15	
Severinson, Doc	Music	10			20	Tonite Show

Name	Field	SIG	DS	ALS	SP	Remarks
Sevier, John 1745-1815	RevWar	600		750		
Sewall, David	RevWar	25	50	100		
Sewall, Samuel 1652-30	Political	350		950		Salem Witchcraft Trials
Sewall, Samuel 1757-14	Political	25		60		
Seward, Frederick Wm.	Political	30	50	75		Ass't Sec'y State
Seward, William H.	Political	75	125	150		1801-72
Sewell, William J.	Civil War	40	90	125		Union General/1835-1901
Sexton, Walton R.	Military	10	30	45	30	Adm. US Navy. WWII
Seymour, Jane	Ent	15			40	Dr. Quinn
Seymour, Stephanie	Ent	20			45	Super-Model
Seymour, Truman	Civil War	75	100	200		Union General/1824-91
Shackelford, Ted	Ent	5			15	
Shackleton, Ernest H.	Explorer	200		400	450	Br Antarctic Explorer
Shaffer, Paul	Music	5			15	David Letterman Show
Shaffer, Peter L.	Author	10	20		15	
Shafter, William R.	Civil War	15	40	75		Union General/1835-1906
Shafter, William R.	Civil War	35	75	125	150	Union General/War Dated
Shaftesbury, A.A.C.	Political	25	75	150		
Shah, Zahir	Royalty	50				King Afghanistan
Shahn, Ben	Art	50	125	200	150	Am.Painter-Graphic Artist
Shalamar	Music	20	50		50	
Shaler, Alexander	Civil War	35	60	100		Union General
Shalikashvilli, John	Military	10	25		20	Chm. Joint Chiefs of Staff
Shamir, Yitzhak	Political	25		60	70	Prime Minister Israel
Shamroy, Leon	Ent	25				Director
Shandling, Gary	Ent	25	50		50	Larry Sanders Show
Shannon, Del	Music	35	60		75	
Shannon, Wilson	Political	25	65	100		
Shapiro, Karl	Author	10	30	50	20	
Shapiro, Robert	Political	15			35	OJ Simpson Attorney
Shapley, Alan	Military	15	35	50		
Shapley, Harlow	Science	50	150	150		Astronomer
Sharan, Shri C.	Political	25	45		75	Pres. India
Sharett, Moshe (Shertok)	Political	50		200		Israeli Prime Minister
Sharif, Omar	Ent	25	25	60	75	
Sharkey, Ray	Ent	10			30	
Sharnova, Sonia	Music	10			25	Am. Contralto
Sharon, Ariel	Military	20	50	75	50	Israeli General
Sharon, William	Business	50	100	200		Banker and Financier
Sharp, U. S. Grant	Military	10	25	35	15	
Sharp, William	Art	15	45	90		
Sharpe, George H.	Civil War	20	45			Union General/1828-1900
Sharpe, William, Dr.	Science	15	30		25	Nobel Enconomics 1990
Shatner, William	Ent	30	75		65	Star Trek's Captain Kirk
Shaud, Grant	Ent	20			45	Murphy Brown
Shaunessy, Charles	Ent	5		25	15	
Shaw, Anna Howard	Political	35	80	145		1847-1919
Shaw, Artie	Music	25			60	Big Band Leader
Shaw, Bernard	Ent	10			25	TV Broadcast Journalist

Name	Field	SIG	DS	ALS	SP	Remarks
Shaw, George Bernard	Author	400	650	800	1,500	Ir. Playwright/Nobel
Shaw, Irwin	Author	25	60		45	Am. Novelist
Shaw, Lemuel	RevWar	15	40	75		
Shaw, Leslie M. 1848-32	Political	30		50		Sec'y Treasury 1902
Shaw, Robert	Ent	60			150	Jaws/The Sting
Shaw, Robert	Ent	65			125	Jaws/James Bond/...
Shaw, T.E.	Author	150			500	Real Life Lawrence of Arabia
Shawn, Dick	Ent	40			100	
Shawn, Ted	Ent	50			100	Am. Dancer-Choreographer
Shay, John	Ent	5			10	
Shayne, Robert	Ent	10			30	
Shazar, Zalman	Political	25			60	Israel
Shea, John	Ent	10			25	
Shear, Rhonda	Ent	5			10	Up All Night host
Shearer, Moira	Ent	25	50		75	Ballet
Shearer, Norma 1902-83	Ent	90	200		275	AA Winner
Shearing, George	Music	20			45	Jazz Pianist
Sheedy, Ally	Ent	10	20		25	
Sheehan, John	Ent	10			25	
Sheen, Charlie	Ent	10	25		25	
Sheen, Martin	Ent	15	30		30	AA Winner
Sheffer, Chris	Ent	10			15	
Sheffield, Johnny	Ent	10			20	Boy/Bomba
Shelby, Isaac 1750-1826	RevWar	300	350	500		
Shelby, Joseph 0.	Civil War	300		1,200	2,000	CSA General/1830-97
Shelby, Joseph 0.	Civil War	450		RARE	RARE	CSA General/War Dated
Sheldon, Gene	Ent	10			20	
Sheldon, Sidney	Author	5		25	15	Am. Novelist
Shelley, Mary W.	Author	900		1,600		Frankenstein
Shelley, Percy Bysshe	Author	1,200		2,750		
Shelton, Deborah	Ent	10			20	Miss USA
Shepard, Alan B.	Space	60	150		195	Moonwalker
Shepherd, Cybill	Ent	20	45		50	Cybil/Moonlighting
Sheridan, Ann	Ent	40			90	
Sheridan, Nicollette	Ent	20			45	SuperModel
Sheridan, Philip H.	Civil War	200	600	600	1,750	Union General/1831-88
Sheridan, Philip H.	Civil War	300	1,200	RARE	2,400	Union General/War Dated
Sheridan, Richard B.	Author	65	120	250		Ir. Dramatist
Sherman, Allan	Ent	10			20	
Sherman, Forrest P.	Military	20	50	75	50	WWII Adm.
Sherman, Frederick C.	Military	20	45	60	35	
Sherman, George	Ent	10			25	
Sherman, James S.	Vice Pres	75	175	275	200	
Sherman, John 1823-00	Political	100	450	750	200	Sherman Anti-Trust Act
Sherman, Roger 1721-93	RevWar	200	600	900		
Sherman, Thomas West	Civil War	30	55	75		Union General/1813-79
Sherman, William	Civil War	450	2,500	4,500	2,500	Union General/War Dated
Sherman, William T.	Civil War	400	550	750	1,250	Union General/1820-91
Sherriff, Robert C.	Author	45		125	80	Playwright/Novelist

Name	Field	SIG	DS	ALS	SP	Remarks
Sherwood, Bobby	Ent	5			15	
Sherwood, Madeleine	Ent	10			20	
Sherwood, Percy	Music	25			60	German Composer
Sherwood, Robert E.	Author	30	75	125	50	Plays/Speeches FDR
Shields, Brooke	Ent	20	50		50	Suddenly Susan
Shields, James	Civil War	50	75	125		Union General/1806-79
Shillaber, Benjamin P.	Author	25	50	100		Humorist-Editor/1814-90
Shimmerman, Armin	Ent	15	25		25	Star Trek DS9/Quark
Shippen, Edward	RevWar	50		150		Chief Justice PA.
Shiras, George, Jr.	SuprCt	100	250	350		
Shire, Talia	Ent	15			35	
Shirer, William L.	Author	15	35		20	
Shirley, Anne	Ent	15		35	30	
Shirley, William 1693-71	Political	350	1,000	1,200		Colonial Gov. MA
Shockley, William, Dr.	Science	45	100	150	100	Nobel Physics 1956
Shoemaker, Bill	Sports	35			75	Willie"/Jockey
Shoma, William	Aviation	15	35	50	45	WWII ACE
Shoop, Pamela Susan	Ent	5	20		15	
Shor, Bernard Toots	Business	20	45	50	35	
Shore, Dinah	Ent	25	60	100	50	Singer-Actress-TV Host
Shore, Pauly	Ent	15			25	
Short, Bobby	Music	10			20	
Short, Martin	Ent	20	45		50	Sat Nite Live
Shostakovich, Dmitri	Music	300	575	850	RARE	Composer
Shoumatoff, Elizabeth	Art	25	50	75		
Shoup, David M.	Military	15	35	60	35	
Shoup, Francis, A.	Civil War	100		300		CSA General/1834-96
Show, Grant	Ent	10			20	
Shrimpton, Jean	Ent	5	20		10	
Shriner, Herb	Ent	5			15	
Shriver, Edmund	Civil War	20	40			
Shriver, Maria	Ent	5			15	Broadcast Journalist
Shriver, Sargent	Political	10		25	20	Created Job Corps
Shroyer, Sonny	Ent	5			10	
Shrum, Cal	Ent	5			25	Cowboy Actor
Shubert, John	Ent	5			15	
Shubert, Lee 1873-1953	Ent	25	60	75	40	Theatrical Mgr.-Producer
Shue, Andrew	Ent	15			35	
Shue, Elizabeth	Ent	25			50	AA Winner
Shugart, Alan	Science	10	20		20	Computer Disk Drive
Shulman, Max	Author	10			20	Creator Dobie Gillis
Shultz, George P.	Political	10	25	55	30	Sec'y State 1982
Shuman, Eleanor J.	Celebrity	85				Titanic Survivor
Shuster, W, Morgan	Business	10		35	15	
Sibelius, Jan 1865-1957	Music	400	750	1,250	1,000	Composer
Sibley, Henry H.	Civil War	150	300	450		Union General/1811-1891
Sickles, Daniel E.	Civil War	75	125	150	175	Union General/1825-1914
Siddons, F. Scott, Mrs.	Ent	25			50	
Siddons, Sarah Kemble	Ent	200		600		

Name	Field	SIG	DS	ALS	SP	Remarks
Sidmouth, Viscount	Political	35	65	100		Prime Minister
Sidney, George	Ent	25			50	Director
Sidney, Sylvia	Ent	10	25		25	
Siegbahn, Kai Manne	Science	30	55	100	90	Nobel Physics 1981
Siegbahn, Karl Manne	Science	35	65	125	100	Nobel Physics 1924
Siegel & Shuster	Cartoonist	175			400	Superman/Signed by Both
Siegel, Don	Ent	20	50		40	Film Director
Siegel, Jerry 1915-96	Cartoonist	25			75	Superman Co-Creator
Siegel, Joel	Ent	5			10	TV Film Reviewer
Siegfried and Roy	Ent	20			40	Magicians
Siegmeister, Elie	Music	25	75		40	Composer
Siems, Margarethe	Music	45			125	Opera
Sigall, Joseph	Art	100	200	400		Pres and Royal Portraits
Sigel, Franz 1824-1902	Civil War	75	125	200		Union General
Sighele, Mietta	Music	15			30	Opera
Signac, Paul	Art	75	150	300		Watercolor Seascapes
Signoret, Simone	Ent	65	125		150	AA Winner
Sigsbee, Charles D.	Military	40	90	150	75	Capt. USN The Maine
Sihanouk, Norodom	Political	35	75	125	75	Cambodia
Sikes, Cynthia	Ent	5			15	
Sikorsky, Igor 1889-1972	Aviation	85	225	300	275	Designed 1st Helicopter
Silja, Anja	Music	15			40	Opera
Silliman, Benjamin	Science	30	65	100		Am.Chemist
Sills, Beverly	Music	15			35	Am. Soprano
Sills, Milton 1882-1930	Ent	30	40	75	80	Silent Films
Silver, Ron	Ent	15			40	Veronica's Closet
Silvera, Frank	Ent	10			20	
Silverheels, Jay	Ent	200	300		350	Tonto/Lone Ranger
Silverman, Fred	Business	5	20		10	Broadcasting Executive
Silverman, Jonathan	Ent	10			25	The Single Guy
Silverman, Robert	Music	15			45	Contemporary Pianist
Silvers, Phil 1912-85	Ent	40	65	125	175	Sgt. Bilko
Silverstone, Alicia	Ent	30			65	Batgirl/Batman Movie
Simenon, Georges	Author	65	125	275	125	1903-1989
Simmons, Gene	Music	25			45	KISS member
Simmons, Jean	Ent	10		20	20	
Simmons, Richard	Business	5			15	Excercise Guru
Simmons, Richard	Ent	15			35	
Simms, Ginny	Music	10			20	Band Vocalist
Simms, William G.	Author	35	90	125		Lawyer
Simon and Garfunkel	Music	50			100	Signed by Both
Simon, Carly	Music	20	50		50	
Simon, Claude	Author	150				Nobel Literature 1985
Simon, Herbert A.	Science	20	35	50	25	Nobel Economics
Simon, Neil	Author	25	50		50	Playwright, Screenwriter
Simon, Paul	Music	25	50		50	
Simon, Simone	Ent	20			45	
Simpson, James H.	Civil War	35	75			Union General/1813-83
Simpson, James Y.	Science	25	75	150		

Name	Field	SIG	DS	ALS	SP	Remarks
Simpson, Louis	Author	25			65	Am. Poet
Simpson, O.J.	Sports	25			65	1985 Football HOF
Simpson, Russell	Ent	50			100	
Simpson, Wallis W.	Political	150		550		Duchess of Windsor
Simpson, William H.	Military	25		200	75	Gen. WWII
Sims, William S. 1858-36	Military	30		125	50	Adm. USN WWI/Pulitzer
Sinatra, Frank	Ent	200	500		500	Rat Pack
Sinatra, Nancy	Ent	5	20		20	
Sinbad	Ent	10			20	
Sinclair, Harry F.	Business	125	175	300	200	Teapot Dome
Sinclair, Upton	Author	50		150	125	Am. Writer
Sinding, Christian A.	Music	50		175		
Singer, Isaac Bashevis	Author	45		225	150	Nobel Literature 1978
Singer, Isaac M. 1811-75	Science	600	2,000	RARE	RARE	Singer Sewing Machine
Singer, Lori	Ent	15			30	
Singer, Marc	Ent	10			30	
Singlaub, John K.	Military	10	25	35	20	General WWII
Singleton, Penny	Ent	5	20		20	Blondie
Sinise, Gary	Ent	25			50	AA Winner
Sinopoli, Giuseppe	Music	15			35	Conductor
Sioli, Franco	Music	5			15	Opera
Siple, Paul A.	Aviation	20	45			
Sirica, John J.	Political	20	35		50	Watergate Judge
Siroky, Villiam	Political	50				Premier Czech.
Sirtis, Marina	Ent	15			35	Star Trek/ Next Generation
Siskel, Gene	Ent	5			15	Film Critic
Sisley, Alfred 1839-99	Art	175	400	1,200		Fr. Impressionist
Sissle, Noble	Music	25			50	Big Band Leader
Sitgreaves, John	RevWar	35	75	125		
Sitting Bull 1831-1890	Western	5,750	RARE	RARE	15,000	Sioux Indian Leader
Sitwell, Edith Dame	Author	65	125	175		British Poet
Sitwell, Osbert Sir	Author	35	75	150		Playwright/Novelist
Skaggs, Ricky	Music	10			20	
Skala, Lilia	Ent	10	25		30	
Skelly, William Grove	Business	300				Founder Skelly Oil
Skelton, Red	Ent	35	100	100	85	
Skerrit, Tom	Ent	10			30	
Skinner, B. F.	Author	25		50	75	Behavioral Psychology
Skinner, Cornelia Otis	Ent	15			25	1901-1950
Skinner, Cortlandt	Military	50	75	150		Born NJ. Loyalist General
Skinner, Otis	Ent	35	45	75	65	
Skinner, Stella	Art	25	40	75		
Skipworth, Alison	Ent	15		30	25	
Skorzeny, Otto 1908-75	Military	250		450	500	Nazi SS Officer & Adventurer
Skouras, Spyros 1893-71	Business	50			175	Fndr/20th Century Fox
Skovhus, Boje	Music	10			25	Opera
Skye, Ione	Ent	15			30	
Slater, Christian	Ent	20	50		50	
Slater, Helen	Ent	20			45	SuperGirl

Name	Field	SIG	DS	ALS	SP	Remarks
Slaughter, Frank G.	Author	10		35	20	
Slayton, Donald K.	Space	35	150		185	Mercury Seven "Deke"
Sledd, Patsy	Music	5			15	
Slezak, Leo 1873-1946	Music	45	60		125	Tenor/Opera
Slezak, Walter	Ent	35			75	
Slick, Grace	Music	25			50	
Slidell, John 1793-1871	Civil War	75		200		Statesman/CSA Diplomat
Slim, Wm. Joseph, Sir	Military	30	75	125	60	Br. General WWII
Sliwinski, Josef	Ent	25		100	75	Pianist
Sloan, Alfred P. Jr.	Business	40		90	60	Sloan-Kettering Inst.
Sloan, John	Art	100	200	400		Am Painter/Illustrator
Sloan, John 1779-1856	Political	25		95		Fillmore Treasurer of U.S.
Sloane, Everett	Ent	30			50	
Sloat, John Drake	Civil War	50	95	130		Union Naval Officer
Slocum, Henry Warner	Civil War	75		150		Union General/1827-94
Slough, John P.	Civil War	200		600		Union General/1829-67
Smallens, Alexander	Music	20			50	Conductor/Porgy and Bess
Smallwood, Norma	Ent	20			50	Miss America 1926
Smart, Jean	Ent	15			45	Designing Women
Smedley, Richard	Ent	5			10	
Smetana, Bedrich	Music	1,500	RARE	RARE	RARE	Composer
Smiley, Delores	Music	10			20	
Smirnoff, Yakov	Ent	10			15	Comedian
Smith, Anna Nicole	Ent	20			50	Playboy/Model
Smith, Al	Cartoonist	15			45	Mutt & Jeff
Smith, Alexis	Ent	15	30		35	
Smith, Alfred E.	Political	50			125	Presidential Candidate
Smith, Armistead B.	Aviation	10		25	30	WWII Navy ACE
Smith, Ashbel	Civil War	150		450		
Smith, Bernie	Ent	10			15	
Smith, Betty	Author	40			75	
Smith, Bubba	Sports	10			25	Football
Smith, Buffalo Bob	Ent	35			75	Howdy Doody
Smith, Buffalo Bob	Ent	20			60	w/Howdy Doody
Smith, C. Aubrey	Ent	35			75	
Smith, C.R.	Military	25		75		Adm. Flagship Fleet
Smith, Caleb 1808-64	Political	50	150	250		Lincoln Attorney General
Smith, Carl	Music	5			15	
Smith, Charles E.	Political	15		25	20	P.M. General 1898
Smith, Charles M.	Ent	10			25	
Smith, Connie	Music	5			15	
Smith, Edmund K.	Civil War	400	900	1,250		CSA General/War Dated
Smith, Edmund Kirby	Civil War	300		600		CSA General/1824-93
Smith, Elinor	Aviation	50	100	150	125	
Smith, Elizabeth Oakes	Political	100	200	325		Womens Suffrage
Smith, Francis Hopkinson	Art	15	20	35		Am. Engineer/Artist
Smith, Francis M. Borax	Business	30	60	75		Founder U.S. Borax Co.
Smith, Frederick W.	Business	15	30	45	25	Fndr Federal Express
Smith, Garrett	Political	25		100		Abolitionist

Name	Field	SIG	DS	ALS	SP	Remarks
Smith, Gerrit 1797-1874	Political	100		300		Abolitionist
Smith, Green Clay	Civil War	50	65	125		Union General/1832-95
Smith, Gustavus W.	Civil War	125	250	550		CSA General/1822-96
Smith, Hamilton	Science	15	35	45	25	Nobel Medicine 1978
Smith, Harry	Ent	5	15		10	Broadcast Journalist
Smith, Hoke 1855-1931	Political	10	35		30	
Smith, Ian	Political	15		45	30	
Smith, Ida B. Wise	Political	30	50	75		Temperance Advocate
Smith, Jaclyn	Ent	10	20		20	Charlie Angels
Smith, James 1719-1806	RevWar	250	750	1,600		Signer Decl. of Indepen.
Smith, James Y.	Civil War	35	55			Civil War Gov. RI/1809-76
Smith, Joe	Ent	15			45	
Smith, John	Political	RARE	RARE	RARE	RARE	
Smith, Joseph 1805-44	Clergy	750	1,500			Founder Morman Church
Smith, Julia Holmes, Dr.	Science	100		300		
Smith, Kate 1909-1986	Music	50	125	175	100	God Bless America Singer
Smith, Keely	Music	10			30	Band Vocalist
Smith, Kent	Ent	5			15	
Smith, Maggie	Ent	15	30	35	30	AA Winner
Smith, Margaret Chase	Political	10	25	45	25	
Smith, Martha	Ent	5			15	
Smith, Martin Luther	Civil War	75	125	200		CSA General/1819-66
Smith, Martin Luther	Civil War	125		350		CSA General/War Dated
Smith, Matthew	RevWar	25	75			
Smith, Melancton	RevWar	75	125			Continental Congress
Smith, Michael J.	Space	200			300	Died on Challenger
Smith, R.T.	Aviation	15		45	35	WWII Flying Tiger ACE
Smith, Rex	Ent	10			20	
Smith, Richard	RevWar	50	125	250		Continental Congress
Smith, Robert 1757-1842	Political	55	170	290		Att'y Gen./Sec'y Navy
Smith, Robert H. Snuffy	Aviation	15	35	45	35	WWII Flying Tiger ACE
Smith, Roger	Ent	10			20	
Smith, Samuel 1752-1839	RevWar	50	125	200		Senator MD
Smith, Samuel Francis	Music	200		450		America"/1808-1895
Smith, Stanley	Ent	10		25		
Smith, Sydney	Cartoonist	30			60	The Gumps
Smith, Thomas A.	Military	100		250		General
Smith, Thomas Church	Civil War	30	55	75		Union General/1819-97
Smith, Tom E.	Business	10	25	30	25	Pres. Food Lion Grocery
Smith, Truman 1791-1884	Political	10	25	40		
Smith, Walter Bedell	Military	35	50	75	45	WWII General
Smith, William	Civil War	175		RARE	RARE	CSA General/War Dated
Smith, William 1797-1887	Civil War	100	225	300		CSA General
Smith, William Farrar	Civil War	50		175		Union General/1824-1903
Smith, William S.	RevWar	45		175		RevWar Soldier
Smith, William Sidney	Military	50		160		Br.Adm. Napoleonic War
Smith, Willie The Lion	Music	75			125	Jazz
Smithers, Jan	Ent	5			15	
Smits, Jimmy	Ent	15			45	NYPD Blue

Name	Field	SIG	DS	ALS	SP	Remarks
Smothers Brothers	Ent	15	45		35	Signed by Both
Smothers, Dick	Ent	10			20	Smothers Brothers
Smothers, Tommy	Ent	10			20	Smothers Brothers
Smucker, Paul	Business	10			25	Smuckers Jams & Jellies
Smuts, Jan Christian	Political	50	100	300	250	Fld. Marshal. Pres.
Smythe, Reg	Cartoonist	10			30	Andy Capp
Snell, George D., Dr.	Science	15	30	45	45	Nobel Medicine 1980
Snipes, Wesley	Ent	25	75		50	
Snow, Charles Percy	Author	25	80	150	60	British Novelist
Snow, Hank	Music	20			45	
Soddy, Frederick, Dr.	Science	65	150	225	125	Nobel Chemistry 1921
Soglow, Otto	Cartoonist	25			75	The Little King
Sohn, Lee	Music	10			20	Singer
Sokoloff, Vladimir	Ent	25			60	
Solow, Robert M., Dr.	Science	20	30		25	Nobel Economics 1987
Solti, Georg, Sir	Music	30	45		75	Conductor
Solzhenitsyn, Alex.	Author	100	275		175	Sov. Novelist. Nobel Lit
Somers, Suzanne	Ent	20			45	Three's Company
Somervell, Arthur, Sir	Music	25	50	75		Composer
Somervell, Brehon B.	Military	35	100			Gen.WWII
Sommer, Elke	Ent	10	20		25	
Sommers, Joanne	Ent	5			10	
Somoza, Anastasio	Political	25			75	Nicaragua
Sondergaard, Gale	Ent	30			65	AA Winner/1899-1985
Sondheim, Stephen	Music	50	100		125	Composer
Sonic Youth	Music	25			50	Signed by all
Sonny & Cher	Music	100	200		200	Signed by Both
Sontag, Henrietta Rossi	Music	100			375	Opera
Sontag, Susan	Author	10	25	45	20	
Soo, Jack	Ent	100	150		150	Barney Miller/Scarce
Sopwith, Thos. Sir	Aviation	50		150	100	British Pioneer
Sorbo, Kevin	Ent	25			50	TV's Hercules
Sorrel, Gilbert M.	Civil War	300	RARE	RARE	RARE	CSA General/War Dated
Sorrel, Gilbert Moxley	Civil War	150	300	400		CSA General/1838-1901
Sorrvia, Agnes	Music	20			45	Opera
Sorvino, Mira	Ent	25			50	AA Winner
Sorvino, Paul	Ent	15			35	Mira's Father
Sosa, Sammy	Sports	50			150	Baseball
Sothern, Ann	Ent	20		35	35	
Sothern, E. A.	Ent	35	75	125		19th Century Romantic Idol
Soto, Talisa	Ent	25			50	
Soucek, Appolo, Lt .	Aviation	15			25	World Altitude Records
Soul Asylum	Music	45			95	Signed by Entire Group
Soul, David	Ent	10	25		25	Starskey and Hutch
Soule, Pierre	Civil War	75	150	250		CSA General/1802-70
Soult, Nicolas Jean de	Military	100	225	300		Nap.Marshal of France
Sousa, John Philip	Music	125	400	400	900	Composer/1854-1932
Soustelle, Jacques	Political	5	20	30	15	
Souter, David H.	SuprCt	40			60	

Name	Field	SIG	DS	ALS	SP	Remarks
Southampton, 1st Earl	Royalty	75	200	350		
Southey, Robert 1774-43	Author	100	225	350		Br. Poet Laureate
Sovine, Red	Music	15			35	
Soyer, Raphael 1899-87	Art	25	50	125	100	
Spaak, Paul-Henri	Political	15	30	40	25	
Spaatz, Carl Tooey	Military	75	100		125	General WWII
Spacek, Sissy	Ent	15			40	AA Winner/Carrie
Spacey, Kevin	Ent	20			50	AA Winner
Spader, James	Ent	15			30	
Spahn, Warren	Sports	10			20	1973 Baseball HOF
Spaight, Richard Dobbs	RevWar	100	250			Signer Constitution
Spalding, Albert	Music	35			75	Violinist/1888-1953
Spalding, J. Walter	Business	25		100	50	
Spallanzani, Lazzaro	Science	150	300	600		Artificial Insemination
Sparks, Jared 1789-1866	Author	20	35	65		US Historian
Sparks, Ned	Ent	25	35	75	65	
Sparks, William E.	Military	20	35	50		
Spate, Wolfgang	Aviation	50			85	German WWII ACE
Spaulding, Albert	Music	25			65	Composer
Spaulding, R.Z.	Business	15	40	50	25	
Speaks, Oley	Music	50	75	100		Composer
Spector, Phil	Music	60	100		75	
Speed, James 1812-87	Political	50	75	125		Lincoln Att'y Gen.
Speer, Albert 1905-1981	Military	50	150	225	150	Hitler's Architect
Speidel, Hans	Military	35	90		75	Nazi General
Spelling, Aaron	Ent	10			25	Film Producer
Spelling, Tori	Ent	25	55		50	
Spencer, George E.	Civil War	40	75	150		Union Officer
Spencer, Herbert, Sir	Author	50	125	200		Br. Philosopher
Spencer, John C.	Political	25	60	100		Tyler Sec'y War
Spender, Stephen	Author	50	150	200	75	British Poet
Spenser, Tim	Music	15			35	Sons of the Pioneers
Sperry, Elmer A,	Science	125	350	450	225	Inventor Gyroscope
Sperry, Roger W.	Science	20	30	35	30	Nobel Medicine 1981
Spice Girls	Music	65			125	Signed by All FIVE
Spice Girls	Music	75			150	Signed by all five
Spiegle, Dan	Cartoonist	35			75	Hoppy cartoon strip
Spielberg, Steven	Ent	40	150		75	Director
Spillane, Mickey	Author	40	75	100	125	Detective Fiction
Spin Doctors	Music	35			65	Signed by all
Spiner, Brent	Ent	15			35	Star Trek/Next Gen/Data
Spinner, Francis E.	Political	25		45		Treasurer for 4 Presidents
Spitz, Mark	Sports	10			30	Olympic Swimmer
Spivak, Charlie	Music	20			40	Big Band Leader-Trumpet
Spock, Benjamin, Dr.	Science	35	75	100	50	Am. Pediatrician
Spofford, Harriet P.	Author	15	25	40		Am. Poet/Novelist
Spong, Hilda	Ent	15			40	
Spontini, Gaspare	Music	100		300		Composer
Sprague, Frank Julian	Science	50	100	150	100	Asst. to Edison

Name	Field	SIG	DS	ALS	SP	Remarks
Sprague, William	Civil War	75		100		Union General/1830-1915
Springfield, Rick	Music	20			40	
Springfield, Sherry	Ent	20			50	ER
Springsteen, Bruce	Music	35			75	The Boss
Spruance, Raymond A.	Military	25	125	125	65	1886-1969
Squibb, Edward R.	Business	75	150	200		Pharmaceuticals
St. Clair, Arthur 1734-18	Military	150	250	700		Pres Continental Congress
St. Cyr, Lily	Ent	15			30	
St. Denis, Ruth 1878-1968	Ent	50	125	225	300	Dancer, Choreographer
St. Jacques, Ramond	Ent	15			45	
St. John, Isaac M.	Civil War	100		250		CSA General
St. John, Jill	Ent	10			20	
St. Johns, Adela Rogers	Author	10	25	35	25	Star Hearst Reporter
St. Laurent, Louis	Political	20			45	P. M. Canada
St. Vincent, John Jervis	Military	35	65	125		Br. Adm. 1735-1823
Stabile, Dick	Music	20			40	Big Band Leader
Stacey Q	Music	15			30	
Stack, Robert	Ent	10	20		20	Untouchables
Stael, Anne-Louise	Author	75	150			Fr. Writer
Stafford, Jo	Music	5	20		15	Country
Stafford, Susan	Ent	10			25	
Stager, Anson	Civil War	20	60	100		Union Officer/1825-85
Stahl, Leslie	Ent	5			10	TV's 60 Minutes
Stalin, Joseph 1879-1953	Political	3,500	7,500	20,000	RARE	USSR
Stalin, Svetlana	Political	35	90	150	65	Daughter of Stalin
Stallone, Sylvester	Ent	25	75		55	
Stamos, John	Ent	15			35	Full House
Stamp, Terence	Ent	20			35	
Stanbery, Henry	Political	10		45		Att'y General 1866
Stander, Lionel	Ent	20	30		35	Hart To Hart
Standing, Guy Sir	Ent	25			50	
Standish, Miles	Political	RARE	RARE	RARE	RARE	Mayflower Colonist
Stanford, Leland 1824-93	Business	225	1,750	2,500	400	Calif. Gov.
Stang, Arnold	Ent	5			15	Voice of Top Cat
Stanhope, Edward	Military	10	20	30		
Stanhope, Hester, Lady	Political	15	45	65		
Stanhope, Phil.H.5th Earl	Author	10	20	25		
Stanhope, Phil.H.7th Earl	Author	10	20	35		
Stanhope, Philip D.	Author	125				4th Earl Chesterfield
Stanislavski, Konstantin	Ent	275				
Stanislaw, Augustus P.	Royalty	100	300	600		Last King of Poland
Stanley, David Sloane	Civil War	25	65	75		Union General/1828-1902
Stanley, Freelan	Science	350		1,200		Stanley Steamer/Auto
Stanley, Henry M. Sir	Explorer	275		550	750	Am Journalist
Stanley, Wendell M.	Science	20	25	60	30	Nobel Chemistry 1946
Stanton, Edwin M.	Political	100	160	300		Sect of War/1814-69
Stanton, Elizabeth Cady	Political	150	225	400		Pres. Womans Suffrage
Stanton, Frank L.	Author	5	15	25		Am. Poet/Journalist
Stanton, Frank, Dr.	Business	15	45	65	30	Pres. CBS

Name	Field	SIG	DS	ALS	SP	Remarks
Stanton, Harry Dean	Ent	10			20	
Stanwyck, Barbara	Ent	30	100		85	1907-1990
Stapleton, Jean	Ent	5	20		20	Edith/All in the Family
Stapleton, Maureen	Ent	10			25	
Stapp, Olivia	Music	15			35	Opera
Stark, Harold R.	Military	15	45	75	40	
Stark, John	RevWar	400	600	1,250		Often Quoted General
Starr, Belle	Western	2,500	RARE	RARE	RARE	Early West Bandit Queen
Starr, Blaze	Ent	15		45	30	
Starr, Kay	Music	20			30	Big Band Singer
Starr, Leonard	Cartoonist	25			40	Little Orphan Annie
Starr, Ringo	Music	125	250		200	Beatles Drummer
Starrett, Charles	Ent	25	45		65	Cowboy Star "Durango"
Statlers, The	Music	25			50	
Stead, Wm. Thomas	Author	30	75	100		Died on Titanic
Steber, Eleanor	Music	25			75	Opera
Stedman, Edmund C.	Author	20	35			Poet/Publisher
Steel, Danielle	Author	10			25	Novelist
Steele, Barbara	Ent	20			35	
Steele, Bob	Ent	25			55	Cowboy Star
Steele, Frederick	Civil War	50	100	150		Union General/1819-68
Steele, Richard, Sir	Author	200	600	1,200		1672-1729
Steele, Tom	Ent	15			25	
Steely Dan	Music	25			50	Signed by Both
Steenburgen, Mary	Ent	15			40	
Stefani, Gwen	Music	25			50	No Doubt
Stefansson, Vilhjalmur	Explorer	75	150	225	275	Arctic Explorer
Steffens, Lincoln 1866-36	Author	40	100	150		Journalist
Stegner, Wallace	Author	20		45		Am. Novelist. Pulitzer
Steichen, Edward J.	Art	100	200	300	400	Pioneer Photgraphy as Art
Steig, William	Cartoonist	20			40	New Yorker Cartoonist
Steiger, Rod	Ent	10			25	
Stein, Gertrude 1874-46	Author	400	550	750	675	Expatriot Am. Writer
Stein, Jules	Political	50	100			Founder MCA
Steinbeck, John 1902-68	Author	400	1,450	2,250	1,250	Pulitzer and Nobel in Lit.
Steinem, Gloria	Political	15	25	30	25	Editor
Steinhoff, J. 'Mickey'	Aviation	15	25	40	30	
Steinmetz, Charles P.	Science	75	150	300		Electrical Engineer
Steinway, Henry Z.	Business	20	50	75	35	Steinway Piano
Stella, Antonietta	Music	25			50	Opera
Stemple, Robert	Business	25			40	Pres. General Motors
Sten, Anna	Ent	15		30	35	
Stengel, Casey	Sports	100			200	1966 Baseball HOF
Stephanie, Princess	Royalty	10			25	Princess of Monaco
Stephen, Adam 1730-91	RevWar	75	150	250		General
Stephens, Alexander H.	Civil War	250		500		VP CSA/1812-83
Stephenson, George	Science	225	350	750		Steam Locomotive
Stephenson, Henry	Ent	35			75	
Stephenson, Robert	Science	100	200	350		Br. Railroad Engineer

Name	Field	SIG	DS	ALS	SP	Remarks
Steppenwolf	Music	75	125		125	Signed by Entire Group
Sterling, Andrew B.	Music	25	50	100		Composer
Sterling, Robert	Ent	10			20	
Sterling, Robert	Ent	10			20	
Stern, Daniel	Ent	15			25	
Stern, Howard	Ent	25			55	Syndicated Radio Show
Stern, Isaac	Music	20	35	45	60	
Sterrett, Cliff	Cartoonist	35			65	Polly And Her Pals
Stettinius, Edward R. Jr.	Political	30	100	150	55	FRD & Trumans Sect/State
Steuben, Friedrich von	RevWar	1,400	RARE	RARE	RARE	1730-94
Stevens, Albert W., Capt.	Aviation	25	35			Aviator-Balloonist
Stevens, Andrew	Ent	10	20		20	
Stevens, Brinke	Ent	5			15	Scream Queen
Stevens, Cat	Music	35	100		75	
Stevens, Clement H.	Civil War	250	1,500	2,500		CSA General/1821-64
Stevens, Connie	Ent	5			15	
Stevens, Craig	Ent	10			20	
Stevens, Ebenezer	RevWar	75	175			Boston Tea Party
Stevens, Fisher	Ent	15			25	
Stevens, George	Ent	30			60	Director
Stevens, Inger	Ent	75			150	Scarce
Stevens, James F.	Author	125	250			Paul Bunyan Stories
Stevens, John 1748-1838	RevWar	25	45	75		Engineer/Steam Engine
Stevens, John Paul, III	SuprCt	40	90		150	
Stevens, K.T.	Ent	5			10	
Stevens, Onslow	Ent	30			65	
Stevens, Ray	Music	5			10	Country
Stevens, Rise	Music	20			40	Opera
Stevens, Stella	Ent	5			20	Nutty Professor
Stevens, Thaddeus	Political	35	100	150		
Stevens, Wallace	Author	250	750	RARE	RARE	Am. Poet/Pulitzer
Stevens, Walter Husted	Civil War	250				CSA General
Stevens, Warren	Ent	5			15	Forbidden Planet
Stevenson, Adlai E.	Vice Pres	50	150	200	150	Cleveland Vice Pres.
Stevenson, Carter L.	Civil War	100	200	400		CSA General/1817-88
Stevenson, McLean	Ent	35	65		65	MASH
Stevenson, Parker	Ent	15			25	Hardy Boys
Stevenson, R. H.	Civil War	10		30		Union Officer
Stevenson, Robert Louis	Author	300	750	1,400	RARE	Novelist
Stewart, Alexander P.	Civil War	250		600		CSA General/War Dated
Stewart, Alexander P.	Civil War	150	300	350		CSA General/1821-1908
Stewart, Catherine Mary	Ent	5			15	
Stewart, Charles	Military	100	250			Cmdr. USS Constitution
Stewart, Elaine	Ent	5			10	
Stewart, James (Jimmy)	Ent	45	150	225	130	
Stewart, James C.	Aviation	15	25	40	30	WWII ACE
Stewart, Jon	Ent	15			25	
Stewart, Lisa	Ent	5			15	
Stewart, Paul	Ent	10			30	

Name	Field	SIG	DS	ALS	SP	Remarks
Stewart, Peggy	Ent	5			10	
Stewart, Potter	SuprCt	35			90	
Stewart, Rex	Music	75	100		150	
Stewart, Rod	Music	25	65		55	
Stewart, William	Political	30	45	65		Drafted US Mining Law
Stewart, Wynn	Music	10			20	
Stiborik, Joe	Aviation	30			50	Enola Gay Radar Operator
Stieglitz, Alfred 1864-46	Art	200	450	600		Rev. Camera Techniques
Stiers, David Ogden	Ent	40			75	MASH/Scarce Signer
Stigler, George J.	Science	20	25	40	25	Nobel Economics 1982
Still, William Grant	Music	125		300	250	
Stills, Stephen	Ent	40			65	
Stilwell, Joseph W.	Military	175			400	WWII General
Stimson, Henry L.	Political	40	125		50	1867-1950
Sting	Music	25			50	
Stirling, Linda	Ent	20			45	
Stirling, Wm. Alex.	RevWar	450		1,500		General Continental Army
Stock, Frederick A.	Music	25	50		45	
Stockdale, James B.	Military	20			25	WWII Adm.
Stockton, Frank R.	Author	25			35	Juvenile Fiction
Stockton, Richard	RevWar	500	1,000	RARE	RARE	Signer Decl. of Indepen.
Stockton, Robert Field	Military	125	250	350		
Stockwell, Dean	Ent	15			30	Quantum Leap
Stockwell, Guy	Ent	10			30	
Stockwell, Harry	Ent	50			100	
Stoddard, Richard H.	Author	20	30	45		Poet/Writer
Stoddart, James H.	Ent	20			40	Vintage Actor
Stoddert, Benjamin	RevWar	100	250	400		lst Sec'y Navy 1798
Stoica, Chivu	Political	50				Romanian Premier
Stoker, Bram 1847-1912	Author	200		450		Dracula
Stokes, William	Civil War	75				Union Officer
Stokowski, Leopold	Music	65	125	150	150	Conductor
Stollery, David	Ent	10			20	
Stoloff, Morris	Music	10			30	Conductor
Stoltz, Eric	Ent	10		20	25	
Stolz, Robert 1880-1975	Music	25	75			Conductor/Composer
Stolz, Teresa	Ent	40	75			
Stone Temple Pilots	Music	40			90	Signed by Entire Group
Stone, Ezra	Ent	25	40		50	
Stone, Fred	Ent	30		50		Scarecrow in Broadway Oz
Stone, George E.	Ent	20			45	
Stone, Harlan Fiske	SuprCt	75	200	250	225	Chief Justice
Stone, Irving	Author	20	45	100	40	Historical Novelist
Stone, Lewis	Ent	30	40	75	65	
Stone, Lucy (Blackwell)	Political	100		350		Womans Rights/Suffragette
Stone, Marcus	Art	15		30		Illustrated for Dickens
Stone, Matt	Cartoonist	25			50	Co-Creator of South Park
Stone, Milburn	Ent	75	100		125	Doc in TV's Gunsmoke
Stone, Oliver	Ent	10	25		25	AA Film Director

Name	Field	SIG	DS	ALS	SP	Remarks
Stone, Paula	Ent	25			40	Western Heroine
Stone, Sharon	Ent	25	75		50	
Stone, Thomas 1743-87	RevWar	500	775	1,400		Signer Decl. of Indepen.
Stoneman, George	Civil War	75	200			Union General/1822-94
Stooges, The Three	Ent	1,500			3,500	Signed by Orig Three
Stoopnagle, Colonel L.	Ent	15		30	30	Radio
Stoppard, Tom	Author	30	75	125	35	Br Playwright
Storch, Larry	Ent	5			15	F Troop
Stordahl, Axel	Music	25			65	Conductor
Storey, June	Ent	15			45	Western Actress
Storm, Gale	Ent	10			20	Star of Early TV Series
Storm, Tempest	Ent	10		30	25	
Story, Joseph	SuprCt	100	175	250		1779 - 1845
Stoughton, William	Political	450	950			1632-1701
Stout, Rex 1886-1975	Author	35	100	200	45	Nero Wolf
Stowe, Harriet Beecher	Author	275		550	RARE	1811-96/Uncle Toms Cabin
Stowe, Madeline	Ent	25			50	
Strachey, Lytton	Author	75	150			
Stradlin, lzzy	Music	20			45	Guns N' Roses
Straight, Beatrice	Ent	10			20	AA Winner
Strait, Donald G.	Aviation	15		40	35	WWII ACE
Strait, George	Music	20			45	Country
Stranahan, Robert A, Jr.	Business	5			10	CEO/Champion Spark Plugs
Strand, Paul	Art	25	75	200		
Strange, Glenn	Ent	150	200	250	250	Frankenstein
Strangis, Judy	Ent	10			20	
Strasberg, Lee 1901-82	Ent	25	35		75	
Strasberg, Susan	Ent	15		35	20	
Stratas, Teresa	Music	25			50	Opera
Stratemeyer, George F.	Military	30			50	
Stratten, Dorothy	Ent	125			250	Playboy Model/Killed
Stratton, Chas. S.	Ent	250		375	450	General Tom Thumb
Straus, Nathan 1848-1931	Business	100				Owner R.H. Macy Co. Dept
Straus, Oscar 1870-1954	Music	150		250	200	The Chocolate Soldier
Strause, Charles	Music	10		30	25	
Strauss, Franz Josef	Political	15	45	75	35	
Strauss, Johann 1804-49	Music	250	450	1,200	RARE	Aus. Waltzes
Strauss, Johann, Jr.	Music	450	750	900	RARE	The Waltz King
Strauss, Levi	Business	RARE	RARE	RARE	RARE	1850 Establ'd Levi Strauss
Strauss, Peter	Ent	15			45	
Strauss, Richard	Music	225	450	750	700	
Strauss, Robert	Ent	25			45	
Stravinsky, Igor 1882-71	Music	325	550	750	750	Composer
Strawberry, Darryl	Sports	35			75	Baseball
Stray Cats	Music	40	100		75	Signed by Entire Band
Strayhorn, Billy	Music	RARE	RARE	RARE	RARE	Jazz Musician
Streep, Meryl	Ent	20	30	45	50	AA Winner
Street, Julian	Author	25			75	
Streib, Werner	Aviation	25			60	German ACE WWII

Name	Field	SIG	DS	ALS	SP	Remarks
Streich, Rita	Music	10			25	Opera
Streicher, Julius	Political	50	125			Nazi Anti-Semetic, Hanged
Streight, Abel	Civil War	50	150			Union Gen. Escaped Libby
Streisand, Barbra	Ent	150	400		250	
Stribling, Thomas S.	Author	15		45		Am. Novelist/Pulitzer
Strindberg, August	Author	275		750	900	1849-1912
Stringfield, Sherry	Ent	20			40	ER
Stringham, Silas Horton	Civil War	50	100			Union Admiral
Stroheim, Eric von	Ent	150	300		450	Classic Film Director
Stroll, Edson	Ent	10			20	
Stromberg, Hunt	Ent	10			30	Film Producer, Director
Strong, Caleb 1745-1819	RevWar	75	200	400		1st US Senator
Strong, George C.	Civil War	350	550			Union General/KIA
Strong, Susan	Ent	10			20	Vintage Actress
Strong, William	SuprCt	80	160	250		
Stroud, Robert	Criminal	200	RARE		550 RARE	Birdman of Alcatraz
Strouse, Charles	Music	15			30	Composer
Struck, Heinz	Science	10			35	Rocket Pioneer
Struthers, Sally	Ent	15	25		25	All in the Family
Stryker	Music	30			65	Signed by All Four
Stuart, Alexander H. H.	Political	25	60	75		Fillmore Sec'y Interior
Stuart, Gilbert 1755-1828	Art	200	500	750		Pres and Royalty Portraits
Stuart, Gloria	Ent	20			50	Titanic
Stuart, J. E. B. 1833-64	Civil War	2,500	4,500	RARE	RARE	CSA General
Stuart, J.E.B.	Civil War	RARE	RARE	RARE	RARE	CSA General/War Dated
Stuart, Marty	Music	10			25	Country
Studebaker, Clement	Business	200	500	650		Studebaker Bros.
Studebaker, Jr., Clement	Business	40	80	150	75	Studebaker Bros. Mfg. Co,
Studer, Cheryl	Music	15			35	Opera
Stultz, Wilmer	Aviation	75			250	Pioneer Aviator
Stump, Felix B.	Military	25			50	WWII Adm.
Sturge, Joseph	Political	10	20	45		1793 - 1859
Sturgeon, Daniel	Political	25	75	125		
Sturges, John	Ent	5		15	15	
Sturges, Preston	Ent	20			50	Director/Writer
Sturgis, Samuel D.	Civil War	50	100			Union General/1822-89
Styne, Jule 1905-1994	Music	25			50	Composer
Styron, William	Author	15	35		60	
Styx	Music	40			80	Signed by Entire Band
Suchet, David	Ent	10			30	Br. Actor. Poirot
Suchet, Louis G. Duc	Military	100	200	300		Marshal of Napoleon
Sucre, Antonio de	Military	300	650			
Sues, Alan	Ent	5			15	Laugh In
Sugar Ray	Music	25			50	
Sullivan, Anne (Annie)	Science	200		400		
Sullivan, Arthur, Sir	Music	175	400	650	1,000	1842-1900
Sullivan, Barry	Ent	10			25	
Sullivan, Ed 1902-1974	Ent	30	50	65	125	Columnist, TV Host
Sullivan, Francis L.	Ent	10	25		25	

Name	Field	SIG	DS	ALS	SP	Remarks
Sullivan, James	RevWar	50	100	200		Continental Congress
Sullivan, John 1740-95	RevWar	150	400	550		Continental Congress/Gen
Sullivan, John L.	Sports	600			1,250	Boxer
Sullivan, Kathleen	Ent	10			20	TV Hostess
Sullivan, Kathryn D.	Aviation	10	25	45	30	
Sullivan, Margaret	Ent	60	75		125	Suicide
Sullivan, Pat	Cartoonist	75			250	Felix The Cat
Sullivan, Peter John	Civil War	60	100	150		Union General/1821-83
Sullivan, Susan	Ent	5		20	15	
Sullivan, William	Author	20	40	75		Politician
Sully, Alfred	Civil War	50	100	100	150	Union General/1821-79
Sully, Thomas 1783-1872	Art	175	350	450		Portraits
Sully-Prudhomme, Ren.	Author	50	125	200		Fr. Poet/Nobel
Sulzberger, Art Ochs, Jr.	Business	10	25	30	20	NY Times
Summer, Donna	Music	20			45	Disco Queen
Summerall, Charles P.	Military	15	25	35	25	Gen/Pres.Citadel 1931-53
Summerfield, Arthur E.	Political	15		30	25	
Summers, Yale	Ent	10			25	
Summersby, Kay	Military	75			125	D.D. Eisenhower's WWII
Sumner, Charles 1811-74	Civil War	100		225		Abolitionist
Sumner, Increase	Political	75	175			Rev. War Jurist /1746-99
Sumter, Thomas	RevWar	400	900			Soldier
Sun Yat-Sen 1866-1975	Political	6,000	900	1,250	2,000	lst Pres. Chinese Republic
Sunday, William A.	Clergy	100		200	400	Evangelist
Sung, Kim II	Political	50			150	North Viet Nam
Supertramp	Music	40			75	Signed by Entire Group
Susann,Jacqueline	Author	20	35	45	40	Valley of the Dolls etc.
Sutherland, Donald	Ent	10	20		20	MASH movie
Sutherland, George	SuprCt	75	150		250	
Sutherland, Joan	Music	15		35	35	Opera
Sutherland, Keifer	Ent	15			45	
Sutro, Adolph H. J.	Business	35	90	150		Mining Magnate
Sutter, John A. 1803-80	Western	1,200	RARE	2,700	RARE	Ca. Gold Rush on his Farm
Sutton, Frank	Ent	75	100		100	Sgt. Carter/Gomer Pyle
Sutton, Grady	Ent	10			15	
Sutton, John	Ent	10			25	Suave Br. Co-Star
Svanholm, Set	Music	20			45	Opera
Svenson, Bo	Ent	5			10	
Swaggart, Jimmy	Clergy	10		35	30	Evangelist
Swan, James	RevWar	200	450	600		Financial Speculator
Swanson, Gloria 1897-83	Ent	50	100		150	
Swanson, J.	Civil War	75	125	175		
Swanson, Kristy	Ent	20			50	
Swarthout, Gladys	Music	25	75		75	Opera and Film Star
Swasey, Ambrose	Business	50	75			
Swayne, Noah H.	SuprCt	45	125	200		
Swayne, Wager	Civil War	25	50	100		Union General/1834-1902
Swayze, John Cameron	Ent	5			10	TV Newsman
Swayze, Patrick	Ent	25			50	Dirty Dancing/Ghost

Name	Field	SIG	DS	ALS	SP	Remarks
Sweeney, Walter C.	Military	5	15	25	15	Gen/Tactical Air Command
Sweet, Blanche	Ent	20		35	35	
Sweet, John H.	Business	5			10	
Swenson, Ruth Ann	Music	10			25	Opera
Swett, James E.	Aviation	15	30		45	WWII ACE
Swift, Frederic W.	Civil War	65	125	175		Union Officer
Swift, George B.	Political	10	25			Mayor of Chicago
Swift, Harold Higgins	Business	20	50	75	35	Swift and Co.
Swift, John W. 1750-1819	RevWar	75	150			Soldier/Merchant
Swift, Jonathan 1667-45	Author	2,500	RARE	RARE	RARE	Poet
Swigert, John L. Jr.	Space	40	75		125	Astronaut
Swinburne, Algernon C.	Author	150	200	450		British Poet
Swinnerton, Frank	Author	25	50	85		British Novelist
Swinton, Ernest D.	Military	50	100	200		British Inventor of Tank
Swit, Loretta	Ent	15			30	MASH/Hotlips
Switzer, Carl "Alfalfa"	Ent	400	RARE	RARE	900	Our Gang
Swope, Herbert Bayard	Author	10		60	25	War Correspondence
Swope, James S.	Aviation	15		40	30	WWII ACE
Sykes, Jerome H.	Music	15			30	Opera
Sylvia	Music	15			30	
Symmes, John Cleves	RevWar	125	275	450		Patriot/Cont. Congress
Szell, George	Music	25			75	Hungarian Conductor
Szent-Gyorgyi, Albert	Science	30	65	100	50	Nobel Medicine 1937
Szigeti, Joseph	Music	75			200	Violinist
Szold, Henrietta 1860-45	Political	150	450	600		
Szymanowski, Karol M.	Music	150		450		Composer

Albert Schweitzer

Paul Scofield

Omar Sharif

Percy B. Shelley

Terrence Stamp

Red Skelton

John Philip Sousa

Name	Field	SIG	DS	ALS	SP	Remarks
Taft, Charles P.	Business	10		25	10	
Taft, Helen Herron	First Lady	100	200	450	850	1861-1943
Taft, Helen Manning	First Lady	75	150	300	500	Daughter
Taft, Lorado 1860-1936	Art	60	125			Am Sculptor/Author
Taft, William Howard	President	175	450	650	450	1857-1930
Taft, William Howard	President	225	550	2,500	600	As President
Tagliabue, Carlo	Music	50			150	Opera
Tagliavini, Feruccio	Music	35			75	Opera
Taglioni, Marie 1804-1884	Music	300		RARE	RARE	It. Premier Ballerina
Tagore, Rabindranath	Author	100	250	350	350	Poet/Nobel
Takei, George	Ent	15		40	30	Star Trek
Talbot, Gloria	Ent	10			20	
Talbot, Helen	Ent	10			25	
Talbot, Lyle	Ent	10	25	25	20	
Talbot, Nita	Ent	10			20	
Talbot, Wm. Henry Fox	Science	300		900		Inv. Photographic Process
Talcott, Joseph	Political	35	75	150		Colonial Gov.CT/1669-1741
Talese, Gay	Author	10			25	Am. Novelist
Taliaferro, William B.	Civil War	175	400	650		CSA General/War Dated
Taliaferro, William B.	Civil War	90		300		CSA General/1822-98
Talking Heads	Music	35			65	Signed by Entire Group
Tallchief, Maria	Ent	15	20	35	30	Ballerina
Talley, Marion	Music	15		45	50	Am. Soprano
Talleyrand, Charles M.	Political	200	600	750		Chancellor of Napoleon
Talmadge, Benjamin	RevWar	225	400			1754-1835
Talmadge, Constance	Ent	35			75	Silent Star
Talmadge, Norma	Ent	75			175	
Talman, William	Ent	50	75	150	125	Perry Mason
Talvela, Marti	Music	30			75	Opera
Tamblyn, Russ	Ent	10			20	
Tambor, Jeffrey	Ent	10			20	
Tamiroff, Akim	Ent	30	45	75	75	
Tandy, Jessica 1904-94	Ent	25	45	60	60	AA Winner
Taney, Roger B.1777-64	SuprCt	100	275	350		
Tanner, Henry Ossawa	Art	275		600		Religious Subjects
Tansman, Alexandre	Music	50	125		250	
Tappan, Arthur	Political	25	65	100		Merchant/1786-1865
Tappan, James C.	Civil War	35	75	100		CSA General
Tarantino, Quentin	Ent	20			50	AA Writer/Director
Tarbell, Ida M. 1857-1944	Author	20	45	75	30	
Tarkington, Booth	Author	45	150	175	125	Playwright/Nobel
Tarleton, Banastre, Sir	RevWar	150	300	600		British General
Tashlin, Frank	Ent	25			35	Director

Name	Field	SIG	DS	ALS	SP	Remarks
Tashman, Lilyan	Ent	30	45	75	75	
Tassigny, J.M.G. de	Military	35	75	125		
Tate, Allen 1899-1979	Author	10	30	75		Am.Poet/Biographer
Tate, Henry, Sir	Business	50	100	175		
Tate, Jackson R.	Military	10		30	25	Adm. WWII
Tate, Sharon	Ent	275		550	775	Murdered/Manson Gang
Tattersall, Richard	Business	25	50	75		1724-95
Tattnall, Josiah	Civil War			650		CSA Naval Captain
Tatum, Edward L.	Science	45	75	125		Nobel Medicine 1958
Taube, Henry, Dr.	Science	20	35		30	Nobel Chemistry 1983
Tauber, Richard	Music	50			150	Opera
Taufflieb, Gen.	Military	50	125	150	100	
Taurog, Norman	Ent	50			150	Film Director
Taveling Wilbury's	Music	100	200		200	Signed by all four
Tayback, Vic	Ent	35	60		50	Alice
Taylor, Bayard 1825-78	Author	25	75	125		Journalist
Taylor, Deems	Music	40	75		60	Musicologist
Taylor, Don	Ent	10			20	Actor/Director
Taylor, Dub	Ent	15			40	
Taylor, Elizabeth	Ent	175	400		350	AA Winner
Taylor, Estelle	Ent	15		45	45	
Taylor, George 1716-81	RevWar	7,500	20,000	45,000	RARE	Signer
Taylor, James	Music	35	100		65	Singer/Writer
Taylor, Joseph P.	Civil War	65	150			Union General
Taylor, Kent	Ent	5			15	
Taylor, Laurette	Ent	15		40	35	
Taylor, Margaret	First Lady	RARE	RARE	RARE	RARE	
Taylor, Mary	Music	10			20	
Taylor, Maxwell D.	Military	25	75	100	65	Gen. WWII
Taylor, Meshach	Ent	15			35	Designing Women
Taylor, Niki	Ent	20			50	Super-Model
Taylor, Richard	Civil War	375	1,400			CSA General/War Dated
Taylor, Richard 1826-79	Civil War	225	675			CSA General
Taylor, Richard E., Dr.	Science	20	50			Nobel Physics 1990
Taylor, Robert 1911-69	Ent	50	100	125	150	
Taylor, Rod	Ent	5	20	20	20	
Taylor, Thomas H.	Civil War	75	100	200		CSA General/1825-1901
Taylor, Thomas H.	Civil War	125	200	450		CSA General/War Dated
Taylor, Vaughn	Ent	20			50	
Taylor, Walter H.	Civil War	50	100			Aide to Robt E. Lee
Taylor, Zachary	President	525	1,500	3,000		1784-1850
Taylor, Zachary	President	950	4,500	6,500		As President
Taylor-Young, Leigh	Ent	5	20		15	
Tchaikovsky, Piotr I.	Music	2,000	3,000	RARE	RARE	Russian Opera/1840-93
Tchernihovsky, Saul	Author	175		450		Poet
Teagarden, Charlie	Music	10			25	Jazz Trumpet
Teagarden, Jack	Music	65	100		125	Big Band Leader
Teal, Ray	Ent	50			150	
Tearle, Conway	Ent	15			40	Vintage Br. Actor

Name	Field	SIG	DS	ALS	SP	Remarks
Tearle, Godfrey, Sir	Ent	20			50	British Actor
Tebaidi, Renata	Music	20			45	Opera
Telfair, Edward	RevWar	40	80	150		Continental Congress
Teller, Edward, Dr.	Science	35	125	250	90	1908-1994
Telva, Marion	Music	15			45	Opera
Temin, Howard M., Dr.	Science	20	35	56	35	Nobel Medicine 1975
Tempest, Marie	Ent	25	45	50	75	
Temple, Shirley	Ent	200	450	600	450	Signature as a Child
Temple, Shirley (Black)	Ent	20	75	75	45	Adult Signature
Templeton, Alec	Music	20			50	Br. Blind Jazz Pianist
Templeton, Ben	Cartoonist	10			20	Motley's Crew
Templeton, Faye	Music	25	50		65	
Temptations	Music	45	125		125	Signed by Entire Group
Ten Broeck, Abraham	RevWar	100	125			General/Judge
Tenant, Victoria	Ent	10			25	
Tenniel, John, Sir	Art	75	150	250		Illustr. Alice in Wonderland
Tennille, Toni	Music	5			15	Captain and Tennille
Tennyson, Alfred, Lord	Author	200		700	950	Br. Poet Laureate
Tennyson, Jean	Music	10			20	Am. Soprano
Teresa, Mother 1910-97	Clergy	125	250	RARE	275	Nobel Peace Prize
Tereshkova, Valentina	Space	200	250		250	1st Woman in Space
Terfel, Bryn	Music	15			35	Welsh Operatic Baritone
Terhune, Alfred Payson	Author	25	65	75	50	Writer of Dog Stories
Terhune, Max	Ent	100			225	
Terkel, Studs	Author	10		25	20	TV Biographer
Ternina, Milka	Music	25		125		Opera
Terry, Alfred Howe	Civil War	150	350	475		Union General/1827-90
Terry, Ellen, Dame	Ent	35	65	100	75	
Terry, Fred 1864-1933	Ent	15		25	25	Br. Stage & Film Star
Terry, Henry D.	Civil War	45	100	150		Union General/1812-69
Terry, Paul	Cartoonist	50			100	Animator-Mighty Mouse
Terry, Phillip	Ent	5		20	15	
Terry, William H.	Civil War	73		225		CSA General/1824-88
Terry, William Richard	Civil War	75	150	250		CSA General/1817-97
Tesla, Nikola, Dr.	Science	400	850	1,250	1,250	Physicist
Tetard, J.	Aviation	50	75	150	100	
Tetrazzini, Luisa	Music	75	125	200	225	Opera/1871-1940
Teyte, Maggie	Music	50			125	Opera
Thacher, James, Dr.	RevWar	50		250		Revolutionary War Surgeon
Thackeray, Wm. M.	Author	100	300	550		Br. Novelist/1811-63
Thalberg, Irving	Ent	250	450	600	450	MGM Producer
Tharp, Twyla	Ent	20	25		40	Dancer-Choreographer
Thatcher, Henry Knox	Civil War	50	100	150		Union Naval Commander
Thatcher, Margaret	Political	50	150	225	135	Prime Minister
Thaw, Harry K.	Business	50	100	200	75	
Thaxter, Celia 1835-94	Author	25	45	90	125	Am. Poet
Thaxter, Phyllis	Ent	10			25	
Thayer, Abbott	Art	15	35	65		Am. Landscapes
Thayer, Celia	Author	5		15		Am. Novelist

Name	Field	SIG	DS	ALS	SP	Remarks
Thayer, John Milton	Civil War	45	75	150		Union General
Thayer, Silvanus	Military	75	125	200		
Thebaw	Political	125				Burma
Thebom, Blanche	Music	25	45		75	Opera
Theissen, Tiffany Amber	Ent	20			50	
Thelen, Bob	Aviation	15		40	35	WWII ACE
Theron, Charlize	Ent	25			50	
Thicke, Alan	Ent	15	25		25	Growing Pains
Thiers, Louis-Adolphe	Military	35	65	150		lst Pres. 3rd Republic
Thieu, Nguyen Van	Political	25	60	125	45	South Vietnam
Thinnis, Roy	Ent	5		20	15	
Thomas, Ambroise	Music			450		Composer/1811-1896
Thomas, B.J.	Music	10	20		15	Writer
Thomas, Betty	Ent	5		15	10	
Thomas, C.-L.-Ambroise	Music	75	125	250		Composer
Thomas, Charles	Military		600			Union General/1840-1878
Thomas, Clarence	SuprCt	25			40	
Thomas, Danny	Ent	25	55		60	1914 - 1991
Thomas, Dave	Business	10	25		25	Founder of Wendy's
Thomas, Dave	Ent	10			20	Grace Under Fire
Thomas, Dylan 1914-53	Author	500		1,500	1,500	Welsh Poet/Playwright
Thomas, E. Donnall, Dr.	Science	15	25		30	Nobel Medicine 1990
Thomas, Frank	Sports	10			25	Sports
Thomas, Frankie	Ent	10			20	
Thomas, George Henry	Civil War	125	300	500		Union General/1818-70
Thomas, Heather	Ent	15	30		35	
Thomas, Isaiah 1749-31	Business	150	300	750		
Thomas, Jess	Music	15			40	Opera
Thomas, John 1724-76	RevWar	500	750	1,400		Am. Physician & Gen.
Thomas, John Charles	Ent	25	45	55	45	Am. Baritone
Thomas, Jonathan T.	Ent	20			50	Home Improvement
Thomas, Kurt	Ent	5			15	
Thomas, Lorenzo	Civil War	75	140	250		Union General/1804-75
Thomas, Lowell	Ent	35			125	
Thomas, Marlo	Ent	10	20		20	That Girl
Thomas, Michael Tilson	Music	20			45	Am. Conductor
Thomas, Norman	Political	35	100	200	75	6 Presidential Attempts
Thomas, Richard	Ent	5			15	
Thomas, Robert Bailey	Author	25	45	80		
Thomas, Samuel	Civil War	45				Union General
Thomas, Seth E.	Business	125	250	400		Fndr Seth Thomas Clock
Thomas, Seth E. Jr.	Business	75	175	350		Cont'd Seth Thomas Clock Co.
Thomas, Terry	Ent	50		100	150	
Thomas, Theodore	Ent	15			30	Conductor
Thompson Twins	Music	30			65	Signed by Both
Thompson, Benj. von	RevWar	275	450	1,400		Br.Physicist/Inventor
Thompson, Denman	Ent	10			30	Stage Actor
Thompson, Dorothy	Author	35	50	75	75	Journalist/1894-1961
Thompson, Emma	Ent	25			50	Br. Actress-Playwright AA

Name	Field	SIG	DS	ALS	SP	Remarks
Thompson, Ernest Seton	Author	50	100	200		Wild Life Stories
Thompson, Gordon	Ent	10			20	
Thompson, Hank	Music	5			15	
Thompson, J. Walter	Business	100	750			Father/Modern Advertising
Thompson, Jacob	Civil War	150	300	RARE	RARE	CSA Secret Service Agent
Thompson, John P.	Business	15	35	50	25	Pres. Southland Corp.
Thompson, John T.	Science	100	300	RARE	RARE	Arms Inventor
Thompson, Lea	Ent	20			45	Caroline in the City
Thompson, Linda	Ent	5			10	
Thompson, Merriwether	Civil War	125	275	400		CSA General/1826-76
Thompson, Richard W.	Political	25	45	65		Sec'y Navy 1809
Thompson, Ruth Plumly	Author	450		RARE	RARE	
Thompson, Smith	SuprCt	75	150	175		1768 - 1843
Thompson, Wm. H. Big	Political	125				
Thomson, Charles	RevWar	700	1,400			1729-1824
Thomson, Elihu 1853-37	Science	500	950			Electrical Engineer-Inventor
Thomson, Geo. Paget	Science	50				Nobel Physics 1937
Thomson, Virgil	Music	50	75	150	125	1896-1989
Thor, Jerome	Ent	10			20	
Thorborg, Kerstin	Music	25			75	Opera
Thoreau, Henry David	Author	3,000	6,000	8,500	RARE	Am. Naturalist
Thorndike, Sybil, Dame	Ent	30	45		75	
Thornhill, Claude	Music	15			45	Bandleader
Thornton, Billy Bob	Ent	25			50	AA Winner
Thornton, Matthew	RevWar	625	1,400	1,650		Signer/1714-1803
Thornton, William	RevWar	150	300			Am. Architect
Thornton, William A.	Civil War	35				Union General/1803-66
Thorpe, Jim	Sports	400			1,250	1963 Football HOF
Thorvaidsen, Bertel	Art	100	250			Sculptor Lion of Lucerne
Three Stooges, The	Ent	1,400	2,750		2,550	With Moe, Curly and Larry
Thruston, Gates P.	Civil War	25		55		Union General
Thurber, James	Cartoonist	100		450	400	New Yorker Illustrator
Thurman, Uma	Ent	25			50	
Thurmond, J. Strom	Political	10		25	15	SC Senator
Thurston, Howard	Ent	200	600	600	475	Magician/1869-1936
Tibbett, Lawrence	Music	50	100		125	Opera
Tibbetts, Paul W.	Aviation	25		100	75	Pilot of Enola Gay
Tidball, John C.	Civil War	60	125	175		Union Officer
Tiegs, Cheryl	Ent	10			20	Model
Tierney, Gene	Ent	25		50	45	
Tierney, Harry	Music	50	100	200		Composer
Tietjens, Therese	Music	45			125	German Soprano/Opera
Tiffany, Charles Lewis	Business	200	400	RARE	1,500	Founder Tiffany and Co.
Tiffany, Louis Comfort	Art	400	750	RARE	1,500	Stain Glass Artist
Tiffin, Pamela	Ent	5		20	15	
Tilden, Samuel J.	Political	75	150	250		Presidential Candidate
Tilghman, James	RevWar	40	75	150		
Tilghman, Lloyd 1816-63	Civil War	150	300	450		CSA General/KIA/RARE
Tilghman, Matthew	RevWar	200		650		Cont. Congress

Name	Field	SIG	DS	ALS	SP	Remarks
Tilghman, William M.	Western	200	850	1,250		Early Western Sheriff
Tilkin-Servais, Ernest	Music	35			85	Opera
Tillinghast, Charles C.	Business	10	20	30	15	
Tillis, Mel	Music	5			15	Country
Tillis, Pam	Music	15			35	
Tilly, Jennifer	Ent	15			35	
Tilly, Meg	Ent	15			35	
Tilton, Charlene	Ent	15	35		40	
Tilton, Wm. Stowell	Civil War	50	100			Union Officer
Tim, Tiny	Music	20			45	Tiptoe through the Tulips
Timken, William Robert	Business	30	75	100	60	
Ting, Samuel C., Dr.	Science	20	35	50	25	Nobel Physics 1976
Tingey, Thomas	Military	60	150	200		Continental Navy
Tinker, Grant C.	Ent	10			15	TV Film Producer
Tiny Tim	Music	25	35		45	Tiptoe Thru the Tulips
Tiomkin, Dimitri	Music	45		175	100	Composer/1894-1979
Tippett, Michael Sir	Music	50			150	Composer
Tisch, Laurence A.	Business	15			35	CEO of CBS
Tissot, James	Art	75	150	225		
Tito, Marshal	Political	80	175	250	250	1892 - 1980
TLC	Music	35			65	Signed by all three
Tobey, Ken	Ent	10	25		25	
Tobias, George	Ent	50			150	
Tobin, Genevieve	Ent	15		35	35	
Tocqueville, Alexis de	Author	50	125	275		Fr. Writer/Politician
Todd, Alexander R.	Science	30	75		45	Nobel Chemistry 1957
Todd, Ann	Ent	20			40	
Todd, Richard	Ent	75			125	
Todd, Robert	Aviation	15	30	45	25	
Todd, Thelma 1905-35	Ent	175	250	350	475	Mysterious Death at 30
Togo, Heihachiro	Military	100	300	450	200	Jap. Adm. Sino-Jap. War
Togo, Shigenori	Political	250			400	
Tojo, Hideki 1884-1948	Military	250	550	1,500	1,500	Jap Adm/Pearl Harbour
Toklas, Alice B. 1877-67	Author	50	100	RARE	RARE	
Tokody, Ilona	Music	10			25	Opera
Tokyo Rose (Iva,Toguri)	Military	250			400	WWII
Toler, Sidney	Ent	150			300	Charlie Chan
Tolkien, John R.R.	Author	500	1,500	2,500	RARE	Br. Lord of the Rings
Tolstoy, Leo, Count	Author	1,200	RARE	RARE	2,200	Rus. Novelist
Tombaugh, Clyde W.	Science	30	65	125	125	Astronomer/Discov. Pluto
Tomei, Marissa	Ent	25			50	AA Winning Actress
Tomlin, Lily	Ent	10	20		20	
Tomlin, Pinky	Music	15			35	Scat Singer
Tompkins, Angel	Ent	10		20	25	
Tompkins, Daniel	Vice Pres	100	125	150		Monroe's VP
Tone, Franchot 1905-68	Ent	25	50	55	50	
Toombs, Robert A.	Civil War	125	200	200		CSA General/1810-85
Toomey, Regis	Ent	15	25		45	
Toones, Fred Snowflake	Ent	150			300	

Name	Field	SIG	DS	ALS	SP	Remarks
Topal	Ent	15			30	
Topp, Erich	Military	35			100	Ger. U Boat Cmdr. WWII
Topping, Dan	Business	10		30	15	Owner NY Yankees
Torisu, Kennosuke	Military	50		150	75	
Tork, Peter	Music	20			45	The Monkees
Torme, Mel	Music	25			50	Singer/Writer
Torn, Rip	Ent	15			35	Easy Rider
Torrance, Ernest 1878-33	Ent	75			150	Silent Films
Torrence, Ridgely	Author	25	35	75		Am. Poet/1875-1950
Torres, Raquel	Ent	25			45	
Tors, Ivan	Ent	15			35	Producer-Director
Toscanini, Arturo	Music	300	550	750	700	Conductor/1867-1957
Tosti, Paolo	Music	25	60	125		Composer
Toto	Music	65			150	Signed by Entire Band
Totten, Jos. G.	Civil War	20	35	65		Union General/1788-1864
Totter, Audrey	Ent	5	15		15	
Toucey, Isaac 1792-1869	Political	25	75	125		
Toulouse-Lautrec, Henri	Art	1,200	2,500	RARE	RARE	
Toumanova, Tamara	Ent	35			100	Rus-Am Ballerina
Tourel, Jennie	Music	25			50	Opera
Tourgee, Albion W.	Author	15	25	40		Lawyer/Judge
Tower, Zealous B.	Civil War	20	35	50		Union General/1819-1900
Townes, Charles Hanson	Science	25	35	65		Inventor
Townsend, Edward D.	Civil War	30	55	60		Union Officer/1817-93
Townsend, Francis E.	Science	50			150	Physician
Townsend, Frederick	Civil War	15	30	45		Union General
Townsend, George A.	Author	15		40		War Correspondent
Townsend, Lynn	Business	10		35	20	CEO Chrysler Corporation
Townsend, Pete	Music	30			65	The Who
Townsend, Robert	Ent	10			20	Director
Toynbee, Arnold 1852-83	Author	25	105	190	75	Br, Historian, Sociologist
Tozzi, Giorgio	Music	20			40	Opera
Tracy, Doreen	Ent	5			15	Mouseketeer
Tracy, Edward Dorr	Civil War	150	450	750		CSA General/KIA
Tracy, Lee	Ent	10			25	
Tracy, Spencer 1900-67	Ent	125	250	350	300	AA Winning Actor
Train, Arthur	Author	10		35		
Trapier, James H.	Civil War	125	200	325		CSA General/1815-65
Trask, Diana	Music	10			20	
Traubel, Helen 1899-72	Music	40			90	Opera
Trautloft, Hannes	Aviation	25			50	Ger. Ace WWII
Travalena, Fred	Ent	5			15	Comedian
Travanti, Daniel J.	Ent	10			20	
Traven, Berwick	Author	275	650	1,250		German Novelist
Travers, Henry	Ent	250	RARE	RARE	400	Angel/Its a Wonderful Life
Travers, Patricia	Ent	5			15	
Traverso, Giuseppe	Music	15			45	Opera
Travis, Kylie	Ent	10			20	
Travis, Merle	Music	20			40	

Name	Field	SIG	DS	ALS	SP	Remarks
Travis, Nancy	Ent	20			45	
Travis, Randy	Music	20			40	Country
Travis, Richard	Ent	10			20	
Travis, William Barret	Military	2,500	RARE	RARE	RARE	Co-Cmdr Alamo
Travolta, John	Ent	25			50	
Treacher, Arthur	Ent	20			45	1894 - 1975
Treadwell, John	RevWar	25	60	75		
Trebek, Alex	Ent	10		20	25	Host/Jeopardy
Tree, Herbert Beerbohm	Ent	35	75	100	75	
Treen, Mary	Ent	5		30	25	
Treilhard, Jean-Baptiste	Military	15	25	50		Fr. Politician
Trelawny, Edward	Author	175	400	750		Br.Author-Adventurer
Trenholm, George A.	Civil War	95	170	450		CSA Sec'y Treasury
Trettner, Henrich 'Heniz	Aviation	20	45		50	
Trevelyan, George Otto	Author	15	35	75		Br. Historian
Treves, Frederick, Dr.	Science	200		400		Dr. To Elephant Man
Trevor, Claire	Ent	30	45		45	AA Winner
Trilling, Lionel	Author	10	25	45		Am. Lit. Critic. Professor
Trimble, Isaac R.	Civil War	400		1,200		CSA General/War Dated
Trimble, Isaac Ridgeway	Civil War	175		400		CSA General/1802-88
Tripler, Charles E.	Science	75	150			Inventor Liquid Air
Tripplehorn, Jeanne	Ent	15			45	
Tritt, Travis	Music	20			45	Country
Tritton, William Ashbee	Science	25	65	100	45	Developed Military Tank
Trollope, Anthony	Author	100	225			Br. Novelist. 50 Novels
Trollope, Frances	Author	35	100	200		Br. Novelist
Trollope, Thomas A.	Author		25	45		Novelist/1810-92
Trotsky, Leon 1879-1940	Political	650	1,500	2,250	950	Communist Leader
Troubridge, Thomas, Sir	Military	75		250		Br Admiral
Troup, Bobby	Music	10			20	Composer
Trow, Bob	Ent	10			20	
Trower, Robin	Ent	15			30	
Troyanos, Tatiana	Music	15			40	Opera
Truax, Ernest	Ent	10		40	30	
Trudeau, Gary	Cartoonist	30			65	Doonesbury
Trudeau, Pierre	Political	25	65	90	65	Prime Minister Canada
Truffaut, Francois	Ent	50	150			
Trujillo, Rafael 1891-1961	Political	75			250	Dominican Republic
Truman, Bess W.	First Lady	75	125	200	175	1885-1982
Truman, Harry S.	President	150	450	1,200	400	1884-1972
Truman, Harry S.	President	300	1,200	3,500	800	As President
Truman, Margaret	Political	25	65	80	30	Daughter of Truman
Trumbo, Dalton	Author	50			75	Blacklisted Oscar Winner
Trumbull, John 1750-31	Author	75		200		CT Poet & Lawyer
Trumbull, John 1756-43	Art	100	300	750		
Trumbull, Jonathan	Military	125	300	450		Sec'y Washington's Staff
Trumbull, Jonathan	RevWar	300		900		1710-85
Trump, Donald J.	Business	15	50	75	40	Millionaire Entrepreneur
Trump, Ivana	Business	10			35	Ex Mrs. Donald Trump

Name	Field	SIG	DS	ALS	SP	Remarks
Truth, Sojourner	Political	30,000	RARE	RARE	RARE	Abolitionist
Truxton, Thomas	RevWar	125	300	550		Cmdr. USS Constellation
Truxton, William Talbot	Civil War	20	45	75		Union Admiral
Tryon, William	RevWar	150	300	600		Colonial Governor NC/NY
Tsiolkovsky, Konstantin	Science	RARE	RARE	2,500	RARE	Rus. Space Program
Tubb, Ernest	Music	15			35	
Tuchman, Barbara W.	Author	35	100	150	45	Historian
Tucker, Forrest	Ent	25		40	45	
Tucker, John R.	Civil War	125	200			CSA Commdr. 1812-83
Tucker, Orrin	Music	15			25	Big Band Leader
Tucker, Richard	Music	35	75		120	Opera
Tucker, Samuel	RevWar	125	250	550		Am. Naval Hero
Tucker, Sophie	Ent	25		60	60	Vaudeville
Tucker, Tanya	Music	20			50	Country
Tucker, Thomas T.	RevWar	50	150	175		Soldier/Statesman
Tucker, Tommy	Music	20			45	Bandleader
Tudor, Anthony	Ent	35	45		90	Dancer/Choreagrapher
Tufts, Cotton 1734-1815	RevWar	75	150	250		Physician
Tufts, Sonny	Ent	20	25		35	
Tully, Tom	Ent	25			45	
Tune, Tommy	Music	10			20	Dancer/Choreagrapher
Tunney, Gene	Sports	125			250	Boxer
Turgenev, Ivan 1818-33	Author	200	450	900	1,200	Russian Novelist
Turkel, Ann	Ent	5			15	
Turkel, Studs	Author	10	25	35	20	TV Commentator
Turlington, Christy	Ent	20			45	Super-Model
Turner, Edward	Science	25		125		Chemist/Atomic Weight
Turner, Frederick J.	Author	50		200		Pulitzer Prize. Historian
Turner, J. M. W. 1775-51	Art	200	500	900		Br. Landscape Painter
Turner, Janine	Ent	25			60	
Turner, John Wesley	Civil War	100	125	300		Union General/1833-99
Turner, Kathleen	Ent	15			35	
Turner, Lana	Ent	40	75	100	80	
Turner, Philip	RevWar	65	125	225		Surgeon During War
Turner, Roscoe, Col.	Aviation	75			125	Pioneer Aviator
Turner, Ted	Business	10		40	30	
Turner, Tina	Music	25			50	
Turpin, Ben	Ent	150			375	
Turreau de Garambouville	Military	25		75		French Revolution
Turtles	Music	35			75	Signed by Entire Group
Turturro, Nick	Ent	10			25	
Tusmayan, Barsag	Music	10			25	Opera
Tuttle, Lurene	Ent	5		20	15	Radio Dramatic Star
Tuttle, Wes & Marilyn	Music	15			30	
Tutu, Desmond, Bishop	Clergy	45	100	200	75	Nobel Peace Prize
Tuve, Merle Antony	Science	35	75	150	50	Radar...
Twain, Mark	Author	500		1,500		
Twain, Shania	Music	25			50	Country/Pop Star
Tweed, Shannon	Ent	10		30	25	

Name	Field	SIG	DS	ALS	SP	Remarks
Tweed, William Marcy	Political	125	200	350	750	
Twiggs, David E.	Civil War	150	300	750		CSA General/1790-1862
Twiggy (Leslie Hornsby)	Ent	15		40	35	60's Brit. Fashion Model
Twining, Nathan F.	Aviation	45	125	175	65	General WWII
Twiss, Peter	Aviation	10		30	20	
Twitty, Conway	Music	40	60		65	Country
Two Guns White Calf	Western	750	RARE	RARE	2,000	Buffalo Nickel Model
Tyler, Bonnie	Music	15			35	
Tyler, Daniel 1799-1882	Civil War	35	75	125		Union General
Tyler, Edward Burnett	Science	15	35	50		
Tyler, Gerald E.	Aviation	15		40	30	ACE WWII
Tyler, John 1790-1862	President	400	750	1,200		
Tyler, Judy	Ent	10			20	
Tyler, Julia Gardiner	First Lady	200	450		650	
Tyler, Liv	Ent	25			50	
Tyler, Moses Coit	Author	10		25		Am. Historian
Tyler, Robert 1816-77	Military	100		250		President's Son. Mex War. CSA Register
Tyler, Robert C.	Civil War	250	500	800		CSA General
Tyler, Royall	RevWar	25	50	100		Jurist/Author
Tyler, Tom	Ent	100	200		200	GWTW...Phantom
Tyndale, Hector	Civil War	35	55	75	150	Union General/1821-80
Tyndall, John 1820-93	Science	50	125	150		Physicist/Philosopher
Tyner, James N.	Political	15	40	75		P. M. General 1876
Tyner, McCoy	Music	10	20		30	Jazz Pianist-Composer
Tyson, Cicely	Ent	10		30	20	
Tyson, Mike	Sports	30			75	Boxer

Margaret H. Thatcher

Mark Twain
(Samuel L Clemens)

Name	Field	SIG	DS	ALS	SP	Remarks
U-2	Music	75			175	Signed by entire group
Udet, Ernst 1896-1941	Aviation	225	375	450	500	WWI German ACE
Ueberroth, Peter	Business	10	25	25	15	
Uggams, Leslie	Ent	10	20		20	
Ullman, Liv	Ent	15		40	35	
Ullman, Tracey	Ent	25			50	
Umberto I	Royalty	60	150	275		King Italy
Umeki, Miyoshi	Ent	200			400	
Underwood, Blair	Ent	15			25	
Underwood, J. T.	Science	45	125	200		Underwood Typewriter
Undset, Sigrid 1882-1949	Author	100			300	Nobel Prize Winner
Unger, Jim	Cartoonist	15			25	Henry
Ungher, Caroline 1803-77	Music	50		150		Opera
Unitas, Johnny	Sports	15			45	1979 Football HOF
Unreal, Minerva	Ent	25			60	
Unser, Al	Sports	10			30	Auto Racing
Unser, Bobby	Sports	10			25	1990 Racing HOF
Untermeyer, Louis	Author	20	40	75	25	Am. Poet/Critic
Updike, John	Author	25	75	125	45	Am. Novelist
Upjohn, E. Gifford, Dr.	Business	125	250			Upjohn Pharmaceuticals
Upshaw, Dawn	Music	10			25	Opera
Upshur, Abel Parker	Political	25	50	75		Tyler Sec'y Navy
Upton, Emory	Civil War	25	50	75		Union General/1839-81
Urbanowicz, Witold A.	Aviation	35	70	125	60	WWII Polish ACE
Urey, Harold C. 1893-81	Science	100		350		Nobel in Chemistry 1934
Urich, Robert	Ent	10	25		30	
Uris, Leon	Author	30	75	125	65	Am. Novelist
Urso, Camilla	Music	25			40	Fr. Violinist
Urvanowicz, Witold A.	Aviation	25		75	50	WWII Polish ACE
Usher, John P.	Political	40	90	175		Sec'y Interior 1863-65
Ustinov, Peter	Ent	25	65		65	AA Actor/Author
Utrillo, Maurice 1833-55	Art	450	550	650		Fr. Paris Scenes

Name	Field	SIG	DS	ALS	SP	Remarks
Vaccaro, Brenda	Ent	5	20	15	10	
Vadim, Roger	Ent	20			50	
Vague, Vera	Ent	35			65	Disney Voice
Valdengo, Giuseppe	Music	15			40	Opera
Vale, Virginia	Ent	15			35	

Name	Field	SIG	DS	ALS	SP	Remarks
Valens, Richie	Music	450			900	
Valenti, Jack	Ent	5	10		15	Pres/Motion Pix Assoc.
Valentine, Karen	Ent	10	20		20	Room 222
Valentine, Lewis	Political	35	75		50	
Valentino, Rudolph	Ent	900	1,500		2,000	
Valenzuela, Fernando	Sports	10			25	Baseball
Valery, Paul A, 1871-45	Author	50	100	150		Poet/Philosopher
Valette, A.J.M.	Military	25		75		French Revolution
Valetti, Cesare	Music	25			50	Opera
Vallandigham, Clement	Civil War	125		250		Civil War Copperhead
Vallee, Rudy	Ent	15	35	45	35	1901 - 1986
Vallejo, Mariano G.	Military	150	350			
Valli, Frankie	Music	15			45	
Valli, Virginia	Ent	15			40	Films From 1915-1931
Van Allan, Richard	Music	10			25	Opera
Van Allen, James	Science	40	100	200	100	Nobel Physics
Van Ark, Joan	Ent	5	15		15	
Van Buren, Abigail	Author	10	20	30	20	Am. Syndicated Columnist
Van Buren, Angelica	First Lady	RARE	RARE	RARE	RARE	
Van Buren, Hannah	First Lady	RARE	RARE	RARE	RARE	
Van Buren, Martin	President	350	900	900		1782 - 1862
Van Buren, Raeburn	Cartoonist	10			30	Abbie & Slats
Van Cleef, Lee	Ent	25			45	
Van Dam, Rip 1662-1736	Political	75	175	300		Colonial Governor
Van Devanter, Willis	SuprCt	40	125	150	75	
Van Dine, S.S.	Author	45	100	150	2,000	Created Philo Vance
Van Dongen, Kees	Art	30	45	90		Fauvist Painter
Van Doren, Carl	Author	15	45	60	25	Pulitzer in Biography
Van Doren, Mamie	Ent	10	20	25	25	
Van Doren, Mark 1894-73	Author	10	50	45	25	Poetry/Pulitzer
Van Dorn, Earl	Civil War	350		RARE	RARE	CSA General/Assasinated
Van Dorn, Earl 1820-63	Civil War	250		700		CSA General/Assasinated
Van Dresser, Marcia	Ent	15			40	
Van Druten, John W.	Author	10	20	35	15	Novelist/Playwright
Van Dyck, M, Ernest	Music	15	25		40	Tenor
Van Dyke, Dick	Ent	15	40		35	Dick Van Dyke Show
Van Dyke, Henry 1852-33	Political	25	50	75		
Van Dyke, Jerry	Ent	10	20		20	Coach
Van Dyke, Nicholas	RevWar	125	250	450		Statesman/1738-89
Van Fleet, James, Gen.	Military	25	65	75	45	Gen. WWII
Van Fleet, Jo	Ent	15	20	40	35	AA Winner
Van Halen	Music	45			100	Signed by Four members
Van Halen, Alex	Music	20			50	Van Halen Musical Group
Van Halen, Eddie	Music	25	60		50	
Van Heusen, James	Music	50	75	150	75	Composer
Van Hoften, James D.	Space	10			20	Astronaut
Van Horne, David	RevWar	20		75		
Van Kirk, Theodore	Aviation	50	85		100	
Van Loon, Hendrik W.	Author	15	40	60	40	Historian/Journalist

Name	Field	SIG	DS	ALS	SP	Remarks
Van Loon, William	Author	15		50		Journalist
Van Patten, Dick	Ent	5	20	20	15	Eight is Enough
Van Patten, Joyce	Ent	5			15	
Van Sloon, Edward	Ent	125			250	
Van Stade, Frederica	Music	15			45	Opera
Van Sweringen, Otis P.	Business	15	45	75	35	
Van Vechten, Carl	Author	40	80	150	65	Am. Novelist
Van Vleck, John H., Dr.	Science	30	50	75		Nobel Physics 1977
Van Vliet, Stewart	Civil War	50		200		Union General/1815-1901
Van Wyck, Charles Henry	Civil War	40	70	90		Union General/1824-95
Van Zandt, Philip	Ent	50			150	
Van Zant, Ronnie	Music	35			75	
Van Zealand, Paul	Political	15			35	Premier Belgium
Van, Bobby	Ent	10			20	
Van, Gloria	Ent	5			15	
Vance, A.T., Capt.	Aviation	15	25		35	Record Polar Flight
Vance, Cyrus	Political	10	20	35	25	Sec'y State/Sec'y Army
Vance, Jack	Author	10		20	15	Sci-Fi Writer
Vance, Louis Joseph	Author	15	35	65		Am. Novelist
Vance, Robert Brank	Civil War	85	145	225		CSA General/1828-1899
Vance, Vivian	Ent	150	200		225	I Love Lucy/Ethel
Vance, Zebulon Baird	Civil War	175		450		Gov NC/Opposed Davis
Vandamme, Dominique	Military	75	150	200		Battle of Waterloo
Vandamme, Jean-Claude	Ent	25			50	
Vandenberg, Hoyt S.	Aviation	25			75	
Vander Pyl, Jean	Ent	10			20	Voice/Wilma Flintstone ...
Vanderbilt, Alfred G.	Business	15	35	65	25	
Vanderbilt, Amy	Author	15	25	40	35	Authority on Manners
Vanderbilt, Cornelius	Business	600	2,000	3,500	3,000	Financier/1794-1877
Vanderbilt, Cornelius, Jr.	Business	200	750	1,500	450	Journalist/1843-1899
Vanderbilt, George W.	Business	200	500	900	350	Biltmore House/1862-1914
Vanderbilt, Gloria	Business	20	45	65	35	Fashion Designer
Vanderbilt, Jacob H.	Business	500	1,500	2,500		Brother of Cornelius
Vanderbilt, William H.	Business	250	750	1,500	500	Railroad Executive
Vanderbilt, William K.	Business	200	550	1,200	400	RR Exec/Financier
Vandergrift, Alexander	Military	40	85	125	60	Marine Corps Gen. WWII
Vanderlyn, John 1775-52	Art	250		550		Am. Pres. Portraits
VanDien, Caspar	Ent	20			40	
Vane, John R., Dr.	Science	20	30	50	25	Nobel Medicine 1982
Vaness, Carol	Music	15			35	Opera
Vanili, Milli	Music	30			65	Both Signed
Vanilla Ice	Music	20			40	
Vanity	Ent	10			25	
Vanzetti, Bartolomeo	Criminal	600	1,500	RARE	RARE	Convicted Murderer
Varese, Edgard	Music	200	400	575		
Vargas, Alberto	Art	150		350	250	
Vargas, Getuilio	Political	50	100		75	Revolutionary Pres. Brazil.
Varick, Richard	RevWar	75	150	200		Soldier
Varmus, Harold E., Dr.	Science	25	50		35	Nobel Medicine 1989

Name	Field	SIG	DS	ALS	SP	Remarks
Varney, Astrid	Music	10			25	Opera
Varney, Jim	Ent	10			20	
Vasarely, Victor	Art	40	125			
Vasquez, Roberta	Ent	5			15	Playboy Centerfold
Vassar, Matthew	Business	200	750	1,500		Founder Vassar College
Vaughan, Benjamin	Political	200	1,000			Br. Diplomat/1751-1835
Vaughn, Alfred J.	Civil War	100		300		CSA General/1830-99
Vaughn, George A.	Aviation	35	55	95	65	WWII ACE
Vaughn, John C.	Civil War	200	300	RARE	RARE	CSA General/War Dated
Vaughn, John C.1824-75	Civil War	100	200			CSA General
Vaughn, Robert	Ent	15	25		25	Man from UNCLE
Vaughn, Sarah	Music	45	75	150	125	Jazz Vocalist-Pianist
Vaughn, Stevie Ray	Music	150			300	Died in air crash
Vaughn, Vince	Ent	20			40	Psycho re-make
Vaughn-Williams, Ralph	Music	75	200	350	150	
Vedrines, Jules	Aviation	175	300		275	
Vee, Bobby	Music	5			15	
Veidt, Conrad 1893-1950	Ent	75	150		250	
Velez, Lupe 1908 - 1944	Ent	70	125	200	175	Mexican Spitfire
Venable, Evelyn	Ent	65			85	Disney Voice
Vendela	Ent	20			45	SuperModel/Actress
Vendome, L.J., Duke de	Military	150		450		Marshal of France
Ventura, Charlie	Music	25			75	Bandleader
Vera Ellen	Ent	20			45	Dancer
Verdi, Giuseppe	Music	1,200	1,500	2,400	RARE	Composer/1813-1901
Verdin, James, Lt.Cdr.	Aviation	10	25			
Verdon, Gwen	Ent	5		20	15	
Verdugo, Elena	Ent	15			30	The Wolfman
Verdy, Violette	Music	10			30	Opera
Vereen, Ben	Ent	10			20	
Vereshchagin, Vassili V.	Art	50		150		Paintings of Russian Wars
Vergennes, Chas. G.,Le	Political	175	300			Fr Ambassador
Verlaine, Paul 1844-96	Author	175		500		Fr. Symbolist Poet
Vermehren, Werner	Aviation	20	35	55	60	Ger. Capt. WWI Zeppelin
Verne, Jules 1828-1905	Author	250	650	900	RARE	20K Leagues Under Sea...
Vernier, Theodore	Military	35	100			French Revolution
Vessey, John W.	Military	10			30	
Vetch, Samuel 1668-1732	Political	100	225	400		Colonial Governor
Veverka, Jaroslav	Music	20			45	Opera
Vezzani, Cesare	Music	50			150	Opera
Vickers, Jon	Music	25			50	Opera
Victor and Mussolinni	Royalty		600			Signed by Both
Victor Emmanuel I	Royalty		350			King of Sardinia
Victor Emmanuel II	Royalty	100	250	450		
Victor Emmanuel III	Royalty	40				King Italy 1900-46
Victor, Claude Perrin	Military	125		150		Marshal of Napoleon
Victoria, Duchess/Kent	Royalty			125		Mother of Queen Victoria
Victoria, Empress	Royalty	45		125		Eldest Daughter of Queen
Victoria, Mary Louisa	Royalty	45	125	175		Mother of Q. Victoria

Name	Field	SIG	DS	ALS	SP	Remarks
Victoria, Queen 1819-01	Royalty	175	350	550	900	Great Britain etc.
Victors, Henry	Ent	75			200	
Vidal, Gore	Author	10	20	30	20	Am. Novelist/Playwright
Vidor, Florence	Ent	40	35	65	60	
Vidor, King 1894-1982	Ent	30			100	AA Winning Director
Viele, Egbert L.	Civil War	25	40	55	65	Union General/1825-1902
Vigneaud, Vincent du	Science	10	25	45	25	
Vilas, William F.	Political	15	30	45	35	PM General
Viljoenk, B.J.	Military	35		125		
Villa, Francesco	Military	900	1,500	2,500	3,500	Pancho Villa
Villa-Lobos, Heitor	Music	100	200	400	250	Composer/1887-1959
Villechaize, Herve	Ent	40	65		60	Tatoo/Fantasy Island
Villepique, John B.	Civil War	250		550		CSA General/1830-62
Villiers, Frederic	Art	10		35	25	
Vinay, Ramon	Music	75			200	Opera
Vincent, Gene	Music	175			300	
Vincent, Jan-Michael	Ent	10		20	20	
Vincent, Thomas M.	Civil War	30	55	100		Union General/1832-1909
Vinci, Leonardo da	Art	RARE	RARE	RARE	RARE	
Vinson, Carl 1883-1991	Political	20	40		65	
Vinson, Frederick M.	SuprCt	75	150	300	300	Chief Justice
Vinson, Helen	Ent	15		40	35	
Vinton, Bobby	Music	5			15	
Vinton, David 1803-73	Civil War	125	250			Union General/First POW
Virchow, Rudolf 1821-02	Science	250				Founder Cellular Pathology
Vishinsky, Andrei	Political	75		150	125	
Visitor, Nana	Ent	15			35	Star Trek/Deep Space Nine
Vittor, Frank	Art	45		125		
Vivian, Richard H. Sir	RevWar	50	125	250		
Vlaminck, Maurice de	Art	125	200	450	325	Fr. Fauvist Painter
Voelker, John D.	Author	5		15	15	
Voight, Deborah	Music	10			25	Opera
Voight, Jon	Ent	10	30		30	AA Winner
Voisin, Gabriel	Aviation	65	135	225	125	Fr. Airplane Mfg. Pioneer
Vokes, Christopher	Military	15	30	40	25	
Volkov, Viadislav	Space	75			150	Cosmonaut
Voll, John J.	Aviation	20	45	65	45	WWII ACE
Volstead, Andrew J.	Political	75	150	200		1860-1947
Volta, Alessandro	Science	600	1,400	2,500	RARE	Volt Unit Named for Him
Voltaire, Frangois M.	Author	500	1,400	RARE	RARE	Fr. Writer/Philosopher
Von Behr, Henrich	Military	15		30		
Von Braun, Magnus	Science	15		45		Rocket Pioneer
Von Braun, Wernher	Science	150	400	550	400	German Rocket Pioneer
Von Bulow, H.	Music	20		65		German Pianist
Von Debizka, Hedwig	Music	40		150		Opera
Von der Chevaerie	Military	15		40		
Von Edelsheim, M.	Military	20		45		Panzer General
Von Gazen, Waldemar	Military	20		50		Panzer General
Von Gronau, Wolfgang	Aviation	200		500		WWI German ACE

Name	Field	SIG	DS	ALS	SP	Remarks
Von Hesse-Nassau, A.	Royalty	100	200	300		lst Duke of Luxembourg
Von Kleist, Paul	Military	50	100		100	German WWII Tank Comdr.
Von Kretchmer, Otto	Military	45	100			Top German U- Boat Cmdr. WWII
Von Oy, Jenna	Ent	15			35	Blossom/Six
Von Papen, Franz	Military	100	150	250	175	
Von Paulus, Friedrich	Military	175	350			Ger. WWII Field Marshal
Von Sauken, Dietrich	Military	25			75	Panzer General
Von Sternberg, Joseph	Ent	30	75		45	Director
Von Stroheim, Erich	Ent	150			450	Director
Von Tilzer, Albert	Music	30		150	45	Founder ASCAP
Von Trapp, Maria	Music	40	125	200	85	Sound of Music Fame
Von Zell, Harry	Ent	10		25	25	Radio Announcer
Vonnegut, Kurt, Jr.	Author	20	40		50	
Voronoff, Serge 1866-51	Science	25			50	
Vorster, Balthazar J.	Political	25	60	125	55	Prime Minister South Afr.
Voslo, Arnold	Ent	20			50	The Mummy/Darkman II
Vosseller, Aurelius B.	Military	35	75			
Vraciu, Alex	Aviation	15	25	50	35	WWII ACE
Vuillard, Edouard 1868-49	Art	150	300	450		French Painter

Cordially yours,

Rudolph Valentino

Rudolph Valentino

Martin VanBuren

J C VanDamme

Name	Field	SIG	DS	ALS	SP	Remarks
Wachtel, Theodor	Music			195		Opera
Wade, Benjamin F.	Political	50	100	150		OH Senator
Wade, Leigh	Aviation	30	75	100	45	Pilot '24 Round The World
Wadopian, Eliot	Music	10			25	Bassist
Wadsworth, James S.	Civil War	50	100	200		Union General/1807-64
Wadsworth, Jeremiah	RevWar	150	300	450		Army Officer/1743-1804
Waesche, R.R.	Military	20	50			US Coast Guard Command
Wafterson, Henry 1840-21	Author	25		75	100	CSA Army/Pulitzer
Waggoner, Lyle	Ent	10			25	Carol Burnett Show
Wagner, Honus	Sports	450	1,200		1,200	1936 Baseball HOF
Wagner, Jane	Author	10			20	Playwright
Wagner, Lindsay	Ent	10	20		25	Bionic Woman
Wagner, Richard	Music	1,200	1,600	2,500	3,000	Composer/1813-1883
Wagner, Robert	Ent	15		25	35	Hart to Hart
Wagner, Robert F.	Political	30	75	125	50	1877-1953
Wagoner, Porter	Music	10			20	
Wahlberg, Mark	Ent	20			40	Marky-Mark
Wainwright, James	Ent	5			15	Actor
Wainwright, Jonathan	Military	100	225	250	225	Gen. WW II
Waite, H. Roy	Aviation	15	25	40		
Waite, Morrison R.	SuprCt	40	75		65	Chief Justice SuprCt
Waite, Ralph	Ent	5		20	15	
Wakely, Jimmy	Music	45			100	
Waksman, Selman A.	Science	45	75	100	60	Nobel Medicine 1952
Walburn, Raymond	Ent	15		45	35	
Walcott, Charleis F.	Civil War	15		45		Union Officer
Walcutt, Charles C.	Civil War	30	65	75		Union General/1838-98
Wald, George	Science	15	30	50	25	Nobel Medicine 1967
Wald, Jerry	Music	15	25		45	Bandleader
Wald, Lillian D. 1867-40	Political	30	60		50	Reformer
Waldheim, Kurt	Political	15	65	100	40	Prime Minister Austria
Waldo, Janet	Ent	5			15	Voice Judy Jetson...
Waldron, Hicks B.	Business	5			10	CEO Heublein Inc.
Walesa, Lech	Political	25	75		100	President of Poland
Walgreen, Charles R.	Business	35	75	100		Fndr. Walgreens
Walken, Christopher	Ent	20			50	
Walker, Alice	Author	25			50	The Color Purple
Walker, Benjamin	RevWar	100	250			Rev. Army Officer
Walker, Clint	Ent	20			35	Western TV Star
Walker, Francis Amasa	Civil War	45	90	145		Union General/1840-97
Walker, Frank C.	Political	5	15		10	P.M. General 1940
Walker, James J.	Political	25	60		45	Mayor NYC
Walker, Jimmy	Ent	10	20		20	Good Times

Name	Field	SIG	DS	ALS	SP	Remarks
Walker, John Brisben	Author	10	30			Editor Cosmopolitan
Walker, John George	Civil War	75	150	225		CSA General/1822-93
Walker, Leroy Pope	Civil War	250	400	600		CSA General/1817-84
Walker, Mary E. 1832-19	Civil War	300		550	RARE	Union Nurse/Surgeon
Walker, Mort	Cartoonist	15			35	Beetle Bailey
Walker, Nancy	Ent	30	40		45	Rhoda
Walker, Reuben L.	Civil War	100		250		CSA General/1827-90
Walker, Robert J.	Political	25	75	125		Polk Sec'y Treasury
Walker, Robert, Sr.	Ent	50		150	150	
Walker, T. Bone	Music	45			85	Jazz Guitar-Vocalist
Walker, Walton H.	Military	30	55	75	50	Gen./Killed in Korea 1950
Walker, William S.	Civil War	100		250		CSA General/1822-90
Walker, Wm Henry T.	Civil War	150	350	475		CSA General/KIA
Wallace, Alfred R.	Science	75	150	400		Theory of Evolution
Wallace, Dee	Ent	5		20	15	
Wallace, Edgar 1875-32	Author	75	225	300	350	
Wallace, Henry A.	Vice Pres	50	125	150	100	FDR V.P.
Wallace, Irving	Author	25	100	150	75	Am. Novelist
Wallace, Jean	Ent	10		20	25	
Wallace, John	Civil War	100	300			
Wallace, Lewis Lew	Civil War	150	300	450		Union General
Wallace, Marjorie	Ent	10			20	Miss USA/Actress
Wallace, Mike	Ent	5		20	15	60 Minutes
Wallace, William H.	Civil War	100	250			CSA General/1827-1905
Wallach, Eli	Ent	5	20		20	Batman villian "Mr.Freeze"
Wallburg, Donnie	Music	15			45	Marky Mark
Wallenda, Karl 1905-78	Ent	150	250		400	Flying Wallendas Circus
Wallenstein, Alfred, Dr.	Music	25			75	Conductor
Waller, Littleton	Military	100				Marine General 1880-1920
Waller, Thomas Fats	Music	125	275	RARE	400	Jazz Pianist/1904-43
Walley, Deborah	Ent	5		15	30	
Wallis, Barnes, Sir	Aviation	35	75			Br. Aircraft Designer
Wallis, Hal	Ent	20	45		40	Producer
Wallis, Ruth	Ent	10			25	
Walpole, Horace 1717-97	Author	150	450	900		Br. Novelist
Walpole, Hugh Seymour	Author	35	90	125		Novelist/Playwright
Walpole, Robert, Sir	Political	75		300		Prime Minister
Walsh, Blanche	Ent	15			35	
Walsh, John	Ent	5			10	Fox TV Host
Walsh, Kenneth	Aviation	15	25	50	35	WWII ACE
Walsh, M. Emmet	Ent	5			15	
Walsh, Raoul	Ent	35			75	Director
Walsh, Thomas J.	Political	15	40		25	1859-1933
Walston, Ray	Ent	15	25		30	My Favorite Martian
Walter, Bruno	Music	75		150	375	German Conductor
Walter, Jessica	Ent	10			15	
Walters, Barbara	Ent	10		20	20	TV Anchor
Walters, Julie	Ent	5		20	15	
Walthall, Edward C.	Civil War	100	150	250		CSA General/1831-98

Name	Field	SIG	DS	ALS	SP	Remarks
Walthall, Edward C.	Civil War	185	750	RARE	RARE	CSA General/War Dated
Walthall, Henry B.	Ent	25		55	65	
Walton, Ernest T.S.,Dr.	Science	75				Nobel Physics 1951
Walton, George 1740-04	RevWar	350	650	950		Signer
Walton, Sam M.	Business	50			80	Wal-Mart
Walton, William, Sir	Music	75		200	150	Composer/1902-83
Waltrip, Darrell	Sports	5			15	Auto Racing
Wambaugh, Joseph	Author	10		35	25	Novelist/Amercian
Wanamaker, John	Business	45	60	150	100	Department Store Pioneer
Wanger, Walter 1894-68	Ent	30	45			Producer
Wapner, Jos. A., Judge	Ent	5			15	TV Judge
War	Music	30			65	Signed by Entire Group
Ward, Aaron	Military	15	35	50		General/War of 1812
Ward, Artemas	Author	15	35	60	25	Humorist
Ward, Artemas 1727-00	RevWar	350	1,500			RevWar Commander
Ward, Burt	Ent	15	25		25	TV's Batman/Played Robin
Ward, David	Music	10			35	Opera
Ward, Henry 1732-97	RevWar	150	350	700		
Ward, Henry A.	Business	40		125		Merchant
Ward, J.H. Hobart	Civil War	35	60	75		Union General
Ward, John Q. Adams	Art	25	75	100	45	Am. Sculptor/1830-1910
Ward, Joseph, Sir	Political	15	25	60		PM New Zealand
Ward, Rachel	Ent	10			25	
Ward, Richard 1689-1763	Political	20	35			Colonial Governor of RI
Ward, Samuel 1725-1776	RevWar		550	775		Patriot/Merchant
Ward, Sela	Ent	15			30	
Warden, Jack	Ent	5			15	
Warfield, David	Ent	35	50	75	75	
Warfield, Marsha	Ent	10			25	Night Court
Warfield, William	Music	15			45	Baritone
Warhol, Andy 1930-87	Art	150	250	475	275	
Waring, Fred	Music	15	40		25	Big Band
Warner, Adoniram J.	Civil War	25		100		Union General/1834-1910
Warner, Charles Dudley	Author	20	65	100		1829-1911
Warner, H.B.	Business	40	125		125	Warner Brothers
Warner, Harry M.	Business	100	175		150	Fndr. Warner Bros.
Warner, Jack L.	Business	75	175		150	Fndr. Warner Bros)
Warner, Malcolm Jamal	Ent	15	30		30	Cosby Show
Warner, Seth 1743-84	RevWar	250				
Warnow, Mark	Music	10			25	Big Band Leader
Warrant	Music	45			80	Signed by Entire Group
Warren, Chas. Marquis	Author	5		25	10	
Warren, Earl 1891-1974	SuprCt	75	165		250	Chief Justice, Governor CA
Warren, Gouverneur	Civil War	175	450			Union General/War Dated
Warren, Gouverneur K.	Civil War	125	250	400		Union General/1830-82
Warren, Harry	Music	30	75		45	Composer
Warren, James 1726-08	RevWar	125	350	750		Patriot/Merchant
Warren, Jennifer	Music	10			25	
Warren, Joseph 1741-75	RevWar	6,000	RARE	RARE	RARE	Patriot/Doctor

Name	Field	SIG	DS	ALS	SP	Remarks
Warren, Joseph, Sr.	Political	50	125	175		Colonial
Warren, Lavinia	Ent	75			225	Mrs. Tom Thumb
Warren, Leonard	Music	75			275	Opera
Warren, Leslie Ann	Ent	15	25		30	
Warren, Michael	Ent	5			15	
Warren, Robert Penn	Author	35	100	125	75	Am. Poet
Warren, Russell 1783-60	Science	35		150		Architect
Warren, William 1812-88	Ent	10		25		
Warrick, Ruth	Ent	10		20	25	
Warsitz, Erich	Aviation	15	35	45	45	
Washburn, Cadwallader	Civil War	45	75		85	Union General/1818-82
Washburne, Elihu B.	Political	25	50	75		Minister France
Washington, Booker T.	Author	300	450	700	1,500	1856-1915
Washington, Bushrod	SuprCt	125	350	700		1762 - 1829
Washington, Denzel	Ent	25	60		50	
Washington, Dinah	Music	125			200	Vocalist
Washington, George	President	4,500	10,000	14,000		1732-99
Washington, John A.	Civil War	125		450		CSA Lt. Colonel General
Washington, Martha	First Lady	RARE	RARE	RARE	RARE	
Washington, Ned	Music	50			100	
Washington, William	Military	65	165	250		General/Patriot
Wasserman, Dale	Music	15		35	30	
Waterhouse, Benjamin	Science	250	600	1,650		Small Pox Vaccination
Waterhouse, J. W.	Art	15		50		
Waterhouse, Richard	Civil War	150	275	450		CSA General/1832-76
Waterman, F.D.	Business	75	200			Waterman Pen
Waters, Ethel 1896-1977	Music	55	100	125	150	Stormy Weather
Waters, Muddy	Music	100	200		275	Jazz Musician
Waterston, Sam	Ent	15	35		30	Law & Order
Watkins, Henry George	Explorer	125		300		
Watson, Harold F.	Aviation	10	30	45	25	
Watson, J. Crittenden	Civil War	25	60	90		Union Commodore
Watson, James D., Dr.	Science	30	40	50	35	Nobel Medicine 1962
Watson, R.J. Doc	Aviation	15	25	40	30	USAF WWII ACE
Watson, Thomas A.	Science	75	225	275	RARE	
Watson, Thomas J., Jr.	Business	100	550	1,250	200	Chairman IBM
Watt, James	Political	10		20	25	Controversial Sec'y Interior
Watt, James 1736-1819	Science	400	750	1,400		Inventor/Steam Engine
Watt, James, Jr.	Science	40	85	160		
Watterson, Bill	Cartoonist	25			55	Calvin & Hobbes
Watts, George Frederick	Art	75	150	300		Br. Painter & Sculptor
Watts, Thomas H.	Civil War	50				CSA Att'y Gen./1819-92
Waugh, Evelyn 1903-66	Author	45	150	225	75	Brideshead Revisited
Wavell, Archibald, Sir	Military	50	150	175	65	Br. Field Marshal
Wayans, Keenen Ivory	Ent	15			35	
Wayne, Anthony 1745-96	RevWar		750	1,500	RARE RARE	Mad Anthony" Wayne
Wayne, Carol	Ent	35		125	150	
Wayne, David	Ent	20	45		45	1914 - 1996
Wayne, Henry C.	Civil War	175	275			CSA General/War Dated

Name	Field	SIG	DS	ALS	SP	Remarks
Wayne, Henry C. 1815-83	Civil War	100	200	275	250	CSA General
Wayne, James M.	SuprCt	100	200	350		
Wayne, John 1907-79	Ent	400	800	1,000	800	
Weare, Meshech 1713-86	RevWar	35	100			Pres. of New Hampshire
Weathers, Carl	Ent	10			20	
Weaver, Dennis	Ent	10			25	
Weaver, Doodles	Ent	20	20		30	
Weaver, James B.	Civil War	30		140		Union General/1833-1912
Weaver, Sigourney	Ent	20			50	Aliens movies
Webb, Alexander S.	Civil War	25		55		Union General/1835-1911
Webb, Beatrice Potter	Political	40	125			Reformer
Webb, Charles Henry	Author	10		30		
Webb, Clifton	Ent	35			65	1891 - 1966
Webb, Del	Business	10		25	30	Desert Inn Casino
Webb, Jack	Ent	45	75		100	Dragnet
Webb, Jimmy	Music	25	35		65	Composer
Webb, Richard	Ent	15			35	Capt. Midnight
Webb, Samuel B.	RevWar	125	300	450		1753-1807
Webb, Sidney	Political	35		75	150	Br. Economist
Webb, W.R. Spider	Aviation	15	30	45	35	WWII ACE in One Day
Webber, Andrew Lloyd	Music	65		RARE	175	Br. Musical Theatre
Weber (Joe) and Fields	Ent	85			165	Vaudeville Comedians
Weber, Joe 1867-1942	Ent	20	35	45	45	
Weber, Karl Maria von	Music	375	900	1,200		Composer
Webster, Ben	Music	125				Tenor Sax-Arranger
Webster, Daniel 1782-52	Political	100	250	350	475	
Webster, Jean	Author	15	45	95		Am. Novelist
Webster, Noah 1758-1843	Author	500	750	1,400		Am. Lexicographer
Webster, Paul Francis	Music	25	50	75	45	Composer
Wedell, Jimmie	Aviation	15	30	40	35	
Wedemeyer, Albert C.	Military	45	150		150	Gen.WWII
Weed, Marian	Music	20			50	Opera
Weede, Robert	Music	10			35	Opera
Weeks, John W.	Political	15	35	65		Sec'y War 1921
Weems, Ted	Music	20	30	50	45	Big Band Leader
Weidler, Virginia	Ent	15		20	25	1927 - 1968
Weikl, Bernd	Music	10			20	Opera
Weill, Kurt	Music	250	500	900	375	Composer/1900-1950
Weinberg, Steven, Dr.	Science	25	35		30	Nobel Physics 1979
Weinberger, Casper	Political	5		25	15	Sec'y HEW, Sec'y Defense
Weingartner, Felix von	Music	50		200	150	Austrian Conductor
Weir, Julian Alden	Art	50	125	250		Am. Impressionist
Weir, Robert Walter	Art	50	125	225		
Weisbart, David	Ent	15			35	Director-Producer
Weiser, Jan Conrad	Military	250	750	1,400		French Revolution
Weisiger, David A.	Civil War	100	225			CSA General/1818-1899
Weissmuller, Johnny	Ent	150	300		400	Tarzan/1904-84
Weitzel, Godfrey	Civil War	50	100	150		Union General/1835-84
Weizman, Vera	First Lady	25	75		35	Widow of lst Pres. Israel

Name	Field	SIG	DS	ALS	SP	Remarks
Weizmann, Chaim	Political	450	1,200	2,200	900	lst Pres. Israel
Welby, Amelia	Author	450		RARE	RARE	Poet
Welch, Raquel	Ent	15	45		35	
Weld, Tuesday	Ent	10		30	25	
Welden, Ben	Ent	10			25	
Weldon, Felix de	Art	65				Iwo Jima Memorial Statue
Welk, Lawrence	Music	10		35	25	
Weller, Peter	Ent	10	20	25	35	Robocop
Weller, Thomas H., Dr.	Science	25	35	50	30	Nobel Medicine 1954
Welles, Gideon 1802-78	Political	100	200	300	675	Sect of Navy
Welles, Orson 1915-85	Ent	125	450		350	QQ Winner
Welles, Sumner 1892-61	Political	25	75	100	55	Ambassador
Wellington, 1st Duke of	Political	175	250	375		Prime Minister
Wellman, Manly Wade	Author	35	100		75	
Wellman, Walter	Aviation	60	150	225	75	Aviator-Explorer-Writer
Wells, Kitty	Music	5			15	
Wells, Carolyn	Author	10	25	35	15	
Wells, Carveth	Author	20	45	90	35	Explorer, Author
Wells, Dawn	Ent	10	20		20	Mary Ann/Gilligans Island
Wells, H.G. 1866-1946	Author	175		400	750	War of the Worlds
Wells, Henry & Fargo, J.	Business	850	1,250			Wells Fargo
Wells, Henry & Fargo, W.	Business		1,500			Wells Fargo/Amer Express
Wells, Henry 1805-78	Business	300	750	1,500		Wells Fargo/Amer Express
Wells, Junior	Music	5			10	
Welty, Eudora	Author	35	100	175	100	Am. Novelist
Wendelin, Rudolph	Cartoonist	25			45	Smokey the Bear
Wendorf, E.G. Wendy	Aviation	10	25	40	30	WWII Navy ACE
Wendt, George	Ent	15	30		35	Norm on "Cheers"
Wenrich, Percy	Music	55	100			Composer
Wentworth, Benning	Political	100	250	450		1696-1770
Wentworth, John 1737-20	RevWar	100	225	300		
Wermuth, Arthur W.	Military	15	35	50	25	WWII Hero
Werner, Oskar	Ent	25		45	50	
Werrenrath, Reinald	Music	25		45	50	Opera
Wesley, John	Clergy	500		2,500		Methodist Founder
Wessel, Corydon M., Dr.	Military	45	85	150	65	Missionary China.WWII
Wesselowsky, Aless.	Music	50			150	Opera
Wesson, Daniel B.	Science	400				Gunsmith
West, Adam	Ent	10	25		25	TV's Batman
West, Benjamin 1738-20	Art	200	700	1,250		Am. Historical Painter
West, Dottie	Music	15			40	
West, F. H.	Civil War	40	100			Union Officer
West, Jessamyn	Author	15	30	35	25	Novelist
West, Joseph R. 1822-98	Civil War	40	75			Union General
West, Mae 1892-1980	Ent	55	115		250	
West, Morris L.	Author	15	45	80	30	
West, Rebecca, Dame	Author	15	45	75		Br. Novelist
Westall, William	Art	15	45	95		
Westheimer, Ruth, Dr.	Science	5	15	25	15	Sex Therapist

Name	Field	SIG	DS	ALS	SP	Remarks
Westinghouse, George	Business	300	900			Fndr. Westinghouse Co
Westinghouse, George	Business	500	1,500			Fndr Westinghouse Corp.
Westminster, 2nd Earl	Royalty	25	50			Robert Grosvenor
Westmore, Wally	Ent	25			50	Makeup Director
Westmoreland, Wm. C.	Military	25		75	65	Gen. Korea. Viet Nam
Weston, Edward 1850-36	Business	45	125	300	75	
Weston, Edward 1886-58	Art	35				Am. Western Photographer
Weston, Paul	Music	15			45	Bandleader/Arranger
Westover, Russ 1887-66	Cartoonist	20		40	35	Tillie The Toiler
Weygand, Maxime	Military	40	75	150	125	Fr. Gen./ Chief of Staff
Weyman, Stanley J.	Author	15	35	65		Br. Novelist
Whalen, Michael	Ent	15		35	30	
Wharton, Edith N.	Author	225	475	950		Age of Innocence/Pulitzer
Wharton, Gabriel C.	Civil War	80		175		CSA General/1824-1906
Wharton, John A.	Civil War	200	450	900		CSA General/1828-65
Wharton, Thomas	RevWar	125	275	450		Governor PA
Wheaton, Wil	Ent	25			50	Star Trek/Wesley
Wheatstone, Charles, Sir	Science	100	300	450		Br. Physicist, Inventor
Wheeler, Bert	Ent	25			75	Wheeler and Woolsey
Wheeler, Earle G.	Military	20			50	
Wheeler, Ellie	Ent	10		25	25	
Wheeler, Joseph	Civil War	275	750	1,250		CSA General/War Dated
Wheeler, Joseph	Civil War	125	300	350	950	CSA General/1836-1906
Wheeler, William A.	Vice Pres	75	225			Hayes VP
Whelan, Arleen	Ent	10		25	20	
Whelchel, Lisa	Ent	10			25	Facts of Life
Whipple, Abraham	RevWar	250	750			Fired First Gun in RevWar
Whipple, Amiel Weeks	Civil War	125	225	300		Union General/1816-63
Whipple, George H.	Science	50	75	150		Nobel Medicine !934
Whipple, William	RevWar	750		1,500		Signer Decl. of Ind.
Whipple, William D.	Civil War	25		50		Union General/1826-1902
Whirry, Shannon	Ent	10			25	
Whisner, William T.	Aviation	25	50	75	50	WWII ACE
Whistler, James McNeill	Art	300	450	600		Am. Painter
Whitaker, Johnnie	Ent	10			25	
White, Alice	Ent	25	45		75	
White, Anthony Walton	RevWar	55	150	250		Washington Aide de Camp
White, Betty	Ent	10	15	20	20	MTM/Golden Girls
White, Byron R.	SuprCt	55	125	150	75	
White, E.B.	Author	35	125			Charlotte's Web
White, Edward D.	SuprCt	50	150	200	150	
White, Edward H.	Space	200	250	550	400	1st Am. To Walk In Space
White, George	Ent	60			100	
White, George Stuart	Military	40		75		Br.Fid.Marshal
White, Jesse	Ent	25	50		50	Harvey
White, Jim	Explorer	50		150		Discover Carlsbad Caverns
White, Josh	Music	65			225	Am. Folk Singer
White, Julius	Civil War	25	50	100		Union General/1816-90
White, Paul Dudley, Dr.	Science	45	100		80	Heart Specialist

Name	Field	SIG	DS	ALS	SP	Remarks
White, Pearl	Ent	125		250	275	Silent Film
White, Robert, Maj.	Aviation	10	25		30	Speed & Altitude Record
White, Sanford	Science	100	200		150	
White, Stewart E.	Author	10	20	40	20	Am. Westernn Stories
White, Vanna	Ent	5		20	15	Wheel of Fortune
White, William Allen	Author	35	75	85	75	Pulitzer
White, Windsor T.	Business	125		350		Pioneer Auto-Truck Mfg,
Whitelaw, Billie	Ent	15			30	
Whiteman, Paul	Music	60		160	175	King of JAZZ
Whitestone, Heather	Ent	20			40	Miss America/1995
Whiting, Jack	Ent	5			15	
Whiting, John D.	Political	10		20		Jerusalem
Whiting, Margaret	Music	10			15	Vocalist
Whiting, Richard	Music	50		125	100	Composer
Whiting, William Henry	Civil War	200				CSA General/1824-65
Whitlam, Gough	Political	10			25	Prime Minister Australia
Whitley, Ray	Music	10			35	Cowboy Movies
Whitman, Slim	Music	5			15	
Whitman, Walt 1819-92	Author	1,200	2,000	2,400	2,750	Am. Poet
Whitmore, James	Ent	5		20	15	
Whitney, Asa 1797-1872	Business	35		100		Transcontinental Railroad
Whitney, Casper	Business	10	25	35		Publisher
Whitney, Courtney	Military	15	40	75	35	WWII General
Whitney, Eli 1765-1825	Science	750	2,500	3,500	RARE	Am. Inventor Cotton Gin
Whitney, Grace Lee	Ent	15	25	30	25	Star Trek
Whitney, Josiah D.	Science	75		250		1819-1896
Whitney, Richard	Business	35	50			Pres. NY Stock Exchange
Whitney, William Collins	Political	20	45	65	35	1841-1904
Whittaker, Charles E.	SuprCt	50	75	150	85	
Whitten-Brown, Arthur	Aviation	250	375			Pioneer Aviator
Whittier, John Greenleaf	Author	100	250	350		Quaker Poet
Whittle, Frank, Sir	Aviation	15			45	
Whittlesey, Elisha	Political	15		45		Founder of Whig Party
Who, The	Music	350			600	Signed by Four Originals
Wickersham, George W.	Political	15	45	60	45	Taft Att'y Gen.
Wickes, Mary	Ent	20	30		30	
Wickham, William	Civil War	140	375			CSA General/War Dated
Wickham, William C.	Civil War	80	250			CSA General/1820-88
Wickliffe, Charles A.	Political	30	65	100		P.M. General
Widmark, Richard	Ent	10		20	25	
Widor, Charles Marie	Music	65		150		Composer
Wieghorst, Olaf	Art	75	225	250	200	Dean of Western Art
Wiemann, Ernst	Music	10			20	Opera
Wiesel, Elie	Author	20	45	55	25	Nobel Peace Prize 1986
Wiesel, Torsten S., Dr.	Science	20	30	45	25	Nobel Medicine 1981
Wiesenthal, Simon	Political	20	45	90	35	Famed Nazi Hunter
Wiest, Diane	Ent	20	45		45	AA Winner
Wigfall, Louis T. 1816-74	Civil War	125	225			CSA General
Wiggin, Kate Douglas	Author	95		165	125	

Name	Field	SIG	DS	ALS	SP	Remarks
Wigner, Eugene P. Dr.	Science	15	25	45	25	Nobel Physics 1963
Wihan, Hanus	Music	35		100		Czech Violinist/Cellist
Wilberforce, William	Political	50	145	250		Br. Anti-Slavery Politician
Wilbur, Curtis D,	Political	10	25	35	25	Sec'y Navy
Wilbur, Ray Lyman	Political	20	25	35	25	Sec'y Interior
Wilbur, Richard	Author	5		35	10	U.S. Poet Laureate
Wilcox, Cadmus M.	Civil War	100	200	300		CSA General/1824-90
Wilcox, Cadmus M.	Civil War	175	400			CSA General/War Dated
Wilcox, Ella Wheeler	Author	20	35	75		Journalist/Poet
Wilcoxon, Henry	Ent	20		35	45	
Wild, Edward A.	Civil War	75	150	200		Union General/1825-91
Wilde, Cornel	Ent	15	25	40	35	
Wilde, Oscar 1856-1900	Author	675	1,500	2,500	2,250	Ir. Poet/Playwright
Wilde, Percival	Author	25	50	100		Playwright/Novelist
Wilder, Billy	Ent	20	50		50	AA Winning Director
Wilder, Gene	Ent	15	30		30	Young Frankenstein
Wilder, Thornton	Author	75	150	350	200	Pulitzer/1897-1975
Wilding, Michael	Ent	30			55	
Wilhelm I (Ger) 1797- 88	Royalty	75	250	350		King of Prussia
Wilhelm II (Kaiser)(Ger)	Royalty	175	375	450	300	1859-1941
Wilhelmj, August	Music	25			75	German Violinist
Wilke, Robert J.	Ent	10			25	
Wilkerson, Guy	Ent	25			65	
Wilkes, Charles	Civil War	50	100	200		Union Admiral/1798-1877
Wilkes, Earle	Military	20			50	
Wilkie, David, Sir	Art	40	80	125		Br.Genre Paintings
Wilkins, Geo. Hubert,Sir	Explorer	30	50	90	55	1888-1958
Wilkins, Roy	Political	15	35	45	25	Statesman/Civil Rights
Wilkinson, Geoffrey	Science	15	25	40	25	Nobel Chemistry 1985
Wilkinson, James	RevWar	125	275	350		
Wilkinson, June	Ent	5		20	20	
Willard, Edward S.	Ent	15		35	30	
Willard, Frances E.	Political	40	65	125		Temperence Movement
Willard, Frank	Cartoonist	35			65	Moon Mullins
Willard, Fred	Ent	5			15	
Willard, John	Ent	10			25	Playwright
Willcox, Orlando B.	Civil War	40	75	150		Union General/1823-1907
Willem VI & I, 1772-1848	Royalty			600		King Netherlands
Willett, Marinus 1740-30	RevWar	75	150	250		Cont. Army Officer
William III (Eng)	Royalty	650	1,400	2,250		
William IV (Eng) 1765-37	Royalty	100	300	400		The Sailor King
William, 4th Duke of	Political	75	175	300		Prime Minister 1756
William, Warren	Ent	10		40	45	
Williams, Andy	Music	20			45	
Williams, Barry	Ent	20	50			Brady Bunch
Williams, Ben Ames	Author	15	25	40	25	Am. Novelist
Williams, Bill	Ent	10			25	
Williams, Billy Dee	Ent	10	25		25	Empire Strikes Back
Williams, Cindy	Ent	5		20	20	Laverne and Shirley

Name	Field	SIG	DS	ALS	SP	Remarks
Williams, Clarence	Ent	15			30	Mod Squad
Williams, Edward M.	Business	35	75	125		
Williams, Edy	Ent	10			20	
Williams, Esther	Ent	10		20	20	
Williams, George H.	Political	10	25	40		Attorney General
Williams, Grant	Ent	45			125	
Williams, Gus	Ent	10			25	Showman
Williams, Guy 1924-89	Ent	150	250		250	Zorro/Lost in Space
Williams, Hal	Ent	5			15	
Williams, Hank	Music	650	1,200		1,200	
Williams, Hank Jr.	Music	20	25		35	
Williams, JoBeth	Ent	10			25	
Williams, Joe	Music	15			40	Jazz Vocalist
Williams, John	Music	20	75		50	Composer/Conductor
Williams, Jr., Alford J.	Aviation	35	45	75	125	
Williams, Mary Alice	Author	10			20	TV News Journalist
Williams, Mason	Music	10			20	Guitar Soloist
Williams, Otho	RevWar	150	400	600		1749 - 1800
Williams, Paul	Music	10			20	
Williams, Robin	Ent	20	50		50	
Williams, Roger	Music	10			35	Pianist
Williams, Roy	Ent	10			20	
Williams, Seth 1822-66	Civil War	35	65	85		Union General
Williams, Spencer	Ent	10			20	
Williams, Ted	Sports	75			200	1966 Baseball HOF
Williams, Tennessee	Author	150	300	475	350	Cat on a Hot Tin Roof
Williams, Tex	Music	10			20	Big Band
Williams, Treat	Ent	10	20	25	20	
Williams, Van	Ent	15	25		25	TV's Green Hornet
Williams, Vanessa	Ent	25			50	Miss America
Williams, William	RevWar	300	450	600		Signer Decl. of Indepen.
Williams, William Carlos	Author	275			300	Am. Poet/Novelist
Williamson, Fred	Ent	10			20	
Willing, Foy	Music	10			20	(Riders of the Purple Sage)
Willing, Thomas	RevWar	75	200			Banker/Cont. Congress
Willis, Bruce	Ent	35	125		65	Tough Signer
Willis, Nathaniel P.	Author	20	45	75		1806-67
Willkie, Wendell	Political	35	75		125	Pres. Candidate
Wills, Bob	Music	75			200	
Willson, Meredith	Music	25	75	125	80	Composer/The Music Man
Willys, John North	Business	60	100	125	90	Auto Pioneer, Diplomat
Wilson, Brian	Music	40			85	Beach Boys
Wilson, Bridget	Ent	10			30	
Wilson, Charles E.	Business	20	35	70	30	Pres. GM./Sec'y Defense
Wilson, Charles Edward	Business	20	75			Pres. General Electric
Wilson, Demond	Ent	25			45	Sanford and Son
Wilson, Dennis	Music	35			75	Beach Boys
Wilson, Dooley	Ent	400	500		800	Casablanca Sam
Wilson, Edith Bolling	First Lady	100	200	250	200	1872-1961

Name	Field	SIG	DS	ALS	SP	Remarks
Wilson, Edmund	Author	25	75	150		
Wilson, Edmund B.	Science	350	450			Am. Biologist
Wilson, Ellen Louise	First Lady	100	300	550		1st Wife - Pres. Wilson
Wilson, Flip	Ent	25	50		50	
Wilson, Francis 1854-35	Ent	15			25	
Wilson, Gahan	Cartoonist	15			25	Magazine and Comic Book Artist
Wilson, Harold, Sir	Political	40	75		65	Br. Prime Minister
Wilson, Henry 1812-75	Vice Pres	85		125		Grant VP
Wilson, Jackie	Music	200	300		250	
Wilson, James 1742-98	SuprCt	700	900	1,400		Signer
Wilson, James 1835-1920	Political	25	50	75		Sec'y Agriculture 1897
Wilson, James G.	Civil War	100		275		Union General/1833-1914
Wilson, James H. 1837-25	Civil War	85	175	350		Union General Calvary
Wilson, Julie	Ent	15			35	
Wilson, Kemmons	Business	15	45		50	Founder Holiday Inn
Wilson, Lois	Ent	15		35	45	
Wilson, Marie	Ent	25	35	50	60	My Friend Irma Early TV
Wilson, Robert, Dr.	Science	15	25	35	25	Nobel Physics 1978
Wilson, Sloan	Author	15	35	50	25	Man in Grey Flannel Suit
Wilson, Teddy 1912-86	Music	40		75	100	Pianist-Arranger
Wilson, Tom	Cartoonist	10			30	Ziggy
Wilson, Woodrow	President	200	550	750	775	1856-1924
Wilson, Woodrow	President	375	950			As President
Winchell, Paul	Ent	10	25		35	Ventriloquist
Winchell, Walter	Author	35	40	45	45	1897-1972
Winchester, Oliver F.	Science	400	1,500	1,500		Winchester Repeating Arm
Winder, Charles S.	Civil War	RARE	RARE	RARE	RARE	CSA General/KIA
Winder, John Henry	Civil War	150		450		CSA General
Windgassen, Wolfgang	Music	15			45	Opera
Windsor, Claire	Ent	10			25	
Windsor, Duke/Duchess	Royalty	400			650	Edward & Wallis
Windsor, Marie	Ent	5	20	15	15	
Windsor, Wallis, Duchess	Royalty	125	250	450	175	
Winfield, Dave	Sports	10			30	Baseball
Winfield, Paul	Ent	15	30		35	Afr.-Am. Actor
Winfrey, Oprah	Ent	20			45	
Wing, Toby	Ent	10		25	25	
Wingate, Francis R., Sir	Military	35	75	125	75	Gen. Succeeded Kitchener
Winger, Debra	Ent	15	50		45	
Winkler, Henry	Ent	5	20		20	The Fonz on "Happy Days"
Winner, Septimus	Music	100	200	350		Composer
Winninger, Charles	Ent	25		50	60	
Winningham, Mare	Ent	10			30	
Winslow, Edward	RevWar	25	50	100		Loyalist/1714-84
Winslow, John 1753-19	RevWar	25	50	100		Soldier/Hero
Winslow, John Ancrum	Military	100	275	375		Union Naval Officer
Winslow, John F.	Civil War	75	150	225		Builder of the Monitor
Winters, Jonathan	Ent	10	25	25	25	
Winters, Roland	Ent	30	45	75	75	Charlie Chan

Name	Field	SIG	DS	ALS	SP	Remarks
Winters, Shelley	Ent	5	20		20	
Winthrop, John 1714-79	RevWar	200	600			Science
Winthrop, John, The	Political	800	1,600	RARE	RARE	Colonial Governor
Winthrop, Thomas L.	RevWar	25	50	90		Merchant
Winwood, Estelle	Ent	15	35		35	1883 - 1984
Wire, Calvin C.	Aviation	15		30	25	WWII ACE
Wirt, William 1772-1834	Political	40	90	125		Attorney General 1817
Wirz, Henry Hartmann	Civil War	600	RARE	RARE	RARE	CSA Officer
Wise, Henry A.	Civil War	100	200	250		CSA General/1806-76
Wise, Robert	Ent	15	30		30	Director
Wiseman, Joseph	Ent	35			65	Dr. No/James Bond film
Wister, Owen 1860-1938	Author	50	150	200	75	Novelist/The Virginian
Withers, Jane	Ent	10		25	20	Shirley Temple Sidekick
Withers, Robert E.	Civil War	25		75		CSA Colonel
Witherspoon, Jimmy	Music	15			30	Jazz Musician
Witherspoon, John	RevWar	600	1,500	RARE	RARE	Signer Decl. of Indepen.
Witt, Katarina	Sports	25			50	Figure Skater
Witte, Serge	Political	30		100		1st Premier of Russia
Wittig, Georg F.K.	Science	25	50		40	Nobel Chemistry 1979
Wixell, Ingvar	Music	20			45	Opera
Wodehouse, P. G.	Author	150		300	450	British Novelist
Wolcott, Derek	Author	15	20		25	Poet/Nobel
Wolcott, Oliver 1726-97	RevWar	200	450	1,200		Signer Decl. of Ind.
Wolcott, Oliver, Jr.	Political	75	250	350		Washington Sec'y Treas.
Wolf, Gary	Author	10			25	Who Framed Roger Rabbit?
Wolf, George	Political	35	75	150		Gov. PA 1829, Statesman
Wolf, Hugo 1860-1903	Music	250	RARE	RARE	RARE	Austrian Composer
Wolfe, James 1727-59	Military	1,500	RARE	RARE	RARE	Br.Gen/French/Indian War
Wolfe, Thomas 1900-38	Author	500	2,000	RARE	RARE	
Wolfe, Tom	Author	15	45	65	35	Am. Novelist
Wolff, Karl	Military	175		550		German SS General
Woll, Matthew	Political	20		75		Am. Labor Leader
Wolper, David	Ent	5			15	
Wolseley, Garnet J.	Military	25	75	100	35	Br.Field Marshal
Wolsey, Thomas	Political	RARE	7,500	RARE	RARE	Cardinal/Statesman
Wonder, George	Cartoonist	15			35	Terry & The Pirates
Wonder, Stevie	Music	RARE	200	N/A	150	Only "Signs"w/Thumbprint
Wong, Anna May 1907-61	Ent	75	150	150	175	Chinese Film Star
Wood, Edward F.L.	Political	15	35	50	25	Diplomat/1881-1959
Wood, Evelyn, Sir	Military	20		55		Br.Fld.Marshal (Boer War)
Wood, Fernando 1812-81	Civil War	20	55	75		Civil War Mayor NYC
Wood, Garfield 'Gar'	Science	60		80	75	Boat Designer/Builder
Wood, Grant	Art	150	400	550		American Gothic
Wood, Haydn	Music	20	55	75	35	Composer
Wood, James 1750-1813	RevWar	50	75	125		Governor VA
Wood, Lana	Ent	10	20		25	James Bond Girl
Wood, Leonard, Dr.	Military	25	45	75	150	Roosevelt's Rough Riders
Wood, Murray	Ent	25	35		50	Munchkin in Wiz of Oz
Wood, Natalie 1938-81	Ent	150			400	Died Young

Name	Field	SIG	DS	ALS	SP	Remarks
Wood, Peggy	Ent	20			35	
Wood, Robert	Space	5			15	Astronaut
Wood, Robert E.	Military	20	75			General WWII
Wood, Robert W.	Science	10	25		25	Manhatten Project
Wood, Sam	Ent	40			90	
Wood, Sterling Alex.	Civil War	100	200	300		CSA General
Wood, Thomas J.	Civil War	50	100	100		Union General/1823-1906
Wood, Thomas W.	Art	10	25	50		
Woodbury, Levi 1789-51	SuprCt	65	150	250		
Woodcock, Amos Walter	Military	10			20	General
Woodfill, Samuel	Military	10	30	50	25	WWI
Woodford, Stewart L.	Civil War	35	100	200		Union Officer/1835-1913
Woodhull, Victoria C.	Political	125	250	450		1870's Feminist
Woodring, Henry H.	Political	20	45	70	30	FDR Sect of War
Woods, Charles Robert	Civil War	30	50	75		Union General/1827-85
Woods, Donald	Ent	15	20	35	35	
Woods, James	Ent	20		25	45	
Woods, Phil	Music	15			45	Jazz Alto Sax-Clarinet
Woods, Rose Mary	Political	15		30		Nixon Sec'y. Watergate
Woods, Tiger	Sports	100			300	Golf
Woods, William B.	SuprCt	40	85	150	125	
Woodward, Bob	Author	10	20	35	25	Watergate
Woodward, Edward	Ent	10	15	25	20	
Woodward, Joanne	Ent	15	40		30	AA Winner
Woodward, Robert Burns	Science	20	40	75	35	Nobel Chemistry 1965
Woodworth, Samuel	Author	50	150	275		
Wool, John E. 1789-1869	Civil War	100	200	350		Union General/War of 1812 Veteran
Wooley, Sheb	Music	10			20	
Woolf, Virginia 1882-44	Author	450		1,500	RARE	British Novelist
Woolworth, Charles S.	Business	250	750	Scarce	Scarce	F.W. Woolworth Co.
Woolworth, Frank W.	Business	550	2,500	RARE	RARE	Fndr. F.W. Woolworth Co.
Woorinen, Charles	Music	10	25	40		Composer/Pulitzer
Wooster, David 1710-77	RevWar	250	600	RARE	RARE	General: Continental Army
Wopat, Tom	Ent	10			20	Dukes of Hazzard
Worden, Hank	Ent	15				
Worden, John L.	Civil War	125	175	250		Union Naval Commander
Wordsworth, William	Author	225		1,200		Br. Poet Laureatte
Work, Hubert	Political	20	45	90	35	Sec'y Interior 1923
Worley, Jo Ann	Ent	5			15	Laugh In
Worth, Irene	Ent	10			25	
Worth, William J.	Military	35	75	125		General/Mexican War
Wouk, Herman	Author	45	100	150	125	Am. Novelist/Caine Mutiny
Wray, Fay	Ent	25			50	King Kong
Wren, Christopher	Science	1,500	RARE	RARE	RARE	
Wright, Bobby	Music	5			15	
Wright, Frank Lloyd	Science	900	1,550	RARE	RARE	Architect
Wright, Harold Bell	Author	25			50	Am. Novelist
Wright, Henry C.	Political	10	20	35		1797-1870
Wright, Horatio G.	Civil War	50	150	200		Union General/1820-99

Name	Field	SIG	DS	ALS	SP	Remarks
Wright, Marcus J.	Civil War	125	150	175		CSA General/1831-1922
Wright, Orville 1871-1948	Aviation	500	1,250	1,750	2,000	
Wright, Richard	Author	75	225		375	
Wright, Robin	Ent	25	65		50	
Wright, Teresa	Ent	30			60	AA Winner
Wright, Turbutt 1741-83	RevWar	25	60	75		Continental Congress
Wright, Wilbur 1867-12	Aviation	775	2,000	5,000	4,500	
Wrigley, Philip K.	Business	75	150	200	150	Wrigley Gum; Chicago Cubs
Wrigley, William, Jr.	Business	150	350	400	350	Founder Wrigley Gum Mfg.
Wunderlich, Fritz	Music	150			400	Opera
Wunsche, Max	Military	50			125	Hitlers Adj/WWII
Wyant, Alexander H.	Art	100		300		
Wyatt, Jane	Ent	5			20	Spocks Mom/Star Trek
Wyeth, Andrew	Art	250	450	650	950	Am. Painter
Wyeth, Jamie	Art	125		300	300	Andrews Son
Wyeth, John A.	Science	75		250		Noted Surgeon
Wyeth, N. C. 1882-1945	Art	150	400	800		Am. Illustrator & Painter
Wyler, William	Ent	25	35		75	AA Winning Director
Wylie, Elinor	Author	65	125	250		Am. Poet/Novelist
Wylie, Noah	Ent	15			35	ER
Wylie, Robert 1839-1877	Art	50	150			
Wyllys, Samuel 1739-23	RevWar	20		45		Military. Sec'y State of CT
Wyman, Bill	Music	35		RARE	75	Rolling Stones Bassist
Wyman, Jane	Ent	15			35	
Wyman, Willard G.	Military	15	25	40	25	4 Star General WW II
Wyndham, Charles, Sir	Ent	15	35	45	60	1837-1919
Wynette, Tammy	Music	10			30	Country
Wynn, Ed	Ent	50	100		125	1886 - 1966
Wynn, Keenan	Ent	25	35		45	1916 - 1986
Wynter, Dana	Ent	5			15	
Wysong, Forrest R.	Aviation	10		30	20	
Wythe, George 1726-06	RevWar	450	650	RARE	RARE	Signer

Tennessee Williams

Richard Wagner

Eli Whitney

Orville Wright
Wilbur Wright

Name	Field	SIG	DS	ALS	SP	Remarks
Xenia Alexandrova	Political	75		300		Russia

Name	Field	SIG	DS	ALS	SP	Remarks
Yadin, Yigael	Science	55		85		Archaeologist
Yalow, Rosalyn S.	Science	15	25	40	25	Nobel Medicine 1972
Yamamoto, Isoroku	Military	150		450	475	Pearl Harbor Attack
Yamanashi, Hanzo	Military	100	250			
Yamashiro, Katsumari	Military	100			300	
Yamashita, Tomoyuki	Military	125	275	500	275	Jap. General. Hanged
Yang, Chen N.	Science	15	20	35	20	Nobel Physics 1957
Yang, Y. C.	Political	10			20	
Yankovic, Frank	Ent	5			10	
Yardbirds	Music	150	250		275	Entire Band Signed
Yarnell, Harry E.	Military	15	35		25	Adm. Fleet Commander
Yarnell, Lorine	Ent	5			10	Shields & Yarnell
Yastremski, Carl	Sports	15			35	1989 Baseball HOF
Yates, Edmund 1831-94	Author	5		25		Br. Journalist-Novelist
Yates, Peter W., 1747-26	RevWar	45	125	175		Continental Congress
Yates, Richard 1815-73	Civil War	45	125	200		Civil War Governor IL 1861
Yaw, Ellen Beach	Music	45			175	Am. Soprano
Yeager, Chuck	Aviation	25	50	65	50	WWII ACE/Test Pilot
Yeager, Jeana	Aviation	15			35	
Yearwood, Trisha	Music	15			35	Country
Yeates, Jasper 1745-1817	RevWar	15	35	60		Jurist
Yeats, Jack Butler	Art	25	60	125		Brother/ Wm. Butler Yeats
Yeats, Wm. Butler	Author	200	600	900		Novelist/Poet
Yeltsin, Boris	Political	600	1,200			Russia
Yen, C.K.	Political	50	150			Pres. Republic China
Yeoh, Michelle	Ent	25			50	James Bond babe
Yerby, Frank G.	Author	35	75	150	45	Novelist
Yerkes, Charles	Business	35	100			Capitalist
Yes	Music	60	125		125	Signed by Entire Band
Yo Yo Ma	Music	25			45	Concert Cellist
Yokum, Dwight	Music	15			35	Country
York, Alvin, Sgt. 1887-64	Military	175	250	450	425	

Name	Field	SIG	DS	ALS	SP	Remarks
York, Dick	Ent	25	60		50	Bewitched/Darren
York, Michael	Ent	10	25	25	25	Logans Run
York, Susanna	Ent	10			30	
Youmans, Vincent	Music	75	150	200	150	Composer/Tea for Two
Young, Alan	Ent	5	20	20	15	
Young, Art	Cartoonist	20			45	Political Cartoonist
Young, Brigham 1801-77	Clergy	650	1,500	RARE	RARE	Mormon Leader/Scarce
Young, Burt	Ent	10			20	
Young, Charles Augustus	Science	35	125	200		Am. Astronomer
Young, Chic 1901-73	Cartoonist	35			75	Blondie
Young, Clara Kimball	Ent	40			75	Vintage Stage Actress
Young, Cy	Sports	500	1,000		1,000	1937 Baseball HOF
Young, David H.	Aviation	10	25		35	
Young, Faron	Music	5			15	
Young, Gig	Ent	30	50	75	75	1913 - 1978
Young, Henry E.	Civil War	25	45	70		CSA Officer
Young, John	Space	75			250	Moonwalker
Young, Lester	Music	75		150	150	JAZZ
Young, Loretta	Ent	20			45	
Young, Lyman	Cartoonist	10			25	Tim Tyler's Luck
Young, Neil	Music	25			50	
Young, Owen D. 1874-62	Business	15	25	35	20	
Young, Pierce M.B.	Civil War	100		300		CSA General/1836-96
Young, Robert	Ent	15			45	
Young, Roland	Ent	25			50	
Young, Samuel B.M.	Civil War	30	50	75		Union Officer
Young, Sean	Ent	15			35	
Young, Trummy	Music	15			45	Jazz Musician
Young, Whitney	Political	5	20	45	15	Am. Civil Rights Leader
Younger, Cole	Western	2,000		7,500		

Glenda Jackson

Max Planck

Name	Field	SIG	DS	ALS	SP	Remarks
Zadora, Pia	Ent	10			25	
Zaharias, Babe	Sports	750	1,500		1,500	(Didrikson) 1974 Golf HOF
Zane, Billy	Ent	25			50	Titanic/Phantom
Zanuck, Daryl F. 1902-79	Ent	50			85	Producer/20th Cent. Fox
Zapata, Emiliano	Military	500	1,500	RARE	RARE	Mexican Leader/1879-1919
Zappa, Frank 1940-1993	Music	100	200		200	
Zellwegger, Rene	Ent	25			50	
Zeman, Jacklyn	Ent	5			15	
Zemekis, Robert	Ent	20	50		45	Director/Back to the Future
Zemke, Hubert Hub	Aviation	15			45	WWII Triple ACE
Zeppelin, Ferdinand von	Aviation	275	475			Inventor Dirigible Air Ships
Zhukov, Georgi K.	Military	100			300	Soviet Hero in WWII
Ziegfield, Florenz	Ent	200	350	500	300	1869-1931
Ziegler, George M.	Civil War	40		100		Union General
Zimbalist, Efrem Jr.	Ent	5			15	
Zimbalist, Efrem Sr.	Music	50			150	Composer
Zimbalist, Stephanie	Ent	10			35	Remington Steele
Zinneman, Fred	Ent	35			75	Director/AA Winner
Zola, Emile 1840-1902	Author	200		450	1,500	Fr. Novelist
Zollicoffer, Felix K.	Civil War	300		750		CSA General/KIA
Zukor, Adolph 1873-1976	Ent	50		200	150	Founder Paramount Pix
Zumwalt, Elmo	Military	25	75	125	50	Admiral in WWII
Zweigert, Eugen Lt.	Aviation	100			300	German ACE WWII
Zworykin, Vladimir	Science	60			100	Inventor of the TV System
ZZ Top	Music	45			90	Signed by Entire Group

Emile Zola

Camille Pissarro

Fess Parker

Andrew Jackson

Entertainment Facsimiles

Sharon Adar

Kim Bassinger

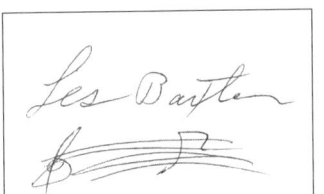

Les Baxter

Harry Belefonte

Milton Berle

Carroll Luna Borland

Peter Boyle

Charles Bronson

Entertainment Facsimiles

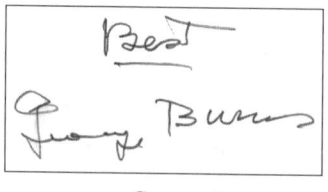

George Burns

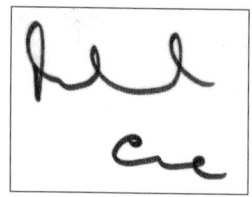

Michael Cain

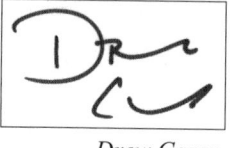

Drew Carey

Johnny Cash

Sid Caesar

Peter Fonda

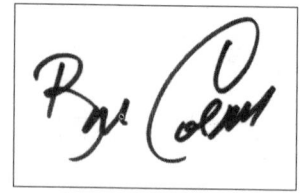

Mae Clarke

Bill Cosby

Entertainment Facsimiles

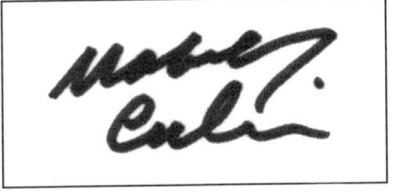

McCauley Culkin

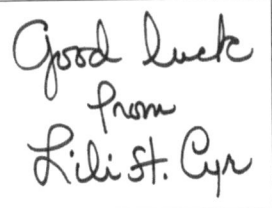

Lili St. Cyr

Douglas Fairbanks, Jr.

Lou Ferrigno

Louise Fletcher

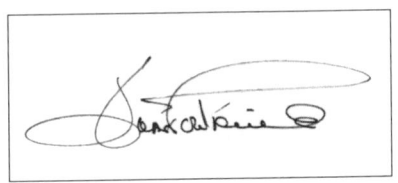

Joan Fontaine

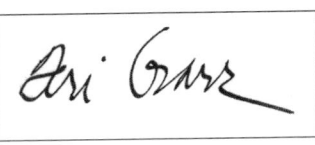

Teri Garr

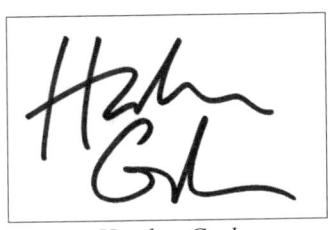

Heather Graham

Entertainment Facsimiles

Charlton Heston

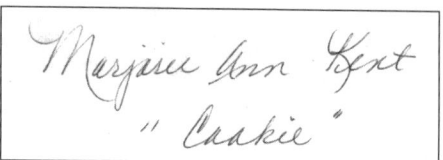

Marjorie Ann Kent

Jack Lemmon

Sophia Loren

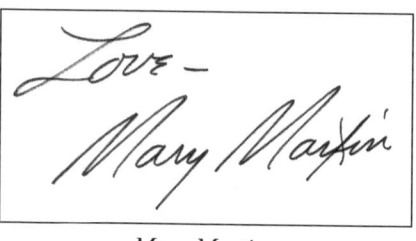

Mary Martin

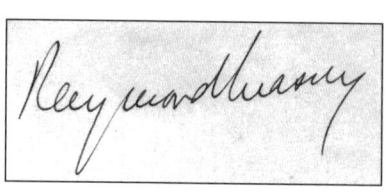

Raymond Massey

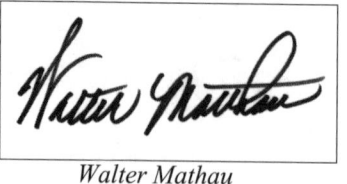

Walter Mathau

Jimmy McCracken

Entertainment Facsimiles

Don McLean

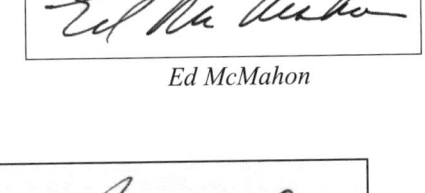

Ed McMahon

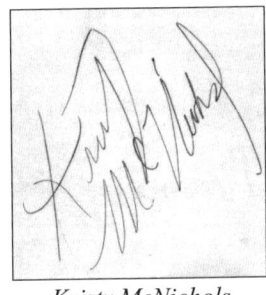

Kristy McNichols

Bill Medley

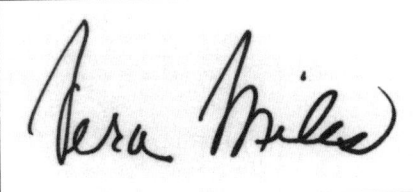

Vera Miles

Liza Minelli

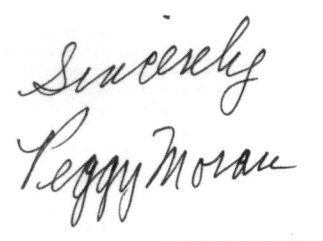

Peggy Moran

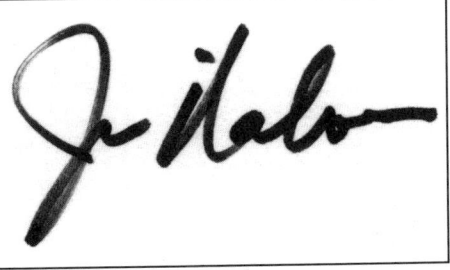

Jim Nabors

Entertainment Facsimiles

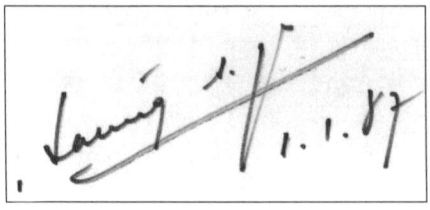

Haing Ngor

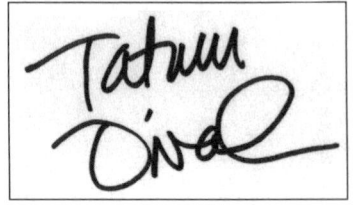

Tatum O'Neal

Pat Paulson

Anthony Quinn

Patricia Richardson

Diana Rigg

John Ritter

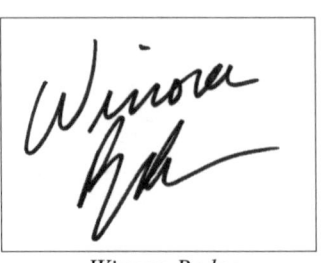

Winona Ryder

Entertainment Facsimiles

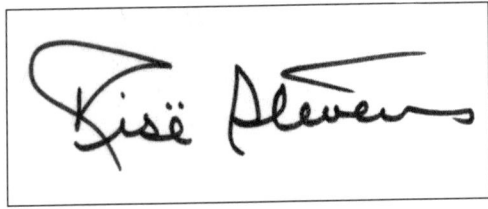

Rise Stevens

Lee Strausman

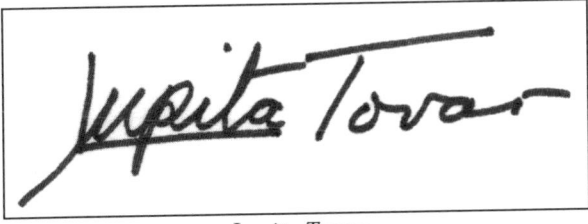

Lupita Tovar

Shannon Tweed

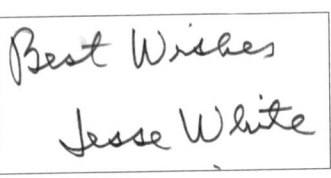

Jesse White

John Williams

Jonathan Winters

Entertainment Facsimiles

Bill Withers

Fay Wray

Jane Wyman

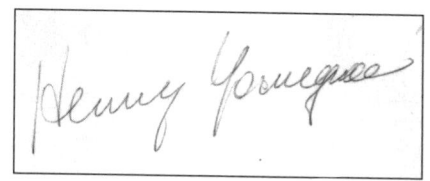

Henny Youngman

Roland Young

Historical Facsimiles

John Jacob Astor

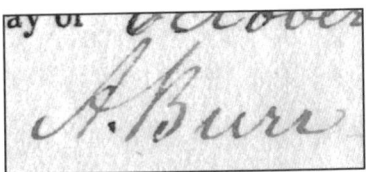

Aaron Burr

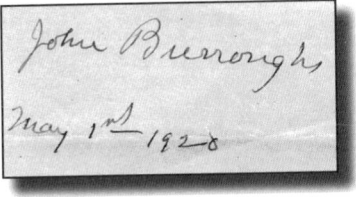

John Burroughs

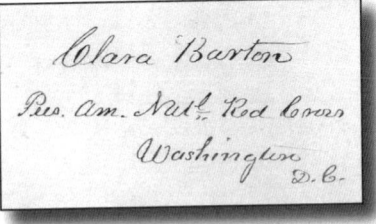

Clara Barton

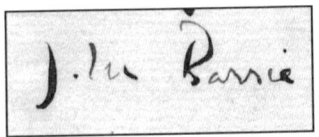

Sir James Barrie

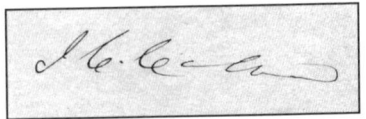

John C. Calhoun

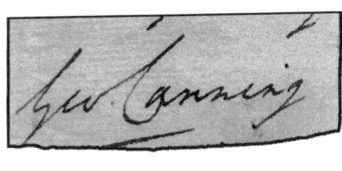

George Canning

Winston Churchill

Historical Facsimiles

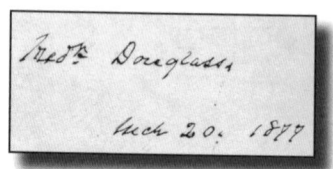

Frederick Douglas

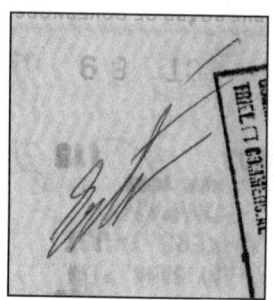

Erte

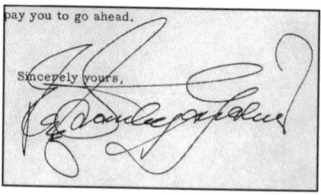

Erle Stanley Gardner

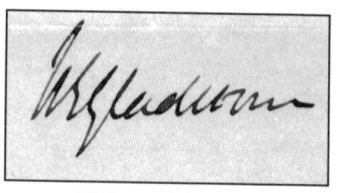

William Gladstone

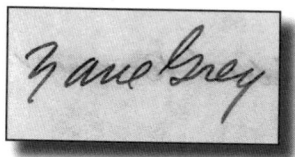

Zane Grey

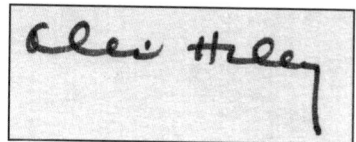

Alex Haley

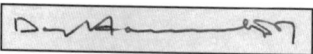

Dag Hammarskjold

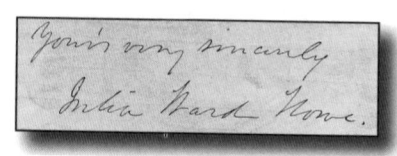

Julia Ward Howe

Historical Facsimiles

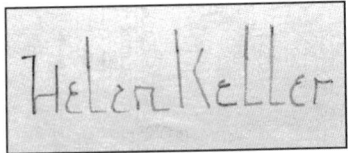

Hellen Keller

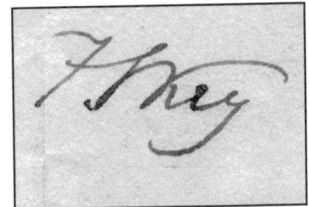

Francis Scott Key

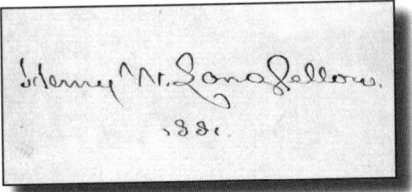

Henry Longfellow

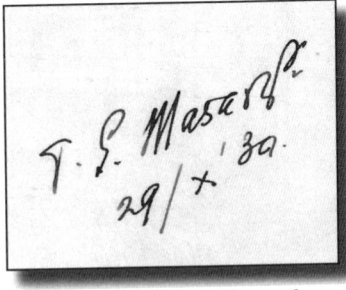

Thomas Masaryk

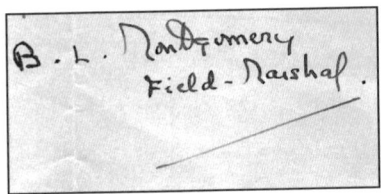

Field Marshall Montgomery

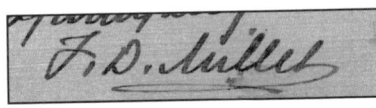

Francis Davis Millet

Picasso

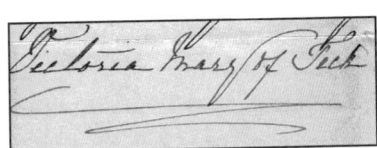

Queen Mary of Teck

Historical Facsimiles

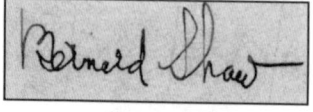

Bernard Shaw

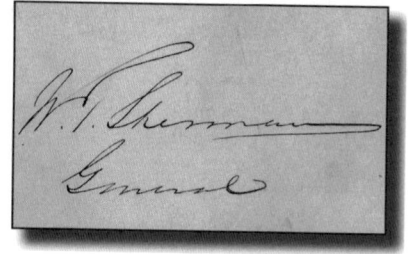

William T. Sherman

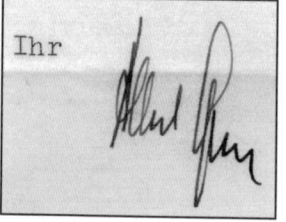

Albert Speer

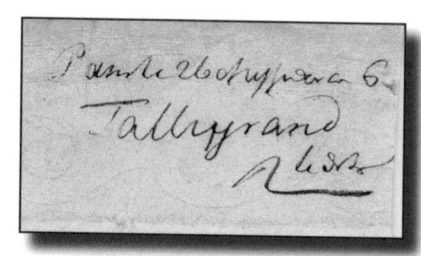

Tallyrand

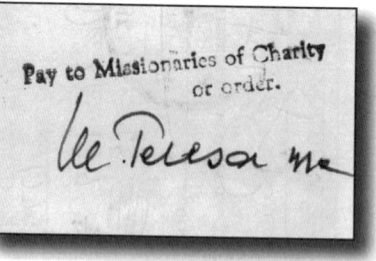

Mother Teresa

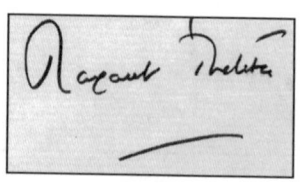

Margaret Thatcher

Space Facsimiles

Buzz Aldrin

Neil Armstrong

Frank Borman

Scott Carpenter

Charles Conrad

Space Facsimiles

Gordon Cooper

Walt Cunningham

Charlie Duke

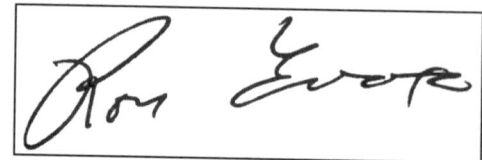

Ron Evans

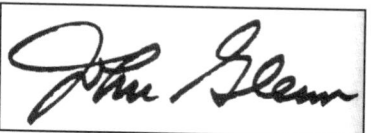

John Glenn

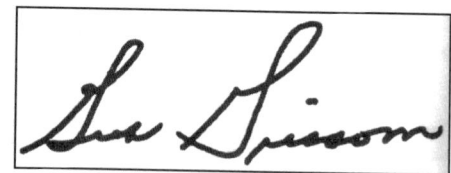

Gus Grissom

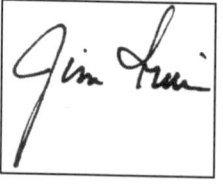

Jim Irwin

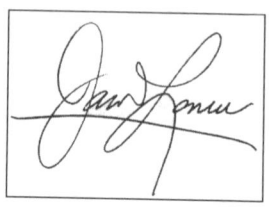

Jim Lovell

Space Facsimiles

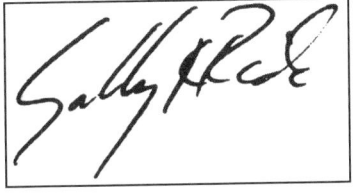

Sally Ride

Wally Schirra

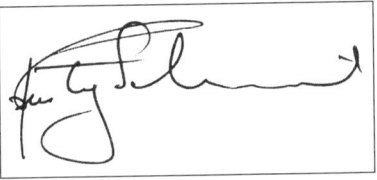

Rusty Schweickart

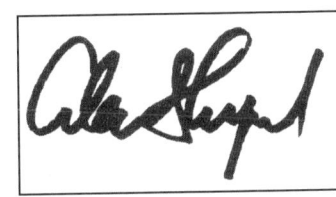

Alan Shepard

Deke Slayton

Edward White

Al Worden

Sports Facsimiles

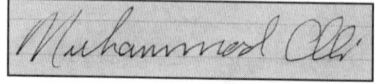

Muhammad Ali

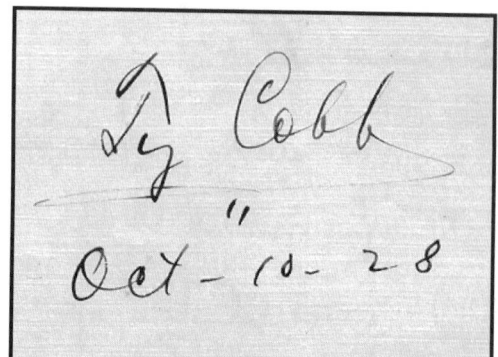

Ty Cobb

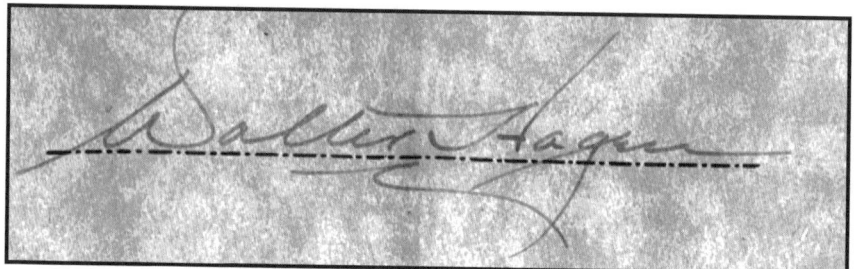

Walter Hagen

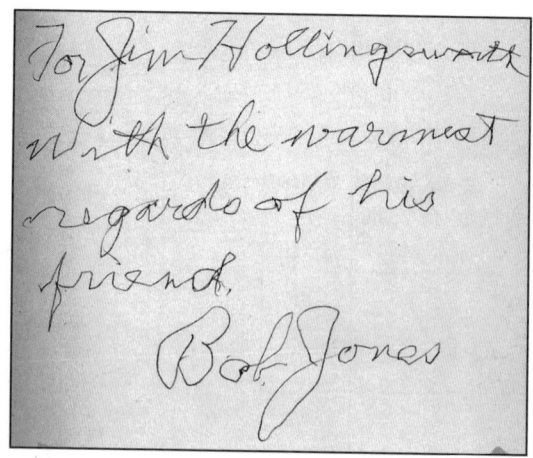

Bob Jones

Sports Facsimiles

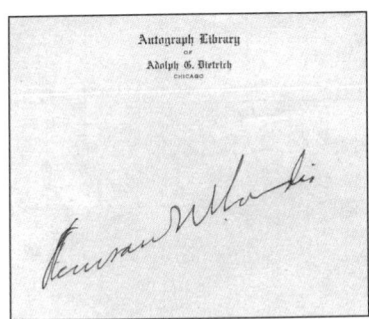

Kennesaw Mountain Landis

Mickey Mantle, Willie Mays, Duke Snider

New York Yankees from the 1955-1967 Season

Jackie Robinson

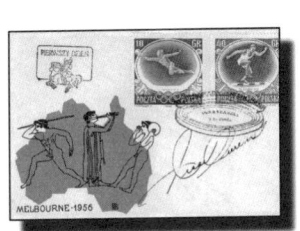

Jessie Owens

Sports Facsimiles

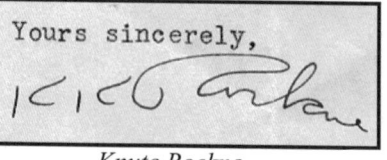

Knute Rockne

Babe Ruth

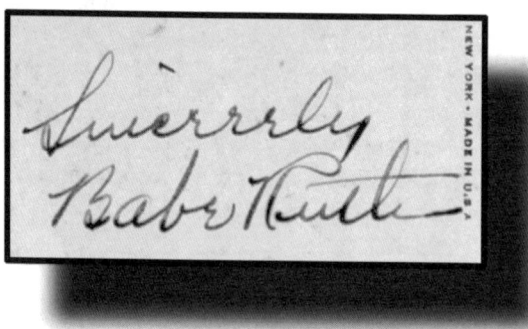

Babe Ruth

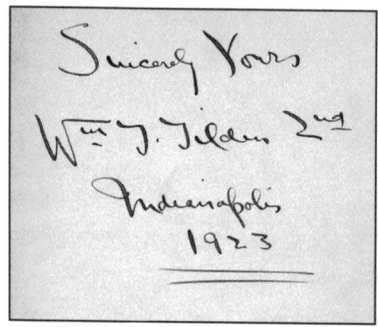

Bill Tilden

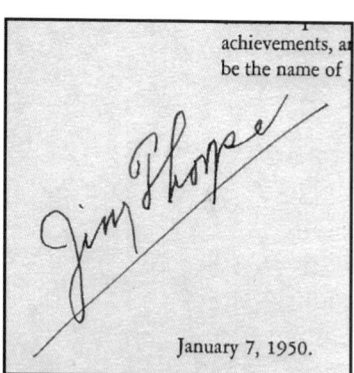

Jim Thorpe

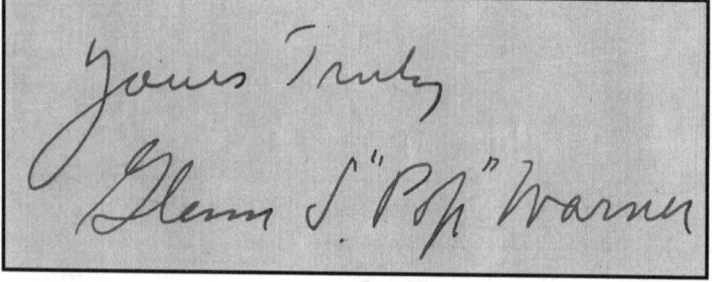

Pop Warner

COLLECTING AUTOGRAPHS THROUGH THE MAIL
by Tony Urban

You want to collect autographs of your favorite stars In Person but you don't live in New York or Los Angeles where there are more opportunities than any other town.

You could buy the ones you admire from a reputable dealer but, you need'nt give up in your quest to get things straight from the star - Here's how I did it with a little money, a little effort and a lot of patience.

In today's high tech world, letter writing has fallen by the wayside, replaced by beepers, faxes, emails, and voice mail. So, pick up the lost art of letter writing and come with me on a fabulous journey.

WHO DO I WRITE ?

The most important question I had to ask myself first when I began collecting autographs in 1991 was who did I want to collect. At the time I was obsessed with baseball so, after being bitten by the autograph bug, I dashed off letters to Ken Griffey Jr., Mark McGwire, Roger Clemens, Greg Maddux, etc... Nearly four months later, I received my first autograph from ... Dave Dravecky. WHO YOU ASK? Well, if your not

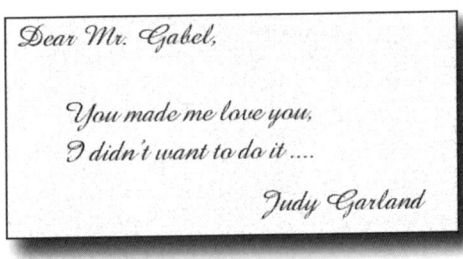

a baseball fan, the name likely does not ring any bells. He was a pitcher for the San Francisco Giants whose off field battle with cancer ended his career and cost him his arm. It is still the most treasured piece in my autograph collection but, it also proved a good point quickly to me. Dravecky was in fact the ONLY one of the over twenty requests that i sent out that I got ANY response to.

With my success rate under five percent, many would have given up.

Lesson? Do NOT write to the superstars in any given field and expect a quick response, any response or authentic responses, in many cases.

Whether its Ken Griffey Jr. (baseball) or Michael Jordon (basketball) or

Steve Young (football), Brad Pitt in movies or Bill Clinton our illustrious leader, if you shoot for the moon, you're probably going to crash and burn.

That's the downsize to collecting autographs through the mail. The top celebrities can get ten thousand requests a week and more !

They have busy lives and we can NOT expect them to answer all of their mail. If they did, they couldnt be out hitting home runs, scoring goals, filming movies or leading the free world.

So, what's an inventive collector to do? Research !!! Most superstars rise up in their careers like everyone else startingg at the bottom and working up the ladder rung by rung. If you are into sports, subscribe to some magazines and find out who the top college athletes are and write to them. Today's all American could be tommorrows most valuable player.

If you are into movies, write to the supporting actors, especially TV stars or soap stars. While Kelsey Grammer, Ricky Martin, Anne Heche or Catherine Zeta-Jones are all already superstars they all started with small roles on screen. Write to Governors and Cabinet Members BEFORE they become the next President..stay one step ahead of the game.

WHERE DO I FIND THE ADDRESSES ?

This is easy. So easy I should send you to a library to do your own leg work but as I am a nice guy, Ill give it to you on a silver platter.

Buy "Autograph Collector" maga-zine where each month they list over 100 celebrity addresses in the magazine. They also have advertisements for address lists, all available for less than one good reponse will be worth to you later.

Buy the "Information Please Almanac" and the "Information Please Sports Almanac" two great resources which an autograph collector MUST have. Inside you will find addresses for every major TV network, sports team, college team, Hall of Fame, and dozens more.

And if your so cheap that you don't want to do any of the above, surf the internet instead. But the old phrase "You get what you pay for" is appropriate here. Beware also of bad addresses. Most internet sites are rarely updated, so the hard earned money you saved by not buying an address list can be lost in the dreaded RTS (Return to Sender)

WHAT DO I SAY IN THE LETTER?

You know now who you are going to write and have found their address, the letter you write now is by far the most important aspect of collecting autographs in the mail. First, here are some general guidelines on etiquette.

Should you write the letter by hand or type it? If your handwriting is hards to read you should type it but a handwritten letter does tell the celebrity that you took those extra minutes and that you are not using a form letter.

> Dear Madonna,
>
>   I hoped you could sign your album "Thriller" for my nephew.
>
>   Yours,
>   A truly stupid person

If you do plan on typing the letter, again, don't use one of those fancy fonts instead use something big and easy to read, like Times Roman or Courier. If your printing the letter from a computer, make sure your ribbon is fresh not pale and hard to see. PLEASE PLEASE DO NOT make your letter a form letter where all you change is the celebritys name. It is tacky and insulting to use a form letter and gives autograph collectors a bad name !

Now the most important part of the letter is its content. What you say depends of course on who you are writing and why. If you are writing former President George Bush because you are also 75 years old and seeing him parachute recently on his birthday inspired you to do the same, then tell him that in your letter. Heck, enclose a picture of you in your jumpsuit even. The more personal your letter is the more chance of a response.

But, do NOT get too personal. Tell Cindy Crawford she is beautiful but not the parts of her anatomy you admire most..your letter could end up in the stars "special" files and believe me they do exist.

If your writing to Charlton Heston, don't say things like "you're my favorite actor". Even if thats true, it sounds corny and he hears it all the time. Instead tell him that "Ben Hur" was the first film you saw at a theatre or that every Easter your family watches the "Ten Commandments". Put thought into it. After all, if you are writing for a persons autograph you should have a good reason.

Make the letter short and sweet. While there are dozens of celebrities that I could write five page letters to, I do not. Why? It's a time issue, would YOU read a five page rambling letter from a stranger? Especially if you received stacks every day? You'd probably throw them in the trash can and while doing just that your eyes fall upon a half page letter..oh the joy, the person who writes one like that must understand how busy you are and you just might reward them with your autograph.

How do you ask for the autograph? Coming right out and asking is not rude, just ask. Something like "Would you please autograph the enclosed card or photo for my collection?" works wonders. Your being polite which matters most.

Ready to write your letter now? Not so fast..double check to make sure your facts are correct. Don't tell Neve Campbell you loved her in "Two to Tango" when the film was called "Three to Tango". Little things count and even a minor mistake can destroy your credibility.

Last, but not least, is grammer and spelling. Use a program to check it or a friend to proof read it and keep a dictionary by your side but most importantly SPELL the celebrity's name correctly! It seems silly to stress but you would not believe the people who write to Cathy Bates or Kevin Kostner. People have even written to me asking for the address of Jody Foster and William DeFoe. Look it up and check it twice.

WHERE DO I SEND IT AND HOW DO I SEND IT ?

Prepare the package right or dont bother to do it at all. First use TWO envelopes and TWO stamps for every request you send out. One for the items you mail and one for the celebrity to return it in. Be SURE you enclose a SASE which means a stamped self addressed envelope for the celeb to use. Without a SASE your chances are slim on getting ANY responses at all.

Make sure your postage is calculated correctly on BOTH envelopes so all your effort doesn't end up in the Post Office Dead Letter box.

What do you enclose with your letter for them to sign?

What you send is a matter of personal preference. I know of collectors who send out only 8x10 photographs to everyone they write.

But, most of us cant afford to do that so what else can you send? Magazine photographs, trading cards, and more. At the very least, send a blank index card (cheap at $1.00 per 100) That way, you've given the celebrity something to autograph just in case they don't have anything of their own to send you.

You can always ask the celebrity to send you a signed photograph of themselves and many will oblige but if you do always remember to enclose a 9x12 SASE with 78 cents postage on it. (Check with your post office as this may be outdated).

You are about to drop your package in the mail so do this last minute check list.

1. Write Photos/Do Not Bend on the outside of Both of your envelopes. This should give you a little extra protection from the post office handlers.

2. Double check the address of the celebrity and be sure it is error free.

3. Put YOUR return address in the upper left corner of the envelope. Celebrities move on average more often than regular folk but even if they have moved, as long as your return address is listed, you will atleast get your precious package and SASE back to use in another request.

Now What ?

Remember how I said in the beginning you needed patience too?

Now is the time for that..the Wait !

The bane of every collectors existence and I can not tell you how long the wait will be either. Ive had responses in only THREE DAYS and Ive had them take FOUR YEARS. Quite a range huh? But do not despair you will survive the wait. I know you can do it !

Write lots of letters as the more you mail the better your chances of responses.

My personal record was to write seventy letters in one day ! But it was worth it as I started getting more than one response per day in my mailbox!

You now have autographs sticking out of your mailbox when the most important question begins to cross your mind..is it real?

You are bound to receive both real and non-genuine responses. It happens to us all so dont feel badly.

For a beginning collector determining the legitemacy of an autograph can be tough.

The more you read on the subject and more authentic examples you collect up to compare yours to the better chance you will have of authenticating it.

Besides being genuine it might be :

1. An Autopen - This is a machine which perfectly reproduces a person's signature. Some signs you have one are a heavy glob of ink at the beginning and end of a signature, an overall shakiness, a few dots at the beginning of the signature (although these traits may not be present at all). Also any TWO autographs made by an autopen machine will match PERFECTLY.

2. Rubber Stamp - Just like it sounds, a rubber stamp signature is made by pressing the rubber stamp to the card, photograph etc.. and is easily detected by looking carefully at the signature (use a magnifying glass to make this easier) and you will see that there are no strokes, that it isn't fluid like a real signature.

3. Steel Stamp - Similar to a rubber stamp it also has tell-tale signs like often leaving an indentation that can be seen on the back of the photograph.

4. Secretarial - The toughest to discern as it is a real autograph just not by the person you had hoped ! The only way to tell this from a real one is by comparison to known authentic examples.

5. Preprinted - This is a common one these days. The celebrity signs an actual photograph and then makes prints from this one. The magnifying glass should show you there are no depths to these looking very flat unlike a real one.

In Closing,

Once you begin to get autographs frequently, it will become an addiction. The more autographs you receive, the more you need to have. You'll watch for the mail to come with great anticipation. You'll start trying to determine who sent you a response just based on the postmark. You'll get to know everyone at your post office on a first name basis. You will think of better and more ingenious ways to get those tougher signers to answer YOUR letter. The longer you collect the better you get. You'll never tire of tearing open those envelopes !

So, What are you waiting for ?

Mr. Urban can be reached in care of :
Odyssey Publications, Inc.
510-A So. Corona Mall. Corona, California 91719
where he is a monthly columnist for Autograph Collector magazine.
Go to http://www.Autographs.com for free addresses and start writing!

SPECIALIZING
by Kevin Martin

It's an ugly word to some collectors who want one of everything but the fact is deciding to specialize is a question all of us must face eventually. (maybe not Malcolm Forbes but any of us without unlimited funds).

Many collectors start out believing in ernest that they will collect the top names in many fields and soon learn that this is a tougher task than it originally appears to be. Specializing limits your focus but certainly need not limit the variety of names in your collection or the fun in obtaining them all.

Some more popular specialties include all the US Presidents, every Oscar winner, every Congressman, Rock and Roll Hall of Famer, Hall of Famers in various sports fields, country music legends, mystery writers, animators and cartoonists, directors, opera stars, military leaders (you might even want to pick one conflict) etc.

Even narrowing your prospects down to these examples will leave you needing hundreds or thousands of examples in your collection or hundreds and thousands of dollars to obtain the ones you need.

These days more and more dealers have begun to specialize also realizing that if they deal in all fields they certainly can not be considered an expert in them all.

Some dealers and collectors have even narrowed their focus to one celebrity like The Beatle's or Harry Houdini or John F. Kennedy (as opposed to all rock bands, all magicians or all Presidents).

If you should ever decide to sell your collection at auction or privately to a dealer or another collector, you will find that a focused well thought out collection will bring more interest and often more money then a collection consisting of a little bit of this and a little bit of that.

There are almost limitless fields in which to specialize so I will close by giving you a few more that I am often encountering with collectors.

Western Stars
Musicians who have had number one records
Gone with the Wind cast members as well as
Casablanca and Wizard of Oz
Women who have starred opposite Elvis Presley in movies
Heavy weight Champions
People who have played Tarzan
Our Gang/Little Rascal children stars

The cast over the years of Saturday Night Live (over 100)
Television casts
Vice-Presidents
First Ladies
Financial Barons
Artists
Cartoonists
Signers of the Declaration of Independence
Civil War Generals in Grey or in Blue
Authors in various fields
and as much more as the imagination will allow you!

Happy Collecting !

Kevin Martin is the editor of this price guide as well as the author of numerous other books and articels in the field of autograph collcting. His comapny, Piece of thePast, Inc. offers monthly no minimum bid auctions as well as fixed price catalogs.
He can be reached by calling toll free 1-888-689-7079 or by going to www.pieceofthepast.com

REFERENCE TABLES FOR COLLECTORS
100 Greatest Movies
Of All Time

Many people try to create this tough list every year, from video stores to the venerable American Film Institute. No matter who takes the poll or who contributes to its content there are always arguments as to why a particular film made the list or didn't !

This is the 100 Greatest Movies of All Time according to an informal poll of dealers and collectors taken over the past year. As an autograph collector this is an invaluable list for focusing your collecting. Wouldn't it be great to own complete casts signatures form each one? And very fun to collect as well !

(I hope your favorite is on this list)

1. Gone with the Wind
2. The Godfather
3. Star Wars
4. ET
5. Schindlers List
6. Snow White and the Seven Dwarfs
7. 2001 A Space Odyssey
8. Sunset Boulevard
9. The Maltese Falcon
10. The Wizard of Oz
11. It Happened One Night
12. Alien
13. Casablanca
14. Chinatown
15. The Grapes of Wrath
16. The Wizard of Oz
17. Philadelphia Story
18. Taxi Driver
19. Some Like it Hot
20. Psycho
21. Dr. Strangelove
22. On the Waterfront

100 Greatest Movies Of All Time (cont.)

23. Gone with the Wind
24. Raging Bull
25. Lawrence of Arabia
26. North by Northwest
27. The Bridge on the River Kwai
28. The Third Man
29. To Kill a Mockingbird
30. Tootsie
31. Annie Hall
32. Jaws
33. King Kong
34. Silence of the Lambs
35. Bonnie and Clyde
36. Last of the Mohicans
37. Mildred Pierce
38. Great Expectations
39. Hello Dolly
40. Notorious
41. It's a Wonderful Life
42. Raging Bull
43. Citizen Kane
44. Mr. Smith Goes to Washington
45. Vertigo
46. Singing in the Rain
47. The Manchurian Candidate
48. Duck Soup
49. The Adventures of Sherlock Holmes
50. The Adventures of Robin Hood
51. Close Encounters of the Third Kind
52. Dracula
53. Frankenstein
54. The Mummy
55. The Graduate
56. The Wild Bunch
57. Gunfight at the OK Corral
58. Airplane

100 Greatest Movies
Of All Time (cont.)

59. Henry V
60. Harvey
61. Back to the Future
62. Rocky
63. Pulp Fiction
64. The Gold Rush
65. Cat on a Hot Tin Roof
66. Miracle on 34th Street
67. Guess Whose Coming to Dinner?
68. Ghostbusters
69. One Flew Over the Cukoos Nest
70. The African Queen
71. From Here to Eternity
72. Breakfast at Tiffany's
73. Raiders of the Lost Ark
74. Animal House
75. Saturday Night Fever
76. Streetcar Named Desire
77. A Star is Born
78. Halloween
79. Ten Commandments
80. West Side Story
81. Grand Hotel
82. My Fair Lady
83. Sound of Music
84. Mutiny on the Bounty
85. The Best Years of Our Lives
86. The Sting
87. Patton
88. Butch Cassidy and the Sundance Kid
89. Amadeus
90. Titanic
91. Rain Man
92. Risky Business
93. Terms of Endearment
94. On the Waterfront

100 Greatest Movies Of All Time (cont.)

95. All Quiet on the Western Front
96. Batman
97. Lethal Weapon
98. Terminator
99. Dr. No
100. Pink Panther

100 Greatest Entertainers

Like the last Table of the greatest movies to collect, this one taken from informal collector/dealer polls may help the investor know what to have in a collection or the in the mail enthusiast know who to write to try and get a response from..it is meant as fun food for thought ! We allowed our "Greatest" list to include a few behind the scenes folk like Directors.   Enjoy !

1. The Beatles
2. The Rolling Stones
3. Elvis Presley
4. The Beach Boys
5. Marilyn Monroe
6. James Dean
7. Steven Spielberg
8. Frank Sinatra
9. Madonna
10. John Belushi
11. Lucille Ball and Desi Arnaz
12. Bob Dylan
13. Michael Jackson
14. John Wayne
15. Marlon Brando
16. Orson Welles
17. Mae West
18. Prince
19. Barbra Streisand
20. Alfred Hitchcock
21. Jimmy Stewart
22. Katherine Hepburn
23. Audrey Hepburn
24. Roy Rogers
25. Gene Autry
26. Elizabeth Taylor
27. Greta Garbo
28. Al Pacino
29. Robert Deniro

James Dean

Alfred Hitchcock

James Stewart

Audrey Hepburn

Greta Garbo

100 Greatest
Entertainers
(cont.)

30. Jack Nicholson
31. Robert Redford
32. Demi Moore
33. Bruce Willis
34. Paul Newman
35. Gary Oldman
36. Kevin Spacey
37. Woody Allen
38. Clint Eastwood
39. Charles Bronson
40. Humphrey Bogart
41. James Brown
42. Harrison Ford
43. William Shatner
44. Richard Pryor
45. Meryl Streep
46. Tom Hanks
47. Francis Ford Coppola
48. Nicolas Cage
49. John Travolta
50. Johnny Carson
51. Jackie Gleason
52. Red Skelton
53. Tom Cruise
54. Jimi Hendrix
55. Janis Joplin
56. Jim Morrison
57. Dustin Hoffman
58. Milton Berle
59. Bob Hope
60. George Burns
61. Jerry Seinfeld
62. Dick Van Dyke
63. Jim Henson

Woody Allen

Francis Ford Coppola

Nicolas Cage

Milon Berle

Jim Henson

100 Greatest Entertainers (cont.)

64. Errol Flynn
65. Jim Carrey
66. Julia Roberts
67. Jodie Foster
68. Sean Connery
69. Carol Burnett
70. The Supremes
71. Robin Williams
72. The Grateful Dead
73. Mel Brooks
74. Garth Brooks
75. James Cameron
76. Arnold Scwarzenegger
77. Gene Kelly
78. Vincent Price
79. Vivien Leigh
80. Clark Gable
81. Johnny Cash
82. Spencer Tracy
83. Bela Lugosi
84. Boris Karloff
85. Judy Garland
86. Lon Chaney Jr.
87. Lon Chaney Sr.
88. Jennifer Jones
89. Joan Crawford
90. Bette Davis
91. Jimmy Cagney
92. Grace Kelly
93. Anthony Hopkins
94. Henry Fonda
95. Kirk Douglas
96. Sylvester Stallone
97. Burt Lancaster

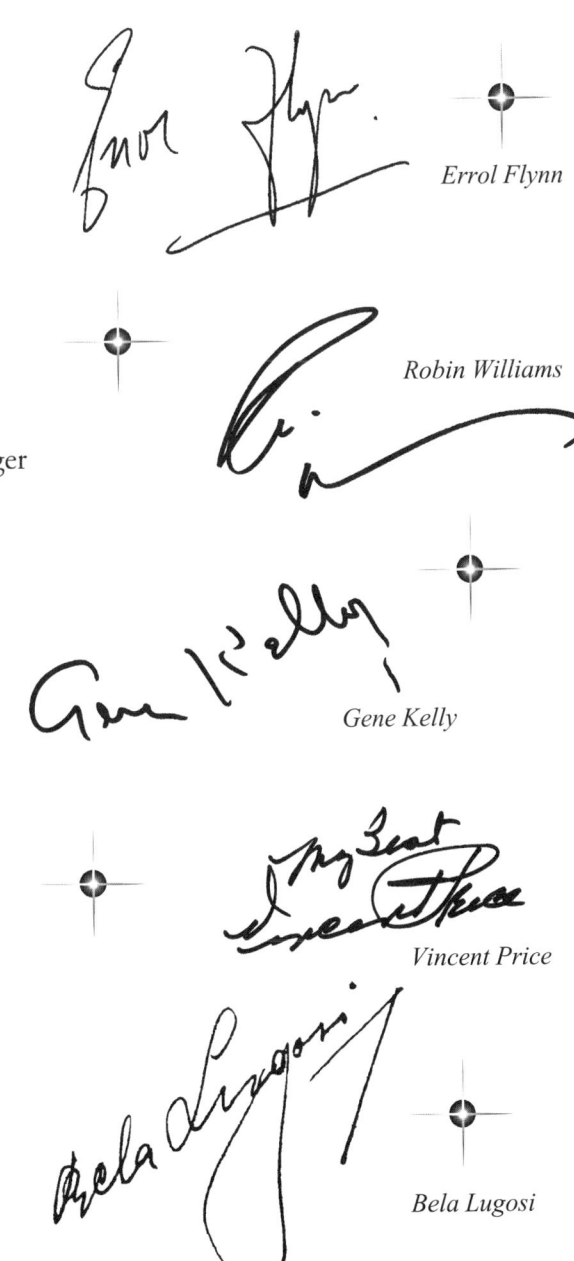

Errol Flynn

Robin Williams

Gene Kelly

Vincent Price

Bela Lugosi

100 Greatest
Entertainers
(cont.)

98. Johnny Weismuller
99. Brad Pitt
100. Leonardo DiCaprio

Johnny Weismuller

Brad Pitt

Kirk Dougls

Bette Davis

Henry Fonda

Boris Karloff

REVOLUTIONARY WAR GENERALS

George Washington of course was our Commander in Chief aided by the following Generals:

Allen, Ethan
Armand, Charles T.
Armstrong, John Sr.
Arnold, Benedict
Baylor, George
Borre, Prudhomme de
Broadhead, Daniel
Butler, Richard
Clark, George Rogers
Clark, Thomas
Clinton, George
Clinton, James
Conway, Thomas
Crane, John
Davidson, William
Dayton, Elias
DuCoudray, Phillipe
Duportail, The Chevalier
Elbert, Samuel
Febiger, Samuel
Frye, Joseph
Gadsden, Christopher
Gates, Horatio
Gibson, John
Gist, Mordecai
Glover, John
Greaton, John
Green, Nathaniel
Gunby, John
Haas, John Philip de

Hand, Edward
Hazen, Moses
Heath, William
Hogan, James
Howard, John E.
Howe, Robert
Huger, Isaac
Humpton, Richard
Huntington, Jedediah
Irvine, William
Jackson, Henry
Jackson, Michael
Kalb, Baron John de
Knox, Henry
Kosciuszko, Thaddeus
Lafayette, Marquis de
Lamb, John
Laumoy, Monsieur de
Learned, Ebenezer
Lee, Charles
Lee, Henry
Lewis, Andrew
Lincoln, Benjamin
Marion, Francis
Matthews, George
Maxwell, William
McDougall, Alexander
McIntosh, Lachlan
Mercer, Hugh
Mifflin, Thomas

REVOLUTIONARY WAR GENERALS

Montgomery, Richard
Moore, James
Morgan, Daniel
Moultrie, William
Moylan, Stephen
Muhlenberg, Peter M.
Nash, Francis
Neuville, The Chevalier
Nevil, John
Nicola, Lewis
Nixon, John
Ogden, Mathias
Parsons, Samuel Holland
Paterson, John
Pickens, Andrew
Pinckney, Charles
Poor, Enoch
Pulaski, Count Casimir
Putnam, Israel
Putnam, William
Reed, James
Reed, Joseph
Rochefermoy, Chevalier
Russell, William
Schuyler, Philip
Scott, Charles
Sheldon, Elisha
Shepard, William
Smallwood, William

Spencer, Joseph
St. Clair, Arthur
Stark, John
Stephen, Adam
Steuben, Baron von
Stewart, Walter
Stirling, Lord
Sullivan, John
Sumner, Jethro
Sumter, Thomas
Swift, Herman
Thomas, John
Thompson, William
Tupper, Benjamin
Van Cortland, Philip
Van Schaick, Gozen
Varnum, James M.
Vose, Joseph
Ward, Artemus
Warren, Joseph
Wayne, Anthony
Weedon, George
Webb, Samuel B.
Wilkinson, James
Williams, Otho Holland
Woedtke, Baron de
Woodford, William
Wooster, David

Signers of the United Nations Charter

In San Francisco, on June 26, 1945, delegates from 50 nations met at the now legendary United Nations Conference and signed the final charter that would make history in establishing the United Nations.

Six delegates that were on the "official" list to sign the charter did not, making the actual document signed by only 147 of the 153 that where to sign.

From one to seven delegates signed representing their individual countries.

Incidentally, a space for the country of Poland was included in the original document but was not signed by a delegate that day. (It was signed by a representative of Poland on October 15, 1945)

Here are the names in the order in which they appear on the charter document.

1. CHINA - V.K.Wellington Koo, Wang Chung-Hui, Wai Tao-ming, Miss Wu Yi-fang, Li Hwang, Chun-mai Carson Chang, Tung Pi-wu, Hu Lin.
2. USSR (Russia) - A.A. Gromyko, A.I.Lavrentiev, K.V. Nokikov, S.K. Tsarapkin, S.A. Golunsky, S.B. Krylov, Rear Admiral K.K. Rodionov
3. United Kingdon - The Earl of Halifax, The Viscount of Cranborne.
4. United States of America - Edward Stettinius, Tom Connally, Arthur Vandenberg, Sol Bloom, Charles Eaton, Harols E. Stassen and Virginia C. Gildersleeve.
5. France - Joseph Paul-Boncour
6. Argentina - Miguel Angel Carcano, Oscar Ibarra Garcia, Juan Carlos Bassi, Alberto C. Brunot.
7. Australia - Francis Michael Forde, Herbert Vere Evatt.
8. Belgium - Auguste de Schryver
9. Bolivia - Victor Andrade, Eduardo Arze Quiroga, Carlos Salamanca.
10. Brazil - Pedro Leao Velloso, Cyro de Freitas Valle, Estevo Leitao de Carvalho, Antonio Camillo de Oliveira, Dr. Bertha Lutz.
11. Byelorussia - Kuzma Benedzitkovich Kiselev, Anton R. Zhebrak, Vladimir N. Pertsev, Georgi I. Baidakov, Frol P. Shmygav
12. Canada - William Lyon Mackenzie King, Louis Stephen St.Laurent
13. Chile - Joaquin Fernandez, Marcial Mora, Jose Maza, Gabriel Gonzalez-Videla, Carlos Contreras-Labarca, Feliz Nieto del Rio, Enrique Alcalde, German Vergara, Julio Escudero.
14. Colombia - Alberto Lleras Camargo, Alberto Gonzalez Fernandez, Eduardo Zuleta Angel, Silvio Villegas, Jesus Maria Yepes.
15. Costa Rica - Julio Acosta Garcia, J. Rafael Oreamuno.

16. Cuba - Guillermo Belt Ranmirez, Ernesto Dihigo Lopez Trigo.
17. Czechoslovakia - Jan Masaryk.
18. Denmark - Henrik Kauffman, Hartvig Frisch, Erik Husfeldt.
19. Dominican Republic - Manuel Pena Batlle, Emilio Garcia Godoy, Gilberto Sanchez Lustrino, Tulio Franco y Franco, Minerva Bernardino
20. Ecuador - Camilo Ponce Enriquez, Galo Plaza Lasso, Carlos Tobar Zaldumbride
21. Egypt - Abdel Hamid Pasha Badawi, Ibrahim Pasha Abdel Hadi
22. El Salvador - Hector David Castro, Carlos Leiva
23. Ethiopia - Ato Aklilou Abte-Wold, Ato Ambaye Wolde Mariam, Blatta Ephrem Tewelde Medhen
24. Greece - John Sofianipoulos
25. Guatemala - Guillermo Toriello, Manuel Noriega Morales, Eugenio Silva Pena
26. Haiti - Gerard E. Lescot, Andre Liautaud
27. Honduras - Julian R. Caceres, Marcos Carias Reyes, Virgilio R. Galvez.
28. India - Sir A. Ramaswami Mudaliar, V.T. Krishnamachari
29. Iran - Mostalfa Adle
30. Iraq - Fadhil Jamali
31. Lebanon - Wadih Naim, Abdauah Yafi, Joseph Salem, Charles Habib Malik
32. Liberia - C.L. Simpson, Gabriel L.Dennis, Lemuel Gibson, Richard Henries, Moses Grant
33. Luxembourg - Hugues Le Gallais
34. Mexico - Ezequiel Padilla, Francisco Castillo Najera, Manuel Tello
35. Netherlands - Alexander Loudon
36. New Zealand - Peter Fraser, Carl Berendsen
37. Nicauagua - Mariano Arguello Vargas, Luis Manuel de Bayle
38. Norway - Wilhelm Munthe Morgenstierne
39. Panama - Roberto Jimenez
40. Paraguay - Celso R. Velazquez, Juan Batista Ayala
41. Peru - Manuel C. Gallagher, Victor Andres Belaunde, Luis Fernan Cisneros
42. Phillipines - Carlos P. Romulo, Francisco Delgado
43. Saudi Arabia - HRH Faisal Ibn Abdul Aziz
44. Syria - Faris Al-Khouri, Naim al-Antaki, Nazim al-Kodsi
45. Turkey - Hasan Saka, Huseyin Ragip Baydur, Feridun Cemal Erkin.
46. Ukranian Republic - Dmitro Z. Manuilsky, Ivan S. Senin, Alexander V. Palladin, Mikola N. Petrovsky
47. South Africa - Jan Christian Smuts
48. Uraguay - Jose Serrato, Jacobo D. Varela, Hector Luisi, Cyro Giambruno, Juan F. Guichon, Hector Paysse Reyes
49. Venezuela - Caracciola Parra-Perez, Gustavo Herrera, Alfredo Machado-Hernandez, Rafael Ernesto Lopez.
50. Yugoslavia - Stanoje Simic

BIBLIOGRAPHY

The Autograph Collector Celebrity Autograph Guide, by Kevin Martin
Authentic Examples of over 1,000 Celebrity Autographs,

        288pages , 8.5" x 11" format
        ISBN# 0-9669710-1-9 $22.95
         (in bookstores or order from publisher)
        Publisher : Odyssey Publications
              510A S. Corona Mall
              Corona, CA 91719
          (Phone 1-800-996-3977)
       *If ordering from publisher additional Shipping &
       Handling will be added.

Signatures of the Stars, by Kevin Martin
An Insider's Guide to Celebrity Autographs,
208pages, 6" x 9" format
ISBN# 0-930625-93-5 $16.95
(in bookstores or order from author)
Publisher : Antique Trader Books
Direct Order Information   1-888-689-7079
                       Piece of the Past, Inc.
                       9709 Tumble Lake CT.
                       Las Vegas, NV 89117

Collecting Autographs & Manuscripts, by Charles Hamilton
ISBN# 0-929-246-05-5
Published by: Modoco Press, Inc.
        Santa Monica, CA

Signature House

We will guarantee you will be happy in dealing with us. We are pleased to offer our:

You have to be happy with your purchase of any lot or send it back in the same condition within seven business days. We will refund your full purchase price including commission.

Because of our lifetime guarantee of authenticity, should your purchase of any autographs, documents, letters or collectibles prove not authentic, we will refund the full purchase price plus the commission ... providing it comes back to us in the same condition.

You can feel safe with a Signature House auction through our Catalogue, Internet, or Private Treaty sales. You can be sure with our GOLDEN GUARANTEE. Plus, our bidders receive a free catalogue.

Call or write TODAY to get a complimentary catalog.

CONSIGNORS! We have one of the most competitive commission rates in the industry. And now with our GOLDEN GUARANTEE, you can be assured of more sales. And our quick payment means:

A low-cost to you for sale of your items

A higher chance to sell your item with our GOLDEN GUARANTEE

A faster pay-off to you.

407 Liberty Avenue
Bridgeport, WV 26330
Phone (304) 842-3386 • Fax: (304) 842-3001
Webpage: www.signaturehouse.net

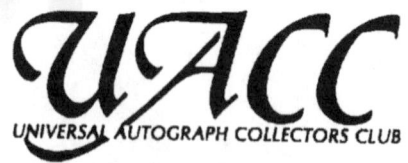

AN INVITATION TO JOIN

The Manuscript Society

The Manuscript Society is an international society
whose members cover all fields of
autograph collecting. Members receive our
quarterly journal, *Manuscripts*, our newsletter,
and have the opportunity to attend annual
conventions held each May in a city rich
with manuscript resources.

Austin - 2000   **New York - 2001**

Annual Membership Fee: $35

**Members joining after July 1
may pay half the annual rate.**

**Send check with name and address to:
David R. Smith
Executive Director
The Manuscript Society
350 N. Niagara St.
Burbank, CA 91505-3648**

website: www.manuscript.org

ATTENTION ALL AUTOGRAPH COLLECTORS

International
autograph collectors club

P.O. Box 848486
Hollywood, FL 33084

The Original Autograph Collector/Dealer Association

Web Site: www.iacc-da.com

PRESIDENT
Lynne E. Keyes
P.O. Box 6542
West Palm Beach, FL 33405

VICE PRESIDENT
John Reznikoff
University Archives
49 Richmondville Rd.
Westport, CT 06880

TREASURER
Mike Frost
4575 Sheridan St.
Suite #111
Hollywood, FL 33021

EXECUTIVE DIRECTOR
Stephen Koschal
P.O. Box 1581
Boynton Beach, FL 33425

**DIRECTOR
INTERNATIONAL
RELATIONS**
Gerard A.J. Stodolski
Gerard A.J. Stodolski, Inc.
555 Canal St.
Manchester, NH 03101

ETHICS BOARD
Larry Rosenbaum
EAC Gallery
99 Powerhouse Rd., Ste. 204
Roslyn Heights, NY 11577

Harris Schaller
P.O. Box 746
Dubuque, IA 52004

AUTOGRAPH COLLECTORS
YOUR INVITATION TO JOIN THE IACC

The IACC is the most unique and progressive autograph organization in existence today. A non-profit corporation, it is the first organization of its kind which includes separate categories for collectors and dealers. We feel this marriage is a vital one; as it assures that collectors and dealers can join forces in ways previously impossible. Additionally, we are the largest group **DEDICATED** exclusively to autograph collecting. By keeping this as our focus, we can concentrate our efforts only on this field. In our dedication to educate and inform, we feel that the measures we have taken as an organization will revolutionize the autograph world.

Our club has on hand one of the largest and most comprehensive collection of authentic "standards" for perusal by members. You are invited to interact with board members. We also offer material that is a result of our private signings to our members at prices below market value.

Our club publication *Eyes, Ears and Voice of the Hobby* is published six times annually. It has been called by many "the best in the business" due to the inclusion of informative articles, biographies of member dealers and our landmark signature studies. All news is timely and fresh. The low cost of your membership includes this publication, your membership card, the "2000 IACC/DA Dealers Directory", discount admission at all IACC/DA endorsed events and much more. Educational courses are available at most events and the instructors are among the flagship names in this field.

Membership in the IACC is open to all interested in autographs.

2000 Collector Membership, U.S. zip codes		$20.00
2000 All Foreign Countries	USD	$30.00
Lifetime Membership	USD	$350.00

Please send membership checks to:
IACC, P.O. Box 848486, Hollywood, FL 33084

CELEBRATE A CENTURY OF CELEBRITIES
MOVIES · THEATER · RADIO · TELEVISION
CALL 1·800·526·2724 FOR A FREE COURTESY PACK, DISCOUNT TICKETS & HOTELS

NEW YORK TIMES "The prime weekend for enthusiasts"
WASHINGTON POST "A staggering variety of offerings"
PHILADELPHIA INQUIRER "Go and let yourself be dazzled"

SAN FRANCISCO EXAMINER "Impressive and worth the trip"
CHICAGO SUN TIMES "The antiques capital of the world"
REUTERS LONDON "The ultimate triumph of the big idea"

THE LARGEST INDOOR ANTIQUE & COLLECTIBLES FAIR IN THE WORLD

'ATLANTIQUE CITY.
OVER 1600 FINE BOOTHS
MARCH 25 AND MARCH 26
OCTOBER 21 AND OCTOBER 22

SATURDAY, 10:00 AM · 8:00 PM · SUNDAY, 10:00 AM · 5:00 PM · THE NEW ATLANTIC CITY CONVENTION CENTER
CALL 1·800·526·2724 FOR FREE COURTESY PACK, DISCOUNT TICKETS & HOTELS · WWW.ATLANTIQUECITY.COM

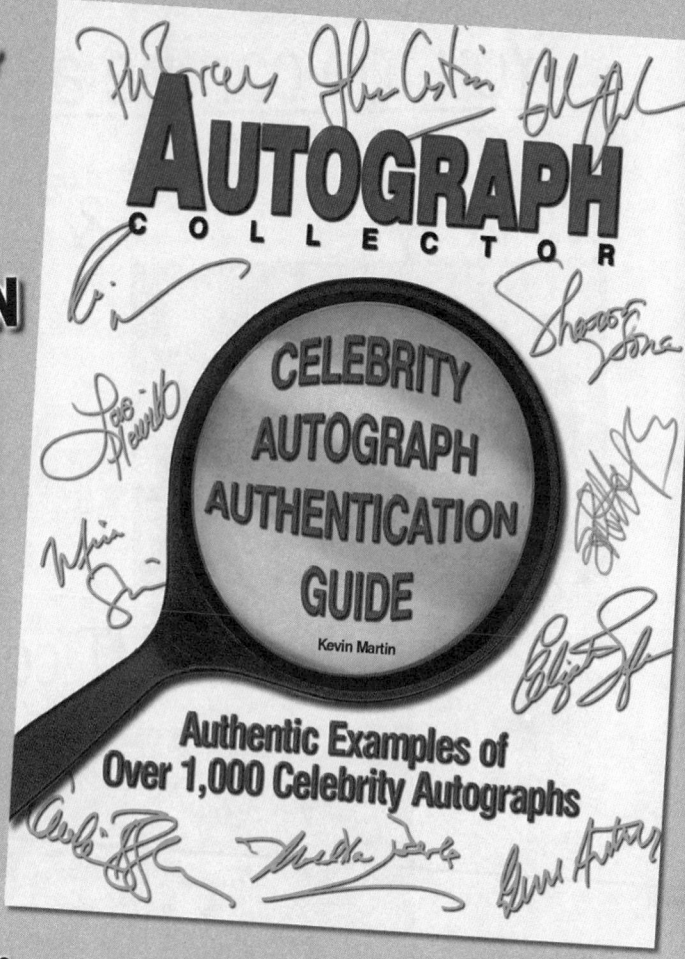

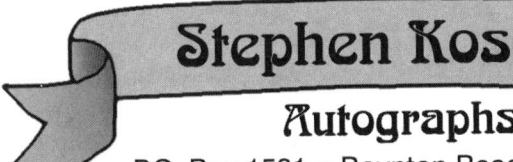

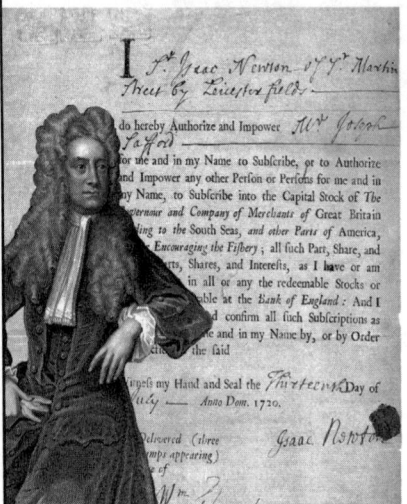